# The World
# Since 1945

EIGHTH EDITION

# The World

# Since 1945

## A History of
## International Relations

Wayne C. McWilliams
Harry Piotrowski

LYNNE
RIENNER
PUBLISHERS

BOULDER
LONDON

*In Memoriam*

*Bill Sladek*
*1938–1993*

*friend and colleague*

Published in the United States of America in 2014 by
Lynne Rienner Publishers, Inc.
1800 30th Street, Boulder, Colorado 80301
www.rienner.com

and in the United Kingdom by
Lynne Rienner Publishers, Inc.
3 Henrietta Street, Covent Garden, London WC2E 8LU

**Library of Congress Cataloging-in-Publication Data**
McWilliams, Wayne C.
  The world since 1945 : a history of international relations / Wayne C.
McWilliams, Harry Piotrowski.—8th ed.
  Includes bibliographical references and index.
  ISBN 978-1-62637-074-6 (pbk. : alk. paper)
  1. World politics—1945–1989. 2. World politics—1989– 3. Military
history, Modern—20th century. 4. Military history, Modern—21st century.
5. Developing countries. I. Piotrowski, Harry. II.Title.
  D8430M363 2014
  327.09'045—dc22                                          2014002633

**British Cataloguing in Publication Data**
A Cataloguing in Publication record for this book
is available from the British Library.

Printed and bound in the United States of America

The paper used in this publication meets the requirements
of the American National Standard for Permanence of
Paper for Printed Library Materials Z39.48-1992.

5  4  3  2  1

# Contents

# Maps

# Introduction

In this eighth edition of *The World Since 1945*, we take the story
to early 2014. Nearly seventy years after the end of World War II, the world
grappled with challenges very much different from those it faced in previous
decades. Arguably the most significant development during the past three
decades was the increasing globalization of the economy, a process that produced an ever-tightening, interlocking economic relationship among nations
and corporations. Globalization brought prosperity to many nations, notably
China (which by 2012 had the world's second largest economy, behind only
the United States) and India (which broke into the top ten). It came, however,
with its own problems, as witnessed during the financial crises and the global
recession that started in 2007, high unemployment rates, and the maldistribution of wealth.

Several old problems continued to roil the globe. The Arab-Israeli conflict
remained unresolved; nuclear proliferation (once thought to have been kept
under reasonable control) reemerged as an issue of concern; militant Islam
gained a shot in the arm during the "Arab Spring." The president of Russia,
Vladimir Putin, announced that his country was no longer on its knees and
served notice that eastward expansion by the European Union and the North
Atlantic Treaty Organization (NATO) could only go so far. The European
Union, meanwhile, was forced to reassess it mission and ability to manage
effectively the economy of its member states. A number of nations—notably
in Latin America, Africa, and Asia—struggled with the challenges of establishing democratic institutions and raising the standard of living of their people.

• • •

1

A survey of current world conditions and a reading of the recent past reveal that the world is neither a fair nor a friendly place. Insurrections and wars abound, and all too many of the world's inhabitants live in misery and hunger while others live in comfort and luxury. In this age of modern science and technology, of space exploration and heart transplants, how does one account for the absence of peace and the continuing prevalence of poverty in a world of plenty? What are the roots of the perilous condition of human affairs? Today's students, young and old, must ask and seek to answer these questions. This book, a history of the world since 1945, was undertaken in order to assist them in that endeavor.

Tribal hostility and wars between nations have been common throughout history, but in modern times, and especially in the twentieth century with the development of modern military technology, wars became increasingly deadly. World War II brought death and destruction on an unprecedented scale, and it ended with the use of a powerful new weapon of mass destruction, the atomic bomb. From the ruins of that war came a cry, expressed even by military leaders, that there must never be another such war. Yet, even as the ashes of World War II were still smoldering, friction developed among its victors, and they—the United States and Britain on one side and the Soviet Union on the other—became locked in a new power struggle that threatened the very peace they had sacrificed so much to attain. The postwar friction between them rapidly hardened into a political Cold War that soon turned into a military confrontation marked by mutual mistrust, suspicion, and hostility. After World War II the Cold War continued for more than forty-five years as a major determinant of international affairs. The two superpowers, the United States and the Soviet Union, aggressively sought to establish and maintain blocs of allies, thus dividing the world into two hostile camps. And since each claimed to be the champion of a superior system, one capitalist and the other Communist, the world became the arena of an ideological conflict that endured for nearly half a century.

Meanwhile, both superpowers engaged in a relentless arms race. Each claimed that security lay in its own military strength and that the other's armaments threatened world peace. Thus they justified the building of massive arsenals containing thousands of nuclear weapons far more powerful than the ones used against Japan in 1945. Their arsenals became, by the end of the 1950s, large enough to destroy each other many times over and possibly extinguish human life on this planet, and yet year after year the superpowers continued to pile up ever more powerful weapons, which they could use only at their own peril. When they decided to scale back their nuclear arsenals, they found out that the genie was already out of the bottle, that even poor nations had the capability to build and launch them.

The military standoff between the nuclear powers brought about a precarious truce between them, but it did not keep them from sponsoring proxy wars—such as in Korea, southern Asia, and Vietnam. The rest of the world became engaged in their own wars, for one reason or another. Since World War II, there have been more than a hundred wars, and many of these lesser wars, though contained geographically and limited to conventional weapons, carried the potential of igniting a larger conflagration.

Another danger to the well-being of humanity was the growing gulf between the world's rich nations and the poor nations, between the industrially advanced nations of the North and the underdeveloped nations of the South (or the Third World, as they were called during the Cold War). In the South, one finds the world's lowest standards of living, lowest economic growth rates, lowest levels of education, lowest rates of life expectancy, and the highest population growth rates and infant mortality rates. Thus, millions of the inhabitants of the South were dreadfully impoverished, malnourished, disease-ridden, and unable to live productively and in dignity. Their governments struggled, usually ineptly, to lift their countries from such impoverishment, and while some made marginal progress, many others were merely marking time or slipping even farther behind. Many of these countries contracted enormous foreign debts they were unable to pay, and their indebtedness threatened the financial stability of the wealthier nations of the North. Economic failure made the South more volatile politically and more vulnerable to intervention and militarization by the superpowers. Nearly every war fought since World War II was fought in the global South, and all were fought with weapons supplied by industrialized nations.

This is the world into which the youth of today were born. Their chances of resolving the immense problems they have inherited, of reducing the nuclear threat, and of alleviating the misery of the majority of humankind, thus making this world a safer and more civilized place, depend to a great extent on what they know of the causes of these problems. The clear-eyed vision needed to come to terms with these difficult problems and to progress toward a resolution of them must be based on an understanding of the past.

Our aim is to provide our readers with an evenhanded, yet critical, explanation of the political history of this troubled world and to expose them to more than one viewpoint. We seek to advance our readers' knowledge of the recent past and to develop a better understanding of the difficult issues and dangerous conditions in the world today. Above all, we hope to instill an appreciation of the need for greater objectivity and for careful, critical thinking about political issues. It is, therefore, our hope that this text will serve as a primer for responsible global citizenship.

It should be noted that we are primarily dealing with political history, except in certain chapters where economic themes are particularly relevant. We do not address many of the social or cultural dimensions of recent world history, as interesting or important as they may be. We also wish to point out that a text with a scope as broad as the world cannot help but be selective. Not every political development around the globe can be discussed within these pages. We have attempted to provide a balanced coverage of global history, rather than a Western—or US-centered—approach.

The study of the recent past is no substitute for studying the longer haul of human history. Obviously, World War II had antecedents, the knowledge of which deepens our understanding of that momentous event, its consequences, and the course of events in the postwar period. Nonetheless, because World War II represents a historic watershed, it is not inappropriate that it be taken as a starting point for the study of recent world history. And because the end of the war ushered in a distinctly a new era with many new features—the advent of nuclear warfare, the development of high-speed aviation, the emergence of two superpowers, and the end of European colonialism, to name just a few—it makes sense to treat it as a distinct historical period. To be sure, for certain topics treated in this text, such as the Arab-Israeli conflict or the revolution in China, it will be necessary to trace historical roots further back in time, but our focus remains on the postwar period.

## Eight Major Consequences of World War II

The enormous consequences of World War II gave shape to the postwar world, and they are treated as major themes in this text. We have identified the following as the most important of those consequences:

1. *The end of the European age.* Europe ceased to be the center of international power. At war's end, Europe was in shambles; its nations were prostrate, its cities in ruins, its people exhausted, and its economies shattered. The total defeat and destruction of Germany created a power vacuum in central Europe, and because nature and politics both abhor a vacuum, the victors inevitably filled it.

2. *The rise of the United States to superpower status.* Having played a decisive role in the global war and emerging from it militarily and economically supreme among the nations of the world, the United States shed for good what was left of its earlier isolationist tendencies and assumed a leadership role in the international arena.

3. *The expansion of the Soviet Union and its rise to superpower status.* Having played the major role in the defeat of Germany, the Soviet Union intended, despite its severe war damage and its dire economic condition, to extend its power, especially in Eastern Europe, and subsequently play a major role in world affairs.

4. *The emergence of the Cold War.* Contention, mistrust, and hostility between the two emerging superpowers, the United States and the Soviet Union, developed quickly and produced an ongoing, global, bipolar power struggle.

5. *The beginning of the nuclear age.* The use of the atomic bomb by the United States and the world's failure to achieve international control of atomic energy resulted inevitably in an ever-growing nuclear arms race, not only by the great powers, but by lesser powers as well.

6. *The rise of nationalism and independence movements in Asia and Africa.* Although the roots of nationalism may be traced back to prewar times, it was not until the postwar period that nationalist movements became strong enough to challenge successfully the colonial order in Asia and Africa. The struggle for independence, stimulated by a number of factors, including Japan's victories over Western colonial powers during World War II and the weakening of the European colonial powers during the war, resulted in an end to Western colonialism in a remarkably short span of time.

7. *A renewed effort to secure lasting peace through international organization.* The United Nations was created in the hope that it might help preserve the global peace and security that the old League of Nations had failed to maintain.

8. *A renewed effort to secure lasting global prosperity.* At the Bretton Woods Monetary Conference in July 1944, the International Monetary Fund and the World Bank came into existence, two agencies that played a major role in managing the global economy.

Most of these—interrelated—themes are discussed in Part 1, "The Origins of the Cold War," where we examine the global state of affairs at the end of World War II and the origins of the Cold War. In Part 2, "Nationalism and the End of Colonialism," we take up the sixth theme. There, we also trace the development of Arab and Israeli nationalism and the conflict arising from them. Part 3, "The Shifting Sands of Global Power," focusing mainly on the 1960s, examines the changing configuration of the Cold War, the strains within the Eastern and Western blocs, the Sino-Soviet split, and the resulting emergence of multipolarity, which replaced the bipolar confrontation of the earlier Cold War period. This section also includes coverage of the Vietnam War and its consequences.

Part 4, "The Global South," takes us back to Asia and Africa to trace their postindependence progress—or lack thereof—and to Latin America. In addition to investigating the political and economic patterns in Southern nations, we devote sections to topics such as the problem caused by their indebtedness and continued ethnic strife (particularly in Africa).

Part 5, "The Emergence of a New Landscape," treats the major global developments since the early 1980s. We have selected for special attention the rise of Japan, China, and the European Community as new economic superpowers and the promise and pitfalls in globalization, in addition to later Cold War issues such as the rise of Solidarity in Poland, the Soviet invasion of Afghanistan, and the nuclear arms race. We also discuss the momentous changes in the Soviet Union and Eastern Europe since the end of the 1980s, changes that signaled the end of the postwar era. We conclude the book with a discussion of the rise of militant Islam, as manifested in the Iranian revolution and its impact on the Arab world.

We urge our readers to join with us in a quest for a fuller, more objective understanding of the world of turmoil in which we live. And we would remind them that history, especially recent political history, is not merely the compilation of dead facts, of factoids as it were; it is alive with controversy and conflicting ideas. We challenge our readers to confront these controversies, to weigh the conflicting ideas and viewpoints, and to formulate their own opinions.

# Part 1

# The Origins of the Cold War

In light of the enormous impact of the Cold War since World War II—the immeasurable human energies it exhausted, the gargantuan amounts of wealth it consumed, the shifting of national priorities it demanded, the attention it diverted from other concerns, the civil liberties it impinged on and the intellectual freedom it constrained, the anguish and fears it caused so many people, the threat it posed to the earth's inhabitants, and the enormous loss of life in the proxy wars (Korea, Vietnam, and Afghanistan)—it becomes necessary to investigate its origins.

The Cold War was for many years so divisive a subject that it was all but impossible to study it with detachment and objectivity. So strong were the feelings and so total the commitment of each side to its cause, and so contemptuous and mistrusting was each of the other side, that each had its own self-serving version of the origin and history of the Cold War.

The United States and the Soviet Union each perpetuated a series of Cold War myths that sustained them over the years. The people of the United States generally felt (1) that the Soviet Union broke its postwar promises regarding Eastern Europe and was therefore responsible for starting the Cold War; (2) that its aggressive action in Eastern Europe was a manifestation of the determination of the Soviet Union to capture the entire world for Communism; (3) that so-called international Communism was a monolithic (i.e., singular) movement centered in and controlled by the Soviet Union; (4) that Communism was enslavement and was never accepted by any people without coercion; and (5) that the great victory of the United States in World War II, as well as its immense prosperity and strength, attested to the superiority of its values and its system—that, in short, the United States represented humanity's best hope.

7

The Soviets argued (1) that the United States and the Western allies purposely let the Soviet Union bleed in World War II, and furthermore lacked gratitude for the role that it played in the defeat of Hitler, as well as for the enormous losses it suffered in that cause; (2) that the United States was committed to the annihilation of Communism in general and to the overthrow of the Communist government of the Soviet Union in particular; (3) that the laws of history were on its side, meaning that capitalism was in decline and Communism was the wave of the future; (4) that the US political system was not really democratic but was controlled by Wall Street, or at any rate by a small clique of leading corporate interests; and (5) that capitalist nations were necessarily imperialistic and thus responsible for colonization across the globe, and that the leading capitalist nation, the United States, was the most imperialistic of them all.[1]

As unquestioned assumptions, these myths became a mental straitjacket. They provided only a narrow channel for foreign policy initiatives by either country. When notions such as these were embedded in the thinking of the two adversaries, it became all but impossible for the two countries to end the Cold War and equally impossible to analyze objectively the history of the conflict.

The myths came into play during the Cold War, and especially in its earliest phase even before the defeat of Nazi Germany—when the Allied leaders met at Yalta in February 1945. For this reason, in the opening chapter, we examine the wartime relationship between the United States and the Soviet Union, and their respective strengths and positions at the end of the war. We also analyze the US decision to use the atomic bomb against Japan and the impact it had on US-Soviet relations. In Chapter 2, we turn to the Yalta Conference and examine its bearing on the beginning of the Cold War. We then trace the hardening of Cold War positions over critical issues in Eastern Europe in the four years following the end of World War II. By 1947, when the US policy of "containment" of Communism was in place, the Cold War myths were firmly entrenched on both sides.

In March 1964, William Fulbright, the chairman of the Senate Foreign Relations Committee, attempted to challenge some of these and other Cold War myths. He questioned whether Communist China's "implacable hostility" to the West was "permanent," whether Fidel Castro in Cuba posed "a grave danger to the United States," and whether there was something "morally sacred" about the US possession of the Panama Canal, which it had seized in 1903. Yet few listened; indeed, Fulbright spoke before a nearly empty Senate chamber.

The Cold War quickly became global, and in fact it was in Asia where it became most inflamed in the first decade after the war. In Chapter 3, we discuss its impact on Asia by treating the Allied Occupation of defeated Japan, the civil war in China, and the Korean War—all Cold War issues. The Allied occupation of defeated Japan was thoroughly dominated by the United States over the feeble objections of the Soviets, and eventually the United States succeeded in converting Japan into an ally in the global Cold War. The Chinese revolution, which brought the Communists to power in 1949, was fought entirely by indigenous forces, but the stakes were great for the two superpowers. The United States responded to the Communist victory in China with still firmer resolve to stem the advance of Communism in Asia. Less than a year later that resolve was tested in Korea, where Cold War tensions grew most intense and finally ignited in the Korean War. The armed conflict between East and West was contained in Korea, but it threatened to explode into the dreaded World War III.

After the standoff in Korea, Cold War tensions oscillated during the remainder of the 1950s. During this period, covered in Chapter 4, new leaders—Dwight Eisenhower in the United States and Nikita Khrushchev in the Soviet Union—exhibited a new flexibility, which made possible some reduction in tensions and the solution of a few of the Cold War issues. But the Cold War myths remained entrenched during this period, as manifested by sporadic crises and the substantial growth in the nuclear arsenals of both countries. The two superpowers came to the brink of nuclear war in 1962 over the deployment of Soviet nuclear missiles in Cuba, an episode that turned into the most dangerous of the many Cold War confrontations.

## Note

1. These myths are an adaptation of a similar set of Cold War myths in Ralph B. Levering, *The Cold War, 1945–1972* (Arlington Heights, IL: Harlan Davidson, 1982), pp. 8–9.

# 1

# The End of World War II and the Dawn of the Nuclear Age

World War II was a cataclysmic event, by far the most deadly and destructive war in history. It raged for almost six years in Europe, beginning with Nazi Germany's attack on Poland in September 1939 and ending with the surrender of Germany to the Allied Powers led by the United States, the Soviet Union, and Great Britain on May 9, 1945. The war lasted even longer in Asia, where it began with the Japanese invasion of China in July 1937 and ended with Japan's capitulation to the Allies on August 14, 1945.

World War II represented something new in recent history: total war. It was total in the sense that it involved or affected the entire population of nations, not just the men and women in uniform. Everyone was drawn into the war effort and everyone became a target. This was not merely a war between armies but between societies. Because a nation's military might rested on its industrial capacity, the civilian workforce contributed to the war effort and thus became targets and victims of new and more deadly modern weapons.

Another major dimension of the war was the introduction of atomic weapons. There are many difficult questions to ponder concerning the US use of atomic bombs against Japan, one of the most important and most controversial issues in modern history. But the fundamental question remains: Was it necessary or justifiable to use the bomb? It is also important to consider what bearing the emerging Cold War had on the US decision to drop the bomb on Japan, and what bearing its use had on subsequent US-Soviet relations.

After the war, the victorious nations—mainly the United States and the Soviet Union—took the lead in shaping the postwar world. In order to understand their respective postwar policies, one must consider the impact of World War II on these two nations, the new "superpowers."

The "Grand Alliance" against Nazi Germany—fashioned during the war by the United States, the Soviet Union, and Great Britain—began to crumble as soon as the war was over and gave way to Cold War hostility. Politicians of these and other nations searched for a new international structure for the maintenance of global peace through collective security—the United Nations (UN). Although the founding of the United Nations was attended by great hope, it was from the beginning severely limited in its capacity to attain its objective of world peace.

## History's Most Destructive War

The carnage of World War II was so great as to be beyond comprehension. Much of Europe and East Asia was in ruins. Vast stretches of both continents were destroyed twice, first when they were conquered and again when they were liberated. It is impossible to know the complete toll in human lives lost in this war, but some estimates run higher than 70 million people. The nation that suffered the greatest loss of life was the Soviet Union. It lost an incredible 27 million people in the war, a figure that represents at least half of the total European war dead. Poland lost 5.8 million people, about 15 percent (perhaps even 20 percent) of its population. Germany lost 4.5 million people, and Yugoslavia, 1.5 million. Six other European nations—France, Italy, Romania, Hungary, Czechoslovakia, and Britain—each lost more than a half million people. In Asia, perhaps as many as 20 million Chinese and 2.3 million Japanese died in the war, and there were large numbers of casualties in various other Asian countries, from India in the south to Korea in the northeast. In Vietnam, the famine caused by the wartime Japanese occupation led to the death of 2 million people. In some European countries and in Japan, there was hardly a family that had not lost at least one member in the war.[1]

Approximately two-thirds of those who died in World War II were civilians—many of them specifically targeted for destruction. In contrast, during World War I much less than half of the dead were civilians, who tended to be incidental victims of the consequences of the war, famine, and disease—"collateral damage," as it were. World War II, however, to an extent not witnessed in modern European history, became a war against civilians, who were deliberately targeted.

Germany's war of conquest in Eastern Europe, under the direction of Adolf Hitler, led to the systematic murder of an estimated 12 million civilians—Jews, Slavs, and gypsies. Other victims included the disabled, conscientious objectors, and political opponents (notably Communists). The Jewish Holocaust—replete with mass executions and gas chambers—reduced Europe's prewar Jewish population from 9.2 million to 3.8 million. In 1945 came the shocking revelations of forced labor and extermination camps in Eastern Europe—Theresienstadt, Auschwitz (where 1.5 million Jews died),

Treblinka, Buchenwald. It raised the vexing question of how German society—heir to a humanist tradition that gave the world Beethoven, Goethe, Bach, and Schiller—descended (willingly or unwillingly, the debate continues) to such a level of depravity.

Another factor leading to the huge toll of civilian lives was the development of airpower—bigger and faster airplanes with longer range and greater carrying capacity. Indiscriminate bombing of the enemy's cities, populated by noncombatants, became common practice during the war.

Aerial bombardment began in earnest in the 1930s, even before the war. Its deadliness was demonstrated by the German bombing of Spanish cities in the Spanish civil war (most famously at Guernica in April 1937) and the Japanese bombing of Shanghai (in 1932) and other Chinese cities. In World War II, Britain carried out bombing raids on Berlin before Germany began its bombardment of Britain, but the latter (the "Blitz" as the British called it) represented the first sustained, large-scale bombing attack on the cities of another country. An estimated 38,000 British citizens died in the Blitz. British and US bombers retaliated with a massive bombardment of Germany. At the end of the war, an Anglo-US bombing raid on the German city of Dresden in February 1945 (when Germany was all but defeated) killed some 135,000 people, nearly all civilians. The Japanese, who also used airpower, suffered the destruction of virtually all of their cities by saturation firebombings by US bombers. And the war ended with the use by the United States of a dreadful new weapon of mass destruction, the atomic bomb, wreaking horrible devastation upon Hiroshima and Nagasaki in August 1945. In the end, the nations that fought in the name of democracy in order to put an end to militarism resorted to the barbaric methods of their enemies. If unrestrained warfare had come to mean sustained, indiscriminate bombing of noncombatants with weapons of mass destruction, what hope was there for humankind should total war ever again occur?

The suffering and sorrow, the anguish and desperation of the survivors of the war lingered long after the last bombs had fallen and the victory celebrations had ended. Never in history had so much of the human race been so uprooted. In Europe alone there were approximately 65 million refugees, a staggering figure. Among them were East Europeans—Poles, Ukrainians, Lithuanians, and others—fleeing the advancing Red Army; 13 million Germans expelled from Poland, Czechoslovakia, and other parts of Eastern Europe; as well as slave laborers—on farms, factories, and construction sites—employed in Nazi Germany.[2]

The ethnic cleansing that the Germans began in 1939 was completed by their victims in 1945. It was based on the eternal principle expressed in W. H. Auden's poem "September 1, 1939" that "those to whom evil is done, do evil in return." The Czechs showed the Germans little mercy as they expelled them from the Sudetenland; the Germans in East Prussia suddenly discovered that, after all, their armies had committed atrocities in the East and the Red Army would respond in kind. (Former German territories, which became parts of Poland, Czechoslovakia, and the Soviet Union, remained for decades among the unresolved issues of the Cold War.)

The figures cited above do not include the uncountable millions of refugees in China plus some 6 million Japanese—half of them military personnel—scattered across Asia at war's end. The United States transported most of these Japanese back home and returned Koreans, Chinese, and others to their homelands. In Manchuria, however, which the Soviets occupied temporarily, several hundred thousand Japanese were never repatriated. They succumbed either to the severity of the Manchurian winter without adequate food, shelter, or clothing or to the brutality of Soviet labor camps in Siberia. In China, cities such as Beijing (Peking) and Shanghai were swollen with weary, desperate people scavenging for food. They were plagued by disease, poverty, inflation, and corruption, all of which ran rampant in China during and well after the war.

The inferno of World War II left many cities gutted and vacant. Dresden, Hamburg, and Berlin in Germany and Tokyo, Yokohama, Hiroshima, and Nagasaki in Japan were virtually flattened, and many other cities in these and other countries were in large part turned to rubble. Some were entirely vacated and devoid of life for a while after the war. The huge and once crowded city of Tokyo, which lay mostly in ruins, saw its population dwindle to only a third of its prewar size. Stalingrad, in the wake of the greatest battle ever, had virtually no people left. In these once bustling cities, survivors scrounged in the debris in hopes of salvaging anything that might help them in their struggle for survival. At war's end homeless people moved into those few buildings that still stood—an office building, a railroad station, a school—and lived sometimes three or four families to a room, while others threw up shanties and shacks made of scraps of debris. Decades later one could still find here and there in many of these cities rubble left over from the war.

The physical destruction wrought by the war, estimated at over $2 trillion, continued to cause economic and social disruption in the lives of survivors long afterward. Not only were cities and towns destroyed but so too were industrial plants and transportation facilities. The destruction of factories, farmlands, and livestock and of railroads, bridges, and port facilities made it extremely difficult to feed and supply the needy populations. Acute shortages of food and scarcity of other life essentials continued well after the fighting was over. In these dire circumstances, many became desperate and demoralized, and some sought to ensure their survival or to profit from others' misfortune by resorting to hoarding goods and selling them on the black market. These were grim times in which greed, vengeance, and other base instincts of humanity found expression.

The widespread desolation and despair in Europe bred cynicism and disillusionment, which in turn gave rise to a political shift to the left, toward socialist solutions. Shaken and bewildered by the nightmarish devastation all about them, many Europeans lost confidence in the old political order and turned to other more radical political doctrines and movements. Many embraced Marxism as a natural alternative to discredited fascism as an ideology that offered hope for the future. The renewed popularity of the left was reflected primarily in postwar electoral victories of the moderate left, such as the Labour Party in Great Britain and the Socialist Party in Austria. Communists, too, were able to make strong showings in elections—if only for the time being—particularly in France and Italy. In Asia the political swing to the left could be seen in China, Indochina, and to a lesser extent in Japan. Alarmed by this trend, US leaders soon came to the view that massive aid was necessary to bring about a speedy economic recovery to eliminate the poverty that was seen as the breeding ground for the spread of Communism.

During the war, in November 1943, the US Congress created the United Nations Relief and Rehabilitation Administration (UNRRA), the purpose of which was the rehabilitation of war-torn areas. By the fall of 1946, many of the transportation facilities and factories in Western Europe were repaired and industrial production began to climb slowly, but the harsh winter of 1946–1947 brought new economic setbacks with a depletion of food supplies, raw materials, and financial reserves. Economic stagnation and attendant deprivation spread throughout nearly all of Europe—in defeated and devastated Germany as well as in victorious Britain. A similar situation prevailed in the war-ravaged nations of Asia, especially China and Japan.

When one considers the death, destruction, suffering, and social dislocation, it becomes clear that World War II was much more than a series of heroic military campaigns and more than a set of war games to be played and replayed by nostalgic war buffs. It was human anguish and agony on an unprecedented scale. And nowhere were the scars any deeper than in the Japanese cities of Hiroshima and Nagasaki.

## The Atomic Bombing of Japan

On August 6, 1945, the United States dropped an atomic bomb on Hiroshima and, three days later, another one on Nagasaki. In each instance a large city was obliterated and tens of thousands of its inhabitants were either instantly incinerated or left to succumb to radiation sickness weeks, months, and even years later. According to Japanese estimates, the atomic bomb strikes killed about 140,000 people in Hiroshima and about 70,000 in Nagasaki. US estimates of the death toll from the atomic bombings are 70,000 in Hiroshima and 40,000 in Nagasaki. The discrepancy in the fatality figures is partly the result of different methods of calculation and partly from differing intentions of those doing the counting. Thus, as World War II was about to end, the nuclear age began with the use of a new weapon, one that a Japanese physicist later called "a magnificent product of pure physics."[3]

The people of the United States and their wartime president, Franklin Roosevelt, were determined to bring about the earliest possible defeat of Japan. Roosevelt, who had commissioned the building of the atomic bomb, was prepared to use it against Japan once it was ready, but he died in April 1945. The decision whether to use the revolutionary new weapon fell to the new president, Harry S. Truman, who had not even been informed of the existence of the atomic bomb program until after he took office. In consultation with the secretary of war, Henry Stimson, Truman set up an advisory group known as the Interim Committee, which was to deliberate on whether to use the revolutionary weapon. The committee recommended that it be deployed against Japan as soon as possible, and without prior warning, on a dual target (meaning a military or war-plant site surrounded by workers' homes, i.e., a Japanese city).[4] The rationale for this strategy was to enhance the atomic bomb's shock value. The bomb was successfully tested in a remote New Mexico desert on July 16, just as Truman was meeting British prime minister Winston Churchill and Soviet leader Joseph Stalin at Potsdam, Germany. Elated by the news of the test, Truman approved the military orders for the bomb's use nine days later, on July 25. The following day, Truman issued the Potsdam Proclamation, which spelled out terms for Japan's unconditional surrender and warned of "prompt and utter destruction" for noncompliance. But it made no specific reference to the new weapon. When the Japanese government rejected the proclamation, the orders for the first atomic bomb strike were carried out as planned.

The Japanese government dismissed the proclamation, for it was silent on the most important question, a guarantee by the victors that Japan would be allowed to retain the most sacred of its institutions: the emperor. The US intelligence community, which from the very beginning of the war had been able to decode Japanese diplomatic and military cables, was well aware that the Potsdam Proclamation had a "magnetic effect" on the emperor, Prime Minister Suzuki Kantaro, and the army. Some Japanese officials thought that Article 10 of the proclamation implied the retention of the emperor and thus could be used as the basis of a surrender; others wanted a clarification. Article 10 suggested that the Japanese government—including the emperor—would play a role in postwar Japan. Only two questions remained: Would Washington clarify Article 10? Would it accept a Japanese surrender before atomic weapons were used?[5]

Many people have since questioned the use of the atomic bomb, and opinions differ sharply. The orthodox view, presented by US officials and generally shared by the US public, is that by cutting short the war and sparing the casualties that would have occurred in the planned invasion of Japan, the atomic bomb actually saved many lives, Japanese as well as US. This explanation concludes that, although use of the bomb was regrettable, it was nonetheless necessary. Japan's diehard military leaders were determined to fight to the bitter end, as they had in the Pacific islands, and they were prepared to fight even more fanatically on their own soil (as exemplified in the late spring of 1945 by the bloodiest battle in the Pacific, on the island of Okinawa, where more than 12,000 US soldiers and Marines lost their lives in less than three months of fighting). To bring about the earliest possible surrender of Japan and an end to the long and costly war, US officials felt compelled to use the revolutionary new weapon at their disposal.

One commonly finds in US literature the figure of 1 million as the estimate of US troops who would have been killed in the invasion of Japan had the atomic bombs not been used. But the figure is grossly exaggerated as it is more than three times the total number of US military deaths resulting from World War II—both in Europe and in the Pacific—in four years of warfare. The 1 million figure was used by Secretary of War Stimson after the war in an article intended to justify the use of the atomic bombs. At a meeting of military officials to discuss the planned invasion of Japan, on June 18, 1945, General George C. Marshall, the army chief of staff, thought it was impossible to give an estimate of the casualties in such an invasion, but surmised that in the first month they would probably not exceed those suffered in the invasion of Luzon—31,000.[6]

The projection of 1 million dead US troops, basically a justification of the atomic bombing of Japan, neglects many important historical facts. First, Japan was all but defeated, defenseless against the sustained US naval and air

*Hiroshima, Japan, August 1945. Located near ground zero, this building with its "A-Bomb Dome" has been preserved as a peace monument.*

bombardments; its navy and merchant marine were sunk, its armies were weakened and undersupplied, and it was already being strangled by a US naval blockade. US leaders, who had underestimated Japan at the beginning of the war, were now overestimating its remaining strength. Although the diehard determination of its military leaders kept Japan from surrendering unconditionally, the nation's capacity to wage war had been virtually eliminated.

Second, before the United States had tested the atomic bomb in mid-July, the Japanese were already seeking negotiations with Washington to end the war. They sought to do this through Soviet mediation, since direct communication between Tokyo and Washington had been broken off during the war; Japan, however, was not at war with the Soviet Union. The US government was fully aware of these efforts and of the sense of urgency voiced by the Japanese in their communications to Moscow. US policymakers chose to ignore these diplomatic overtures, which they dismissed as unreliable and possibly a trick. The major obstacle to Japan's effort to achieve a diplomatic settlement to the war was the US insistence upon unconditional surrender, which called for Japan's acceptance of complete submission to the will of the United States, as opposed to a negotiated settlement to end the war.

The Japanese wanted at least a guarantee of the safety of their sacred imperial institution—which is to say, the retention of their emperor, Hirohito, in whose name the imperial forces had fought the war. The US government steadfastly refused to offer any such exception to the unconditional surrender policy. The Potsdam Proclamation did not offer Japan any guarantees regarding the emperor, and thus the Japanese did not accept it as a basis for surrender. This was the only condition the Japanese insisted upon, and eventually the United States granted it, but only after the nuclear destruction of Hiroshima and Nagasaki, on August 6 and 9, respectively. On August 11, the Japanese government still insisted on surrender that "does not comprise any demand which prejudices the prerogatives of His Majesty as a sovereign ruler."[7] The Truman administration accepted this condition in its reply when it demanded the unconditional surrender of the Japanese forces "on behalf of the Emperor of Japan." Had this condition been granted beforehand, the Japanese may well have surrendered and the atomic bombs would have been unnecessary.

Third, the Japanese might have been spared the horrendous fate of Hiroshima and Nagasaki had the US government provided them with an explicit warning about the nature of the new weapon and possibly an actual demonstration of an atomic blast as well. If Tokyo then still refused to accept the surrender terms, the use of the atomic weapons might have been morally justifiable. The Japanese were given no specific warning of the atomic bombing, other than the vague threat in the Potsdam Proclamation of "prompt and utter destruction." The Interim Committee ruled out a specific warning or a demonstration of the bomb in favor of its direct use on a Japanese city to shock the Japanese into surrender. It was argued that a demonstration would be risky

*Nagasaki before*

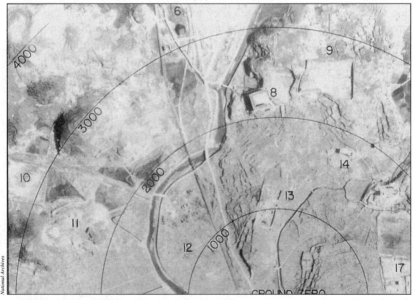

*Nagasaki after*

because of the possibility of the bomb failing to work, thus causing the United States to lose credibility and the Japanese military leaders to gain confidence.

Fourth, an unquestioned assumption of most of those who defend the use of the atomic bombs is that it produced the desired results: Japan quickly surrendered. Still, questions arise. Did the atomic bombings actually cause the Japanese to surrender? And was a second bomb necessary to bring it about? (The plan was for a "one-two punch" using both bombs in rapid succession and then, if necessary, a third, which was to be ready within ten days, so as to maximize the new weapon's shock value and force Japan to capitulate as rapidly as possible.)

Those who specifically protest the bombing of Nagasaki as unnecessary, and therefore immoral, assume that the bombing of Hiroshima was sufficient to cause Japan's surrender, or that Japan should have been given more time to assess what had hit Hiroshima. One may indeed question whether the interval of three days was long enough for the Japanese military to assess the significance of the new force that had destroyed one of their cities. But a more fundamental question is whether the atomic bombings indeed caused Japan's surrender. Japanese newspapers, the testimony of Japanese leaders, and US intercepts of Japanese diplomatic cables provide reason to believe that the Soviet entry into the war against Japan on August 8 was as much a cause for Japan's surrender as the two atomic bombs. The Soviet Union was the only major nation in the world not at war with Japan, and the Japanese leaders were still desperately hoping for continued Soviet neutrality or possible Soviet mediation as a vehicle to end the war. They took heart in the fact that the Soviet Union had neither signed the Potsdam Proclamation nor signified support for it, even though Stalin was meeting with Truman and Churchill when it was issued. But with the Soviet attack the last shred of hope was gone. With Japan's large army in Manchuria subject to an attack by an equally large and well-armed Red Army, Japan could no longer avoid admitting defeat. As for the effect of the atomic bombings on Japanese leaders, Japan's inner cabinet was divided three-to-three for and against accepting the Potsdam Proclamation before the bombing of Hiroshima, and it remained so afterward. It remained equally divided after the Soviet entry into the war and the bombing of Nagasaki, until finally the emperor himself broke the deadlock in favor of ending the war.

At the Yalta Conference in February 1945, Roosevelt and his military advisers had strongly desired an early entry of the Soviet Union into the war against Japan, and he was willing to concede much to Stalin to attain this. But after the Battle of Okinawa (April 1–June 22, 1945, during which an estimated 200,000 Japanese soldiers and civilians died) and after the atomic bomb was successfully tested, leading figures in the Truman administration were not so sure they wanted the Soviet Union to join the war against Japan. Nor did they want the Soviets to know anything about the atomic bomb. In fact, both

Roosevelt and Truman pointedly refused to inform Moscow about the development and planned use of the new weapon (about which Stalin's spies, however, had already informed him).

This last point raises intriguing and important questions about the connection between the US use of the bomb and its policies toward the Soviet Union at the end of the war. One historical interpretation asserts that the United States used the atomic bombs on a defeated Japan not so much as the last act of World War II, but as the first expression of US power in the Cold War. In other words, the bomb was used to coerce the Soviet Union into behaving itself in Eastern Europe, Asia, and elsewhere. This interpretation would explain the hurried use of the bombs before the Soviet Union had entered the war and nearly three months prior to the planned US invasion of Japan. It would explain Truman's refusal to inform Stalin about the new weapon before (or even after) its use against Japan. In this way, it is argued, the United States sought to maintain its nuclear monopoly (shared with Britain) and to engage in what became known as "nuclear diplomacy" as a means to curb Soviet ambitions.

This interpretation by revisionist historians, based on substantial evidence and logic, remains speculative. Those who hold the traditional view, of course, reject it and offer counterarguments. They emphasize the fanaticism and intransigence of the Japanese military leaders, who even resorted to suicidal kamikaze airplane attacks on US ships. And they argue that the atomic bomb was needed to subdue an irrational enemy who seemed determined to fight to the bitter end. Therefore, in this view, it was solely for military purposes that Truman decided to use the atomic bomb. They also argue that Truman, as commander in chief, had the responsibility to use every military means at his command to produce the earliest possible defeat of Japan. If he had not used the atomic bomb and more US military personnel had died in the continuing war, they assert, he would surely have been condemned as being politically and morally liable for their deaths.

Those who hold this view also argue that Truman could hardly have decided against use of the atomic bomb. As a new occupant of the White House following the popular Roosevelt, Truman inherited Roosevelt's cabinet, his policies, and specifically his resolve to treat the atomic bombs as a legitimate weapon of war. General Leslie Groves, head of the Manhattan Project (the code name of the secret program to build the atomic bomb), fully expected that the bomb would be used as soon as it became operational. The military planning for its use was well under way by the time the first test was conducted. Many of the scientists and military personnel involved in the project anticipated the successful deployment of the weapon they had brought into being after four years of expensive and herculean effort. Truman could hardly have stemmed the momentum. General Groves was especially determined to deploy the new weapon to determine its destructive force. Military planners picked out a set of Japanese cities as targets and ordered that they be spared from conventional bombing so that they would remain unspoiled for the nuclear experiment.

## The Political Fallout

Historians are also in disagreement over the impact of the atomic bomb on the Cold War. If the Truman administration actually attempted nuclear diplomacy after the war, it is safe to say it did not work. The nuclear threat, implicit in the exclusive Anglo-US possession of the atomic bomb, did not produce any significant change in Soviet behavior or policies anywhere. But it did, no doubt, affect attitudes on both sides that contributed to Cold War mistrust. US possession of the bomb caused its leaders to be more demanding and less flexible in dealing with Moscow, and the US possession and use of the bomb surely caused Stalin to increase his suspicions of the West.

It is fairly certain that the secretive manner of the United States in building and then using the atomic bomb made a postwar nuclear arms race likely, if not inevitable. Truman's secretary of state, James Byrnes, who also served on the Interim Committee, contended that it would take the Soviet Union at least ten years to develop an atomic bomb and that in the interim the United States could take advantage of its "master card" in dealing with the Soviet Union. Leading US nuclear scientists, however, including lead scientist Robert Oppenheimer, predicted that the Soviet Union could build the bomb within four years.[8] Several of the Manhattan Project scientists attempted to warn the Truman administration that the atomic monopoly could not be maintained for long and that a nuclear arms race would surely follow if the US government did not inform the Soviet Union about this revolutionary new weapon of mass destruction and did not attempt to bring it under international control. This advice, given both before and after the Hiroshima and Nagasaki bombings, went unheeded, and the result was exactly what the scientists had predicted. Indeed, Oppenheimer's prediction that the Soviets would have their own atomic weapon in four years was right on target.

The US government did, however, after months of careful study of the complicated issues involved, offer a proposal for international control of atomic power. This proposal, the Baruch Plan, presented to the United Nations in June 1946, was unacceptable to the Soviet Union because, among other reasons, it permitted the United States to retain its nuclear arsenal indefinitely while restricting Soviet efforts to develop one. The Soviets countered by proposing the immediate destruction of all existing nuclear weapons and the signing of a treaty outlawing future production or use of them. The United States, understandably unwilling to scuttle its atomic monopoly, flatly rejected this proposal. Talks continued for the next three years at the United Nations, but they proved fruitless. In the meantime, the Soviet Union's frantic effort to build an atomic bomb did bear fruit as early as the US atomic scientists had predicted—July 1949. The nuclear arms race was thus joined.

### The United States and the Soviet Union at War's End

The two nations that emerged from the war as the most powerful shapers of the postwar world, the two new superpowers, the United States and the Soviet Union, had very different wartime experiences. No nation has ever suffered as many wartime casualties as the Soviet Union, and no major nation in World War II suffered as few as the United States.

In June 1941, the German army of more than 2 million soldiers invaded the Soviet Union, destroying immense areas and leaving some 1,700 cities and 70,000 villages in ruins and some 70 percent of its industries and 60 percent of its transportation facilities destroyed. During the war, the Germans took several million Soviet prisoners, many of whom did not survive their ordeal, and several million others were forcibly conscripted to labor in German factories and on farms until the end. The horrors of the German invasion and the assault on Soviet cities (notably Leningrad, Moscow, and Stalingrad) aroused the patriotism of Russians as well as non-Russian peoples of the Soviet Union, who fought heroically to defend the nation in what became known as the Second Great Patriotic War (the first one being against the Napoleonic invasion of 1812), celebrated ad infinitum in songs, memorials, literature, film, and paintings.

Ultimately, the Soviet people endured, and the Soviet Red Army chased the German army back to Berlin. But the cost in lives was enormous: an estimated 7.5 million military deaths and twice—possibly three times—as many civilian lives. There were perhaps twice as many Soviet battle deaths in the Battle of Stalingrad alone as the United States suffered in the entire war (330,000); another estimated 1 million (largely civilians) died in the siege of Leningrad. In contrast, the United States emerged from the war largely unscathed. Except for the Japanese attack on Pearl Harbor at the outset of the war and the brief Japanese occupation of Attu and Kiska at the far end of the Aleutian Islands, it was not invaded or bombed. For every US death resulting from the war there were more than 80 Soviet deaths.

Any discussion of postwar policies of the Soviet Union and its relations with the United States must begin with a recognition of the incredible losses it suffered in the war against Nazi Germany and the insistence that there be no repetition of this history.

In comparison to the immense physical destruction sustained by the Soviet Union, the US infrastructure suffered no damage. On the contrary, the US economy experienced a great wartime boom, which brought it out of the Great Depression. While the Soviet Union's industrial output fell by 40 percent during the war years, that of the United States more than doubled. And while the Soviet Union sorely needed economic rehabilitation to recover from the ravages of war, the United States possessed unparalleled economic power. Indeed, no nation ever achieved such economic supremacy as that achieved by the United States at the end of World War II. In a war-ravaged world where every other industrial nation had suffered extensive damage and declining production, the US economy, with its wartime growth, towered over all others like a colossus. What is more, the United States had the capacity to greatly extend its huge lead. It possessed in great abundance every resource necessary for sustained industrial growth in the postwar era: large, undamaged industrial plants; skilled labor; technology; raw materials; a sophisticated transport system; and, last but not least, a huge supply of capital for investment.

The United States came through the war with another important although intangible asset: a greatly inflated national ego. The nation was brimming with renewed confidence and optimism, and the pessimism spawned by the Great Depression became a thing of the past. The US people saw their victory in war as proof of the superiority of their way of life. With their nation standing tall at the pinnacle of power in the war-torn world, the people exhibited what has been called an "illusion of American omnipotence."[9] Here we have, indeed, what Henry Luce, the publisher of *Time* and *Life* magazines, had predicted five years earlier, the dawn of the "American Century." Bolstered by this new confidence and sense of supremacy, the United States now displayed a new determination to play the role of a great power and to exercise its leadership in shaping the postwar world. It was astonishing to see, therefore, its self-confidence so rapidly shaken once the Cold War got under way.

### The Quest for Collective Security

The task of establishing a new world order after the defeat of Germany and Japan fell to the victors, the United States, the Soviet Union, and to a lesser degree Great Britain. During the war, the leaders of these "Big Three" countries—Franklin Roosevelt, Joseph Stalin, and Winston Churchill—met not only to coordinate war plans but also to lay plans for a postwar settlement. Roosevelt, in particular, was confident that the harmony and—relative—trust developed during the war would endure and that through personal diplomacy the Big Three could settle the enormous problems of the postwar world, such as the futures of Germany, Eastern Europe, Japan, and other parts of East Asia. Before the war ended, however, two of the three were no longer in power: Roosevelt died in April 1945, and Churchill was defeated in the election of July of that year. But it was already apparent even before Roosevelt's death that the wartime alliance would not outlast the war. In retrospect, it became clear that the Big Three had little in common other than a common enemy, and once the enemy was defeated their conflicting interests came to the fore.

Wartime solidarity could not be counted on to guide the postwar world to safety and security and would not, in any case, endure beyond the war. The Big Three did endeavor, however cautiously, to erect a new international structure designed to settle international problems. The Big Three were in general agreement on the concept of maintaining peace through collective security. Roosevelt was most ardent in advocating a new international peacekeeping organization to replace the defunct League of Nations. Early in the war, he began sounding out Churchill on this idea and then found occasion to discuss it with Stalin as well. All three were concerned about maintaining a postwar working relationship among the "united nations," as the Allied powers were sometimes called. Roosevelt wished to avoid a return of his country to isolationism, and Stalin did not want the Soviet Union to be diplomatically isolated as it had been prior to World War II.

There was much discussion about what shape the new collective security organization should take—its structure, functions, and authority. The most difficult issue was the conflict between a commitment to internationalism, on the one hand, and nationalist concerns, on the other. Specifically, the question was how much of any member nation's sovereignty was to be surrendered to the new supranational body in the interest of maintaining world peace. Would the new international organization have enough authority to enforce its decisions on member nations and yet permit each the right to protect its national interests? Another key question was the relationship of the major powers to the many smaller nations of the international body. From the outset the Big Three were in agreement that they would not sacrifice their power to majority rule.

*The Big Three. Soviet marshal Joseph Stalin, US president Franklin D. Roosevelt, and British prime minister Winston Churchill at the Tehran conference in November 1943.*

They insisted that their own nations, which had played the major role in World War II, should be entrusted with the responsibility to maintain the postwar peace, and that the new international organization should invest authority in them to exercise leadership unobstructed by the collective will of the smaller, but more numerous, member states.

These issues were resolved at a series of wartime conferences. At a meeting in Moscow in October 1943, the Allied foreign ministers agreed in principle to the creation of the organization that would come to be known as the United Nations. In August 1944, as victory in the war approached, representatives of the Big Three, now joined by Nationalist China, met at Dumbarton Oaks (in Washington, DC) to hammer out the shape of the new international body. At the Yalta Conference in February 1945 (see Chapter 2), the Big Three came to terms on the matter of securing for each of the major powers the right to veto decisions by the new international body. This cleared the way for convening a conference in San Francisco in April 1945, where the United Nations charter, which spelled out the principles, authority, and organizational structure, as well as a commitment to human rights, was signed by representattives of the new organization. In September 1945, the United Nations officially opened its headquarters in New York City.

The principal organs of the United Nations were the Security Council, the General Assembly, the Economic and Social Council, the International Court of Justice, and the Secretariat. The most powerful and important of these was the Security Council, which was given the responsibility to keep the peace. It was empowered to determine whether an action such as armed aggression by a member nation constituted a breach of the United Nations Charter and to recommend corrective measures or sanctions, including the use of force under the principle of collective security. The Council was composed of five permanent members (the Big Five: the United States, the Soviet Union, Great Britain, Nationalist China, and France) and six other nations elected for two-year terms. The permanent members were given absolute veto power, which is to say the Council could not enact a binding resolution unless unanimity existed among the Big Five. In this manner the Big Five intended to protect themselves from actions by the world body against their own interests. It must be noted that both the United States and the Soviet Union insisted on this veto power, and without it they would not have joined the United Nations. It should also be noted that it was this same provision that soon rendered the United Nations Security Council ineffective because in the ensuing Cold War unanimity among the major powers became all but impossible to attain. In the early years of the United Nations, the Soviet Union, which often stood alone against the other four major powers, resorted again and again to the veto.

The UN General Assembly was composed of all of the member nations, each with an equal voice and a single vote. It acted as an open forum in which international problems and proposed solutions were discussed. The Assembly passed resolutions by majority vote, but these were treated merely as recommendations and were not binding on the member nations, particularly the Big Five. The General Assembly was important mainly for giving the smaller nations a voice—albeit generally ignored—in world affairs.

The UN Secretariat was the permanent administrative office concerned primarily with the internal operations of the organization, which was to be headed by a secretary-general, the highest and most visible officer of the United Nations. He was appointed by the General Assembly on the recommendation of the Security Council. In effect, it meant finding a compromise candidate from a neutral country acceptable to the two sides in the Cold War. As such, the secretary-general's authority tended to be limited since he took his marching orders from the Security Council.[10]

The other bodies of the United Nations, especially the specialized agencies (e.g., the World Health Organization) under the Economic and Social Council, functioned more effectively than the Security Council precisely because they were more operational than political in nature and the problems they addressed could be separated from Cold War polemics. This also was true for such UN bodies as the International Court of Justice, the highly effective World Health Organization, UNESCO (United Nations Educational, Scientific, and Cultural Organization), and UNHCR (the UN High Commissioner for Refugees, an agency that, in 1951, took over the functions of UN Relief and Rehabilitation Administration, or UNRRA).

The founding of the United Nations was an expression of hope by the survivors of a catastrophic world war, the fulfillment of dreams for an organization dedicated to international peace and order. It was not long, however, before the United Nations proved unable to fulfill those dreams and even became an object of derision for many. The United Nations did on several occasions intervene to settle or moderate international disputes when and where the interests of both the United States and the Soviet Union were either minimal or not in conflict. Bigger issues, however—such as ending the Berlin blockade of 1948, ending the First Indochina War, or the Austrian settlement (see Chapters 2, 4, and 5)—were resolved outside UN jurisdiction. The veto power that both superpowers had insisted on and the Cold War context rendered the Security Council all but powerless to keep the peace in the postwar era.

## Notes

1. The magnitude of the slaughter was such that no exact figures are possible. For the aftermath of the war, see Ian Buruma, *Year Zero: A History of 1945* (New York: Penguin, 2013). For a breakdown of the figures in East Asia, see John W. Dower, *War Without Mercy: Race and Power in the Pacific War* (New York: Pantheon, 1986), pp. 295–301.

2. United Nations High Commissioner for Refugees (UNHCR), *The State of the World's Refugees, 2000: Fifty Years of Humanitarian Action* (New York: Oxford University Press, 2000), chapter 1, "The Early Years."

3. Dr. Yoshio Nishina, "The Atomic Bomb," Report for the United States Strategic Bombing Survey (Washington, DC: National Archives), p. 1, Record Group 243, Box 56.

4. "Notes of the Interim Committee," Record Group 77, Manhattan Engineering District Papers, Modern Military Branch, National Archives (Washington, DC: National Archives, May 31, 1945), pp. 9–10.

5. Pacific Strategic Intelligence Section, intelligence summary of August 7, 1945, "Russo Japanese Relations (28 July–6 August 1945)," National Archives, Record Group 457, SRH-088, pp. 3, 7–8, 16. For the Japanese attempts to surrender, beginning on July 13, 1945, see "Magic Diplomatic Extracts, July 1945," Military Intelligence Service (MIS), War Department, prepared for the attention of General George C. Marshall, National Archives, Record Group 457, SRH-040, pp. 1–78.

6. Herbert Feis, *The Atomic Bomb and the End of World War II* (Princeton, NJ: Princeton University Press, 1966), pp. 8–9.

7. Harry S. Truman, *Memoirs, I, 1945: Year of Decisions* (New York: Signet, [orig. 1955] 1965), p. 471.

8. "Notes of the Interim Committee," May 31, 1945, pp. 10–12; Gregg Herken, *The Winning Weapon: The Atomic Bomb in the Cold War, 1945–1950* (New York: Random House, 1981), pp. 109–113. Byrnes was apparently less influenced by the views of the scientists than he was by General Groves, who speculated that it would take the Soviet Union from ten to twenty years to produce an atomic bomb.

9. Sir Denis Brogan, cited in Louis Halle, *The Cold War as History* (New York: Harper and Row, 1967), p. 25.

10. The first secretary-general was Trygve Lie of Norway (1946–1952), who was followed by Dag Hammarskjöld of Sweden (1953–1961), U Thant of Burma (1961–1971), Kurt Waldheim of Austria (1972–1981), Javier Pérez de Cuéllar of Peru (1982–1991), Boutros Boutros-Ghali of Egypt (1992–1996), Kofi Annan of Ghana (1997–2006), and Ban Ki-moon of South Korea (2007).

# 2

# The Cold War Institutionalized

At the end of 1944, it became clear that it was only a matter of time until the Allies would defeat Nazi Germany. It also became evident that the reason for the wartime alliance—always a marriage of convenience—was coming to an end. Postwar considerations were beginning to play an ever-increasing role in the relations between the Allies. Throughout the war, the Allies repeatedly had made clear that they fought for specific aims and not merely for the high-sounding principles of liberty and democracy. In 1945, the moment thus came to consider the postwar world. For these reasons the Allied heads of state—Franklin Roosevelt of the United States, Joseph Stalin of the Soviet Union, and Winston Churchill of Great Britain—met in February 1945 in the Soviet resort of Yalta on the Crimean peninsula on the Black Sea. It was here that the Big Three attempted to sort out four central issues.

## The Yalta Conference

The main topic at Yalta was the status of postwar Eastern Europe, mainly that of Poland, which had been—and still was at the time of the conference—an ally in the war against Germany. It was on behalf of the government of Poland that Great Britain and France had declared war on Germany in 1939, thereby turning the German-Polish war into a European conflict, which then spilled over into the Atlantic, the Mediterranean, and North Africa, and with the Japanese attack on Pearl Harbor in December 1941, into the Pacific and Asia. In short, the governments of France and Great Britain had taken the momentous decision to go to war—and thus risk the lives and fortunes of their people—to prevent the German conquest of a nation in Eastern Europe.

As the war drew to a conclusion and the Germans were expelled from Poland, the fate of that nation became the overriding political concern of the Allies. To complicate matters, the prewar government of Poland, virulently anti-Russian and anti-Communist, had fled Warsaw in the wake of the German invasion and had taken up residence in London, waiting to return to power at the end of the war. The Polish leaders in London insisted that the West had an obligation to return them to Warsaw as the legitimate government of Poland. The Western leaders, Churchill and Roosevelt, wanted to oblige, but it was the Red Army of the Soviet Union that was in the process of occupying Poland. It became increasingly clear that Stalin, not Roosevelt or Churchill, would determine the nature of the government in postwar Poland.

The second issue at Yalta was one of prime importance for the US armed forces, which at that time were still engaged in a bitter war with Japan that promised to continue perhaps into 1946. The sustained bombing of Japanese cities was under way, but Japanese resistance was as fierce as ever and the Battle of Okinawa (where the United States first set foot on Japanese soil) had not yet taken place. For the US Joint Chiefs of Staff, therefore, Yalta was primarily a war conference designed to bring the seasoned Red Army into the war against the Japanese army ensconced in Manchuria.

The third question was the formation of the United Nations to replace the old League of Nations, a casualty of World War II. Roosevelt sought an organizational structure that was acceptable to Churchill and Stalin, as well as to constituents back home. Roosevelt firmly believed that there could be no effective international organization without US and Soviet participation.

Finally, there was the question of what to do with the German state, whose defeat was imminent. The Allies would soon control the devastated lands of once powerful Germany, whose uncertain future was in their hands.

### The Polish Question

The first question, the status of Poland, proved to be the thorniest. It came up in seven of the eight plenary (full, formal) sessions. Roosevelt and Churchill argued that Poland, an ally, must be free to choose its own government. Specifically, they sought the return of the prewar—pro-West, anti-Communist, and anti-Russian—government of Poland, in exile in London.

This "London government" consisted of Poles who did not hide their strong anti-Moscow sentiments, the result of age-old struggles between Russians and Poles. Their animosity toward the Communist government in Moscow was so great that on the eve of the war with Germany they had refused even to consider an alliance with the Soviet Union. Stalin then made his famous deal in 1939 with Hitler whereby the two agreed to a Non-Aggression Pact, by which Stalin hoped to sit out the war.[1] As part of the bargain, Hitler offered Stalin the eastern region of Poland, a large piece of territory that the victorious Poles had seized from a devastated Soviet state in

1921. The Polish conquest (1921) of what the Soviets considered part of their empire and the subsequent Soviet reconquest (1939) of these lands (with Hitler's complicity) were but two events in the long and bloody relationship between Russians and Poles going back centuries. In 1941, Hitler used Poland as a springboard to invade the Soviet Union and at the end of the war the Soviets returned to Poland once more.

Stalin understood only too well the nationalistic and bitterly anti-Russian attitudes of the Poles, particularly that of the prewar government, which had sworn eternal hostility to his government. As the Soviet soldiers moved into Poland they became targets of the Polish resistance, which took time out from fighting the Germans to deal with the invader from the east. Stalin well understood the nationalistic and religious divisions in Eastern Europe. As an ethnic Georgian, Stalin was, after all, a product of the volatile ethnic mix of the old tsarist empire. He knew, as he told his Western allies at Yalta, that the "quarrelsome" Poles would be difficult to control.[2]

Stalin could not forget that Hitler's invasion had cost the Soviet Union an estimated 27 million lives. At Yalta, he was determined to prevent the reestablishment of a hostile Poland along his western border. Stalin had no intentions, therefore, to permit the London Poles to take power in Warsaw, a major concern he repeatedly conveyed to Roosevelt and Churchill, who grudgingly accepted in principle the reality that Eastern Europe in general, and Poland in particular, already had become part and parcel of the Soviet Union's sphere of influence. To this end, even before Yalta, Stalin had created his own Polish government, with its seat in the eastern Polish city of Lublin, one that consisted of Communists and socialists.

Roosevelt and Churchill faced a dilemma. World War II had been fought for the noble ideals of democracy and self-determination. But in postwar Poland there would be neither. Britain, moreover, still had a treaty obligation with the London Poles. The treaty with the Polish government in London, however, consisted of an obligation on the part of Britain to defend its ally only against Germany, not the Soviet Union, a point the British government stressed in April 1945, when it released a secret protocol of the 1939 treaty. With this release, Britain's legal obligation to the Polish government came to an end. But there was still the moral duty to defend a former ally against Stalin's aspirations. Yet that moral obligation was trumped by the Red Army's control of Poland.

The Polish question pitted the demands of Roosevelt and Churchill for self-determination against Stalin's insistence on a government answerable to Moscow. Specifically, it came down to an argument over the composition of a provisional (interim) government of Poland. Stalin argued for recognition of the Lublin regime as the provisional government; Roosevelt and Churchill wanted it to include "democratic" (that is, pro-Western) politicians. Finally, the two sides arrived at an ambiguous agreement that papered over their broad differences. The Polish government was to be "reorganized on a broader democratic basis with the inclusion of democratic leaders from Poland itself and Poles abroad."[3] This reorganized government was to be provisional until the "free election" of a permanent government.

After the conference, Roosevelt and Churchill chose to accentuate Stalin's concession to allow "free elections" so as to claim that they had won at Yalta a victory for the London Poles and for democracy. Stalin, however, had no intention of allowing "democratic" politicians—that is, the Western-oriented and anti-Soviet London Poles—into the government or of permitting them to run for office. In any case, his definition of free elections was so narrow that the supposed promise of free elections became meaningless. When elections were finally held, the slate of candidates was restricted to "safe" political figures who posed no threat to the Soviet domination of Poland.

Stalin apparently was under the impression that the Western powers had essentially yielded at Yalta to the Soviet Union's presence in Poland and that their complaints were largely cosmetic and for domestic consumption. He thus considered the question resolved. But in Britain, and in particular the United States, the Soviet Union's control of Poland never sat easily. There were no free elections in Poland, a country that was now safely in the hands of Communists loyal to Moscow. In the meantime, the Red Army pushed through Poland all the way to Berlin, carrying Stalin's political and military influence into the center of Europe.

From these events came the following arguments, which Roosevelt's Republican critics often made: (1) Roosevelt had yielded Poland (as well as the rest of Eastern Europe) to Stalin; and (2) Stalin had broken his promise at Yalta to hold free elections, and this act of infidelity precipitated the Cold War. The Democrats, stung by these charges, replied that Roosevelt had done no such thing as ceding Eastern Europe to Stalin. Geography and the fortunes of war, they contended, had put the Red Army into Eastern Europe, not appeasement on the part of Roosevelt or of his successor, Harry Truman, who became president upon Roosevelt's death on April 12, 1945.

### The Ghost of Munich

At this juncture the two major allies in World War II became locked into positions that were the result of their peculiar readings of the lessons of history—particularly, the "lessons of Munich." This refers to the event that is considered the single most important step leading to World War II.

In the autumn of 1938, Adolf Hitler insisted that a part of western Czechoslovakia—the Sudetenland, with a population of 3 million ethnic Germans—must be transferred to Germany on the basis of the principle of national self-determination, a principle dear to the victors of World War I, who had created the sovereign state of Czechoslovakia. Germans must live in Germany, Hitler threatened, otherwise there will be war. France had a treaty of alliance with Czechoslovakia that committed France to its defense in case Germany attacked it. But the French government was psychologically and militarily incapable of honoring its treaty and sought, therefore, a compromise solution. At this point England's prime minister, Neville Chamberlain, stepped in. The result was the Munich Conference, by which the Western powers avoided war, if only for the time being, and Hitler obtained the Sudetenland without firing a shot. At the same time, Hitler, who had already annexed Austria, promised that this was his last demand in Eastern Europe. It permitted Chamberlain to return to London famously proclaiming that he had "brought peace in our time."

Events quickly showed that Hitler had lied. In March 1939, he annexed the rest of Czechoslovakia and then pressured the Poles to yield on territory Germany demanded. When the Poles refused to budge, the British, and later the French, determined that the time had come to take a stand and offered the Poles a treaty of alliance. When Hitler invaded Poland, a European war was in the making.

The lessons of Munich for the West were clear. A dictator can never be satisfied. Appeasement only whets his appetite. In the words of the US secretary of the navy, James Forrestal, there were "no returns on appeasement."[4] When Stalin imposed Communist governments in Eastern Europe after the war, the West quickly brought up the lessons of Munich and concluded that acceptance of the Soviet Union's expanded influence would inevitably bring further Soviet expansion and war. Western leaders proved to be psychologically incapable of accepting the Soviet Union's control of Eastern Europe: There could be no business-as-usual division of the spoils of victory.

The Soviets had their own reading of these same events. To them, Munich meant the first decisive move by Hitler (in collusion with the capitalist West) against the Soviet Union. The men in the Kremlin long believed that the Soviet Union, and not the West or Poland, had been Hitler's main target. Throughout the latter half of the 1930s, the Soviet Union had repeatedly called for an alliance with the West against Germany, but the pleas had always fallen on unreceptive and suspicious Western ears. From Moscow's perspective, the West's deal with Hitler at Munich deflected Hitler toward the East. In rapid order Hitler then swallowed up Czechoslovakia and a host of other East European nations, confirming the Soviet leaders' deep suspicions. By June of 1941, when Hitler launched his invasion of the Soviet Union, he was in control of all of Eastern Europe—not to mention most of the rest of Europe as well—and proceeded to turn it against the Soviet Union.

For the Soviets the lessons of Munich were obvious. Eastern Europe must not fall into the hands of hostile forces. Stalin would tolerate neither the return to power of the hostile Poles in London nor that of the old regimes in Hungary, Romania, and Bulgaria, which had cooperated with the Nazis. No foreign power must have the opportunity to do what Hitler had done and turn Eastern

**Central and Eastern Europe:**
**Territorial Changes After World War II**

Europe against the Soviet Union. The old order of hostile states aligned with the enemies of the Soviet Union must give way to a new reality that served Moscow's interests.

From the same events the two antagonists in the Cold War thus drew diametrically opposed conclusions. The West focused on the military containment of the Soviet Union accompanied by its unwillingness to legitimize the Kremlin's position in Eastern Europe. A lack of resolve, it was argued in the West, would surely bring war. The Soviets were just as adamant in insisting that the buffer they had created in Eastern Europe, at a tremendous cost, must now serve to keep the capitalist West at bay. These opposing visions of the lessons of history were at the core of the conflict between the West and the Soviet Union.

### Polish Borders

At Yalta, Stalin also insisted on moving Poland's borders. He demanded a return to the Soviet Union of what it had lost to the Poles in the Treaty of Riga in 1921 (after the Poles had defeated the Red Army). At that time Lord Curzon, the British foreign secretary, had urged the stubborn Poles to accept an eastern border 125 miles to the west because that line separated more equitably the Poles from the Belorussian and Ukrainian populations of the Soviet Union. But in 1921, the victorious Poles rejected the Curzon Line and imposed, instead, their own line upon the defeated Soviets. In 1945, it became Stalin's turn to redraw the border.

To compensate the Poles for land lost on the east to the Soviet Union, Stalin moved Poland's western border about 75 miles farther west into what had been Germany, to the Oder and Western Neisse Rivers. At Yalta, Stalin sought his allies' stamp of approval for the Oder-Neisse Line but without success.

A third readjustment of Poland's border called for the division between the Soviets and the Poles of East Prussia, Germany's easternmost province, as part of the spoils of war. On that score Stalin and the Poles were in agreement. The Soviet Union and Poland, they agreed, had suffered injury at the hands of Germany and thus deserved compensation. The West grudgingly acceded to Stalin's border readjustment, which, in any event, had already been accomplished. Since 1945, the Soviets and Poles considered the border changes at the expense of Germany a fait accompli. A fair number of Germans, however, were not ready to accept these consequences of the war.

When the Western powers and the Soviet Union failed to reach an agreement on a unified Germany, the result was the division of that nation into the US-sponsored Federal Republic of Germany (commonly known as West Germany) and the Soviet creation, the Democratic Republic of Germany (or East Germany). The East German government had little choice but to accept the new German-Polish border. The West German government, however, insisted that it was the sole legitimate German government; that it spoke for all Germans, East and West; and that Germany's proper borders were that of 1937 (before Hitler began to annex new territory, starting with Austria in March 1938). The first West German government of Chancellor Konrad Adenauer—a determined champion of German territorial integrity—refused to accept the new, Soviet-imposed boundaries.

In the late 1960s, the West German government, this time under the leadership of Willy Brandt, began to acknowledge the reality of the new borders, but for the first forty-two years of its existence, no West German government (not even that of Brandt) formally accepted the loss of German territory. Until the reunification of Germany in 1990, it remained one of the unresolved consequences of the war.

### The Japanese Issue

The second issue at Yalta was more straightforward. The US Joint Chiefs of Staff wanted the Soviet Red Army to enter the war against Japan. The Soviets, as it turned out, needed little prodding. Stalin promised to enter the war ninety days after the end of the war in Europe. The Japanese had handed Russia a humiliating defeat in the Russo-Japanese War of 1904–1905 and took the island of Sakhalin, which previously had been under Russian control. In the wake of the Bolshevik Revolution of 1917 and the civil war that followed, the Japanese had invaded eastern Siberia and remained there until 1922.[5] In the 1930s, it seemed for a while as if the Soviet Union might become Japan's next target after the Japanese annexation of the northeastern Chinese region of Manchuria. In fact, in late summer 1939, the Red Army and the Japanese army became engaged in a bloody battle along the Mongolian-Chinese border at Khalkin Gol. Japan's thrust southward—which ultimately brought it into conflict with the United States—and the Soviet Union's preoccupation with Nazi Germany kept the two from resuming their old rivalry. When the Soviets attacked the Japanese army in Manchuria at the very end of World War II, it marked the fourth Russo-Japanese conflict of the twentieth century. From the Soviet point of view, here was a golden opportunity to settle past scores and to regain lost territories.

### The UN Question

The third major topic at Yalta dealt with the organization of the United Nations. Roosevelt proposed, and Churchill and Stalin quickly accepted, the power of an absolute veto for the world's great powers over any United Nations action they opposed. In 1919, when President Woodrow Wilson unsuccessfully proposed the US entry into the League of Nations, his opponents argued that in doing so, the foreign policy of the United States would be dictated by the League. A US veto at the United Nation would prevent such an eventuality. The United States, however, could not expect to be the only nation with a veto. Roosevelt thus proposed that each of the Big Five—the United

States, the Soviet Union, Great Britain, France, and China—be given the power to veto a UN action. It also meant that the United Nations could act only when the Big Five were in concert—and that proved to be a rare occasion. The weakness of the United Nations was thus built into its charter.

An example of what this sort of arrangement meant in practice may be seen in this exchange between Stalin and Churchill at Yalta (concerning the issue of Hong Kong, a colony Great Britain had taken from China in the nineteenth century):

> Stalin: Suppose China . . . demands Hong Kong to be returned to her?

> Churchill: I could say "no." I would have a right to say that the power of [the United Nations] could not be used against us.[6]

### The German Question

The fourth question, the immediate fate of Germany, was resolved when the Big Three decided that, as a temporary expedient, the territory of the Third Reich—including Austria, which Hitler had annexed in 1938—was to be divided into zones of occupation among the three participants at the Yalta Conference. Shortly, the French insisted that as an ally and a major power they, too, were entitled to an occupation zone. Stalin did not object to the inclusion of another Western, capitalist power, but insisted that if France were to obtain a zone, it must come from the holdings of the United States and Great Britain. The result was the Four-Power occupation of Germany and Austria, as well as of their respective capitals, Berlin and Vienna.

As the Big Three returned home from Yalta, they were fairly satisfied that they had gotten what they had sought. As events would show, however, Yalta immediately became the focal point of the Cold War. Poland and its postwar borders, the United Nations, the Red Army's entrance into the war against Japan, and the German and Austrian questions all became bones of contention between East and West in the months and years ahead.

## The Potsdam Conference

By late spring 1945, with Berlin in ruins and the defeat of Japan all but a certainty, the Grand Alliance fell apart with remarkable speed once the quarrel over Eastern Europe picked up in intensity, with wartime cooperation turning into mutual suspicion. Still, the two sides agreed to meet again in July 1945, this time for a conference in Berlin, the capital of Hitler's Third Reich. The near-total destruction of the city led to a change in venue to nearby Potsdam.

The Big Three at Potsdam were Joseph Stalin, Harry Truman (who had succeeded Roosevelt in April 1945), and Winston Churchill (who later in the conference would be replaced by Britain's new premier, Clement Attlee).

This meeting accomplished little. The Polish question came up at once, particularly the new border drawn at the expense of Germany, which the Western leaders reluctantly accepted. The Western leaders also grudgingly recognized the new socialist government in Poland, but they repeatedly voiced their objections to other client governments Stalin had set up in Eastern Europe, particularly those of Romania and Bulgaria. Stalin, however, considered the transformation of the political picture in Eastern Europe a closed issue, comparing it to the creation of the new government in Italy under Western supervision, which had replaced the previous fascist government, an ally of Nazi Germany. The sharp exchanges at Potsdam heightened suspicions and resolved nothing.

Another source of disagreement was the issue of reparations from Germany. Stalin insisted on the large sum of $20 billion and the West agreed in principle. The problem was that reparations would have to come from a German state that was utterly destroyed and could not possibly pay such a huge amount. Stalin's demand meant stripping Germany of whatever industrial equipment it still possessed and sending it to the Soviet Union. This scenario presented several disadvantages to the West. It would leave Germany impoverished, weak, and dependent on outside help. It was feared that a helpless Germany, moreover, would only be an invitation to further Soviet expansion westward. An impoverished Germany, besides conceivably succumbing to Communism, would be neither an importer of US goods nor an exporter of its own goods (a central component of its economic reconstruction). As the United States was already contemplating economic aid to Germany, its assistance would simply pass through Germany to the Soviet Union as reparations.

The Soviets insisted that at the Yalta Conference their allies had promised them the sum of $20 billion. US representatives replied that this figure was intended to be the basis of discussion, depending upon conditions in Germany after the war. The devastation of Germany meant the Soviets would have to settle for far less.

To Truman the solution was simple. The Soviets would have to find whatever reparations they could come up with in their Eastern zone. They did so by plundering the eastern—the poorer, mostly agricultural—part of Germany. The reparations question marked the first instance of the inability of the wartime allies to agree on how to govern Germany. It established the principle that in each zone of occupation the military commander would have free rein. As such, the occupying powers never came up with a unified policy for Germany, thereby setting the stage for the long-enduring division of Germany. Within three years there was no point in pretending that a single German state existed.

The only thing on which Truman and Stalin agreed at Potsdam was on Japan. Neither, it seems, was willing to let the Japanese off the hook. Surrender could only be unconditional. While at Potsdam, Truman received word that the first atomic bomb had been successfully tested at Alamogordo, New Mexico. Truman knew of Japanese efforts to end the war through negotiations, but with the atomic bomb he could now end the conflict on his own terms and keep the Soviet Union out of postwar Japan. Stalin, similar to Truman, did not want a quick Japanese surrender. At Yalta he had pledged to enter the war ninety days after hostilities against Germany had ended, and he had every intention of doing so. It would give him the chance to redress old grievances against Japan and to extend his influence in the Far East. Truman did not tell Stalin about the atomic bomb—of which Stalin already was well aware—and his plans to use it against Japan. Stalin was led to believe that Truman still wanted the Soviet Union to attack Japan. With the United States secretly planning to drop atomic bombs on Japan, and Stalin secretly planning to attack its forces in Manchuria, Japan was doomed.

The defeat of Japan brought no improvement in East-West relations. Indeed, the bombings of Hiroshima and Nagasaki gave the Soviets still more reason to distrust and suspect the intentions of the United States. Each point of disagreement was magnified; each misunderstanding became a weapon; each hostile act was positive proof of the other side's evil intentions.

But one could not yet speak of a full-blown, irreversible Cold War. This came in 1947, when the conflict reached a new plateau. In fact, many historians, in the Soviet Union as well as in the West, see that year as the true beginning of the Cold War. It was then that the United States declared its commitment to contain—by economic as well as military means—all manifestations of Communist expansion wherever it occurred. In the same year, a Soviet delegation walked out of an economic conference that concerned itself with the rebuilding of Europe under US auspices. With this act East-West cooperation came to an end and the battle lines were more clearly drawn.

## The Truman Doctrine

"The turning point in American foreign policy," in the words of President Truman, came early in 1947 when the United States faced the prospect of a Communist victory in a civil war in Greece.[7] The end of World War II had not brought peace to Greece. Instead, it saw the continuation of a bitter conflict between the right and the left, one that in early 1947 promised a Communist victory. The British, who for a long time had played a major role in Greek affairs, had supported the right (the army and the Greek monarchy), but exhausted by the war and unable to go on, they ended their involvement in Greece, dumping the problem unceremoniously into Washington's lap: If the United States wanted a non-Communist government in Greece, it would have to see to it and would have to go it alone. Truman, a man seldom plagued by self-doubt, quickly jumped into the breach. He also understood, however, that the US public would be slow to back such an undertaking. At the end of World

*President Harry S. Truman and General Dwight Eisenhower, January 1951. Two years later, the general would succeed Truman as president.*

War II, the public had expected that within two years the US military presence in Europe would end. Truman's involvement in Greece, instead, would extend it and postpone a disengagement from Europe indefinitely. In fact, it meant an increased, continued US military presence in Europe. To achieve his aim, Truman knew he would have to "scare the hell out of the American people."[8] And he succeeded admirably.

In March 1947, Truman addressed a joint session of Congress to present his case. In his oration, one of the most stirring Cold War speeches by a US political leader, Truman insisted that the war in Greece was not a matter between Greeks; rather, it was caused by outside aggression. International Communism was on the march and the orders came from its center, Moscow. It was the duty of the United States "to support free peoples who are resisting attempted subjugation by armed minorities or by outside pressures." The United States must play the role of the champion of democracy and "orderly political processes." A Communist victory in Greece, Truman declared, threatened to set off similar events in other countries, like a long row of dominoes or pearls slipping off a string. "If Greece should fall under the control of an armed minority, the effect upon its neighbor, Turkey, would be immediate and serious. Confusion and disorder might well spread throughout the entire Middle East."[9] This speech, which became known as the Truman Doctrine, firmly set US foreign policy on a path committed to suppressing radicalism and revolution throughout the world. All US interventions since that day invoked what became known as the "domino theory": If country X falls, then Y and Z will surely follow.

But there was no clear evidence that the guiding hand of Stalin was behind the Greek revolution. Stalin, it seems, kept his part of the bargain he made with Churchill in October 1944, by which the two agreed that after the war Greece would fall into Britain's sphere of influence. Churchill later wrote that Stalin adhered to this understanding.[10] If anything, Stalin wanted the Greek revolt to "fold up . . . as quickly as possible" because he feared precisely what ultimately happened.[11] He told the Yugoslav vice president, Milovan Djilas: "What do you think? That . . . the United States, the most powerful state in the world will permit you to break their line of communications in the Mediterranean Sea? Nonsense, and we have no navy."[12] But to Truman and most of the US public it was a simple matter: All revolutions in the name of Karl Marx must necessarily come out of Moscow.[13] The Republican Party, not to be left behind in the holy struggle against "godless Communism," quickly backed Truman. Thus, a national consensus was forged, one that remained intact until the divisive years of the Vietnam War.

The first application of the Truman Doctrine worked remarkably well. US military and economic aid rapidly turned the tide in Greece; the Communists were defeated and the monarchy was spared. All this was achieved without sending US troops into combat. There appeared to be no limits to US power. This truly appeared to be, as Henry Luce, the influential publisher of *Time* and *Life* magazines, had said earlier, the "American Century."[14] Yet, at about the same time, events in China showed that there were in fact limits on the ability of the United States to affect the course of history, when the US-supported government and its army there began to unravel.

## The Marshall Plan

Three months after the pronouncement of the Truman Doctrine, the Truman administration took another step to protect its interests in Europe when it unveiled the Marshall Plan. It was named after General George Marshall, Truman's secretary of state, who first publicly proposed a program intended to provide funds for the rebuilding of the heavily damaged economies of Europe. The Marshall Plan was in large part a humanitarian gesture for which many Europeans expressed their gratitude for decades to come. It was also intended as a means to preserve the prosperity the war had brought to US society. At the end of the war, the United States took the lead in establishing an international system of "free trade"—or at least relatively unrestricted trade. But international commerce—in this case access to European markets—demanded a strong and prosperous Europe that was capable of purchasing US goods. The United States proved to be extremely successful in helping to shore up the financial system of the Western, capitalist world. In this sense, the Marshall Plan well complemented the Truman Doctrine as a potent political weapon in the containment of Soviet influence. The Marshall Plan, Truman explained, was but "the other half of the same walnut."[15]

The Marshall Plan helped to stymie the ambitions of the Communist parties in Western Europe. After initial strong showings, particularly in France and Italy, their fortunes declined rapidly under the impact of the Marshall Plan.

At the end of World War II, the US wartime Lend-Lease program for the Soviet Union—war matériel valued at $11 billion—came to an end. Moscow applied for continued economic assistance from the United States, but nothing came of it. Officially, Washington was willing to extend Marshall Plan aid to Eastern Europe, including the Soviet Union. But it would come with preconditions. For one, aid was dependent on proper Soviet behavior in Eastern Europe. Moreover, the aid would have to be administered, as in Western Europe, by the United States, not by its recipients.

Several East European states were receptive to the plan, particularly Poland and Czechoslovakia, both of which were governed by coalitions of Communist and non-Communist parties. The Soviet Union, too, at first appeared ready to participate in the rebuilding of Europe under the auspices of the Marshall Plan. Its foreign minister, Viacheslav Molotov, came to Paris with a large entourage of economic experts to discuss the implementation of the plan. But shortly afterward, he left the conference declaring that the US conditions were unacceptable as their implementation would entail the presence of US officials on East European and Soviet soil and would, therefore, infringe upon his country's national sovereignty. Molotov did not say publicly that the presence of US representatives in Eastern Europe would reveal the glaring weaknesses of the Soviet Union and its satellites. The Marshall Plan was a gamble Stalin apparently felt he could not afford. Stalin then pressured the governments of Poland and Czechoslovakia to reject the Marshall Plan.

Stalin went beyond merely applying pressure on Czechoslovakia. In February 1948, a Communist coup in that country ended its coalition government and brought Czechoslovakia firmly into the Soviet orbit. This act regenerated in the West the image of an aggressive, brutal, and calculating leadership in Moscow. Once again, Czechoslovakia fell victim to the machinations of a dictator. The Communist coup in Czechoslovakia, only ten years after Hitler had brought it under his heel, did much to underscore in the West the lessons of Munich. During the coup, Czechoslovakia's foreign minister, Jan Masaryk, died under mysterious circumstances, an act generally attributed in the West to Stalin. The coup had a deep impact on public opinion in the West and became prima facie evidence that one could not do business with the Soviets.

Stalin's rejection of Marshall Plan aid also meant that the East European countries would have to rebuild their war-torn economies with their own limited resources, under Moscow's umbrella and without US aid and Western technology. In response to the consolidation of Soviet power in the center of Europe, Churchill, in a speech in Fulton, Missouri, in 1946, reminded his audience that an "Iron Curtain" had descended across Europe—from Stettin on the Baltic Sea to Trieste on the Adriatic Sea—a dividing line that lasted for more than forty years.

## Limits of Soviet Power

Immediately after Stalin appeared to have consolidated his position in Eastern Europe, however, the first crack appeared in what had been a monolithic Communist facade. The Yugoslav Communist leadership, under the direction of Josip Tito, broke with the Kremlin over the fundamental question of national sovereignty. Moscow insisted that the interests of any and all foreign Communist parties must be subordinate to those of the Soviet Union, officially the center of an international movement. The Yugoslav Communists insisted, however, on running their own affairs as they saw fit. In the summer of 1948, this bitter, smoldering quarrel became public. Tito refused to subordinate the interests of his state to those of Stalin, and consequently Yugoslavia became the first Communist nation in Eastern Europe to assert its independence from the Soviet Union.

In the West, the prevailing view was that "Titoism"—a nationalist deviation from the international Communist community—was a unique, singular incident. Stalin knew better, however. He understood that Titoism was no isolated phenomenon, that other East European nations—given the chance—could readily fall to the same temptation. To forestall such an eventuality, he launched a bloody purge of East European "national Communists," a purge so thorough that, until his death in March 1953, Eastern Europe remained quiet.

In 1948, it also became evident that the division of Germany and Berlin would become permanent. All talks on German reunification had broken down, and the West took steps to create a separate West German state, with West Berlin, a city 110 miles inside the Soviet sector, becoming a part of West Germany. When, during World War II, Stalin had agreed on the division of Berlin among the allies, he had not bargained on such an eventuality. The last thing he wanted was a Western outpost inside his zone. Berlin had little military value for the West since it was trapped and outgunned by the Soviet army, which occupied East Germany, but it served as a valuable political, capitalist spearhead pointing into Eastern Europe, eventually becoming a showplace of Western prosperity. Moreover, West Berlin was invaluable as a center of espionage operations. In June 1948, Stalin took a dangerous, calculated risk to eliminate the Western presence in that city when he closed the land routes into West Berlin in the hope of convincing the West to abandon Berlin. The West had few options. It neither wanted World War III nor could afford—for political and psychological reasons—to abandon West Berlin and its 2 million people to the Communists. The result was the "Berlin Airlift," by which the West resupplied West Berlin with transport planes flown over East Germany.

*West Berlin children on rubble mounds cheer the arrival of a US aircraft filled with food during the airlift, 1948*

During the next ten months, over 270,000 flights carried an average of 4,000 tons of supplies a day to the beleaguered city. Stalin dared not attack the planes for neither would he risk World War III. Finally, in May 1949, Stalin yielded by reopening the highways, linking the city once again with West Germany. Stalin had lost his gamble and there was no point in perpetuating the show-down. The first Berlin crisis was over.

Throughout the late 1940s, US policymakers assumed that the Soviet Union was preparing for an attack on Western Europe, a supposition based largely on fear rather than on fact. The image of an expansionist, aggressive Soviet Union was the result of three factors. First, the Soviet army was ensconced in the center of Europe. Second, its position there was seen not so much as the logical consequence of the war but as the fulfillment of Soviet propaganda predicting the triumph of socialism throughout the world. Third, the differences of opinion between the Soviet Union and the West had taken on the character of a military confrontation, and people began to fear the worst.

Once the specter of an inevitably expansionist Soviet state gripped the Western imagination, it became almost impossible to shake this image. This view of Soviet intentions buttressed the US arguments that the Soviet Union must be contained at all costs. The subsequent "containment theory," first spelled out in 1947 in a lengthy essay by George Kennan, a State Department expert on the Soviet Union, seemed to be working reasonably well with the application of the Truman Doctrine and the Marshall Plan. In his essay, however, Kennan had not make clear the sort of containment of the Soviet Union he had in mind. Later, he explained that he had meant a political, and not a military, containment. Yet the central feature of Truman's containment policy was its military nature. In 1949, the United States created NATO, the North Atlantic Treaty Organization, an alliance that boxed in the Soviet Union along its western flank, followed by additional alliances elsewhere. One person's containment theory is another person's capitalist encirclement. Stalin—and his successors—responded by digging in.

## Notes

1. Often called the Molotov-Ribbentrop Pact, after the foreign minister of Nazi Germany, Joachim Ribbentrop, and the Soviet Union's commissar for foreign affairs, Viacheslav Molotov, who worked out the details.

2. Winston S. Churchill, *The Second World War, VI, Triumph and Tragedy* (New York: Bantam, [orig. 1953] 1962), p. 329.

3. Quoted from "The Yalta Declaration on Poland," as found in US Department of State, *Foreign Relations of the United States: The Conferences at Malta and Yalta, 1945* (Washington, DC: US Government Printing Office, 1955), p. 938.

4. Quoted from a cabinet meeting of September 21, 1945, in Walter Millis, ed., *The Forrestal Diaries* (New York: Viking, 1951), p. 96.

5. The US president, Woodrow Wilson, also sent troops into eastern Siberia at that time, ostensibly to keep an eye on the Japanese. Earlier, at the end of World War I, Wilson had sent troops into European Russia, ostensibly to protect supplies that had been sent to the Russian ally—led at the time by Tsar Nicholas II—to keep them from falling into German hands. The Soviets have always rejected this explanation and have argued that US intentions were to overthrow the fledgling Communist government.

6. James F. Byrnes, *Frankly Speaking* (New York: Harper and Brothers, 1947), p. 37.

7. Harry S. Truman, *Memoirs, II, Years of Trial and Hope* (Garden City, NY: Doubleday, 1956), p. 106.

8. The words are Senator Arthur Vandenberg's, cited in William A. Williams, *The Tragedy of American Diplomacy*, rev. ed. (New York: Delta, 1962), pp. 269–270.

9. "Text of President Truman's Speech on New Foreign Policy," *New York Times*, March 13, 1947, p. 2.

10. Churchill's report to the House of Commons, February 27, 1945, in which he stated that he "was encouraged by Stalin's behavior about Greece." *The Second World War, VI*, p. 334. In his "Iron Curtain" telegram to Truman, May 12, 1945, Churchill expressed concern about Soviet influence throughout Eastern Europe, "except Greece." Lord Moran, *Churchill: Taken from the Diaries of Lord Moran, The Struggle for Survival, 1940–1965* (Boston: Houghton Mifflin, 1966), p. 847. Churchill to the House of Commons, January 23, 1948, on Greece: "Agreements were kept [by Stalin] when they were made." Robert Rhodes James, *Winston S. Churchill: His Complete Speeches, 1897–1963, VII, 1943–1949* (New York: Chelsea House, 1974), p. 7583.

11. Milovan Djilas, *Conversations with Stalin* (New York: Harcourt, Brace and World, 1962), pp. 181–182.

12. Ibid., p. 182.

13. After World War II, the most militant Communist head of state was Josip Tito of Yugoslavia. It was Tito, rather than Stalin, who openly supported the Greek

Communist insurgency by providing them weapons and refuge in Yugoslavia. Tito's actions were seen in the West as evidence of Stalin's involvement via a proxy; yet even Tito, once he broke with Stalin in 1948, shut his border to the Greek Communists and abandoned them.

14. Henry Luce, "American Century," in W. A. Swanberg, *Luce and His Empire* (New York: Dell, 1972), pp. 257–261.

15. Quoted in Walter LaFeber, *America, Russia, and the Cold War, 1945–1984*, 5th ed. (New York: Knopf, 1985), pp. 62–63.

# 3

# The Cold War in Asia: A Change of Venue

The Cold War, which had its origins in Europe, where tensions mounted between East and West over the status of Germany, Poland, and other East European countries, became even more inflamed in Asia. In 1945, US policy in East Asia was focused primarily on the elimination of the menace of Japanese militarism and on support of the Nationalist government of China under Jiang Jieshi (Chiang Kai-shek)[1] as the main pillar of stability in Asia. But within five short years the United States was confronted with a set of affairs very different from what Washington had envisioned just after the war.

In China, under the leadership of Chairman Mao Zedong (Mao Tse-tung), Communists defeated the Nationalist regime and then proclaimed the People's Republic of China (PRC) on October 1, 1949. The largest nation on earth, in terms of population, was now under Communist rule. Only nine months later, the Communist forces of North Korea invaded anti-Communist South Korea. By this time, the United States and the Soviet Union had withdrawn from the Korean peninsula, leaving behind two Korean zones, both of which claimed the right to unify Korea. The North Korean invasion immediately brought the United States back to Korea on a permanent basis. For the first time the super-powers in the Cold War clashed on the field of battle, if only by way of prox-ies. The Korean War had a great impact on the US-led military occupation of defeated Japan, which became a US military outpost directed against the Soviet Union and Communist China.

## The Allied Occupation of Japan
The Allied Occupation of Japan, between September 1945 and May 1952, was unique in the annals of history. As the US historian and diplomat Edwin

**East Asia (1945)**

Reischauer noted, "never before had one advanced nation attempted to reform the supposed faults of another advanced nation from within. And never did the military occupation of one world power by another prove so satisfactory to the victors and tolerable to the vanquished."[2] From the outset, the US policy in Japan was benevolent and constructive, although it had its punitive aspects as well. The Japanese, who had never in their long history been defeated and garrisoned by foreign troops, expected the worst. Not only did their fears of US brutality prove unfounded, but so also did US fears of continued hostility by Japanese diehards. The two nations, which had fought each other so bitterly for almost four years, made amends, and in a remarkably short time they established enduring bonds of friendship and cooperation. This was partly the result of the generous treatment by the US occupation forces, and partly the result of the receptivity and goodwill of the Japanese themselves. They welcomed the opportunity to rid themselves of the scourge of militarism that had led their nation into the blind alley of defeat and destruction. And they appreciated the sight of US GIs brandishing not rifles, but chocolate bars and chewing gum. Even more important for securing the active support of the Japanese was the decision by US authorities to retain the emperor on the throne rather than try him as a war criminal, as many in the United States demanded. Indeed, one important reason why the Japanese were so docile and cooperative with the US occupation forces was that their emperor, whom they were in the habit of dutifully obeying, had implored them to be cooperative.

Prior to the defeat of Japan, officials in Washington were already planning a reform program under a military occupation. The Allied Occupation of Japan was, as the name implies, supposedly an Allied affair, but it was in fact dominated by the United States, despite the desire of the Soviet Union and other nations to play a role in it. Thus, unlike Germany, Japan was placed under a single-power occupation. General Douglas MacArthur was appointed Supreme Commander of Allied Powers (SCAP), and under his authority a broad-ranging reform program began. The government of Japan was not abolished and replaced by a military administration as was the case in defeated Germany; rather, the Japanese cabinet was maintained as the instrument by which the reform directives of SCAP were administered.

The principal objectives of the US-controlled occupation program were demilitarization and democratization. Japan's army and navy were abolished, its military personnel brought home from overseas and dismissed, its war plants dismantled, and its weapons destroyed. Some 3 million Japanese soldiers were repatriated to Japan from all over Asia and the Pacific mainly by US ships, as were almost as many Japanese civilians. Also, as a measure to rid Japan of militarism, Japanese wartime leaders were put on trial at an international military tribunal in Tokyo. In court proceedings similar to the Nuremberg trials of Nazi war criminals, twenty-eight leading figures were accused of "planning a war of aggression" and "crimes against humanity," found guilty, and given severe sentences. Seven of them were hanged and seventeen others were sentenced to prison for life. Additionally, several thousand other Japanese military officers were tried and found guilty of a variety of wartime atrocities.

The United States sought to rid Japan of its ultranationalist ideology, steeped in Shintoism and emperor worship. On January 1, 1946, the emperor was called upon to make a radio speech to the nation renouncing imperial divinity. SCAP sought to abolish "State Shinto," the aspect of Japan's native religion on which the divinity of the emperor was based. Textbooks were censored to rid them of such ideas and other content considered militaristic.

Democratization of Japan was a more complex matter and would take longer to achieve, but the first major step in that direction was a new constitution promulgated in May 1947. Drafted by MacArthur's staff, it provided for a fundamental political reform. It provided Japan with a parliamentary system similar to that of Britain, an institution consistent with Japan's prewar political experience. The people of Japan were made sovereign (meaning, in effect, that government power ultimately rested on the consent of the governed, the people). The emperor, who had been sovereign in the old constitution, became no more than a symbol of the state, which is to say he would no longer have any political authority. All laws were to be passed by a majority in the popularly elected House of Representatives in the Diet (Japan's parliament). The constitution also included extensive provisions spelling out the civil rights of Japanese citizens. The most striking feature of the new constitution—one in keeping with the demilitarization objective—was Article Nine, which outlawed war and forbade Japan to maintain land, sea, or air forces. MacArthur himself ordered that this provision be put into the constitution, but the idea was enthusiastically endorsed by Japan's political leaders and a war-weary nation.

As the occupation continued under the watchful eye of MacArthur, a host of other reforms were imposed upon the Japanese. The economic reforms included the dismantling of the old *zaibatsu* (the huge financial cartels that dominated Japan's prewar economy), a land reform that redistributed farmland for the benefit of poor farmers and at the expense of wealthy landowners, and a labor reform creating Japan's first genuine trade union movement. There were also far-reaching social and educational reforms, all of which were intended to make Japan a more democratic society. Generally, these various reform programs were remarkably successful, largely because they addressed real needs in Japan and because the Japanese themselves desired the reforms.

One of the anomalies of the occupation was that democracy was implanted in Japan by a military command, that is, by General MacArthur and his staff. SCAP censored the Japanese press, disallowed free speech, ruled by fiat, and issued directives to the Japanese government. Also anomalous was the character of General MacArthur as a reformer. In Japan he was aloof, arrogant, and almighty. The defeated Japanese seemed to need an august authority figure—a shogun behind the throne as it were—and the imperious MacArthur seemed destined to play just such a role. Although he claimed to like the Japanese people, his manner toward them was condescending, and he often expressed contempt for their culture. In his view, the Japanese were but twelve-year-old children who must be shown the way from "feudalism" to democracy.[3] But despite MacArthur's arrogance and the military cast of the occupation, he and his staff possessed a genuine reformist zeal, and their sense of mission contributed greatly to the successful rooting of democratic ideas and institutions in Japan.

The menace of Japanese militarism was thus eliminated and supplanted by democracy, but US minds soon perceived a larger menace looming on the horizon: the spread of Communism in East Asia. The Communist victory in the civil war in China in 1949 and Communist aggression in Korea in the following year caused the US government to recast its policy in Japan reflecting Cold War exigencies. Safely under US control, Japan was to be prepared to play a key role in the US policy of containment of Communism.

It is difficult to arrive at a final assessment of the occupation of Japan, for opinions differ greatly according to one's ideology and nationality. That the occupation program, with its various reforms, was in every instance a grand success is certainly debatable. Many Japanese historians as well as revisionist historians in the United States have argued that the US exercise of power in postwar Japan was excessive, that the "reverse course" policies negated many of the democratic reforms, and that Japan was victimized by zealous US anti-Communist policies. But there is little question that Japan emerged from the experience with a working democratic system of government and a more democratic society, a passionate pacifism, the beginnings of an economic recovery, and a large measure of military security. And the United States emerged with a new, potentially strong ally strategically located in a part of the world confronted with the spread of Communist revolution.

## The Civil War in China

The victory of the Chinese Communists over the Nationalist government of China in 1949 was the culmination of a long struggle between two revolutionary parties—the Communists and the Nationalists—that began back in the 1920s. After winning the first round of that struggle in 1928, the Nationalist Party, under its domineering leader Jiang Jieshi, sought to exterminate the rural-based Communist Party led by Mao Zedong. In 1935, the Communists barely escaped annihilation by embarking on the epic "Long March," a trek of over 6,000 miles, after which they secured themselves in a remote area in northwestern China. When the war with Japan began in mid-1937, Mao persuaded Jiang to set aside their differences and form a united front to defend China from the Japanese invaders. During the war against Japan (1937–1945), the Chinese Communist Party (CCP) and its army grew enormously while the Nationalist regime deteriorated badly. The Communists' success was the product of inspired leadership, effective mobilization of the peasantry for the war effort, and skillful use of guerrilla warfare tactics against the Japanese. By the end of the war the Communists controlled nineteen "liberated areas," rural regions mainly in northern China, with a combined population of about 100 million, and the size of their army had increased tenfold from about 50,000 to over half a million. In contrast, the Nationalist government and army had retreated deep into the interior to Chongqing (Chungking) during the war and failed to launch a successful counteroffensive against the Japanese. Meanwhile, wartime inflation was rampant, as was corruption in Jiang's Nationalist government and army. Jiang barely used his army, supplied and trained by the United States, against the Japanese, but rather used it to guard against the spread of Communist forces or left it to languish in garrison duty.

When World War II ended with the US defeat of Japan, civil war in China was all but a certainty as the Nationalists and Communists rushed to fill the vacuum left behind by the defeated Japanese. Both sought to expand their areas of control and particularly went after the major cities in northern China. Jiang issued orders, sanctioned by Washington, that Japanese commanders were to surrender only to Nationalist military officers rather than to the Communists.

The United States continued to support Jiang's government as it had during the war, but it wished to avert the impending civil war and thus urged Jiang to find a peaceful solution with the Communists. Even before the war ended, Washington had sent a special envoy, Patrick Hurley, to China to serve as a mediator between the two sides. He succeeded in bringing Mao and Jiang to the negotiating table in August 1945, but could not get them to agree to stop fighting. President Harry Truman tried again to find a negotiated solution, and to that end he sent General George C. Marshall to China in December 1945 to mediate the dispute. The sixty-five-year-old general, who had dreams of retiring, spent more than a year in China only to come away empty-handed. While he was in China, the Mao-Jiang rivalry escalated into a full-fledged civil war that began in the spring of 1946.

Mao had been willing to get his foot in the door by agreeing to join a coalition government, but Jiang would have none of it. He would not share power with the Communists. Meanwhile, the United States continued to provide military and economic aid to the Nationalists. The civil war resumed after Jiang concluded that the only solution to the problem was a military one and that it was obtainable.

At the outset of the war, the Nationalists had good reason to be confident of victory. The Nationalist Army still had a numerical superiority of three to one over the Communist forces. It was much better equipped by virtue of huge amounts of US military aid that included artillery pieces, tanks, and trucks, as well as light arms and ammunition. Moreover, the Nationalists also had available the use of US airplanes and troop ships to move their forces. In contrast, the Communist People's Liberation Army (PLA), was relatively poorly equipped and had practically no outside support. Given the Nationalist edge, it is not surprising that Jiang's armies were victorious in the early months of the war, defeating the PLA in almost every battle in northern China. But within a year, the tide began to shift.

The battle for China took place mainly in Manchuria, the northeastern area of China, which had been under Japanese control since the early 1930s.

It was prized by both for its rich resources and as the most industrialized area of China (thanks to the Japanese and to the earlier imperialist presence of Russia). Immediately after World War II, Manchuria was temporarily under the control of the Soviet Union, whose Red Army had attacked the Japanese forces there in the closing days of the war and "liberated" the area. On August 14, 1945, the Soviet Union concluded a treaty of friendship with the Nationalist government of China, which included provisions for the withdrawal of Soviet forces from Manchuria to be completed within three months after the surrender of Japan. Before the Nationalist Army could occupy the area, the Red Army hastily stripped Manchuria of all Japanese military and industrial equipment that was not nailed down and shipped it—together with Japanese prisoners of war—into the Soviet Union in order to support its own economic rehabilitation. Meanwhile, Chinese Communist forces had begun entering Manchuria immediately after the surrender of Japan. A poorly equipped PLA force of about 100,000 troops surrounded the major cities of Manchuria. Against the advice of his US military advisers, Jiang sent his best divisions to remote Manchuria, where they could be reinforced only with great difficulty. When the battle for Manchuria began, Jiang's Nationalist forces held the major cities, railways, and other strategic points, while the PLA held the surrounding countryside. The Communists were not assisted by the Red Army in Manchuria (or elsewhere), but before the Soviets left Manchuria they did provide the PLA with a much needed cache of captured Japanese weapons (mainly light arms—rifles, machine guns, light artillery, and ammunition).

The PLA won the major battles in Manchuria in late 1947 and 1948. Nationalist Army combat casualties ran into the hundreds of thousands, but it lost almost as many soldiers to the other side either as captives or defectors. As the PLA advanced, it captured large amounts of US weapons from the retreating Nationalist Army. In the end, it was the better-disciplined and mobile PLA, not the Nationalists, who took the offensive. The Nationalists, their forces spread thin, were unable to hold open the transportation lines needed to bring up reinforcements and supplies.

After the last battle in Manchuria, the momentum shifted to the Communists. The last major engagement of the war was fought in the fall of 1948 at Xuzhou (Hsuchow), about 100 miles north of the Nationalist capital of Nanjing (Nanking). Trying to hang on, Jiang deployed 400,000 of his best troops, equipped with tanks and heavy artillery. After two months of fighting, however, in which the Nationalists lost 200,000 men, the larger and more mobile Communist army won a decisive victory.

It became a matter of time before the complete Nationalist collapse. In October 1949, Jiang fled with the remainder of his army to the Chinese island of Taiwan. There the embattled Nationalist leader continued to claim that his Nationalist regime (formally titled the Republic of China) was the only legitimate government of China, and he promised to return to the mainland to drive

*Mao Zedong (Mao Tse-tung), chairman of the Chinese Communist Party, October 1, 1950, the first anniversary of the founding of the People's Republic of China*

off the "Communist bandits." In the meantime, on October 1, 1949, Mao Zedong and his victorious Communist Party proclaimed the founding of the PRC with Beijing (Peking) as its capital.

The continuing Chinese civil war became a part of the global Cold War. The new Communist government in Beijing insisted it would never rest until its rival on Taiwan was completely defeated; conversely, the Nationalist government was determined never to submit to the Communists. The continued existence of "two Chinas," each intent on destroying the other and each allied to one of the superpowers, would remain for decades a major Cold War issue and source of tension in East Asia.

The Communist victory was the product of many factors, but direct outside intervention was not one of them. Neither superpower, nor any other nation, was engaged militarily in the conflict once it began in 1946. After Jiang launched the full-scale civil war in mid-1946, General Marshall made clear to him that the United States would not underwrite his war. Thereafter, Washington turned down Jiang's urgent requests for additional aid and provided only a reduced amount of assistance after 1946. If military aid had been a factor, the Nationalists surely should have won, for the United States provided them far more assistance, military and otherwise, during and after World War II than the Soviet Union provided the Chinese Communists. Since 1941, the United States had provided Nationalist China with massive military and economic aid, amounting to more than $2 billion.

The postwar policy of the Soviet Union toward Nationalist China was ambivalent, as was its attitude toward the Chinese Communists. It is noteworthy that at the end of World War II, Stalin signed a treaty with the Nationalist government of China and publicly recognized Jiang's rule of China. The Soviet Red Army did little to deter the takeover of Manchuria by Jiang's Nationalist Army, and it withdrew from Manchuria not long after the date to which the two sides had agreed.

The Soviet Union's looting of Manchuria for "war booty" benefited neither of the combatants in China and was objectionable to both. Moreover, Stalin made no real effort to support or encourage the Chinese Communists in their bid for power, except for turning over the cache of Japanese arms in Manchuria. (The transfer of these weapons may have been at the initiative of the local Red Army commander.) On the contrary, Stalin is known to have stated in 1948, when the victory of the Chinese Communists was all but certain, that he had counseled the Chinese Communists not to fight the Nationalists because their prospect for victory seemed remote. It may well have been that Stalin would have been happier to deal with a weak Nationalist Chinese government than with a new and vigorous Communist government.

Chinese domestic factors were the major determinant of the civil war's outcome: peasant support for the Communists (85 percent of the population), the PLA's high morale and effective military strategy, the corruption of the Nationalist regime, the low morale and ineffective strategy of its army, and the inept political and military leadership of General Jiang Jieshi. The Nationalist government also had to deal with runaway inflation, corruption, and a demoralized Chinese population. The Communists, by contrast, enjoyed much greater popular support, especially from the large mass of peasants, because of their successful land redistribution programs. The Nationalists, in contrast, had neither a land reform program nor offered protection for tenant farmers against greedy and overbearing landowners.

The turn of events in China had immediate political repercussions in the United States. Shortly before the civil war ended, the US Senate Foreign Relations Committee heard testimony from US teachers, businesspeople, journalists, and missionaries who had lived in China for years. They were unanimous in their criticism of Jiang's regime and warned that any additional aid would only fall into the hands of corrupt officials or the Communists. Truman understood this, but knew that to cut off all aid to its anti-Communist client promised to invite the inevitable political charge that he had abandoned a worthy ally, albeit a hopelessly corrupt one, in the struggle against international Communism. The Republicans, who had been sharpening their knives for several years, did precisely what Truman had feared. No sooner had the Chinese civil war ended, than they were blaming the Democrats for "losing China." Republican senator Joseph McCarthy went so far as to blame the "loss of China" on Communists and Communist sympathizers in the State Department.

It mattered little that McCarthy's charges proved to be unfounded. The Democrats were nonetheless saddled with the "loss of China" to international Communism.

The "loss of China," as if it ever belonged to United States to begin with, drove the Truman administration farther to the right in its foreign policy. Truman, who had already invoked his Communist "containment policy," became ever more vigilant to check the spread of Communism to other parts of Asia. And when, immediately afterward, he was faced with a Vietnamese Communist victory over French colonialism in Indochina, Communist aggression in Korea, and the prospect of "losing" Korea, he responded immediately and forcefully.

## The Korean War

On June 25, 1950, nine months after the Communist victory in China, the armed forces of Communist North Korea launched a full-scale attack on South Korea. The United States and its major allies responded swiftly and decisively to halt what they perceived to be the forceful expansion of international Communism and a blatant violation of the United Nations Charter. Korea thus became the first real battleground of the Cold War and the first major threat of an all-out war between the East and West. Even though it remained a limited war and resulted in a stalemate, it proved to be a bitter and bloody conflict that lasted over three years, resulted in over 2 million fatalities, and left Korea devastated and hopelessly divided.

The roots of the war go back to the last days of World War II, when the United States and the Soviet Union divided the Korean peninsula at the thirty-eighth parallel. The division, which was agreed to by US and Soviet diplomats at Potsdam in July 1945, was meant to be a temporary arrangement for receiving the surrender of Japanese forces in Korea. Soviet occupation of northern Korea and the US occupation of the southern half were to last only until a unified Korean government could be established—an objective agreed to by both parties.

However, before any steps were taken to achieve that objective, Korean Communists, who during the war had been in exile in either the Soviet Union or northern China, established in the north a Soviet-styled government and speedily carried out an extensive land reform program. Meanwhile, in the south, US occupation authorities attempted to bring order to a chaotic situation. Korean nationalists opposed the US military occupation and agitated for immediate independence. Rival nationalist parties, some of them virulently anti-Communist, contended with each other in a political free-for-all.

US and Soviet diplomats agreed in late 1945 to set up a provisional government for both parts of Korea, scheduled to operate for the next five years under joint US-Soviet trusteeship. But the two sides could not agree on the particulars. Failing to solve the impasse, Washington took the issue to the United Nations in September 1947. The UN General Assembly passed a nonbinding resolution calling for free elections throughout all of Korea and a UN commission to oversee these elections. In May 1948, National Assembly elections were held under UN supervision, but in the south only, since the Communist regime in North Korea refused to permit the UN commission into the north. Syngman Rhee, who had spent the war years in exile in the United States, became the first president of South Korea (officially known as the Republic of Korea), which purported to be the only legitimate government of all of Korea. Shortly thereafter, in September 1948, the Communist regime in the north, led by Kim Il Sung, formally proclaimed the Democratic People's Republic of Korea, which, similarly to South Korea, claimed to be the rightful government of all of Korea. With the peninsula now divided between two rival regimes, the hope of peaceful unification was dashed. Despite this and despite the steadily mounting tensions between the two opposing regimes, the Soviet Union and the United States both began withdrawing their forces from the peninsula. By mid-1949 the withdrawal was completed. (There remained in North Korea a 3,500-troop Soviet military mission and in South Korea a 500-troop US military advisory group.)

Under Syngman Rhee, South Korea joined the US-led "free world." It would take another forty years, however, before democracy was established. In the meantime, he ruled by force. The "April 3 Cheju [Jeju] Incident" was a case in point. In March and April 1948, on the island of Jeju, off the southern coast of Korea, socialist "people's committees" organized demonstrations against the US presence and the upcoming elections designed to legitimize Rhee's government limited to the South, and thereby accepting, in effect, a divided country. As US troops and local police attempted to put an end to the demonstrations, they killed several people. The US military branded Jeju as a "second Moscow" and its people as Communists. When a general insurrection began on April 3, order was restored only after an estimated 14,000 were killed (according to the official South Korean count, which was bound to be low). US estimates ran to 30,000, while the islanders (who were bound to exaggerate) claimed 80,000. Another 40,000 fled to Japan. Under penalty of the National Security Law of December 1948, it became forbidden to mention the Jeju massacre. Not until after a democratic government had come to power forty-five years later could it be discussed in public. At the fiftieth anniversary of the massacre, in 1998, South Korean president Roh Moo-hyun profusely apologized to the residents of the island.[4]

Tensions were mounting not only in Korea but elsewhere as well. By the end of the 1940s, the US containment of the Soviet Union began to show signs of cracks, especially when, in August 1949, the US public was hit with twin shocks. First, the Soviet Union successfully tested an atomic bomb, thus breaking the US monopoly in four short years. Second, only two months later, the civil war in China ended with a Communist victory in the world's most populous nation. Predictably, policymakers in the United States believed that the Communist triumph in China was not a local event but rather had been engineered by Moscow. International Communism appeared to be on the march.

The Republicans charged that Truman had lost China to the Communists just as Roosevelt had lost Eastern Europe to the Soviets. It served to create a perception of Communist dominoes falling one after another. The relentless Republican criticism of the Democrats for being "soft on Communism" caused the Truman administration (and especially Secretary of State Dean Acheson, a favorite target of McCarthy) to strengthen even more its resolve to stand up to the Communists.

• • •

In April 1950, Truman received and accepted a set of recommendations from his National Security Council (NSC), the president's own advisory committee. These recommendations, known as NSC-68, were based on the premise that there could be no meaningful negotiations with the Kremlin until it "changed its policies drastically." According to NSC-68, Stalin understood only force, and it recommended, therefore, that the United States develop the hydrogen bomb to offset the Soviet Union's atomic bomb, and that it rapidly increase its conventional forces. The cost of such programs would have to be borne by a large increase in taxes. The US public would have to be mobilized; the emphasis must be on "consensus," "sacrifice," and "unity." NSC-68 also expressed the hope of making "the Russian people our allies in this enterprise" of ridding the world of "Communist tyranny." This hope, however, was based on the questionable assumptions that people never willingly accepted Communism, that it is always forced on them, and that they will always welcome US troops as liberators. This set of assumptions later produced fatal consequences for poorly thought-out US ventures in Cuba and in Vietnam, where the local populations refused to rally to the US cause.

The NSC, created in 1947, duplicates much of the work of the State Department. During the Kennedy administration (1961–1963) a tendency emerged where presidents began to consult primarily with the politically appointed NSC rather than the career professionals in the State Department. The discussion in 1950 on the nature of the Soviet threat proved to be one of the first instances where the professionals in the State Department played second fiddle to the NSC. The State Department's experts on the Soviet Union, Charles Bohlen and George Kennan, both of whom later served as ambassadors to Moscow, challenged the argument that Stalin had a master plan of conquest. They saw the Soviet threat largely as a potential political problem in Western Europe. But they were overruled by Dean Acheson, who sided with the hard-liners on the National Security Council.

• • •

The first test of the mobilization of the US people came two months after Truman approved NSC-68, when the Korean War broke out. At this point, the remilitarization of the United States began in earnest. It should be noted that earlier in the year top US military leaders (including the Joint Chiefs of Staff and Generals Dwight Eisenhower and Douglas MacArthur) had concluded that Korea was not of sufficient importance to US national interests to be included within its defensive perimeter. This assessment was based mainly on the higher priority given to defending Europe and Japan and on the insufficiency of US ground forces at the time. Secretary of State Acheson stated publicly in January 1950 (as MacArthur had done earlier) that the US defense perimeter ran from Alaska through Japan to the Philippines, and that Korea was outside that perimeter. In making this statement Acheson can hardly be faulted for inviting the North Korean attack on the south, as his critics would later charge, because he was merely stating what was already quite clearly US policy. North Korea and the Soviet Union were well aware of US strategic priorities and troop limitations. US military doctrine at the time emphasized preparation for "total war" (and not so-called brushfire wars) and focused primarily on resisting the Soviet threat in Europe, not in Asia.

When the North Korean invasion came in June 1950, Washington acted as if it had been caught off guard and denounced it as an unwarranted surprise attack. In fact, both MacArthur's military intelligence and that of Syngman Rhee had monitored North Korean troop movements and preparations and had abundant evidence of the impending attack. It appears that both Rhee and MacArthur withheld this information to maximize the psychological impact of what they called a "surprise attack."[5]

It is not altogether clear what roles the Soviet Union and Communist China played in the North Korean decision to attack the south, but neither Soviet nor Chinese troops were involved initially. Nor were they deployed near Korea prior to the war. North Korea, however, was a Communist state that received substantial Soviet political, economic, and military support and was considered in the West to be under Soviet control. The Truman administration concluded, therefore, that this was another case of Soviet aggression, and it was quick to lay the blame at Joseph Stalin's feet.

Testimony by men who were close to Stalin, which came to light only after the collapse of the Soviet Union, makes clear that Kim Il Sung, whose nationalist convictions were as strong as his Communist ones, met with Stalin in Moscow in March 1949 and again in March 1950, lobbying for the Soviet Union's support for an invasion of South Korea. Stalin, someone not given to reckless adventures abroad, opposed throughout 1949 a North Korean attack on the south, repeatedly telling Kim that "the 38th parallel must remain peaceful." Stalin feared that a war would give Washington a pretext for getting

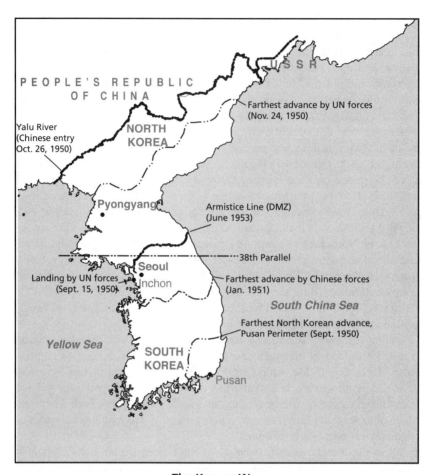

**The Korean War**

involved in Korean affairs. Kim, however, continued to lobby for a green light from Stalin. It was not until April 1950 that Stalin accepted Kim's view that the war could be contained in the Korean peninsula and would not draw foreign intervention.

By some accounts Stalin acknowledged Kim's plans for war and wished him success but did not offer specific instructions, much less orders for carrying out such plans. Stalin neither blocked Kim's preparation for war nor gave it enthusiastic support. He did advise Kim to consult first with Mao Zedong, which Kim did in Beijing in May 1950. It seems that Kim was there merely to inform the Chinese leader of his plans and that Mao, although skeptical, raised no objections and speculated that the United States was not likely to intervene in such a distant and small country.[6] On the evidence available, it is reasonable to conclude that the decision for war—specifically the strategy and timing of the attack—was made by Kim himself in Pyongyang, the North Korean capital, after he had secured at least general acquiescence from both Stalin and Mao. Stalin and Mao may not have been enthusiastic about a war in Korea, but a North Korean victory would have strengthened their hands in East Asia.

Kim was convinced that his army was strong enough to gain a swift victory by launching a full-scale offensive. He also assumed that the United States lacked either the will or the means to come to the rescue of South Korea. It proved to be a serious miscalculation.

Far from standing by idly while North Korean units were heading toward the southern tip of Korea, Truman rapidly swung into action. He immediately ordered US naval and air support from bases in nearby Japan to bolster the retreating South Korean army. After that, he took the issue of North Korean aggression to an emergency session of the UN Security Council. In the absence of the Soviet delegate, who was boycotting the United Nations in protest against its refusal to seat the People's Republic of China in the world body, the Security Council, on June 25, passed a resolution (by a 9-0 vote, with one abstention) condemning the invasion by North Korea and calling for the withdrawal of its forces from South Korea. In the course of three additional resolutions, the last one on July 31, the Security Council called for UN member nations to contribute forces for what became known as a UN "police action" to repel the aggression. Throughout, the Soviet ambassador to the United Nations, Yakov Malik, did not bother to return to New York. It seems unlikely that the Soviet delegate to the United Nations would not have been at his seat in the Security Council—or even in New York—if Moscow had known in advance of, much less had planned, the North Korean attack on the south.

Since the United Nations authorized US involvement in Korea, Truman did not need to go to Congress to ask for a declaration of war. In any case, the United States was at war even before the Security Council deliberated on what steps to take. Truman already had ordered US ground troops (in addition to air and naval support) into action in Korea. Moscow complained that the UN operation in Korea was actually a mask for US aggression, that it had been South Korea that had started the war, and that the authorization of UN forces was in violation of the UN Charter.

Although some sixteen nations ultimately contributed to the UN forces in Korea, the bulk of UN troops, weapons, and matériel were from the United States. The UN operations were largely financed by the US government, the UN forces were under the command of US Army general Douglas MacArthur, and the military and diplomatic planning for the war was done mainly in Washington.

The authors of NSC-68 welcomed the outbreak of war as an opportunity to roll back Communism on the Korean peninsula.[7] The swift and resolute US response to halt Communist aggression in Korea reflected the thinking of NSC-68, and not Acheson's statement of January 1950 that Korea was outside the US defensive perimeter. Truman determined that the defense of South Korea was vital to the defense of US interests in Asia, especially since the prospect of a Soviet-controlled Korea could threaten the security of Japan, which had suddenly become the major US ally in Asia. Truman, moreover, saw the defense of Korea as important to the maintenance of US credibility and defense commitments elsewhere in the world, and thus to the maintenance of the NATO alliance. He likened the situation in Korea in June 1950 to Nazi aggression in the late 1930s and invoked the lesson of Munich: Appeasement of an aggressor does not bring peace but only more aggression. Korea represented a test of US will, which the United State could not afford to fail.

The South Korean army, which lacked tanks, artillery, and aircraft, was no match for the heavily armed North Korean forces, and it therefore took a beating in the early weeks of the war. The first units of US ground troops coming to its rescue were also undermanned, ill-equipped, and poorly trained, but still they succeeded in holding the Pusan perimeter in the southeastern corner of Korea. Then, in September 1950, MacArthur engineered a dramatic reversal of the war with his successful landing of a large US/UN force at Inchon several hundred miles behind the Communist lines. Taken by surprise by this daring move, the North Korean forces then beat a hasty retreat back up the penin-

*US Army trucks at the thirty-eighth parallel, crossing into North Korea, October 1950, heading toward a showdown with the People's Liberation Army of Communist China*

sula. By early October the North Koreans were driven across the thirty-eighth parallel. The US/UN forces had won a spectacular victory.

At this juncture the Truman administration had to make a critical decision: whether or not to pursue the retreating enemy across the thirty-eighth parallel. MacArthur, however, riding the wings of victory, was raring to go, and so, of course, was Syngman Rhee, who hoped to eliminate the Communist regime in the north and bring the whole of Korea under his government. But the use of military force to achieve the unification of Korea had not been part of the UN resolution, which had called only for repelling the North Korean invasion. Moreover, a push into North Korea ran the risk of intervention by Communist China and possibly the Soviet Union.

At first, Truman authorized the entry of the South Korean army into the north and ultimately granted the same authority to MacArthur's UN forces—on condition they would halt their advance northward if either Chinese or Soviet forces entered the war. By entering North Korea, however, the US objective was now significantly altered. The goal was no longer limited to repelling an attack but was extended to eliminating the Communist regime in the north and militarily unifying the whole of Korea. MacArthur, sensing the imminent collapse of the North Korean army, pressed on, rapidly advancing his forces toward the Yalu River, the boundary between Korea and China. In doing so he ignored the repeated warnings from skeptics in Washington and those from Beijing, which threatened intervention if MacArthur pursued his course. To Beijing, with its memory of Western imperialism in China over the past century, the prospect of a hostile "imperialist" military presence across the border of Manchuria, its most industrialized region, was intolerable.

MacArthur's aggressive pursuit of the enemy raised a few eyebrows among Truman's advisers. In mid-October, Truman and MacArthur met on Wake Island in the Pacific, where the president urged caution against provoking Chinese or Soviet entry into the war. By that time, however, the cat was already out of the bag. MacArthur's units had already crossed the thirty-eighth parallel. MacArthur confidently assured Truman of an imminent victory, adding that if the Chinese dared to intervene, they could get no more than 50,000 troops across the Yalu and the result would be "the greatest slaughter."[8] Back in Korea, MacArthur continued with the offensive, which, he predicted, would have his soldiers home in time for Christmas.

With US forces rapidly advancing toward the Chinese border, China did exactly as it had warned it would do: It sent the PLA into battle in Korea. Beijing insisted that these troops were "volunteers," thereby disclaiming official involvement in the war in order to ward off a possible retaliatory attack by UN forces on China itself. After an initial surprise attack on October 25, the Chinese made a strategic retreat for about a month, only to come back in much greater numbers. MacArthur's intelligence reports badly underestimated the number of Chinese troops involved and China's capacity to increase the size of its forces. Suddenly, on November 26, a vast Chinese army of more than 300,000 soldiers opened a massive counteroffensive. Overwhelmed by this superior force, MacArthur's UN forces swiftly retreated over 250 miles to a line 50 miles south of the thirty-eighth parallel. It was the longest military retreat in US history.

The Chinese intervention with a force much larger than MacArthur thought possible made it, in his words, "an entirely new war," and it also provoked a sharp dispute with Truman over political and military policy. Frustrated by having an imminent victory denied him and by the limitations placed on him by his superiors in Washington, MacArthur favored widening the war, including using Chinese Nationalist forces from Taiwan, bombing Chinese Communist bases in Manchuria, and blockading the coast of China. The president, his military advisers, and his European allies feared that such steps might touch off World War III—possibly a nuclear war with the Soviet Union—or that sending increasing numbers of US troops to an expanded Korean War would leave Europe defenseless against a possible Soviet attack. MacArthur, ordered to follow a strategy of limited war, nonetheless voiced his opposition to it, famously declaring in March 1951 that there is "no substitute for victory."

MacArthur exceeded his authority when he publicly threatened China with nuclear destruction if it refused to heed his demand for an immediate disengagement from Korea. MacArthur's unauthorized ultimatum led Truman to dismiss him from his command. Truman, who later stated that this was the most difficult decision he had ever made, felt it necessary to reassert presidential authority over the military and make clear to both enemies and allies that the United States spoke with a single voice. Moreover, there was good reason to fear that MacArthur's insubordination could lead to an all-out war between East and West. For his part, MacArthur minimized such a prospect and argued that the West was missing an opportunity to eliminate Communism not only from Korea but from China as well.

It has been frequently alleged that it was MacArthur's advocacy of use of the atomic bomb against the Chinese that contributed to his dismissal. Although there may be some truth to the allegation, it must be pointed out that on at least three separate occasions US presidents considered the use of the bomb in the Korean War. Truman threatened its use in a press conference in November 1950, just after Chinese soldiers entered the war in large numbers; he even suggested that the decision rested with his field commander, MacArthur. That concession to MacArthur caused so much consternation among US allies and Truman's own advisers that he quickly modified his statement, saying that the final decision to use the bomb rested, after all, with the president. Several months later, when Chinese forces stymied a new UN offensive near the thirty-eighth parallel, Truman conferred with his advisers on the possibility of using the bomb. And near the end of the war, in June 1953, when armistice talks were deadlocked, the new US president, Dwight Eisenhower, seriously considered using the atomic bomb to break the stalemate.

The dismissal of MacArthur on April 11, 1951, brought no significant change in the war. His replacement, General Matthew Ridgway, held against a new Chinese offensive in late April, and several weeks later he forced the Chinese to retreat to near the thirty-eighth parallel. The war was now stalemated in the general vicinity of the thirty-eighth parallel. For the next two years, neither side launched a major new offensive. Still, casualties mounted as patrol actions on the ground continued. All the while, the United States conducted devastating bombing attacks on North Korea, destroying virtually every city as well as hydroelectric plants and irrigation dams. The toll on the civilian population of North Korea of these bombing attacks was enormous.

The military deadlock in the spring of 1951 led to tentative peace talks. In June of that year, Moscow and Washington agreed to negotiate a cease-fire, and both Beijing and Pyongyang concurred. Talks began in July and continued on and off for two years at Panmunjom, a town situated along the battle line. Two main issues that divided the negotiators were the cease-fire line and the exchange of prisoners. The Communist side insisted on returning to the thirty-eighth parallel but finally agreed to the existing battle line, which gave South Korea a slight territorial advantage. The second issue proved thornier, the Communists insisted on a complete exchange of all prisoners, but the US negotiators called for allowing the prisoners to decide for themselves whether they wished to be returned to their homelands. The truce talks remained deadlocked on this issue, which carried great propaganda value for the United States. Indeed, many North Korean captives—perhaps as many as 40,000—did not wish to be repatriated, and the United States wanted to exploit this matter as much as the Communists wanted to prevent this mass defection and thereby deny the United States a major propaganda victory.

The inauguration of Eisenhower in January 1951 and the death of Stalin six weeks later resulted in a more flexible approach (particularly in Moscow) needed to break the impasse. On June 8, 1953, the negotiators at Panmunjom signed an agreement that made repatriation of prisoners voluntary, but allowed each side the opportunity (under the supervision of a UN commission) to attempt to persuade their defectors to return home. For a while, the truce settlement was delayed because of a drastic attempt by South Korean president Syngman Rhee to sabotage it. Rhee, who desired to continue the fight to unify the country under his regime, released some 25,000 North Korean prisoners, who rejected repatriation to the north. The Chinese responded with a new offensive against South Korean units. Finally, after US negotiators offered assurances to restrain Rhee, the two sides signed a truce on July 23, 1953. The fighting ended with the final battle line as the truce line, which was widened to become a two-and-a-half-mile-wide demilitarized zone (DMZ). The truce, however, did not mean an official end of the war; it merely meant a halt in the fighting by the exhausted adversaries. Officially, a state of war continued and the truce line between North and South Korea remained the most militarized border anywhere in the world. For over fifty years it remained a potential flash point in the Cold War. (For years to come, Pyongyang repeatedly asked for a peace treaty, only to be rebuffed by Washington).

Even though the Korean War ended roughly along the same line where it began, its costs and its consequences were enormous. The United States lost 34,000 army soldiers in combat (and more than 55,000 in all); South Korea, an estimated 300,000; North Korea, 52,000; and China, 900,000 (Washington estimates). The historian Bruce Cumings estimated that the total number of fatalities may have been as high as 2 million.[9] While the outcome represented something short of victory for either side, both could claim important achievements. The United States, with the help of its allies, stood firm against Communist aggression. The war brought greater security to Japan and contributed to the strengthening of NATO as well. The Chinese emerged from the Korean conflict with greatly enhanced prestige, especially insofar as its now battle-hardened army had stood up to technically superior Western armies in a manner that no Chinese army ever had. Indeed, the Chinese considered it a victory.

For Korea, however, the war was a disaster. Korean soldiers, whether from the North or South, did not hesitate to inflict vicious punishment on their enemies—not only enemy soldiers but civilians thought to be informers or collaborators. Consequently, both sides committed atrocities. Bitterness and resentment persisted for decades. The war codified the division of Korea. There was no reduction of tensions and animosity between the Communist regime in the north and the anti-Communist regime in the south. The war produced millions of refugees, and when the fighting ended, several hundred thousand Korean families remained separated. Nowhere did Cold War attitudes remain as deeply entrenched as in Korea.

### The United States and the Cold War in Asia

The Communist victory in China represented a major setback for US foreign policy. The threat to US power in East Asia was made all the greater when the new Communist government of China promptly signed with the Soviet Union a thirty-year military alliance aimed at the United States, and vehemently denounced US "imperialism." The United States faced a Communist bloc that, with the addition of China's 463 million people, had more than doubled—to 750 million people, one-third of the world's population. The *New York Times* foreign correspondent Anne O'Hare McCormick ominously warned of a "muddied tide" of Communism that "will continue to flow and overflow."[10]

The turn of events in China meant that the US immediate postwar Asian policy, which had envisioned the emergence of a strong, united, democratic

China to serve as the main pillar of stability in Asia, was completely shattered. Instead, the Truman administration was forced to extend its "containment policy" into East Asia.

In 1948, when it was apparent that the Chinese Communists would defeat the Nationalists, US occupation policy in Japan took a strong turn to the right. The new policy, known as the "reverse course," called for rebuilding the former enemy, Japan, so that it could play the role of Washington's major ally in Asia, acting as a bulwark against the spread of Communism. Beginning in 1948, Washington, which heretofore had made no effort to assist Japan economically, now began to pump economic aid into Japan and assist its economic recovery in other ways. The reverse course was evidenced by a relaxation of the restrictions against the *zaibatsu*, a new ban on general labor strikes, and the purge of leftist labor leaders. With the outbreak of war in Korea in 1950, the security of Japan became an urgent concern to the United States. In order to maintain domestic security in Japan, MacArthur authorized the formation of a 75,000-person Japanese National Police Reserve, thus reversing his earlier policy for an unarmed Japan. It was the beginning of the rearmament of Japan, and it was bitterly disappointing to many Japanese who were sincere in their conversion to pacifism.

In the midst of the intensified Cold War, the United States not only groomed Japan to become its ally, but also took the lead in framing a peace treaty with Japan in 1951 that would secure the new relationship. The treaty, crafted by the US diplomat John Foster Dulles (in perfunctory consultation with Western allies), formally ended the Allied Occupation and restored full sovereignty to Japan. The Soviet Union, which was not consulted, objected to the final terms of the treaty and refused to sign it. The treaty was accompanied by the US-Japan Mutual Security Pact, which provided that the United States would guarantee Japan's security and went into effect in May 1952. It also permitted US military bases to remain in Japan to be used to contain Communism in East Asia. To that end, the Pentagon retained control of the Japanese island of Okinawa, on which it built huge military installations. The reborn nation of Japan thus became a child of the Cold War, tied militarily and politically as well as economically to the apron strings of the United States.

Within Japan the Cold War was mirrored by political polarization between the right and the left. The right (the conservative political parties, which governed Japan for the next four decades) accepted the Mutual Security Pact and favored strong political and military ties with the United States. Moreover, they were fully aware of Japan's economic dependence on the United States and did not wish to jeopardize these vital ties. The left (labor unions and many—probably most—of Japan's intellectuals and university students) was bitterly opposed to the Mutual Security Pact, to US military forces remaining on Japanese soil, and to the rearmament of Japan. It favored instead unarmed neutrality rather than Japan becoming a party to the Cold War. But since the conservatives remained in power, Japan continued to be a close partner of the

United States in the international arena, and more than 40,000 US forces remained on US military bases in Japan.

Beyond the fact that the Korean War had been fought to a standstill, it occasioned a large military buildup by both East and West. The Cold War, which had begun as a political dispute over Eastern Europe, had turned into a military confrontation. "Defense" budgets of both the United States and the Soviet Union skyrocketed during the Korean War and remained at that high level even after the fighting ended. The military budget of the People's Republic of China also grew commensurately.

A less tangible, but no less important, consequence of the Korean War was the great intensification of hostility between the United States and the People's Republic of China. The Chinese could not forget that US airplanes bombed the bridges across the Yalu River, right up to mid-channel. Another yard or so and they would have bombed Chinese territory. The possibility for accommodation between the United States and China, which had existed before they crossed swords in Korea, vanished. Both continued to accuse each other of aggression. For the PRC, the increased US military presence in East Asia meant a rising threat of US "imperialism," and for decades to come this perceived threat remained the central point of Chinese diplomacy, military preparedness, and propaganda. For the United States, the continuing threat of "Chinese Communist aggression" required a greatly strengthened commitment to the containment of Communist China, and this became the central feature of US Asia policy for the next twenty-five years. US policy was reflected in the turning of Japan into the major US ally and base of operations in East Asia, the decision to guarantee the security of South Korea and maintain US forces there, a commitment to defend the Nationalist Chinese government on the island of Taiwan against an attack from the mainland, and a growing US involvement in Vietnam in support of the French in their efforts to defeat a Communist-led independence movement. In their turn, the Communists in East Asia—China, North Korea, Vietnam, and others—strengthened their own resolve to resist US intervention and "imperialism." The Cold War battle lines in East Asia were drawn by the early 1950s, and for the next four decades the two sides maintained their respective positions in mutual hostility.

## Notes

1. One finds in English-language materials on China two different spellings of Chinese names depending on when they were published. In the People's Republic of China, the Wade-Giles system of romanization of Chinese names and words was replaced in 1979 by the pinyin system and subsequently adopted by US publishers. After 1979, Chiang Kai-shek's name was rendered as Jiang Jieshi, and that of Mao Tse-tung as Mao Zedong; Peking become Beijing, and so on. This text uses the pinyin system, but in most instances the old spelling of Chinese names is also provided in parentheses. Also note that personal names for Chinese, Japanese, Vietnamese, and Koreans

are given in the manner native to their countries, that is, the surname or family name precedes the given name.

2. Edwin O. Reischauer, *Japan: The Story of a Nation*, 3rd ed. (New York: Knopf, 1981), p. 221. Reischauer left out Germany, but his omission is understandable.

3. MacArthur's testimony to the joint committee of the US Senate on the military situation in the Far East in April 1951, cited in Rinjiro Sodei, "Eulogy to My Dear General," in L. H. Redford, ed., *The Occupation of Japan: Impact of Legal Reform* (Norfolk, VA: The MacArthur Memorial, 1977), p. 82.

4. Chalmers Johnson, *Blowback: The Costs and Consequences of Empire* (New York: Henry Holt, 2000), pp. 98–100. US authorities, too, participated in the cover-up.

5. The first to make this case was I. F. Stone, *The Hidden History of the Korean War* (New York: Monthly Review Press, 1952), pp. 1–14. Also see Bruce Cumings, "Introduction: The Course of Korean-American Relations, 1943–1953," in Bruce Cumings, ed., *Child of Conflict: The Korean American Relationship, 1943–1953* (Seattle: University of Washington Press, 1983), pp. 41–42.

6. See Natal'ia Bazhanova, "Samaia zagadochnaia voina XX stoletniia," *Novoe vremia* no. 6 (February 1996), pp. 29–31; also, Sergei N. Goncharov, John W. Lewis, and Xue Litai, *Uncertain Partners: Stalin, Mao, and the Korean War* (Stanford: Stanford University Press, 1993), pp. 136–146.

7. Cumings, "Introduction: The Course of Korean-American Relations, 1943–1953," pp. 29–38.

8. Quoted in Richard Rovere and Arthur Schlesinger Jr., *The General and the President* (New York: Farrar, Straus, 1951), pp. 253–262.

9. Bruce Cumings, *The Origins of the Korean War, II, The Roaring of the Cataract, 1947–1950* (Princeton, NJ: Princeton University Press, 1990).

10. Anne O'Hare McCormick, "While Moscow Charts a Course for Asia" and editorial "At China's Border," *New York Times*, January 23, 1950, 22.

# 4

# Confrontation
# and Coexistence

For centuries the nations of Europe had waged war against each other. France and Britain had been enemies in past centuries, and in modern times the strife between France and Germany has been even bloodier. Within the span of seventy-five years, they fought in three wars. Twice in the first half of the twentieth century, European nations divided into warring camps and fought each other with ever more destructive consequences. During and immediately after World War II, leading Western politicians spoke fervently of the necessity of burying the violent past and embarking on a search for peace and unity among Europeans.

The closing of the Iron Curtain, thereby relegating Eastern Europe to the Soviet sphere of influence, meant that Western designs for European unity would be limited to Western Europe. Indeed, the East-West division of Europe and the perceived threat posed by the Soviet Union to the security of West European nations served to reinforce the need for greater unity among them. To counter the Soviet Union's hegemony in Eastern Europe, the United States and its allies began to take steps in the late 1940s to secure the integration of Western Europe. In its turn, Moscow set out to create its own unified empire in Eastern Europe. The result was the rigid political division of the continent.

### West European Economic Integration
After 1945, the focal point in the East-West power struggle was Germany, a nation divided into four occupation zones. Disagreements over reparations to be extracted from Germany and other issues led to a closing off of the Russian zone in East Germany from the US, British, and French zones in West

70

Germany. By early 1947, less than two years after the conclusion of the war, it became clear that the chances for a settlement of the German question had vanished in the Cold War climate of acrimony, suspicion, and fear. The United States consolidated its position in Western Europe, a community of nations with common economic and political systems and security interests. In essence, it meant the military integration of the parliamentary, capitalist nations of Western Europe—Great Britain, France, Italy, Belgium, the Netherlands, Luxembourg, Denmark, and Norway (but excluding the dictatorial states of Spain and Portugal)—into a defensive alliance. Within a decade, West Germany, by virtue of its location, size, and economic potential, also joined this community and was destined to play a major role in it. In the late 1940s, West Germany, like Japan in East Asia, became the first line of defense for the United States against Soviet expansion.

The creation of a separate West German state and its economic recovery became matters of high priority for US officials. With the concurrence of Britain and France, the United States took the lead in creating a parliamentary government in West Germany, officially known as the Federal Republic of Germany. From the moment of its formation in May 1949, the West German government insisted that it spoke for all of Germany, including what at the time was still the Soviet zone of occupation. West Germany's choice of a capital, the small provincial city of Bonn, signified its provisional and temporary status. The traditional German capital, Berlin (which was divided into East and West German sectors), was within East German territory.

In rapid order, the United States integrated West Germany into a system of international trade, supplied it with generous amounts of economic aid (through the Marshall Plan), helped to introduce a new currency, and eventually brought West Germany into the US-led military alliance, the North Atlantic Treaty Organization (NATO). Under such circumstances, West German democracy flourished, as did its economy. Indeed, West Germany was the first of the world's war-torn industrial nations to attain an economic recovery, and by the late 1950s its postwar growth was described as an economic miracle, or *Wirtschaftswunder*.

When the government in Bonn introduced the new currency, the deutschmark, into West Berlin, it underscored the fact that the new West German state had an outpost 110 miles inside the Soviet zone. During the war, the Soviets had agreed to the Allied occupation of Berlin, but had not expected a permanent Western outpost inside their zone. In June 1948, Stalin attempted to force the West to abandon Berlin by closing the overland routes into West Berlin. Unable to reopen the roads by military means and unwilling to abandon West Berlin, the Allies responded with the Berlin Airlift. (For details, see Chapter 2.) When Stalin finally relented by lifting the overland blockade in May 1949, it was a tacit recognition that West Berlin would remain part of West Germany.

Once West Germany came into existence in May 1949, its chancellor, Konrad Adenauer, doggedly sought to integrate it into the community of West European nations. He insisted that West Germany develop democratic, liberal institutions under the aegis of the West. In fact, there is ample evidence to suggest that Adenauer, who came from the westernmost part of Germany—the Rhineland—and whose credentials as an opponent of the Nazi regime were impeccable, did not trust the German people. He feared that, left alone, they would succumb once more to the lure of political, economic, and, in particular, military power. Germans, he felt, needed to be under the lengthy tutelage of the Western democracies. When, in March 1952, Stalin sought talks with the West about the possibility of establishing a unified neutral and demilitarized Germany, it was Adenauer who lobbied strenuously—and successfully—with his Western allies to reject Stalin's diplomatic note without even bothering to discuss it.[1] For Adenauer, the inclusion in the company of Western nations was more important than German unification. The unification of Germany had to wait, and it had to be accomplished on Western, not Stalin's, terms. A unified Germany would continue to be tied to the West.

What endeared the Roman Catholic Adenauer to the West was his conservatism and staunch opposition to Communism. The West German voters, not inclined to another round of social experimentation, gave their votes to Adenauer's conservative Christian Democratic Union. *Der Alte* ("The Old Man") Adenauer, already seventy-three years old at the time of his first election as chancellor, held that post until 1963. By the time he stepped down, he had put West Germany firmly onto its postwar path.

During Adenauer's tenure, West Germany experienced rapid economic recovery, established viable democratic institutions, and tried to come to grips with its recent past. It acknowledged Germany's responsibility for World War II and the Jewish Holocaust and paid large sums in reparations to Jewish victims, running to ninety billion dollars. (As recently as May 2013, it agreed to another one billion dollars to elderly survivors of the Holocaust.)[2] It took steps to purge the nation of its Nazi past. The Nazi Party and its symbols were outlawed, and students were taught the causes and consequences of the rise of Nazism.

When dealing with the West, Adenauer always said the right things, but he and many Germans had a more difficult time acknowledging the crimes the German armies committed in the East. Not only did Adenauer insist that Poland and the Soviet Union return German lands they had seized at the end of the war, but his government refused to pay reparations to the millions of Poles, Russians, and others in Eastern Europe who had been forced to work in Nazi slave labor camps or had family members murdered. Under Adenauer, there was no diplomatic or economic contact with Eastern Europe, except with the Soviet Union. Stalin had created the Iron Curtain, but politicians such as

Adenauer also played a role in maintaining the partition of Europe. (For details, see Chapter 11.)

West European economic integration had its beginnings in the Marshall Plan, the US economic aid program announced in June 1947, which was intended to rescue Europe from the economic devastation of the war. However, insofar as the Marshall Plan was rejected by Moscow, which spoke for most of Eastern Europe, the aid and the integrative impact of the program were limited to Western Europe.

In short order, several countries in Western Europe took bold steps toward greater economic integration. In April 1951, six nations—France, West Germany, Italy, and the Benelux countries (Belgium, the Netherlands, and Luxembourg)—signed a treaty establishing the European Coal and Steel Community. This program, designed primarily by the French economist Jean Monnet and French foreign minister Robert Schuman (both of whom have been referred to as the "father of Europe"), called for the pooling of the coal and steel resources of the member nations. On the basis of majority vote, its High Authority was empowered to make decisions regulating the production of coal and steel in the member countries. Its impact was especially pronounced in the highly industrialized Saar and Ruhr regions of West Germany. It also became the basis on which to build the later economic and political integration of much of the rest of Western Europe.

So well did the integrated coal and steel program work that six years later, the same nations formed the European Economic Community (EC), also known as the Common Market, to further integrate their economies. The Treaty of Rome of March 1957 brought a more comprehensive organization formally into existence. A central feature was a customs union for the purpose of lowering tariffs among the member states and of establishing one common tariff rate on imports from outside countries. This easing of trade restrictions greatly increased the flow of goods within the EC, which in turn stimulated production, provided jobs and capital accumulation, and increased personal income and consumption. Western Europe began to reemerge as one of the thriving economic regions of the world. In fact, the economic growth rate of the Common Market countries surpassed that of the United States by the end of the 1950s and remained significantly higher for many years thereafter.

Britain initially chose not to join the Common Market. It already enjoyed the benefits of a preferential tariff system within its own community of nations—the British Commonwealth—and it could not reconcile its Commonwealth trade interests with those of its European neighbors in the Common Market. Other reasons for Britain's rejection of the Common Market included its conservative inclination to retain the old order rather than join a new one. Britain, moreover, was reluctant to give up a measure of its national sovereignty to a supranational body whose decisions were binding on member nations. However, after its economy faltered in the 1950s, Britain saw fit in

1961 to apply for membership in the Common Market, only to find that admission now was not for the mere asking. The issue was hotly debated both in Britain, where the Labour Party opposed it, and in France, where President Charles de Gaulle had his own terms for British admission. After over a year of deliberation, de Gaulle, critical of Britain's close political and economic ties with the United States and with its Commonwealth nations, suddenly announced in January 1963 his firm opposition to British membership in the EC. Since EC decisions required unanimity—a point de Gaulle had insisted upon—the French president's veto unilaterally kept Britain out. When Britain renewed its application to join the EC in 1966, de Gaulle still objected, and it was only after his resignation as president of France in 1969 that Britain gained entry. After lengthy negotiations, Britain finally joined the EC in January 1973 (together with Denmark and Ireland).

From its inception, the EC was divided between the "supranationalists," who desired comprehensive integration, and the "federalists," who wished to retain for each nation essential decisionmaking powers. The tug-of-war between the two camps remained unresolved. Moreover, because decisions on key issues were binding for all member states, certain members (most notably France and later Britain) successfully insisted on unanimity rather than majority vote on issues such as expansion of the membership, a common currency, social legislation, and so on. (For more on the EC, see Chapter 17.)

## NATO: The Military Integration of Western Europe

In April 1949, a number of nations heeded a call by the United States to create an alliance against the Soviet Union. The result was NATO, the North Atlantic Treaty Organization, a collective security system for Western Europe and North America. It was the military counterpart to the Marshall Plan. The ten European member states (Britain, France, Iceland, Norway, Denmark, Belgium, the Netherlands, Luxembourg, Portugal, and Italy), together with the United States and Canada, signed a treaty of mutual assistance: An attack on one was an attack on the others. (NATO remained intact even after the demise of the Soviet Union. It was invoked for the first time after al Qaeda's September 11, 2001, assault on the World Trade Center in New York and the Pentagon in Washington.) NATO brought US airpower and nuclear weapons to bear as the primary means to prevent the Soviet Union from using its large land forces against West Germany, the main target. Each of the NATO members pledged to contribute ground forces to a collective army under a unified command, always headed by a US general.

Once again, the main obstacle was the force of nationalism, especially as personified by France's Charles de Gaulle. The first serious question facing NATO was whether to include West Germany. Its territory was covered by the initial NATO security guarantee, but it was not a treaty member. In fact, it remained under Allied military occupation until 1952 and had no armed forces of its own. After the outbreak of the Korean War, however, US officials immediately urged the rearmament of West Germany and membership in NATO. But the French and other Europeans, fearing the return of German militarism, were reluctant to allow German rearmament.

The fear of potential Soviet aggression, however, overshadowed the fear of German militarism. German troops were badly needed to beef up the under-strength NATO ground forces. At the urging of the United States, Britain, and West Germany itself, the NATO members agreed by the end of 1954 on West Germany's entry into NATO—on the conditions that it supply twelve ground divisions and that it be prohibited from developing nuclear, bacteriological, and chemical weapons, as well as warships and long-range missiles and bombers.

The Soviet Union, too, opposed the rearmament of West Germany and made an eleventh-hour attempt to block its entry into NATO. That was the reason for Stalin's March 1952 proposal of a demilitarized, neutral, unified Germany. Stalin's proposal was too late. By that time the die had been cast: A German army would be reconstituted. Western leaders—particularly Adenauer—rejected Stalin's proposal as a propaganda ploy aimed at disrupting the Western military alliance.

In NATO's first decade, the weak link in the collective security system was France. France was unable to supply its share of ground troops to NATO because they were needed first in Indochina and later in Algeria, as it sought desperately to cling to its colonial empire. De Gaulle eventually decided on cutting France's losses in Algeria to try to regain a dominant position in Europe. De Gaulle, France's great World War II hero and always the supreme nationalist, sought to elevate his country's role in a reinvigorated Europe. It was the cardinal point of his political philosophy, which came to be called Gaullism—national independence in foreign affairs and social conservatism at home. (*Gaullism* was a play on words, a reference to de Gaulle himself and also the Roman name for France, Gaul).

De Gaulle's assertive nationalism was reflected in his view of the security needs of France (and Europe). Because he sought to strengthen France's posture in Europe and to reassert European power in global affairs, de Gaulle wished to put the United States at a greater distance from Europe. He felt that Western Europe and NATO were dominated by the United States and its closest ally, Great Britain. De Gaulle also questioned, moreover, the commitment of the United States to the defense of Europe. He thought that while the United States might wage a nuclear war in its own defense, it could not be counted to defend Western Europe from an invasion by conventional Soviet ground forces.

De Gaulle rejected an offer of US nuclear weapons stationed in France. Instead of depending on the United States, he preferred to rely on a French

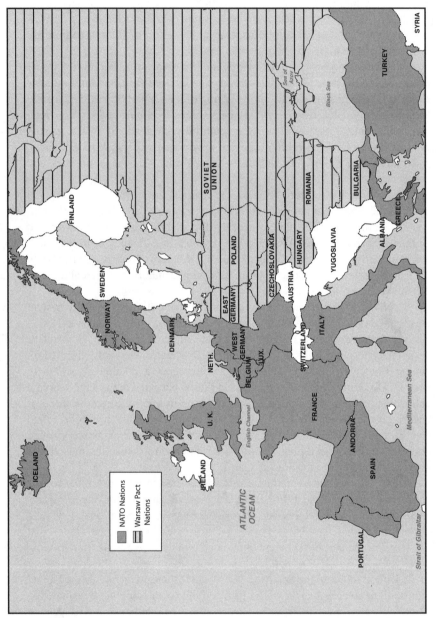

**Europe (1990)**

*force de frappe,* or "strike force," a nuclear triad of land, sea, and air-borne nuclear weapons. France thereby joined the exclusive club of nuclear powers. De Gaulle felt that, even if France's nuclear force were far smaller than that of the superpowers, it still would serve as a deterrent. He turned a deaf ear to foreign critics when he refused to join other nations in signing a series of nuclear arms control agreements or to halt France's atomic bomb testing program in the Pacific Ocean.

All this was prelude to de Gaulle's withdrawal, in 1966, of all French troops from NATO (although he did not formally withdraw France from the alliance) while at the same time calling for the withdrawal of all US forces from French soil. French security, the general insisted, must remain in French hands. The NATO headquarters, located in Paris, was then relocated to Brussels, Belgium.

Occasionally, de Gaulle also conducted a foreign policy at odds with that of the United States. He conducted his own diplomacy with the Soviet Union and, in 1964, he extended diplomatic recognition to the People's Republic of China. He disliked the confrontational approach taken by the United States in the Cold War, especially during the 1962 Cuban missile crisis (to be discussed later), and he did not want to be left out of diplomatic meetings between the superpowers where decisions might be made affecting the security and interests of France. De Gaulle, who had played a major role in the French quagmire of its Indochina War, had no difficulty in lecturing the United States on its war in Vietnam.

De Gaulle was more interested in an *entente* (understanding) with West Germany, the most powerful West European state, than with Washington. West Germany's aged chancellor, Konrad Adenauer, accepted an invitation to meet de Gaulle in Paris in July 1962; two months later, de Gaulle undertook a well-received tour of West Germany. The Franco-German summit meetings set the table for the signing of a Franco-German treaty aimed at strengthening their relations. From de Gaulle's perspective, the treaty was meant to check the Anglo-US domination of the Western alliance. It did not, however, put a greater distance between West Germany and the United States, as de Gaulle had wished. Nonetheless, it did symbolize the marked improvement of postwar relations between two powerful European nations with a long history of mutual hostility.

## East European Integration

Moscow had its own program of political and economic integration for Eastern Europe. What had begun in 1944–1945 as a military occupation by the Red Army shortly became a social, political, and economic experiment with Stalin's Soviet Union serving as the model. In 1949, in response to the Marshall Plan, Stalin's foreign minister, Viacheslav Molotov, introduced the

Council of Mutual Economic Aid, commonly known as COMECON. Its purpose was to integrate the economies of the East European nations of Poland, Hungary, Romania, Czechoslovakia, and Bulgaria (and later Albania) with that of the Soviet Union. It was meant to aid in the postwar reconstruction of the Soviet Union and in the industrial development of Eastern Europe, which was still largely an agricultural region. It also extended the Kremlin's political control of Eastern Europe by giving it an economic lever.

The transformation of the East European economies took place along Soviet lines. The emphasis was on heavy and war industries, with consumer goods taking a backseat. Expropriation decrees, issued as early as September 1944 in Poland, led to the confiscation of the estates of nobles and the churches. These measures eliminated the "landlord" classes and paved the way for collectivization of agriculture.

The economic transformation of Eastern Europe was accompanied by sweeping political changes. In Bulgaria, Albania, Yugoslavia, and Romania, the monarchies were officially abolished. Moscow's East European satellites followed the Soviet example by adopting constitutions similar to the 1936 Stalin constitution. Everywhere, parties in opposition to the new political order were either declared illegal or merely served as window dressing.

In response to the inclusion of West Germany in NATO, the Soviet Union created, in 1955, its own military alliance, the Warsaw Treaty Organization, commonly known as the Warsaw Pact. Its membership included Albania, Bulgaria, Czechoslovakia, East Germany, Hungary, Poland, Romania, and the Soviet Union. Unlike NATO, its members did not have the right to withdraw from the organization, an act the Kremlin considered the supreme political sin its satellites could commit. Albania, by virtue of its geographic position and relative lack of importance, did manage to leave the Warsaw Pact in 1968, but when Hungary flirted with neutrality in 1956, the Soviet Army forced it back into the fold. When Czechoslovakia in 1968 and Poland in the early 1980s moved dangerously close to a position similar to that of Hungary in 1956, the Soviet leadership made clear that it would not tolerate the disintegration of its military alliance.

Officially, Eastern Europe consisted of one happy family of fraternal Communist states. Nationalist sentiments, however, ran deep. People there could not forget past grievances against neighboring nations, even though they were now fellow Communist states. The examples are legion. Poles resented Russians, Germans, and Lithuanians; Hungarians resented Slovaks and Romanians. The most interesting manifestation of the force of nationalism was that of Romania, which since the mid-1960s sought to carve out a measure of independence from Moscow. Under the leadership of Nicolae Ceaușescu, the Romanian Communist Party successfully maneuvered to secure limited economic and political independence, particularly in its dealings with Western Europe. Over the years, Romania retained diplomatic ties with Israel after all other East European nations had broken relations after the 1967 Six Day War. Romania did not leave the Warsaw Pact but at times refused to participate in Warsaw Pact maneuvers. It maintained good relations with the People's Republic of China at a time of ever-increasing hostility between Moscow and Beijing. It gave warm receptions to visiting US presidents, and sent its athletes to the 1984 summer Olympic Games in Los Angeles in defiance of the Soviet boycott of these games. The Kremlin cast a wary eye on the Romanian maverick but refrained from taking drastic action. There was no pressing need to discipline Ceauşescu as long as he remained a member of the Warsaw Pact. Perhaps even more important for the Kremlin, Ceauşescu showed absolutely no tendency toward any sort of political reform. Moscow always considered political reforms—whether in Warsaw, Budapest, or Prague—a greater threat to its hegemony in Eastern Europe than Ceauşescu's actions, which, although an irritant, did not pose a major problem.

Despite the Kremlin's insistence on maintaining its hegemony over Eastern Europe, nationalist tendencies repeatedly made clear that Eastern Europe contained restless populations with whom the Kremlin's control did not sit easily. In the face of repeated Soviet pronouncements that Eastern Europe was a closed issue (notably General Secretary Leonid Brezhnev's statement in 1968 that the Soviet Union's defensive borders were at the Elbe River separating East and West Germany), the solidarity remained a problem.

## The First Attempts at Détente

Immediately after World War II, the United States and the Soviet Union nations reduced their armed forces. US intelligence agencies did not believe that a Soviet attack was in the cards—unless an uncontrolled chain of events led to miscalculations on the part of the leaders in the Kremlin. By early 1947, US forces dwindled from a wartime strength of 12 million troops to fewer than 1 million. When NATO was formed it did not have the means to stop a potential Soviet ground attack against West Germany. Should it happen, US troops in Western Europe were ordered not to fight but to find the quickest way across the English Channel or into Italy to the Mediterranean Sea.

The Soviets showed no inclination to initiate World War III on the heels of the just-concluded World War II. Stalin reduced the Soviet Army to its prewar level of about 3.5 million soldiers, a large number of whom were used to clear the rubble in Soviet cities in need of rebuilding. Then there was always the US trump card, the atomic bomb. In essence, Washington did not consider it likely that Stalin would attack in Central Europe; similarly, Moscow did not contemplate a US attack, at least not until the Korean War. For the next five years the protagonists maintained their forces at a level just sufficient to repel a potential attack. The Korean War was the catalyst for the rapid remilitarization of both sides.

In April 1950, nine weeks before the outbreak of the Korean War, a National Security Council directive (NSC-68) recommended to President Harry Truman a drastic increase in the military budget. The prospects of attaining this were slim, however, for popular sentiment was against it, if only for the reason it would have meant an increase in taxes. The opportunity to implement NSC-68 came in June 1950 when, as Secretary of State Dean Acheson put it, "Korea came along and saved us."[3] Sacrifice, unity, and consensus became the order of the day. Eventually, the 1950s became known as the "consensus decade" (contrasting them with the turbulent 1960s).

In the Soviet Union a similar scenario played out. Starting in the late 1940s, that is, even before the Korean War, Stalin renewed his insistence on unity and sacrifice to defend the socialist, Soviet fatherland at any cost. A renewed emphasis on ideological rigidity and conformity was accompanied by purges of individuals suspected of ideological nonconformity. When the war in Korea broke out, Stalin rapidly increased the size of the Red Army from 3.5 million to about 5–6 million troops, the approximate level the Soviet armed forces retained until the late 1980s. The five-year period after World War II during which both sides had reduced their armed forces and had curtailed their military expenditures was at an end.

Truman retired from political life in January 1953 and Stalin suddenly died six weeks later. The departure of the two chief combatants during the initial stages of the Cold War made it possible for the new leaders to try a different tack, for they were not locked into the old positions to the same degree their predecessors had been.

President Dwight Eisenhower and Nikita Khrushchev, who had emerged as the Soviet Union's new leader by September 1953, began a dialogue that led to a lessening of tensions. It was in this context that the word *détente* (from the French, the easing of tensions of strained international relations) first entered the vocabulary of the Cold War. Eisenhower, the hero of World War II, had no need to establish his anti-Communist credentials. He had greater latitude in dealing with the Soviets than did Harry Truman or his secretary of state, Dean Acheson, whom Republicans (notably Senator Joseph McCarthy and Richard Nixon) had berated time and again for being "soft on Communism." In fact, McCarthy went far beyond that. He accused Acheson's State Department of harboring Communist subversives.

Khrushchev and his colleagues began to move away from the Stalinist pattern of conduct at home and abroad. Khrushchev was determined to avoid a military showdown with the West and declared, by dusting off an old Leninist phrase, that "peaceful coexistence" (the Soviet euphemism for détente) with the West was possible. He thereby rejected the Stalinist thesis of the inevitability of war between the socialist and capitalist camps.

In short order, the great powers convened at Geneva in 1954 to deal with the central problems of the day. The more relaxed climate made possible the

"Spirit of Geneva." Its most tangible result was to end the four-power military occupation of Austria that had been in place since the end of World War II. It proved to be the first significant political settlement by the belligerents in the Cold War. In May 1955, Austria gained its independence as a neutral state, a nonaligned buffer in the heart of Europe, separating the armies of the superpowers. The stubborn fact that it took the two sides ten years and new leadership to agree on the Austrian solution—and on little else—was testimony to the intensity of the Cold War.

With the Austrian settlement, the Iron Curtain shifted eastward to the southern borders of Czechoslovakia and western Hungary. Western and Soviet troops disengaged along a line of about 200 miles. In return, Austria pledged its neutrality in the Cold War, a condition that suited the Austrian temperament perfectly. In particular, Austria was prohibited to join in any alliance—particularly military, but also economic—with West Germany. Austria quickly became a meeting ground between East and West. Its capital, Vienna, became a neutral site for international gatherings. Similar to Berlin, it also had one of the largest concentrations of foreign spies in the world.

A solution similar to the Austrian settlement had once been envisioned for Germany. But once the two German states came into existence, it proved to be impossible to unify them until Mikhail Gorbachev abandoned East Germany in 1989. In contrast to Germany, Austria had the good fortune of being officially treated at the end of the war as a liberated nation, not a conquered enemy. It also had a relatively small population of just over 7 million with relatively little economic clout. However, this may also be said of Korea and Vietnam in the mid-1950s, yet no one in the West considered their unification.

Oddly, it had been Stalin who, in April 1945, had taken the first preparatory steps leading to Austrian unification. He appointed the moderate socialist Karl Renner as the new head of Austria, and in this fashion Austria—unlike Germany, Korea, and Vietnam—was from the very beginning under one government, which all of the occupying powers eventually recognized. Churchill and Truman were initially unhappy with Stalin's unilateral action, not because they objected to Renner, but because he had acted without consulting them. Renner then guided his nation carefully on a middle course between the superpowers. When the occupying powers left Austria in May 1955, it already had a neutral government in existence for ten years.

The partial rapprochement between the United States and the Soviet Union enabled Nikita Khrushchev to visit the United States in 1959. His itinerary took him to New York City, a farm in Iowa, Los Angeles, and the Camp David presidential retreat in the hills of western Maryland, where he and Eisenhower conferred in private. The "Spirit of Camp David" produced recommendations for disarmament and an agreement to hold a summit meeting in Paris in May 1960, to be followed by an Eisenhower visit to the Soviet Union.

The Austrian settlement and talks between the heads of state did not mean that the Cold War was over. Nor did it mean that a comprehensive process of disengagement had begun. Détente was always tempered by a heavy residue of mistrust and a continued reliance on military might. Even at the high point of détente in the 1950s, the Cassandras were always in the wings warning of dire consequences.

Khrushchev spoke of peaceful coexistence, but he also made it clear that the ideological struggle would continue. Nor would détente mean the abandonment of the Soviet sphere of influence. Khrushchev's critics at home, particularly the old Stalinist Viacheslav Molotov, who remained foreign minister until Khrushchev replaced him in 1956, kept a jaundiced eye on his doings.[4] When challenged in Eastern Europe, Khrushchev's Politburo did not hesitate to act. The Kremlin accepted the defections of Yugoslavia and Albania, at the fringes of their sphere of influence, but after that it drew the line. When rebellions broke out in East Germany in 1953 and in Hungary in 1956, the Soviet Army acted quickly.

A conflict between détente and the entrenched Cold War mindset was also evident in the United States. While the Republican president, Eisenhower, pursued the high road of compromise and negotiations, his secretary of state, John Foster Dulles, was an uncompromising anti-Communist. Containment of the Soviet Union, a policy initiated by his Democratic predecessors George Marshall and Dean Acheson, was not enough for Dulles, for it suggested tolerance of an evil, godless system. To Dulles, the Cold War was not merely a struggle between two contending economic and political orders; it was also a clash between religion and atheism. Dulles, therefore, proposed the "rollback" of the Soviet Union's forward position and the "liberation" of lands under Communist rule. It was all part of Dulles's "New Look" in foreign policy. But as events showed, particularly in Hungary in 1956, it is the president who ultimately determines foreign policy, and Eisenhower had no desire to start World War III over Hungary. Despite Dulles's rhetoric, US foreign policy had to settle for containment in Europe.

It was in Asia and Latin America where Dulles was able to act more vigorously to preserve US interests. When in 1954 the Communist Vietminh triumphed over the French in Indochina (see Chapter 5), he moved to preserve the southern half of that country for the Western camp. When the United States felt its interests threatened in Iran in 1953 and in Guatemala in 1954, the US Central Intelligence Agency (CIA), under the direction of his brother, Allen Dulles, quickly moved into covert action and pulled off its most successful coups. In Iran, the CIA returned the shah to power when it engineered the overthrow of Premier Mohammed Mossadegh, who had nationalized the nation's oil industry in order to take it out of the hands of British and US companies. In Guatemala, the CIA ousted the socialist Jacobo Arbenz, who had proposed the nationalization of lands held by US corporations, replacing him with a military junta.

## Moscow's Response to Containment

In the mid-1950s, Khrushchev took the first steps to counter the US-led system of regional alliances designed to contain the Soviet Union. Until that time the Soviet Union and its satellites had resembled a beleaguered fortress, digging in its heels against any attempt to dislodge it. In addition to NATO, the United States created other military alliances. In 1954, it pledged to defend Taiwan should the People's Republic of China attack it. In the same year, it created the Southeast Asia Treaty Organization (SEATO). Much was made of SEATO, but in effect it had no teeth since any involvement in Southeast Asia had to be unanimous, and the British and the French, as Dulles knew, wanted no part of it. SEATO's role was mostly symbolic, another emblem of Communist containment. SEATO's other members included the Philippines, Thailand, Pakistan, New Zealand, and Australia. When the United States sent combat troops to South Vietnam, in 1965, it did so unilaterally, without bothering to consult with SEATO. Nonetheless, by virtue of training and equipping the South Vietnamese army, Washington now had a foothold in what once had been French Indochina.

The Baghdad Pact, formed in 1955, was more ambitious than SEATO. It sought to organize a Middle Eastern alliance of Arab states, yet the only such state to join was Iraq. Its other members were the United States, Britain, Turkey, Pakistan, and Iran.

By the mid-1950s, the Soviet Union was surrounded on all sides. To the north was the Arctic Ocean, ice-bound for much of the year (the sole exception was the ice-free port of Murmansk above the Arctic Circle). NATO stood watch in Western and Southeastern Europe (including the Turkish Straits); in the Far East the United States had military ties with South Korea, Japan, and Taiwan. Further south was SEATO, which reached westward all the way to Pakistan. If there was a gap, it was of India, which refused to join a US military alliance. (It was one of the reasons why Moscow cultivated a friendship with India.) But even in South Asia, the Soviet Union was contained by the rugged Karakorum mountain range, the western extension of the Himalayas. In the Middle East was the Baghdad Pact.

From the end of World War II until Stalin's death, the Soviet Union conducted a relatively conservative foreign policy. Stalin had refused to yield to the West on a number of central issues, notably Eastern Europe, but he had not challenged the West elsewhere. The successful Communist insurgencies in China and Vietnam, for instance, had not been of his making. Shortly after Stalin's death, the CIA, in a special report to Eisenhower and the National Security Council, described Stalin as a man "ruthless and determined to spread Soviet power," who nevertheless "did not allow his ambitions to lead him to reckless courses of action in his foreign policy." The report warned, however, that Stalin's successors might not be as cautious.[5]

Events quickly bore out the CIA's prediction. In 1954, a bitter debate took place in the Kremlin over the Soviet Union's foreign policy. One faction, led by Prime Minister Georgi Malenkov and Foreign Minister Viacheslav Molotov, urged caution, favoring a continuation of the Stalinist pattern of defiance and rearmament. The majority in the Presidium of the Central Committee of the party,[6] led by Nikita Khrushchev, who was the first secretary of the party and thus its leader, argued for a more active foreign policy, one calling for a breakout from what they called capitalist encirclement. They argued that those who stood still, those who accept the status quo, will inevitably suffer defeat at the hands of the enemy. Interestingly, this position echoed that of John Foster Dulles, who could not tolerate the mere containment of the Soviet Union. The conflict, both sides argued, must be taken to the enemy.

Molotov and his allies warned that should the Soviet Union challenge the United States in the Middle East, it was bound to fail. The British and US navies controlled the Mediterranean Sea and were bound to stop all shipments, as the United States had intercepted a Czechoslovak arms shipment to Guatemala earlier in 1954. But Khrushchev and his faction prevailed, and the Soviet Union began early in 1955 to provide weapons in secret to the armed forces of Gamal Abdel Nasser, Egypt's military dictator. The arms agreement, Moscow's first with a non-Communist state, was revealed to the world later that year.

In return for its support of Nasser, the Soviet Union obtained a client in the Middle East, and it was thus able partially to offset the effects of the Baghdad Pact, an alliance that, at any rate, did not last long, nor accomplish much. Khrushchev's support of Nasser had primarily a symbolic value: The Soviet Union had become a global player.

For the first time the Soviet Union had a foothold in a region beyond the Communist world. The person largely responsible for this significant departure in Soviet foreign policy and who reaped handsome political dividends at home was Khrushchev. He had challenged the West in what had formerly been a Western preserve. It marked the beginning of a contest for the hearts and minds of the nonaligned world. With this in mind, Khrushchev undertook in 1955 a much-publicized journey to South Asia. He visited India and on his way home stopped in Kabul, the capital of Afghanistan, to forestall apparent US designs on that country. "It was . . . clear that America was courting Afghanistan," Khrushchev wrote in his memoirs, for "the obvious purpose of setting up a military base."[7] In 1960, Khrushchev paid a second visit to Asia. Eisenhower, concerned with the growing Soviet influence in southern Asia, followed in 1960 in Khrushchev's footsteps when he visited India and other nonaligned nations where he drew large crowds.

The Soviet Union's foray into the Third World had little to do with ideology, but everything to do with balance-of-power politics. Nasser, contrary to Western charges, was hardly a Communist. In fact, Nasser had outlawed the Egyptian Communist Party. The Soviet Union turned a blind eye to Nasser's jailing of Communists in order not to jeopardize its new relationship with the

Arab world. Similarly, when the Soviets began to sell arms to the Sukarno government of Indonesia, the powerful Indonesian Communist Party complained bitterly. The party's fears were well founded. In October 1965, the Indonesian army launched a bloodbath, killing up to half a million actual and suspected Communists. The Soviet Union, however, first and foremost, wanted clients outside its sphere of influence to challenge the West. What those clients did to their Communist comrades was of secondary concern.

The United States sought to bring Nasser to heel by withdrawing funding for the Aswan High Dam on the upper Nile River. Nasser then turned to the Soviet Union to help him complete the project. By that time he had already concluded his arms agreement with the Soviet Union. When, in the summer of 1956, Nasser nationalized the Suez Canal, which had been in British hands since 1887, the stage was set for a retaliatory strike.[8] In October 1956, France and Britain joined Israel in an attack on Egypt. Once again, the Cold War spilled over into the Third World.

Relations between the Soviet Union and the United States took a sudden turn for the worse in 1960, when a CIA spy plane, a U-2, was shot down deep inside the Soviet Union. The Soviet Rocket Force Command had finally been able to bring down one of the high-flying planes, which had periodically violated Soviet airspace since 1956. The downing of the U-2 wrecked the summit between Khrushchev and Eisenhower later that month and led to the cancellation of Eisenhower's scheduled goodwill visit to the Soviet Union. Khrushchev's vehement denunciation of Eisenhower overstepped the boundaries of both common sense and good manners. Western historians have often speculated that Khrushchev had to placate the hard-liners at home, who had never been happy with his rapprochement with the West. U-2 flights, of which the Soviet military was well aware, had proved to be an embarrassment for Khrushchev. After all, the Soviet military and scientific establishment had launched the first earth satellite and the first intercontinental missile, yet it had been unable to bring down a US plane at 75,000 feet until engine trouble apparently forced one to a lower altitude.

The U-2 incident also embarrassed Eisenhower, who had first lied about it and then had to acknowledge that he had approved the spy mission. In the United States, 1960 was a presidential election year. During the campaign, the "outs," in this case John Kennedy and his Democratic Party, accused the "ins," Richard Nixon (Eisenhower's vice president) and the Republicans, of having fallen asleep on the job. They charged that the Soviets had opened a "missile gap" that endangered the security of the United States. The Cold War was back in full bloom, the "spirit" of Geneva and Camp David a fading memory.

Since the Korean War, the superpowers were feverishly engaged in an open-ended arms race—both conventional and nuclear—in preparation for a military showdown that neither wanted. In conventional land forces, the Soviet bloc always held the lead, while the West relied primarily upon the US nuclear umbrella. The US nuclear monopoly, however, was short-lived. In 1949, Stalin tested the Soviet Union's first atomic weapon, "Joe-One" as it became known in US intelligence circles. In the early 1950s, the Soviet Union exploded its first thermonuclear bomb (or hydrogen bomb, vastly more powerful than atomic bombs), and by 1955, it had the capability of delivering these weapons by means of intercontinental bombers. By the end of the 1950s, both the Soviet Union and the United States had successfully tested intercontinental missiles. Essentially, the nuclear arms race was deadlocked. A nuclear exchange was bound to lead to what became known as Mutually Assured Destruction (MAD). But it did not keep the two sides from adding to their arsenals. The focus of the nuclear standoff shifted in October 1962 to a most unlikely place: Cuba. The confrontation—the most dangerous episode in the Cold War—grew out of the Cuban revolution of the 1950s that brought Fidel Castro to power.

### The Cuban Missile Crisis

Cuba's war for independence against Spain, ended in 1898 with US assistance, came with a high price, the overbearing presence of the "colossus of the north." Cuba's national hero, José Martí, had warned that US support for Cuban independence would lead to that. Indeed, after 1898, the most power-ful man in Cuba's capital of Havana was the US ambassador. When one Cuban dictator after another made his peace with Washington, it came at the expense of Cuban sovereignty.

A military coup in March 1952 returned to power the dictator Fulgencio Batista (who had governed Cuba between 1933 and 1944). Under Batista, who had good relations with the CIA, US influence grew considerably. US busi-nesses—both legitimate (farming, mining, tourism) and illegitimate (the mafia with its reach into hotels, nightclubs, prostitution, and narcotics)—dominated the Cuban economy. Indeed, the mafia—accustomed to demanding protection money from others—paid the obliging Batista to protect its investments. It was a symbiotic relationship that served both very well. Batista made sure it worked smoothly by brandishing both the carrot (such as bribes and the grant-ing of licenses) and the stick (strong-arm tactics by the police and army). The brutality and venality of the Batista regime—which had sold Cuba to foreign and criminal interests accompanied by an unequal distribution of wealth—bred resentment among Cubans of all walks of life.

Resentment, however, failed to produce an organized resistance, and dis-senting voices remained amorphous and thus ineffective. And even when meaningful resistance began to take shape under the direction of Fidel Castro, he managed to organize no more than 300 comrades under arms at any one time. In time, however, the Cuban population became more receptive to Castro's message, which he broadcast by a mobile radio transmitter. When Castro came to power in January 1959, it was not so much that he had gained power by force of arms but that Batista had lost his hold on it. Castro himself admitted that had Batista enjoyed a measure of popular support, his revolution would easily have been crushed. At the end, however, there was no one willing to defend Batista, not even his military.

Castro's revolution began on July 26, 1952, in a supreme act of recklessness, an attack on the Moncada military barracks in Santiago, in the southeastern corner of Cuba. Everything went wrong from the outset: the planning, the dearth of arms, the fact that Castro's 120 men were outnumbered by a factor of ten to one. Castro's forces were decimated; he was captured, tried, and sentenced to a fifteen-year prison term. Popular revulsion against Batista (on the part of the Roman Catholic Church, students, the middle class) led to an amnesty of political prisoners. In May 1956, a defiant Castro walked out of prison and went into exile in Mexico to plot his next step. It was there he and his brother, Raúl, met Ernesto Ché Guevara of Argentina. Guevara, who had been in Guatemala City at the time of the 1954 CIA-backed military coup that overthrew Jacobo Arbenz, had been appalled by Arbenz's lack of resolve. He and Castro would have to be of sterner stuff to succeed where Arbenz had failed.

Unable to raise substantial sums of money from the Cuban community-in-exile in south Florida, Castro returned to Cuba in a shaky, used thirty-eight-foot cabin cruiser that had seen better days, the *Granma*, named after its US owner's grandmother. In November 1956, *Granma*, with eighty-one rebels aboard, in a re-creation of José Martí's fateful return to Cuba in 1895, set sail for Cuba's Oriente Province. There, they immediately ran into an ambush that devastated their ranks. Havana newspapers declared Castro dead, his revolution crushed. Castro was down to sixteen men, but among the survivors were Ché Guevara and Raúl Castro, who set out to rebuild their organization and recruit new fighters.

This time Castro refrained from frontal assaults against a stronger enemy. Operating out of the rugged Sierra Maestra Mountains of southeastern Cuba, his guerrillas attacked lightly defended military outposts, gathering weapons, supplies, and experience in the process. In May 1957, eighty Castro guerrillas scored a significant psychological victory over the undermanned garrison at Uvero. The seizure of Uvero signified (in Guevara's words) that the revolution had "reached full maturity." As the confidence of the rebels waxed, that of Batista's military waned. The rebels' radio messages had their intended effect. When, in May 1958, Batista dispatched 10,000 troops into the Sierra Maestra, Castro's 300 guerrillas halted their advance and captured a large cache of weapons. The last battle took place at the end of December 1958 for control of Cuba's fourth largest city, Santa Clara, straddling the road to Havana. Batista's army, which should have strenuously defended the city, simply gave up. Abandoned by his military (some of whom were plotting against him) and encouraged by the US

*Soviet leader Nikita Khrushchev and Cuban president Fidel Castro at the United Nations, New York, November 1960*

ambassador to leave the country, Batista fled in the middle of the night. It was New Year's Day, 1959.

Castro's rebels immediately began the "purification" of Cuba. "The dead shout out for justice," Castro declared. Justice included the execution of Batista's top officials for "treason, rebellion, sedition, desertion, malfeasance, robbery and fraud." It meant the closing of crooked numbers games, casinos, and news offices in the pay of Batista, and the mass dismissal of officials, all without due legal process.[9]

Castro aimed to establish Cuba's sovereignty—political and economic—at the expense of the overbearing US influence. To that end, he insisted on the nationalization—with compensation, initially—of US investments estimated at just under $1 billion. With the Cuban treasury virtually empty and much of the nation's assets deposited in accounts abroad (Batista alone plundered Cuba of an estimated $300 million), the nationalization process would have to be underwritten by international banking institutions. In case there would be compensation, US businesses now claimed assets of $2 billion. Castro reminded them that for the purpose of taxation, they had previously grossly undervalued their investments. At stake, however, was something much more than money. US businesses were less interested in compensation than in maintaining their profitable businesses. The mafia, as well, had no intention of abandoning its golden goose in Havana.

Castro's revolution soon felt the full brunt of the US business community, the mafia, the CIA, the State Department, and the Pentagon. Initially, the

CIA did not believe Castro to be a Communist (unlike his brother, Raúl), but merely one of the many Cuban rebels, inspired by José Martí, who had railed against the United States only to come around (as Batista had done) and, in the end, continue business as usual. As pressure mounted, Castro found an unlikely patron in the Kremlin.

Shortly, the Eisenhower administration charged that Castro was a Communist. (It is difficult to pinpoint when his conversion to Communism took place, but apparently it was after the revolution.) Either way, Castro had to be overthrown. There were solid reasons to believe that the CIA could duplicate its successes in Iran and Guatemala.

• • •

The crisis in Iran was the consequence of a decision in April 1951 by Iran's parliament, the *majlis*, to nationalize the property of the Anglo-Iranian Oil Company (AIOC), Britain's most profitable business anywhere. Not only had the AIOC taken Iran's wealth out of the country, but its workers in Abadan suffered the indignities of surviving on wages of fifty cents a day, living in a shantytown (called "paper city"), and battling pollution, rats, and disease. In May, the *majlis*, led by Iran's nationalist prime minister, Mohammed Mossadegh, forced the shah, Mohammed Reza Pahlavi, to establish the National Iranian Oil Company, the first step toward the nationalization of the oil industry. Britain's prime minister, the old imperialist Winston Churchill, then appealed to the CIA to help him get rid of Mossadegh. The Truman administration, however, was hesitant to become involved in the dispute. Churchill had to wait until the Eisenhower administration, with its "New Look" came to power. Secretary of State John Foster Dulles and his brother, Allen, the director of the CIA, were more than willing to try and overthrow Mossadegh, a man already much demonized in the US press.

In August 1953, street demonstration forced the shah, fearing for his life, into exile in Rome. At that point, the CIA and British intelligence scrambled to bring him back. The CIA spent large sums of money to foment pro-shah street demonstrations (some of it going to individuals who only days before had demonstrated against the shah), paid off religious leaders, and bribed army officers. The army arrested Mossadegh and the shah returned home after only three days in exile. The CIA got its man back. When the leading CIA operative in Iran, Kermit Roosevelt (Theodore Roosevelt's grandson), briefed John Foster Dulles on the agency's success, Dulles "purred like a giant cat."

But that was not the end of the story. As a critic of the operation later explained, "nations . . . cannot be manipulated without a sense on the part of the aggrieved that old scores must eventually be settled." The day came in 1979, when demonstrations forced the shah into exile once again and when Iranian students took possession of the US embassy in Tehran. While Dulles purred back in 1953, many in the CIA understood that the United States might pay a price someday.[10] In the month after the overthrow of Mossadegh, a CIA report spoke for the first time of "blowback."[11]

In the following year, in Guatemala, the CIA moved into action once more. A revolution in 1944 had overthrown Guatemala's military dictatorship and had brought to power civilians who sought to address the country's social and economic problems. In 1950, 2.2 percent of landowners owned 70 percent of the land (of which they cultivated but one-quarter) and the annual income of agricultural workers was $87. Most of the economy was in foreign—mostly US—hands and, consequently, large profits went abroad. The greatest employer was the United Fruit Company, *El Coloso*, with its vast landholdings, 85 percent of which consisted of excess, uncultivated land.

In March 1951, the nationalist Jacobo Arbenz won the presidency in a democratic election. Arbenz and his congress—which had but a handful of Communist deputies with little influence—limited the power of foreign corporations, notably United Fruit. They nationalized unused land and supported strikes against foreign businesses. In March 1954, Arbenz told his congress that this was a matter of protecting the "integrity of our national independence." In Washington, John Foster Dulles raised the specter of international Communism. The Dulles brothers decided to act for reasons of national security, ideology, and the fact that they owned stock in United Fruit and had previously provided legal services to the company. To deal with Arbenz, the CIA organized and armed disaffected elements of the Guatemalan army, led by Colonel Carlos Castillo Armas, who earlier, in November 1950, had sought (unsuccessfully) to overthrow the civilian government and then had fled into exile. This time he succeeded, in July 1954, when Arbenz's own army abandoned him.

For Washington, the crisis was over. For Guatemala, it was the first step of a descent into hell. Castillo Armas, who was assassinated in July 1957, never did bring order or prosperity to Guatemala. Instead, a revolutionary movement began to gain strength. In the early 1960s, a succession of military regimes—some of them extraordinarily brutal—launched a series of campaigns in an attempt to return the country to the "quiet days" before 1944.[12]

For more than three decades, the military killed an estimated 200,000 Guatemalans, most of them indigenous Mayans. Of particular viciousness was the reign of General Efrain Rios Montt, a born-again Christian who became the darling of the US religious right in the early 1980s. During his seventeen-month reign, his army killed an estimated 70,000 people, mostly Mayan peasants, and razed thousands of villages. Rios Montt's scorched-earth policy, directed primarily against an ethnic group, came close to the definition of genocide. Rios Montt was the worst human rights abuser in Latin American history since the days of the Spanish *conquistadores*. Guatemala's civil war produced more fatalities than the "dirty wars" of El Salvador, Nicaragua, Argentina, and Chile combined.

• • •

There was little reason to believe that the United States could not duplicate the Iranian and Guatemalan scenarios in Cuba. The first weapon Washington employed was economic. It closed the US market to Cuba's main source of income, the export of sugarcane. The US market previously had taken half of Cuba's exports and had provided nearly three quarters of its imports. As anticipated, the US trade embargo had severe repercussions for the Cuban economy.

Castro, however, refused to yield to US pressure and instead turned to the Soviet Union for economic, political, and military support. Also, he saw his revolution as a model for other countries in Latin America, which were challenging US hegemony there. When Castro's strong-arm methods and reform acquired an increasingly socialist flavor, it produced an exodus of thousands of Cubans. They settled mainly in Florida, waiting to return to their native land.

In March 1960, a frustrated Eisenhower administration turned the Cuban problem over to the CIA and subsequently to the new president, John Kennedy. Cuba became Kennedy's first foreign policy challenge. In the spring of 1961, Allen Dulles assured him that Castro could be removed with little difficulty. After all, the CIA had dealt successfully with similar problems before. Dulles worked out a plan that called for Cuban exiles, trained and supplied by the CIA, to land on the beaches of Cuba and appeal to the Cuban population to rise against Castro. It was based on the assumption that Castro's regime had scant popular support. All that was needed was a push and the corrupt house of cards would come tumbling down.

Kennedy, although skeptical of the plan, decided to put it into operation in April 1961, if only because by that late date it could not be called off without charges of betrayal by the Cubans in Florida. Kennedy had good reason to be skeptical, for the operation stood little chance of success. The population did not rise against Castro. In the course of seventy-two hours, Castro's army destroyed the contingent of 1,500 Cuban exiles on the beaches at the Bay of Pigs. A vague understanding between the CIA and the Cuban exiles had led the exiles to believe that the United States would come to their assistance in case they ran into difficulties. When Kennedy did not respond militarily to the fiasco at the Bay of Pigs, many Cubans in the United States felt betrayed. But Kennedy had never contemplated such a step. Moreover, direct US involvement would have been in violation of international law and promised international and domestic repercussions.

A month after Kennedy's assassination, Harry Truman tried to address the growing problem of using CIA covert operations as a tool of US foreign policy. It was not something he had in mind when the CIA was organized during his administration in 1947. The purpose of the CIA, he explained in a *Washington Post* op-ed piece, was to gather intelligence, not to become "a policymaking arm of the Government." He never thought that when he set up the CIA, it would become involved in "cloak and dagger operations" that caused problems abroad. As a result, the CIA became a "symbol of sinister and mysterious foreign intrigue—and a subject for cold war enemy propaganda."[13]

By now, however, the horse was already out of the barn, and with Truman's help at that. It was true that since the days of Eisenhower, the CIA had expanded its political operations across the globe—notably in Iran, Guatemala, Cuba, and Vietnam. But it had been Truman who had opened the barn door when he used the CIA to intervene in the elections in Italy, sought to recruit Tibetans against the Communist Chinese, and meddled in Middle Eastern affairs.

Kennedy, stung by the defeat at the Bay of Pigs, blamed Allen Dulles for the fiasco. Castro became an obsession with Kennedy that made it difficult for him to accept the new government of Cuba. Three days after the Bay of Pigs, he delivered to Castro a warning: "Let the record show that our restraint is not inexhaustible."[14]

The Soviet Union could do little to aid Castro. It did not have the means to challenge the United States in the Caribbean, where the US navy enjoyed a vast superiority. The United States also had a huge lead in the nuclear arms race, by a ratio of 17 to 1. When Kennedy entered the White House, it possessed over 100 intercontinental and intermediate-range ballistic missiles, 80 submarine-launched missiles, 1,700 intercontinental bombers, 300 nuclear-armed airplanes on aircraft carriers, and 1,000 land-based fighters with nuclear weapons. In contrast, the Soviets had 50 intercontinental ballistic missiles, 150 intercontinental bombers, and an additional 400 intermediate-range missiles capable of reaching US overseas bases.[15]

In the presidential election of 1960, Kennedy had charged that the Eisenhower administration had been responsible for a "missile gap" to the detriment of the United States. But that myth was laid to rest shortly after Kennedy became president. In October 1961, his deputy secretary of defense, Roswell Gilpatric, announced that there was no missile gap favoring the Soviet Union; on the contrary, there was a large gap favoring the United States. "We have a second-strike capability," Gilpatric stated, "which is at least as extensive as what the Soviets can deliver by striking first."[16]

Nikita Khrushchev understood all too well that his boasts of Soviet military might had only masked the unyielding reality that the Soviet Union trailed badly in the nuclear arms race. But one day in 1962, a solution came to him in a flash. He reasoned that if he could establish a Soviet nuclear presence in Cuba, he could solve several problems in one bold stroke. First, he would be able to present himself as the defender of a small and vulnerable state. Second, and more important, medium-range missiles in Cuba would essentially give the Soviet Union nuclear parity—if only symbolically—with the United States. The missile gap, which favored the United States, would be no more.

Third, nuclear parity with the United States would greatly enhance the international prestige of the Soviet Union.

In 1955, Khrushchev had argued for a secret arms shipment to Nasser's Egypt, and it had proven to be a bold and successful initiative. In Cuba, he could perhaps do the same. Success promised impressive dividends. Khrushchev—a man of action, rather than reflection—decided to make his move. His memoirs suggest that neither he nor his advisers spent much time considering the consequences of such a rash step. In the past, Khrushchev had taken decisive yet potentially dangerous steps that nevertheless had brought him political rewards. Success in this high-stakes gamble promised to bring great gains, but failure promised dire consequences. Two years after the Cuban missile crisis, when his party turned Khrushchev out, it accused him of unspecified "hare-brained" and "wild schemes, half-baked conclusions and hasty decisions," none too subtle reminders of what had gone wrong in the Caribbean.[17]

When the CIA became aware of the construction of Soviet missile sites in Cuba, Kennedy had to act. Political considerations demanded it. The Joint Chiefs understood that the presence of perhaps ninety Soviet intermediate-range missiles in Cuba, while posing a formidable threat to much of the eastern United States, did not change what was known as the nuclear "balance of terror." Both sides already had the capability to annihilate the other. At the height of the crisis, Secretary of Defense Robert McNamara told National Security Advisor McGeorge Bundy: "I'll be quite frank, I don't think there is a military problem here. . . . This is a domestic, political problem. . . . We said we'd act. Well, how will we act?"[18]

One option was to launch preemptive air strikes against the missile sites, which would bring about the deaths of Soviet troops, humiliate a great power, and conceivably touch off a nuclear war. Two of Kennedy's advisers, the Air Force chief of staff, General Curtis LeMay, and the commander of the Strategic Air Command, Thomas Power—both of whom for over a decade had advocated a preemptive nuclear war against the Soviet Union—now took the opportunity to urge a nuclear resolution of the crisis. In the unlikely event of a Soviet nuclear retaliation, they argued, the Kremlin would be able to inflict only minimal damage on the United States. "The Russian bear," LeMay said, "has always been eager to stick his paw in Latin American waters. Now we've got him in a trap, let's take his leg off right up to his testicles. On second thought, let's take off his testicles too." Somehow, LeMay thought the bear would accept his castration without trying to reclaim his manhood. After the crisis was over, a disappointed LeMay publicly berated Kennedy for having "lost" the showdown.[19]

The Joint Chiefs and the CIA had a more sanguine assessment. They told Kennedy that in an all-out war the Soviet nuclear arsenal was capable of destroying the United States, even without the Cuban missiles. This bleak

*This low-level reconnaissance photograph, taken by the United States on October 23, 1962, provided evidence that the Soviet Union was setting up missile bases in Cuba.*

assessment had a sobering impact on Kennedy and his advisers, who met around the clock in an effort to find a political solution to the confrontation.

A second alternative was the invasion of Cuba, but that option was as dangerous as the first. The destruction of Soviet forces in Cuba would leave Khrushchev with few options. He could accept a defeat, contemplate a nuclear exchange, or attack the West's isolated and vulnerable outpost in Berlin, where the Soviet army had a marked advantage.

Kennedy decided on a third option, a blockade of Cuba (which he called a "quarantine" since a blockade is an act of war) that would give both sides additional time to resolve the issue. The blockade was limited to Soviet ships carrying missile components. In the face of Kennedy's resolve, Khrushchev was prepared to back down. But he, similar to Kennedy, had his own domestic political problems. He could not afford to come away empty-handed from the confrontation. He insisted on the Soviet Union's right to place defensive missiles in Cuba since, after all, the United States had done the same in Turkey, along the Soviet Union's southern border. At the least, the United States should remove its missiles from Turkey. Kennedy, however, refused publicly to discuss this demand. He, too, could not afford to appear to back down, even though the missiles in Turkey were by now obsolete and already had been scheduled for removal. As a second concession, Khrushchev wanted a pledge from the United States not to invade Cuba and to respect its sovereignty.

The standoff was resolved with the help of two unlikely intermediaries. Soviet journalist Alexander Feklisov, who was also a Russian secret police (KGB) agent, and US journalist John Scali, who had contacts in the White House, met in a restaurant in Washington on October 26 to discuss a solution. Feklisov pointed out that it was "mutual fear" that drove the superpowers: Moscow feared a US invasion of Cuba, and Washington feared the rockets in Cuba. A US pledge not to invade Cuba would resolve the matter. Feklisov contacted his embassy, while Scali notified the White House. They met again for dinner that same day, and Scali informed Feklisov that "the highest power"—namely, John Kennedy—had accepted the deal to trade the Soviet rockets for a public pledge that the United States would not invade Cuba.[20]

Kennedy ignored Khrushchev's previous belligerent statements and replied instead to a conciliatory letter in which Khrushchev had expressed his desire to resolve the dilemma:

> We and you ought not to pull on the ends of the rope in which you have tied the knot of war. . . . [The] moment may come when that knot will be tied too tight that even he who tied it will not have the strength to untie it. . . . Let us not only relax the forces pulling on the ends of the rope; let us take measures to untie that knot.[21]

Robert Kennedy, the president's brother and closest adviser, met with Soviet ambassador Anatoly Dobrynin to tell him that the United States was prepared to pledge not to invade Cuba in the future and that after a sufficient interval it would remove the missiles from Turkey. But there would be no official US acknowledgment of this second concession. On the next day, Dobrynin told Robert Kennedy that the Soviet missiles would be withdrawn. The crisis was over.

After the first Soviet ships were turned back by the US blockade, Secretary of State Dean Rusk famously remarked that "we looked into the mouth of the cannon; the Russians flinched."[22] That statement became the basis of the widely held view in the United States that Kennedy had stared down Khrushchev. It suggested that US warships had forced Soviet freighters carrying missile components to turn around. But in reality, the Soviet freighters had turned around more than 500 nautical miles (575 miles) from the nearest US warships, the result of a diplomatic solution.[23]

It had not only been the Soviets who had flinched. Both sides realized that the arms race had driven them to the brink of nuclear war. Both concluded that the time had come for a sobering, constructive dialogue. And, indeed, relations between the United States and the Soviet Union improved markedly shortly thereafter. The most notable, immediate achievement was the partial Nuclear Test Ban Treaty of 1963, which forbade nuclear testing in the atmosphere. It set the stage for further East-West discussions and the beginning of the détente of the late 1960s.

In the aftermath of the crisis, historians, politicians, and military officers studied the lessons of the confrontation. A view commonly held in the United States emphasized that the crisis showed that the Soviets yielded only in the face of determination. Force was the only thing they understood. Khrushchev, indeed, had surrendered to Kennedy's demands by removing the Soviet missiles from Cuba. But this explanation has several serious flaws. On balance, the victory did go to Kennedy. Until the very end, however, Khrushchev insisted on a quid pro quo—something in return—and he continued to hold out for two concessions Washington had never contemplated granting Moscow prior to the missile crisis: abandoning its dubious right to invade Cuba and its equally dubious right to deploy nuclear missiles in Turkey.

Until Kennedy yielded on these issues, the Soviets continued to work on the Cuban missile sites and challenged the CIA U-2 spy planes continuing their surveillance flights. A Soviet tactical ground-to-air missile—fired by Cubans at the express order of Fidel Castro—shot one down and killed its pilot, Major Rudolph Anderson, the sole fatality in the crisis. And when a US intelligence plane entered Soviet airspace, the Soviet air force chased it back.

The missile crisis was first and foremost a political test of wills that demanded a diplomatic solution based on a quid pro quo. That is how it was resolved, not by one side dictating a settlement to the other. In his memoirs, Khrushchev dwelled on the political nature of the compromise, as he spared no words in thanking Kennedy for taking that road rather than going to war.[24] Khrushchev had good reason to be grateful, for Kennedy had saved him from his own recklessness.

The crisis also revealed the Soviet Union's relative weakness in the face of US military might. This imbalance favoring the United States was in part the result of a modest military build-down on the part of the Soviets, which had begun under Khrushchev in the late 1950s. When Kennedy and his secretary of defense, Robert McNamara, continued to push for an increase in the already bloated US nuclear arsenal, the Soviet leaders felt they had no choice but to pursue a genuine—and not just symbolic—nuclear parity with the United States. After the missile crisis, they vowed that the United States would never again humiliate them. The result was a renewed—this time successful—Soviet effort to establish nuclear parity with the United States.

The United States honored Kennedy's verbal pledge not to invade Cuba. Castro, however, remained an obsession to the Kennedy brothers, who turned to organized crime to do what the CIA had failed to accomplish. The mafia had the best of reasons for trying to eliminate Castro. Their profits had been of such magnitude before Castro's revolution ruined everything that they had been willing to pay Batista a monthly bribe of $1.28 million.[25] It was not surprising they sought to assassinate Castro.

## Notes

1. For details, see Rolf Steininger, *Eine Chance zur Wiedervereinigung? Die Stalin-Note vom 10. März 1952: Darstellung und Dokumentation auf der Grundlage unveröffentlichter britischer und amerikanischer Akten* (Bonn: Neue Gesellschaft, 1985).

2. "Holocaust Reparations: Germany to Pay 772 Million Euros to Survivors," *SpiegelOnline*, May 29, 2013; Melissa Eddy, "For 60th Year, Germany Honors Duty to Pay Holocaust Victim," *New York Times*, November 17, 2012.

3. Cited in Walter LaFeber, *America, Russia, and the Cold War: 1945–1990*, 6th ed. (New York: McGraw-Hill, 1991), p. 98.

4. In 1957, Andrei Gromyko became foreign minister; he retained his post until July 1985, when Mikhail Gorbachev kicked him upstairs to take the ceremonial post of president of the Soviet Union.

5. CIA special estimate, advance copy for National Security Council, March 10, 1953, "Probable Consequences of the Death of Stalin and the Elevation of Malenkov to Leadership in the USSR," p. 4, in Paul Kesaris, ed., *CIA Research Reports: The Soviet Union, 1946–1976* (Frederick, MD: University Publications of America, 1982), reel II, frames 637–648.

6. The Presidium (known as the Politburo during 1966–1991) of the Central Committee of the Communist Party was the decisionmaking body, which consisted of approximately a dozen individuals. The number was not fixed; it varied frequently.

7. N. S. Khrushchev, *Khrushchev Remembers: The Last Testament* (Boston: Little, Brown, 1974), pp. 299–300.

8. The Suez Canal was owned by a joint-stock company in which British and (to a lesser extent) French money had been invested.

9. "Purification," *Time*, February 9, 1959.

10. Stephen Kinzer, *All the Shah's Men: An American Coup and the Roots of Middle East Terror* (Hoboken, NJ: John Wiley and Sons, 2003), pp. 2, 5–6, 67, 161–163, 209. The citation is by William Roger Louis, p. 215.

11. Chalmers Johnson, "Abolish the CIA!" *London Review of Books*, October 21, 2004, p. 25.

12. Stephen Schlesinger and Stephen Kinzer, *Bitter Fruit: The Untold Story of the American Coup in Guatemala* (New York: Anchor Books, 1990), pp. 49–63, 76, 108, 253–254.

13. Harry S. Truman, "Limit CIA Role to Intelligence," *Washington Post*, December 1962, p. A11.

14. Cited in Richard J. Walton, *Cold War and Counter-Revolution: The Foreign Policy of John F. Kennedy* (Baltimore: Viking, 1972), p. 50.

15. David Horowitz, *The Free World Colossus: A Critique of American Foreign Policy in the Cold War*, rev. ed. (New York: Hill and Wang, 1971), pp. 342–345. Also, Edgar M. Bottome, *The Balance of Terror: A Guide to the Arms Race* (Boston: Beacon Press, 1971), pp. 120–121, 158–160.

16. "Gilpatric Warns US Can Destroy Atom Aggressor," *New York Times*, October 22, 1961, pp. 1, 6.

17. "Nezyblemaia leninskaia general'naia linia KPSS," *Pravda*, October 17, 1964, p. 1.

18. Kai Bird and Max Holland, "Dispatches," *The Nation*, April 28, 1984, p. 504.

19. See Richard Rhodes, *Dark Sun: The Making of the Hydrogen Bomb* (New York: Simon and Schuster, 1995), pp. 571, 574–575.

20. See A. S. Feklisov, "Neizvestnoe o razviazke karibskogo krizisa," in M. V. Filimoshin, ed., *KGB otkryvaet tainy* (Moscow: Patriot, 1992), pp. 118–132.

21. Robert F. Kennedy, *Thirteen Days: A Memoir of the Cuban Missile Crisis* (New York: Norton, 1969), pp. 89–90.

22. Ibid., p. 18.

23. Michael Dobbs, *One Minute to Midnight: Kennedy, Khrushchev, and Castro on the Brink of War* (New York: Knopf, 2008).

24. Khrushchev, *Khrushchev Remembers*, pp. 513–514.

25. For Batista and the mafia, see T. J. English, *Havana Nocturne: How the Mob Owned Cuba—and Then Lost It to the Revolution* (New York: William Morrow, 2008), pp. 16, 58–59, 132–133, 266–267, 318, passim.

# Part 2

# Nationalism and
# the End of Colonialism

After World War II, a wave of nationalism swept across Asia and Africa, and in its wake a host of new nations proclaimed independence from their European colonial masters. Within two decades about one-third of the world's population was freed from colonial rule. The scope and the speed of the dismantling of the colonial empires were unforeseen. By 1960, it had become clear to even the more conservative rulers of the European colonial powers that they could no longer stem the tide. None stated it better than British prime minister Harold Macmillan in his famous "Wind of Change" speech delivered at the end of a tour of Africa in January 1960:

> We have seen the awakening of national consciousness in peoples who have for centuries lived in dependence upon some other power. Fifteen years ago this movement spread through Asia. . . . Today the same thing is happening in Africa and the most striking of all the impressions . . . is the strength of this African national consciousness. The wind of change is blowing through the continent, and whether we like it or not this growth of national consciousness is a political fact.[1]

Several historical developments merged to give birth to this phenomenon. First, the war itself had weakened the European imperial powers. Some of them had lost their colonies during the war and found it difficult to restore control of them afterward, and others were so exhausted by the war that they came to view the maintenance of a colonial empire as a burden greater than it was worth. Another factor was the emergence of a Western-educated elite among the natives of the colonies, who took seriously the lessons they had learned in the Western universities and now demanded popular representation leading to national sovereignty. In many cases the colonial peoples took part as allies in the war and, having contributed to the victory of the "four freedoms" (Franklin Roosevelt's not too subtle swipe against colonialism), they now demanded a measure of that freedom for themselves.

Still another factor with relevance to Asia was the role of Japan in bringing an early end to European colonialism. Japan had promoted and provoked nationalist movements in various Asian countries. Britain responded to the strength of the independence movement with greater alacrity than France and the Netherlands and took the lead in decolonization. Once it granted independence to India, long its most important colony, the grounds for maintaining its rule over lesser colonies were greatly weakened. France, however, refused to grant independence to its colonies, for it saw in the restoration of the French empire a means of compensating for its humiliating defeats in World War II. In the end, France proved unable to stem the tide of anticolonialism when it lost to a determined Vietnamese nationalist-Communist movement led by Ho Chi Minh and then to the revolutionary movement in Algeria.

In Africa, decolonization came later than in Asia largely because national consciousness and strong nationalist movements were slower to develop. The persistence of ethnic divisions in Africa was a major obstacle to the development of nationalism. In general, Britain did more to prepare its African colonies for self-rule and independence than France, Belgium, or Portugal. In fact, the abrupt departure of France and Belgium from Africa left their former colonies particularly ill prepared for either political or economic independence. Moreover, France refused to abandon Algeria, which many French citizens called home and which their government considered a province of France and not a colony, despite its large Muslim majority. The result was that France had on its hands another long and bitter revolutionary struggle it was unable to win.

Nationalism was a key ingredient in the postwar struggles in the Middle East as well. Here, two peoples with dreams of established their own nations, Jews and Arabs, clashed over their claims to the same land. The Jews, fortified by their particular brand of nationalism—Zionism—returned to settle a land they had parted from centuries before, while the Palestinians, who had occupied this same land for centuries, were determined to establish their own state. The state of Israel came into being in 1948, at the expense of the Palestinians, and ever since it remained embattled by its Arab neighbors.

## Note

1. James J. McBath, ed., *British Public Addresses, 1828–1960* (Boston: Houghton Mifflin, 1971), pp. 75–83.

# 5

# Decolonization in Asia

Independence movements in Asia had been brewing since the beginning of the twentieth century and by the end of World War II could no longer be contained. In some cases, independence was achieved peacefully, because the imperial nation became resigned to the termination of its colonial rule, as was the case of the United States in the Philippines and Great Britain in India and Burma. In other cases, colonial powers were determined to resist the nationalist movements, granting them their independence only after long and bloody attempts to suppress them, as was the case of the French in Indochina and the Dutch in the East Indies.

The primary ingredient in all independence movements was nationalism. By drawing on their precolonial traditions, the colonized peoples developed a sense of national consciousness mixed with strong anti-imperialist sentiment. They were outraged by colonialist domination, by being treated as inferior citizens in their own native lands. They would point out to their European overlords the blatant contradiction between their professed ideals of democracy and self-government—of *liberté*, *égalité*, *fraternité*, in the case of the French—and their denial of the same to their colonies, which they treated under a different set of laws. Indeed, the French had a separate legal code for the indigenous peoples, the *indigenat*, that confirmed their inferior legal status and denied them rights the European residents enjoyed—such as freedom of speech, assembly, and travel. After witnessing the destruction European nations had wrought upon one another in World War I, the Asian colonial peoples began to doubt the superiority of their colonial masters. During World War II, that sentiment only grew.

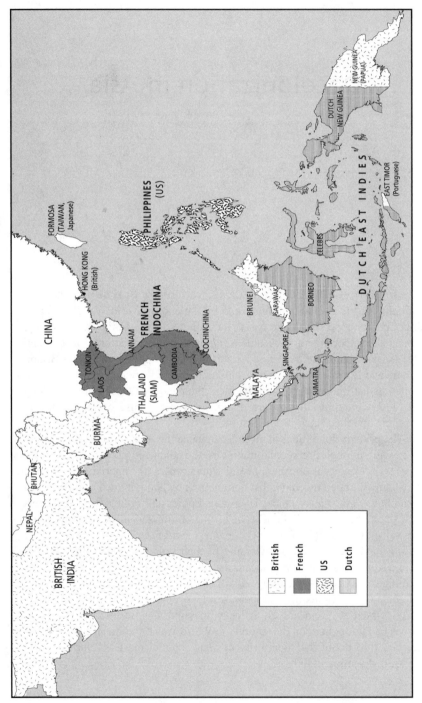

**Colonial Asia (1940)**

British
French
US
Dutch

CHINA

FORMOSA (TAIWAN, Japanese)

HONG KONG (British)

PHILIPPINES (US)

NEPAL

BHUTAN

BRITISH INDIA

BURMA

FRENCH INDOCHINA

ANNAM

TONKIN

LAOS

THAILAND (SIAM)

CAMBODIA

COCHINCHINA

MALAYA

SINGAPORE

SUMATRA

BRUNEI

SARAWAK

BORNEO

CELEBES

DUTCH EAST INDIES

DUTCH NEW GUINEA

NEW GUINEA (PAPUA)

EAST TIMOR (Portuguese)

## The Impact of World War II

World War II, and especially the role played by Japan, greatly stimulated Asian independence movements. During the war, several of the imperial powers of Europe were either overrun by Nazi Germany, as were France and the Netherlands, or were fighting desperately for survival, as was Great Britain. These nations were unable to defend their colonies once Japan set out to bring Southeast Asia into its own colonial orbit. The Japanese claimed that they came as liberators, fighting to free Asians from the chains of Western imperialism and to make Asia safe for Asians. While it is true that under Japanese rule Asian colonies merely faced a replacement of one master for another, Japan did much to strengthen nationalist movements in Southeast Asia. The swiftness and apparent ease by which the Japanese defeated the Europeans in Asia signaled to Vietnamese, Indonesians, Burmese, Indians, and others that their former European masters were not as powerful as they had thought.

In Indonesia the Japanese released native political prisoners from the jails and threw the Dutch colonial officials into the same cells. They banned the use of the Dutch language and promoted the use of native languages. In Indochina, under French rule for sixty years, they granted Vietnam its independence, albeit under Japanese tutelage. They also granted nominal independence to the Philippines and to Burma in 1943, and promised it to others. In some cases, such as in India and Burma, Japan helped arm and train national armies to fight the British. By the end of the war, when Japan was forced out, the nationalist organizations Japan had assisted stood ready to oppose the efforts by the European powers to reimpose their colonial rule. This was especially the case in Indonesia, where nationalist leaders issued a declaration of independence at the time of Japan's surrender.

The United States, too, played a role in hastening the end of colonialism in East Asia. During the war, President Franklin Roosevelt had been outspoken in his opposition to the continuation of European colonialism; indeed, after the war, the United States became the first Western nation to relinquish its colonial power in Asia. It had long promised independence to the Philippines, a colony since 1898, and no sooner was the war over than plans for the transfer of power were made. In 1946, with great fanfare, the Republic of the Philippines was proclaimed on an appropriate date, July 4.

## Independence and the Partition of India

The decolonization of British India has deep historical roots. Resistance to British rule began in the nineteenth century with the founding of the Indian National Congress (a political party usually known as Congress). When World War II broke out, the British Raj (rule) faced a well-organized independence movement led by Jawaharlal Nehru and Mohandas Gandhi.

While Nehru was the leading political figure, Gandhi represented a moral argument against British colonialism, which found expression in passive resistance to British colonial laws. (Gandhi drew upon the writings of the nineteenth-century US political activist Henry David Thoreau and, in turn, he influenced the US civil rights leader Martin Luther King Jr.) Gandhi became a unique force to be reckoned with because of his long-suffering and selfless pursuit of national independence using such nonviolent methods as refusing to pay British-imposed taxes, organizing work stoppages, and engaging in hunger strikes. Britain's viceroy (the crown's representative in India) described him as a "terribly difficult little person," while Prime Minister Winston Churchill called him a "half naked" fakir, something Gandhi took as a compliment.[1] They had good reason to fear Gandhi, who inexorably undermined Britain's pretentions of moral and legal authority to control India.

It did not help that when World War II broke out in Europe in September 1939, the British viceroy—without consulting with Indian leaders—declared war on Germany on behalf of India. Churchill had no intention of even discussing Indian independence, but he found that the exigencies of war demanded a more flexible position. In March 1942, his government dispatched a special envoy, Sir Stafford Cripps, on a mission aimed at placating the Indian nationalists. In August 1942, at a time when the Japanese armies appeared to be moving inexorably toward India (Britain's major military base in Southeast Asia, with Singapore having fallen in February), Cripps offered India dominion status (self-government but continuing membership in the British Commonwealth) and an election for a native constituent assembly to draft an Indian constitution—*after* the war. Congress responded with the Quit India Resolution demanding, as Gandhi put it, that Britain leave India "to God, or to anarchy."

The British response to the Quit India Resolution was to arrest tens of thousands, including Gandhi and Nehru. Congress followers rebelled but were quickly suppressed. One expatriate Indian nationalist leader, Subhas Chandra Bose, went so far as to put an army in the field (with Japanese assistance) to fight the British. Toward the end of the war, the British viceroy repeatedly advised London that the demand for independence in India was so strong that it could be postponed no longer. Churchill, the guardian of Britain's empire, however, disliked Indians, had little tolerance for their nationalist sentiments, and had no intention of granting them independence. In his public reaction to the Quit India Resolution he famously declared:

> We intend to remain the effective rulers of India for a long and indefinite period. . . . I have not become the King's First Minister in order to preside over the liquidation of the British Empire. . . . Here we are, and here we stand, a veritable rock of salvation in this drifting world.[2]

Churchill offered two alternatives: The British could either stand and rule or they could cut and run, and he did not seriously consider the latter. In the end, however, he was unable to prevent the inevitable. In June 1945, in anticipation of the end of the war, British authorities in India convened a conference of Indian leaders (several of whom were released from prison so that they could take part) aimed at creating an interim coalition government pending the granting of independence after the war. These talks, however, were complicated by the presence of a third party, the Muslim League. Muslims made up the largest religious minority in India, and they feared political domination on the part of the far more powerful Hindu majority. They feared becoming a helpless minority in an Indian nation in which the Hindu-Muslim population ratio was about five to one. Centuries of Hindu-Muslim antagonism could not easily be resolved, and the Muslim League, led by Mohammed Ali Jinnah, insisted on nothing less than a separate state for the Muslims. Gandhi and Nehru were staunchly opposed to such a division, and they tried—without success—to reassure Jinnah and the British that Muslim autonomy and safety would be guaranteed in the proposed Union of India. The British, too, wished to preserve the unity of India, but Jinnah remained adamant in his demands for a separate Muslim state.

In London, the new prime minister, Clement Attlee, whose Labour Party had unseated Churchill's government in July 1945, agreed to the transfer of power to an Indian government as soon as possible, while at the same time trying to preserve the unity of the country. In an effort to resolve the Muslim-Hindu dispute, Attlee dispatched, in March 1946, a cabinet mission to India, where tensions were rapidly mounting. Indian nationalism was made manifest in a mutiny by Indian sailors against their British naval officers, and by the outpouring of the inspired nationalist rhetoric of Gandhi and Nehru. Jinnah was equally articulate and passionate in his demand for a separate nation for the Muslims. When the British mission released its report, it rejected partition as impractical. It proposed, instead, a formula for ensuring the autonomy of Muslim provinces within a greater Indian state. The efforts to implement this compromise, however, were forestalled by mutual mistrust and quarreling. With the outbreak of communal violence between Hindus and Muslims (and among other minorities), there was too little time to work out a peaceful solution.

The tense situation in India caused the British government to advance the timetable for independence. It appointed a new viceroy of India, Lord Louis Mountbatten, Britain's popular wartime hero, who arrived in India in March 1947. Mountbatten announced July 1948 as the new deadline for the transfer of power from the British to the Indians. Instead of pacifying the Indians—both Hindus and Muslims—as he had intended, his announcement had the opposite effect. Fearful and mistrustful of each other, Hindus and Muslims initiated a new cycle of violence.

Although Mountbatten at first reaffirmed the British desire to preserve the unity of India, he could not satisfy the Muslim League with anything less than partition, and he therefore decided to settle the matter speedily by establishing two successor states to British rule. The result was a hasty agreement on the independence and partition of India to go into effect on a new, earlier date, August 15, 1947.

Thus, not one but two nations came into being: India and Pakistan, the new Muslim state. The problem was compounded by the new maps—drawn up in haste by a London judge, Cyril Radcliffe, who was granted only forty days to draw up the so-called Radcliffe Line—which suddenly placed people into regions where they were now a religious minority. He well understood that his hurried handiwork antagonized both parties. He wrote at the time: "There will be roughly 80 million people with a grievance looking for me. I do not want them to find me." The partition of India led to a flood of some 15 million refugees, one of history's largest. Radcliffe departed for home, never to return to India, explaining, "I suspect they'd shoot me out of hand—both sides."[3]

The transfer of the refugees was accompanied by unbridled violence, particularly in the provinces of Punjab and Bengal, which had been cut in half. Trains carrying nothing but corpses were but one symptom of it. Hysterical mobs of Hindus, Muslims, Sikhs, and others savagely attacked one another in acts of reprisal, bitterness, and desperation. In many cities, terrorism raged out of control for days when arson, looting, beatings, murder, and rape became common. Villages became battlegrounds of warring groups, and massacres were frequent along highways clogged with poor and usually unprotected refugees. Before all was over, an estimated 1 million people lost their lives. The result was a legacy of bitterness that has plagued Indian-Pakistani relations since that day.

Violence ultimately claimed even the life of Mohandas Gandhi, the supreme symbol of nonviolent resistance. In January 1948, a Hindu extremist, believing that Gandhi had been too conciliatory to the Muslims, shot him to death. Between 1937 and 1948, Gandhi had been nominated five times for the Nobel Peace Prize, only to be denied the honor because "he was neither a real politician nor a humanitarian relief worker." Nonetheless, nonviolent dissident movements across the globe continue to carry the imprint of Gandhi's legacy.

The agreement on the partition of India did not specify the future status of the Sikhs, another religious minority, nor of the 565 small, independent princely states scattered throughout India. It was presumed, however, that they would look to one or the other of the two new governments for protection and thus become integrated into either India or Pakistan.

The new nation of Pakistan—made up almost exclusively of Muslims (whereas India retained a sizable Muslim minority, who a half century later became hostages to Hindu extremists)—came into being in a strange configuration. It consisted of two parts—West Pakistan and East Pakistan—situated on Indian's western and eastern flanks, separated by 1,000 miles. (For the fate of East Pakistan, see Chapter 16).

## The British and Dutch in Southeast Asia

Decolonization in Southeast Asia—the region stretching from Burma to the Philippines, which includes Thailand, Vietnam, Indonesia, and Malaysia—varied from country to country. In general, it was more orderly in the US and British colonies (excepting, of course, the violence involved in the partition of India) than in the French and Dutch colonies. The British granted independence to Ceylon (now known as Sri Lanka) in 1947 and to Burma (later called Myanmar) in 1948. They were prepared to transfer power to a Malayan union in 1948, but this was delayed for a decade by internal strife between the majority Malays and the minority Chinese. An unsuccessful ten-year Maoist-inspired Communist insurgency by ethnic Chinese further complicated matters. Finally, in August 1957, after the Maoists were defeated and after a semblance of ethnic tolerance between the Malays and the Chinese was attained, the British granted independence to the Federation of Malaya. Singapore, made up largely of Chinese, separated from Malaya in 1965 and became a sovereign state.

In contrast to Britain, the Netherlands had no intention of granting independence to the Dutch East Indies, a colony comprising 8,000 ethnically diverse islands, which the Dutch had exploited for three centuries. Dutch intransigence was met by equally strong resistance on the part of Indonesian nationalists. During World War II, the Japanese military rulers of Indonesia gave their active support to an anti-Dutch nationalist organization known as Putera. As the war ended, this organization, under the leadership of Achem Sukarno, boasted a 120,000-troop army. When news of Japan's surrender reached the capital of Jakarta, Sukarno, who had been under intense pressure from the more radical student element in Putera, quickly drafted a declaration of Indonesian independence and, on August 17, 1945, read it to a huge crowd that had gathered to celebrate the event. At about the same time, the British landed an occupying force to receive the Japanese surrender and to maintain order until Dutch forces could arrive.

The Dutch intended to restore colonial rule, only to be confronted by a strong nationalist movement with a large, well-equipped army and by an even more hostile Communist movement. Negotiations produced a compromise in late 1946 whereby the Dutch would recognize Indonesian independence only on the islands of Java and Sumatra, but on condition that this new truncated Indonesian republic remain within the Dutch colonial empire in a "Union of Netherlands and Indonesia." Indonesian leaders rejected this plan, however, and when the Dutch resorted to force to quell demonstrations in July 1947, they were met by armed resistance. Despite UN efforts to arrange a cease-fire, and diplomatic pressures on the Dutch by the United States and Britain, the Indonesian war of independence continued for another two years, with thousands of casualties on both sides. Finally, in 1949, the Dutch conceded, and a fully independent Federation of Indonesia came into being with Sukarno as its president.

## The French in Indochina

After World War II, the French government was resolutely opposed to granting independence to its Asian colonies. Their retention was a matter of *honneur* and commitment to their *mission civilisatrice*.

France's colonial presence in Vietnam dates back to 1858, when its troops first arrived. It took a quarter of a century, but in 1883 the ruling dynasty submitted to French rule. The Vietnamese nationalist resistance began literally the very day the emperor surrendered his country's sovereignty to France. It took the French another dozen years to establish a sense of stability, but they never did extinguish Vietnamese resistance, something the Vietnamese had honed for 2,000 years against any and all foreigners, primarily the Chinese to the north. For the next half-century, French rule appeared to be secure. Military might, imprisonment, and the public use of the guillotine had their intended impact.

The central figure in the Vietnamese independence movement was Ho Chi Minh who, since his teenage days, questioned the moral and legal authority of France to be in Vietnam. He happened to be living in Paris when the victors of World War I met to decide the fate of the losers. US president Woodrow Wilson had come to the 1919 Paris peace conference as the champion of national self-determination, as someone who spoke for the rights of all subjugated peoples. To make his case for Vietnamese independence, Ho humbly submitted a petition to the US delegation asking for Vietnamese self-rule, amnesty for all political prisoners, equal justice, freedom of the press, and the implementation of "the sacred right of all peoples to decide their own destiny."[4] The US delegation ignored it. The diplomats at the conference had more pressing issues to consider, and the French, whose overriding concern was the punishment of Germany, were in no mood to abandon their prized colony (which by then had become a money-making enterprise through the ruthless exploitation of Vietnam's people and resources).

In the following year, Ho became one of the founders of the French Communist Party, because he saw Communism as the only political movement in France that concerned itself "a great deal with the colonial question." For Ho, Communism thus became a vehicle for national liberation of his native land from French colonialists who professed the principles of liberalism and democracy. Ho's identity as a Marxist and anticolonialist took him to

Moscow in 1923, just as the Kremlin began to focus on domestic problems and all but abandoned its commitment to international revolution. By the late 1920s, he made his way to China, where revolutionary ferment threatened to spread to the rest of Asia. For nearly thirty years, he remained a man without a country, living in exile and waiting for a chance to return to his native Vietnam to challenge the French.

The opportunity came during the early years of World War II. The French army, one of the world's best on paper, had collapsed in the face of the German attack. In September 1940, when the Japanese swept over Southeast Asia, the French again offered no resistance. Japan had humbled one of Europe's great powers, but it proved to be little solace for the Vietnamese, since they merely exchanged one exploitative master for another. The Japanese conquest of Southeast Asia, however, had put into sharp focus the vulnerability of the European colonial presence in Asia, a lesson that was not lost on the Vietnamese.

In the meantime, Ho returned to Vietnam in 1941 to create a native resistance movement, the Vietminh (the League for the Independence of Vietnam). When he turned against the Japanese, who now controlled Vietnam, the Vietminh and the United States, by a strange twist of fate, became allies during World War II. The US military recognized the usefulness of the Vietminh, and in fact officers of the US Office of Strategic Services (the forerunner of the CIA), generally anti-French and quite sympathetic to the Vietnamese rev-

*Ho Chi Minh at Dien Bien Phu, May 1954*

*National Archives*

olution, offered the Vietminh troops training, weapons, and supplies—even medical assistance when they nursed the chronically ill Ho back to health.

When the war ended in 1945, it was Ho and his men who controlled most of Vietnam. France's colonial ambitions in Southeast Asia seemed to be at an end. During the war, Roosevelt had urged the French to follow the US example in the Philippines and grant Vietnam its independence. But the French, humiliated in World War II, insisted on returning to Vietnam as one of the world's great powers and refused to accept the loss of their prized colony. Equating colonialism with national prestige, they insisted on reasserting France's authority. They had done so in the past, and could not imagine they would not be able to do so again.

In the meantime, the poorly armed Vietminh stepped into a power vacuum (France having been routed by Japan and Japan having surrendered to the United States) and forced the abdication of Bao Dai, the last emperor of Vietnam. On September 2, 1945, before a massive throng in Hanoi's main square, Ho declared the independence of Vietnam. In his proclamation, he drew on hallowed French and US political documents—the 1789 French Declaration of the Rights of Man and Citizen and the US Declaration of Independence—to justify a Vietnam free from colonial rule. The governments in Paris and Washington, however, turned a deaf ear to Ho's pleas. Subsequent talks between Ho and the French achieved little. At a minimum, Ho insisted on a genuine measure of autonomy within the French empire. Ho did agree, however, on the return of the French army to Tonkin (the northern third of Vietnam) to deal with the rapacious Chinese Nationalist army, which had arrived there in September 1945 to disarm the Japanese army. Ho had his work cut out to convince his followers that the Chinese were the primary threat to Vietnamese independence (indeed, the Chinese head of state, Jiang Jieshi, claimed Tonkin as part of China) and that they could be forced out only with French help. The French, Ho felt, could be dealt with in due time.

As tensions between the Vietnamese and the French rose, the French navy replied with a classic example of gunboat diplomacy. In November 1946, it bombarded the Vietnamese sector of the port of Haiphong, killing, according to French estimates, 6,000 civilians. In December 1946, the Vietminh, fearful that the French would replicate the Haiphong scenario in Hanoi, launched an attack on the French garrison in that city. The first Indochina war was under way.

### The First Indochina War

Initially, the Vietminh proved to be no match for the French army, which possessed superior weapons as well as more troops. As the French were able to put into battle airplanes, tanks, trucks, and heavy artillery, they were destined to win in a conventional head-to-head clash. The Vietminh had no choice except to pursue (at least at the beginning) the tactics of the weak against the strong: guerrilla warfare.

Guerrillas (from the Spanish meaning "little war") have little chance of defeating their more powerful enemy in a single decisive battle. They rely instead on a series of small campaigns designed to tie down enemy soldiers without engaging them directly. Once the enemy brings superior power into play, the guerrillas break off the fight and withdraw, leaving the battlefield to the conventional forces, who then plant their banners and proclaim victory.

Such a scenario is misleading. Ché Guevara, one of the better-known practitioners of guerrilla warfare and who had fought alongside Fidel Castro in Cuba in the 1950s, compared a guerrilla campaign to the minuet, the eighteenth-century dance. In it, the dancers take several steps forward and then back.[5] The "steps back" are central to guerrilla warfare since the guerrillas cannot afford to try to hold their ground lest they be decimated. Instead, they gather their dead, their wounded, and their supplies and reorganize to fight another day. Little wonder that the conventional forces are able to claim "victories," that they are winning the war and argue that it will only be a matter of time until the guerrillas suffer their "final" defeat.

The guerrillas' ultimate victory comes after a prolonged struggle that wears down the enemy physically and psychologically. Of utmost importance for the guerrillas is the sophisticated conduct of political action necessary to attract support. For conventional forces, the conflict is frequently of a purely military nature; successful guerrilla movements, in contrast, always focus on the psychological and political nature of the conflict. The French colonel Gabriel Bonnet reduced this to a quasi-mathematical formula: "RW = G + P (revolutionary warfare is guerrilla action plus psychological-political operations)."[6]

The sanguine French, certain of victory, were constantly able to discern "light at the end of the tunnel" (an unfortunate phrase the US military later borrowed). The Vietminh, however, always reappeared to fight again. Thus, what was intended as a short punitive action by the French turned into a long and costly war of attrition. And because all wars have political and economic repercussions, successive French governments were beginning to feel the heat. At the beginning, the French public had supported the suppression of yet another anticolonial rebellion. But as the years went by, as the financial burden and the number of casualties rose, public dissatisfaction grew apace.

In the spring of 1950, the United States became involved—indirectly—in the Indochina war and—directly—in the Korean War. Washington considered both wars as manifestations of a general Communist offensive in East Asia. President Harry Truman became concerned with the increasingly precarious French position in Vietnam, and he thus became the first US president to involve the United States in that region when he offered the French military and financial aid. At the end of the war, in 1954, it was the US taxpayer who underwrote most of the French expenditures in Vietnam. Along the way, Truman and his staunchly anti-Communist secretary of state, Dean Acheson, came down on the side of French colonialism, and Vietnam, a relatively small nation, became a focal point of the Cold War for the next twenty-five years.

Cold War orthodoxy in Washington insisted that Communist revolutions were fomented from the outside. The Soviet Union, however, offered the Vietminh no aid. Indeed, Ho's revolution—the formation of the Vietminh, the seizure of power in Hanoi, and the attack on the French garrison in that city— was carried out without Moscow's advice, support, or even knowledge. When the Chinese Communists came to power in 1949, Ho Chi Minh emphatically rejected the idea of using Chinese troops against the French, although he did accept Chinese matériel assistance, particularly artillery. Age-old Chinese-Vietnamese enmity was such that Ho feared the Chinese, their Communism notwithstanding, even more than he did the French. He believed, correctly, that the days of the white colonizers in Asia were numbered, but if the Chinese came they would stay for 1,000 years (as they had done in the past).

After years of fighting, the French were bogged down with little chance of winning the war. To suppress a guerrilla insurrection, conventional armies need vast troop superiority, somewhere between four and ten conventional soldiers for every guerrilla soldier. But in some of the important contested regions in the north, notably in the Red River delta, the Vietminh were able to match the French one to one. It is a truism of guerrilla warfare that as long as the guerrillas are not defeated, they are winning. In retrospect, by 1953 the French had already lost the war in Indochina.

French public support for the war was coming to an end. Predictions of victory by French generals and politicians had proven to be hollow promises. In desperation, the French military command hoped to entice the elusive Vietminh guerrillas to stand their ground and engage a final, conventional battle at the remote outpost of Dien Bien Phu, near the border of Laos. If the Vietminh took the bait and attacked Dien Bien Phu, it would lead to a conventional showdown, one that the French—in possession of superior firepower as well as control of the air and the roads—felt certain they would win.

General Vo Nguyen Giap, the military genius of the Vietminh, decided to oblige the French, but only after making adequate preparations for the battle. With extraordinary difficulty he brought into combat heavy artillery (courtesy of the Chinese Communists). To the surprise of the French, Giap was able to isolate the French garrison and deploy his heavy artillery on the hilltops overlooking it. When the French realized their position was doomed, they appealed for US intervention.

As Truman had done before him, the new US president, Dwight Eisenhower, was ready to come in on the side of French colonialism, but his options were severely limited. Some of Eisenhower's advisers urged a nuclear strike, but he rejected their advice. It made no sense to incinerate Dien Bien

Phu—killing French and Vietnamese alike—to "save" it. Eisenhower decided against directly becoming involved in Vietnam, particularly after the Senate majority leader, Lyndon Baines Johnson, told him that the US people would not support another war in Asia, particularly in light of the fact that the cease-fire in Korea had been signed only the previous year.[7] Eisenhower did, however, offer the French clandestine assistance at Dien Bien Phu. The CIA flew 682 airdrop missions, and two of its pilots were killed, the first US combatants to die in Vietnam in hostile action.[8]

The battle of Dien Bien Phu ("hell in a very small place," in the words of the French historian Bernard Fall) took place in the spring of 1954. The French fought heroically facing tremendous odds against nearly 50,000 Vietminh who pounded their fortifications as they inexorably inched ever closer in the tunnels and trenches they dug. The French commander, Henri Navarre, safely ensconced in Hanoi, demanded that there be no surrender. Despite his orders, white flags appeared over the French fort in early May. Two thousand of France's finest soldiers lay dead; 10,000 were taken prisoner (along with 4,000 indigenous soldiers), and only seventy-three managed to escape (nearly all of them indigenous troops who knew the area well).[9] The Vietminh lost perhaps as many as 15,000 of their best soldiers. But the French role in Indochina was over. A new French government and the public both welcomed the end of the war.

By coincidence, the world's leading powers—both Communist and capitalist—were engaged at that time in discussing several issues in Geneva and had agreed to take up the question of Indochina. Even before the battle of Dien Bien Phu commenced, the French and Vietnamese had agreed to take their dispute to this forum. It was thus incumbent for Ho and Giap (as well as the French) to attain a victory before the talks began. At the conference, however, the Vietnamese Communists received no support from the other Communist powers, the Soviet Union and China, both of which were more interested in normalizing relations with the West. As a consequence, the talks produced a strange agreement—which none of the parties signed and which left most parties dissatisfied. The only parties to be satisfied with the final document were the Soviet Union and, particularly, China. The Geneva Agreement called for a Vietnam temporarily divided along the 17th parallel with a Communist government in the north and an anti-Communist government in the south. The division was to last until a nationwide election, scheduled for July 1956 at the latest, meant to give the country a single government and president and thus finally bring about the "unity and territorial integrity" of Vietnam. In the meantime, the agreement demanded the neutrality of both parts of Vietnam, north and south.

The US delegates at Geneva were hypnotized by the specter of a global monolithic Communism. But they need not have worried. Both the Communist Chinese and the Soviets were more interested in cutting a deal with the French than in coming to the aid of their Vietnamese comrades. It appears that it was the Chinese foreign minister, Zhou Enlai (Chou En-lai), much to the surprise of the French, who first proposed a division of Vietnam. The Vietminh grudgingly yielded, but not before insisting on a dividing line along the 13th parallel, which would have left them in control of two-thirds of the country. Under Chinese and Soviet pressure, the Vietnamese backed down and accepted the 17th parallel, which cut the country in half. At the farewell banquet, Zhou hinted to the South Vietnamese delegation that he favored a permanent partition of Vietnam. Zhou's comment reflected China's centuries-old animosity toward Vietnam rather than solidarity among fraternal Communist nations. A divided Vietnam suited the Chinese just fine.

The Vietminh also yielded on the question of the timetable for the scheduled election. They wanted an election as soon as possible to cash in on their stunning defeat of the French. It was the Soviet foreign minister, Viacheslav Molotov, who asked rhetorically: "Shall we say two years?"[10] The French and the US delegates quickly endorsed Molotov's proposal. It was the best deal the US delegation (which had hoped for a six-year interval) could hope to obtain. Secretary of State John Foster Dulles knew that any southern, anti-Communist candidate stood little chance against the popular Ho Chi Minh. Earlier in the conference, Dulles had cabled his ambassador in Paris:

> Thus since [it is] undoubtedly true that elections might eventually mean unification of Vietnam under Ho Chi Minh this makes it all more important that they should be held only as long after cease-fire agreement as possible. . . . We believe important that no date should be set now.[11]

As it was, losing even half of the nation to Communism did not sit well with Dulles. US representatives refused to sign the Geneva Agreement, but in a separate statement the chief US negotiator, General W. Bedell Smith, acting on behalf of Eisenhower, pledged US adherence to it.

Washington made clear it wanted no part of the elections, even two years down the road. In a development reminiscent of Korea and Germany, two separate governments came into being: a pro-Western dictatorship in the South (with its capital city of Saigon) and a Communist dictatorship in the North (with the capital in Hanoi). The United States then propped up the anti-Communist government in the South, which it dubbed as "democratic" and which refused to abide by the Geneva Agreement. It refused to participate in the nationwide election and claimed to be the heir to all of Vietnam. As Washington supported the South Vietnamese government, it became increasingly tied to its unpopular and repressive regime, headed by Ngo Dinh Diem. Its military assistance and economic aid programs proved to be the precursors to direct intervention once the very existence of the Diem regime was threatened.

In the eyes of Washington, South Vietnam became the "guardian" of the "free world." Once that metaphor took root in popular thought, the survival of the anti-Communist regime in South Vietnam was linked to the survival of the United States. For psychological, geopolitical, and domestic political reasons, therefore, US–South Vietnamese relations became a Gordian knot that a succession of US presidents did not dare to cut. When the Diem regime was challenged by an insurgency in the late 1950s, the Second Indochina War began.

## Notes

1. For this and other citations below, see Pankaj Mishra, "Exit Wounds: The Legacy of Indian Partition," *The New Yorker*, August 13, 2007, pp. 80–84.

2. Cited in Francis G. Hutchins, *India's Revolution: Gandhi and the Quit India Movement* (Cambridge, MA: Harvard University Press, 1973), p. 143.

3. Basharat Peer, "The View from Jantar Mantar," *The Nation*, November 19, 2007, p. 42; Mishra, "Exit Wounds," p. 84.

4. Jean Lacouture, *Ho Chi Minh: A Political Biography* (New York: Random House, 1968), pp. 24–25; Chalmer M. Roberts, "Archives Show Ho's Letter," *Washington Post*, September 14, 1969, p. A-25.

5. Ché Guevara, *Guerrilla Warfare* (New York: Vintage Books, 1969), p. 13.

6. Bernard B. Fall, *The Two Vietnams: A Political and Military Analysis*, 2nd rev. ed. (New York: Frederick A. Praeger, 1967), pp. 349–350; Bernard B. Fall, *Last Reflections on a War* (Garden City, NY: Doubleday, 1967), pp. 209–223.

7. David Halberstam, *The Best and the Brightest* (New York: Random House, 1969), p. 141; also Stanley Karnow, *Vietnam: A History* (New York: Viking, 1983), p. 197.

8. James Bamford, *Body of Secrets: Anatomy of the Ultra-Secret National Security Agency* (New York: Doubleday, 2001), p. 286. The names of the pilots, however, are not inscribed in the Vietnam War Memorial in Washington.

9. Bernard B. Fall, "Dienbienphu: A Battle to Remember," in Marvin E. Gettleman, ed., *Vietnam: History, Documents, and Opinions* (Greenwich, CT: Fawcett, 1965), p. 107.

10. Karnow, *Vietnam*, pp. 198–204.

11. Neil Sheehan et al., eds., *The Pentagon Papers* (New York: Bantam, 1971), p. 46. Dulles also sent a copy of the cable to the head of the US delegation at Geneva, Bedell Smith. Eisenhower wrote in his memoirs that Ho Chi Minh would have defeated the last emperor, Bao Dai, with 80 percent of the vote.

# 6

# Decolonization in Sub-Saharan Africa

**Africa was the last bastion of European colonialism. At the close of** World War II, the European powers—Britain, France, Belgium, Portugal, and Spain—still firmly held their colonies, virtually the entire continent. But once decolonization began, it was carried out in a relatively short time. In the early 1950s, there were only three independent nations in Africa (Ethiopia, Liberia, and South Africa); by 1980, there were more than fifty such states.

The British government, already having lost India and Palestine in the late 1940s, recognized the inevitability of decolonization and began preparing for it. By the end of the 1950s, the French, too, had resigned themselves—even in Algeria, where they took their last stand—to the new historic reality. In the early 1960s, Africa was full of excitement and expectation as power changed hands from the white colonial masters to new African rulers who were flush with nationalistic pride and eager to face the new challenges of nationhood. The transition was relatively smooth in many colonies (albeit not in all) and was achieved faster and with less bloodshed than had been thought possible. Yet it was also a process that many European colonialists—notably in Algeria and Kenya—bitterly resisted.

## The Rise of Nationalism

The idea that Africans belonged to a particular nation was difficult to instill among peoples who, as a rule, identified with their tribe or ethnic group, not a centralized state. The colonies had boundaries that the Europeans had artificially created in the previous century without giving much thought to the fact that their inhabitants belonged to diverse ethnic groups, which in many cases were spread over more than one colony. In sub-Saharan Africa, no colony came close to containing a majority ethnic group. A sense of nationalism, however, required that loyalty to one's ethnic group be shifted to loyalty to the nation. The timing of decolonization in the colonies therefore depended, to a great extent, on the growth of a national consciousness and a sense of political unity. It was a slow and difficult process, barely begun in the 1950s. After independence, the persistence of ethnic loyalties continued to plague the new nations.

Prior to World War II, European colonial rule was hardly challenged by the subject peoples of Africa. The colonial administrations seemed so secure that they needed little military force to protect them. In some cases, especially in British and French colonies, this was achieved by use of the protectorate system, whereby local rulers were permitted to retain considerable autonomy under the military, political, and financial umbrella of their colonial overlords. The African population, the majority of whom were illiterate, generally viewed the Europeans with mixed awe and fear, and they were hesitant to attempt armed insurrection. And since political consciousness remained relatively low, there seemed little prospect of effective, organized anticolonial action.

Gradually, the situation changed as more Africans received an education—ironically, at the hands of the Europeans—and gained more experience in and exposure to the European world. Indeed, the very presence of Europeans in Africa fundamentally altered African society. In the cities the Europeans created educational (and to a lesser degree economic) opportunities for a select number of Africans. Colonialism carried within it the seeds of its own destruction. As the Europeans espoused democracy and civil liberties, they espoused ideas that were antithetical to colonialism, a system based on force, racial superiority, a professed desire to civilize the backward natives, economic exploitation, and the rule of the few. After generations under colonial rule, a native elite emerged, marked by a Western education and at times by Western values. Many of the early leaders tended to be lawyers or officers in the colonial armies. It was this educated class that first developed a sense of grievance, frustration, a political and historical consciousness, and a strong desire to put an end to colonialism.

Although signs of African restiveness appeared in the prewar period, especially as Africans felt the effects of the Great Depression of the 1930s, it was not until World War II that the demand for independence gained strength. Some African leaders pointed out that their people, who had been called upon to participate in that war to help defeat tyranny and defend liberty, deserved their just reward, a greater measure of that liberty. In the wake of World War I, they had made similar such arguments, which, however, had fallen on deaf ears. This time they determined it would be different. They were stimulated by the example of colonies in Asia winning their independence from the same Europeans who ruled them. The French defeat at Dien Bien Phu, in particular,

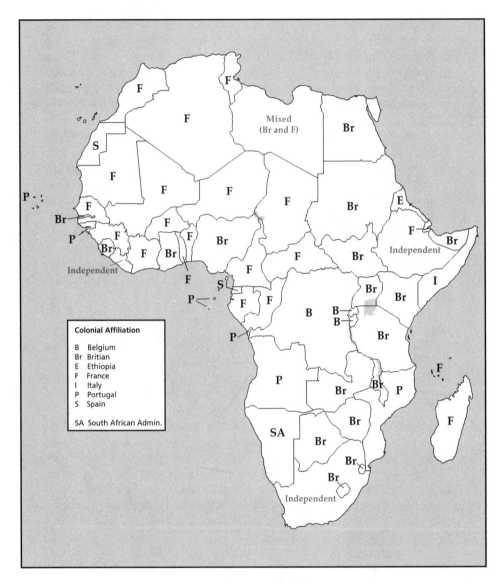

**Colonial Africa (1945)**

had an electrifying impact on African independence movements. And in India, Jawaharlal Nehru vigorously championed the cause of decolonization at the United Nations and other international forums. The founding of the United Nations also gave heart to the African nationalists, who looked forward to the day when their new nations would join its ranks as full-fledged members. The two superpowers, the United States and the Soviet Union, as professed champions of oppressed peoples everywhere, also urged early decolonization (in part because it did not affect them directly).

## The British Departure

The British were the first to understand that their direct rule in Africa was coming to an end, and thus, step-by-step, they permitted greater participation by the native peoples in governing of their colonies. They established executive and legislative councils to advise the British governors and began to appoint a few well-educated black Africans to these councils. Next, black political leaders were permitted to seek election to the legislative councils. Once this was granted, the nationalist leaders began convening congresses and political parties, which became their organs of nationalistic, anti-imperialist propaganda. They also agitated for universal suffrage—the right to vote. According to the parliamentary system that operated in British colonies, the party that gained the majority seats in the legislature earned the right to appoint the prime minister. The first native Africans elected to national office were usually charismatic figures blessed with great oratorical and organizational ability. The vast majority of them had spent their youth in Western schools and their adult years in Western prisons.

This process was first played out in West Africa, in the Gold Coast, the first of Britain's sub-Saharan colonies to gain independence. There, the able nationalist leader Kwame Nkrumah (who had attended universities in the United States and Britain) organized an effective political movement that took advantage of the legal political process. But he did not shrink away from using illegal political methods, which he called "positive action"—civil disobedience, strikes, and boycotts. On the first day of "positive action," in January 1950, the British authorities arrested him. In 1951, Nkrumah managed his party's election campaign while sitting in a British prison. After Nkrumah's party won a large majority, the British governor had little choice but to release him, now a national hero, and grant him a seat on the executive council. When the colony gained its independence, in March 1957, Nkrumah became its first prime minister. Henceforth, the Gold Coast became known as Ghana, after an ancient empire that once controlled much of West Africa.

Ghana became the model for other African independence movements, and Nkrumah became the continent's most outspoken champion of liberation of all of Africa. Nkrumah invited leading African politicians to two conferences in Accra, the capital of Ghana, for the express purpose of creating the Organization of African Unity (OAU). (Established in 1963, the OAU was disbanded in 2002 and replaced by the African Union.) Its purpose was to complete decolonization, end white minority rule, and forge pan-African cooperation. Nkrumah's call for independence spread rapidly across Africa. In

Nigeria, the most heavily populated British colony, self-rule came in October 1960, in the form of a federation that granted the major regions substantial autonomy. Mistrust among the various ethnic groups, however, had a destabilizing impact and soon Nigeria found itself in a civil war. (For details, see Chapter 13.)

In East Africa, Kenya's independence was forestalled by the European settlers' demand to retain the status quo. Kenya was one of several so-called "settler colonies" in Africa—such as Algeria, South Africa, and Southern Rhodesia—with an entrenched permanent class of Europeans, many of whom had been born in Africa and who, indeed, called themselves Africans. Their status was at the expense of the once independent native African farmers, who now were reduced to serving the Europeans. In Kenya, the 40,000 white settlers living mostly in the central highlands possessed the best lands and controlled the economic and political levers of power. Their opposition to independence ran deep.

The largest tribe in Kenya (one of three dozen), the Kikuyu, took the lead in demanding independence. In World War II, 75,000 Kenyans had served in the British army and now they expected fairer treatment. In 1952, the hitherto peaceful Kikuyus launched a movement known as the "burning spear," or Mau Mau. Their primary aim was to return the land to its original owners, who had not only been dispossessed, but were also forbidden to compete with the white farmers. The British demanded that cash crops for export—such as coffee, tea, and sisal—be grown only by Europeans.

Between 1952 and 1960, the Mau Mau indeed terrorized white settlers (as the press claimed), but in fact it directed most of its violence against other blacks. The Mau Mau insurrection was primarily a civil war between the Mau Mau and those loyal to Britain (such as local chiefs and Christians). The Mau Mau killed approximately 2,000 black Africans, thirty-two European settlers, and fewer than 200 British soldiers and police.

The British response was out of proportion to the uprising. They saw Kenya as their most important remaining colony, and to hold on to it they used any and all means—arbitrary arrests, hard labor, the bribing of judges to obtain convictions, torture of every conceivable sort (including dogs mauling prisoners, castration, men forced to sodomize each other), collective punishment of entire villages (some set on fire), the resettlement of nearly the entire Kikuyu population of 1.5 million in 800 "new villages" (detention camps surrounded by barbed wire), and the strafing of villages from airplanes. Kenya became a police state in the proper sense of the word. In all, the British killed, at a minimum, 100,000 Kikuyus. Between 1953 and 1958, they hanged 1,090 Kikuyus. Nowhere in the annals of British imperialism had the authorities executed so many.

At first, the British dismissed the accounts of their own stark brutality as rumormongering or as the acts of a few individuals who had strayed from the norms of civilization. But an investigation into the deaths of eleven Kikuyus at the Hola prison in March 1959 revealed the prisoners had been systematically clubbed to death. The Hola murders marked the end of Britain's "civilizing mission" in Kenya.[1]

The Kikuyu and other tribes eventually formed a national party under the leadership of the relatively moderate Jomo Kenyatta. A London-educated member of the Kikuyus, Kenyatta had languished in a British jail for over seven years as a political prisoner (the result of the mistaken assumption that he headed the Mau Mau uprising). In May 1960, while still in prison, he led his party, the Kenyan African National Union, to political victory, and when Kenya gained its independence in December 1963, he became its first prime minister. Kenyatta and the outgoing British colonial authorities worked out a political formula, embodied in a new constitution, designed to provide for majority rule and yet protect the white minority.

A small number of Europeans left, but those who remained were not victimized by Kenya's black majority or the new government. Indeed, Kenyatta made sure that there would be no land reform, as the Mau Mau had insisted. Europeans and black loyalists kept their government jobs. Kenyatta and the British, moreover, came to a tacit agreement not to dwell on the atrocities Britain had committed. Kenyatta, at pains to bury this sordid episode in British colonial history, declared the Mau Mau "a disease which has been eradicated, and must never be remembered again." To this day, there is no official memorial in the capital of Nairobi to the Mau Mau, the architects of Kenyan independence.

Three other British settler colonies in south-central Africa—Nyasaland, Northern Rhodesia, and Southern Rhodesia—formed a federation in 1953, partly for economic reasons and partly as a means of retaining white minority rule. In response to increasing pressure by the majority black populations, the British dissolved the federation and imposed on Nyasaland and Northern Rhodesia constitutions guaranteeing majority rule, thus ending white political supremacy. In 1961, Nyasaland became independent Malawi, and in 1963, Northern Rhodesia became the independent Zambia.

In Southern Rhodesia, however, a white minority regime, led by Ian Smith, defied the British government and its own black majority by rejecting the British-sponsored majority-rule constitution. Southern Rhodesia unilaterally declared its independence in 1965 and withdrew from the British Commonwealth. Only after prolonged guerrilla attacks by African nationalist parties from bases in neighboring countries and sustained international pressure did Smith finally relent and, in 1976, accept majority rule, to become reality in two years' time. Continued fighting among rival nationalist parties delayed until 1980 the formation of a black majority government in what became known as Zimbabwe. The hero of the resistance, Robert Mugabe, became the nation's first prime minister elected by popular vote; he then made sure to stay in power via a series of fixed elections. (See Chapter 13.)

## The French Departure

France's colonial policy was different from that of Britain in that its official aim was the assimilation of its subject peoples, that is, to turn them into French citizens. The colonial peoples were enjoined to abandon their heritage in favor of France's "superior" culture as expounded by its *mission civilisatrice*. Those who attended French schools were taught the French language and the elites among them received their higher education at French universities. No attempt was truly made to prepare them for independence.

The problem with assimilation was that it assumed that the peoples of the French colonies wanted to become and in fact were somehow capable of becoming "French." In all cases, notably in Algeria where the assimilation of the broad masses of Muslim Arabs proved to be virtually impossible, the European settlers and Africans both rejected it. Similar to the Arabs and the peoples of French Indochina, black Africans understood that they were, first and foremost, conquered subjects. There was no point for their schoolchildren to recite the lessons written for French children in Paris: "Our ancestors the Gauls had blue eyes and blond hair." At its worst, assimilation as Paris envisioned it was racist; at its best, it was unabashedly ethnocentric.

Until the mid-1950s, none of the short-lived cabinets in postwar France—desperately trying to suppress an anticolonial rebellion in Indochina—responded to African demands for self-rule. After abandoning Indochina, however, France faced another massive uprising in Algeria coupled with a growing demand for independence in its other African colonies. With the exception of Algeria, where the French refused to budge, the African colonies were surprised to find a new French receptiveness to change.

African nationalists in the French colonies, similar to Nkrumah in Ghana, worked within the colonial system to attain independence. The most successful was Félix Houphouët-Boigny, a medical doctor from the Ivory Coast. Shortly after World War II, Houphouët-Boigny took the lead in forming a political party championing independence. As a member of the French National Assembly (as well as president of the colonial assembly and mayor of Abidjan), he played a leading role in drawing up legislation designed to lead to self-government. The effect of his historic "Reform Act," which the French National Assembly passed in June 1956, was to permit greater autonomy for the separate French colonies, which heretofore had been under one centralized colonial administration, the Ministry of Overseas France. Each colony was to have an ethnic French prime minister and African vice-ministers, as well as elections for legislative assemblies under universal suffrage.

Still, France intended to maintain a measure of indirect control over its African colonies, and to that end, President Charles de Gaulle, after he came to power in Paris in May 1958, endorsed a plan for continued association. Later that year, he offered France's twelve sub-Saharan colonies the option of membership in the French Union or immediate and full independence. The former meant self-rule coupled with continued association with France that included, most importantly, economic and military aid. It was the preference of all the colonies except Guinea, which opted instead for independence. In response to Guinea's decision, France immediately pulled out all of its personnel and equipment and terminated its economic aid in hopes of forcing the maverick back into the fold. French Guinea (renamed simply as Guinea), however, stuck with its decision.

In 1960, after two years of agitation and negotiations, de Gaulle, with his hands full in Algeria (see Chapter 7), abruptly granted independence to the French colonies in sub-Saharan Africa. These new nations were relatively unprepared either politically or economically for independence, and consequently they tended to remain politically unstable and economically dependent on France for years to come.

## The Belgian and Portuguese Departures

The Belgian government paid virtually no attention to prepare its prized possession, the Belgian Congo, for independence. Once the private domain of Belgian King Leopold II, the Congo was one of the largest and richest of the African colonies. Between 1885 and 1908, Leopold controlled what he called euphemistically the Congo Free State, where he exercised complete control, referring to himself as its "proprietor." He never visited his possession, however, preferring to live off his fortune (estimated at more than $1 billion in current dollars) on yachts and luxury villas on the French Riviera. His legacy was a rule of terror and exploitation leading to the deaths of perhaps up to 10 million Africans—nearly half of the population—during the next forty years, either killed outright, ravaged by disease, or worked to death mining ore and harvesting rubber.[2] The novelist Joseph Conrad called it the "heart of darkness." Belgian colonial policy changed little in the twentieth century.

In response to the outbreak of an insurrection in the capital of Leopoldville (today's Kinshasa) in early January 1959, the Belgian government hastily issued plans for granting the colony its independence. The new government was to be based on universal suffrage and civil rights for all people. In January 1960, Belgium made the stunning announcement that in only six months' time it would formally transfer power to the sovereign state of the Republic of the Congo.

The turbulent events that followed independence showed that the Congo was ill prepared for self-rule and that it had been too hastily abandoned by Belgium. The Belgians left behind but a handful of university-trained Congolese; among the 5,000 senior administrators, only three were native Congolese. The Belgians had made no effort to educate a broad range of the population. Kwame Nkrumah aptly described the Belgians' motto as "no elite, no trouble."[3]

The sudden Belgian departure contributed to an explosion of ethnic rivalry and separatist wars, the result of the Congo having over 200 different ethnic groups. A national consciousness, the notion of being a citizen of a unified state, was for all intents and purposes nonexistent. Even before the Belgians exited, a rift had developed between the two leading nationalist leaders: Patrice Lumumba and Joseph Kasavubu. Lumumba traveled throughout the Congo exhorting people to see themselves as citizens of a unitary state with a strong central government. Kasavubu, instead, wanted a loose federation to protect the autonomy of ethnic groups, such as his own Bakongo (or Kongo), after whom the country was named, who had their own strong sense of nationalism.

In the Congo's first and only democratic national election, in May 1960, Lumumba's all-union party (the National Movement of the Congo) outpolled Kasavubu's Abako Party, the cultural and political association of the Bakongo. With nearly twenty parties competing, neither came close to gaining a majority in the legislature, the Chamber of Representatives. In an uneasy compromise, Lumumba became prime minister (the more important position) and Kasavubu settled for the presidency.

In the meantime, the separatist leader of the rich copper-mining province of Katanga, the pro-Western Moise Tshombe, announced the secession of that province from the new republic. The result was a complicated, three-sided political struggle that soon involved outside forces, including Belgian and UN troops, the CIA, Soviet advisers, and Ché Guevara, fresh from the Cuban revolution. The subsequent extraordinarily violent civil war lasted over two years and left tens of thousands dead.

The Congolese army, weakened by the mutiny of black soldiers against their white officers and divided in loyalty between Lumumba and Kasavubu, was unable to maintain order. Nor could either leader match the Katangan forces of Tshombe, whose army remained under the command of Belgian officers. Tshombe, who had the support of the Union Minière, the huge corporation that controlled the copper mines, and of the white settlers, invited Belgian reinforcements into Katanga to defend its independence. Desperate to maintain Congolese national unity, Lumumba requested military assistance from the United Nations. The UN Security Council called upon Belgium to withdraw its forces from the Congo and dispatched a peacekeeping force. The United Nations, however, proved to be impotent because the Big Five were in disagreement over its role in the Congo.[4] Frustrated by the UN failure to act decisively against secessionist Katanga, and unable to defeat Katanga's Belgian-led forces, Lumumba then turned to the Soviet Union for support. This complicated the situation all the more as the Western powers then moved to check the Soviet influence. Kasavubu, with the help of Colonel Joseph Mobutu and the CIA, handed Lumumba over to his Katangan enemies, who murdered him. The democratic experiment in the Congo was over.

Kasavubu, who had sought autonomy for his own ethnic group, was no more ready than Lumumba to accepted Katanga's independence. For three years, the Katangan secessionist war, which was only possible with the assistance of Belgian industrial companies and 6,000 Belgian troops, severely damaged the credibility of African nationalists who had touted their readiness for self-government. It also further exposed the weakness of the United Nations as a neutral peacekeeping body.

In November 1965, Katanga's independence became moot after both Kasavubu and Tshombe were overthrown in a military coup by their erstwhile ally Mobutu, by now a general. Mobutu established a long-lasting, brutal, and dreadfully corrupt regime in the Congo, which he renamed Zaire in 1971 as part of his Africanization campaign. Under Mobutu, the country reverted to its status under King Leopold as Mobutu similarly treated it as his private preserve. As Leopold before him, Mobutu became one of the richest men on earth, even acquiring villas on the Riviera not far from those that once had belonged to Leopold. Meanwhile, Zaire descended further into poverty and degradation. By the time of Mobutu's ouster in 1997, the infrastructure the Belgians had left behind was in utter ruin.

• • •

By the end of the 1960s, Portugal still stubbornly clung to its colonies of Angola and Mozambique in southern Africa. A small country under the dictatorship of António Salazar from 1929 to 1968, Portugal regarded its African possessions—which together amounted to twenty times the size of Portugal itself—as "overseas provinces," that is, as integral parts of the nation and not colonies at all. Portugal savagely suppressed a nationalist insurrection in Angola in 1961, killing about 50,000 people, and quashed a similar uprising in Mozambique in 1964. Throughout, the Salazar regime ignored UN condemnation and continued to battle guerrilla resistance troops. Not until the overthrow of the Salazar dictatorship in April 1974 (Salazar himself having died in 1970) did Portugal take steps to grant independence to its African colonies. The transfer of power to an independent Angola in 1975, however, was accompanied by the eruption of warfare among rival nationalist parties, each of which had international supporters (Cuba, the United States, and the Soviet Union), and the country remained a scene of violence and East-West contention for many years. Exhausted by the conflict in Angola, Portugal decided in June 1975 to grant independence to Mozambique as well.

African solidarity, as envisioned by Nkrumah's pan-African union, remained an impossible dream. It was stymied by ethnic and national differences, rulers who had their own national and personal agendas, and the question of what, specifically, it was meant to accomplish. In the early twenty-first century, when the African Union sought to deal with genocide in the Darfur region of Sudan, it had only modest success in mitigating the violence.

The African nationalists who had led the struggle for independence also championed the cause of democracy, but to achieve the latter was easier said than done. Those who had gained power by the democratic electoral process were all too often loath to risk their positions in another election. The principle of a loyal opposition (i.e., tolerance of opposing political parties) remained an abstraction. Eventually, the overwhelmingly large majority of elected African heads of state clung to power as long as they could. When Nelson Mandela, the democratically elected president of South Africa, stepped down after only one five-year term in office, he was the exception to the rule.

The rulers of the newly independent African nations, especially the former French colonies, found it difficult to maintain a sound economy and raise the standard of living of their people —as they had promised. They found out that independence brought no magic solution to the struggle against poverty. The former colonies remained far more dependent economically on their former rulers than they had expected. One unanticipated financial burden on the new governments was the ever-increasing cost of maintaining armed forces, which they deemed necessary to safeguard internal security. But the armies proved to be a double-edged sword. On the one hand, they maintained internal security; on the other, they were used to topple the very same rulers who had spent lavishly on building up the military forces.

### Apartheid in South Africa

The first genuine European settler colony in Africa was founded in the mid-seventeenth century in what three centuries later became the Republic of South Africa. It proved to be the last African colony to gain its independence.

Between 1949 and 1994, South Africa stood apart from the rest of Africa, not only as the most economically developed nation but also as one ruled by an intransigent white minority. In defiance of world opinion and the demands of its black majority, the white National Party maintained political power by means of a policy known as apartheid, literally "apartness." It was a legal system that demanded the most rigid form of racial segregation anywhere. The laws forbade the most elementary contact among the four racial groupings in South Africa: blacks (also known as Bantus), whites (mostly of Dutch, French, and English descent), coloreds (of mixed black-white parentage), and Asians (largely Indians).

In 1948, the whites of Dutch (and in part French)[5] origin replaced another group of European settlers, the English, as the dominant political force in governing a country they considered to be theirs. Having settled on the South African coast as early as 1652 for the purpose of establishing a new religious commonwealth, the Dutch saw it as their native land and, in fact, called themselves "Afrikaners," Dutch for Africans. (They also called themselves "Boers," or farmers, and are often referred to by that name.) They based their claim to the land on discovery, conquest, economic development, and, ultimately, the will of God.

Apartheid was steeped in the teachings of the Dutch Reformed Church. The Afrikaners saw themselves as God's chosen, a righteous people destined to dominate the land and those who inhabited it. It was no coincidence that the most fervent defenders of apartheid were ministers of the church. Apartheid was also based on the principle of racial superiority. The Bantus, Afrikaners argued, had contributed nothing to civilization; their existence was one of savagery. The twin pillars of apartheid—religious determinism and racial superiority—grew out of the Afrikaners' long struggles against the Catholic Church and other heresies in the Netherlands, Western liberalism, and the black native population of South Africa.

By the end of the eighteenth century, the Dutch had deep roots in the South African soil. In 1795, however, the British gained control of the South African cape and with it came a long struggle between the established Dutch and the newly arrived English. As the outside world was again closing in on them, the Afrikaners decided on yet another exodus, this one into the hinterlands away from the coast. The Afrikaners opposed in particular the English ban of slavery, which in 1833 had become the law of the British Empire. In 1835, the Boers set out on the "Great Trek" northward into the high plains of Natal and Transvaal. The journey was filled with bitterness, determination, and a deep religious fervor. The trek became a triumphant religious procession by which God's elect, a people with a very narrow view of salvation, determined to build a New Jerusalem. God's favor shone on them when, on December 16, 1838—in a scene straight out of the Old Testament—470 Boers decisively defeated a force of 12,500 Zulu warriors, killing 3,000 of them on the banks of what became known as the Blood River.[6] After the Afrikaners came to power, December 16 became a national holiday, the Day of Covenant between God and his people.

Later in the nineteenth century, when the British again encroached on Boer territory, the Boers stood and fought two bloody and brutal yet losing wars that ended in 1902. From that day on, they prepared for the day of liberation and redemption. That day came in 1948, when their National Party, under the leadership of D. F. Malan—a minister of the Dutch Reformed Church—won a narrow electoral political victory. At this juncture, the modest British efforts to maintain racial harmony were abandoned, and segregation became the law of the land. Driven by an intense sense of religious and cultural self-preservation, the Afrikaners rejected all proposals for social and racial integration. They insisted instead that the races be kept apart by law and that no one had the right to cross the color line. It led to the political isolation of South Africa, yet isolation bred defiance and reinforced the outlook of a people long accustomed to adversity and determined to go it alone. A stiff-necked people, the Boers had stood up to the British, the Bantus, and now the world.

The first of the segregation laws—enacted in 1949, four years after Hitler's death—forbade miscegenation, the marriage or cohabitation of persons of different color. Whites and nonwhites were not permitted to spend the night under one roof. The Population Registration Act classified individuals on the basis of race, which was the deciding factor in where people were permitted to live. Schools, jobs, and pay scales were determined on the basis of color. Political organizations and strikes by nonwhites were outlawed. All public facilities—from hospitals to park benches and beaches—were segregated. Every aspect of sexual, social, religious, and economic intercourse between the races was regulated, not only among the living but also the dead. Even the cemeteries were segregated. The number of apartheid laws ran well over 300.

Race became an obsession in South Africa. A classification board assigned every individual to a racial category, but the science of distinguishing skin color, facial features, and hair texture is not exact. Often the result was as follows:

> In one typical twelve-month period, 150 coloreds were reclassified as white; ten whites became colored; six Indians became Malay; two Malay became Indians; two coloreds became Chinese; ten Indians became coloreds; one Indian became white; one white became Malay; four blacks became Indians; three whites became Chinese.

The absurdity knew no end. Chinese were classified as a white subgroup and Japanese as "honorary whites."[7]

Apartheid turned the once oppressed Afrikaners into oppressors. In 1980, blacks outnumbered whites by a ratio of three to one, 18 million to 6 million; the coloreds numbered about 3 million and the Asians nearly 1 million. It was little wonder that a siege mentality permeated white society. And, in fact, white settlements were frequently referred to as *laagers*, literally "camps," a term taken from the Great Trek of the 1830s.

The segregation laws were also the linchpin of economic exploitation. The laws excluded nonwhites from the better-paying jobs and positions of authority. In the construction industry in the late 1980s, whites earned twice the salary of Asians, three times that of coloreds, and five times that of blacks. A white miner earned $16,000 a year, a black miner $2,500. The combination of rich natural resources, industrial planning, and cheap black labor turned South Africa into Africa's only modern, industrialized state—but only for the white population. The defenders of apartheid pointed out that the wealth trickled down to the black population, whose standard of living was the highest of any blacks in Africa. Blacks regarded this argument as irrelevant. The blatant system of economic exploitation, psychological oppression, and political domination could only be maintained by force.

## The Struggle Against Apartheid

In 1959, the government set aside ten regions for the black population, the so-called "homelands" or Bantustans, on 13 percent of the nation's land. These "homelands" were the official residential areas of the native black population, who were denied legal access to the rest of South Africa. Although blacks, who made up much of the nation's essential workforce, could find work and a temporary residence permit in areas officially set aside for whites, their families had to remain behind. Officially, blacks were but temporary visitors at the pleasure of the white hosts, aliens in their native land. The "homelands" officially signaled the completion of the system of apartheid. The government hoped to obtain international recognition of the "homelands" as the national homes of the blacks of South Africa, yet no country recognized them as such. They had no legal international standing, if only because they never became viable entities, remaining financially dependent on the South African government.

The government's position became still more rigid in 1960, the official UN "Year of Africa," during which a number of sub-Saharan nations gained their independence. In February, British prime minister Harold Macmillan went to Capetown to remind the South African parliament that a "wind of change" was blowing through Africa. Black nationalism, he said, was a force that had to be recognized, if only to prevent the newly independent African nations from being drawn into the Communist camp. The government of Hendrik Verwoerd ignored whatever winds were blowing through Africa and made clear that there would be no accommodation of native African nationalism in South Africa. Six weeks later, on March 21, Verwoerd's government gave his reply to Macmillan when, in Sharpeville, police shot and killed sixtynine demonstrators who had protested the creation of the Bantustans and the "pass laws" that required them to carry identification documents that restricted their right of movement.

The Sharpeville massacre had an extraordinary psychological impact on black Africans, who saw it as a watershed. The time had come to move from peaceful agitation to armed revolution. The apartheid laws left them two choices: either accept their status as second-class citizen or rebel. Shortly after Sharpeville, highly publicized disturbances took place in Soweto (short for South-West Township), a black ghetto of 1 million people thirty minutes from Johannesburg, the elegant financial capital of South Africa. In April 1960, the government banned the political parties of the still-moderate African National Congress (ANC) and the militant Pan-Africanist Congress.

At this juncture, South Africa's oldest and most influential civil rights organization, the ANC—an umbrella organization of blacks, whites, Asians,

*Embassy of the Republic of South Africa*

*Nelson Mandela, leader of the African National Congress and first nonwhite president of the Republic of South Africa*

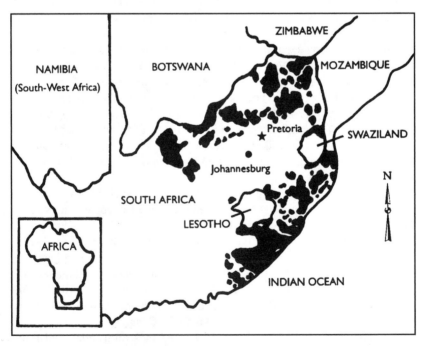

**South Africa's "Homelands"**

coloreds, and liberals—reassessed its strategy. Since its formation in 1912, the ANC had sought the peaceful establishment of a nonracial democracy. Its leader, Nelson Mandela, explained at his trial in 1964 that until the late 1950s his organization had "adhered strictly to a constitutional struggle."[8] But events between 1959 and 1961 made clear that this approach had reached a dead end.[9]

In 1961, the ANC, concluding that legal, nonviolent actions had been exhausted, adopted armed struggle as one of the means to bring an end to apartheid and formed its armed wing, Umkhonto we Sizwe—the "Spear of the Nation." Mandela, one of the founders of Umkhonto, explained that nonviolence had brought the black Africans "nothing but more and more repressive legislation, and fewer and fewer rights." On December 16, 1961, Umkhonto carried out its first acts of sabotage. The date was carefully chosen; it was the anniversary of the 1838 Afrikaner victory over the Zulus at the Blood River, the Afrikaners' Day of Covenant. The ANC marked that date as its Heroes' Day to honor those who had died in the struggle against apartheid.

The armed conflict between Umkhonto and the National Party had the effect Macmillan had feared. The ANC made common cause with the Communist Party, and consequently South Africa was drawn into the global Cold War. The Soviet Union provided money and weapons to the ANC, and the United States supported the South African apartheid regime. The ANC, however, did not espouse Marxist economic theory. In fact, it advocated a capitalist South Africa in which private property was more equitably distributed.

A tip from the CIA led to the arrest of Nelson Mandela in 1963. At his 1964 trial, Mandela justified the formation of Umkhonto as an act of self-defense. The court sentenced him to life in prison at hard labor.

### Black Consciousness and Zulu Nationalism

The early 1970s saw the emergence of a "black consciousness" movement in South Africa, a trend influenced in part by the US civil rights movement. Its leading advocate was Steve Biko, who preached that blacks must no longer rely on liberal whites to speak for them but must deal with whites as equals. "Whites must be made to realize that they are only human, [and] not superior," he declared, and blacks "must be made to realize that they are also human, [and] not inferior."[10] Biko's demand of racial equality as his birthright made him a dangerous and marked man. The authorities arrested him on a pass violation—his refusal to carry a passbook. He died in police custody in September 1977, his skull repeatedly fractured. After Biko's death, the radical Azanian People's Organization (Azapo), the militant wing of the Pan-Africanist Congress, declared itself the heir of Biko's "black consciousness" and then went much farther than Biko ever did. It demanded the expulsion of all whites from South Africa and declared war on them under the slogan "one settler, one bullet." Azapo also became engaged in an ideological—and soon bloody—conflict with the ANC and its allies, who promoted a nonracial democracy.

At the same time, the ANC also faced opposition from another black organization, the Inkatha Freedom Party, the political base of Zulu chief Mangosuthu Buthelezi. In their younger days, Buthelezi and Mandela had been comrades, but over the years Buthelezi became the champion of narrow Zulu aims rather than broad national interests. Buthelezi became a defender of the status quo in the form of the Afrikaner-created Zulu "homeland," KwaZulu, in the province of Natal. An integrated South Africa threatened his base of power, and thus he sought to perpetuate the continued existence of KwaZulu, either as a "homeland" or an entirely independent Zulu state. Biko and Mandela both criticized Buthelezi for accepting the Afrikaner formula for the separation of the races.

## The Dismantling of Apartheid

In the mid-1980s, the government slowly began to question the wisdom of continuing with apartheid. The financial, psychological, and human costs were becoming too high. June 1976 saw an uprising in Soweto that started as a student rebellion against the use of Afrikaans (a version of Dutch) as the language of instruction. The police established a semblance of order after killing several hundred demonstrators. In 1985, during demonstrations commemorating the twenty-fifth anniversary of the Sharpeville massacre, the police killed nineteen people at one demonstration alone, and scores also died in other clashes. The funeral processions for those killed served as protest demonstrations and brought yet more violence. At summer's end, for the first time white residential areas became the scenes of racial confrontations. There were 1,605 outbreaks of political violence in January 1986, and the numbers kept climbing in subsequent months. The anti-apartheid uprising of the mid-1980s claimed 1,650 black lives and nearly 30,000 were arrested.[11]

As violence escalated, the government began to consider the unthinkable: a political dialogue with the banned ANC and Mandela. In 1985, it offered Mandela release from prison provided that the ANC pledge to refrain from violent activity and that Mandela live in the "homeland" set aside for his ethnic group, the Xhosa. Mandela rejected the conditions as unacceptable. He insisted that as a free man he had the right to live wherever he chose and as long as the government resorted to violence, that ANC had the right to defend itself.

In 1985, President P. W. Botha came to acknowledge that apartheid was breaking down. His new slogan was "adapt or die." Demographics alone, in a nation where the black population was growing much more rapidly than the ruling white population, demanded a new approach. A split developed in Botha's government between the "enlightened" ministers and the conservatives fearful of any change. Determined to quell disturbances and to put an end to worldwide press and television coverage of the carnage in the streets, Botha imposed a nationwide state of emergency in June 1986. Botha, however, did scrap the hated pass laws and thereby abandoned the Boer stance that South

Africa was a white-only preserve. He understood that the old days were over, without having a clear idea of what would come next.

International pressure began to have a telling effect. Under the aegis of a UN-sponsored trade embargo, the United States government (over the veto of president Ronald Reagan) and most European nations imposed economic sanctions and foreign corporations began withdrawing their assets from South Africa. From 1986 to 1988, South Africa suffered a net capital outflow of nearly $4 billion, resulting in increased unemployment, inflation, and interest rates. Economic growth declined from a sturdy 5 percent to 2 percent. The price of apartheid had become too high.[12] A growing number of whites, especially in the business community, urged change. Many whites also felt a sense of isolation from the world community. Since the late 1960s, South Africa, a nation proud of its world-class athletes, had been banned from the Olympic Games and other venues of international competition, such as the soccer World Cup.

Botha gradually moderated the apartheid system. Some of the more superfluous restrictions were lifted. Certain public facilities—such as drinking fountains, movie theaters, and public parks and swimming beaches—were desegregated, and mixed residency was permitted in certain previously segregated urban residential areas.

### De Klerk and Mandela

In September 1989, Frederik W. de Klerk succeeded Botha as president of South Africa. In his inauguration speech he pledged to work for "a totally changed South Africa . . . free of domination or oppression in whatever form."[13] De Klerk took a remarkably conciliatory posture toward the outlawed ANC. Anti-apartheid protesters were permitted to hold a mammoth rally in Soweto at which released ANC leaders were permitted to address a throng of some 60,000 people. Even more surprising was the lifting of the political ban on the ANC, followed by the unconditional release of the seventy-one-year-old Mandela, in February 1990. De Klerk declared an end to Botha's state of emergency and promised to free all political prisoners. International investors responded swiftly by making money available to the South African economy, and the Johannesburg Stock Exchange industrial index rose 7.2 percent in two days.

As the newly freed Mandela took the first steps to negotiate with de Klerk for an end to apartheid, old issues came to the fore. One was the continued political rivalry between Mandela's ANC and Buthelezi's ethnic Zulu-based Inkatha movement. In contrast to Buthelezi, Mandela, although a descendant of Xhosa kings, had long since moved beyond ethnic politics and was committed to the abolition of the Bantustans.

Despite his lofty stature, Mandela was unable to halt black-on-black bloodletting. Between 1985 and 1996, ANC-Inkatha violence claimed 10,000 to 15,000 lives. Much of the violence was perpetrated by young radical blacks, the "Young Lions," who sought economic and political power in the black townships. Impervious to pleas for moderation, the Young Lions became notorious for "necklacing" their victims (placing tires around their necks and setting them on fire). Mandela's appeal to them to throw their guns and knives into the sea fell on deaf ears.

In 1991, the government abolished all apartheid laws—including the Population Registration Act, the legal underpinning of apartheid—and prepared to negotiate a new constitution. As it had done in the past, the ANC insisted on "one man, one vote"—that is, majority rule. If implemented, it would mean the election of a black majority government and, therefore, would produce a strong reaction from the Afrikaner right wing, such as the Conservative Party and the Afrikaner Resistance Movement. Nonetheless, a national referendum by white voters gave de Klerk an overwhelming mandate (68 percent for, 32 percent against) to continue negotiations with Mandela.

In 1992, the last obstacle, the "homelands," became a focal point of the ANC's political agenda. Pretoria still considered four of them—Ciskei, Bophuthatswana, Transkei, and Venda—independent entities. The ANC insisted they be reincorporated into South Africa. The leaders of these "homelands," where elections and opposition parties (including the ANC) were banned, insisted on maintaining their autonomy. They made clear they would defend that autonomy by force if necessary. Only after repeated, bloody clashes with ANC supporters did they finally yield to incorporation into a unified South Africa. Buthelezi and KwaZulu remained defiant, however, holding out for independence for the Zulu population of 7.5 million, South Africa's largest ethnic group. Not until the eve of the April elections did Buthelezi finally order his Inkatha Freedom Party to accept a unitary South African state.

### Mandela's Victory

Everyone knew that South Africa's first free multiparty and multiracial parliamentary election—slated for April 27, 1994—would mean a transition from white-minority to black-majority rule. As expected, Mandela's ANC was the big winner in the historic election, garnering 62 percent of the vote and 252 seats (out of 400) in the National Assembly. The National Party obtained but 20 percent of the vote and 82 seats. On May 27, 1994, the now seventy-five-year-old Mandela, who had spent twenty-seven years of his life as a political prisoner, was elected by the assembly as the first nonwhite president of his country. "The time for the healing of wounds has come," he declared. "Never, never, and never again shall it be that this beautiful land will again experience the oppression of one by the other. . . . Let freedom reign. God bless Africa!"[14]

This remarkable turn of events was the result of several factors: the South African government's inability to produce a stable society under apartheid; effective international economic sanctions; the end of the Cold War, which ended deleterious outside meddling by the superpowers; and the roles of de

Klerk and Mandela. For their efforts, de Klerk and Mandela shared the Nobel Peace Prize in 1993. The roles of old-guard National Party leaders, who had begun behind-the-scenes initiatives for change a decade earlier, should not be overlooked. At the time of the 1994 elections, several members of the former Botha government revealed that they had become convinced in the 1980s that apartheid could not be sustained and that they should strike a deal with the ANC for a peaceful transition to majority rule. It took another two and a half years after the election to reach an agreement on a permanent constitution. It was only fitting that Mandela sign this new consitution in Sharpeville in the presence of survivors of the 1960 massacre.

Mandela's inauguration, however, could not disguise the hard realities of unresolved divisive political issues and persistent economic and social inequalities. The dismantling of apartheid and the changing of the guard did not erase the miserable living conditions for the bulk of the black population or provide them with proper education opportunities.

Under Mandela's persistent demand, South Africa, which had one of the world's highest rates of capital punishment, abolished the death penalty. The question remained of how to deal with those responsible for past acts of violence. In July 1995, Mandela's government established a Truth and Reconciliation Commission, which sought—as its name implied—not to punish the guilty but to try to bring about national reconciliation between peoples who only recently had been killing each other. The head of the commission was the retired Episcopalian archbishop Desmond Tutu, a recipient of the Nobel Peace Prize in 1984—a man whose life had been dedicated to peaceful reconciliation.

The commission granted amnesty to the few who acknowledged their past crimes. The families of the victims—understandably—were generally opposed to amnesty, but there appeared to be no workable alternative. If punishment were to be meted out, then to whom? The new defense minister, Joe Modise, once the head of Umkhonto? Former defense minister Magnus Malan, who had organized anti-ANC death squads manned by Zulus? The guilty parties in the ANC-Inkatha violence, which had claimed as many as 15,000 lives over a ten-year span and who continued to kill each other even as the commission was holding its hearings? Could the state, even if it wanted to, bring some of the Inkatha leaders—not to mention Buthelezi—into the dock? And what was one to do about the charges that implicated P. W. Botha in acts of violence?[15]

After two and a half years of hearings, the Truth and Reconciliation Commission issued, in October 1998, its long-awaited final report. The 2,750-page document presented in gruesome detail thousands of instances of human rights violations perpetrated by both blacks and whites. Whites, especially those associated with right-wing organizations, denounced the report as biased against them; blacks criticized it for dwelling on ANC abuses. The report did not implicate former president de Klerk, but it did implicate former president Botha, who accused the commission of engaging in a witch hunt.

In the meantime, the new government had to tackle the mundane daily tasks of governance. Rampant crime was one of the biggest problems. Police officers were often poorly trained and departments were affected by corruption, absenteeism, and lack of discipline. Many crimes were not properly investigated; only 32 percent of murder suspects were convicted—this in a country with the highest murder rate in the world. Another urgent problem was the AIDS epidemic. In 2000, the Health Ministry calculated that AIDS already had claimed 250,000 lives and that the nation faced 1,600 new AIDS cases daily.

In December 1998, Mandela turned over the reins of the ANC to his old comrade-in-arms, Thabo Mbeki, who then succeeded Mandela as president of South Africa. Mandela's peaceful transfer of power stood in contrast to so many African leaders who had clung to power until they breathed their last. Mandela left behind an impressive legacy. He had led the fight against apartheid, achieved the transfer of power to the black majority, and laid the foundation for a society with a critical free press, integrated universities, political pluralism, and a private economy. "We have confounded the prophets of doom and achieved a bloodless revolution," he said. "We have restored the dignity of every South African."[16] The revolution, however, had by no means been bloodless; still, there had been far less violence than thought possible.

At Mandela's ninetieth birthday celebration, in July 2008, he expressed fear that his legacy was eroding. With the National Party barely hanging on, the ANC governed what was now essentially a one-party state. The head of the National Party announced in August 2004 that he was joining the ruling ANC and advised his followers to do the same, explaining that "the real debate about the future of the country is within the ANC and not outside."[17] Absent an effective opposition party, the system of checks and balances in South Africa was breaking down. The upshot was increased political corruption and the failure to effectively deal with society's woes—the world's highest crime and AIDS rates, poverty, a struggling economy—even while South Africa prepared to showcase the 2010 World Cup games, the first time the competition was held in an African nation.

An opposition party to the ANC, the Democratic Alliance (DA), slowly gained in strength. South Africa, the DA reminded the voters, was beset by a host of lingering problems beyond the ANC's ability to solve—among them, corruption, shoddy public services, and unemployment measured at 37 percent.

At Mandela's funeral in December 2013, foreign dignitaries rightfully hailed his legacy, notably his rare ability to forgive those who had trespassed against him. Other blacks, however, were preparing for a struggle over a more equitable distribution of South Africa's wealth, a problem that Mandela's unfinished revolution had ignored. When the brash, young populist Julius Malema called for a radical redistribution of South Africa's riches, he declared political war on president Jacob Zuma (and the ANC in general), Mandela's legacy, foreign investors, and particularly white Afrikaners, who were equally adamant there would be no redistribution of the nation's assets.

## Notes

1. David Anderson, *Histories of the Hanged: The Dirty War in Kenya and the End of Empire* (New York: W. W. Norton, 2005); also Caroline Elkins, *Imperial Reckoning: The Untold Story of Britain's Gulag in Kenya* (New York: Henry Holt, 2005).

2. Revelations of Leopold's greed and brutality prepared the way for the first great human rights crusade—augmented by the writings of Mark Twain and Joseph Conrad—of the twentieth century. See Adam Hochschild, *King Leopold's Ghost: A Story of Greed, Terror, and Heroism in Colonial Africa* (Boston: Houghton Mifflin, 1999).

3. Kwame Nkrumah, *Class Struggle in Africa* (New York: International Publishers, 1970), p. 38.

4. Secretary-general of the United Nations Dag Hammarskjöld made great efforts to resolve conflicts among the disputants both in the Congo and among member states of the United Nations. On the last of his frequent trips between New York and the Congo, while traveling to Katanga in September 1960, he died in an airplane crash.

5. In the late 1680s, French Calvinists, the so-called Huguenots, left France after their government revoked in 1685 the Edict of Nantes of 1598, a decree of religious toleration. The Huguenots were shortly absorbed into the Dutch Afrikaner community.

6. C. F. J. Muller, ed., *Five Hundred Years: A History of South Africa* (Pretoria: Academia, 1969), pp. 166–167.

7. David Lamb, *The Africans* (New York: Random House, 1982), pp. 320–321.

8. This and other statements by Mandela later in the chapter are from his defense from the dock in Pretoria Supreme Court, April 20, 1964, cited in *Nelson Mandela: The Struggle Is My Life* (New York: Pathfinder Press, 1986), pp. 161–181.

9. The Nobel Peace Prize committee acknowledged the peaceful nature of the ANC when in 1960 it awarded its medal to Chief Albert J. Luthuli, the ANC's president since 1952.

10. Biko, cited in Donald Woods, *Biko* (New York: Paddington Press, 1978), p. 97.

11. Rian Malan, *My Traitor's Heart: A South African Exile Returns to Face His Country, His Tribe, and His Conscience* (New York: Atlantic Monthly Press, 1990), p. 333. For black-on-black violence, see pp. 323–334.

12. World Bank, *World Development Report, 1989* (Washington, DC: World Bank, 1989), pp. 165, 167, and 179, has the following figures: The percentage of average annual growth rate, 1965–1987, stood at a mere 0.6 percent; the average rate of inflation, 1980–1987, was 13.8 percent. During 1980–1987, there was a decline in average annual growth rate in industry and manufacturing of –0.1 and –0.5, respectively. Gross domestic investment, 1980–1987, declined by 7.3 percent.

13. Peter Honey, "De Klerk Sworn in, Promises 'Totally Changed' S. Africa," *Baltimore Sun*, September 21, 1989.

14. "Mandela's Address: 'Glory and Hope,'" *New York Times*, May 11, 1994, p. A8.

15. Tina Rosenberg, "Recovering from Apartheid," *The New Yorker*, November 18, 1996, pp. 86–95.

16. Terry Leonard, "Mandela Has a Legacy of Peace," Associated Press, June 1, 1999.

17. Cited in "The Party of Apartheid Departs," *The Economist*, August 14, 2004, p. 44.

# 7

# Decolonization in the Arab World

While sub-Saharan Africa sought to free itself from European control after World War II, a similar drama played out in much of the Arab world—the stretch of land from the Arabian Peninsula westward, along the southern shores of the Mediterranean Sea, all the way to Morocco. Again the dominant powers were Britain and France. Most of their colonial possessions (Morocco excluded) had been wrested from Ottoman Turkey, a declining empire under pressure from Arab nationalism. In the years between the two world wars, Britain and France managed to keep Arab aspirations of nationhood in check. But after 1945, as decolonization became the order of the day, they faced an untenable position. By 1962, direct European control of Arab states was a thing of the past.

## The French Exit from Algeria

France's determination to retain control over Algeria must be viewed in the historical context of rising Arab nationalist aspirations and its war in Indochina. The war there drained the French people emotionally, physically, and economically. When the end came, in 1954, French society accepted the loss of Indochina without bitter recrimination. Instead they saw Indochina as a burden, which was finally lifted from their shoulders. There were few dissenting voices when Prime Minister Pierre Mendès-France accepted Indochina's independence. (For the details, see Chapter 10.)

Yet, five months later, France once again faced the prospect of losing a colonial possession. This time it was Algeria. Again, at stake were France's honor and its role as a great power. Having lost Indochina, the French were in no mood to accept another defeat.

139

What distinguished Algeria from France's other colonies was its official designation as an integral part of France, a province across the Mediterranean Sea, in the same manner that Brittany, Alsace, and Lorraine were provinces. (US president Dwight Eisenhower compared it to Texas, that is, an integral part of the United States.) Equally important, Algeria was the home of 1 million Europeans who considered themselves living in France. Mendès-France, the prime minister who had taken France out of Vietnam, now insisted that Algeria was "part of the republic." Algeria had "been French for a long time," he declared. "Between it and the mainland, no secession is conceivable. . . . Never will France . . . yield on this fundamental principle." His minister of the interior, François Mitterrand, added: "Algeria is France."[1]

France's presence in Algeria dated back to 1830 when its army first arrived. It took the French seventeen years to complete the conquest of a people with whom they had nothing in common, who spoke Arabic and professed the faith of Islam, a religion remarkably impervious to Christian missionaries. (For a summary of Islam, see Chapter 21.) In 1848, the first French Roman Catholic settlers arrived, setting the stage for a bitter struggle between two cultures and two religions. In 1870–1871, in the wake of France's defeat in its war with Prussia, the Arab population rose in rebellion, which was put down in blood, followed by the widespread confiscation of Arab lands. Algeria became a land divided between the settlers (from various parts of Europe, not just France), who seized the best lands along the coast and who enjoyed the rights and protection of French citizenship, and the native Algerians, for whom the law offered little protection. The French justified their conquest as part of their *mission civilisatrice*, yet the blessings of French democracy were meant only for Europeans, not for the indigenous Arab (and minority Berber) and Muslim population.

In the years between the two world wars (1918–1939), the French government had grappled repeatedly with the question of the status of native Algerians. Liberals urged the integration of Muslim Algerians into French society by offering them citizenship without first having to convert to Catholicism. To that end, French premier Leon Blum proposed in 1936 a bill granting a number of select Arabs—such as soldiers with distinguished military records in World War I, teachers, graduates from French institutes—the privilege of French citizenship even though they continued to profess the faith of their fathers. Unrelenting opposition killed the bill—and with it the opportunity of integrating Algeria with France.

A synthesis of Algerian and French societies was a pipe dream pursued only by a liberal minority back in France. The European settlers in Algeria resolutely refused to consider it. The same can be said of most Muslims, who also could not envision themselves as French. As one Muslim scholar put it: "The Algerian people are not French, do not wish to be and could not be even if they did wish." Children in Muslim schools were taught to recite: "Islam is my religion. Arabic is my language. Algeria is my country."[2]

World War II was fought for the noblest of reasons: against fascism, racism, and colonialism, and for human dignity. It was inevitable that at the end of the war the Algerians demanded the implementation of these ideals for which many of their compatriots had died while fighting in the French army.

The first manifestation of Algerian militancy appeared even before the guns fell silent in Europe. On May 1, 1945, during the May Day celebrations in Algiers, demonstrators staged an unauthorized march carrying banners denouncing French rule and demanding independence. The French attempt to halt the demonstration led to the deaths of ten Algerians and one European. The French then boasted that they had ended all disorder. But days later, on May 8, 1945, the V-E (Victory-in-Europe) Day parade in the city of Setif turned into a riot. The French marched under their victorious flag, the *tricolor*; Algerian nationalists countered with their own flags and banners as they called for independence. One young man defiantly carried Algeria's forbidden green-and-white flag emblazoned with the red crescent. A police officer shot him dead, touching off a spontaneous anticolonial rebellion—and one of the bloodiest repressions by a European power.

The heavy-handed French response included aerial and naval bombardments of Algerian villages. The British, as they did later that year when they helped the French to return to Vietnam, provided airplanes to carry French troops from France, Morocco, and Tunisia. When the fighting was over, the French conducted wholesale arrests—the traditional European policy after colonial outbreaks. The French claimed to have killed 1,165 Arabs; Algerians put the number at 45,000.[3] The Office of Strategic Services, the US wartime intelligence-gathering organization, put the number of Algerian casualties between 16,000 and 20,000, including 6,000 dead, a figure that is still generally accepted.[4] The violence claimed the lives of 103 Europeans. On May 13, the French staged a military parade in Constantine to impress upon the Algerians the decisive nature of their victory. The Algerians found that World War II had been a war for the liberation of the French from German occupation, not for the liberation of the French colonies from French domination.

In France, politicians of all stripes, including the Communist Party—whose official position was one of anticolonialism—strongly supported the suppression of the uprising. The French authorities in Algiers blamed the violence on food shortages and fascist elements, all the while refusing to acknowledge its underlying cause, a deep-seated resentment of French racism and colonial rule.

For the next nine years relative stability prevailed in Algeria. When the next rebellion broke out, however, it was not a spontaneous uprising as had been the case in 1945. This time it was organized by the FLN (Front de Libération Nationale), which turned to the traditional weapons of the weak— terror and guerrilla warfare. Terrorists and guerrillas have little hope of defeating a formidable military. They seek, instead, to intimidate and to keep the struggle alive in the hope of breaking the other side's will. As long as the guerrillas continue to fight, it is often said, they are winning.

The distinction between terrorism and guerrilla warfare has always been blurred. Guerrilla action is frequently accompanied by terror; terror is a form of political propaganda. The FLN in Algeria was primarily a terrorist organization. The guerrillas of the National Liberation Front (NLF) in Vietnam, no stranger to the uses of terror, went into combat. All guerrillas have been labeled by their opponents as terrorists, bandits, and the like. None of the studies on contemporary terror have yet to come up with a generally accepted definition of the term. To complicate matters further, no one ever admits to being a terrorist. One study defines terrorism as "politically motivated violence engaged in by small groups claiming to represent the masses."[5] That would include both the FLN and the French army.

The war in Algeria became one of extraordinary brutality. The FLN bombed European targets; the Europeans then, predictably, bombed Muslim establishments. French military officers concluded that they had lost in Indochina because they had not applied sufficient force and vowed not to make the same mistake again. The French tortured and executed prisoners in order to uncover the FLN's organizational structure. In 1956, France's parliament—with the express support of the Communist Party—granted General Jacques Massu of the Tenth Parachute Division absolute authority to do whatever was necessary. The subsequent "Battle of Algiers" ended with the destruction of the FLN's leadership. Brute force had triumphed over brute force. Within a year the uprising appeared to be over.

But the rebellion continued as new leaders emerged. Algerians such as Ferhat Abbas, who had devoted their lives to cooperation with the French, joined the rebellion. With the million European settlers demanding an increase in protection, the size of the French army, initially at 50,000, rose to 400,000, a figure that does not include the number of Algerians who fought on the French side. Still, the vastly outnumbered resistance, estimated at 25,000 armed rebels, continued the fight. In the end, 2 to 3 million Arabs (out of a population of 9 million) were driven from their villages to become refugees, and perhaps as many as a million were dead.

Gradually, many in France began to comprehend the unpalatable truth that Algeria would never be French. By the late 1950s, the French, who initially had been unified on the Algerian question, began an intense debate of the subject. The war divided French society to the point that it threatened to touch off a civil war. One of the telling arguments against the continued French presence in Algeria was that it corrupted the soldiers who were serving in an army guilty of repeated atrocities. Many French (not unlike many of their US counterparts during the war in Vietnam) became more concerned about the effect that brutality (notably torture) had on their society than the effect on the Arab victims.

The moral and economic costs were outweighing the benefits. The time had come for France to quit Algeria.

It took an exceptional political leader, General Charles de Gaulle—who had emerged from World War II as the supreme symbol of French resistance to Nazi Germany and of French honor—to take a deeply divided France out of Algeria. The settlers in Algeria continued to insist that as French citizens they had the right of military protection; the army, too, was determined to stay. By 1957, the gravest issue before France was no longer the Algerian uprising, but a sequence of domestic "white rebellions," led by military officers who sought to assassinate de Gaulle.[6] They threatened to topple the constitutional government of France and plunge the nation into civil war.

A decade earlier, de Gaulle, still in the thrall of defending the empire, had tied the fate of Algeria to France's status as a great power: "We must never allow the fact that Algeria is our domain to be called into question." But conditions had changed, and so had de Gaulle's position. After he became president in June 1958, he sought at first to resolve the conflict by offering the Algerians what previous French governments had refused. By granting the Algerians the right to vote without renouncing Islam, de Gaulle hoped Algeria would remain part of France. Arab nationalists, however, rejected this solution, which might have worked before hostilities had commenced in 1954. Now nothing short of independence would do. De Gaulle's choices were narrowed down to either more bloodshed or withdrawal. He chose the latter. In the summer of 1960, he publicly spoke of an "*Algérie algeriénne*" which, he declared, would have "its own government, its institutions and its laws."[7] When he took an inspection trip to Algeria in December 1960, European residents organized a general strike to protest his policies, demanding an "*Algérie française!*"

In July 1962, de Gaulle quit Algeria in the face of intense opposition in his own army and from the settlers in Algeria, nearly all of whom left for France and never forgave de Gaulle for his betrayal. When Algeria formally declared its independence in July 1962, only 170,000 French citizens remained. The withdrawal marked the end of France as a colonial power.

The leaders of the FLN had been educated in French schools, and many of them had fought with distinction in the French army during World War II. Indeed, at the time of the FLN's creation in Cairo in March 1954, Ahmed Ben Bella, one of the legendary nine founders of the FLN, profusely apologized to an Egyptian audience for his inability to address them in Arabic.[8] The FLN's leaders had little regard for Islam and had no intention of establishing an Islamic republic. Algerian women who joined the rebellion did so in opposition to both French colonialism and the Islamic veil. Nor did the FLN's leaders truly seek a social revolution, although they described themselves as socialists—in line with the prevailing trend in Western Europe and in the colonial world. Nearly all independence leaders after World War II—from Mao to

Nehru, Ho Chi Minh, Castro, and so on—professed one form of socialism or another.

The new leaders of Algeria were interested, first and foremost, in the exercise of power. Ben Bella, who became independent Algeria's first president, was soon overthrown by his defense minister and imprisoned. The revolution was over. The military then sought—successfully—to preserve one-party rule. When, in 1991–1992, under the influence of the Islamic revolution in Iran and the rise of Islamic fervor throughout the Arab world, the Islamic Salvation Front party was about to win the elections, the military cancelled them. What followed was an exceptionally bloody civil war during which an estimated 100,000 people perished, one in which both the army and the Islamic militants committing untold atrocities. Journalists were prevented—by means of censorship and assassination—from investigating independently the army's complicity in massacres that it attributed to the insurgents. Throughout, the army remained in control of selecting political candidates. In 1999, it settled on Abdelaziz Bouteflika as their new front man for the continuing military dictatorship. In 2001, US president George W. Bush welcomed Algeria as an ally in his global war on terror.

## Morocco

France's retreat from Morocco and Tunisia proved to be less problematic than in Algeria. Under the 1912 Treaty of Fez, Morocco became a French protectorate—a euphemism for foreign control. Officially, Morocco remained a sovereign state ruled by its sultan. But it was the French resident-general, civil servants, and settlers (who had bought up the best agricultural lands) who wielded power. World War II, professedly fought for the rights of peoples to form their own governments, strengthened the simmering Moroccan independence movement. In the wake of street demonstrations and riots in the capital of Rabat, Casablanca, and other cities in 1952, France exiled to Madagascar the sultan Mohammed V, a descendant of the prophet Mohammed. But with its hands full in neighboring Algeria, France saw little recourse but to bring the sultan back and grant independence to Morocco, now dubbed a "constitutional monarchy."

The constitution, however, granted Mohammed V (proclaimed king in 1957) wide powers to engage in politics (unlike in Europe, where constitutional monarchs play only a ceremonial role severely proscribed by law and custom). Mohammed V used his powers to improve Morocco's human rights record, ban polygamy, and introduce a civil divorce law (hitherto a religious matter). But the king remained Morocco's central political figure, someone completely above reproach. He retained control over the press, the army, and the courts and the power to issue decrees.

With Morocco on the western fringe of the Maghreb (literally "the [Arab] West"), Mohammed V and his successors had no intention of being drawn into the anti-Israel wars, which consumed the time and energy of their distant cousins. They preferred to maintain excellent relations with the West, particularly with France. On the surface, Morocco remained stable, but the kings kept a watchful eye on dissidents, particularly those drawn to radical Islam at the end of the twentieth century. It was not surprising that after 9/11, Mohammed VI willingly joined the United States in its war against militant, anti-Western Islam.

## Tunisia

The central figure in the independence movement for Tunisia, a French protectorate similar to Morocco, was Habib Bourguiba. Famous for his passionate speeches denouncing French colonialism, Bourguiba spent much of the 1930s in prison for allegedly inciting "racial hatred." After World War II, the French blamed him for the recurring unrest and arrested him once more. Bourguiba's arrest, however, only caused further disturbances. In the end, as in Morocco, unable to contain the unrest, France was left little choice but to release Bourguiba. In 1956, it granted Tunisia its independence.

A product of France's *mission civilisatrice*, Bourguiba was an unlikely candidate to lead the Tunisian independence movement. He had studied law and political science in Paris and had married a French woman. He greatly admired the West and did not hesitate to say so, declaring, "I hate colonialism, not the French." He saw himself as a social reformer in the French tradition, who championed education (including that of females), family planning, women's rights (ending polygamy, raising a woman's marrying age to seventeen, and famously referring to the Muslim veil as "that odious rag"), and a modern state health care system. He paid close attention to economic development, particularly in the impoverished regions. Tunisia's culture remained a mix of French and moderate Islamic influences, its beaches a favorite vacation spot for scantily dressed Europeans and Tunisians.

In time, however, Bourguiba's rule evolved into a cult of personality. As early as 1958, he had begun to complain about the people's "preoccupation with liberty." In 1974, his legislature, the Chamber of Deputies, bestowed on him the title of president-for-life. His reign ended in 1987 when his newly appointed prime minister, army general Zine el-Abidine Ben Ali, declared the eighty-four-year old Bourguiba mentally unfit to rule and dismissed him from office. Despite its shortcomings, Bourguiba's relatively benign dictatorship was one of the more successful ones in the postcolonial world.

## Libya

In the 1920s, the Italian fascist leader Benito Mussolini claimed Libya—already a protectorate of Italy—as part of Rome's ancient legacy. Instead of "protecting" it, however, Mussolini subjected Libya to the full brunt of his *riconquista* of territory he considered part of Rome's patrimony. In the course of several punitive campaigns, Mussolini's army drove an estimated 100,000 Libyans off their land and replaced them with Italian settlers (who ultimately made up 12 percent of the population.)

Not surprisingly, during World War II, Libyans assisted the British army fighting the Germans in North Africa. After the war, the grateful British turned over Libya to their former ally, Sidi Idris, the emir of Cyrenaica, the eastern third of the country.

Idris, proclaimed king in 1957, maintained close ties with the West (even as Britain went to war against Egypt in 1956). Libya's considerable wealth came from its newly discovered oil fields, developed by Western companies and protected by Wheelus US Air Base (now Mitiga International Airport) on the edge of Tripoli. But the West could not protect the king against his domestic foes.

In September 1969, a faction of the Libyan army, led by Colonel Muammar Qaddafi, took advantage of anti-Western riots in Tripoli and Benghazi and declared the end of the reign of Idris (who happened to be in Turkey for medical reasons). Qaddafi abolished the monarchy and established in its stead an "Islamic socialist" republic. Whereas Idris had excellent relations with London and Washington, Qaddafi's strong antipathy toward the West ushered in an era of confrontation. (See Chapter 21.)

## Egypt

Egypt had been under Britain's tutelage since 1882, when its warships bombarded the port of Alexandria. At stake were Britain's commercial interests, notably the strategic Suez Canal, its way station into the Red Sea and from there to the Indian Ocean. On some maps of Africa, Egypt was depicted as quasi-independent, but it was the British who ruled, not the *khedive* (originally, the viceroy who ruled on behalf of the Ottoman Empire). In 1922, the *khedive* was elevated to king of Egypt, albeit under British tutelage. British rule lasted until 1952 when an Egyptian army coup, led by Gamal Abdel Nasser, overthrew the ineffectual King Farouk. Farouk's ouster coincided with the independence struggles in Morocco and Tunisia, where nationalists sought to end their nation's status as French protectorates. It was inevitable that, sooner or later, Egypt would follow suit.

To shake off the British yoke, Egypt needed someone who was made of sterner stuff than the ineffectual king, who by now had become an embarrassment to his people. Farouk, who had come to the throne in 1936 at the age of sixteen, never outgrew his childhood. Dozens of palaces and a hundred cars were never enough for him. On state visits abroad, he stole priceless objects, including a ceremonial sword form the shah of Iran and a pocket watch from Winston Churchill. As if that were not enough, he also became a highly skilled pickpocket. A favorite of European tabloids, the "thief of Cairo" was famous for his highly publicized escapades involving women, his irrational behavior, and his gluttonous appetite. He literally ate himself to death at the age of forty-five.

Nasser, as did most of the post–World War II Arab heads of state, saw himself as a socialist. The definition of socialism, however, runs the gamut from West European social democracy to the Khmer Rouge's attempt to take Cambodia back to its ancient agrarian past. Nasser's definition of socialism left Nikita Khrushchev baffled when he visited Egypt in 1958. Nasser's focus was on improving Egypt's primitive agricultural sector, developing an industrial capacity (a major reason for the Aswan Dam on the upper Nile River), providing social services, and strengthening his military for the inevitable next war with Israel. As much as Nasser sought to solve Egypt's social needs—the economy, education, health care—they remained the stepchildren of his revolution, who took a backseat to his favorite child, the military. When Nasser suddenly died in 1970, the army did not skip a beat. It continued to rule Egypt—with the exception of a brief, one-year interlude during the "Arab Spring." (See Chapter 23.)

First and foremost, Nasser was a pan-Arab nationalist who sought to unify the Arab world and to eliminate the last vestiges of the European colonial presence, whether British or French. The bloody Algerian uprising against France, for instance, began in 1954 with Nasser's financial and logistical support. Nasser's antiforeign sentiment was directed initially primarily against Britain, which had meddled in Egyptian affairs. Britain's control of the Suez Canal remained an affront to Egyptian nationalist sensibilities; this was the reason why Nasser nationalized it, that is, placed it under Egypt's control.

Nasser's worsening relations with London had a spill-over effect in his dealings with Washington. When Western lending agencies, under US pressure, refused to fund the Aswan Dam, Nasser turned to Moscow. Not only did the Soviet Union build the dam, but it also became the supplier of weapons to Egypt. In the process, Moscow established a foothold of nearly two decades' duration in the most populous and most strategically located country in the Arab world.

Nasser further raised the hackles of the West (and Israel) when he engineered in 1958 the political unity of Syria and Egypt under the umbrella of what became known as the United Arab Republic (UAR). The measure was initially popular in both countries, but not to the extent, as the official tally proclaimed, that 100 percent of their people had voted for it. It soon became evident, however, that the force of Arab regionalism was stronger—the union lasted only three years (although officially it continued for another ten). Syrians discovered that, after all, they would rather run their own affairs without outside interference.

Once Nasser emerged as the self-proclaimed voice of pan-Arabism, it logically followed that he would declare there was no place for a Jewish state in the Arab world. It was Nasser, more than any other Arab leader, who threatened to destroy Israel. It was thus inevitable that, during Nasser's presidency, Egypt fought two wars against Israel, both of which it lost. The second one in particular, the Six Day War of 1967, left Nasser psychologically shattered.

## Lebanon

By the terms of the secret Sykes-Picot Agreement (May 1916), Asia Minor—the region east of the Mediterranean Sea, at that time still under Ottoman Turkish rule—was divided between Britain and France. In 1922, the League of Nations gave legal sanction to what became known as the French and British "mandate" system. The French took control of a stretch of land that contained today's Syria and Lebanon; the British inherited what became Israel, Jordan, and Iraq. The division came at a time of rising anti-colonial sentiment that dated back to the days of Turkish control. During World War I, it was directed against Ottoman Turkey; after it, Arab nationalists targeted Britain and France and the presence of European Jews in the Arab world.

In 1943, the old imperialist Charles de Gaulle, as the head of the French government-in-exile, granted Lebanon its independence. He did so not because he had a change of heart, but to keep Lebanon from joining the German side in World War II. When the last French troops departed Lebanon in 1946, they left behind a heterogeneous nation in which Maronite Catholic Christians[9] and Sunni and Shiite Muslims shared power. Beirut became known as the "Paris of the Middle East," a prosperous trading and financial center and a favorite of French tourists. Reality, however, soon began to intrude on the fragile tranquility of Lebanon. Sunnis, Shiites, and Christians continued to jockey for power, with no group trusting the others. Even more destabilizing were the flood of Palestinian refugees from Israel and Syria's claim to Lebanon as one of its provinces.

The French had arbitrarily put the border between Syria and Lebanon on the eastern edge of the broad, fertile Beqaa Valley, historically part of the province of nearby Damascus. The French, who favored their Christian co-religionists, did not do them any favors by making the valley part of Lebanon, since it altered the demographic makeup of the country. It reduced the percentage of Christians, while Muslims saw their percentage of the population increase. The demographic shift toward the Muslims (who, moreover, had a high birth rate) was a contributing factor in the civil strife in years to come. Moreover, Syria sought to regain its influence in Lebanon while continuing to claim the Beqaa Valley as one of the provinces of "Greater Syria."

## Syria

At the same time that France granted Lebanon its independence in 1946, it accorded the same to Syria. From the beginning, Syria's military played the predominant role in the country's politics. After the humiliating 1948 Arab-Israeli War, the socialist Ba'ath (Resurrection) Party—which was more military, however, than socialist in nature—gradually gained in influence. Since independence, Syria (similar to most Arab nations) has been under military control in the form of the Assad regime.

In 1970, a small faction of the military composed of Alawites—generally, albeit incorrectly, described in the West as Shiite Muslims—took power. Forty years later, in the face of strong opposition during the "Arab Spring," the Alawites remained determined to cling to power at all cost, touching off a vicious civil war that began in March 2011. (See Chapter 23.)

## Jordan

By the Sykes-Picot Agreement, Britain inherited Palestine, an amorphous region stretching from the Mediterranean Sea to Iraq. Having made promises in World War I to both Zionists and Arabs, it promptly divided Palestine into two parts. The western part was set aside as a Jewish "homeland" while the land beyond the Jordan River became the emirate of Trans-Jordan (today's Jordan). Its Hashemite[10] emir, Abdullah, a descendant of the prophet Mohammed, also happened to be the son of Hussein, the sharif and emir of Mecca (later crowned "King of the Arabs"), Britain's ally during World War I. From the beginning, Jordan had a majority Palestinian population. From that fact came the Zionist argument that a Palestinian state already existed. The rest of Jordan's people consist predominantly of desert-dwelling Bedouins who make up an estimated 30 percent of the population.

## Iraq

In Iraq, the British installed Abdullah's brother as King Faisal I. As Hashemite kings, outsiders from Mecca, both were much resented. After Abdullah's de facto recognition of Israel and annexation of the West Bank, Palestinian nationalists assassinated him. Faisal's son suffered a similar fate. In the course of the 1958 "14 July Revolution," Ba'athist troops, at the behest of Abd al-Karim Qassim, murdered Faisal II, the twenty-three-year-old, British-educated king (along with his prime minister, son, wife, other family members, and servants). No sooner had Qassim seized power than other Ba'athist officers, the ambitious Saddam Hussein among them, sought to assassinate him. In the aftermath of the botched attempt, Hussein was forced to flee to Syria. But after Ba'athist officers succeeded in assassinating Qassim in 1963, Hussein returned home. Iraq continued to be roiled by coups and countercoups, the perfect environment for an inveterate plotter such as Hussein.

In July 1979, Hussein and his supporters seized power by dismissing the ineffectual prime minister. Hussein's first order of business was to restore order by putting an end to the fratricide in the ranks of the Ba'ath Party. Henceforth, the party would speak with one voice. To that end, he orchestrated a spine-chilling theatrical event, which he put on film as an object lesson for all who for a moment thought of challenging him. In a hall filled with 200 of the party's luminaries, he ominously announced there were "traitors among us." As a functionary read off the names of all those in attendance, he paused for dramatic effect before passing judgment on their guilt or innocence. Those deemed guilty were at once taken out by bodyguards to meet their fate, usually at the hand of the executioner. As they left the hall, Hussein shouted after them to "get out, get out." Some of the trembling Ba'athists, even before their names were called out, openly wept and proclaimed their undying loyalty to Hussein, shouting, "Long live Saddam Hussein!" Others, even as their fate hung in the balance, praised him for the show trial. It was a perfect example of what sheer terror was able to accomplish. Such scenes were usually carried out behind the curtain, but Hussein wanted Iraqis to see what happened to traitors. Several of those arrested were released after having been tortured, a favorite tactic of Hussein. They now served as a visible reminder of an opposition he had broken physically and psychologically. Whether their opposition had been real or imagined did not matter.[11] The issue was to mete out terror, not justice.

After Hussein purged the Ba'ath Party, he terrorized the majority Shiite Muslims, as well as the Kurds (who were of Indo-European rather than Arab descent) in northeastern Iraq, a people constantly clamoring for autonomy, if not outright independence. Unlike his predecessors, Hussein was so successful in holding on to power—for nearly a quarter of a century—that it took the world's greatest military power to topple him, which occurred in 2003.

## Notes

1. Mendès-France and Mitterand cited in John Talbott, *The War Without a Name: France in Algeria, 1954–1962* (New York: Random House, 1980), p. 39.

2. Abdelhamid Ben Badis, one of the founders in 1931 of the Society of Reformist Ulema, in Tanya Matthews, *War in Algeria: Background for Crisis* (New York: Fordham University Press, 1961), p. 20.

3. Frantz Fanon, *A Dying Colonialism* (New York: Monthly Review Press, 1965), p. 74.

4. "Moslem Uprisings in Algeria, May 1945," Record Group 226, OSS Research and Analysis Report 3135, May 30, 1945, pp. 1–6, National Archives, Washington, DC.

5. Richard E. Rubenstein, *Alchemists of Revolution: Terrorism in the Modern World* (New York: Basic Books, 1987).

6. In the European political lexicon, red is the color of revolution seeking to upend the status quo; a *white revolution* is a counterrevolution in defense of the old order.

7. Samuel B. Blumenfeld's epilogue in Michael Clark, *Algeria in Turmoil: The Rebellion, Its Causes, Its Effects, Its Future* (New York: Grosset and Dunlap, 1960), pp. 443–454.

8. Gamal Nkrumah, "Ahmed Ben Bella: Plus ça change," *Al-Ahram Weekly Online*, May 10–16, 2001.

9. Named after Marun, a fourth century Syrian-Aramaic monk, these Eastern rite Catholics are in full communion with the Vatican. In fact, its current patriarch is a member of the Catholic Church's College of Cardinals.

10. Named after an Arab clan from the Hejaz, a region along the Red Sea. Its descendants gave the Arab world an untold number of caliphs, emirs of Mecca, and kings of the Hejaz, Saudi Arabia, Syria, Iraq, Jordan, Morocco, Tunisia, Somalia, and Yemen.

11. Discovery Channel, "The Real Saddam," January 31, 2003.

# 8

# The Arab-Israeli Conflict

**Anticolonial resistance in the Middle East in the early twentieth** century was initially directed against the Ottoman Turkish Empire, which had controlled the region for centuries. But with Turkey's defeat in World War I, the region fell under the dominion of other outside forces, Britain and France. Thus, the Arab states merely exchanged one master for another and, predictably, resistance against outside control continued. Ultimately, France and Britain began to understand that they would have to leave. The Arab world had long been impervious to European cultural penetration, a lesson hammered home to the French during their bloody attempt to suppress the Algerian revolution. Arab nationalism and culture, steeped in Islamic tradition, gradually yet irrevocably undermined French and British authority in the Middle East.

Yet, by a twist of fate, at the same time Arab nationalism began to assert itself, the Middle East saw the introduction in the 1880s of another cultural and political element: the first attempts to re-create a home for Jews, to reestablish the biblical Zion in Jerusalem, in a region populated largely by Arabs. The Zionists, primarily of European background, launched their experiment at a time when the European presence in the world beyond Europe was under direct challenge and retreat.

## The Rebirth of Zionism

Contemporary Zionism has its origins in the rebirth of European nationalism, which soon became transformed—in Germany and elsewhere—into virulent manifestations of racism. The nineteenth century witnessed the revival of romantic national consciousness among Europeans who sought to define their histories, origins, and contributions to civilization. The result was an increased fragmentation of what is commonly called "European civilization." The Germans, Italians, Russians, and Irish, to mention just a few, discovered their uniqueness in their ancient histories and traditions and professed cultural superiority over their neighbors. They all had one thing in common: They sought to find their proper places in the context of European civilization, their "place in the sun."

The Jews of Europe were another case in point. Their religion set them apart from the rest of Christian Europe and generally made it difficult to achieve cultural and political assimilation. Moreover, the nineteenth century was an extraordinarily race-conscious age. The relative toleration of Jews during the previous century, the Age of Reason, was no more. The legal status of Jews was beginning to deteriorate, particularly in Eastern Europe. European Jews began to contemplate the re-creation of the ancient Jewish state in the biblical land of Zion. The result was the rebirth of Jewish nationalism, an escape from the destructive fury of a rejuvenated anti-Semitism during the last decades of the nineteenth century.[1]

Appropriately, the father of modern Zionism was Leon Pinsker, a Jew from Russia, a nation where anti-Semitism had become state policy. The assassination of Tsar Alexander II in 1881 was blamed on the Jews and touched off anti-Semitic pogroms (or massacres). Jews made up a large percentage of the revolutionary movement, and even though it was ethnic Russians who carried out the murder of the tsar, the assassination let loose anti-Semitic passions of unprecedented scope and intensity. Self-preservation demanding the creation of a Jewish state, Pinsker published in 1882 a pamphlet, *Auto-Emancipation: An Appeal to His People by a Russian Jew*. His appeal was instrumental in creating the Lovers of Zion, an organization responsible for launching the first wave of emigrants to Palestine. At the time, the region contained virtually no Jews; by the end of the 1880s, however, the Jewish population was 30,000–40,000, about 5 percent of the total population.

Theodor Herzl, an Austrian Jew, became the best-known publicist of the Zionist cause after he organized the First World Zionist Congress and published, in 1897, a pamphlet entitled *The Jewish State*. Herzl knew that the creation of such a state faced numerous obstacles. Palestine was well in the hands of the Ottoman Empire, a power that sought to suppress all manifestations of nationalism, whether Jewish or Arab. It was little wonder that Herzl called the first Zionists "beggars . . . with dreams."[2]

The nationalist movements of modern times (that is, since the end of the Middle Ages) arose mainly as reactions to foreign imperialism. The Napoleonic Wars gave birth to German nationalism; the Mongol invasion of Russia gave rise to Russian nationalism; American nationalism came with the wars against the British. Modern Jewish nationalism was the product of an assault on the culture and, ultimately, on the very existence of the Jews. Similarly, the resurgence of Arab nationalism coincided with the resistance

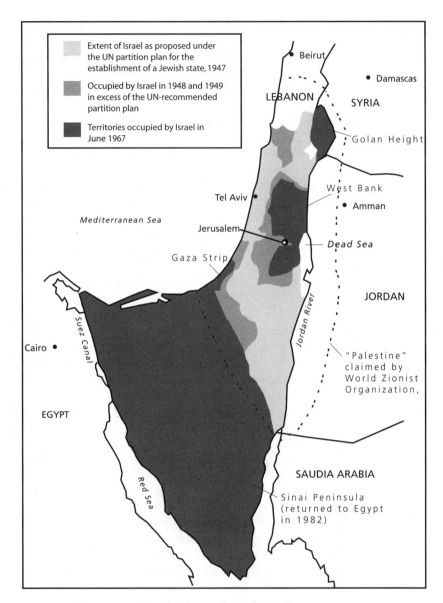

**The Expansion of Israel**

against the Turkish Ottoman Empire. Jewish and Arab nationalism reappeared in Palestine at about the same time. Arabs sought to reclaim their lands from Turkish control; desperate Jews, seeking a safe haven from the gathering fury of anti-Semitism, claimed the same land.

The early Zionists were slow to grasp that their struggle would ultimately be against the Arabs. Soon, however, it became clear to them that the defeat of Turkey would be but the first step of a long journey. David Ben-Gurion, one of the early Zionist settlers and later Israel's first prime minister, overlooked the Arabs until 1916. It was a friend, a Palestinian Arab, who awakened him to the prospect of an Arab-Jewish conflict. The Arab expressed his concern over Ben-Gurion's incarceration in a Turkish military prison. "As your friend, I am deeply sorry," he told Ben-Gurion, "but as an Arab I am pleased." "It came down on me like a blow," Ben-Gurion later wrote, "so there is an Arab national movement *here*."[3]

The possibility of a Jewish state surfaced during World War I, when Britain was at war against Turkey, an ally of imperial Germany. In December 1916, the British advanced from Egypt, and in the following month they entered Jerusalem. By this time, Britain and France had already agreed to carve up the Middle East after Turkey's defeat. By the secret Sykes-Picot Agreement of May 1916, Britain claimed Palestine, Iraq, and what shortly became Trans-Jordan, while France claimed Lebanon and Syria.

The British did not foresee the troubles ahead. While fighting the Turks, they had enlisted Arab support (most famously organized by one of their compatriots, "Lawrence of Arabia") and had promised the Arabs nationhood after the war. These pledges had contributed to anti-Turkish rebellions in Jerusalem, Damascus, and other cities long controlled by the Turks. At the same time, however, the British government also enlisted Jewish aid and in return "viewed with favour" the creation of a "national home for the Jewish people" in Palestine. This pledge came in November 1917 in the Balfour Declaration (named after the British foreign secretary) in a one-page letter to Baron Lionel Rothschild, a leading figure of the Jewish community in England. The declaration also insisted, however, that "nothing shall be done which may prejudice the civil and religious rights of the existing non-Jewish communities in Palestine."[4] The declaration and its later endorsement by the League of Nations gave international sanction to what since 1881 had been a haphazard experiment to create a homeland for Jews.

The Arabs rejected the Balfour Declaration. The promises made by the British, they argued, were at best limited and conditional. A Jewish "national home" in Palestine, they insisted, did not constitute a Jewish state. Moreover, Great Britain had no right to give away Palestine over the heads of its inhabitants. If anything, Britain earlier had promised Palestine to the Arabs in the Hussein-McMahon Letters of 1915–1916. This exchange of letters had led to the Hussein-McMahon Agreement of 1916 (between Sharif Hussein, the emir of Mecca, and Henry McMahon, Britain's high commissioner in Egypt), whereby the Arabs, in exchange for Britain's recognition of a united Arab state between the Mediterranean and Red Seas, joined Britain in the war against Turkey.

The best that can be said about the British policy is that the authorities in London did their best to satisfy all claimants to the lands of the Middle East that became a part of the British postwar "mandate." To satisfy the Arabs, they granted Abdullah, the second son of Sharif Hussein, a stretch of territory east of the Jordan River. The British thereby transferred the easternmost portion of Palestine to what became the Emirate of Trans-Jordan, today's Kingdom of Jordan. The creation of this artificial realm constituted the first partition of Palestine. The remainder of Palestine west of the Jordan River, with its restless Arab and Jewish populations, remained under British rule.

The British soon found out that one cannot serve two clients with conflicting claims without arousing the animosity of both. Arabs and Jews both suspected that the British were backing away from the commitments they had made. Arabs feared the British sought to establish a Zionist state; Jews feared the British favored the numerically superior Arabs and thus had no intention of honoring the Balfour Declaration. The British had no clear policy except to try to keep the antagonists apart. The consequence of this fence-straddling was that the British came under fire from both Jews and Arabs.

After World War I, the clash between the Zionists and the Palestinians was a conflict fueled by passion, anger, and hatred between two movements insisting on their historic and religious rights to the same land. Violence bred retaliatory violence. Particularly bloody were the riots of 1929, the first instance of large-scale bloodshed between Jews and Arabs. In a dispute in Jerusalem over the Wailing Wall and the Dome of the Rock, 133 Jews and 116 Arabs lost their lives. In Hebron, the Jewish inhabitants, a people with an ancient linear connection to biblical times in that city, were expelled in the course of a riot that claimed 87 Jewish lives. The British authorities sought to keep the peace but had only limited success. Both sides felt the British had betrayed them for not fulfilling the promises made during the war. To placate the Arabs who had risen in rebellion (1936–1939), Britain issued in 1939 a controversial "white paper," or position paper. With it, the British authorities sought to limit the Jewish population of Palestine to one-third and severely curtail the transfer of land to Jews. (The Jewish population at that time was already at 30 percent of the total population, up from 10 percent in 1918.)

The British directive came at a time when life in Nazi Germany had become perilous for Jews. Yet no country would take them in. Within two years, Hitler initiated his program of extermination of Jews. Militant Zionists began to suspect the worst, namely, collusion between the British and the Nazis. The British decision, indeed, closed the door to Palestine for Jews who sought a safe haven trying to escape the Nazi jackboot. It created a lingering legacy of bitterness among Zionists against British rule in Palestine. After World War II, it contributed to violence between the British army and militant Jewish organizations, such as the Irgun (Irgun Zvai Leumi, or National Military Organization, headed by Menachem Begin). The Irgun captured and executed British soldiers and blew up the King David Hotel in Jerusalem in July 1946, killing ninety-one, including twenty-eight British citizens.

The murder of 6 million European Jews at the hands of Nazi Germany during World War II, all too frequently with the collusion of peoples—Poles, Ukrainians, French, and others—who themselves had been conquered by the Germans, seared the consciousness of Jews. More than ever before, it underscored the necessity of a Jewish state as a matter of self-preservation, as the only place where Jews could be assured a sanctuary against the fury of anti-Semitism. Years later, when Egyptian president Gamal Abdel Nasser spoke of the destruction of Israel, its citizens could not help but invoke the memory of Hitler's attempt to annihilate the Jews.

After World War II, the British decided to wash their hands of Palestine, handing the problem over to the fledgling United Nations. It was clear by then, however, that a single Palestinian state consisting of Arabs and Jews, as the Balfour Declaration had suggested, was an impossibility. Few Zionists or Arabs were interested in such a solution. Too much blood had been shed already; besides, both sides saw themselves as the legitimate heirs to Palestine. In November 1947, the United Nations, therefore, called for the creation of separate states, one Israeli and one Arab. Jerusalem, a holy city for Jews and Muslims (as well as Christians), was to have international status with free access for members of all faiths. The UN decision marked the second partition of Palestine, of what had remained after the British had granted the eastern bank of the Jordan River to the emir of Trans-Jordan.

Nearly all Arabs rejected the UN resolution that called for a fifty-fifty split of Palestine. The Arabs harbored the suspicion that Zionism in control of half of Palestine—and the fact that the heart of Zion, Jerusalem, was slated to remain a separate entity, apart from the state of Israel—would ultimately satisfy few Israelis and inevitably lead to additional Jewish expansion. Most Jews were generally willing to accept the borders the United Nations had drawn, even though they fell far short of what the Zionist movement had originally envisioned. David Ben-Gurion, who once had argued that Israel's eastern border must reach the Jordan River, rejected pressures for expansion in the hope of gaining Arab recognition of what in his youth had been but a dream—the state of Israel. The more militant Zionists, such as Begin, whose Irgun military organization had as its logo a map of Israel with borders beyond the Jordan River, had a much larger Israel in mind than the one the UN plan defined.

The Arabs remained adamant in their refusal to recognize Israel's existence. At best, some were willing to accept the presence of a Jewish minority in an Arab state. More significant, many Arabs were convinced that they could prevent the establishment of the Israeli state by military means and could drive the Zionists into the Mediterranean Sea.

*The Dome of the Rock, Jerusalem*

*The Western Wall—or Wailing Wall—in Jerusalem*

The Zionist dream had finally borne fruit. The state of Israel (no longer merely a homeland for Jews) had gained international sanction. The first country to extend diplomatic recognition was the United States; the Soviet Union and several Western nations quickly followed suit. No Arab state, however, recognized Israel. Indeed, after King Abdullah of Jordan met in secret talks with Zionists in 1949, it cost him his life at the hand of a Palestinian assassin. Arab intransigence—coupled with the threat of another event like the Holocaust a scant three years after Hitler's defeat—made clear that Israel's right to exist would have to be defended by the sword.

## The Arab-Israeli Wars

The British were slated to withdraw from Palestine in May 1948, and both sides prepared for that day. Violence between Arabs and Jews, already endemic, escalated. On April 9, 1948, Begin's Irgun killed between 116 and 254 Palestinians (depending upon whose account one credits) in the village of Deir Yassin, and three days later an Arab reprisal caused the deaths of 77 Jews. The acts of violence became etched into the collective memory of both peoples. Each massacre had its apologists who defended the bloodletting as a just action in a just war. In this fashion the first Arab-Israeli war began.

The 1948 war was essentially over in four weeks. A number of Arab states—Jordan, Syria, Egypt, Lebanon, and Iraq—invaded Israel, but their actions were uncoordinated and ineffectual. The Israeli victory resulted in the third partition of Palestine. Israel wound up with one-third more land than under the UN partition plan when it seized West Jerusalem, the Negev Desert, and parts of Galilee. King Abdullah of Jordan made the best of his defeat at the hands of the Israelis by annexing the West Bank and East Jerusalem. The Palestinians, defeated by Israel and betrayed by the kingdom of Jordan, saw the dream of a state of their own vanish into thin air.

The war led to a refugee problem that continued to plague the Middle East. By the end of April 1948, even before the outbreak of the war, Israeli forces expelled 290,000 Palestinian Arabs. During the war, the Israelis expelled another 300,000 Palestinians. By 1973, the number of refugees topped 1.5 million; in 2004, their number plus those of their descendants stood at 4 million, many of them wards of the UN relief organizations. Most of the refugees fled across the Jordan River into Jordan. As a result, 70 percent of the population of the Kingdom of Jordan consisted of Palestinians, from which came the argument in some quarters in Israel that a Palestinian state already existed.

The flight of the Palestinians guaranteed that Israel would be a Zionist state dominated by a Jewish majority at the expense of the remaining Arab minority. Whatever property the Arabs had abandoned, if only to seek shelter elsewhere during the war, was confiscated by Israel.[5] The displaced

Palestinians—holed up in refugee camps in Jordan, Lebanon, and Gaza—considered their status as temporary and looked to the day of return to lands and homes that had once belonged to them.

When the war ended, the Israelis considered the armistice lines, which gave them the additional lands, to be permanent and refused—in violation of international law—to permit the refugees to return. For Arabs, the new borders and the refugees were a humiliating reminder of their defeat, and they remained incapable of accepting the consequences of the war. These factors, coupled with Arab intransigence on the question of Israel's right to exist, remained at the core of the continuing deadlock in Arab-Israeli relations.

The partitions of Palestine were the result of actions taken by Great Britain, the United Nations, Israel, and Jordan with the complicity of the nations of Europe, both capitalist and Communist. From the beginning, the United States and other major Western powers offered the Israelis diplomatic support; the Soviet bloc had provided most of the weapons for the Jewish victory in the first Arab-Israeli war. The 1948 war exposed the Arabs' weaknesses and their inability to unite. Israeli forces outnumbered those of the Arabs by a ratio of roughly two to one. Arabs spoke fervently of fighting another war against Israel to drive the Israelis into the sea, but their rhetoric only masked their impotence and frustration.

A palace revolution in Egypt in 1952 swept aside the ineffectual King Farouk, who was replaced by one of the conspirators, Gamal Abdel Nasser. Nasser envisioned a pan-Arab movement uniting all Arabs, and for a short time Egypt and Syria were in fact merged into one nation, the United Arab Republic. Nasser's rejuvenation of Arab pride was coupled with a call for the ouster of the Western presence—notably that of the British, French, and Israelis—responsible for the humiliation of the Muslim world. Another war between Israel and the Arabs seemed inevitable. Instead of accepting the existence of Israel, Nasser was busy putting another Arab-Israeli war on the agenda.

As tensions in the Middle East increased, so did the arms race. Nasser turned to the Soviet Union, and in September 1955 announced a historic weapons deal by which Egypt became the recipient of Soviet MiG-15 fighter planes, bombers, and tanks. The Soviet Union, in turn, gained for the first time a client outside its Communist sphere of influence. Israel immediately renegotiated an arms agreement with France. The Middle East was now on a hair-trigger alert waiting for the next crisis. The wait was not long. In July 1956, Nasser boldly seized the Suez Canal, thus eliminating British and French control and operation of the strategic waterway.

The British and French prepared a counterattack to retake the Suez Canal. They were joined by the Israelis who had had enough of Nasser's bloodcurdling rhetoric promising the destruction of their state. This was their chance to deal with Nasser's military threat and to halt the border raids by Arab *fedayeen* (literally "those who sacrifice themselves"). The raids had produced an unbroken circle of violence, a series of incursions and reprisals, which in turn led to further raids and reprisals.

In preparation for the second Arab-Israeli war, Britain, France, and Israel signed the secret Treaty of Sèvres in October 1956. Israel swept all the way to the Suez Canal and to the southern tip of Egypt's Sinai Peninsula at Sharm el-Sheikh. British and French naval, air, and land forces joined the battle against the outgunned Egyptians. The war lasted only a few days, from October 29 until November 2, 1956. Egypt's defeat on the battlefield—not to mention its humiliation—was complete.

When the British and French launched their assault to retake the Suez Canal, they ran into an international roadblock. President Dwight Eisenhower's declared opposition to the war, Soviet threats of intervention, and UN condemnations persuaded Britain, France, and Israel to halt the attacks. Israel eventually agreed to withdraw from the Sinai after Egypt pledged not to interfere with Israeli shipping through the Strait of Tiran, Israel's outlet to the Red Sea. Nasser remained in control of the Suez Canal, which, however, remained bottled up with war-damaged ships for several years. UN troops patrolling on the Egyptian side of the Israeli border managed to preserve an uneasy truce that lasted for more than ten years.

The 1956 Sinai War resolved none of the grievances held by the Israelis and Arabs. Officially, the state of war between the Arab nations and Israel continued. Israel still was unable to obtain recognition from any Arab government, and the Arabs continued to call for the destruction of Israel. Both sides held little doubt that another war was in the offing, and thus took steps to prepare for it.

In the spring of 1967, Nasser closed the Strait of Tiran to Israeli shipping despite Israeli warnings that such an act constituted a *casus belli*, a cause for war. Inevitably, tensions rose rapidly. Nasser demanded that the UN troops leave Egyptian territory along the Israeli border and concluded a military pact with King Hussein of Jordan. When Iraq joined the pact, the Israelis struck, initiating the Six Day War of June 1967.

In less than a week Israeli forces decimated those of Egypt, Syria, and Jordan and in the process rearranged the map of the Middle East. The political repercussions still haunt the region. Once again—as it had done in the 1956 war—Israel conquered the Sinai all the way to the Suez Canal. It also seized from Egypt the Gaza Strip, a small stretch of land inhabited by Palestinian refugees. It then turned against Syria and stormed the Golan Heights, a seemingly impregnable 20-mile-wide strategic plateau rising 600 feet above Galilee from which the Syrian army had fired repeatedly on Israeli settlements below. But most significant, Israel also took what had been under Jordan's administration, the lands west of the Jordan River and the Dead Sea—a region generally known as the West Bank (that is, west of the Jordan River). With it, Israel took possession of the entire city of Jerusalem.

Israel returned the Sinai to Egypt in 1982 and handed Gaza over to the Palestinians in 2005, even though it was governed by Hamas, a militant Islamist organization. The other conquered territories—the Golan Heights, the West Bank, and Jerusalem—remained, from the Arab perspective, unresolved issues.

In November 1967, the great powers again sought the offices of the United Nations to resolve the conflict. The United States and the Soviet Union, each backing one of the belligerents, feared being drawn into the Arab-Israeli wars. Thus, in a rare display of US-Soviet cooperation, UN Security Council Resolution 242 called for an Israeli withdrawal from territories conquered in the Six Day War, accompanied by a political settlement that would include Arab recognition of Israel and a fair deal for the Palestinian refugees. After some hesitation, Egypt and Jordan accepted Resolution 242, but Syria and the militant Palestinians rejected it. The Israelis, in their turn, were not inclined to give up all the spoils of victory, and they, too, rejected it. In the decades to come, there was occasional talk in the West of using Resolution 242 as a basis for a political solution. Israel, however, saw no pressing need to return to its pre-1967 borders. It later gave up the Sinai and Gaza, but it never contemplated the return of East Jerusalem to the Arabs. The Arabs, however, always insisted that according to Resolution 242, "the territories occupied [by Israel] in the hostilities" meant "all territories."[6] General Moshe Dayan, one of the architects of Israel's victory in the Six Day War, expressed the extremist conviction when he said, "I would rather have land than peace," to which King Hussein of Jordan prophetically replied, "Israel can have land or peace, but not both."[7] The resultant deadlock was yet another manifestation of how in the Middle East the militants nearly always carried the day.

With the acquisition of the West Bank, Israel came into possession of land containing 750,000 hostile Arabs. Three days after the war ended, on June 13, 1967, the first Jewish settlers arrived at the village of Gush Etzion, from which Jews had been expelled in 1948. Other Jews began to reclaim property in East Jerusalem.[8] The Israeli election of 1977 brought to power Menachem Begin, who had always insisted that the West Bank was not merely conquered Arab territory or a bargaining card to be played eventually in exchange for Arab recognition of Israel's right to exist. It was under Begin that the widespread Israeli settlement of the West Bank began. Begin refused to refer to that region as the West Bank, insisting instead that it consisted of the biblical lands of Judea and Samaria, part of historic Zion. Despite objections from Arab states, the United Nations, United States, and other nations, Begin considered the annexation of Judea and Samaria a closed matter. His government also officially annexed the Golan Heights and considered that matter closed as well.

The problem of the West Bank was complicated by the fact that its largest city, Hebron, contains the tomb of Abraham, who is revered by both Jews and Muslims. Both groups consider Abraham as God's messenger and their spiritual—and even biological—patriarch. Jews consider themselves the direct descendants of one of Abraham's sons, Isaac; Arabs claim descent from his other son, Ishmael.

The 1967 Arab defeat had another unexpected result. It strengthened the hand of Palestinian liberation/terrorist movements. After the war, a recently established umbrella organization, the Palestine Liberation Organization (PLO), led by Yassir Arafat, united the various splinter groups. It was the PLO, rather than Arab national armies, that henceforth played a major role challenging Israel's occupation of the West Bank. During the 1972 Summer Olympics in Munich, for instance, Palestinian terrorists dramatized their cause before a worldwide audience by taking hostage Israeli athletes and coaches, eventually killing eleven of them. The hostage taking—played out before a global audience—propelled the smoldering Palestinian question to the front and center. But this example of "propaganda by the deed" (to use a phrase from the Russian revolutionary movement of the nineteenth century) strengthened the hands of extremists on both sides and continued to impede any and all efforts to resolve the conflict.

The third Arab-Israeli war, the Yom Kippur War, took place in October 1973. The Egyptians could not forget that the Israeli army had mauled their forces three times and was now in possession of the Sinai Peninsula. Egypt's president Anwar Sadat, who had succeeded Nasser in 1970, launched an offensive against the seemingly impregnable Israeli positions across the Suez Canal. The surprise attack garnered Egypt initial success, but Israeli forces counterattacked and threatened to destroy the Egyptian army. The United Nations, United States, and Soviet Union hastily intervened to stop the war. Neither Israel nor Egypt was to be permitted to destroy the other's army. According to the terms of the cease-fire, Egypt was permitted to retain a foothold on the eastern side of the Suez Canal while the United Nations created a buffer zone to keep the two sides apart.

The Egyptian offensive proved to be the first time an Arab state had been able to wrest any territory—however small—from the Israelis. After suffering one humiliation after another for a quarter of a century, an Arab army had finally proven its battleworthiness. Sadat felt he could now negotiate with Israel as an equal. With encouragement from Washington, Egypt became the first Arab state to extend diplomatic recognition to Israel. In an act of supreme political (and physical) courage, Sadat responded to an invitation to give an address to the Knesset, Israel's parliament, in Jerusalem in November 1977, in which he expressed a willingness "to live with you in permanent peace."

It set the stage for a September 1978 summit meeting between Sadat and Begin at the US presidential retreat at Camp David, Maryland, mediated by US president Jimmy Carter. The so-called Camp David Accords led to an Egyptian-Israeli peace treaty in 1979 that ended a state of war of thirty years' duration and brought about Egypt's diplomatic recognition of Israel. In turn,

*Egyptian president Anwar Sadat, US president Jimmy Carter, and Israeli prime minister Menachem Begin after signing the Middle East peace treaty at Camp David, Maryland, March 27, 1979*

Israel agreed to return the Sinai to Egypt and did so by April 1982. It marked the first instance in which an Arab state managed to regain substantial territory lost to Israel. Sadat had achieved through negotiation what no Arab leader had achieved by war. For their efforts, Begin and Sadat—former terrorists turned diplomats—were awarded the Nobel Peace Prize. Inexplicably, however, Carter was excluded.

The Camp David Accords, however, did not adequately address the thorny questions of Jerusalem, the West Bank, and the Palestinian refugees. Begin spoke vaguely of Palestinian "autonomy" within the state of Israel, but he was more interested in peace with Egypt and diplomatic recognition than in discussing the fate of the inhabitants of what he considered to be an integral part of Israel and thus an internal matter. Sadat, similarly, showed little interest in the fate of the Palestinians. Nor did the Camp David Accords settle the issue of Jerusalem, Israel's capital. Virtually all Israelis insisted Jerusalem must remain one and indivisible. But the Palestinians, too, envisioned Jerusalem as the capital of their future state.

The PLO was neither consulted nor interested in these negotiations. Sitting down with Begin would have meant the de facto recognition of Israel. Inevitably, many Arabs saw Sadat as a man who had betrayed the Palestinian and Arab causes. His new relationship with Israel added to his domestic problems. As critics became more vocal, his regime became increasingly dictatorial and his opponents, in turn, became increasingly embittered. Radical Muslims, members of the Egyptian Islamic Jihad, assassinated Sadat in October 1981.[9]

The festering Palestinian problem continued to vex the region. In 1970, King Hussein of Jordan drove the PLO leadership from his country after it had become clear that its presence posed a threat to his regime. Searching for a home, the PLO found a new base of operation in Lebanon, a nation already divided between a politically dominant Christian minority and the majority Muslim population, who at that time were already on the edge of civil war. Lebanon's political factions operated their own private armies, and it was into this volatile environment that the Palestinians introduced their armed insurgents.

From their bases in southern Lebanon, PLO fighters periodically launched raids into northern Israel. The Israelis responded in kind. Raids and reprisals became the order of the day along the Lebanese-Israeli border. In July 1981, however, a special US envoy to the Middle East, Philip Habib, worked out a cease-fire that both sides honored for nearly a year, until June 1982. The cease-fire was broken after Menachem Begin set out to eliminate the Palestinian threat in Lebanon once and for all.

The Israeli government's official explanation for its invasion of southern Lebanon was to secure "Peace for Galilee" (the code name of the operation) by rooting out the Palestinians threat across the border. This rationale for the invasion had a hollow ring to it since there had been no Palestinian attacks across that border for nearly a year. The scope of the operation, the Begin government announced, would be limited. The Israeli army would go no farther than 40 kilometers (25 miles) into Lebanon. Events proved, however, that Begin and his defense minister, Ariel Sharon, had more ambitious plans.

In December 1981, Sharon outlined a scenario to Philip Habib that called for a strike into Lebanon in the hope of quickly resolving several problems at once. Sharon would dislodge the Syrians, who had been invited several years earlier by the Lebanese government to restore order at a time when the country had begun to disintegrate into civil war. Once invited, however, the Syrians had stayed. Sharon considered the Syrians, with whom the Israelis had been on a war footing since 1948, to be the real masters of Lebanon. Next, Sharon intended to destroy the PLO, a "time bomb" in his words, in southern Lebanon and with it subdue the restless Palestinian population in Israel, numbering about half a million.[10] When Habib asked of the fate of the 100,000 Palestinians in Lebanon, Sharon told him that "we shall hand them over to the Lebanese. . . . Fifty-thousand armed terrorists won't remain there, and the rest will be taken care of by the Lebanese." Habib protested the impending violation of the cease-fire that he had worked out.

US president Ronald Reagan warned Prime Minister Begin against any moves into Lebanon, but to no avail.

The invasion of Lebanon did bring about the military (although not the political) defeat of the PLO. In its wake, Israeli bombardment created havoc in the areas of Beirut containing Palestinian populations. The invasion set the stage for the massacre of an estimated 700–2,000 Palestinian civilians at the refugee camps of Sabra and Shatila. The slaughter—first with knives, then with firearms—was the handiwork of Lebanese Maronite Christian Phalangist (fascist) militia forces, with the approval and assistance of the Israeli armed forces who witnessed the massacres.[11] Israeli forces also crippled Syrian forces in Lebanon and destroyed much of the military hardware the Soviets had provided them. The Syrians, however, quickly recovered their losses and remained as deeply entrenched in Lebanon as ever. Instead of withdrawing, Israel left behind some of its forces in a buffer zone in southern Lebanon.

The cost of the invasion was considerable. The greatest losers were the Palestinians, who suffered at the hands of first the Israelis, then the Christian Phalangists, and finally the Shiite Muslims in Lebanon. The war also pitted the Israelis against the Shiites; the Shiites against the Maronite Christians and their army, the Phalangists; and a faction of the PLO (the rebels supported by the Syrians) against Arafat's faction. The war led to the evacuation of the PLO guerrillas (who found a haven far from Palestine, in Tunis, Tunisia), the deaths of over 600 Israeli soldiers, and a deep emotional split among Israelis. The volatile political debates in Israel centered on whether the invasion had been necessary, for this was the first war initiated by Israel in which its survival had not been an immediate issue.

There were additional costly consequences. Soon afterward, the US and French peacekeeping forces trying to play the role of an honest broker in the continuing Lebanese civil war ran head-on into an opposition of fury and anger few in the West were able to understand. Once the *USS New Jersey* opened fire on Muslim quarters in Beirut, the US "peace keepers" found themselves directly in harm's way. Two Shiite Hezbollah (Army of God) suicide bombers blew up trucks filled with explosives, killing 242 US troops (mostly Marines) and 59 French paratroopers. At that point, Reagan announced that the US mission had been accomplished, without truly explaining the nature of it.

## The Israeli-Palestinian Impasse

In the mid-1980s, the PLO was no closer than before to achieving its goal—the destruction of Israel followed by the creation of a Palestinian state. After its 1982 expulsion from Lebanon, it was in disarray. For the next several years, its nominal leader, Yassir Arafat, now based in Tunis, struggled to maintain the unity of the organization.

Little changed until December 1987, when the Palestinian population took matters into its own hands. The so-called *intifada* (literally, "shaking off" the Zionist yoke) began in Gaza after an Israeli truck collided with two cars, killing four Palestinians. The protests escalated and spread to the West Bank. Israel was put into the uncomfortable position of using armed soldiers against stone-throwing Palestinians. By early 1990, Israeli soldiers had killed more than 600 Palestinians. Israeli hard-liners blamed the violence on the PLO.

The intifada spurred debate in Israel over the future of Gaza and the West Bank. It also generated a debate in the PLO over strategy and tactics. At a November 1988 meeting in Algeria, the PLO passed a resolution proclaiming its willingness to recognize Israel on the condition that it officially endorse UN Resolutions 242 and 338, which called for Israeli withdrawal—both its military and settlers now numbered 70,000—from the Occupied Territories. For the PLO, this was a remarkably conciliatory position. Arafat also declared, "We [the PLO] totally and absolutely renounce all forms of terrorism."[12] Israeli prime minister Yitzhak Shamir and his party, the right-wing Likud, did not believe his peaceful protestations. There would be no talks with the PLO and no Palestinian state. Shamir could not forget that the PLO had vowed to destroy Israel and that, in fact, several of its factions still held this position.[13]

The end of the Cold War in 1990 led to a significantly improved relationship between Israel and the Soviet Union. The two nations reestablished diplomatic relations (which the Soviet Union had broken off after the 1967 Six Day War), and when Moscow opened its doors for the emigration of Jews, Israel welcomed them. The mass immigration of Jews into Israel (200,000 in 1990 alone) had consequences beyond the domestic issues of providing housing and jobs. Many Soviet Jews were settled in the West Bank and East Jerusalem, areas the Palestinians claimed. Although intifada violence subsided, the influx of the Soviet Jews into the occupied lands again inflamed Arab passions. Shamir, however, reiterated his pledge to preserve the borders of "Greater Israel," which included all areas under Israeli control.

## The Search for a Political Solution

The Arab-Israeli dispute became a factor in the events leading up to the Persian Gulf crisis occasioned by Iraq's invasion of Kuwait in August 1990 (see Chapter 21). Earlier in the year Iraqi ruler Saddam Hussein had threatened to "scorch half of Israel" in reprisal of any Israeli action against Iraq. In his efforts to secure support from Arab countries, Hussein proclaimed his willingness to withdraw from Kuwait if Israel withdrew from all the Occupied Territories.

The defeat of Iraq by the US-led coalition in the Gulf War in early 1991 improved conditions for a breakthrough in the Middle East. The PLO already had announced a willingness to recognize Israel in exchange for the land it had taken in 1967. Syrian president Hafez Assad, deprived of Soviet backing, ceased pretending that he had the military capability of regaining the Golan Heights. Many Israelis, seeking an end to the costly confrontation, believed that the time had come to sit down and talk.

In June 1992, in a tight race for Israeli prime minister, Labor Party leader Yitzhak Rabin defeated Shamir. Rabin had promised greater flexibility in the search for peace and suggested he was willing to trade some land for peace. Rabin was a military man who in January 1964 had become the chief of staff of the Israeli Defense Forces (IDF). His hawkish position had contributed to rising tensions in the years leading up to the Six Day War of 1967. During that war, he was as responsible as anyone for the Israeli conquest of Arab lands. Yet it was he who now had to deal with the consequences of that war. Rabin declared that the most urgent task was to negotiate self-rule for Palestinians in the West Bank and Gaza. Toward that end he announced a curb on building new settlements in the Occupied Territories, but he was not willing to return to the 1967 borders.

### The Oslo Accords

At the end of summer 1993, secret talks in Oslo, Norway, between PLO functionaries and members of Israel's "Peace Now" movement (acting at first independently of the Rabin government) offered hope for a solution to the Arab-Israeli conflict. The negotiations produced a remarkable breakthrough when Arafat and Rabin accepted the broad outlines of an agreement. Oslo called for an Israeli military withdrawal from Gaza (except for the Jewish settlements there) and from the West Bank city of Jericho, with further withdrawals sometime in the future. Political control of these regions would fall to the Palestinian Authority headed by Arafat. The signing ceremony took place on the White House lawn in Washington, on September 13, 1993, where a reluctant Rabin shook Arafat's outstretched hand.

Yet a final settlement proved to be as elusive as ever. The key defect of Oslo was that it failed to define the shape of a permanent peace. It said nothing about the fate of Jewish settlements in Gaza and the West Bank, the status of East Jerusalem, where the population was still almost exclusively Palestinian, or the refugees and a Palestinian state. Most important, it had virtually no effect on the ongoing expansion of Jewish settlements in the West Bank. Without a halt of the expansion, there could be no peace.

Moreover, the two sides had different visions of what Oslo meant, something that was apparent at the signing ceremony. Rabin spoke vaguely of the two sides "destined to live together on the same soil, in the same land." Arafat, in contrast, spoke of the Palestinians' "right to self-determination" and "coexistence" with Israel on the basis of "equal rights," calling for the implementation of UN Resolutions 242 and 338, which demanded an Israeli withdrawal from lands conquered in 1967.[14]

Oslo prompted Jordan's King Hussein to act. Secret talks with Israel soon produced a peace treaty, signed in Washington in July 1994, officially ending a forty-six-year state of war.

Not surprisingly, there was strong opposition to the agreement from radical elements in both Israel and among Palestinians. Rabin's foreign minister, Shimon Peres, explained his government's dilemma. "A peace negotiation is [by necessity] with your own people as well as with the other one."[15] Jewish militants, particularly those who had set up residence in Hebron, deep inside the West Bank, wanted no part of Oslo.

Palestinian and Israeli leaders who dealt with the enemy knew that many of their compatriots saw them as traitors negotiating away their patrimony. To complicate matters for Israel, it now faced another Palestinian social, political, and military force, namely, Hamas ("zeal" in Arabic), a militant Islamic organization based in Gaza, which had gained considerable support with its uncompromising call for the destruction of Israel. Hamas, the Palestinian branch of the Muslim Brotherhood (see Chapter 21), had been founded in 1987, in opposition to the PLO. Led by its spiritual leader, Sheik Ahmed Yassin, Hamas emerged, slowly yet surely, as an alternate voice opposing the increasingly corrupt and ineffective PLO leadership. It wanted nothing to do with Oslo. It charged that Arafat had obtained too little and that he had betrayed the Palestinian cause.

The Israelis had their own militants. In February 1994, a US-born Zionist, Baruch Goldstein, shot and killed twenty-nine Muslim worshippers at the Cave of the Patriarchs (the resting place of Abraham and other Old Testament figures) in Hebron. Goldstein was a member of an extremist organization whose views were capsulized by one of its rabbis in a eulogy to Goldstein: "One million Arabs are not worth a Jewish fingernail."[16]

But as long as the Oslo Accords remained in force, the possibility continued that some of the intractable issues could be resolved. It was for this reason that the Nobel Peace Prize committee, as it had done several times in the past, presented its award for 1994 to former enemies—Rabin, Arafat, and Peres—who had attempted to resolve their differences at the conference table rather than on the battlefield.

Arafat, as the head of the Palestinian Authority (PA), now had to shoulder the work of governing a quasi-autonomous region. Poverty was especially severe in Gaza, where the unemployment rate was around 50 percent. By the end of 1994, the World Bank and several nations contributed the small sum of $180 million in developmental aid to the PA, but the amount was far less than was needed. In addition to having to fend off complaints about the economy, Arafat faced critics of his autocratic and corrupt rule. Most serious was the challenge posed by Hamas. In October 1994, a Hamas suicide bomber blew up a crowded bus in Tel Aviv, killing twenty-one people. A rally in Gaza drew more than 20,000 Hamas supporters who hailed the bomber as a martyr and denounced the PLO's agreement with Israel.

In September 1995, Arafat and Rabin affixed their signatures to a detailed plan that established a timetable for the withdrawal of Israeli soldiers from about 30 percent of the West Bank (including its major cities and about 400 towns) and put the PA in charge of public services for most of the residents of the West Bank. Yet no progress was made on the more crucial questions of halting Jewish settlements or the formation of a Palestinian state.

The militants in Israel stepped up their criticism of Rabin. Benjamin Netanyahu, the new leader of the opposition Likud Party, went so far as to accuse Rabin of treason. One of Netanyahu's campaign posters showed Rabin wearing the *kaffiyeh*, Arafat's trademark Arab headdress. In November 1995, a twenty-one-year-old Israeli extremist, Yigal Amir, assassinated Rabin. He justified his violent act on religious grounds: A Jew who harmed Jewish society must be killed. Rabin's successor was his foreign minister, Shimon Peres. One of the architects of the Oslo peace process, Peres was committed to moving it forward, but first he had to face Netanyahu in the upcoming election.

### Return to Impasse

The first direct election of an Israeli prime minister took place in May 1996 under the shadow of escalating violence. The election became a referendum on the nearly three-year-long peace process. By a razor-thin margin, the victory went to Netanyahu, a hard-liner who had opposed the Oslo process every step of the way. Instead of Rabin's "land for peace" formula, Netanyahu promised "peace with security."

Netanyahu was reluctant to meet with Arafat, whom he considered a terrorist and not a worthy negotiating partner. When Netanyahu and Arafat did meet, however, in January 1997, to sign an agreement on an Israeli military pullback from Hebron, it was telling that they did so in the middle of the night, at 2:45 A.M., away from the glare of publicity. Netanyahu continued to demolish Palestinian homes and authorize the building of additional Jewish settlements and Jewish-only access roads in the West Bank. In the seven years after the signing of the Oslo Accords, settlement construction had increased by more than 50 percent and the settler population by 72 percent, their numbers reaching 380,000 amid more than 3 million Palestinians.[17] Moreover, economic conditions for the Palestinians steadily declined. In February 2000, Egyptian president Hosni Mubarak warned that Palestine had become a time bomb.

In the May 1999 election, Ehud Barak, the centrist candidate of the Labor Party and a former career military man who had risen to the post of IDF chief of staff as a protégé of Rabin, defeated Netanyahu by promising to revive the stalled Oslo Accords. But Barak was unable to come to a final agreement with Arafat. Instead, he focused on the withdrawal of Israeli troops from southern Lebanon, where they had been since 1982. Once that was achieved, in July

2000, Barak turned his attention to Syria in the hopes of coming to an understanding over the Golan Heights. The new leader of Syria, Bashar Assad, however, showed little interest in negotiations. He insisted, instead, on a maximalist position, the unconditional withdrawal of Israel's 18,000 settlers and its military from the Golan Heights.

Barak convinced US president Bill Clinton to convene a Palestinian-Israeli meeting at Camp David in July 2000. In the course of their discussion, Barak offered Arafat concessions that went beyond the Israeli consensus. He promised Arafat most—but not all—of the West Bank, the potential return of an unspecified number of the 3.5 million Palestinian refugees, and the withdrawal of an unspecified number of Israeli settlers from the West Bank and Gaza.

A sticking point again was Jerusalem. Arafat continued to insist on Palestinian sovereignty over its eastern half. When Barak refused to discuss the issue, Arafat returned home to a hero's welcome. Before he left Camp David, he told Clinton: "If I make concessions on Jerusalem, I will be killed, and you will have to talk to Sheikh [Ahmed] Yassin," the head of Hamas.[18]

Barak and Clinton blamed Arafat for the breakdown. The head of Israel's military intelligence, however, thought that Arafat wanted a diplomatic solution but could not accept the loss of 9 percent of West Bank territory and of East Jerusalem. Nor could he ignore the Palestinian refugee problem or the fact that Jewish settlers in the West Bank, Gaza, and East Jerusalem now numbered more than 400,000.[19]

In September 2000, Ariel Sharon—the man primarily responsible for the 1982 Israeli invasion of Lebanon that had resulted in the slaughter of Palestinians there, who had participated in a massacre of Palestinians in 1953, who once had referred to Palestinians as "cockroaches," and who as cabinet minister had overseen the building of Israeli settlements in the Occupied Territories—paid a visit to a most sensitive site, the Temple Mount in the Old City of Jerusalem. It was there that the temple of Solomon once had stood. The last remnant of the Temple Mount, the Western Wall (commonly referred to in the West as the Wailing Wall) at the foot of the mount is the holiest place in the Jewish faith. At the end of the seventh century, however, Muslims had built two mosques on the top of the Mount, which they call the Haram al-Sharif (Noble Sanctuary). The Dome of the Rock and the al-Aqsa Mosque, among the holiest shrines in Islam, are also located there. According to Muslim tradition, it was from the Dome that the Prophet Mohammed took his "Night Journey" to heaven, where he received Allah's command of five daily prayers. After the Six Day War, General Moshe Dayan, one of the architects of Israel's victory, had granted the Muslims sovereignty over the Temple Mount but at the same time had granted Israelis the right to visit it. (In an odd twist, Jews could visit it, but not pray there. Their prayers there had to be done surreptitiously in order not to offend Muslim sensibilities.)

The Temple Mount/Haram al-Sharif has long been a focal point of Arab-Israeli tension. The bloody riots of 1929 were the result of the Palestinians' belief that Zionists were about to seize control of it. In 1990, an Israeli group, the Temple Mount Faithful, sought to lay a cornerstone there for a future temple. In the violent aftermath, Israeli forces killed seventeen Palestinians, whose memory is honored in the museum of the Haram al-Sharif. Over the years, Israeli zealots called for the establishment of a new temple, even threatening to blow up the mosques.

Under heavy guard from 1,000 Israeli soldiers and police, Sharon ascended the Temple Mount to underscore that it belonged to the Jews. Predictably, it touched off the time bomb Mubarak had predicted. Thus began the second intifada, which pitted mostly young Palestinians against Israeli soldiers and citizens. It featured the lynching of two Israeli soldiers and the death of a thirteen-year-old Palestinian boy caught in the cross-fire, both acts caught on videotape and replayed endlessly on television.

Oslo was dead, and Sharon, the candidate promising the restoration of order, became the next Israeli prime minister. Order, however, eluded Sharon. During the next four years, Palestinians carried out more than 170 suicide attacks, most of them by Hamas. One-third, however, were carried out by the al-Aqsa Martyrs' Brigade, an offshoot of Arafat's Fatah organization. The Martyrs' Brigade may have been out of Arafat's control, but he showed little interest in reining it in.

Israel responded with helicopters, tanks, and bulldozers, demolishing even more Palestinian homes in the West Bank and in Gaza. In March 2004, Sharon's agents assassinated Sheikh Ahmed Yassin and his immediate successor, and threatened the same fate for Arafat. All the while, the number of Jewish settlers in Gaza and the West Bank increased. Between the beginning of 1997 and the end of June 2004, 150,000 took up residence in East Jerusalem. The uninterrupted building of new settlements turned any and all talks about peace into a receding mirage. During the first four years of the second intifada (September 2000–September 2004), 1,002 Israelis and 2,780 Palestinians lost their lives.

Sharon and Arafat, two old men, were engaged in their last battle. Arafat, seventy-five years old and suffering from Parkinson's disease, was trapped in his bombed-out compound in Ramallah in the West Bank and was threatened with expulsion by the seventy-six-year-old Sharon. Meanwhile, Hamas challenged Arafat for the hearts and minds of the Palestinians.

To prevent suicide bombers from entering Israel from Gaza and the West Bank, Sharon began construction of a security wall. Arafat replied that he had no problem with such a wall provided it was built on Israeli territory. The wall, scheduled to run 410 miles, cut deep into the West Bank, thereby transferring nearly 17 percent of its territory to Israel. It had a direct impact on the lives of 38 percent of the West Bank population[20]—cut off from other Palestinian communities, schools, hospitals, and farmlands. Arabs charged that what was left of Palestine was now of a collection of *Bantustans*, reminiscent of what white settlers had done to blacks in South Africa.

The administration of President George W. Bush in Washington, busy with the war on terror and the invasion of Iraq, made a few pronouncements calling for a "roadmap" for peace that included the dismantling of Israeli settlements as a step toward Palestinian nationhood. Bush labored under the illusion that a political transformation in Iraq would force the Palestinians to accept whatever Israel had in store for them. The only thing Sharon was willing to do, however, was to eliminate Jewish settlements in Gaza, where 8,100 settlers required the costly protection of 6,000 demoralized soldiers. That still left 450,000 settlers in the West Bank and Jerusalem.

In the autumn of 2004, Sharon's chief negotiator at the "roadmap" negotiations declared they were already "dead." He went on to say that Israel had come to an understanding with the Bush administration that there would be no talks with the Palestinians until they "turn into [peaceful] Finns." The issue of a Palestinian state "has been removed indefinitely from our agenda . . . all with a [US] presidential blessing and the ratification of both houses of Congress."[21]

In November 2004, Yassir Arafat, a man without a country, died in a Paris hospital. After the Egyptian government honored him with a state funeral, he was interred in his compound in Ramallah in the West Bank to which he had been forcibly confined during the last three years of his life. (Many Arabs always suspected Israeli foul play. After Arafat's body was exhumed in 2013, a Swiss forensic team suggested that the cause of death had been Polonium 210, a toxic radioactive substance. A French forensic team, too, found traces of Polonium in Arafat's system but concluded that he had died of natural causes.)

Fair and free Palestinian elections in January 2006 produced a seismic political shift when Hamas not only gained political control of Gaza but also gained an absolute majority of the seats (74 out of 132) in the Palestinian Authority parliament. Hamas's victory came at the expense of the PLO's Fatah party—corrupt, spineless, and without a sense of purpose—now led by Arafat's successor, Mahmoud Abbas, to whom Ariel Sharon once referred—contemptuously yet accurately—as a "plucked chicken." Over the years, Fatah's leadership had failed to achieve anything of substance. Israel continued to build settlements in the West Bank and showed no signs of accepting an independent Palestinian state.

It was precisely for these reasons that Bush and the Israeli leadership were willing to deal with Abbas. Talks with Hamas, however, remained out of the question. Instead, the Israeli government of Ehud Olmert, who had succeeded Sharon, arrested Hamas parliamentary deputies in Ramallah.

Olmert then turned his attention to Lebanon, where Shiite Hezbollah, under the charismatic leader Hassan Nasrallah, held sway. Hezbollah, well funded by Iranian petrodollars, represented the largest religious faction in Lebanon, deeply entrenched as a political (twelve members in the legislature as well as a cabinet minister), social (running schools, hospitals, and orphanages and providing radio and television services), and military force (having gained the right to maintain its well-armed private army after Israel's withdrawal in 2000). After Hezbollah kidnapped two Israeli reservist soldiers in July 2006, Olmert sent the Israeli army into Lebanon.

Hezbollah was stunned by the strong Israeli response, but held its ground. In 1982, the Israeli forces had reached Beirut within a week; this time, despite massive aerial bombardments, the going was much tougher. After thirty-three days, Israel called off the attack without having gained its objectives, neither the destruction of Hezbollah's military capability nor the release of its two soldiers (who, in any case, unbeknown to the Israelis, were already dead). The invasion of Lebanon only increased the prestige of Hezbollah for having stood up to the Israeli assault by the effective use of antitank rockets and shorter-range missiles, which it launched into northern Israel. An estimated 1,200 Lebanese died, more than 4,000 were injured, more than 100,000 were rendered homeless, and three-quarters of Lebanon's roads and bridges were severed. Israeli losses amounted to 116 soldiers and more than forty civilians killed.

Expecting an easy victory, the Bush administration had given its blessing to the Israeli attack on Hezbollah even before the soldiers' kidnapping. When the war was over, Bush described it as an Israeli victory. His secretary of state, Condoleezza Rice, went further, declaring that the Middle East had just experienced the "birth pangs" of a "new" democratic age. But that was wishful thinking. Instead, the war strengthened those who opposed a Pax Americana in the Middle East.

Israelis increasingly understood that they needed to find a political solution to the Palestinian problem. Israel's 5.4 million Jewish citizens had to contend with 1.3 million Arab citizens and another 3.4 million Arabs in the West Bank and East Jerusalem. The Arab population's birthrate, being three times that of the Jews, pointed to the prospect that by 2020, Jews would be outnumbered, making up but 47 percent of the population in the land between the Jordan River and the Mediterranean Sea. Then there were the moral, economic, political, and military implications of controlling a sullen, resentful Arab population.

Israelis, however, were divided on how to resolve the issue. The prime minister's own family was a microcosm of Israel's political deadlock. Olmert's wife was sympathetic to "Peace Now" (which advocated a withdrawal to the 1967 borders), while their four children opposed the father's incursion into Lebanon. One son, a reservist, refused to serve in the Occupied Territories, and the other avoided the military draft altogether. Olmert wistfully acknowledged that at the dinner table, "I am a minority of one." Olmert, who had once urged Jewish control over all of Jerusalem, now urged a return to the 1967 borders, including joint Israeli-Palestinian control of Jerusalem.[22]

In the meantime, there was still the problem of Hamas and its control of Gaza, the result of its 2006 election victory. A number of nations hostile to Hamas refused to accept the legitimacy of the election, among them Egypt (long at war with the Muslim Brotherhood that had given birth to Hamas), Israel, the United States, European Union, Saudi Arabia, and Jordan, as well as the Palestinian Authority in the West Bank. Diplomatically and economically isolated, Gaza, one of the most densely populated pieces of real estate on earth, barely survived, subjected to a tight Israeli blockade—an act of war according to international law. Palestinians in Gaza gained direct access to the outside world only after constructing a series of tunnels along the southern Gaza border with Egypt, through which they smuggled needed supplies, including weapons.

In April 2008, Hamas announced a six-month truce with Israel, one that held until November 4, when Israel bombed Gaza, killing six Palestinians. Hamas responded by launching missiles against southern Israel. Israel countered with a massive bombardment of Gaza. During the previous seven years, Hamas rockets had killed no more than three Israelis, and between July 2008 and the resumption of violence in November, one Israeli died at the hands of Hamas.[23] A cease-fire that had held up reasonably well now gave way to all-out war.

The Israeli goal was to destroy Gaza's infrastructure in the vain hope of turning the population against Hamas. The sustained bombing campaign, which began at the end of December, targeted rocket launchers, residences of Hamas leaders, government buildings, police stations, roads and bridges, schools and universities, mosques, water, and sanitation and power facilities. A week later Israel followed up with a ground invasion. The seventh Arab-Israeli war—and the fourth Israeli conquest of Gaza—was testimony to an intractable conflict. Israel was certain that the Bush administration would not object, while at the same time giving notice to the incoming Barack Obama administration not to expect too much from a resumption of the peace process.

The Israeli invasion of Gaza had more to do with domestic matters than security. It was calculated to affect the election of a new prime minister, which was scheduled for February 10, 2009. In Israel, where public opinion overwhelmingly supported the invasion, it became known as the "election war." It stood to reason that it would benefit the Labor Party candidate, Defense Minister Ehud Barak, the architect of the invasion, one he had carefully planned over several months.[24] None of the three major candidates, however, was able to garner a majority. After lengthy negotiations, Benjamin Netanyahu (Likud) formed a coalition government with Labor and the ultranationalist Yisrael Beiteinu party. Ehud Barak retained his post as defense minister while the head of Yisrael Beiteinu, Avigdor Lieberman, became foreign minister. Lieberman, a resident of the West Bank, was an advocate of a two-state solution without, however, abandoning the Israeli settlements on the West Bank. A Palestinian state would have to be a severely truncated entity.

Barak had harbored the hope of eliminating Hamas once and for all. By now, however, Hamas was more than a fighting force—it had become a religious and social organization with deep roots among the Palestinians. In the end, Israel settled on weakening the military capability of Hamas. When the war was over, much of the infrastructure was in ruins. Palestinian fatalities ran to 1,300, as compared to thirteen Israelis killed.

The newly elected US president, Barack Obama, briefly considered becoming engaged in the "peace process," but then thought better of it. He knew he would receive no help from the Republican Party, which had pledged not to cooperate with him on anything, even on matters that it had once championed. It was not until his second term that Obama took tentative steps, but he then lost interest in an exercise certain to lead to another dead end. Five Israeli and Palestinian negotiators had won the Nobel Peace Prize for their attempts to cut the Gordian knot, only to have little to show for their effort. Indeed, two of them were assassinated because of it. Moreover, Israeli prime minister Benjamin Netanyahu mistrusted Obama's motives. Netanyahu was more interested in attacking Iran's nuclear facilities, but for that he needed US help and Obama would not give it to him. Obama was more interested in finding a political solution to the Israel-Iran standoff over Iran's insistence on the right to nuclear power.

When Iran, in August 2013, elected its new president, Hassan Rouhani, it set the stage for the first substantial contacts between Iran and the United States in thirty-four years. When they reached a tenuous preliminary agreement, whereby Iran acquiesced to dismantle its nuclear weapons program and subject it to daily UN inspections, Netanyahu wasted no time calling it a "historic mistake." (See Chapter 20.)

## Notes

1. Jewish nationalism has existed ever since the diaspora, the dispersion of the Jews, which began in the sixth century B.C. with the destruction of Solomon's temple and culminated with the destruction of the second temple in Jerusalem in A.D. 70 and the defeat of Bar Kochba in A.D. 135. British philosopher Bertrand Russell, in reminding his readers that modern nationalism is a relatively new concept, pointed out that at the end of the Middle Ages "there was hardly any nationalism except that of the Jews."

2. Quoted in Amos Elon, *The Israelis: Founders and Sons* (New York: Holt, Rinehart and Winston, 1971), p. 106.

3. Palestinian Arab and Ben-Gurion cited in ibid., p. 155 (emphasis in the original).

4. "Balfour Declaration," in *Times* (London), November 9, 1917, p. 7.

5. Charles Glass, "'It Was Necessary to Uproot Them,'" *London Review of Books*,

June 24, 2004, pp. 21–23; Ari Shavit, "Lydda, 1948: A City, a Massacre and the Middle East Today," *The New Yorker*, October 21, 2013.

6. "UN Resolution 242," *Yearbook of the United Nations: 1967* (New York: United Nations, 1969), pp. 257–258.

7. Moshe Dayan and King Hussein quoted in Dana Adams Schmidt, *Armageddon in the Middle East* (New York: John Day, 1974), p. 249. For a discussion of the views of Dayan and Hussein, see Bernard Avishai, *The Tragedy of Zionism: Revolution and Democracy in the Land of Israel* (New York: Farrar, Straus and Giroux, 1985), pp. 275–278.

8. Tom Segev, "A Bitter Prize," *Foreign Affairs* 85, no. 3 (May/June 2006), p. 145.

9. Hosni Mubarak, Sadat's successor, jailed a number of suspects, among them Sheik Omar Abdel Rahman and Ayman al-Zawahiri, both of whom eventually were released. Once freed, they joined Osama bin Laden's al Qaeda. In 1993, Rahman led an attempt to blow up one of the towers of the World Trade Center in New York City; Zawahiri became one of the leading figures in al Qaeda.

10. "What can be done," Sharon told Habib, "and this is not actually a plan, but it is practicable, is a swift and vigorous strike of 24 to 48 hours, which will force the Syrians to retreat and inflict such heavy losses on the PLO that they will leave Lebanon." Sharon also expected the Lebanese government to regain control of the Beirut-Damascus highway, thus driving the Syrians farther north. From a report of a US diplomatic summary of the conversation between Sharon and Habib, published by the Israeli Labor Party newspaper *Davar*. The US ambassador to Israel, Samuel W. Lewis, and the State Department confirmed the basic outlines of the conversation. Thomas L. Friedman, "Paper Says Israeli Outlined Invasion," *New York Times*, May 26, 1985, p. 15.

11. John Fisk, *Pity the Nation: The Abduction of Lebanon*, 4th ed. (New York: Thunder's Mouth Press/Nation Books, 2002), chapter 11, "Terrorists," pp. 359–400. In 1983, an Israeli commission declared that Sharon was not fit as defense minister, that he bore personal responsibility for the massacres. That did not prevent him from becoming the minister of housing and construction who oversaw the expansion of settlements in the West Bank. In 2001, he became prime minister.

12. Text of Arafat statement, *Baltimore Sun*, December 15, 1988.

13. Yitzhak Shamir, "Israel at 40: Looking Back, Looking Ahead," *Foreign Affairs* 66, no. 3 (1988), pp. 585–586.

14. The speeches of Rabin and Arafat, in Walter Laqueur and Barry Rubin, eds., *The Israel-Arab Reader: A Documentary History of the Middle East Conflict*, 5th rev. ed. (New York: Penguin, 1995), pp. 613–614.

15. Peres, cited in Connie Bruck, "The Wounds of Peace," *The New Yorker*, October 14, 1996, p. 64.

16. Cited in William Pfaff, "Victory to Extremists," *Baltimore Sun*, March 7, 1994, p. 14A.

17. According to the estimates of Arie Arnon of Peace Now; Graham Usher, "Middle East Divide," *The Nation*, December 25, 2000, p. 6.

18. Cited by Ben Macintyre, "Arafat: If I Sign, I'll Be Killed," *Times* (London), July 27, 2000, p. 17.

19. Amos Malka, cited in Robert Malley, "Israel and the Arafat Question," *New York Review of Books*, October 7, 2004, p. 23.

20. From the website of B'Tselem, the Israeli human rights organization, www.btselem.org. See also John Ward Anderson and Molly Moore, "Israel Blunts Uprising's Impact," *Washington Post*, October 5, 2004, p. A22, and "A Bloody Vacuum," *Economist*, October 2, 2004, pp. 23–25.

21. Dov Weisglass, one of Sharon's closest advisers, cited in John Ward Anderson, "Sharon Aide Says Goal of Gaza Plan Is to Halt Road Map," *Washington Post*, October 7, 2004.

22. Olmert interview in *Yedioth Ahronoth*, reprinted in *New York Review of Books*, December 4, 2008, pp. 6–8.

23. The precise numbers are murky, but nearly all of the thirty-one Israeli terrorist victims in 2008 (according to Israeli government figures) died at the hands of non-Hamas terrorists. "Where Will It End?" *The Economist*, January 10, 2009, p. 24; Human Rights Watch, "Letter to Hamas to Stop Rocket Attacks," November 20, 2008, www.theisraelproject.org.

24. Barak Ravid, "Disinformation, Secrecy, and Lies: How the Gaza Offensive Came About," *Haaretz*, December 31, 2008.

# Part 3

# The Shifting Sands of Global Power

**The Cold War created a bipolar world in which the two contending** superpowers pulled other nations toward one pole or the other. But gradually the bipolar East-West confrontation underwent a transformation marked by divisions within each camp and the emergence of other centers of power. The first years of the Cold War were marked by a straightforward adversarial relationship featuring the hard-nosed diplomatic combat of Joseph Stalin and Harry Truman. It also featured the US containment policy, the division of Europe, the creation of two military alliances (NATO and the Warsaw Pact), a war in Korea, persistent ideological attacks and counterattacks, and the massive rearmament of both sides. Despite conciliatory gestures by the successors of Stalin and Truman and talk of peaceful coexistence, the bipolar struggle carried over into the 1960s, even to the point of the superpowers coming close to a nuclear exchange during the Cuban missile crisis.

By that time, however, it became clear to the superpowers that they could not make military use of their huge nuclear arsenals and that the day of direct confrontation was over. Indeed, the Cuban settlement was testimony to that reality. Additionally, by the early 1960s, the superpowers could no longer take for granted the solidarity of their respective alliances. The bipolar world began to give way to multipolarity.

To explain this process, Joseph Stalin's political legacy is our point of departure in Chapter 9. Here we trace the efforts of his successor, Nikita Khrushchev, to put to an end the excesses of Stalinism, the terror, and the arbitrary and abusive use of state power, and to institute reforms aimed at restoring orderly and legal procedures to Soviet rule and revitalizing the economy. The consequences of this reform effort and the pattern of Soviet politics under

Khrushchev's successors are also discussed. We also examine the stresses and strains within the Communist bloc and particularly the impact of Khrushchev's criticism of Stalin in Eastern Europe. Khrushchev managed to keep de-Stalinization at home within carefully set boundaries, but that was not the case in Poland and Hungary, where it rekindled nationalist sentiments and unleashed pent-up desires for political liberalization and liberation from Moscow's control.

The revolts in Poland and Hungary and later in Czechoslovakia were snuffed out by the Soviet Union. A recalcitrant Communist China, however, could not be so easily dealt with. In Chapter 9 we also analyze the causes and the course of the Sino-Soviet split, which divided the Communist world. Their bitter and long-lasting feud signified that ideological bonds were weaker than the force of nationalism and that international Communism was not the monolithic movement it was generally thought to be in the West.

Meanwhile, in the 1960s, the US government, still convinced that Communism was monolithic, went off to war in distant East Asia to stop its spread. In Chapter 10, we explain how and why the United States took up the fight in Vietnam, and why it lost. The staunch anti-Communist logic prevalent in Washington caused a misreading of the Vietnamese revolution, its causes and strengths, coming up with the erroneous conclusion that its source was Beijing-based Communist aggression rather than Vietnamese nationalism. We discuss the war's escalation and the difficulty the United States had in extracting itself from it. We also examine the war's tragic consequences and impact on the remainder of Indochina, especially Cambodia, and the plight of the refugees, the "boatpeople."

In the late 1960s, despite the fact that the United States was still mired in Vietnam, progress was made in lowering East-West tensions elsewhere. New leadership in West Germany, specifically that of Chancellor Willy Brandt, took bold steps to try and break up the twenty-year-old Cold War logjam in Central Europe. In Chapter 11, we examine Brandt's conciliatory policy toward the Communist nations of Eastern Europe and the role his *Ostpolitik* played in bringing détente—the relaxation of tension—to East-West relations. By the early 1970s, détente became the basis of Soviet-US diplomacy as well. The new relations between Washington and Moscow left Beijing isolated. In fact, the US-Soviet détente at first brought jeers from China, which suspected an anti-Chinese conspiracy but, as we show in Chapter 11, the Chinese leaders came to realize the dangers of China's continued isolation and judged that they had more to gain by normalizing relations with the United States. In a dramatic diplomatic turnabout, the United States and Communist China, two nations that had been the most intransigent of ideological foes for over two decades, suddenly buried the hatchet in 1972.

With US-Soviet détente and the normalization of US-Chinese relations, a new era of delicate tripolar power relations had arrived. Moreover, with the resurgence of Western Europe and the emergence of an economically power-ful Japan, the international arena was now multipolar. The simpler world of East versus West, of the struggle between the "free world" and the "Communist world," gave way to a more complex world of power-balancing diplomacy, one that called for greater political flexibility.

# 9

# The Communist World
# After Stalin

**When Stalin died in March 1953, he had ruled the Soviet Union for** nearly thirty years and in the process left his imprint on the Communist Party and the nation. In the late 1920s, Stalin and his party had launched a program of rapid industrialization with a series of Five-Year Plans. In order to feed the growing proletariat (the industrial workforce), he introduced a program of rapid collectivization whereby the small and inefficient individual farms were consolidated into larger collectives. In effect, it made the Soviet peasant an employee of the state. The state set the price that collective farms received for their agricultural commodities, a price kept low so that the countryside wound up subsidizing the cities, where an industrial revolution was taking place. In this way, agriculture became one of the "stepchildren" of the Communist revolution.

At the time of the Communist revolution in 1917, the peasants had realized an age-old dream, the private and unrestricted ownership of their land. Predictably, they resisted the Stalinist drive toward collectivization. Faced with intense opposition, Stalin had two choices: curtail the collectivization and industrialization program or pursue it with force. He chose the latter. Collectivization became a bloody civil war during the late 1920s and early 1930s, in which several million peasants perished, accompanied by the widespread destruction of equipment and livestock. In such a wasteful and brutal manner, the countryside was forced to subsidize the industrial revolution and the growth of the city.

Stalin subordinated Soviet society to one overriding quest: to create an industrial state to bring to an end Russia's traditional economic backwardness, the root cause of its military weakness. At a conference of factory managers in 1931, he addressed the question of whether the mad dash toward industrialization would be slowed. He offered his audience this capsule history of Russia:

> To slacken the tempo would mean falling behind. And all those who fall behind get beaten. . . . One feature of the history of old Russia was the continual beatings she suffered because of her backwardness. She was beaten by the Mongol khans . . . the Turkish beys . . . the Swedish feudal lords . . . the Polish and Lithuanian gentry . . . the British and French capitalists . . . the Japanese barons. All beat her—because of her backwardness, military backwardness, cultural backwardness, political backwardness, industrial backwardness. . . . Such is the law of the exploiters, to beat the backward and the weak. . . . Either we do it [catch up with the capitalist West], or we shall be crushed. . . . In ten years we must make good the distance which separates us from the advanced capitalist countries. . . . And that depends on us. Only on us![1]

Stalin's Five-Year Plans gave the Soviet Union a highly centralized economy capable of withstanding the supreme test of fire, the German attack in World War II. In fact, during the war the Soviet economy, despite massive destruction at the hands of the Germans, outproduced that of Germany. Studies conducted after the war for the US Joint Chiefs of Staff repeatedly paid tribute to Stalin's industrial revolution, which had transformed the Soviet Union from a weak, backward country into a formidable opponent that in short order broke the US nuclear monopoly (1949) and later was the first to venture into the frontiers of space (1957).

All of this did not come without a heavy price. The Soviet Union's "dictatorship of the proletariat" became a dictatorship of the party over the proletariat and the peasantry, and eventually a dictatorship of the secret police over the proletariat, the peasantry, and the party itself.[2] In 1937, Stalin initiated the bloodiest of a series of purges of the party by which he eliminated all opposition. The Bolshevik Revolution of 1917, which had begun as an uprising supported by the proletariat, rank-and-file soldiers, and peasants, had become a monument to the triumph of the secret police.

### Khrushchev and Stalin's Ghost

When Stalin died in 1953, the party immediately took steps to reassert the position of preeminence it had enjoyed in the days of Vladimir Lenin, the architect of the Bolshevik Revolution, who had led the Soviet Union until his death in 1924. Within a week after Stalin's death, the party forced Stalin's designated successor, Georgi Malenkov, to choose between the two posts he held—first secretary of the party (that is, the head of the party) or that of prime minister (the head of the government). Malenkov, inexplicably, decided to hold on to the weaker position, that of prime minister. A lesser member of the ruling circle, the Politburo, Nikita Khrushchev, became the new first secretary of the party. The party then took another step to prevent the consolidation of power in the hands of one person. It established a collective leadership, a *troika* (Russian for a sled pulled by three horses) consisting of Prime Minister Malenkov, Foreign Minister Viacheslav Molotov, and the head of the secret police, Lavrentii Beria. Beria, who had been an agent of Stalin's terror, remained a threat to the party. In the summer of 1953, the party, with the help of Soviet army generals (who also had suffered greatly during the secret police's unchecked reign of terror), arrested Beria. It charged him with abuse of power and then had him shot.

The party continued in its attempts to come to terms with the Stalinist legacy. The reformers repeatedly clashed with those who sought to maintain the status quo. By the mid-1950s, however, the reformers gained the upper hand. A general amnesty freed the political prisoners. Writers, many of whom had been "writing for the desk drawer," now saw their works in print. Détente with the West now became a possibility. Western visitors began to arrive in Moscow.

The most dramatic assault on Stalin's legacy came in February 1956 at the Communist Party's Twentieth Congress, when Khrushchev took the opportunity to deliver a scathing attack on Stalin's crimes. It became known as the "Secret Speech," but it did not remain secret for long—since any address before an assembly of hundreds of delegates, many of whom had much to gain by making it public, would certainly reach the light of day. The speech was the

*Soviet leader Nikita Khrushchev, flanked by Foreign Minister Andrei Gromyko and Marshal Rodion Malinovski, at a press conference in Paris, May 16, 1960*

result of a commission the party had set up to report on Beria's—and thus Stalin's—crimes against the party. In his speech, Khrushchev focused on Stalin's destruction of the party's role as the revolution's guiding force. "Socialist legality" was to take the place of one-man rule.

The speech was an attempt by the party at self-preservation. And it was limited to just that. It did not address the larger question of Stalin's terror directed against peasants, religious organizations, writers, and composers—in short, the public at large. One of Khrushchev's Western biographers wrote that the Secret Speech was a smokescreen as well as an exposure.[3] It tackled the question of one-man rule, but not one-party rule by the "vanguard of the proletariat." Neither did it challenge the Stalinist system of agriculture, which the party admitted at the time was in ruins, or the system of industrial organization, which still worked reasonably well. Instead, Khrushchev's speech focused on the dictatorship of the police over the party.

The Secret Speech signaled the end of the arbitrary terror of Stalin's time. The secret police was brought under the party's control and its wings were clipped, particularly in dealing with party members. Arbitrary arrests largely ended. Censorship restrictions were partially lifted, breathing new life into the Soviet Union's intellectual community. Khrushchev continued to wage war against the memory of Stalin to the point that, in 1961, he ordered the removal of Stalin's body from the mausoleum it shared with Lenin's remains. Stalin's new resting place along the Kremlin wall was a grave nearly thirty feet deep, with concrete poured over the coffin. Khrushchev then proceeded to rename cities and institutions named in Stalin's honor. The city of Stalingrad, for example, the supreme symbol of the Red Army's resistance to Hitler, where an entire German army perished, became merely Volgograd, the "city on the Volga."

After Khrushchev's ouster in October 1964, the party made no concerted effort to rehabilitate Stalin's image, although overt criticism of Stalin was brought to an end. It was clear, however, that one day Soviet society again would have to come to grips with Stalin's legacy. The transformation of Stalin's image from a hero and generalissimo, to a murderous tyrant in violation of "Leninist legality," and finally to a shadowy figure who appeared scarcely to have existed, simply would not do. In 1961, the party published the long-awaited second edition of its *History of the Communist Party of the Soviet Union*. The first edition, published in 1938 under Stalin's direct editorship, had heaped voluminous praise on Stalin. The second edition was an example of revisionist history with a vengeance. It never mentioned his name. A quarter-century later, under the impetus of Mikhail Gorbachev's reforms, Soviet society once more was brought face-to-face with Stalin's legacy.

To many observers in the West, these changes were of little consequence. The party still retained its control and the economy remained unchanged. But in the context of Russian and Soviet history, the changes were significant. This was something on which both Khrushchev and his opponents agreed. Khrushchev needed to tread carefully without stirring up major repercussions, for, as Alexis de Tocqueville (the French political writer of the nineteenth century) noted, harking back to the French Revolution, the most difficult time in the life of a bad government comes when it tries to reform itself. Khrushchev soon found that out.

Khrushchev thought that art should not be censored. But the flood of writings portraying Soviet reality as it in fact existed, warts and all, soon overwhelmed the party, and Khrushchev himself took on the role of a censor. In 1962, Khrushchev permitted the publication of Alexander Solzhenitsyn's exposé of Stalin's labor camps, *One Day in the Life of Ivan Denisovich,* the literary sensation of the post-Stalin age. Yet several years earlier, he had supported "administrative measures" to prevent the publication of Boris Pasternak's *Doctor Zhivago,* admittedly without having read it. Late in life, a repentant Khrushchev wrote that "readers should be given a chance to make their own judgments" and that "police measures shouldn't be used" in the context of controversial literature.[4] As the head of the party, however, he never managed to come to grips with his contradictions. As a result, he was unable to bring the restless writers under control. The task fell to his successor, Leonid Brezhnev, a man lacking all subtlety.

By the early 1960s, Khrushchev had worn out his welcome. The majority of the party increasingly viewed his erratic moves and innovations as harebrained schemes. The classic case in point was his rash, spur-of-the moment attempt, in 1962, to station Soviet nuclear missiles in Cuba. Poorly thought out and hasty reforms in agriculture and industry also came back to haunt him.

In 1958, Khrushchev demanded a drastic increase in meat production to surpass the United States in that category. The ambitious first secretary of the party in Riazan, A. N. Larionov, publicly pledged a doubling of meat production in 1959. Khrushchev then ordered that other regions follow the Riazan example. In February 1959, before Larionov could even get started, Khrushchev went to Riazan to bestow on him personally the prestigious Order of Lenin. A desperate Larionov fulfilled his pledge by slaughtering whatever livestock was available. Eventually, he went outside the region to purchase milk cows and breeding stock. In December 1959, Larionov declared a hollow "victory" for which he was once again decorated. In 1960, meat production declined by 200,000 tons, a downtrend that took years to reverse. At the end of 1960, Larionov, a Hero of Socialist Labor, shot himself in his office.[5]

When Khrushchev initiated a shakeup in the party, in October 1964, it proved to be the last straw, for it threatened the exalted positions of many. By then he had lost the support of the majority in the Central Committee, officially the major decisionmmaking body of the Communist Party. In a vote of no confidence, the party sent him out to pasture with the stipulation that he stay out of politics. Leonid Brezhnev succeeded him as the head of the party.

Khrushchev's demise proved to be his finest hour. He had dealt with his opponents within the bounds of "socialist legality," that is, by using the rules and procedures written into the party's statutes. But when his behavior became increasingly reckless—and embarrassing, such as pounding the table with his shoe at the United Nations—the party turned against him. Once he faced the cold, hard fact that he had lost the support of the majority, he stepped down. There was never a question of using the military or the secret police.

Khrushchev's successors gave the Soviet Union twenty years of stability, a significant increase in the standard of living, and rough military parity with the West. At the same time, the emphasis was on the retention of the status quo. A freewheeling discussion of Stalin's role in Soviet history had no place in the scheme of the Brezhnev vision of Soviet society. Nor was he interested in sweeping experiments.

Under Brezhnev, the intellectuals were brought under control by intimidation, jailing, and, in several cases, notably that of Solzhenitsyn, expulsion from the country. Brezhnev's prime minister, Alexei Kosygin, sought to continue the economic reforms Khrushchev had begun, which, had they been concluded, could have given the Soviet Union a mixed socialist and small-scale capitalist economy. The discussions led to trial runs, but they were shelved when it became apparent that too many factory managers were more interested in retaining the old system, which depended on production quotas set at the top.

By the time Brezhnev died in 1982, the party was beginning to accept the need for another round of reform. Brezhnev's successors, Yuri Andropov and Konstantin Chernenko, initiated the first modest steps, but both were hampered by what turned out to be incurable illnesses. In 1985, Mikhail Gorbachev, the new first secretary of the party, inherited his nation's economic problems. In a direct challenge to Brezhnev's political, economic, and intellectual inertia, Gorbachev committed the Soviet Union to a wide-ranging discussion of its shortcomings and to the restructuring of the economy (see Chapter 19).

## Eastern Europe: The Satellites

As the Communist Party in the Soviet Union wrestled with Stalin's ghost, a similar drama began to unfold in Moscow's East European satellites. There, the conflict was fought with much more intensity and conviction. The reformers there were more numerous and willing to go much farther than their counterparts in the Kremlin. Moscow, however, made clear that changes must remain within certain parameters, which, although not rigidly defined and constantly shifting, the reformers could not cross. Moscow did not hesitate to brandish the big stick, its army, just in case someone stepped out of line.

The West saw Soviet postwar expansion as a threat to its security and as a source of Soviet strength. Stalin, however, saw it in a different light. His East

European glacis, or defensive buffer, offered his state a forward position in a future confrontation with the capitalist West, but he understood that it was also a potential headache. At the Yalta Conference he had described the Poles as "quarrelsome." He had a much better understanding than, say, Truman of the volatile mix of nationalism, religion, and anti-Russian sentiments in Eastern Europe.

By 1948, Stalin appeared to have consolidated his position in Eastern Europe. The Communist parties there were for the most part the creation of the Soviet Union, and on the surface loyal members of the Communist camp lined up in solidarity against the West. But nationalist currents ran deep. It became clear that East European Communists were more interested in pursuing their own national interests, rather than serving those of the Kremlin.

## Yugoslavia

The classic example of such "nationalist deviation" was that of Joseph Tito, the Communist ruler of Yugoslavia. In the late 1930s, Tito had spent time in Moscow under Stalin's tutelage, and during World War II he had fought with the Red Army (as well as the Western Allies) against Nazi Germany. His loyalty to Stalin and international Communist solidarity appeared beyond reproach. Soon after the war, however, the Yugoslav and Soviet Communists had a falling-out over the question of who was to play the dominant role in running Yugoslavia. The upshot of this noisy and public quarrel was that Tito established his independence from Moscow. He did not, however, move into the capitalist camp. He accepted aid from the West (and from the Soviet Union after Stalin's death), but always remained neutral during the Cold War.[6] The Tito-Stalin split pointed to a lingering problem the Soviets faced in Eastern Europe, the volatile force of nationalism.

The immediate consequence of Tito's defection was Stalin's reorganization of the Communist governments of Eastern Europe. He executed and jailed Communists (such as Poland's Wladyslaw Gomulka, of whom more later) whom he suspected of nationalist (or Titoist) tendencies. The loyalty of foreign Communists, Stalin insisted, must be to the Soviet Union, not to their native lands. Stalin's definition of a loyal Communist was one who faithfully served the interests of the Kremlin. An international "revolutionary," he wrote in 1927, is one "who is ready to protect, to defend the U.S.S.R. without reservation, without qualification."[7] In short, the interests of the Soviet Union outweighed the considerations of all other Communist governments. Stalin never budged on this definition of an international revolutionary. Only one Marxist was permitted to be a nationalist, namely, Stalin himself.

The damage Stalin did to Communist movements abroad was seldom adequately appreciated or understood in the West. By subordinating the foreign Communist parties to the interests of the Soviet, Stalin painted them with a brush wielded by a foreign power. As such, these parties struggled for support, their association with Moscow a millstone dragging them down, and their thunder stolen by moderate reformist socialists in the West. After World War II, the political shifts to the left were the result of wars, poverty, and disillusion with the old order, not the creation of Stalin; the left's demise, however, was in large part Stalin's responsibility.

Stalin's brutal cleansing ("purging") of the East European Communist parties did have its desired effect. Until his death in March 1953, these parties were outwardly loyal to the Soviet Union, and Eastern Europe remained calm.

## Poland

Soon after Stalin's death, however, the East European Communist parties sought to distance themselves from Moscow, if only ever so slightly. It did not mean that they sought to leave the socialist camp or to legalize capitalist parties, but they did insist on dealing with their own internal problems without direct intervention by Moscow. An element of self-preservation played a large part in the restructuring of the relationship between the East European Communist parties and Moscow. The East Europeans sought to do away with Moscow's repeated and arbitrary purges of their ranks and interference in their internal affairs. The Polish party took the lead when it quietly released from house arrest (December 1954) and later readmitted (August 1956) into the party the nationalist Wladyslaw Gomulka.

Stalin had good reason to mistrust Gomulka. As early as 1945, Stalin's agents in Poland had warned him that the "deviationist" Gomulka had repeatedly and publicly advocated a "Polish road" to Communism, a form of "Polish Marxism." Gomulka's variation of Communism, unlike the Soviet version, sought a peaceful rather than a bloody transformation of society. It rejected the collectivization of agriculture, spoke of a "parliamentary democracy" for Poland, and even suggested that the Polish Communist Party had seized political power in 1945 in its own right—as it was "lying in the street" ready to be picked up—thus failing to show proper gratitude for the role of the Red Army. What we are dealing with here, Stalin's agents pointed out, was more a case of "Polish nationalism" than of Communism based on the Soviet model.[8]

By denouncing Stalin, Khrushchev had sought to discredit his Stalinist political opponents at home, not the East European Stalinist hard-liners. Inadvertently, however, he opened up a Pandora's box in Eastern Europe. By dwelling on Stalin's "mistakes" and "excesses" at home—particularly his crimes against party members—he set the stage for the return to power of East European Communists whom Stalin had imprisoned and expelled from the party.

After Khrushchev attacked Stalin at the Twentieth Congress of the Communist Party of the Soviet Union, it was Polish delegates to the congress who leaked to the West a copy of the Secret Speech. Khrushchev later wrote in his memoirs: "I was told that it was being sold for very little. So

Khrushchev's speech . . . wasn't appraised as being worth much! Intelligence agents from every country in the world could buy it cheap on the open market."[9]

The Poles reasoned that if Khrushchev could denounce Stalinism at home, then they ought to be able to do the same. They used the speech to justify their attempt to travel their own road toward socialism without, however, leaving the Soviet camp.

The reformist wing of the Polish Communist Party had its work cut out. The summer of 1956 saw rioting workers, particularly in Poznan, where seventy-five of them were shot dead in confrontations with police. To deal with the crisis, the party met in October 1956 to contemplate changes. Along the way, it once again elected Gomulka as its first secretary. Gomulka then affirmed Poland's right to follow a socialist model other than the Soviet example. He also insisted on his country's "full independence and sovereignty," as part of every nation's right to self-government. Polish-Soviet relations, he said, must be based on equality and independence.

What particularly had galled the Poles was that their defense minister, Konstantin Rokossovsky, was a Soviet citizen. Rokossovsky, a native of Poland, had served in the Russian tsarist army during World War I, and in 1917 he had joined the Russian Communist Party and later attained the highest rank in the Red Army, that of marshal (the equivalent of a five-star general in the US Army). As Poland's minister of defense he thus served a foreign master. Understandably, Rokossovsky became one of the first casualties of Poland's peaceful "October Revolution" when he was dismissed as defense minister.

The impertinent behavior of the Polish Communists alarmed their Soviet comrades. In October 1956, a high-level Soviet delegation, led by Khrushchev, arrived in Warsaw uninvited, ready to put the Polish house in order. The Poles refused to back down. They made clear they would continue to travel down the socialist road, yet at the same time, they insisted on the right to take care of their own internal problems. To mollify their Soviet counterparts, they pledged loyalty to the Warsaw Pact, the Soviet-led military alliance.

The Soviet Communist Party, here, gave tacit assent to the principle that there were several roads to socialism, that the Soviet model was not the only one and thus not necessarily the correct one. In effect, the Kremlin yielded and accepted the legitimacy of what once was a heresy, the right to nationalist deviation. If the Soviets had the right to find their own path to socialism, so did the other socialist countries. In fact, by then, Khrushchev had already buried the hatchet in the ideological dispute with Tito. In May 1955, he had traveled on a state visit to Belgrade where he and Tito embraced, signaling an end to the intra-Marxist feud. Moscow's monopoly on interpreting the writings of Marx and Engels was no more. The Italian Communist Palmiro

Togliatti coined a word to describe the new reality, "polycentrism." The world now had several centers of Marxist orthodoxy.

The Polish Communist Party embarked on its own road to socialism. It set out to placate the restless population. The gradual process of collectivizing farmland was halted and then reversed. (Unlike the Soviet Union, where the state owned all the land, most farmland in Communist Poland was in the hands of private farmers.) Political parties other than the Communist Party were permitted to exist and received subordinate representation in the government. Small businesses were tolerated. Gomulka released from jail the prelate of the Roman Catholic Church in Poland, Stefan Cardinal Wyszynski, and the church regained the traditional right to administer its own affairs. In turn, Gomulka received the church's endorsement.

## Hungary

Across the border, the Hungarians watched the events in Poland with increasing intensity. If the Poles could eliminate some of the baleful aspects of Stalinism, why couldn't they? Heated discussions took place in intellectual circles and within the Hungarian Communist Party. The upshot was that the Stalinists were forced to resign and Imre Nagy, Hungary's "Gomulka," took over.

Initially, events in Hungary paralleled those in Poland. But Nagy could not control the rebellious mood that was building up in his country. Reformers argued that a reformed party, freed of the Stalinists, was not enough. Nothing short of independence from Moscow would do. Deep-seated Hungarian animosity toward the Russians had its historic roots in the intervention by the Russian army during the revolution of 1848, when Hungarians had sought to free themselves of Austrian domination. Also, the Hungarian secret police, modeled after that of Stalin's days, had bred deep resentment. These factors, as well as economic grievances, contributed to massive volatile street demonstrations that culminated in the public lynching of secret police agents. Budapest became unmanageable. On November 1, 1956, Nagy suddenly announced that Hungary was now an independent nation. Next on the agenda were free elections, which undoubtedly would put an end to Communist Party rule in Hungary and withdrawal from the Warsaw Pact.

The events in Hungary left Nikita Khrushchev few choices, particularly when Radio Free Europe, a station operating out of Munich under the aegis of the CIA, offered the Hungarians vague promises of US help. At this highly charged moment in the Cold War, a neutral Hungary was out of the question. John Foster Dulles, the US secretary of state, had said earlier that in this holy, ideologically charged crusade against the forces of absolute evil, neutrality was the height of immorality.[10] The leaders in the Kremlin held a similar view. Hungary's destiny was to remain a pawn in the Cold War. The question was whether it would continue to serve the interests of Moscow or instead serve the interests of Washington.

For several days, the Soviets hesitated. At first, they saw the disturbances in Budapest as anti-Stalinist (as in Poland) but not anti-Communist. They expected to work with Nagy and even discussed the possibility of withdrawing their troops from Hungary. But then came the news that Communists were being lynched in the streets of Budapest. Any withdrawal, Khrushchev now argued, would "cheer up the imperialists." With the Soviet Union's position in Eastern Europe starting to disintegrate, it was left few palatable options. "We had to act," Khrushchev wrote in his memoirs, "and we had to act swiftly."[11]

The Soviet Army attacked Budapest three days after Nagy's proclamation calling for free elections. After a week of savage fighting, the Soviets reestablished their control. The Kremlin installed János Kádár as the Hungarian party's new first secretary. Kadar became known as the "butcher of Budapest," not only for having come to power by dint of Moscow's violent suppression of the revolution, but also because of his execution of Nagy and others in 1958.

In time, however, Kádár proved to be a cautious reformer. Over the next three decades, he introduced the most sweeping economic reforms anywhere in the Soviet bloc, culminating in the legalization of private enterprises in the early 1980s. This combination of the carrot (tolerance of reforms) and the stick (the Soviet Army) lifted many restrictions, raised the standard of living, and kept Hungary quiet.

The United States could do little but watch with indignation the Soviet suppression of the Hungarian uprising and offer political asylum to many of the nearly 200,000 Hungarians who fled their country. John Foster Dulles, who in the past had repeatedly stated that the aim of the United States was the liberation of Eastern Europe and the rollback of the Soviet presence there, could do no more than watch in frustration. Hungary offered him the opportunity to put his policy into operation, but President Dwight Eisenhower's cautious response revealed that Dulles's rhetoric was just that. It became clear that Washington would not start World War III over Poland or Hungary. The lesson was not lost on the Soviets when they had to deal with Czechoslovakia in 1968.

## Czechoslovakia

Events in Poland and Hungary did not affect Czechoslovakia during the 1950s. The country continued to be ruled by Antonin Novotny, whom Stalin had placed in power in 1952. In the late 1960s, Czechoslovakia appeared to be the least likely candidate for social and political reform. Yet many in Czechoslovakia bitterly resented the unreconstructed Stalinist Novotny, not only the public at large but also members of his own party. When a writers' rebellion began late in 1967, Novotny found himself unable to deal with it because his own party did not support him. It asked him to resign, and he did so in January 1968. After the party dutifully checked with the Kremlin, Leonid Brezhnev responded, "This is your matter." The party then elected Alexander Dubček as its first secretary.

In the meantime, the writers, many of them Communists, raised a number of basic questions—those of civil rights, censorship, and the monopoly of the Communist Party in the political, economic, and social affairs of the nation. After Novotny's ouster, intellectuals and party members continued the discussion. Under Dubček's stewardship, the party introduced numerous reforms at breakneck speed. It attempted to create "socialism with a human face," one that combined Eastern-style socialism with Western-style democracy. One restriction after another was lifted. The result was freedom of the press, freedom to travel, freedom from fear of the police. The public was able to follow the intense and open debate in the uncensored press. The "Prague Spring" was under way in the spring and summer of 1968. Euphoria swept a nation that became oblivious to the inherent dangers of such radical reforms. Soon there was the inevitable talk of leaving the Soviet bloc and of declaring neutrality.

The Soviet leadership kept a close eye on these developments. Several high-ranking delegations arrived from Moscow and other East European capitals. The Communist parties of Eastern Europe urged Dubček and his party to bring the movement under control before it completely got out of hand. Several of the East European governments (particularly those of Yugoslavia, Hungary, and Romania) did not want to give the Soviet Union an excuse for intervention. But it was to no avail. Dubček neither wanted to nor was able to put a brake on the discussions and experiments. The hopeful Prague Spring continued unabated. The border between Czechoslovakia and Austria became an abstract line on a map that Czechs—and visitors from the West—crossed without restriction. The Iron Curtain ceased to exist in this part of Europe.

Until August 1968, the Soviet leadership was divided on what course to take. The hard-liners in Moscow became convinced that Dubček and his party were no longer in control. They viewed the events in Czechoslovakia as a counterrevolution in the making, one Dubček was unable and unwilling to bring to an end. Dubček was well aware that the Soviets had a contingency plan to use force. In a telephone conversation with Brezhnev on August 13, a week before the invasion, Dubček said, "If you consider us traitors, then take the measures which your Politburo considers necessary."[12]

Events in Czechoslovakia also threatened to create repercussions in the Soviet Union. The non-Russian population of the Soviet empire—approximately half of the population—watched the events in Czechoslovakia with growing interest. The party chiefs in non-Russian republics, particularly those of Ukraine and Lithuania, took the lead in urging strong action. Brezhnev convened a plenary session of the party's Central Committee to inform its members that the Warsaw Pact was about to put an end to the Prague Spring. On August 20, 1968, the Soviet Army moved into action. When its tanks rolled into Prague, the Czechs, as expected, did not resist to any appreciable degree. The Soviets then replaced Dubček with Gustav Husak.

The Soviets justified their invasion by claiming that they had to protect Czechoslovakia against a counterrevolution. Brezhnev declared, moreover, that the Soviet Union possessed the inherent right to intervene in all socialist countries similarly threatened. This unilateral Soviet right of intervention in Eastern Europe became known in the West as the "Brezhnev Doctrine." In 1979, Brezhnev used it anew to justify intervention in Afghanistan, when he sent the Soviet army to bail out a bankrupt socialist government. And in 1980, Brezhnev resurrected it to warn Poland's Solidarity movement against going too far.

Ironically, the Soviet Union previously had been able to count on a certain measure of goodwill among the people of Czechoslovakia. It had been only the Soviets Union that declared a willingness to come to the aid of Czechoslovakia when Hitler carved it up in 1938; and it had been the Red Army that had liberated Prague from the Germans in 1945. But whatever goodwill had existed before 1968 was now a thing of the past.

### East Germany

East Germany was unique among the Communist states in Eastern Europe. For one, it was the last of the Communist states Stalin established. It is not clear what Stalin had in mind for Germany after World War II, but after the West formally created West Germany in May 1949, Stalin countered by creating his own German state in October of that year. As late as March 1952, Stalin still proposed to the West a unified—but demilitarized and neutral—Germany. A West German historian concluded that East Germany was "Stalin's unloved child," a burden he wanted to be rid of.[13] Stalin's proposal to unload East Germany came too late, however, as the Cold War by then was in full bloom and attitudes had hardened. By then, West Germany was on its way to rearmament, preparing to join NATO.

Second, East Germany was the Communist state with the least popular support. Its leaders understood that without Soviet backing they would not be able to govern. The West German state considered East Germany as part of a unified nation under its jurisdiction. As a result, East German leaders, such as Walter Ulbricht and Erich Honecker, wanted the Soviets to dig in as deeply as possibly in East Germany. Shortly after Stalin died, the Kremlin leadership again contemplated the abandonment of East Germany. But when widespread uprisings took place on June 17, 1953, the Soviet Communists, after initial hesitation, came to the "fraternal" assistance of their East German comrades in deep political trouble.[14] Soviet tanks put an end to the disturbances in East Berlin and other cities.

Third, the economic gap between West and East Germany steadily grew. As East Germany rebuilt its war-torn economy under Soviet auspices, West Germany experienced a sustained and dramatic economic boom. By the late

*View of the Berlin Wall, part of the "German-German" border, where eighty East Germans lost their lives trying to leave for the West. Another 720 died along the rest of the 850-mile-long border.*

1950s, West Germany had reached its prewar standard of living. As a thriving West German economy suffered from a shortage of skilled workers, many East Germans left their country to take advantage of the economic opportunities in the West. East Germans traveled by public transport to West Berlin, where they automatically received West German citizenship. By the early 1960s, Berlin became the biggest hole in the Iron Curtain. The hemorrhage not only produced a skilled labor shortage in East Germany, it also seriously undermined the moral and political authority of the Eastern Communist bloc. "Will the last person to leave, please turn out the lights" became a common refrain in East Germany. At a loss of how to close that hole, Khrushchev threatened war to expel the West militarily from Berlin.

The Berlin Blockade (1948–1949) and Khrushchev's saber-rattling in the early 1960s proved ineffective in dislodging the Western powers. Another way had to be found to stop the bleeding. Khrushchev's solution was a ten-foot barrier, the "Berlin Wall," surrounding West Berlin. Built in August 1961, the "wall" solved East Germany's most pressing problem by sealing off the last remaining gap in the Iron Curtain. The East Germans left behind were shut off from the rest of the German-speaking world by a wall that became the supreme symbol of the division of Europe, the most visible manifestation of the Iron Curtain.

## The Sino-Soviet Split

After Stalin's death, the Soviet leaders faced another crisis in the Communist world. Shortly after coming to power in October 1949, the Communist leadership of the People's Republic of China (PRC) began to strike out on its own. Before long, it was apparent that the two Communist giants were at loggerheads. The rift between them became more serious with each passing year, and by the early 1960s, relations were openly hostile. The feud between the Communist giants had a great impact on international relations. The Cold War, initially a bipolar struggle between Moscow and Washington, gave way to a triangular contest involving the Soviet Union, China, and the United States.

Initially, the PRC sought close relations with the Soviet Union. It received Soviet military and economic assistance—such as loans, technicians, and advisers. It did not amount to much, however, if only for the reason that Moscow, still recovering from World War II, had little to give. What cemented their relationship was the Western threat. Chairman Mao Zedong's mission to Moscow, in early 1950, confirmed the Western suspicion that Mao and Stalin were comrades united in the cause of international Communism and dedicated to the defeat of the capitalist world. And indeed, in February 1950, Mao and Stalin signed a thirty-year military alliance aimed at the United States.

The Soviet Union subsequently took up the cause of seating the PRC in the United Nations to replace the Republic of China (Nationalist China, that is, Taiwan). By November, Beijing was at war with the US-led forces of the United Nations in Korea. Moscow and Beijing rallied in support of Communist North Korea during the Korean War. And of course they spoke the same Marxist language as they denounced US imperialism. There was little reason to believe that theirs was a troubled alliance. Yet, a scant six years after the PRC had come into existence, the two began to pull apart.

It was little wonder that the United States was skeptical about the early reports of difficulties between the two Communist giants. The US assumption that Communism was a monolith, a single unitary movement directed by Moscow, was much slower to die than the reality of Communist unity.

In retrospect, the signs of friction between Beijing and Moscow were visible from the very outset. The Chinese could hardly be pleased by the rather cavalier manner in which Stalin treated them. The terms of Moscow's assistance (1950) were not at all generous. Stalin offered Mao a development loan of no more than $300 million to be spread over five years and to be repaid by China in agricultural produce and with interest. As a price for that loan, China agreed to continued Soviet use and control of the principal railroads and ports in Manchuria, as well as to the creation of joint Sino-Soviet stock companies to conduct mineral surveys in Xinjiang (Sinkiang), the innermost province of China. It began to appear to some in the West that Stalin was wary of this new

Communist friend and that he would have preferred dealing with a weaker, more vulnerable Nationalist China than with a more vigorous new Communist regime. If the Chinese Communists harbored ill feelings toward Stalin or resented the continued Soviet presence in Manchuria and Xinjiang, they prudently remained silent, publicly accepting Stalin's leadership and extolling their fraternal relationship with the Soviet Union. The backwardness of China's economy was such that Chinese leaders considered Soviet economic assistance and diplomatic support too important to be sacrificed on the altar of national pride.

There is no single reason for the Sino-Soviet split. One can trace its historical roots to tsarist imperialism in the nineteenth century, even to the Mongol invasions of Russia in the thirteenth century. But it would be too simple to argue that the conflict in the late 1950s was the inevitable result of that history. The two sides dredged up the conflicts of the past, such as territorial claims, only after the dispute began to develop over other, contemporary issues in the mid-1950s.

CIA "heretics" (as they became known in the agency) first began to take note of the split in 1952; by 1954, they spoke of a "conflict." The CIA's first analytic study ("Chinese and Soviet Views on Mao as a Marxist Theorist," 1953) noted that Chinese propagandists had claimed, in June 1951, that "Mao had made a new contribution to Marxist-Leninist theory" applicable to the colonial independence movements.[15] Mao, already involved in the First Indochina War, saw Vietnam as a test case of his doctrine of "armed struggle" in the colonial world. Stalin had no fondness for the doctrine but, having no choice in the matter, grudgingly paid lip service to it. At a November 1951 Moscow conference commemorating the fortieth anniversary of the start of the Chinese revolution, however, the academician E. M. Zhukov declared that "one should not fetishize" Mao's doctrine "as a universal 'model' applicable" to other countries in Asia.[16] No one spoke as yet of a Sino-Soviet split, but its faint outlines were already evident.

The strains became even more pronounced after Nikita Khrushchev's Secret Speech in February 1956. The Chinese were caught by surprise by this sudden, scathing attack on Stalin and in particular by Khrushchev's call for peaceful coexistence with the capitalist world. The Chinese had no particular reason to defend the departed Stalin. If anything, they criticized Stalin for his "major mistakes" starting in the 1920s.[17] But the Chinese feared that the attack on Stalin's "cult of personality" might, by implication, undermine Mao's dictatorship in China. Moreover, they questioned the wisdom of peaceful coexistence and disputed the right of Moscow to unilaterally make such a major ideological shift with significant global implications. Earlier, Stalin had not been enamored by Mao's reinterpretation of Marxism; now Mao chafed at Khrushchev's bold reinterpretation of Marxist doctrine, without so much as consulting with him in advance. Mao, who had led the Chinese Communist

Party since 1935, was the world's senior ranking Communist leader, and he had reason to object to being ignored by the brash new leader of the Soviet Union. The Chinese were, in effect, questioning Khrushchev's authority to dictate policy to the Communist world.

"Peaceful coexistence" soon became the major bone of contention between Moscow and Beijing. The Soviet leadership became alarmed about the nuclear arms race in which they lagged behind the United States. Thus, on the one hand, peaceful coexistence was a matter of necessity; on the other, the Soviets worked feverishly to close the gap in the nuclear arms race. In 1957, Soviet scientists achieved two remarkable technological breakthroughs. In August, they launched their first intercontinental ballistic missile (ICBM), and in October they stunned the world with *Sputnik*, the first artificial satellite sent into earth orbit. The strategic significance of these feats was not lost on the Chinese.

While attending a meeting of world Communist leaders in Moscow in November 1957, Mao declared that the Communist world had taken the ideological lead over the capitalist world. "At present," he said, "it is not the west wind which is prevailing over the east wind, but the east wind prevailing over the west wind."[18] He argued that the Communist camp should put its new-found military superiority to work to attain the final victory over capitalism. Khrushchev, however, had no intention of obliging Mao and instead concluded the meeting with a reaffirmation of peaceful coexistence.

The dispute over global strategy split the two Communist giants. The Chinese argued that, by making peace with the capitalists, the Soviet Union was departing from essential Marxist-Leninist doctrine. Peaceful coexistence might suit the Soviet Union, already an industrial power with secure borders and nuclear weapons, but it did not serve China, which had none of these. Mao well remembered that his army had fought a bloody war with the United States in the not too distant past in Korea, a war the imperialists in Washington were apt to resume. He argued that Communist nations should continue the international struggle by assisting Communist forces engaged in wars of national liberation.

Moreover, the PRC sought assurances of Soviet support in China's own unfinished war of national liberation: the civil war against Jiang Jieshi's Nationalist regime, which controlled the island of Taiwan. In 1958, Beijing intensified its pressure on Taiwan by launching a sustained artillery barrage against two small offshore islands occupied by Nationalist forces, Quemoy and Matsu. Mao's purpose was to test the resolve of the United States to defend Nationalist China and to test the Soviet Union's willingness to offer active military support to the PRC. The United States made clear its commitment to the defense of Taiwan, but the Soviets, instead of pledging support, denounced Mao's actions as reckless. Moscow would not be drawn into a nuclear war with Washington over Taiwan.

Moscow and Beijing also disagreed on the means to attain Communism, their final historical stage in human progress. China first adopted the Soviet model for economic development when, in 1953, it launched a Soviet-style Five-Year Plan. But by 1957, the Chinese were beginning to question the appropriateness of the Soviet model for China. In early 1958, China scrapped its Second Five-Year Plan and replaced it with one of its own, the Great Leap Forward, ostensibly a shortcut on the road to Communism. Within a year, however, the Great Leap Forward, with its hastily created communes, produced an economic disaster of historic proportions (see Chapter 15). By now, the international Communist movement was a church divided against itself, its high priests each proclaiming he had found the only road to salvation. From the beginning, Khrushchev criticized the Great Leap Forward. When it failed spectacularly, he heaped all the more scorn on its architect.

In September 1959, Khrushchev gave the ever-suspicious Mao reason to believe that the Soviet Union was plotting against China. At the invitation of President Eisenhower, Khrushchev undertook a two-week visit to the United States. Mao, who remained adamantly opposed to peaceful coexistence, took a dim view of it. He was left to speculate on what was transpiring at Camp David during the private talks between Khrushchev and Eisenhower. He suspected that the two were about to strike some sort of devious bargain at the expense of China.

By 1960, the two sides no longer bothered to hide their disdain for each other. In April, *Red Flag*, an official organ of the Chinese Communist Party, carried an article, "Long Live Leninism," in which it rejected peaceful coexistence as contrary to the precepts of Leninism: "War is an inevitable outcome" of imperialist exploitation. Until the exploiting capitalist imperialist system was swept aside, "wars of one kind or another will always occur."[19]

Khrushchev responded quickly. In July, he abruptly pulled out of China its 1,300 Soviet economic advisers, engineers, and technicians, who took their blueprints with them and left behind many unfinished projects. It was a serious blow to China's industrialization efforts. At the same time, Moscow rescinded an earlier agreement to provide China nuclear technology to build the atomic bomb.

Khrushchev hoped to force Beijing back into line and to coerce it to accept Moscow's leadership in the Communist world. In the year that followed, Beijing seemed to acquiesce, but it proved to be only a brief respite, until the October 1961 Twenty-Second Party Congress of the Communist Party of the Soviet Union. In his opening speech, Khrushchev again lashed out at the Chinese, attacking a range of Chinese policies, including one of Mao's pet projects, the formation of agricultural communes. Industrial development, he said, must precede the poorly thought out experiment of creating communes. In short, Communism could only be reached by following the Soviet lead. In response, Chinese foreign minister Zhou Enlai, who only the day before had laid two wreaths at the base of the Lenin-Stalin mausoleum, led the entire Chinese delegation out of the hall and back to Beijing. The Sino-Soviet split was now official.

When China and India fought a brief border war, in October 1962, Moscow offered India diplomatic support (despite the fact that it still had a military alliance with Beijing), and joined Washington in condemning China for instigating the war. After the Cuban missile crisis, the Chinese mocked Khrushchev as weak-kneed for caving in to the US demand to pull his missiles out of Cuba.

Beijing, rather than Moscow, became the champion of national liberation movements in the Third World. China's identification with the nonaligned nations dated back to its participation in the Bandung Conference in Indonesia in 1955.[20] Increasingly in the 1960s, China sought to befriend the leaders of independence movements, even to the point of providing economic and military aid while it grappled with its own economic problems.

When Khrushchev's Central Committee voted him out of power in October 1964, there was much rejoicing in Beijing. More significantly, on the day the world learned of Khrushchev's ouster, Beijing announced it had successfully tested an atomic bomb. Proudly, the Chinese proclaimed that the PRC, too, was now a superpower. They had defied Khrushchev's efforts to dictate policy and his efforts to deny them nuclear weapons.

The election of Leonid Brezhnev as the new head of the Soviet Communist Party had no impact on Sino-Soviet relations. Nor did the escalation of the US involvement in the Vietnam War in 1965 bring China and the Soviet Union closer together, although they rivaled one another for influence over the Communist regime in North Vietnam (something neither of them ever achieved). Mao would not even permit Soviet aircraft the use of Chinese airspace to resupply North Vietnam.

Mao's tirade against the Soviet Union reached new heights in the summer of 1966 when he launched the Great Proletarian Cultural Revolution, designed to revitalize his revolution by mass mobilization (see Chapter 15). The campaign's political program contained a strong anti-Soviet aspect. Mao called upon his people to purge the Chinese party of functionaries who sought to imitate the Soviet system. These officials, he declared, were guilty of the same crimes as the Soviet leaders: bureaucratic elitism, revisionism, sabotage of the Communist movement, and taking China down the capitalist road. The political and economic chaos caused by his Cultural Revolution gave the Soviet Union still more reason to ridicule Mao. Mao replied that he had set the Chinese revolution back on the track to true Communism.

All that was prologue. The ideological (and personal) conflict turned bloody on the Sino-Soviet border. Clashes had occurred in the early 1960s along the remote Western border of China, but the two sides, not wanting to publicize the depth of their disagreement, kept it a secret. Occasionally, Mao had called into question the legality of Soviet territories in East Asia that had once been part of China. In two separate treaties in 1858 and 1860, China had relinquished to tsarist Russia territory north of the Amur River and east of the Ussuri River. Mao contended that because imperial China had been forced to sign the treaties, they were not legally binding under international law.

As the feud heated up, the two sides fortified their common border. In February and March 1969, the dispute turned deadly when Chinese and Soviet troops fought over several disputed, uninhabited islands on the Ussuri River. After the Chinese launched an assault against Soviet border guards on Damanskii Island (or Zhenbao, as the Chinese called it), the Soviets retaliated with artillery, tanks, and aircraft. The clash left about 800 Chinese troops dead as compared with about sixty Soviet soldiers killed.

A full-scale war between China and the Soviet Union seemed imminent. It was in this context that the Beijing leadership began to consider ending China's diplomatic isolation by improving relations with the United States. Tension along the border continued into the late 1980s as both sides reinforced their positions. Ultimately, the Soviet Union deployed an estimated 2 million troops along its 2,700-mile-long China border and armed them with the most modern of weapons, including tactical and intermediate-range nuclear missiles. China's border forces were thought to be as large as the Soviets' but not as well equipped.

One of the major consequences of the Sino-Soviet split, specifically the military confrontation, was the normalization of relations between the PRC and the United States in the early 1970s. As the PRC moved closer to Washington and farther away from Moscow, it charged the Soviet Union with "socialist imperialism" and "hegemonism." In fact, "antihegemonism" became the main pillar of China's foreign policy in the 1970s.

### The Thirty-Year Feud Is Ended

The estrangement between the Communist giants continued into the mid-1980s. Although Moscow showed signs of desiring a thaw, Deng Xiaoping, the new Chinese Communist ruler who came to power after Mao's death in 1976, showed little flexibility. He insisted that the Soviet Union remove its "three obstacles" before Sino-Soviet relations could be normalized. He demanded a withdrawal (or at least a substantial reduction) of Soviet forces from the Chinese border, an end to Soviet support for the Vietnamese army in Cambodia, and an end to the Soviet invasion of Afghanistan (see Chapters 10 and 19).

As both Beijing and Moscow focused on economic reforms in the 1980s, the prospects for Sino-Soviet rapprochement improved. Mikhail Gorbachev, who came to power in the Kremlin in 1985, brought a dynamic new pragmatism to Soviet diplomacy. Determined to regenerate the faltering economy,

Gorbachev saw it necessary to reduce the size of the Soviet Union's military establishment. With this in mind, in July 1986 Gorbachev traveled to Vladivostok, the largest Soviet city in East Asia, to deliver a speech in which he expressed a desire to establish normal relations with China and other Asian nations. The Soviet Union, he said, was ready to accommodate Beijing on all "three obstacles." He indicated that steps were already being taken toward the evacuation of Soviet forces from Afghanistan, that Soviet troops would withdraw from Mongolia on the Sino-Mongolian border, and that Moscow was prepared to discuss mutual reductions of forces on the Sino-Soviet border. Moscow would also seek a resolution of the Vietnamese occupation of Cambodia.

Deng Xiaoping responded positively. In April 1987, Chinese and Soviet negotiators began to address the border disputes and the Cambodian question. Further negotiations led to confidence-building gestures and agreements. By 1989, the Soviet Union indeed withdrew from Afghanistan, reduced its troops along the Chinese border, and pressured Vietnam to begin evacuation of its troops from Cambodia.

In December 1988, Gorbachev pledged at the United Nations to cut Soviet military forces by half a million, 200,000 of which would be from units in Asia. In the wake of Gorbachev's conciliatory measures, Deng accepted Gorbachev's proposal for a summit scheduled in Beijing in May 1989.

Gorbachev's visit to China signaled the end of the thirty-year-long rift. He arrived in Beijing, however, in the midst of the mammoth student demonstrations in the Chinese capital, and his historic visit was upstaged by this tumultuous event (see Chapter 15). The summit, nonetheless, was a success. Gorbachev acknowledged that the Soviet Union was partly to blame for the deep split between the two countries. The two sides pledged a mutual reduction of troop strength along their long border "to a minimum level commensurate with normal, good-neighborly relations" and to seek expanded trade and cultural relations.[21] Gorbachev aptly described the summit as a "watershed event."

In 1992, the Russian parliament ratified Gorbachev's agreement with China. It recognized that Damanskii Island on the Ussuri River, over which the two sides had clashed in 1969, was indeed Chinese territory. Russian historians at the time estimated that Soviet troop deployment along the Amur and Ussuri Rivers from the onset of hostilities in 1969 to Gorbachev's visit to Beijing cost the state the massive sum of 200–300 billion rubles (in 1960s rubles), roughly the equivalent of $200–300 billion.[22]

## Notes

1. J. V. Stalin, "The Tasks of Business Executives," February 4, 1931; J. V. Stalin, *Works* (Moscow: Foreign Languages Publishing House, 1955), vol. 13, pp. 40–41.

2. A proletarian—a member of the proletariat—is a wage-earner or, more commonly, a factory worker. In Marxist jargon, the words "proletarian" and "worker" are used interchangeably.

3. Edward Crankshaw, *Khrushchev: A Career* (New York: Viking, 1966), p. 228.

4. N. S. Khrushchev, *Khrushchev Remembers: The Last Testament* (Boston: Little, Brown, 1974), p. 77.

5. Roy A. Medvedev and Zhores A. Medvedev, *Khrushchev: The Years in Power* (New York: Norton, 1978), pp. 94–101.

6. Tito's independence from both the Soviet Union and the West led him to take a "third" road. Tito, Nehru of India, and Nasser of Egypt became the early leaders of the Third World, that is, nations that refused to align themselves with either the Western or Communist blocs. The term later lost its original meaning, for it came to designate the world's underdeveloped nations.

7. J. V. Stalin, "The International Situation and the Defense of the U.S.S.R.," speech delivered on August 1, 1927, to the Joint Plenum of the Central Committee and Central Control Commission of the C.P.S.U.; J. V. Stalin, *Works*, vol. 10, pp. 53–54.

8. G. M. Adibekov, *Kominform i poslevoinnaia Evropa* (Moscow: Rossia molodaia, 1994), pp. 90–95.

9. Khrushchev, *Khrushchev Remembers*, p. 351; for the full text of the "Secret Speech" see pp. 559–618.

10. For a summary of Dulles's views on Communism, see his testimony before Congress, January 15, 1953; Walter LaFeber, ed., *The Dynamics of World Power: A Documentary History of United States Foreign Policy, 1945–1973*, vol. 2, *Eastern Europe and the Soviet Union* (New York: Chelsea House, 1973), pp. 465–468.

11. Khrushchev, *Khrushchev Remembers*, pp. 416–420. See also the documents made public at a conference in Budapest commemorating the fortieth anniversary of the uprising: Timothy Garton Ash, "Hungary's Revolution: Forty Years On," *New York Review of Books*, November 16, 1996, pp. 18–22; Reuters, "Soviets Almost Recognized Hungary Revolt, Data Show," *Baltimore Sun*, September 28, 1996, p. 7A; Jane Perlez, "Thawing Out Cold War History," *New York Times*, October 6, 1996, p. 4E.

12. R. G. Pikhoia, "Chekhoslovakiia, 1968 god. Vzgliad iz Moskvy: Po dokumentam TsK KPSS," *Novaia i noveishaia istorii* 1 (January–February 1995), p. 42.

13. Wilfried Loth, *Stalins ungeliebtes Kind: Warum Moskau die DDR nicht wollte* (Berlin: Rohwolt-Berlin, 1994).

14. That day became an official holiday in West Germany, the Day of Unity, commemorating the victims of the uprising and underscoring the commitment to unification. After Germany's unification, in 1990, October 3 became the new official Day of Unity.

15. Harold P. Ford, "Calling the Sino-Soviet Split: The CIA and Double Demonology," *Studies in Intelligence*, Winter 1998–1990, cia.gov; posted April 2007.

16. "On the Character and Specific Features of People's Democracy in the Countries of the East," *Izvestiia Academii Nauk SSSR, Seriia Istorii i Filosofi*, No. 1, 1949; *Revolutionary Democracy*, Vol. IV, No. 2, September 1999; www.revolutionary-democrac.org.

17. Ford, "Calling the Sino-Soviet Split."

18. Mao cited in "At Present It Is Not the West Wind," *Survey of the China Mainland Press*, US Consulate General, Hong Kong, no. 1662, December 2, 1957, p. 2.

19. Mao on Lenin, *Current Background*, US Consulate General, Hong Kong, no. 617, April 26, 1960.

20. At this conference of twenty-nine African and Asian nations, China's representative, Zhou Enlai, shared the spotlight with India's neutralist prime minister, Nehru. China joined with these Third World nations in pledging peace and mutual noninterference.

21. Scott Shane, "Gorbachev Returns Home from 'Watershed' Summit," *Baltimore Sun*, May 19, 1989.

22. Viktor Usov, "'Goriachaia vesna' na Damanskom," *Novoe vremia* 9 (1994), pp. 36–39.

# 10

# The War in Indochina

When the fighting stopped in Korea in 1953, it became an article of faith in the Pentagon that the United States must "never again" become bogged down in a war on the Asian mainland. Yet a scant dozen years later, the United States became tied down in another land war in Southeast Asia.

After the Vietminh defeated the French at Dien Bien Phu, the Geneva Agreement of July 1954 called for France's withdrawal from Indochina and the formation of the independent states of Laos, Cambodia, and Vietnam. Vietnam, however, was to remain temporarily divided along the 17th parallel. In the interim, in the South a new pro-Western and anti-Communist nation, the Republic of Vietnam, came into existence. The northern half became the Communist-led Democratic Republic of Vietnam, headed by Ho Chi Minh, the hero of the Vietnamese revolution.

The Geneva Agreement also called for an internationally supervised nationwide election of a president for a unified Vietnam, to be held by July 1956 at the latest. In the meantime, Geneva permitted the voluntary transfer of peoples across the 17th parallel. The result was an exodus from the North (organized in part by the US Navy) of 860,000 people, the majority of them Catholics fearful of the future under Communism. "God and the Virgin have gone south," priests told their parishioners, and "only the devil remains in the north." From the South, approximately 140,000 Vietminh went North, hoping to return after unification.

The Eisenhower administration immediately became involved in the affairs of South Vietnam, providing it economic and military assistance. The US military and CIA officers replaced the French presence in Saigon, South Vietnam's capital, and began to carry out sabotage and intelligence missions against the North.

The chief of state of South Vietnam was the former playboy emperor, Bao Dai, known as the "Emperor of Cannes." He prudently remained in exile in France, leaving matters to his newly appointed prime minister, Ngo Dinh Diem, the scion of a famous and influential Roman Catholic family. Diem, however, was someone with only a limited following in Saigon. He had not been in Vietnam for most of its long and difficult struggle for independence against the French but instead had resided abroad, including in the United States, where he cultivated contacts with influential Catholic clergy and politicians.

Diem had lobbied long and hard with Bao Dai for his appointment as prime minister. Relations between the two had never been good, however. Diem, a staunch Vietnamese nationalist, thought that Bao Dai had been too ready to compromise as emperor, too ready to serve the French, the Japanese, the Vietminh—whoever was in control of Vietnam. The pliant Bao Dai well understood that Washington was poised to take over from France and thus gave the Eisenhower administration a prime minister to its liking. Years later, Bao Dai wrote that he had selected Diem because he was "well known to the Americans, who appreciated his [anti-Communist] intransigence," his "fanaticism and messianic tendencies."[1]

Diem, however, had not terribly impressed anyone during his lengthy stays in the United States. The fervidly anti-Communist secretary of state, John Foster Dulles, was not sure whether Diem was up to the job. The chief of the CIA mission in Saigon, Edward Lansdale, however, took an immediate liking to Diem. Lansdale, a former advertising executive, had just arrived from the Philippines, where he had played a role in consolidating the power of the nation's new president, the effective and popular anti-Communist Ramon Magsaysay. Upon arriving in Saigon, Lansdale was certain he had in Diem a similar product that he could readily sell to his bosses in Washington. This time, however, Lansdale was peddling merchandise that was highly defective, something he only slowly grasped.

Rigid and righteous, Diem was at heart a mandarin (a high-ranking educated official who ruled at the behest of the emperor) who believed that it was his people's duty to obey him. He rejected the notion that it was his obligation to gain the goodwill of his people; instead, it was up to the people to gain his goodwill. A century earlier, Diem might have been an effective ruler, but his return to Saigon came at a time when a social revolution already had swept away much of the old order (including the monarchy and the mandarinate).

Diem's other problem was his Catholicism. Catholics supported him in overwhelmingly large numbers, but they made up only 10 percent of the population in Vietnam. Diem had to decide whether to reconcile with his (mostly Buddhist) fellow citizens and govern by consensus or by decree. Psychologically incapable of reconciliation, he chose to govern by decree.

Upon arriving in Saigon in June 1954, Diem faced a number of serious problems. His first task was to secure control of Saigon, a city dominated by a powerful crime syndicate, Binh Xuyen, which controlled the narcotics market, prostitution, and gambling. More significant, Bao Dai (in order to pay off his gambling debts) had also consigned the police to Binh Xuyen control. Diem, unwilling to share power with anyone, let alone with organized crime, declared war on Binh Xuyen and in short order routed the organization. He also neutralized several high-ranking French-trained generals who plotted against him, exiling them to Paris. Finally, he turned against religious sects—Cao Dai and Hoa Hao—under the control of warlords with their own private armies. He drove all resistance underground—until they reemerged later as part of the insurrection coalescing around the Vietcong guerrillas.

After ten months in power, Diem had exceeded Washington's expectations. Doubts about him gave way to the certitude that he was the right man to rule South Vietnam. In a popular referendum in October 1955, Diem asked voters to choose between him and Bao Dai. The result was a smashing—albeit fraudulent—electoral victory for Diem by which he became president of South Vietnam, a post with virtually unlimited powers. He obtained an incredible 98.2 percent of the votes cast nationwide, and in Saigon he received 605,025 votes from the 450,000 registered voters, a mathematically implausible 134 percent.[2] During its short existence, South Vietnam never held a free election. Diem's sister-in-law, for example, the widely reviled Madame Nhu, won her seat in the National Assembly with a vote of 99.4 percent in Long An province in the Mekong Delta, which was under Vietcong control.[3]

Diem's next target were the remaining Vietminh, who were tracked down, imprisoned, and often executed. US observers applauded his doings, hailing him as the "Churchill of Southeast Asia," as *Life* magazine dubbed him, the guardian at the gates of the "free world," the savior of South Vietnam. In May 1957, during a highly publicized state visit to Washington, he was granted the honor of addressing both houses of Congress, where he explained that democracy "is neither material happiness nor the supremacy of numbers." By this time Diem had already rejected the Geneva Agreement's call for an internationally supervised nationwide (that is, all of Vietnam) election. He and his patrons in Washington were well aware that in a national election "the supremacy of numbers" favored Ho Chi Minh, the man who had defeated the French (and who, ironically, by defeating the French had made possible Diem's return as prime minister to an independent South Vietnam). Better to keep Vietnam divided than take a chance on an election in which the numbers were sure to go against Diem.

Diem turned on any and all opponents, real or imagined: former Vietminh, Communists, liberals, Buddhists, peasants. His rejection of the elections in 1956 stirred protests, especially by former Vietminh who had remained in the South in the expectation of reunification. Diem's reign of terror (which included the use of the guillotine, the supreme symbol of French colonialism) dealt the Vietminh in the South a near-mortal blow. Diem rescinded the redistributions of land to the landless peasants, which the Vietminh had already carried out, and returned it to the landlords. Other beneficiaries of Diem's land program were newly arrived Catholics from the North who became the largest landowning bloc in South Vietnam.[4]

It was not enough for Diem to persecute the very same individuals who had fought and bled in the struggle against the French. He added insult to injury by desecrating the graves of Vietminh war dead in violation of the sacred Vietnamese tradition of ancestor worship. Diem's desecration was more than a crime; it was a serious mistake, one of many that eventually led to his downfall.

· · ·

In the mid-1950s, the southern Vietminh's desperate appeal for help from Hanoi, North Vietnam's capital, received only a tepid response. North Vietnam was exhausted from the war against the French; its economy was in shambles, the railroad system was in need of reconstruction, foreign technicians and engineers had left, and rice grown in the South was no longer available. In Hanoi an intense political debate took place over whether to assist the southern Vietminh and thus resume the war, this time against the US "puppet regime" of Diem, or focus on domestic concerns. For the time being, the faction that stressed rebuilding the northern economic infrastructure, the so-called "North First" faction, carried the day. The party's sacred quest for unification would have to wait.

Northern economic reconstruction was accompanied by a drastic—and disastrous—"land reform" program that targeted the landlord class. It was carried out despite Ho Chi Minh's warnings against such a measure. Ho had promised, more than once, that the "patriotic elements," including the holders of large estates, had nothing to fear from the new order. Ho lost the debate in the Politburo, however, and it is not certain that he ever regained his once dominant position.

By the end of 1956, the North Vietnamese Communist Party could no longer ignore the dire consequence of its land reform—between 3,000 and 15,000 members of the landlord class killed (the exact number has never been established) as well as widespread physical damage. An uprising in Nghe An Province—once the staunchest of Vietminh bastions—had to be put down by the army. The party now eased off on land reform—without, however, ever truly abandoning it. The beneficiaries of the land reform program, the broad mass of peasants, became the backbone of support for the North Vietnamese regime. Ho Chi Minh, who had opposed the drastic reforms, wound up profusely apologizing to the victims.

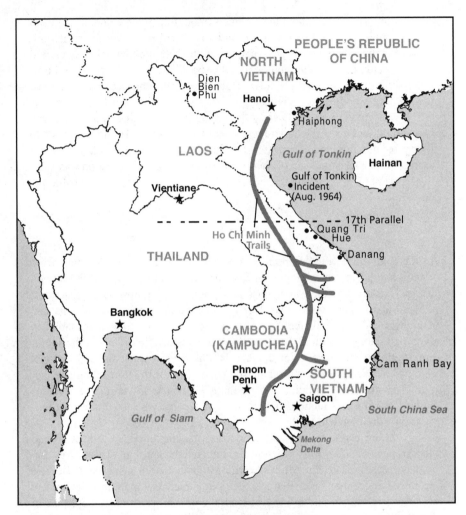

**Indochina: The Vietnam War**

Once land reform was put aside, the party saw its way clear to return to events in the South, where the rebellion was gaining strength. At this point, the "South first" faction in Hanoi became ascendant, and it was this faction—led by Le Duan and Le Duc Tho—that eventually oversaw the unification of Vietnam in 1975. It would take years, however, before the North played a meaningful role in the South. In the meantime, what transpired there was all-out civil war that gradually drew both Hanoi and Washington into the conflict in the South.

• • •

In the late 1950s, the desperate southern Vietminh had virtually no weapons. They did, however, have revolutionary propaganda on their side—a vision of a better future in a unified Vietnam—and they had organizational skills, a carry-over from the war against France. Moreover, despite Diem's attempt to extend his control over all of South Vietnam, the Vietminh still controlled wide stretches of land where they had established themselves during the war against France. That was particularly true in the Mekong River delta, along the Cambodian border, along the provinces surrounding Saigon, and along Route 1, the main road north from Saigon to the 17th parallel, a 250-mile stretch of that the French had dubbed the "street without joy." Along Route 1 also sat the strategic port city of Danang, in the vicinity of which US combat troops first met the enemy in the spring of 1965.

Government terror clashed with guerrilla terror. Starting in the late 1950s, as the resistance grew, rebels managed to capture ever more weapons from the Army of the Republic of (South) Vietnam (ARVN), which was well equipped with US armaments but corrupt and poorly led. The resistance acquired, in early 1960, its first significant cache of arms from an ARVN post in Phu My Hung, just nine miles from Saigon.[5] As the Vietcong became better equipped by virtue of seizing of weapons and supplies from the ARVN, they began to refer to Diem as their "supply sergeant."

In December 1960, various opposition groups and parties, led by former Vietminh and Communists, formed the National Liberation Front (NLF). Diem, encouraged by his US advisers, had already labeled all resistance as Communist in nature. Thus, the NLF became known as the Vietcong (or Vietnamese Communists). At first, the NLF considered the label an insult, but in time its fighters took it as a badge of honor. US soldiers, who originally dismissed them as "VC," "Charlie," or "gooks," eventually paid them a term of respect, referring to them as "Mr. Charles."

Until 1961, the resistance appeared little more than a nuisance. When President-elect John Kennedy met with Dwight Eisenhower to discuss the state of the world, the outgoing president did not deem it important enough to dwell on Vietnam. At that time, the Vietcong were still on their own, receiving no material support from Hanoi, merely advice by the occasional party functionary who had made the difficult, time-consuming, and dangerous trek to the South.

Imperceptibly, the Vietcong grew in size and strength. When Diem replaced locally elected village headmen with his own bureaucrats in an attempt to control the countryside, these interlopers became targets for Vietcong assassinations. To secure the villages of South Vietnam, Diem resorted in 1962 to the drastic and expensive measure of resettling villagers in compounds called "strategic hamlets." It proved to be counterproductive. The peasants, uprooted from their native villages—the soil of their ancestors in which they buried their children's umbilical cords, signifying an eternal bond between the people and the land—became ever more resentful. Diem's heavy-handedness merely pushed the villagers into the resistance.

Diem's government was more popular in the cities, but even here his cult of personality did not sit well. Diem's political theory was based on a vague theory called "personalism," a doctrine steeped in a mixture of Catholic and Confucian traditions that demanded obedience. Individual freedom needed to take a back seat to the collective betterment of society achieved by dutiful loyalty to the morally superior ruler. In practice, it meant absolute obedience to an imperious autocrat. Meanwhile, Diem surrounded himself with a clique of supporters, several of whom were his brothers. The most notorious among them was Ngo Dinh Nhu, the head of the secret police—Diem's "Siamese twin," as the US ambassador called him—without whom Diem was incapable of governing.

Diem never trusted his own armed forces—and for good reason. There were units loyal to him, usually under the command of Catholic generals, but he was unwilling to risk them against the Vietcong, since he needed them to protect the presidential palace against generals he did not trust, such as during the ill-fated coup by paratroopers in November 1960. In February 1962, two disgruntled air force officers—in an attempt to assassinate Diem or, at the least spark a popular uprising against him—bombed the palace. Diem barely escaped being killed. Diem characterized the attack as an "isolated act" and his survival as a manifestation of "divine protection."

### Downfall

In July 1959, the Vietcong infiltrated the huge military base at Bien Hoa, just north of Saigon, where they assassinated two US officers, officially the first of more than 58,000 US troops to die in Vietnam.

At first, in classic guerrilla style, Vietcong attacks consisted of ambushes followed by retreats in the face of the ARVN's superior firepower. In January 1963, however, near the village of Ap Bac in the Mekong Delta, forty miles southwest of Saigon, a well-prepared Vietcong unit engaged the ARVN for the first time in a head-to-head battle. The Vietcong, who knew of the ARVN's battle plans beforehand, suffered eighteen fatalities, but they killed eighty ARVN soldiers and three US advisers and destroyed five helicopters and three armored personnel carriers. The Diem government proclaimed it a victory for the ARVN. US reporters, who rushed to the battle scene, however, were able to see with their own eyes the carnage the Vietcong had inflicted on the well-equipped ARVN troops led by their US advisers. It was a jolting omen of events to come.

It was one thing for Diem to favor the Catholic minority; it was another to engage in an unnecessary confrontation with the Buddhist majority, particularly since its leaders were politically passive and, moreover, looked with a jaundiced eye on the Vietcong and Communists in general. Indeed, Diem and the Buddhists should have been allies against the Vietcong. Instead, Diem went to war against them.

In the city of Hue, in May 1963, during celebrations of Buddha's birthday, the most joyous and most important Buddhist holiday, Diem banned the flying of multicolored Buddhist flags. Only the yellow-and-red South Vietnamese national flag could be flown, even though earlier that month Diem had made an exception for Catholics flying the yellow-and-white papal flag as they commemorated the twenty-fifth anniversary of Ngo Dinh Thuc—Diem's brother—as bishop of Hue. After the army and security forces, without warning, shot and killed nine Buddhist demonstrators, Diem blamed the Vietcong, something no one believed. The protests escalated. An old Buddhist monk resorted to the dramatic act of self-immolation. Seated in a meditative posture in a public square in Saigon, he was doused with a homemade napalm, which was then set aflame. In the weeks to come, other monks followed his example. Graphic depictions of these acts of self-sacrifice, indictments of the Diem regime, were carried around the world in newsprint and on television. Madame Nhu, Diem's sister-in-law and the nation's acting first lady, did not help when she derided the self-immolations as "barbecues." "Let them burn," she said, "and we shall clap our hands."

US officials, including Ambassador Henry Cabot Lodge, were appalled by events in Saigon and concluded that Diem had to be replaced. The CIA thus gave the green light to a group of ARVN officers to do so, which they did in early November 1963. Instead of sending Diem and Nhu into exile as the Kennedy administration had expected, they murdered both, much to the shock of the principals in Washington. Edward Lansdale, who supported Diem until the end, saw his project turn to ashes. In South Vietnam, virtually no one lamented Diem's passing; some celebrated in the streets.

The new junta (a military ruling group) that assumed power was immediately recognized by the Kennedy administration, but it proved to be no more effective than the previous one in dealing with the nation's problems. During the next year and a half the Vietcong grew in strength.

## Johnson's War

During the Kennedy administration, the US presence had grown from nearly 900 advisers (inherited from the Eisenhower administrations) to 16,500, including "special forces." Lyndon Johnson, who succeeded the slain Kennedy as president on November 22, 1963, soon expanded the US presence to more than 20,000, even though he knew it was not enough to counter the growing strength of the Vietcong who, by early 1965, were poised for victory.

A great irony was that Johnson doubted the wisdom of US involvement in Vietnam. In May 1964, in a telephone conversation with his former mentor in the Senate, Richard Russell, a frustrated Johnson thought that Vietnam was "the damndest worst mess that I ever saw . . . and it's going to get worse." "How important is [Vietnam] to us?" Russell wanted to know. Neither Vietnam nor Laos, Johnson replied, were worth "a damn." But he could not withdraw because the Republican Party would denounce him for it. "It's the only issue they've got," Johnson said.[6] That, and the fact that Johnson, a proud son of Texas, refused to become the first president to lose a war, meant that he had little choice but to try to win the war by sending in combat troops.

To sell his escalation of the war, Johnson argued that the revolution in the South was the consequence of Beijing-directed Communist aggression. If South Vietnam fell, other states would fall like a long row of dominoes. It was a scenario first publicly raised by Eisenhower in 1954. The war was portrayed as an international conflict, not a civil war in South Vietnam. For that reason, there could be no retreat from the defense of a "democratic" South Vietnam against "Communist aggression from outside."

During the presidential election of 1964, Johnson faced the Republican "hawk" Barry Goldwater, whose answer to Vietnam was to send the Marines, finish the job, and return home to a victory parade. Johnson played the role of the "dove," assuring the electorate that "we are not going to send American boys nine or ten thousand miles away from home to do what Asian boys ought to be doing for themselves." Still, he spoke of his commitment to "defend freedom" in South Vietnam and stop "Communist aggression." The dove thus had to show he had the talons of a hawk. That opportunity came in early August, during the Gulf of Tonkin incident.

In August of the run-up to the November 1964 election, the Pentagon reported that one of its naval ships, the destroyer *USS Maddox*, had been attacked by North Vietnamese torpedo boats in the Gulf of Tonkin off the coast of North Vietnam. Johnson claimed that the attack had taken place on the high seas (that is, in international waters) and that it was unprovoked. In reality, the destroyer, which was at the disposal of the National Security Agency (NSA), an intelligence arm of the US government, had been inside the twelve-mile territorial limit of North Vietnam gathering electronic intelligence and providing support for covert military operations (including bombing raids) against North Vietnam by South Vietnamese commandos (which had been ongoing since January 1964). Put simply, the *Maddox* had engaged in an act of war against North Vietnam.

On the basis of a reported second "attack" two days later, this one again allegedly in international waters, Johnson went to Congress for authorization to deploy direct military force against North Vietnam. With almost no deliberation, and with virtual unanimity (unanimous in the House of Representatives, and by an 88-to-2 vote in the Senate), Congress passed the Gulf of Tonkin Resolution, which authorized him to take "all necessary measures to repel any armed attacks against the forces of the United States and to prevent further aggression." Johnson's supporters called it a "functional equivalent of a declaration of war." The Democrat Lyndon Johnson and his successor, the Republican Richard Nixon, used it as the legal basis for massive military operations in Vietnam and in neighboring countries. There is no evidence that the second attack had even taken place. North Vietnam always denied it, and it was never confirmed by any investigation, not even by the NSA. Secretary of Defense Robert McNamara wrote in his memoirs, more than thirty years later, that it appeared that no second attack had occurred.[7]

After Johnson defeated Goldwater in a landslide victory in November 1964, Vietnam became "Johnson's war." The president's critics—and they were still rather few at this stage—disputed the claim that South Vietnam was the victim of foreign aggression, that the NLF was a puppet of Hanoi. Hanoi and the NLF had similar objectives and had the same enemies, and the NLF no doubt looked for and received guidance and—eventually—supplies from Hanoi. But the NLF fought its own battles, at least until the bombing of North Vietnam in the wake of the Tonkin confrontation. Massive intervention by US troops in 1965 generated massive North Vietnamese intervention. In June 1966, Democratic senator Mike Mansfield of Montana revealed that when US escalation began in March 1965, only 400 of the 140,000 enemy forces in South Vietnam were North Vietnamese soldiers, figures confirmed by the Pentagon.[8] A lengthy study commissioned by Secretary of Defense McNamara (which became known as the *Pentagon Papers*) pointed to similarly low estimates of North Vietnamese forces. Washington's panicky reaction to events in Vietnam was not in response to what the North was doing, but rather to the weakness of South Vietnamese forces and the fear of a Vietcong victory.[9]

In February 1965, the State Department, headed by the hawkish Dean Rusk, sought to prove that the war in South Vietnam was the result of Communist "aggression from the North." It issued, with great fanfare, its famous but poorly reasoned White Paper. The centerpiece of the paper was the claim that of the weapons captured from the NLF, several were of Communist origin. But the number—179 weapons out of a total of 7,500 during the previous 18 months, a little more than 2 percent—only proved that the NLF depended overwhelmingly on weapons captured from the inept and demoralized ARVN rather than on supplies from external Communist sources.[10]

Shortly after his inauguration in January 1965, Johnson ordered Operation Rolling Thunder, the sustained aerial bombing of North Vietnam. In March 1965, US Marines landed on the beaches of Danang, ostensibly to protect its military airfield, a vital component of Rolling Thunder. It was not long, however, before the Marines began "search-and-destroy" missions, which extend-

*Secretary of Defense Robert S. McNamara and the commander of US forces
(1964–1968) General William C. Westmoreland meeting with South Vietnamese
officers on a visit to South Vietnam, August 1965*

*US Marines during Operation Hastings in a search-and-destroy mission to clear
Quang Tri province, south of the seventeenth parallel, of North Vietnamese troops,
July 1966*

ed the scope of their operations in ever widening circles. Danang and its environs, long a Vietminh-Vietcong stronghold, were not easily pacified, however. With US forces unable to engage the furtive enemy directly, large stretches of the region were declared "free-fire zones" where anything that moved was fair game. Winning over the "hearts and minds" of the population quickly became an afterthought. In November 1965, US troops became engaged for the first time in hand-to-hand combat with the North's People's Army of Vietnam (PAVN) in the bloody battle of Ia Drang Valley.

The enemy "body count" rose ever higher, yet the US commander, General William Westmoreland, asked for additional troops. By the end of 1965, the US contingent numbered 200,000; by the end of 1967, it stood at nearly 550,000, augmented by 1 million ARVN troops. Facing them were an estimated 300,000 Vietcong soldiers (actively supported by another 300,000 South Vietnamese playing auxiliary roles) and 140,000 PAVN troops. The troop ratio favoring the US-Saigon side (approximately 3:1) was not enough considering that it takes, according to conventional wisdom, nearly a ten-to-one advantage to defeat an insurgency, especially one that was organized, dedicated, and well supplied (particularly as Moscow and Beijing stepped up their arms shipments to North Vietnam).

In the meantime, there was no political stability in Saigon. Military coups became the order of the day. In June 1965, yet another coup brought to power Air Marshal Nguyen Cao Ky and army general Nguyen Van Thieu. In September 1967, by virtue of a controlled election, Thieu became president and Ky vice-president. Ky explained that if a civilian won the election, he would respond "militarily" because in a "democratic country you have the right to disagree with the views of others."[11] As if such a perverted definition of democracy was not enough, Ky declared that he had but one hero and that was Adolf Hitler. The rigged election and Ky's comments further dispelled the fiction that Washington was fighting in defense of South Vietnamese democracy.

## The Tet Offensive of 1968

Johnson expected that the bombing of North Vietnam's supply routes into the South (nicknamed the Ho Chi Minh Trail) and the heavy commitment of US forces would bring victory, at the latest, at the outset of the 1968 presidential campaign. The task, however, was much more difficult than expected. At the beginning of 1965, the number of US dead stood at 401; by the end of 1967, when the war had become an escalated military stalemate, it was over 16,400. Hanoi did what Pentagon planners had thought impossible, matching US escalation with its own increased commitment. The Pentagon's war of "attrit" had its North Vietnamese counterpart. Le Duan, the chief of the North Vietnamese Communist Party, was sure that at a certain point, after absorbing 40,000 fatalities, the United States would seek a way out of the war.

US bombing was unable to shut down Hanoi's pipeline bringing increasing numbers of PAVN soldiers and supplies into the South. The PAVN and Vietcong took heavy losses, but they managed to replenish them with men and women willing to fight and die in a war against yet another foreign invader. The Johnson administration, to sell the war to an increasingly skeptical public, insisted that it was being won. In November 1967, General Westmoreland famously declared that a lull in the fighting meant "we have reached an important point, when the end begins to come into view."

The shocking realization that there just might be no victory came in the wake of the Tet Offensive of 1968, during the Vietnamese lunar New Year. It began at the end of January, when the Vietcong and PAVN launched surprise attacks across the breadth of South Vietnam. They were able to take thirty-six of the forty-four provincial capitals, and most surprising of all, they staged a major attack on Saigon, where suicide commandos even penetrated the grounds of the US embassy. The psychological and political impact of the offensive, as Hanoi had calculated, shattered the popular illusion in the United States that victory, the proverbial "light at the end of the tunnel," was within reach.

US forces launched a furious counterattack making full use of their massive firepower. Enemy losses were staggering as they were driven out of Saigon and the other cities and towns. After a month of heavy fighting, Westmoreland claimed that the Tet Offensive had been a military disaster for the enemy, who had surfaced only to be hunted down. This was not an empty claim, for the US counterattack greatly weakened the Vietcong and the PAVN.

During the Tet Offensive, particularly harsh was the fate of the beautiful old imperial city of Hue, the provincial Mekong Delta town of Ben Tre, and the village of My Lai. After the North Vietnamese seized Hue, they immediately rounded up and executed an estimated 3,000 city residents suspected of collaborating with the Saigon government. After US troops reconquered Hue by the end of February, the city was largely in ruins, most of the historic citadel destroyed.

Ben Tre suffered an even worse fate. US artillery destroyed it completely. When asked why the city had been leveled, a US major offered what became the US epitaph in Vietnam: "It became necessary to destroy the town to save it."[12] It was the only answer he could give. The US military's involvement in Vietnam no longer made sense.

It took another year and a half for the My Lai story to break—the massacre of more than 500 Vietnamese villagers, including women, children, and old men, at the hands of US Army troops—graphically retold in color photographs in *Life* magazine. Initially, the Pentagon (as well as Congress) ignored all reports of the massacre, then pinned it on a single lieutenant, whom President Nixon absolved of all wrongdoing and then pardoned. Further investigations revealed that My Lai had not been an isolated incident.

The Tet Offensive was a military setback for the enemy, but it was a psychological and political victory for them. Hanoi gave notice during the 1968

*Marines on the ribs of rice paddies*

presidential election year that the war was far from over. Johnson, faced with mounting opposition to his Vietnam policy, was forced to reassess the war and his own political future. Even his secretary of defense, Robert McNamara, once a true believer in the war, had begun to doubt the wisdom of continuing it. In early March 1968, Johnson replaced him with the still hawkish Clark Clifford, who concluded within a few weeks that the United States had reached a dead end in Vietnam and that the time had come to find a way out.

In March 1968, Johnson received from Westmoreland a request for 206,000 additional soldiers, this despite Westmoreland's consistent claims that his troops were winning the war. In a presidential election year, Johnson was in no position to take the US troop level to 750,000. His advisers prevailed upon him to find a political solution to the war. At the end of the month, in a televised address to the nation, Johnson announced a partial halt to the bombing of North Vietnam and stated that he was willing to sit down with Hanoi to negotiate a settlement. The real surprise came at the end of his address, when he announced that he would not seek reelection as president of the United States.

Hanoi had long been willing to sit down with Johnson, but only on its own terms. Its four-point proposal of April 1965 called for an end to US bombing of the North, withdrawal of all foreign forces from Vietnam, adherence to the Geneva Agreement (notably its call for a unified Vietnam), and the right of the Vietnamese alone to settle their problems. It also insisted, as a precondition for negotiations, that the NLF be recognized and be allowed

*Exhausted troops of the 1st Marine Division after five hours of "humping" to Hill 190, six miles northwest of Danang, late December 1969 or early January 1970*

to take part in the negotiations. The Johnson administration and the generals in Saigon, however, had steadfastly refused to have any dealings with the NLF. In the end, Johnson yielded on that issue, and in October 1968, Hanoi and Washington began to talk in Paris, with the NLF and a reluctant Saigon represented as well.

## Nixon and the Vietnamization of War

In the presidential election of 1968, the Republican candidate, Richard Nixon, defeated by the smallest of margins Johnson's vice-president, Hubert Humphrey, a man tied to the war and despised by the growing antiwar movement. Nixon's appeal to voters consisted primarily of his "secret plan" to end a war in which he had played no direct role. He appeared to be the candidate best suited to extricate the United States from a bloody conflict that already had claimed the lives of 34,000 US troops.

Nixon's great fear on the eve of the election was a negotiated settlement of the war. In Saigon, the South Vietnamese president, Nguyen Van Thieu, also wanted no part of an agreement that, he feared, would come at his expense. Nixon secretly contacted Thieu and offered him a deal (in violation of federal law): If Thieu sabotaged the talks with Hanoi by refusing to participate in any settlement, Nixon, should he be elected president, would continue to support Thieu. Thieu did his part in undermining the talks, and Nixon delivered on his promise and sustained the Thieu regime for another four years—at the expense of an additional 22,000 US war dead.

Years later, Nixon admitted that he had no plan at all on how to end the war. He knew, however, that he had to end direct US involvement by the time the next presidential election rolled around. In the meantime, he and his national security adviser, Henry Kissinger, still pursued an elusive victory. The plan Nixon and Kissinger finally worked out consisted of yet another escalation of the war, followed by what became known as "Vietnamization." Once more, a US president announced, the fighting and the dying would be by Asian boys. As the fighting abilities of the ARVN increased, Washington would decrease its forces. For the time being, Nixon honored Johnson's bombing halt of the North, but he did not spare the South, which took the full brunt of the firepower Nixon had at his disposal. Vietnamization gradually reduced the number of US troops and thus their casualties, but not those of the Vietnamese.

## Negotiations

A third element of Nixon's blueprint for an exit from Vietnam was to put pressure on Hanoi's patrons, the Soviet Union and Communist China. Neither Moscow nor Beijing, however, were interested in helping him out. They welcomed détente with Washington, but they were unwilling to help Nixon achieve victory in South Vietnam. Nixon, during his visit to China in February 1972, brought up Vietnam, but foreign minister Zhou Enlai and party chief Mao Zedong refused to discuss it.

Nixon's election and his pursuit of victory put on hold further talks with Hanoi. It was not until February 1970 that Nixon's negotiator, Henry Kissinger, and the North Vietnamese representative, Le Duc Tho, met in Paris to resume negotiations.

Even though US troop levels were reduced from 542,000 in February 1969 to 139,000 in December 1971, violence in Indochina did not diminish. In fact, an ever more frustrated Nixon expanded the war into Laos and Cambodia in order to destroy Vietcong and PAVN sanctuaries there. Over a period of fourteen months (March 1969 to May 1970), Nixon ordered secret B-52 bombing raids of Cambodia, acts of war illegal under international and US law. A CIA-engineered overthrow of the ruler of Cambodia, the neutralist Prince Norodom Sihanouk, in March 1970 brought to power a pro-US general, Lon Nol. Sihanouk had managed to keep his country out of the Vietnam War but had been unable to prevent the Vietcong and Vietminh from establishing bases in eastern Cambodia; indeed, he had permitted China to supply them through the port of Sihanoukville. He had also been unable prevent Nixon's air strikes. In April 1970, Nixon ordered a joint US-ARVN "incursion" (as he put it) into Cambodia. For more than two months, more than 50,000 US and ARVN troops searched the jungles of eastern Cambodia in a futile effort to find the headquarters of the enemy's southern operations.

The expansion of the war inflamed protest demonstrations by antiwar activists in the United States. By this time, society was already deeply split

*National Archives*

*Antiwar demonstrators confront military police, Pentagon, Washington, DC,
October 21, 1967*

over a host of issues, including civil rights, poverty, women's rights, and cultural issues—what the political right called "amnesty, acid and abortion"—and the war itself. Nixon exacerbated the split by appealing, in a televised address in November 1969, to the "great silent majority," his political base consisting of a resentful, patriotic, God-fearing, socially conservative (mostly southern) white electorate who yearned for simpler, less tumultuous times. After the Cambodian invasion, antiwar students ("bums," Nixon called them) at Columbia University and other campuses sought to shut down their schools in protest. They were intent on "bringing the war home," and in a sense that is what happened on the campus of Kent State University, where members of the Ohio National Guard shot dead four students (and wounded another nine) during an antiwar rally on May 4, 1970.

An incursion into southern Laos in March 1971 demonstrated the failure of Vietnamization. ARVN forces, in an attempt to gain control of the Ho Chi Minh Trail, entered Laos with US air support only to be routed by the PAVN. Television crews sent back images of panic-stricken ARVN troops hanging on to the skids of evacuation helicopters in a desperate effort to escape the North Vietnamese counterattack.

As the 1972 election approached, Nixon had to find a way to bring home the remaining US troops and to decide on a face-saving settlement. To complicate matters, beginning in late March, Hanoi launched its Easter Offensive across the 17th parallel. To stop the offensive, Nixon ordered the most devastating bombing campaign yet against North Vietnam—Operation Linebacker.

Bombing targets included North Vietnam's infrastructure—factories, bridges, harbors, and power stations—as far north as Hanoi.

As the fighting raged, Henry Kissinger and Le Duc Tho resumed their on-again, off-again talks in Paris. This time, they hammered out the broad outlines of a settlement. In the end, Nixon gave Hanoi what it had always demanded: withdrawal of all US troops and the right to retain PAVN troops in South Vietnam. In return, Hanoi promised to release its US prisoners, mostly navy and air force personnel shot down over North Vietnam. What Nixon was unwilling to grant, however, was another of Hanoi's demands, the abandonment of Thieu's government in Saigon. He saw it as a matter of international prestige: A great power does not turn its back on its allies. When Hanoi eventually yielded on this point, meaning that Washington would continue to provide assistance to Saigon, the stage was set for the signing of what is often called a "peace treaty." The agreement, however, merely was designed to eventually lead to peace.

On the eve of the 1972 presidential election, Kissinger announced "peace is at hand." The terms of the preliminary agreement stipulated that within sixty days after a cease-fire the United States would complete the withdrawal of its remaining troops from Vietnam, Hanoi would release all US prisoners, and the political settlement in South Vietnam would be left for the Vietnamese to work out. But one problem remained, essentially the same one that had existed in 1968: Thieu refused to accept these terms. To win over Thieu, Kissinger traveled to Saigon, carrying with him explicit threats and a vague pledge of continued US protection for his government, including $1 billion in additional armaments.

To demonstrate his continuing commitment to defend Thieu's government, Nixon delivered one final savage punishment of North Vietnam—Operation Linebacker II—another round of bombings against Hanoi and Haiphong. The around-the-clock raids (dubbed the "Christmas bombings"), which began on December 18 and continued until the end of the month, turned large parts of these two cities into rubble. The bombings did not bring any significant change in the terms of the agreement finally signed in January 1973. Its terms were essentially those agreed to by Kissinger and Le Duc Tho the previous October. But Nixon, who had a pathological fear of being perceived as weak, was able to claim that he had bombed the enemy back to the conference table.

## Hanoi's Victory

The agreement did not bring an end to the war. The fighting continued. ARVN forces, despite their US-made arsenal, proved to be no match against the PAVN. Public opinion in the United States made impossible a return of troops or even bombing raids. And Congress, reflecting the will of the nation, cut off further aid to South Vietnam.

*National Archives*

*Refugees on Route 1 near Quang Tri, Southern Vietnam, 1972*

Moreover, Nixon was now mired in the Watergate scandal, a direct outgrowth of the war. In June 1971, Daniel Ellsberg, who had once served as a zealous administrator of official US policy in Vietnam and who had since become an equally zealous opponent of it, leaked the *Pentagon Papers* to the media (including the *New York Times* and *Washington Post*), a history of the war in Vietnam, commissioned by the former secretary of defense Robert McNamara. Nixon, furious at this and other leaks of classified information, created a group inside the White House, the "plumbers," whose task it was to plug intelligence leaks and to investigate Ellsberg and other "subversives" undermining his presidency. For reasons still unclear, in June 1972 the "plumbers" broke into the headquarters of the Democratic National Committee at the Watergate, a hotel-office-apartment complex in Washington. They were caught and arrested, and as evidence of wrongdoing began to implicate Nixon himself, he ordered his subordinates to commit perjury, that is, lie under oath. Unfortunately for Nixon, he had tape-recorded his own crimes, and for reasons also still not clear, he had not destroyed the evidence. The upshot was impeachment by Congress. When it became obvious to Nixon that his removal from office was all but a certainty, he resigned and was replaced by his vice-president, Gerald Ford.

Finally, in early 1975, a North Vietnamese attack in the northern highlands cut South Vietnam in half and produced a panic throughout the ARVN, sending generals fleeing ahead of their troops. The expected battle for Saigon never took place. In April 1975, North Vietnamese forces entered the city virtually unopposed. The US embassy became the scene of a frantic airlift of remaining US personnel and as many of their Vietnamese cohorts as they could crowd into the last departing helicopters.

More than 58,000 US troops died in Vietnam and more than 300,000 were wounded. The fiscal cost, an estimated $165 billion, contributed to inflation, the national debt, and balance-of-payments problems. It produced a new activism among the country's young people and a new political consciousness. But it also produced an even more powerful conservative political backlash that was still evident a generation later.

In 1995, Robert McNamara, who had been the US secretary of defense and one of the principal architects of US involvement in Vietnam, published his memoirs in which he confessed that the United States "could and should have withdrawn from South Vietnam" in late 1963. At that point, only seventy-eight US troops had died there. Looking back, McNamara listed eleven major errors on the part of the United States, including misjudging the strength and resolve of North Vietnam, underrating nationalism as a force in Vietnam, failing to understand the history and culture of the country, and failing to recognize the limitations of modern technological warfare.

The cost of the war for the peoples of Indochina was extraordinary. The US estimate of ARVN deaths was over 200,000, and for enemy forces—both NLF and PAVN—almost 500,000. We will never know how many civilians died or how many became refugees. In an interview in 2002, McNamara put the number of dead in Indochina at 3.4 million.[13] The physical mutilation of the country was also staggering. The United States dropped three times more bombs on Indochina than it had dropped on its enemies in the entirety of World War II. In addition, it defoliated over 5 million acres with chemicals such as Agent Orange, a powerful, cancer-causing herbicide.

## The Continuing Tragedy of Indochina

In the wake of the North's victory, the South Vietnamese braced themselves for the terrible, vengeful "bloodbath" that Nixon had predicted. It did not come, yet those identified as high-ranking former government or military officers of the overthrown Saigon regime were singled out for severe punishment, usually involving confiscation of property, arrest, and long sentences to hard labor in remote rural "reeducation" camps. Saigon, renamed Ho Chi Minh City, saw its bars, brothels, and dance halls closed.

Within a year, severe economic problems gripped Vietnam. The government's plan to quickly restore the agricultural productivity of the South to complement the industrial development of the North proved too optimistic. Hundreds of thousands of unemployed city-dwellers were lured to rural "New Economic Zones" with promises of houses, land, and food. Many of them soon fled from the harsh, primitive rural conditions. To compound matters, southern regions experienced three successive years of droughts and devastating floods.

Nor was there international deliverance. Vietnam was unable to attract foreign investment, without which its hopes of economic recovery were dim. The economic assistance that Nixon had once promised never came. Instead, Washington pressured international lending agencies to reject Vietnam's requests for loans. Increasingly, Hanoi was forced to turn to the Soviet Union (which had its own severe economic problems) for assistance. Vietnam's reliance on the Soviet Union contributed to a worsening of its relations with China, which until 1978 had provided a modicum of aid to Hanoi.

### The Plight of Cambodia

Yet a bloodbath did occur, not in Vietnam but in neighboring Cambodia. When the United States disengaged from Vietnam in early 1973, it also reduced its military support for the Lon Nol government in Cambodia, which was embattled by the Khmer Rouge, a native Communist force. In April 1975, just before Saigon fell to the North Vietnamese, the Khmer Rouge swept into Phnom Penh, the Cambodian capital.

Cambodia braced itself for a new order under a Communist government led by Pol Pot, who immediately began a reign of revolutionary terror. In theory, Communist revolutions, upon inheriting the existing capitalist industrial base, transfer ownership from the capitalists to the workers. The Khmer Rouge, however, set out to eradicate the old order completely, root and branch, to reorganize society to a degree no revolutionary regime had ever attempted. Pol Pot's ideal society, in direct contrast to the tenets of Marxism, demanded a return to the land, a return to the glory days of Angkor War during the twelfth century. The entire urban population was evacuated to the countryside. Those who resisted—members of the old regime, the Western-educated elite, city-dwellers, and all real or suspected "enemies of the revolution"—were exterminated. In the space of three years, the Khmer Rouge murdered an estimated 1.7 million Cambodians—almost one-fifth of the population.

Pol Pot also rejected the old borders of Cambodia that the French had drawn up. To redraw the borders, he launched attacks against neighboring Thailand and Communist Vietnam (with which, by necessity, he had cooperated over the years). Vehemently anti-Vietnamese, as were many Cambodians, Pol Pot looked with misgiving upon the substantial Vietnamese population in eastern Cambodia. In 1978, he unleashed a furious attack against them, committing atrocities on a wide scale. The killing of Pol Pot's Cambodians constituted mass murder; that of the Vietnamese (and other ethnic groups) was undiluted genocide.

For a while, Hanoi sought—unsuccessfully—to negotiate with Pol Pot. In January 1979, it sent its battle-tested army into Cambodia, scattered the Khmer Rouge, and then took control of Phnom Penh, where it installed a former Khmer Rouge officer, Heng Samrin, as head of a new pro-Vietnamese government. The Vietnamese conquest of Phnom Penh, however, did not bring peace to Cambodia. A Vietnamese army of about 170,000 continued to battle remnants of Pol Pot's forces who had retreated into the mountainous jungles of western Cambodia.

Even though Vietnam had ended the reign of the Khmer Rouge, the international community was slow in showing its gratitude. Washington and Beijing continued to support the Khmer Rouge as long as Vietnam remained a client of the Soviet Union—the Chinese providing military assistance, the Carter and Reagan administrations diplomatic and economic aid. Beijing even sent its army into Vietnam in February 1979 to "teach it a lesson." That Communist China would be at war with Communist Vietnam, so soon after the US war, proved how utterly wrong was Washington's conviction that a Communist victory in Vietnam would be a victory for Beijing.

By the end of the 1980s, with the Cold War winding down, opportunities arose to resolve the stalemate in Cambodia. The new Soviet leader, Mikhail Gorbachev, disengaged from Third World clients abroad and thus ended economic and military assistance to Vietnam. In 1989, Hanoi withdrew from Cambodia, leaving behind a pro-Vietnamese regime in Phnom Penh.

By the summer of 1991, the Soviet Union unraveled and, with the Soviet threat gone, Washington and Beijing lost interest in Cambodia. The United Nations was thus able to work out a political solution. Sihanouk returned from exile in Beijing, and in 1993 the UN oversaw a nationwide election won by the royalist party. Pol Pot, old and in ill health, was still holed up in the jungle near the Thai border. In April 1998, just as one of his own Khmer Rouge factions was about to hand him over to the government to stand trial for his crimes, Pol Pot cheated the hangman when he died of an apparent heart attack.

Another consequence of the Indochina wars was the desperate flight of refugees from Vietnam, which saw an estimated 1.5 million of its citizens escape by taking to the sea. Many of these "boatpeople" died on the South China Sea from exposure, drowning, and attacks by pirates.

The first wave of boatpeople came in 1975 after the fall of Saigon, when about 100,000 people fled the country. In 1978 and 1979, during the war between Cambodia and Vietnam, a second and much larger wave of refugees fled Vietnam. They arrived in neighboring countries—Malaysia, Thailand, Singapore, the Philippines—which, however, did not want them. In July 1979, the UN secured an agreement with Vietnam to limit the refugee outflow. It also provided relief to nations of "first asylum" (such as Malaysia) and secured promises from other nations to open their doors to refugees.

The majority of those who left Vietnam were ethnic Chinese who had long dominated private business in Vietnam and fell victim to government policies in early 1979 that abolished "bourgeois trade" and introduced a currency reform that rendered their accumulated savings nearly worthless.

Curiously, many were assisted in their flight by Communist authorities who collected exit fees of up to $2,000 in gold from each departing refugee. In northern Vietnam, where a brief Chinese invasion had taken place, 250,000 of the region's approximately 300,000 ethnic Chinese were expelled.

## Notes

1. Cited in Edward Miller, "Vision, Power, and Agency: The Ascent of Ngo Dinh Diem, 1945–1954," *Journal of Southeast Asian Studies* (October 1954), pp. 455–456.

2. Bernard B. Fall, *Last Reflections on a War* (Garden City, NY: Doubleday, 1967), p. 167.

3. David Halberstam, *The Making of a Quagmire: America and Vietnam During the Kennedy Era*, rev. ed. (New York: Knopf, [orig. 1964] 1988), pp. 27, 29.

4. Stanley Karnow, *Vietnam: A History* (New York: Viking, 1983), p. 281.

5. Wilfred G. Burchett, *Vietnam: Inside Story of the Guerrilla War*, 3rd ed. (New York: International Publishers, 1968), pp. 110–111.

6. Johnson's telephone conversation with Russell, May 27, 1964, Lyndon B. Johnson Library, Tape WH6405.10, Side A.

7. Robert S. McNamara, *In Retrospect: The Tragedy and Lessons of Vietnam* (New York: Times Books/Random House, 1995), pp. 128–142.

8. Theodore Draper, "The American Crisis: Vietnam, Cuba, and the Dominican Republic," *Commentary* (January 1967), p. 36.

9. Neil Sheehan et al., *The Pentagon Papers* (New York: Bantam, 1971), documents 61–64, pp. 271–285.

10. For the White Paper "Aggression from the North" and I. F. Stone's reply, see Marcus G. Raskin and Bernard B. Fall, eds., *The Vietnam Reader: Articles and Documents on American Foreign Policy and the Viet-Nam Crisis*, rev. ed. (New York: Vintage, 1967), pp. 143–162.

11. Associated Press, *New York Times*, May 14, 1967, p. 3.

12. Peter Arnett, *Live from the Battle Field: From Vietnam to Baghdad—35 Years in the World's War Zones* (New York: Touchstone Books, 1994), p. 256.

13. Errol Morris (director), documentary, *The Fog of War: Eleven Lessons from the Life of Robert S. McNamara* (2003).

# 11

# Détente and
# the End of Bipolarity

Ironically, the years of direct US military involvement in Vietnam
against international Communism, 1965–1973, saw a gradual improvement in
relations between Washington and the two most powerful Communist states.
Toward the end of that period, the Cold War took several unexpected turns.
Détente eased the tensions between Moscow and Washington followed by the
normalization of relations between the United States and the People's
Republic of China. In the spring of 1972, President Richard Nixon, the quin-
tessential anti-Communist who had always urged strong measures against the
Vietnamese, Soviet, and Chinese Communists—all part of a great conspiracy—paid visits to both Moscow and Beijing. The bipolar world, with Moscow
and Washington at center stage, was coming to an end.

## Washington and Beijing:
## The Normalization of Relations
The split between the Soviet Union and the People's Republic of China gave
the United States a golden opportunity. Monolithic Communism, it became
evident, proved to be an ideological quest that ran aground on the shoals of
nationalist interests. A succession of governments in Washington, tied to the
principle of thwarting an international Communist conspiracy, was slow in
taking advantage of the falling-out between the two most important
Communist states, even though their intelligence agencies had been aware of
it since the early 1950s. Twenty years later, it became high time for
Washington to cash in on the mutually antagonistic relationship between
Moscow and Beijing.

Since 1949, Moscow had played the proverbial "China card." By virtue of the Sino-Soviet military alliance of 1950, Moscow's line of defense in the Far East was on the shores of the Yellow Sea. Twenty years later, however, mutual Soviet-Chinese recrimination and bloody border clashes took their toll on that alliance. With China's security better served by a rapprochement with the United States, it became Washington's turn in the early 1970s to see whether it could play the "China card" against Soviet and North Vietnamese interests.

For more than twenty years the United States and China had no official relations (although its representatives did meet from time to time to discuss pertinent matters). Successive US presidents denounced "Red China" as a menace to the peace-loving peoples of Asia and a reckless, irresponsible, aggressive regime unworthy of diplomatic recognition or UN membership. The United States maintained relations instead with the Nationalist regime on Taiwan, adhering to the fiction that it was the legitimate government of China and pledging to defend it against "Communist aggression." To that end, the United States and Taiwan signed a mutual defense pact in December 1954. Beijing denounced the alliance and the US military presence on Taiwan as "imperialist aggression" and interference in the internal affairs of China. Meanwhile, the United States effectively blocked the PRC from gaining admission into the United Nations, all the while containing it within an arc of military bases—running from South Korea to Japan, Taiwan, the Philippines, and South Vietnam. The United States also maintained a rigid embargo on all trade with China, and denied its citizens the right to travel there.

Nor was this merely a bilateral feud. Both antagonists called upon their respective Cold War allies for support. Supporting China, at least in the first decade, was the Soviet Union, its satellite states in Eastern Europe, and Communist parties in other parts of the world. The Soviet Union had supported from the outset the PRC's bid to replace the Republic of China (Jiang Jieshi's government) in the United Nations. The United States, speaking for the "free world," applied diplomatic pressure on its friends and allies for support of its uncompromising China policy. Britain and France, however, broke ranks with the United States and extended diplomatic recognition to China, in January 1950 and January 1964, respectively. In 1949, only Communist countries recognized China; in the 1950s and 1960s, newly independent former European colonies followed suit, thereby gradually lifting China's isolation.

Washington tirelessly denounced "Red China" and its brutal enslavement of the Chinese people. Beijing regarded the United States as its "Number One Enemy" and argued persistently that US imperialism was the major threat to world peace. As proof of aggressive US designs, the Chinese pointed to the arc of US military bases on their eastern periphery. The United States, in turn, pointed to Chinese intervention in the Korean War and China's border war with India in 1962 as examples of Chinese aggression. Beijing (and some observers in the West) countered that in both cases China acted legitimately to protect its borders.

The Sino-Soviet split did not lead to an improvement in Sino-US relations. Instead, relations worsened since it was China, not the Soviet Union, which argued for a stronger anti–United States line. As Washington and Moscow began to move toward détente in the late 1960s, Beijing's anti-imperialist, anti-US rhetoric charged that the Soviet Union had grown soft on capitalism. Beijing complained bitterly of Moscow's "socialist imperialism," accusing it of being linked with US "capitalist imperialism" to encircle China. In response, Mao emerged as the champion of revolutionary movements engaged in wars of national liberation, such as in Vietnam. He even taunted the United States to make war on China, saying that the atomic bomb was merely a "paper tiger" and that China would prevail in the end. Mao's inflammatory rhetoric made it easy for Moscow and Washington to condemn Beijing's recklessness as the greatest threat to world peace.

The seemingly interminable hostility between China and the United States ended quite suddenly in the early 1970s, in one of the most dramatic turnabouts in modern diplomatic history. On July 15, 1971, the US Republican president and diehard anti-Communist Richard Nixon made a surprising announcement. At the invitation of China's government, he would travel to Beijing for the purpose of developing normal relations. He revealed that his national security advisor, Henry Kissinger, had just returned from a secret trip to Beijing, where he and premier Zhou Enlai had made arrangements for the visit.

The Nixon administration had begun making subtle overtures to the PRC in the previous year. In Warsaw, Poland, where their ambassadors had periodically met for secret talks, the US side intimated its desire for improved relations. In his February 1971 televised "State of the World" address, Nixon referred to the Beijing government as the People's Republic of China, instead of the usual "Red China" or "Communist China." The Chinese took note of the fact that for the first time the US government had publicly used the proper name of their country. These gestures opened the door to what became known as "ping-pong diplomacy." A US table-tennis team was invited to play an exhibition tournament in Beijing, where Zhou gave them a warm reception and noted that their visit "opened a new page in the relations between the Chinese and US peoples."[1] Nixon responded by announcing a relaxation of the US trade embargo with China, and Beijing reciprocated by facilitating Kissinger's secret trip to Beijing.

In February 1993, Nixon made his heralded two-week visit to China, where he was welcomed with great fanfare. At the Beijing airport he made sure to extended his hand to Zhou, the very same leader whom John Foster Dulles had pointedly snubbed eighteen years earlier at Geneva by refusing to shake hands. A large retinue of US journalists and television camera crews recorded the historic event and gave the US people their first glimpse of life inside Communist China. For two weeks they were treated to photo opportunities of China and its friendly, smiling people. And they also were treated to the extraordinary spectacle of Nixon, known for his trenchant anti–Chinese Communist pronouncements, saluting the aged and ailing Mao Zedong and toasting the new bond of friendship with China's most able diplomat, Zhou Enlai. For both the United States and China, it was a mind-boggling, 180-degree turnabout.

At first blush, it appeared ironic that Nixon, a conservative, Communist-hating Republican, would be the one to go to China and establish contact with its Communist government. But the task required just such a politician. A Democratic president would have found it extraordinarily difficult to do so. The Democrats still carried the scars of allegedly having "lost China" to Communism in the first place. A Republican president whose anti-Communist credentials were beyond question would encounter much less opposition for reversing Washington's policy toward China.

In any case, the normalization of Sino-US relations was an event whose time had come and, indeed, was long overdue. Both sides understood that they had more to gain by ending their mutual hostility than by continuing it. Nixon, trying to disengage from Vietnam "with honor," wanted the Chinese to put the North Vietnamese on a short leash. The Chinese, however, had no intention of doing so. Moreover, they made clear to him that their control of the stubborn Vietnamese had its limits. On Vietnam, the main reason for his visit, Nixon came away empty-handed.

The Chinese needed to end their isolation in the face of a growing Soviet threat after the March 1969 Ussuri River border clash. Since then, the Soviets had greatly increased their ground forces along the northern Chinese border and equipped them with tactical nuclear weapons. The Chinese hoped that closer ties with the United States would decrease the prospect of a preemptive Soviet nuclear attack. Beijing also saw it as a means to gain entry into the United Nations and to solve the Taiwan question. Nixon and Kissinger envisioned a new global balance of power, with China playing a major role. They hoped that in their dealings with Moscow, they would be able to play the "China card."

The major obstacle to improving relations between the United States and China was the status of Taiwan. Beijing saw Taiwan as part of China under its control, while Washington recognized the Taiwanese government in Taipei as the legitimate government of all of China. Moreover, Washington had a treaty to defend Taiwan. Nixon's so-called "two-China formula" called for diplomatic recognition of both Chinese governments. Beijing and Taipei, however, firmly rejected that formula. Neither would give up its claim as the legitimate government of the whole of China.

Taiwan appeared to be an intractable problem that, as it turned out, proved to be easily resolved. After Kissinger and Zhou repaired to Shanghai to hammer out a solution, the Chinese dusted off a long-standing proposal of theirs that went back to September 1958. They again proposed that Washington recognize Taiwan as part of China and the island's ultimate "liberation" as a purely Chinese affair, to be completed peacefully over an unspecified time span. Under that arrangement, moreover, the United States would have to end its military alliance with Taiwan. The Eisenhower administration rejected the proposal as "unacceptable," declaring Taiwan was a "sovereign state and trusted ally."[2]

This time, however, Kissinger and Nixon quickly accepted Beijing's solution. There was no question of it being "unacceptable." Washington finally accepted the Communist victory in the Chinese civil war, leaving the last unresolved issue to the Chinese themselves. As for Taiwan's continuing independence, Washington neither supported nor opposed it.

In the carefully worded Shanghai Communiqué at the end of Nixon's visit, the United States acknowledged that all Chinese believed that "there is but one China and that Taiwan is part of China." It would not challenge that position. Having accepted that there was but one China, the Nixon administration hoped for "a peaceful settlement of the Taiwan question by the Chinese themselves." Communist China, however, never specifically pledged to refrain from using force.[3] In the years to come, it repeatedly threatened Taiwan with force, particularly when talk turned to "one China, one Taiwan."

In the past, the United States had voted against the PRC replacing the Republic of China in the United Nations. Even before Nixon's visit, however, Washington had made it known that it would not block such a move. In October 1971, the PRC was admitted to the United Nations on its terms, namely, as the single legitimate government of China and as the rightful claimant of the seat that had been occupied by the Republic of China.

The Nixon-Mao summit was not the end but the beginning of the normalization process. Full normalization of relations, involving the formal recognition of the PRC by the United States and the breaking off of US diplomatic ties with Nationalist China, was yet to come. In the meantime, in accordance with the Shanghai Communiqué, the two countries established liaison offices in each other's capitals and began a series of exchanges in the fields of science, technology, culture, journalism, sports, and ultimately trade.

It was not until January 1979 that full diplomatic relations were established. There were two main reasons for the seven-year delay: political leadership problems in both countries and the matter of the US military alliance with Taiwan. In Washington, Nixon was hamstrung by the Watergate scandal. Political instability in Beijing was greater yet. The deaths of Mao and Zhou in 1976 left behind a struggle for succession that remained unresolved until Deng Xiaoping's consolidation of power in 1978.

It was now up to President Jimmy Carter and Deng to work out the last details. Negotiations produced an agreement in December 1978, the terms of which included the termination of official US diplomatic and military ties with Taiwan, followed by the restoration of full diplomatic relations between the United States and the PRC. It did allow, however, for continued US commercial and cultural ties with Taiwan as well as arms sales. On the latter point, the Chinese agreed to disagree, which is to say that they did not formally agree to such arms sales but would set aside that issue so that the normalization agreement could go into force without further delay. The end of the US-Taiwanese military alliance, on December 31, 1979, was followed immediately by the full diplomatic recognition of the PRC and Deng's state visit to Washington. The United States conceded much by breaking off its military alliance, but it came away with an understanding that the PRC would not attempt to take over Taiwan by force.

The agreement was a severe blow to Taiwan, which remained in the hands of the anti-Communist Nationalist government now headed by Jiang Jingguo (Chiang Ching-kuo), son of Jiang Jieshi, who had died in 1975. Washington sought to soften the blow by passing the Taiwan Relations Act, which affirmed the resolve of the United States to maintain good relations with the people (not the government) of Taiwan and to consider any effort to resolve the Taiwan issue by force as a "grave concern to the United States."

The United States thus ended the anomaly of recognizing a government that ruled only 17 million Chinese in favor of one that governed over 900 million. Normalization led to a significant reduction of tensions in East Asia and opened the way to a vast increase in trade for Communist China followed by an inflow of much-needed capital and technology. In the United States it was hoped that China's large market would serve to offset the mounting US trade deficit with other world markets. That hope vanished when, as early as 1996, China ran up the largest trade surplus of any nation trading with the United States (thereby overtaking Japan).

The abrupt breakthrough in Sino-US relations brought in its wake an equally abrupt turnaround in Sino-Japanese relations. Initially, the Japanese were stunned by Nixon's surprising announcement that he would visit China, not because they opposed the move but because they were caught off guard and felt they should have been consulted beforehand. The Japanese prime minister, Sato Eisaku, had for years touted the mutual trust between his government and Washington. In order not to jeopardize Japan's strong ties with the United States, he had consistently resisted popular pressure for normalizing relations with China. The Japanese saw the reversal of Washington's China policy without consulting them—its major Asian ally—as a diplomatic slap in the face.

Once the Japanese got over what the called the "Nixon shock," they worked out their own rapprochement with China. Prime Minister Tanaka

Kakuei followed in Nixon's footsteps when he accepted a historic invitation to visit Beijing, in September 1972. Tanaka's was the first visit to China by any Japanese head of state. Moreover, it came after almost a century of hostile Sino-Japanese relations. In Beijing, Tanaka contritely expressed his regret over the "unfortunate experiences" between the two nations in the past. He declared that Japan was "keenly aware of . . . [its] responsibility for causing enormous damage in the past to the Chinese people through war and deeply reproaches itself."[4]

Talks between Tanaka and Zhou Enlai produced an agreement on full diplomatic relations. By the terms of the agreement, Japan affirmed its recognition of the PRC as the sole legal government of China and that Taiwan was an inalienable part of the territory of the PRC. China waived its claim to war reparations of several billion dollars and agreed to halt its protest against the US-Japan Mutual Security Pact and to drop its insistence that Japan end its trade relations with Taiwan. The two countries also agreed to negotiate a new treaty of peace and friendship that went into effect in August 1978. China and Japan reaped enormous benefits from their improved relations, particularly from the huge volume of trade that developed between them in years to come. The two were natural trading partners; China had raw materials to offer resource-poor Japan, and in exchange, Japan had technology, machinery, and finished goods.

Taiwan again felt slighted. Its government accused Washington and Tokyo of having been duped by the Communists in Beijing. Having little choice in the matter, however, Taiwan made sure to retain its remaining ties—particularly its all-important commercial relations—with the United States, Japan, and Western nations. Taiwan's diplomatic setback had no impact on its continued high rate of economic growth, which produced a far higher standard of living for its people than the Chinese on the mainland.

Taiwan's government, still dominated by the Nationalist Party, stubbornly rebuffed every overture by the PRC for a peaceful reunification. Meanwhile, the PRC, careful not to risk damaging its relations with the United States, patiently refrained from forceful gestures and waited for a softening of Taiwan's position. But, insofar as the raison d'être of the Taiwanese government was to overthrow the Communist rulers of the mainland, it neither wavered in its resolute anti-Communist policy nor moderated its strident anti-Beijing propaganda. Not until the late 1980s, when the global Cold War ended, did the Taiwan government soften its rhetoric.

## Détente Between East and West

The rapprochement between Washington and Beijing took place in an era of thawing of frozen relations across a wide front. It reflected significant changes in the Cold War mentality in both camps. Originally, both sides had held the position that there could be no improvement of relations until issues such as the division of China, Germany, Korea, and Vietnam had been resolved. In the mid-1960s, however, the belligerents backtracked when they concluded that a normalization of relations—in areas such as trade, international travel and contact, and arms limitations—could contribute to resolving the greater issues—the unification of divided nations, the nuclear arms race—and perhaps even put an end to the Cold War. The result was détente, the lessening of tensions in international relations.

• • •

The Cold War created two Germanys—a West German state aligned with the West and ultimately part of the North Atlantic Treaty Organization, and an East German state whose government had been installed under Soviet auspices and which then joined the Soviet Union's military organization, the Warsaw Pact. The conservative anti-Communist West German governments of the 1950s and the early 1960s, particularly that of Chancellor Konrad Adenauer, considered East Germany as illegitimate and refused to recognize or deal with it. The West German leaders treated Germany as a whole, claimed to speak for all Germans, and automatically granted citizenship to East Germans who made it across the border into West Germany. They considered the West German capital, Bonn, a provisional seat of a provisional state. The true political heart of Germany was Berlin.

Adenauer's position was spelled out in the 1955 Hallstein Doctrine (named after the state secretary of the West German Foreign Office). It declared that West Germany would not recognize any state (with the exception of the Soviet Union) that had diplomatic relations with East Germany. It meant that West Germany would have no dealings with the Soviet client states of Eastern Europe. West Germany would make no attempt to raise the Iron Curtain.

Starting in 1966, West Germany's new foreign minister, Willy Brandt, reversed Adenauer's stand when he took the first steps to establish contact with the Communist nations of Eastern Europe. He was willing to recognize the political realities in place for more than two decades, ever since the Red Army had rolled into the center of Europe. Anticipating Brandt's initiative, US president Lyndon Johnson stated that the reunification of Germany could only come about as a result of détente. In other words, Brandt and Johnson saw détente as a precondition for a unified Germany, whereas Adenauer and Hallstein had argued that there must first be a unified Germany before there could be talk of improved relations with the Soviet bloc. Brandt and Adenauer sought the same end, the unification of Germany. Where they differed was over the means.

Brandt's rejection of the Hallstein Doctrine meant he was willing to grant de facto recognition to East Germany. In doing so, he would also have to

*West German chancellor Willy Brandt after placing a wreath at the Tomb of
the Unknown Soldier in the Polish capital of Warsaw, December 1970*

accept the postwar borders of the two Germanies, the consequence of World
War II. Brandt, now chancellor of West Germany, was willing to recognize the
Oder-Neisse Line as the border between East Germany and Poland. The new
border had been in existence since the end of the war, when the Soviet Union
moved Poland's western border about seventy-five miles (into Silesia, a region
that before the war had been German territory) to the Oder and Western Neisse
Rivers. Of the 6 million former German inhabitants of Silesia, many had been
killed during the war, others had fled before the advancing Red Army, and
nearly all of the remaining 2 million were expelled. Germany also had lost
East Prussia, the easternmost province of the German Reich. The Soviet Union
took the northern half, Poland the southern half. In Czechoslovakia, Germany
had to give up the Sudetenland, which the British and the French had granted
Hitler in 1938. The Czechs wasted little time after the war in expelling what
was left of the 3 million Sudeten Germans.[5]

The Adenauer government had been most adamant in its refusal to accept
the loss of German territory to Poland. Brandt, however, was willing to accept
the Oder-Neisse Line. Moreover, there were only a few remaining Germans
east of that line, in what was now Poland. Brandt also saw little hope of
Germany ever regaining East Prussia. To do so would lead to another war and
only drive Poland and the Soviet Union into each other's arms. (If there was
one thing the Poles and the Soviets had been able to agree on in 1945, it was
that Germany must pay for the war with the loss of territory.) Brandt also aban-

doned all claims to the Sudetenland. This was the least controversial of Brandt's steps because the region had been Czechoslovakia's before the war and its transfer to Hitler's Reich was one of the events leading to World War II. That the Sudetenland would be returned to Czechoslovakia after the war had always been a foregone conclusion. What had not been a foregone conclusion was the expulsion of Germans whose ancestors had lived there for centuries.

The Soviet Union and East Germany, however, wanted more than a West German recognition of the borders. They also wanted West German recognition of the East German government, which of course would legitimize it. Such recognition, moreover, would undermine the West German government's claim that it spoke for all Germans. This was not something Brandt—or any other West German leader—was willing to do.

Still, the two German governments began to talk to each other. On March 19, 1971, at a historic meeting in Erfurt, East Germany, Willy Brandt met with his East German counterpart, Prime Minister Willi Stoph. (The power behind the throne in East Germany, however, was the dogmatic Communist Party chief, Walter Ulbricht.) The meeting led to the Basic Treaty of 1972 between the two German states. West Germany did not grant East Germany full diplomatic recognition, but the treaty did call for "good neighborly" relations, and it led to increased contacts of a cultural, personal, and economic nature. The Iron Curtain was partially raised.

Brandt's contacts with Eastern Europe became known as *Ostpolitik* (literally "eastern politics"). It included a thaw in relations with the Soviet Union and other East European countries. In 1968, West Germany established diplomatic relations with Yugoslavia. In 1970, West Germany and the Soviet Union signed in Moscow a nonaggression treaty. Later that year, Brandt went to Warsaw to sign a similar treaty with the Polish government, thereby formally accepting the Oder-Neisse Line.

But not everyone in West Germany was willing to accept the new borders. Critics pointed out that the West German position—which had been spelled out in the early 1950s—had not changed, at least not officially. There could be no final de jure acceptance of the borders until Germany signed peace treaties with Poland and the Soviet Union, officially signifying the end of World War II. Until such treaties were ratified there could be no de jure recognition of the postwar borders. After East-West relations deteriorated in the late 1970s, West German conservatives, including Chancellor Helmut Kohl, dusted off this argument, thereby keeping the question of Germany's borders an open issue.[6]

Détente and Brandt's *Ostpolitik* helped to prepare the climate for a series of US-Soviet arms limitation talks, including SALT I and SALT II (see Chapter 20), which led directly to the European Security Conference of August 1975 in Helsinki, Finland. The Soviets had proposed such a conference as early as 1954 and again in the late 1960s, hoping thereby to ratify the consequences of World War II. Since no formal treaty or conference recognized the redrawn map of Eastern Europe and the new governments there, the Soviets continued to press for such a conference. At Helsinki finally, in 1975, they hoped to obtain that recognition.

The participants at Helsinki included all European states (except Albania) as well as the United States and Canada. The Helsinki Agreement recognized the postwar borders of Europe, but it left open the prospect that the borders could be changed, although only by peaceful means. NATO and the Warsaw Pact agreed to observe each other's military exercises to avoid the misreading of the other's intentions. Last, all signatories of the agreement promised greater East-West contacts and to guarantee the human rights of their citizens. In Eastern Europe, however, the rights of citizens were defined differently than in the West, and this point later became a central issue when détente was shelved by the United States during the late 1970s.

Détente also helped to set into motion the first steps on the road to a limit on the unchecked nuclear arms race. Until 1972, there had been no limits on the nuclear arsenals of the United States and the Soviet Union, both of which had more than enough firepower to destroy the other several times over. There was little point in adding to stockpiles already of grotesque proportions. By 1970, the Soviet Union had concluded its concerted effort to catch up with the United States and had achieved a rough sort of parity. The US strategic nuclear arsenal consisted at that time of 3,854 warheads; the Soviet total was 2,155.

The year of the Helsinki Agreement, 1975, saw the high point of détente. After that, relations between the United States and the Soviet Union began to deteriorate, and by 1980, détente was a thing of the past. Détente never sat well with a number of influential US policymakers, who saw it as a snare and a delusion. One cannot do business, they warned, with an ideological system that professes world revolution. They seized every opportunity to sabotage détente. Eventually, a number of liberals joined their chorus. The liberals—together with the old hard-liners—became known as the neoconservatives, or simply "neocons," who heavily influenced the foreign policy of presidents from Ronald Reagan to George W. Bush.

With the intensification of the Cold War came a reassessment of Soviet military strength and intentions. In 1976, the head of the CIA, George H. W. Bush, brought in a group of Cold War warriors (known as the "B Team"), who overruled a CIA estimate of Soviet military spending. According to the B Team, the Soviets were spending nearly twice as much on their military as the CIA had reckoned. Their ominous conclusion placed Soviet intentions and capabilities in a new light. Reporters, editorial writers, politicians, and academicians quickly accepted their new figures, which then became part and parcel of the new orthodoxy in this latest phase of the Cold War. This was not the last time the neocons would challenge CIA findings. Their greatest success came when they beat the drums for war against Iraq in 2003.

The professionals in the CIA, in a 1983 report to Congress, cast off the shackles of George H. W. Bush and the B Team when they restated the validity of their original estimates of Soviet military spending. They cut the B Team's estimates by more than half. But while the B Team's findings received much publicity, the CIA's declaration of independence from meddling outsiders received scant attention. Nor did a NATO study of January 1984, which concluded that Soviet military spending since 1976 had, in fact, declined to less than 2.5 percent of the Soviet Union's gross national product (GNP), as compared to 4–5 percent during the early 1970s.

These reassessments of Soviet military spending notwithstanding, the B Team's estimates of Soviet military spending had great staying power. Between 1976 and 1980, Republican presidential hopeful Ronald Reagan got considerable mileage out of an argument in one of his stump speeches that the Soviets had opened up a lead on the United States in the nuclear arms race. He promised to restore US military might, a pledge that, probably more than anything else, gained him the presidency in 1980, particularly after the incumbent Jimmy Carter could not obtain the release of the US hostages in Iran until after the November election (see Chapter 21). The B Team's findings and the Iranian hostage crisis, replete with the burning of US flags in full view of television cameras, had their effect. A new militancy set in.

The Soviets, too, contributed to the scuttling of détente. Their definition of détente had always been different from that of the West. They insisted on the right to conduct their foreign and domestic affairs as they had in the past. What they did in Africa, they insisted, had nothing to do with Soviet-US relations. But many in the West perceived the Soviet activities in Africa differently. As the Brezhnev government signed the Helsinki Agreement in 1975, in the same breath it began sending arms to clients in Angola, Somalia, Ethiopia, and Mozambique, while Cuban soldiers arrived in Soviet planes in Angola and Ethiopia to train African soldiers.

Close Soviet ties with the Marxist leader of Somalia, Siad Barre, dated to the early 1970s. Starting in late 1976, however, Moscow began to send arms shipments to the Marxist head of Ethiopia, Mengistu Haile Miriam. When, in 1978, the Communist governments of Somalia and Ethiopia went to war against each other over a stretch of desert in the Somalian border province of Ogaden, the Soviets had to choose. They decided to stay with Ethiopia. (Washington then became the supplier of weapons to Siad Barre. That he was a professed Marxist was of little importance to the Carter administration.)

Moscow also had a client in Vietnam who, in December 1978, marched its troops into Phnom Penh, the capital of professedly Communist Cambodia. In December 1979, the Soviet army moved into Afghanistan to prop up a bankrupt Communist government. Then, in 1981, the Polish Communist government invoked martial law to bring to heel the only independent labor union in the Soviet bloc. To the West, Moscow and its surrogates appeared to be on the march, even though in each instance it was a case of Communists fighting each other. But with perception being more important than reality, under such circumstances, détente could not survive.

Soviet domestic actions also undermined the spirit of détente, particularly as Jewish emigration was drastically curtailed. Jews who had wished to leave the Soviet Union had been bargaining chips in East-West relations. During the 1970s, about 270,000 Jews emigrated. With the end of détente, emigration slowed to a trickle. Dissidents, moreover, the most famous of whom was the nuclear physicist Andrei Sakharov, were either jailed or exiled, in violation of the Helsinki Agreement. Not surprisingly, détente became a memory of the not too distant past. Ronald Reagan, who became the US president in January 1981, had no intentions of improving US-Soviet relations. He preferred to demonize the Soviet Union as an "evil empire." Only when Mikhail Gorbachev took the helm in Moscow in 1985, did relations improve.

## Notes

1. Immanuel C. Y. Hsu, *The Rise of Modern China*, 3rd rev. ed. (New York: Oxford University Press, 1983), p. 373.

2. Foreign Relations of the United States (FRUS), *China, 1958–1960*, Volume 19, pp. 190–191, 193–195, 209–216.

3. Joint Statement, February 27, 1972, FRUS, *1969–1976*, Vol. 17, *China, 1969–1972*, Document 2013.

4. Cited in ibid., p. 751.

5. For a map of the transfer of land after World War II, see p. 34 in Chapter 2, "The Cold War Institutionalized."

6. Bernt Conrad, "How Definite Is the Oder-Neisse Line?" *Die Welt*, December 24, 1984; reprinted in *The German Tribune: Political Affairs Review* (a publication of the West German government), April 21, 1985, pp. 15–16. See also *The Week in Germany*, a weekly newsletter of the West German Information Center, Washington, D.C., June 21, 1985, p. 1.

# Part 4

# The Global South

**The East-West confrontation was surely the dominant theme in** international relations in the postwar period, but since the 1970s, another cleavage, the North-South divide, became increasingly important. "North" refers to the modern industrialized nations, most of which happen to be located in the temperate zones of the Northern Hemisphere, and "South" signifies the poorer nations, most located in the equatorial region or in the Southern Hemisphere. The nations of the South are scattered throughout Africa, Latin America, and along Asia's, southern fringe. They are sometimes euphemistically called "developing countries," even though some were hardly developing at all, or "underdeveloped countries."

Until recently, they were referred to collectively as the "Third World," but they are now commonly known as the "global South." (The two terms are essentially synonymous in designating nations lacking sustained economic development, notably in the area of industrialization.) Indeed, the principal identifying characteristic of the nations in the South was, and remains, widespread poverty.

The economic dilemma of the global South is the theme of Chapter 12. First we examine the gap between North and South and the reasons for the retarded economic development of the latter. We particularly focus on the population factor and problems in agricultural and industrial development. In the remainder of the chapter, we examine a predicament that strongly affected many Southern nations and became especially acute in the 1990s: the foreign debt crisis. Many of these nations—even those with an industrial base such as Brazil, Mexico, and Argentina—amassed foreign debts so large they were unable to pay either the principal or the interest on their loans.

Economic and political development are interrelated, one being a function of the other, and this was surely the case in Africa, which is the focus of Chapter 13. It is necessary, therefore, to seek political reasons for the economic problems in the South as well as economic reasons for its political problems. We examine the political patterns of postindependence sub-Saharan Africa, where the demise of fledgling, initially democratic governments and the rise of militarism were common. We also take note of a new push for democracy in the early 1990s that ultimately bore little fruit.

The militarization of politics, new to Africa after independence, has a long history in Latin America. There, in countries large and small, postwar economic development was disappointing, and the disaffected classes—mainly laborers and landless farmers—continued to be victimized by a system of entrenched privilege that has endured for centuries. In Chapter 14, we examine the patterns of politics—the swings between democratic rule and militarism, particularly in Argentina, Brazil, Chile, and Peru. Next we turn to the struggle for economic progress and the opening up of the political process in Mexico. The problems were even more acute in Central America, where several Central American nations—notably Nicaragua and El Salvador—became hotbeds of revolution, a major concern for Washington. Finally, we take up the issue of the Latin American narcotics trade, centering on Colombia, and its connection to the US intervention in Panama.

In Chapter 15, we turn to East Asia to study the twists and turns of the Communist rule in the People's Republic of China as it attempted to put that huge nation on the track of economic development. China, the world's largest nation—with over 1 billion people in 1990—faced the problems of feeding a burgeoning population and maintaining political order. China was unique not only because of its size but because for almost three decades while under the rule of Mao Zedong, the political goal of creating a Communist society was given higher priority than economic development. From the late 1970s, however, China's new leader, Deng Xiaoping, gave priority to economic growth. We discuss Deng's economic liberalization as well as the lack of corresponding political liberalization, as seen in the crushing of the student demonstration in Tiananmen Square in Beijing in 1989. Next we turn to the other China—Taiwan—and its economic and political development and ongoing rivalry with Communist China.

The focus shifts in Chapter 16 to South Asia and Southeast Asia, where the trials and tribulations of India—the world's second-most-populous nation—Pakistan, and Bangladesh are given primary attention. We also examine briefly the politics and the economic surge of the Southeast Asian countries of Indonesia, Thailand, and Malaysia, and the problems of the Philippines, where a corrupt dictatorship was overthrown in 1986.

# 12

# The Challenges of Economic Development

In addition to the East-West ideological division, the world was also divided between the rich nations and the poor nations. Many of them were part of the Third World movement, which sought a semblance of political neutrality between the United States and the Soviet Union. Eventually, the term *Third World* became synonymous with poverty.

In the mid-1950s, French journalists coined the term *Third World* to describe nations that were neither part of the Western world nor of the Communist bloc (although time and again they tended to gravitate to one or the other). In April 1955, the leaders of these nations met for the first time at an Afro-Asian conference in the Indonesian resort of Bandung. The spiritual father of the nonaligned Third World movement was prime minister of India Jawaharlal Nehru. As early as 1947, after India had just gained its independence from Britain and the Cold War was already in bloom, Nehru declared that "we will not attach ourselves to any particular group," neither to the Communist nor the Western camp.[1] Seven years later, at Bandung, he called for an "unaligned area" as a buffer between the two camps, if only to lessen the danger of war between them.[2] When delegates at Bandung criticized "colonialism in all of its manifestations," it was a direct swipe at the remaining Western colonial presence in Asia and Africa, as well as the Soviet Union's presence in Eastern Europe.

Among the leading figures in attendance, besides Nehru, were Gamal Abdel Nasser (Egypt), Kwame Nkrumah (Ghana), Achem Sukarno (Indonesia), Zhou Enlai (China), and Josip Tito, the head of Yugoslavia, a Communist state that in 1948 had declared its independence from the Soviet Union without joining the US side. The representatives, who spoke for more than one-half of the world's population, had much in common. They had emerged as heroic figures in the postwar struggles for independence from colonial control. But now they had to devote their attention to the more mundane task of raising their peoples' standard of living. They tended to reject capitalism, the economic model of the former colonial powers, and instead opted for some variant of socialism. Officially, they were nonaligned in the Cold War, although some leaned toward the Soviet bloc and some toward the West. The tilt to one or the other bloc often depended on the assistance they received from either Washington or Moscow. Genuine neutrality was difficult to maintain, particularly because the superpowers constantly bid for the nonaligned nations' loyalty.

• • •

Increasingly, the term *Third World* gave way to what became known as the *global South*. Since about three-quarters of the world's wealth was produced and consumed by a relatively small proportion of the people in North, the focus increasingly was on a North-South division of the globe. The concept was popularized starting in the late 1960s by the West German foreign minister (and later chancellor) Willy Brandt, who argued that the East-West division could readily be overcome; the division between the haves in the North and the have-nots in the South, however, was much more difficult to resolve.

The disparity in wealth between the North and the South during the early 1990s may be seen in the figures in Table 12.1 on per capita gross national product (GNP).

The alarming increase in the gap between the impoverished South and the more prosperous North was the focus of an international conference in

**Table 12.1 Per Capita Gross National Product, 1990**

| | |
|---|---|
| *North* | |
| United States | $21,790 |
| Switzerland | $32,680 |
| Japan | $25,430 |
| West Germany (before unification) | $22,320 |
| | |
| *South* | |
| Sub-Saharan Africa | $340 |
| East Asia and the Pacific (without Japan) | $600 |
| South Asia | $330 |
| Middle East and North Africa | $1,790 |
| Latin America and the Caribbean | $2,180 |
| | |
| *World* | $4,200 |

*Source:* World Bank, *World Development Report 1992*, pp. 196, 218–219.

**Table 12.2  North vs. South, 1985**

|  | North | South |
|---|---|---|
| Population | 1.18 billion | 3.76 billion |
| Annual per capita GNP | $9,510 | $700 |
| Life expectancy | 73 years | 58 years |
| Annual rate of population growth | 0.6% | 2.0% |

*Source:* Population Reference Bureau, *1986 World Population Data Sheet.*

Cancún, Mexico, in September 1981. Figures presented at the conference indicated that the 140 countries that classified themselves as "developing nations" comprised 75 percent of the world's population but had only 20 percent of the world's income. These nations were developing, yet the gap between them and the North continued to grow larger in the 1980s (see Table 12.2).

The statistical average of $700 annual per capita GNP for the South in 1985 masked the great disparity in wealth among its member nations. In fact, per capita GNP for most sub-Saharan African countries was far below $700. According to World Bank figures, in 1984, Ethiopia had a per capita GNP of only $110—the lowest among African nations—followed by Mali ($140), Zaire ($140), and Burkina Faso ($160).[3] Moreover, most of the nations of Africa had low economic growth rates. At least fourteen African nations registered "negative growth," that is, a decline of the per capita GNP. Zaire, for example, had a negative growth rate of –1.2 percent and Uganda one of –3 percent for the decade between 1972 and 1982. The poor were getting poorer.

Adding to the problem was the great disparity in income. The maldistribution of wealth in the underdeveloped Southern nations was greater than that in the industrialized nations of the North.[4] Poverty was widespread among the rural workers, particularly the landless peasants, but hundreds of millions city-dwellers were similarly affected. The national per capita figures, which economists tend to cite, consist of averaging the wealth of the very rich with the pittance of the poor whose children go malnourished. In the mid-1980s, at least one-fifth of the earth's inhabitants lived in dire poverty and suffered from chronic hunger and malnutrition. Since then, poverty rates have diminished. The diminishing rates, however, are based on artificially low criteria. According to the World Bank, one is only truly poor if one had to subsist at the equivalent of $1.25 or less per day.

## The Population Factor

Population growth was a major factor in the persistence of poverty. In the twentieth century, the world's population grew at an alarming rate, but nowhere as rapidly as in the South. It took about 5 million years for the world's population to reach 1 billion, around the year 1800. The second billion was reached in about 130 years, by 1930; the third billion in 30 more years, by 1960; the fourth billion in 15 years, by 1975; and the fifth billion in only 11 years, by 1986. (See Figure 12.1.) That it took fourteen years (until 2000) to reach the 6 billion mark suggested a decline in the rate of growth. Yet the 7 billion mark came only twelve years later, in 2012.

The rate of population growth decreased since the mid-1960s. The rate peaked at 2.4 percent annually in 1964. By the mid-1990s, it fell to about 1.5 percent and to 1.1 percent in 2012.

Demographers are in agreement that one day the world will reach zero population growth, if only because it will have to, but no one knows the day. In 1968, the biologist Paul Ehrlich revived an argument popularized in 1798 by Thomas Malthus that population growth will lead to unmitigated disaster as the world runs out of food and scarce resources.[5] Along the way, Ehrlich became an international media celebrity. But there were skeptics. In 1980, Ehrlich and the economist Julian Simon made their famous bet on the future price of five commodity metals. Simon permitted Ehrlich to select the metals and the time frame. Ehrlich wagered that their increased scarcity over the next ten years would drive up their price; Simon bet prices would decline. Simon won the bet handily. When Ehrlich sent the "doomslayer" Simon the check it came without a note and without acknowledgment that he may have been wrong. In 2013, Ehrlich still defended his thesis, even saying that his doomsday scenario had been "much too optimistic."[6] The cause for widespread malnutrition and starvation, however, was not the result of overpopulation but poverty, the inability to purchase the food that was readily available.

In the global South, population growth rates were much higher than in the North. After World War II, the South witnessed a veritable population explosion, an increase at historically unprecedented rates. During the late 1980s in Africa, for example, many nations had growth rates of more than 3 percent, with some even exceeding 4 percent. It meant a doubling, even a tripling, of the population in less than a generation. During the 1970s and 1980s, Africa's growth rate of 3 percent was about nine times that of Europe and about three times that of the United States and Canada. In contrast, some industrialized nations—notably East Germany, West Germany, Austria, and Japan—attained a stable population (no growth at all) or even negative growth. As a case in point, see the comparison in Table 12.3 between Niger and the Netherlands in 2013. Industrial and agricultural output, never large to begin with, was all too often swallowed up by relentless population growth. In a span of twenty-three years, Africa's population of 450 million doubled; in 2013, it pushed past the 1 billion mark. The population growth rate in Kenya, in the 1970s, stood at 3.5 percent; by the mid-1980s it rose to 4.2 percent. Kenya's fertility rate (the

**Figure 12.1  Past and Project World Population, CE 1–2150**

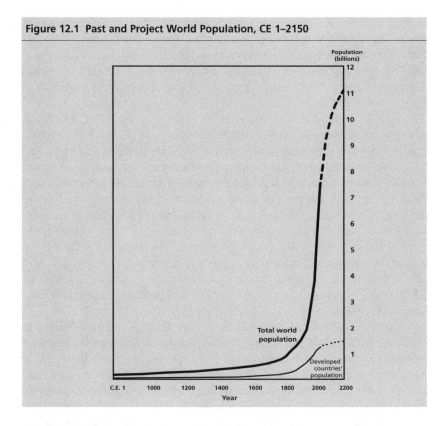

**Table 12.3  The Demographic Divide: Niger and the Netherlands**

|  | Niger | Netherlands |
|---|---|---|
| Population (2013) | 16.9 million | 16.8 million |
| Projected Population (2050) | 65.8 million | 17.9 million |
| 2050 Projected Population as a Multiple of 2013 | 3.9 | 1.1 |
| Lifetime Births per Woman | 7.6 | 1.7 |
| Annual Births | 845,000 | 176,000 |
| Annual Deaths | 195,000 | 141,000 |
| % of Population Below Age 15 | 50% | 17% |
| % of Population Ages 65+ (2013) | 3% | 16% |
| % of Population Ages 65+ (projected 2050) | 3% | 27% |
| Life Expectancy at Birth (all) | 57 years | 81 years |
| Infant Mortality Rate (per 1,000 live births) | 51 | 3.7 |
| Annual Number of Infant Deaths | 43,000 | 650 |

*Source:* Population Reference Bureau, "World Population Data Sheet, 2013"

average number of children born to a woman) was 8.0. These figures were among the highest in recorded history. In the forty years between 1969 and 2009, Kenya's population soared from 11 million to 39 million, a three-and-a-half-fold increase. But Kenya was not alone. Rwanda, Burundi, Zimbabwe, Tanzania, Uganda, Ghana, and Libya all had annual population growth rates approaching 4 percent.

How is the population explosion in the South to be explained? In briefest terms, the death rate fell while the birthrate either rose or remained constant. The introduction of modern medicines, the eradication of communicable diseases (such as smallpox), and improved public health and education all contributed to a reduction in infant mortality and increased life expectancy. But there was no corresponding decrease in fertility. In most developing countries, most families had at least four children and in rural areas often more than five. In these countries—similar to the developing European countries in the nineteenth century—the larger the number of children in a family, the greater the number of hands in the fields or in the factories, where they were able to earn money to supplement their parents' meager income. Having large families was a means to escape poverty and was, therefore, considered economically rational.

The responsibility for overpopulation in the South is often attributable to men, who tended to disdain artificial birth control and for whom having many children (particularly sons) was a sign of virility and moral rectitude. Yet, it was the women who bore the children and wound up caring for the large families. It was also true, however, that in much of the South, women typically shared the men's desire for many children.

Programs by governments and international agencies to control population growth initially met with mixed success. The most dramatic reduction of the birthrate occurred in China, where the Communist government instituted a stringent birth control program that included paramedical services, free abortions (even at near full term), public education, social pressure, and economic sanctions. Government-supported family-planning programs were moderately successful in a number of other countries, notably South Korea, Colombia, Mauritius, Sri Lanka, Argentina, Uruguay, and Egypt. In India, birth control programs had mixed results. They were generally more effective in regions where public education was more widespread.

Overpopulation in the South was compounded by an ongoing exodus of people from the countryside into already overcrowded cities in quest of a better life. In 1940, 185 million people lived in the South's cities; by 1975 the number rose more than fourfold, to 770 million. In the early 1970s, 12 million people a year—an estimated 33,000 a day—were arriving in the cities of the South.[7] At the beginning of the twentieth century, the world's largest cities had been the great industrial and commercial hubs (such as New York, Chicago, and London). By the end of the century, Southern cities supplanted them—Mexico City, São Paulo, Buenos Aires, Seoul, Calcutta, and Cairo. Most were so large that no accurate population count was possible, particularly as thousands of new squatters descended on them on a daily basis. In Africa in 1950, only three cities had a population of 500,000; thirty-five years later there were twenty-nine cities of at least that size. The urban population of Kenya doubled in a decade. The population of Lagos, Nigeria, grew incredibly from 300,000 in 1970 to over 3 million in 1983. Lists of the world's one hundred largest cities, in 2013, contain predominantly Southern cities.

Although the cities typically offered more and better employment opportunities, medical services, and education than the villages, they could not readily accommodate the massive influx of newcomers. They did not provide adequate employment, housing, sanitation, and other services for the numerous new inhabitants—many of whom remained unemployed and impoverished. A case in point was Mexico City. Its population doubled in a decade to over 18 million, with more than one-third of the new arrivals living in squatter settlements in one the world's largest slums. This scene was duplicated in other Southern cities. Many of the slums were world famous, such as the jerry-built *favelas* in Rio de Janeiro. In Cairo, an estimated half-million people lived in an ancient necropolis, millions more in Manshiyat Naser, also known as "Garbage City"; in Calcutta, nearly 1 million of the city's 10 million inhabitants lived in the streets; the shantytown on the outskirts of Lima, Peru, reached as far as the eye could see. The concentration of such huge numbers of disaffected peoples, living in the shadows of the edifices of the opulent class and often within marching distance of the centers of political power (many of the largest Southern cities are capital cities), heightened the potential for political unrest. In Mumbai (formerly Bombay), half of its 20 million residents lived in slums, trying to eke out a living by picking through the city's discarded garbage. Mumbai is also the site of *Antilia* (named after a mythical island), the house of India's wealthiest man, a twenty-seven-story-high, 400,000 square foot, 570-feet-high skyscraper, with every conceivable amenity, including nine elevators, helipads, a swimming pool, and a fifty-seat theater.

One of the most critical problems associated with overpopulation was how to feed the people. In the 1960s, television began to bring home to people in the North the tragedy of mass starvation in Ethiopia and Somalia, but most viewers remained unaware that hundreds of thousands of people in other African countries—including Sudan, Kenya, Mozambique, Chad, Mali, and Niger—also suffered from starvation. Estimates of the extent of world hunger varied greatly, depending in part on how hunger was defined, but there was little doubt that an enormous number of people in the South—perhaps 1 billion—were chronically malnourished.

In the late 1980s, international agencies singled out overpopulation as a leading factor threatening the quality of life. The UN Population Fund, in its Amsterdam Declaration of November 1989, emphasized that "women are in the center of the development process" and that their freedom to make choices "will be crucial in determining future population growth rates."[8] Without rights for women—legal, social, educational, and reproductive—there was little hope of solving the problem of rapid population growth. The Organization for Economic Cooperation and Development (OECD), in 1989, voiced a similar concern. It stressed that "women must be fully involved as decision makers in the planning and implementation of population programs."[9]

The World Bank's fifteenth annual *World Development Report* (1992) linked for the first time unchecked population growth with environmental degradation, slow economic growth, declining health care, and declining living standards. International agencies understood that to implement effective family-planning programs would not be easy because they frequently clashed with deeply entrenched cultural and religious values held particularly (but not exclusively) by adherents of Islam, Hinduism, and Roman Catholicism. Pope John Paul II, for instance, in his encyclical "On the Hundredth Anniversary of Rerum Novarum" (May 1991), denounced, as he had done before, all measures "suppressing or destroying the sources of life." Birth control, he declared, was responsible for "poisoning the lives of millions of defenceless human beings, as if in a form of 'chemical warfare.'"[10]

Still, since the mid-1960s the world witnessed another demographic trend, a considerable *decline* in the population growth rate, from 2.4 percent to 1.5 percent by the end of the century. The world was moving, if ever so slowly, toward the zero-growth fertility rate of 2.1 infants per female.

Conventional wisdom declared that a falling birthrate went hand-in-hand with prosperity. But the increasingly wider availability of birth control in many poorer countries upset this theory. One example was Bangladesh, which not only ranked among the poorest of nations, but was also overwhelmingly Muslim. The tenets of Islam prohibit family planning, yet 40 percent of that country's women used some sort of birth control. This trend produced a shift from the view that "development is the best contraceptive" to "contraceptives are the best contraceptives."[11] At a UN conference on population control in April 1994, Southern feminists produced statistics showing a correlation between higher female education and a lower fertility rate.[12]

By the end of 2013, the world's population stood at 7.2 billion. China, at 1.35 billion people, was still the most populous nation, followed closely by India with 1.22 billion and destined to overtake China in the not too distant future.[13] Africa remained the fastest growing continent, its population of 1 billion estimated to more than double by 2050. Of the twenty-one countries with the highest birthrates, nineteen were in Africa; of the seventeen countries with the highest fertility rate, fifteen were in sub-Saharan Africa.[14]

## The Agrarian Dilemma

Between the late 1960s and the late 1980s, food production in the South increased at about 3.1 percent annually, but population growth ate up this increase almost entirely. Although most Asian nations made considerable progress in agricultural production, fifty-five Southern nations—again most of them in Africa—registered a decline in food production per capita after 1970. In the early 1970s, the nations of the South collectively had been net exporters of food, but by the early 1980s they were net importers.

There were several major causal factors why many nations of the South, all of them primarily agrarian, were unable to increase their food production to a level of self-sufficiency.

1. *Natural causes.* Most Southern nations are in the tropics, where the climate is often very hot and where extended droughts, torrential rainstorms, cyclones, and flooding occur. Desertification is a major problem in Africa, where the Sahara Desert has pushed its frontier southward into the Sahel, a stretch of land running from West Africa eastward into Sudan. Parts of eastern and southern Africa have suffered from prolonged drought.

2. *Abuse of the land.* Great amounts of topsoil are lost to wind and water erosion every year, in part because of climate conditions, in part because of human activity such as deforestation, overgrazing, and overcultivation, all of which exhaust the land's nutrients.

3. *Primitive farming methods.* Most peasants in the South work with simple tools, many with nothing more than a hoe, and much of the plowing is still done with draft animals. Peasants are usually too poor to afford modern equipment. In some instances, intensive farming with traditional methods and tools is efficient, especially in the case of paddy farming (rice growing) in Asia, but in many other areas—especially in Africa—toiling in parched fields with hand tools is an inefficient mode of production. In some parts of Africa, agricultural work was done by women. Traditionally, African men were hunters and herdsmen, and women worked in the fields. With the depletion of wild game, few men continued to hunt. Too proud to toil in the fields, however, men either supervised women or sought other employment. A 1985 UN report, *State of the World's Women*, estimated that between 60 and 80 percent of farmwork in Africa was still done by women.[15]

4. *Inequality of landholdings.* Throughout the South, agricultural production often suffered because the majority of the peasants had too little land and many were tenants burdened with huge rent payments. In 1984, an international study concluded that in Latin America 80 percent of the farmland was owned by 8 percent of landowners, and the poorest peasants—66 percent of all landowners—were squeezed onto only 4 percent of the land.[16]

5. *Lack of capital for agricultural development.* Southern food-producing farmers all too often lacked irrigation, modern equipment, chemical fertilizers,

storage facilities, and improved transport. Yet all too often, their governments were unwilling or unable to supply the capital needed to provide these essentials.

6. *One-crop economies.* In many Southern nations, the best land with the best irrigation belonged to wealthy landowners (including multinational corporations), who grew cash crops—peanuts, cocoa, coffee, and so on—for export rather than food for domestic consumption. It was based on the widely held dogma that economic progress depended on the sale of cash crops to the developed countries. It made United Fruit and Nestlé wealthy, but at the expense of food sufficiency. Dependence on a single cash crop for export, moreover, placed the developing nations at the mercy of the world market, where competition was fierce and where prices fluctuated greatly. This situation proved disastrous when prices of agricultural exports sharply dropped while prices of necessary imports (especially petroleum, fertilizers, and finished goods) rose.

These problems tended to be caused by the political leaders rather than the farmers. To solve them, governments needed to initiate programs of land redistribution, diversification of agriculture, and the building of irrigation systems, roads, storage facilities, fertilizer plants, and agricultural schools. But these efforts required a large amount of capital, political stability, and strong and able political leadership—all of which were frequently lacking. There were easier ways to find money for skyscrapers and jet planes than for the impoverished agricultural sector.

A number of Southern nations obtained relief in the form of shipments of food from abroad to feed their people. Although such aid was beneficial and humane, it did not go to the root of the problem and, in fact, often did not reach the intended recipients who needed it most.

## Prerequisites for Industrialization

Upon gaining independence, the former colonies looked forward to rapid progress as independent nations, hoping to close the gap that separated them from the wealthier nations. They saw industrial development as the primary road to economic modernization. Along the way, however, they tended to neglect agriculture and its role in economic development. They expected progress to be rapid, but found to their dismay that industrial development was a difficult process. The following prerequisites—the minimal necessary conditions for industrialization—were often lacking in the Southern countries.

1. *Capital accumulation.* Money for investments to build plants and buy equipment has to come from somewhere: the World Bank, foreign powers (which usually seek to gain political or military leverage), heavy taxation

(often falling upon people who can least afford it), or the export of raw materials or cash crops. This last method of capital accumulation often led to an anomaly: With the focus on cash crops and the attendant neglect of growing food, agrarian nations found themselves importing expensive food, often from the developed nations. Thus money tended to flow out of their economies rather than in.

The South received substantial sums of capital from abroad for many years, but too often it was mismanaged, squandered on unproductive projects, used to strengthen the military (the main function of which was to control the population), or simply siphoned off by corrupt leaders who became fabulously wealthy. Available capital was spent time and again on expensive imports for those in power—luxury items of every sort, weapons, automobiles, showcase airports, hotels, and the like—and not on the economic substructure for industrial and agricultural growth, which would benefit the population as a whole. Thus, in the cities of the South, ostentatious display of wealth coexisted with grinding poverty—elegant mansions in one part of town and tin-roof hovels in another.

Moreover, overreliance on outside financial aid came with strings attached. It led to foreign intrusions into national sovereignty. The loans led to excessive indebtedness, turning the developing nations into debtors beholden to their former colonial masters.

2. *Technology.* To compete with the industrial world, developing nations must rapidly incorporate new technology. But technology transfer is a complicated matter, and its acceptance and implementation in tradition-bound societies can be a slow process. Meanwhile, technological change in developed nations was rapid, and developing countries too often fell farther behind.

3. *Education.* An industrialized society requires an educated, literate workforce—assembly-line workers, engineers, and managers. Mass education in the South remained a costly long-term and incomplete process.

4. *Favorable trading conditions.* The system of international trade designed by the industrial West after World War II was meant primarily to serve its interests—rather than the developing world. Southern nations sought trade agreements that would underwrite their exports with guaranteed minimum purchases at prices not to fall below a fixed level. At the same time, however, they wanted to maintain higher tariffs on imports to protect their native industries.

5. *Political stability.* Economic growth requires stability. Domestic strife and wars are disruptive and costly, draining off the meager resources for economic development. (Nearly all of the wars since 1945 were fought in Southern countries. The list seems endless: China, Korea, Vietnam, Iran, Iraq, Afghanistan, Ethiopia, Angola, Chad, Nigeria, Lebanon, India, Pakistan, El Salvador, Nicaragua, and so on.) Even Southern nations not engaged in wars spent an extraordinary amount on sophisticated weapons, which they did not

need nor were readily able to afford. By necessity, the expensive weapons had to be from the industrialized powers—primarily the United States and Soviet Union.

## Debt and the Global South:
## Africa and Latin America

The 1970s saw the emergence of a phenomenon with potentially serious international repercussions: the increasing indebtedness of the South to the industrial First World. Traditionally, nations seeking to develop economically rely upon capital from abroad. This was true of the industrial revolutions in England, the Netherlands, the United States, and Russia. Foreign capital—in the form of profits from sales abroad, loans, or capital investments—has long been a catalyst for speeding up the expensive process of industrialization.

Prerevolutionary tsarist Russia drew heavily upon foreign capital and foreign engineers to begin the industrialization process. Stalin's industrial revolution of the 1930s, in contrast, was accomplished largely without foreign assistance. In the early 1960s it became one of the models considered by a number of newly independent nations of the South. Their economic planners found out, however, that their economic base was so primitive in contrast to what Stalin had inherited from the tsars, that they had little choice but to turn to capital available from the industrialized world.

Until the oil crises of the 1970s, reliance on foreign money was kept in bounds. The money borrowed was doled out in reasoned, and at times sparse, amounts—until the surfeit of "petrodollars" (that is, money invested in Western banks by the oil-rich nations) created a binge of lending by these same banks and an orgy of borrowing by the developing South. There appeared to be no limit to the banks' willingness to extend credit and the recipients' willingness to take it. Foreign capital promised the road out of the wilderness, generating rapid economic development and, with it, the ability to repay the loans (even at high interest rates). By the mid-1980s, the result was a staggering debt among Latin American and African nations in excess of $500 billion, a sum far beyond the capacity of the debtor nations to repay. Many were staring bankruptcy in the face and, if they defaulted, they threatened to cause great damage to lending institutions and the international banking system.

### Africa

The African debt had its roots in the political instability that followed independence, which resulted in frequent government turnovers, secessionist movements, and civil wars. Among the first casualties were the budding democratic institutions. Political and military considerations took precedence over economic development, for the first priority of the dictators was the retention of power. Precious resources were diverted to the military, whose main task was not so much the defense of the nation against a foreign foe, but the suppression of domestic opposition.

Political instability led to the flight of Europeans, who took with them their skills and capital. This was the case particularly in the new states where independence was won by force and where a legacy of bitterness and mistrust remained after the violence subsided. Algeria, Mozambique, Angola, Zimbabwe (formerly Southern Rhodesia), the Belgian Congo, and Kenya readily come to mind. The exodus left many African nations with a badly depleted industrial base and a continued reliance on the primitive agricultural sector.

Until the late 1970s, the African economies limped along, but then the roof began to cave in when a number of deleterious conditions came together. The result was that much of the continent was bankrupted. First came the oil crisis with its accompanying rise in the cost of crude oil. The crisis had a greater impact on the poorer nations than on the industrial West, which had the means of meeting the higher payments. (Although several oil-producing nations of sub-Saharan Africa, such as Nigeria and Cameroon, benefited from the new, higher price tag on oil, most suffered greatly. And when oil prices began to fall in the early 1980s, Nigeria was among the hardest hit, having become saddled with mounting debts and attendant political instability.) In the West, the oil crisis contributed to a global recession, which in turn lessened the demand for raw materials. The prices for copper, bauxite (aluminum ore), and diamonds fell. Prices for agricultural exports fell similarly, as a result of a worldwide glut in agricultural commodities that played havoc with the African economies. Cacao, coffee, cotton, peanuts, and such no longer brought the prices African exporters had been accustomed to. After 1979–1980, prices for African commodity exports declined by as much as 30 percent. All the while, the price for goods manufactured in the West—such as machinery, tools, electronics, and weapons—continued to rise.

Appreciation of foreign currencies, particularly the US dollar, added to the dilemma. Since the debts of nations were calculated in US dollars, the increasing purchasing power of the dollar in the early 1980s played havoc with the pay rate of debtor nations. Debts now had to be repaid in dollars with greater purchasing power. It meant that Southern nations had to export more. Indeed, this condition—as well as high interest payments—forced African nations to repay more than they had borrowed.

As Africa's indebtedness to the industrial world increased during the first half of the 1980s, the poorest continent became a net exporter of capital. On average, African nations used 25 percent of their foreign currency earnings to repay their foreign debts. They were reaching the point where they were cannibalizing their economies and social programs (notably health and education) to meet their debt obligations. After more than three decades, that dilemma remained. Between 1970 and 2003, African countries borrowed $540 billion and repaid $580 billion in debt service (principal and interest), yet remained saddled with a crippling debt of over $300 billion—$108 billion owed by the Arabic-speaking states in the north and $194 billion by sub-Saharan Africa.[17]

Africa reached a point where it could neither repay its debt nor borrow any appreciable sums of money. Significant foreign investment in Africa declined after 1980. The continent was on a treadmill, pledged to come up with interest payments over an indefinite period to the industrialized West and its banks. Under such circumstances, indebtedness to the West became a permanent fixture, as there was no question of making a dent in the principal (that is, the debt itself). The African nations listed in Table 12.4 increased their foreign debts between 1987 and 1990.

Predictably, African leaders pointed an accusing finger at the international banking system. In July 1985, the African heads of government met under the aegis of the Organization of African Unity (OAU) in Addis Ababa, Ethiopia's capital, to address this bleak situation. They placed part of the blame on an "unjust and inequitable [international] economic system," but they also acknowledged that natural calamities such as droughts, as well as "some domestic policy shortcomings," had contributed to Africa's problems. The chair of the OAU, Tanzanian president Julius Nyerere, hinted at the creation of a defaulter's club, which sought the cancellation of government-to-government loans and the restructuring of interest rates in order to avoid default and, with it, national bankruptcy. African politicians considered their national obligations as illegitimate, "odious debts," a principle that indeed can be found in international law. The Western lenders, in their turn, saw the debts as legal, binding national obligations. The task was to find a compromise with which both could live. But the debtors would not be permitted to walk away from their obligations, a common practice in the developed world.[18]

**Table 12.4  African Nations with Foreign Debt Increases, 1987–1990**

| Nation | Debt in 1987 (US$, billions) | Debt in 1990 (US$, billions) | Percentage Increase, 1987–1990 |
|--------|------------------------------|------------------------------|--------------------------------|
| Nigeria | $28.7 | $36.1 | 26 |
| Ivory Coast | 13.5 | 17.9 | 33 |
| Sudan | 11.1 | 15.4 | 39 |
| Zaire | 8.6 | 10.1 | 17 |
| Zambia | 6.4 | 7.2 | 13 |
| Kenya | 5.9 | 6.8 | 15 |
| Tanzania | 4.3 | 5.9 | 37 |

*Source:* World Bank, *World Development Report, 1989,* p. 205; World Bank, *World Development Report, 1992,* p. 258.

It took the Western nations another decade to come around to a discussion of debt relief, even cancellation—but only for the most desperately poor nations. The Club of Paris, an informal group of officials from the wealthiest nations, sought in the mid-1990s to find solutions to the developing nations' insurmountable debts, which ran to $2 trillion. The World Bank and the International Monetary Fund (IMF) followed the lead of the club's 1996 Heavily Indebted Poor Countries (HIPC) initiative to provide relief to 41 of the poorest nations (more than three-quarters of them in Africa). By July 2006, 21 nations received 100 percent IMF–World Bank debt cancellation; others had their debts brought down to more sustainable levels. By 2005, about one-third of the debt was cancelled, which, however, still left the HIPC nations with about $90 billion in debt.[19] In September 2013, 39 "heavily indebted poor countries" qualified for help of one sort or another under the IMF's debt relief program.[20]

### Latin America

In the late 1970s, Latin America witnessed sharp economic downturns similar to the ones in Africa, and for similar reasons. The rapid increase in oil prices in the 1970s and the drop in agricultural commodity prices produced a decline in the standard of living.

Latin America has long been a region of economic promise. This was especially the case with Brazil, a land of seemingly unlimited potential. On the basis of future earnings, Brazil borrowed huge sums of money during the 1970s. Within a decade, the borrowing binge came back to haunt it. By 1987, Brazil's foreign debt was well over $120 billion, and in 2003 it was more than $220 billion. The best that Brazil could do was to make interest payments and thus avoid a declaration of bankruptcy. Should Brazil go bankrupt, it threatened not only its own economic health, but also the international banking system. For that reason, despite its staggering debt, Brazil was able to demand additional loans until the time—sometime in the future—it would begin to repay the principal.

Argentina was another Latin American nation that accumulated a large foreign debt. It had traditionally been a nation with a strong and vigorous economy, which made it relatively easy to borrow money from abroad. But a succession of military regimes (1976–1983) contributed to weaken its economy. The regimes' brutality (see Chapter 14) and a losing war with Great Britain over the Falkland Islands in 1983 brought the return to civilian rule that year. At that time, Argentina's foreign debt was thought to be about $24 billion—a large sum by anyone's yardstick. The new civilian government discovered, however, that the military had in fact run up a debt of twice that amount, some $48 billion, at the time the third-largest foreign debt (after Brazil and Mexico) among the developing countries.

The oil shortages of the late 1970s did not initially harm Mexico's economy. Instead, they appeared to work to its benefit, for Mexico's oil reserves were potentially among the world's largest. Indeed, oil promised to solve Mexico's economic problems, caused in part by its large and rapidly growing population, weak industrial base, and inefficient agricultural system. Mexico was able to borrow large sums in the expectation that oil prices would remain high. In short, Mexico borrowed against future income. At the end of 1981, its foreign debt was at about $55 billion. Four years later, that figure had risen to well above $100 billion.

By 1990, Latin America's leading debtors, unlike those of Africa, had a measure of success in reducing their debts—through a combination of increasing exports, selling off equity, and debt cancellation by lenders. Still, the external debt grew. In the mid-1980s, Latin America's obligation to international lending institutions stood at $360 billion; by 2007, it had ballooned to more than $820 billion. As in the past, the leading borrowers were Brazil (holding steady at $224 billion), Mexico (up to $180 billion), and Argentina (up to $136 billion). Chile, Venezuela, Colombia, South Africa, and Peru owed, in descending order, somewhere between $50 billion and $31 billion.[21] At the end of 2012, Brazil's and Mexico's external debt stood, respectively, at $428 and $352 billion, but with their economies improving, their debts became manageable.[22]

## The South's Continuing Poverty

In the 1960s, when many Southern nations gained independence, there existed already a wide gap between the poor nations and the rich nations. By the end of the century, however, the gap for most of these nations was even wider. While per capita GNP figures for most industrialized countries consistently rose ever higher, those for the South rose only slightly, sometimes not at all. Per capita GNP for the industrialized nations remained as much as 100 times higher than that of the poorest countries in the South.

The GNP figures, it should be noted, did not give a complete picture of the standard of living in developing nations since much of the economy is informal. GNP statistics tend to understate real income in the poorer nations because many of their people meet their needs by barter or payment in kind—such as services in return or a sharecropping arrangement—an informal agreement not measured and thus not reflected in GNP figures. To go beyond measurable economic statistics to assess the quality of life, the UN conducted a "human development" survey, assessing and ranking the world's nations on such matters such as health care, life expectancy, education levels, access to clean water, as well as income. But even in this assessment, published in the annual UN "Human Development Index" released in June 2000, Southern nations generally ranked in the bottom half. At the very bottom of the list were twenty-four African countries. The rankings for 2012 saw virtually no change, yet at the same time they reveal the "Rise of the South," as reflected in economic progress in countries such as Turkey, Mexico, South Africa, and Indonesia.[23]

Not all Southern countries, however, remained mired in poverty at the end of the twentieth century. Some made moderate economic gains, and a few others, particularly in East Asia (notably South Korea and China), made significant progress and were able to reach the ranks of newly industrializing countries.

## Notes

1. Nehru's foreign policy address to India's Constituent Assembly, December 4, 1947, in Dorothy Norman, ed., *Nehru: The First Sixty Years*, vol. 2 (New York: John Day, 1965), pp. 353–356.

2. See Nehru's address to the Bandung Conference, in G. M. Kahin, *The Asian-African Conference* (Ithaca, NY: Cornell University Press, 1956), pp. 54–72.

3. GNP, or gross national product, is the wealth—the total goods and services—a nation produces per year. Another yardstick, the GDP, or gross domestic product, is made up of the market value of goods, services, and expenditures (including wages). The per capita GNP or GDP  is calculated by dividing the figure for wealth generated (calculated in US dollars) by the nation's population.

4. See Paul Harrison, *Inside the Third World*, 2nd ed. (New York: Penguin, 1984), pp. 414–415.

5. Paul R. Ehrlich, *The Population Bomb* (New York: Ballantine Books, 1968); Thomas Malthus, *An Essay on the Principle of Population* (1798).

6. Michael Charles Tobias, "The Ehrlich Factor: A Brief History of the Fate of Humanity, with Dr. Paul R. Ehrlich," *Forbes*, January 16, 2013.

7. Ibid., p. 145.

8. For the text of the Amsterdam Declaration, see *Population and Development Review*, March 1990, pp. 186–192.

9. For the text of the OECD's statement, see "Population and Development—DAC Conclusions," *Population and Development Review*, September 1990, pp. 595–601.

10. "Pope John Paul II on Contemporary Development," *Population and Development Review*, September 1991, p. 559. The citations are from Chapter 4 of the encyclical.

11. The statement is by Bryant Robey of the Johns Hopkins School of Hygiene and Public Health and the editor of *American Demographics*, cited in William K. Stevens, "Poor Lands' Success in Cutting Birth Rate Upsets Old Theories," *New York Times*, January 2, 1994, p. 8.

12. Susan Chira, "Women Campaign for New Plan to Curb the World's Population," *New York Times*, April 13, 1994, pp. A1, A12.

13. CIA, *The World Factbook*, 2013.

14. CIA, *The World Factbook*, 2008.

15. Barber Conable, president of the World Bank, at a joint World Bank–International Monetary Fund meeting, stated that women did two-thirds of the world's work, earned 10 percent of the world's income, and owned less than 1 percent of the world's property. As such, women remained "the poorest of the world's poor."

Clyde Farnsworth, "World Bank Chief Outlines Strategy," *New York Times*, October 1, 1986, p. D23.

16. Harrison, *Inside the Third World*, p. 455.

17. Africa Action, "Africa Action Statement on 100% Debt Cancellation for Africa," September 23, 2005; CIA, *The World Factbook*, 2008.

18. Robert Kuttner, "The Debt We Shouldn't Pay," *New York Review of Books*, May 9, 2013.

19. Jubilee USA Network, "The Unfinished Agenda on International Debt," *Spotlight*, July 2006; "At Last, $350 Billion Debt Write-off in Sight for Africa," *The East African*, April 18, 2005.

20. International Monetary Fund, "Debt Relief Under the Heavily Indebted Poor Countries (HIPC) Initiative," October 1, 2013.

21. CIA, *The World Factbook*, 2008.

22. CIA, *The World Factbook*, 2013.

23. United Nations, "Rankings of World's Nations in Human Development," 2000 and 2013. Among the nations in the South, in 2000, Cuba ranked highest (56th), followed by Belize, Panama, Venezuela, Colombia, and Brazil.

# 13

# Africa

In the early 1960s, when most African nations gained their independence, proud African leaders heralded the dawn of a new age. Freed from the shackles of European colonialism, they looked confidently to a new political and economic order that promised an end to the continent's economic backwardness and its dependence on the West. But the euphoria of the early 1960s soon gave way to a more somber reality. As years went by, economic growth, national self-reliance, and African unity remained elusive. Indeed, forty years later those dreams were in shambles, as most African countries had become increasingly impoverished and more dependent on foreign aid than ever before. Across the continent one found declining economies, grinding poverty, civil strife, corruption, crop failures, hungry and starving people, disease, overcrowded and deteriorating cities, massive unemployment, and growing numbers of refugees.

Many of the problems were man-made, exacerbated by the political turmoil. In one African country after another, democratic rule gave way to military rule, and several countries experienced a series of military coups. Many countries were torn apart by civil wars among ethnic groups. Often the flames were fanned by the rival superpowers who armed the combatants.

Africa had the world's lowest economic growth rates, highest infant mortality rates, and highest population growth rates. In the 1970s, the population of Africa grew at about twice the rate of the increase in food production. Chronic malnutrition and starvation became more common in subsequent years. Perhaps as many as 200,000 people succumbed to starvation in the Ethiopian famine in the early 1970s, and another famine a decade later—more publicized than the earlier one—took an equally large toll.

The focus on Ethiopia diverted attention from the hundreds of thousands of people malnourished and on the verge of starvation in Sudan, Chad, Niger, and Mali, nations affected by the relentless expansion of the Sahara Desert. Farther south, countries such as Kenya, Uganda, Gabon, and Mozambique were also drought-stricken. The Economic Commission for Africa, a UN agency, reported that from 1960 to 1975 there had been no significant improvement in most African nations' economies. In 1960, Africa had been 95 percent self-sufficient in food, but twenty-five years later every African country except South Africa was a net importer of food.

By far the most prosperous nation on the continent was South Africa, which stood as an exception to the economic decline characteristic of the remainder of sub-Saharan Africa. In the 1980s, South Africa's per capita income was more than $12,500, far higher than that of any other African country. Whites had one of the highest standards of living in the world. Blacks, however, who outnumbered whites by three to one, earned only about one-sixth of what white workers were paid. Nigeria, burdened with Africa's largest population and yet blessed with large deposits of oil, prospered following independence, only to find its economy in collapse as a result of political corruption and plummeting world oil prices in the 1970s. An examination of per capita GNP growth rates in the decade after 1973 reveals that black African nations were either struggling to maintain marginal economic progress, marking time, or actually declining. According to World Bank figures, only Benin, Botswana, Cameroon, the People's Republic of Congo, Ivory Coast, and Rwanda had marginal growth. Fourteen countries had a decline in per capita GNP.[1] Most tragic were those states that had displayed the potential for economic growth and had made progress in the first decade of independence only to slide backward, such as Ghana, Nigeria, Kenya, Uganda, Zimbabwe, and Zaire.

## Political Instability in Sub-Saharan Africa

Africa's problems were both economic and political in nature. Political chaos followed economic disaster; conversely, political problems contributed to economic woes. Following independence, African nations witnessed the steady erosion of democratic institutions and the steady militarization of politics. After initial trial runs in parliamentary democracy, elected governments often retained power by eliminating or subverting the electoral process. Subsequently, military coups—not popular elections—became the primary vehicle for the transfer of power. Dictatorships became common throughout Africa, where about three-quarters of the governments were controlled either by one-party regimes or by military strongmen. Only about a half-dozen states in sub-Saharan Africa permitted opposition parties to engage in the political process, and until 1991 no African head of state was ever voted out of office.

Under such circumstances, political repression became the order of the day. In Uganda, Zimbabwe, Zaire, and Guinea political opponents were routinely massacred. And more often than not, African leaders were as corrupt as they were repressive.

## The Colonial Legacy

Many African leaders were quick to blame a century of European colonialism for their nations' problems. It was true that after a century of dependency on Europeans, Africans were ill prepared for the task of nation-building. Time and again, the Europeans had left too abruptly, leaving behind political institutions that few Africans, beyond a small circle of Western-educated elites, appreciated or well understood. Also, the Europeans did little to develop national economies in their colonies. Instead, they had mainly built up enterprises that focused on export commodities such as coffee, cacao, copper, and bauxite. The economic system the newly independent African nations inherited had been designed for export rather than for producing goods for domestic consumption. These export-oriented economies, moreover, were directly linked with the former colonial power instead of with African neighbors.

Perhaps the most baleful legacy of European colonialism was the artificiality of the national boundaries it had created. In the nineteenth century, the Europeans hastily drew new boundaries with little or no recognition of the ethnic makeup of Africa. One British commissioner later joked: "In those days we just took a blue pencil and a rule, and we put it down at Old Calabar, and drew that blue line up to Yola. . . . I recollect thinking when I was sitting having an audience with the [local] Emir . . . it was a very good thing that he did not know that I . . . had drawn a line through his territory."[2] Nonetheless, the new African nations kept these boundaries as they fended off ethnic conflicts and secessionist wars. The boundaries drawn by the Europeans ensured that the newly independent states were much larger than the precolonial units and thus contained many more ethnic groups. Not surprisingly, they were much more difficult to manage than the smaller states. Only two countries in sub-Saharan Africa—Lesotho and Swaziland—retained ethnic uniformity. All others had mixed populations made up of many different ethnic entities. The most extreme cases, such as Nigeria and the former Belgian Congo, had more than 200 diverse ethnic groups with their own distinct languages, histories, and traditions. The new nations were artificial constructs, and their rulers had the difficult task of superimposing a new national identity over the existing ethnic configurations. In most instances ethnic identity prevailed over nationalism—a relatively new and foreign concept—to the detriment of the process of nation-building. The results were bloody civil wars, secessionist wars, and even genocide. Ethnic strife claimed a frightful toll on life in Nigeria during the Biafran War in the

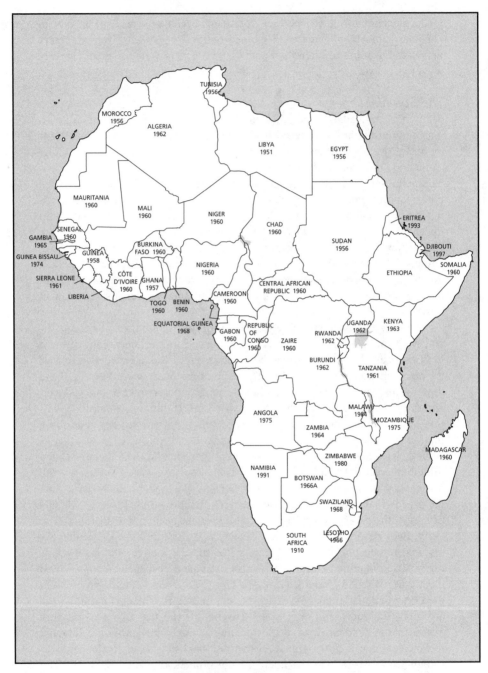

**Africa After Independence**
(with year of independence)

1960s; in Rwanda and Burundi in the 1960s, 1970s, and again in the 1990s; in South Africa in the 1990s; and in Darfur starting in the late 1970s.

Tribalism is a legacy not of colonialism but rather of African history. It persisted during the colonial era—in some places strengthened by colonial policy, in others diluted—and remained strong after independence. Typically, an African's strongest loyalties were to family and ethnic group (tribe). Given the relative lack of geographic mobility in Africa, people of one ethnic group maintained local roots and mixed little with others. Governments often represented one dominant ethnic group to the exclusion and expense of others.

Tribalism and corruption were closely intertwined. In African kinship-based societies, communal elders were entrusted with authority not only to make decisions binding for the group, but also to divide the wealth among its members. Politics often thus degenerated into ethnic contests for the spoils of power. Kenyans, for instance, found out that independence benefited primarily one ethnic group, the Kikuyus.

The combination of unbridled corruption and the cult of personality in Africa produced some of the world's most outrageous displays of extravagance. Not a few rulers lived in regal splendor in fabulous palaces, owned fleets of luxury cars, and stashed vast amounts of money in Western banks. For bizarre extravagance none exceeded Colonel Jean-Bedel Bokassa, emperor of the Central African Republic, who spent about $20 million—one-quarter of his nation's revenue—on his coronation ceremony in 1977. He wore a robe bedecked with 2 million pearls that cost $175,000 and donned a $2 million crown topped with a 138-carat diamond. This in a country that had no more than 170 miles of paved roads. Two years later, Bokassa was deposed.

Most of the newly independent nations inherited a parliamentary system in which executive power was in the hands of a prime minister who was elected by and responsible to a popularly elected legislative body. Typically, prime ministers revised the constitutions to grant themselves broad executive powers and longer terms of office. They made sure to wield power in their own right rather than remain beholden to the legislature. Without an effective check on their new authority, they refused to tolerate political opposition. They argued that opposition parties were divisive, a threat to political stability, even unpatriotic, and thus needed to be abolished. They rejected the principle of a "loyal opposition," namely, an out-of-power political party opposed to the party in power but loyal to the nation and qualified to govern if elected.

African dictators replaced local officials with ruling party members and cronies loyal to them, bought the loyalties of others, made sure to control all outlets of information (the press, radio, television), and subjected their people to a heavy dose of propaganda to construct a cult of personality. When all else failed, they used military force to suppress dissent and to terrorize the population.

## The Militarization of African Politics

African leaders could not always be certain of the loyalty of the military, and this proved to be their Achilles' heel. In many nations, military revolts supplanted presidential dictators with military dictators.[3] The overthrow of Ghana's Kwame Nkrumah in 1966 gave rise to a wave of military coups across Africa, and by 1980, no fewer than sixty coups had taken place. In Benin, between 1963 and 1972, there were five military coups and another ten attempted coups. Ambitious officers had little difficulty in finding cause to overthrow unpopular corrupt rulers. Some promised to restore rule to civilian politicians, but few actually did so. Others, like Zaire's Joseph Mobutu, retired their military uniforms and became presidents; still others became victims of subsequent military coups. Most of the earlier coups were carried out by high-ranking officers, but as time went on, lower-ranking officers and even non-commissioned officers thrust themselves into power behind the barrel of a gun. In Sierra Leone, army generals took power in 1967 but were overthrown several months later by other army officers, who in turn were soon ousted by a sergeants' revolt.

The public would often welcome the new military dictators only to find out that the new crop of leaders was no more prepared to govern effectively than the politicians they had ousted. And as they became more tyrannical and as corrupt as those they had overthrown, they quickly lost popular support and became ripe for overthrow by other military officers.

In Ghana, a nation once looked upon as the pacesetter in Africa's drive for self-determination, its first leader, the charismatic Kwame Nkrumah, inherited a nation that, in the early 1960s, had the second-highest per capita income in Africa. As the leading champion of pan-Africanism, Nkrumah became the spokesman for the liberation and unity of all of Africa. His economic program—based on what he called "African socialist principles" suitable for "Ghanaian conditions" (which he was never able to explain adequately)—entailed the nationalization of industries and state planning.[4] Ghana's economy, however, depended largely on agriculture. By the 1960s, it became the victim of a drastic decline in the world price for cocoa, its principal cash crop. In the decade after independence, its price fell to one-third of its previous level.

In 1964, Nkrumah declared all opposition parties to be illegal. His extravagance, cult of personality, and unwillingness to listen to others did not sit well with many Ghanaians. With the pressures of a struggling economy and popular unrest mounting, the volatile Nkrumah jailed opposition leaders and critics. Finally, when he was away on a visit to Communist China, in February 1966, the army toppled his regime.

In the years that followed, as coup followed coup, Ghana became the epitome of political instability. The officers who grasped power in 1966 made good on their promise to restore civilian rule, but in 1969 a group of junior officers staged another military coup. For a while, Ghana alternated between civilian and military rule. In 1979, a young air force flight lieutenant, Jerry Rawlings, shot his way into power. He made good, however, on his promise to give democracy another chance. He stepped down, only to once again seize power by force at the end of 1981. Despite a host of problems, however, Rawlings remained popular; in 1992 and again in 1996, he won multiparty elections. In 2000, he decided again to leave office—in compliance with the constitutional limit of two terms—provided the election was "fair, genuine and sincere."[5]

Few of Africa's military men exceeded the brutality of Idi Amin of Uganda. In 1971, Amin—an army officer—staged a coup that ended the dictatorship of Milton Obote. Soon Amin found scapegoats for Uganda's economic and social ills, blaming several minority tribes and the country's East Asian (mainly Indian) residents. In 1972, Amin forcefully expelled some 50,000 Asians, an act detrimental to the nation's economy since many of them were merchants and professionals. As conditions worsened, Amin resorted to torture, public execution, and assassination. Before his removal from power, Amin had massacred an estimated 250,000 of his people, caused about as many to flee the country, and left Uganda's economy in shambles. After surviving a number of plots against his life, he was finally overthrown in 1979 by a force from Tanzania, which then installed a civilian government. In 1980, Milton Obote returned to power. Obote's military "cleanup operations" never succeeded in restoring order. In the end, he eventually killed almost as many people as Amin and caused another wave of refugees to flee Uganda.

## The Biafran War

Nigeria provides yet another case of militarization and a stark lesson on the consequences of ethnic warfare. During the early years of independence, no country made greater efforts to overcome ethnic disunity, yet none spilled more blood in ethnic strife in the aftermath of independence. At the time of independence, Nigeria, Africa's most populous nation and one of its wealthiest, was a federal republic of three self-governing regions, each dominated by a major ethnic group—the Hausa-Fulani (mostly Muslim) in the north (approximately 15 million strong), the Yoruba in the west (15 million), and the Ibo in the southeast region (10 million). After independence, tensions remained high among the three factions as each feared domination by the other. The first census in independent Nigeria only added to the suspicion that the northerners were about to abolish the federal system of power-sharing. The census, manipulated by northerners, declared that the north region contained an absolute majority of the population and thus could create a government dominated by Hausas and Fulanis. The census upset the balance of power, charged the political atmosphere, and set the stage for the political crisis that followed.[6]

In January 1966, military officers—mainly Ibos—staged a coup and established a military regime under General J. T. Ironsi. The northerners, who were mainly Muslims, feared and resented the largely Christian and better-educated Ibos, who had enjoyed commercial and political privileges under British rule. The northerners saw the coup as an attempt to destroy the power of the Hausa-Fulani oligarchy.

At the end of May 1966, the northern general, Yakubu Gowon, staged his own coup and kidnapped (and later murdered) Ironsi and members of his government. It was at this point that the first wave of assaults against Ibos took place, first in the north, where tens of thousands were massacred. In all, 2 million Ibos were driven to flight. In July 1966, Ibo soldiers in the Nigerian army were massacred. In an act of self-preservation, an Ibo brotherhood called on compatriots across the country "to come home." On May 30, 1967, at the regional capital of Enugu, the Oxford-educated lieutenant colonel, C. O. Ojukwu, issued the declaration of independence (much of it consciously taken from Thomas Jefferson's declaration) of the Republic of Biafra (named after the Bight of Biafra on the Atlantic Ocean). The independence declaration singled out the Ibos' inalienable right to freedom and security. Now came the difficult task of defending the independence of Biafra.

The Biafran rebels quickly found that they stood alone. Only four of Africa's fifty-odd nations and one European state, France, recognized Biafra. France did so because Biafra was located in the oil-rich southeastern corner of Nigeria and contained the nation's largest oil field and its only refinery. The African nations, even though they had denounced repeatedly the arbitrary borders that the European colonialists had carved out, did not want to see a dangerous secessionist precedent take place.

General Gowon treated the rebellion as an internal Nigerian matter that was not the business of others. The United Nations and the rest of the world accommodated him. When the great powers did become involved, notably Britain and the Soviet Union, they did so in support of a united Nigeria. Britain sought to maintain its political and economic influence in a unified Nigeria. Moreover, a week after the Biafran declaration of independence, the Six Day War in the Middle East closed the Suez Canal, and Nigeria's oil suddenly became more important for Britain. The Soviet Union, in its turn, sought to increase its influence in Africa and thus provided Gowon's army—the likely winner—with modern weapons. This was the first time in modern history that an African nation fought a war with weapons provided by outside powers. It would not be the last, however. Combatants armed by outside powers were later responsible for the destruction of much of Angola, Mozambique, Ethiopia, and Somalia.

Biafra's resistance ended after thirty months. Defeats on the battlefield, bombing raids, and widespread starvation took their toll. In January 1970, the Ibo surrendered. Gowon insisted that no retribution be taken and that Ibos be reintegrated into Nigerian society. A Nigerian colonel described the aftermath to a US reporter: "It was like a referee blowing a whistle in a football game. People just put down their guns and went back to the business of living."[7]

## Foreign Intervention

At the time of independence, African leaders sought to eliminate dependence on foreign powers and insisted on "African solutions to African problems." Political and economic instability, however, made Africa ripe for outside intervention. The Organization of African Unity (OAU), formed in 1963, never achieved a meaningful concert of Africa. Its nations tended to pull apart, with most maintaining closer ties with their former colonial masters than with their neighbors. They continued to rely on Europeans for economic aid and military assistance, and the Europeans continued to intervene in Africa in order to protect investments. France maintained a military presence of more than 15,000, its highly mobile *force d'intervention*. As the gap between African economic development and that of the industrialized nations widened, especially after the oil crises in the 1970s, Africans were forced all the more to depend on foreign aid and became even more vulnerable to meddling by outside powers. These powers were not limited to the former colonial powers of Europe but came to include the United States and the Soviet Union, which, in their global struggle, were eager to make themselves indispensable to their new African friends and to check the influence of the other.

China, too, competed for influence in Africa. Its boldest undertaking was the construction of the 1,200-mile Tanzam "Great Freedom" railroad in the mid-1970s, linking landlocked Zambia with the Tanzanian port city of Dar es Salaam. The $500 million project—which employed some 20,000 Chinese and 50,000 African workers—was undertaken after Britain, Canada, and the United States turned down the project. Previously, the United States had missed an opportunity to expand its influence in Africa when, in 1956, it rejected Egypt's request for financial backing to build the Aswan Dam, leaving the door open for the Soviet Union to build it and thereby temporarily gain Egypt as a client state.

The United States and the Soviet Union offered security arrangements, weapons, and economic aid. At issue was political influence. Although Washington provided much more developmental aid than did Moscow, it did not win more friends. Nowhere was this more evident than in the United Nations, where African nations and the Soviet Union—sharing an anticolonialist viewpoint—often voted the same way, whereas the United States was seldom able to count on the votes of these nations.

Marxism-Leninism was in vogue in the early postindependence years, as new African leaders were attracted to the ideology for its explanation of past colonial exploitation and neocolonialism. The leading theoretician of neocolonialism, Ghana's Kwame Nkrumah, defined it as colonialism by economic means.[8] Nkrumah and others turned to variants of Marxism-Leninism as a model for political organization and state planning. Such governments established close ties with Moscow, such as Guinea and Angola, but found developmental aid from the Soviet Union to be disappointingly meager. Some African leaders—Nkrumah and Tanzania's Nyerere, for instance—conjured up their own brands of "African socialism," a blend of Marxist ideas and indigenous African notions, which were usually vague and had little resemblance to either Marxism or the Soviet system. In any case, it was difficult to distinguish between the states that were nominally socialist and those that claimed to be capitalist, for in all of them state planning and control of the economy were common. "The distinction between socialist and capitalist states in Africa," two noted African specialists explained, "has often proved to be more one of rhetoric than reality." It proved to be less a reflection of ideological commitment than of where the aid came from.[9]

Direct confrontations between the superpowers began in the mid-1970s, with the end of Portuguese colonial rule in southern Africa. Portugal's departure left behind a volatile situation, not only because power was up for grabs, but also because the buffer between black African nations and the white supremacist regime of South Africa had been removed. South Africa found itself threatened by the accession of a Marxist regime in Mozambique in 1975, the transfer of power to a black government in Zimbabwe (formerly Southern Rhodesia) in 1980, and the increasing resolve of Botswana, Zambia, and other black African nations to oppose its racist policies. In response, South Africa started to intervene militarily in Angola, Mozambique, and Lesotho.

In defiance of the United Nations, South Africa continued to occupy nearby Namibia, thereby thwarting its demand for independence. In 1975, South Africa installed a puppet black government in Namibia and promised to grant it independence. The largest Namibian party, the left-leaning South-West Africa People's Organization (SWAPO), was left out of the government and, supported by black African nations, continued guerrilla resistance in its fight for Namibian independence.

Angola represented the most egregious example of foreign intervention. The outsiders came from the United States, the Soviet Union, the People's Republic of China, Cuba, Zaire, and South Africa. When Portugal withdrew from Angola in April 1975, three separate, professedly Marxist Angolan revolutionary groups vied for power. The Popular Movement for the Liberation of Angola (MPLA), a group founded in 1956, controlled the capital of Luanda. The National Front for the Liberation of Angola (FNLA), established in 1962, held the mountainous region in the north. And the National Union for the Total Independence of Angola (UNITA), founded in 1966, represented the Ovimbundu—the largest ethnic group in Angola—in the central and southern regions.

The United States and the Soviet Union accused each other of meddling in Angola, all the while claiming that their own involvement was justified by the actions of the other. The MPLA received Soviet financial and military support, assisted by several thousand Cuban advisers and a Zairean military unit. FNLA and UNITA each received financial support and covert military assistance from the CIA and South Africa. By the end of the year, on the threshold of victory, the MPLA formed a new Angolan government.

In Washington, the administration of Gerald Ford and the US secretary of state, Henry Kissinger, refused to accept what they considered a Soviet victory. Continued US military aid to UNITA rebels and South African military involvement in the years that followed served to perpetuate the Angolan civil war.

## The Worsening Economic Plight of Sub-Saharan Africa

The 1980s saw an increase in living standards throughout much of the globe (other than the nations at war—Afghanistan, Nicaragua, El Salvador, Cambodia, Iran, and Iraq). The great exception was sub-Saharan Africa.

From 1965 until the late 1980s, per capita income in sub-Saharan Africa grew a mere 0.6 percent.[10] Overall, economic growth averaged 3.4 percent per year, barely above the increase in population. Between 1970 and 1987, the rate of growth of agricultural output declined; it grew at a pace of less than half the rate of population growth, 1.4 percent versus 3.3 percent. The increasing drying-up of the Sahel, the climatic transition zone directly south of the Sahara, was in part to blame for the decline in agricultural production.

Moreover, whatever economic gains sub-Saharan Africa had enjoyed since its colonies began to gain their independence were eaten up by the phenomenal rise in population. A World Bank report concluded that "never in human history has population grown so fast." In the half-century since Ghana gained its independence, the population doubled to nearly 1 billion. Often the result of such growth was hunger. Nearly one-quarter of the population faced "chronic food insecurity." Sub-Saharan Africa had the highest rates of maternal and infant mortality in the world. In the poorest countries (Burkina Faso, Ethiopia, and Mali), one-quarter of the children died before they reached the age of five.

During the 1980s, per capita income and food production continued to decrease. The share of sub-Saharan Africa's exports in world markets declined from 2.4 percent in 1970 to 1.3 percent in 1987. The region witnessed, in the terse language of a World Bank report, "accelerated ecological degradation." Several countries—among them Ghana, Liberia, and Zambia—slipped from the middle-income group to the low-income group. In 1987, the region's population of 450 million produced only as much wealth as Belgium's 10 million.

The world's per capita GNP in 1987 was $3,010; for sub-Saharan Africa, it was $330.[11]

Another problem, one that went back to the 1960s, was the high level of public expenditures for standing armies. The World Bank stressed that a direct link existed between low military spending and good economic performance. It also touched for the first time the question of official corruption, although only briefly and gingerly. "Bad habits," it noted, "are hard to undo." Millions of foreign aid dollars continued to be siphoned off into private overseas accounts. An unfettered and vigilant press, playing the role of watchdog, was all too rare. The nations with the best economic performance—Botswana and Mauritius—had low military expenditures, parliamentary democracies, and a free press.

## Africa in the Early 1990s: The Call for Democracy

After the Cold War ended by the early 1990s, Moscow and Washington no longer saw the need to prop up African dictators. The world's leading international lending institutions, notably the International Monetary Fund and the World Bank, increasingly stressed that Africa's economic plight could only be resolved if and when governments became accountable for their actions. Britain's foreign secretary, Douglas Hurd, declared in 1990 that governments "with repressive policies, corrupt management and wasteful, discredited economic systems should not expect us to support their folly with scarce aid resources."[12] French president François Mitterand delivered the same message at a Franco-African summit, saying that there could be "no development without democracy and no democracy without development."[13]

In the early 1990s, political pressure from below—by students and scholars, labor unions (often including government employees), and the poor—challenged dictators who for many years had been impervious to criticism. Demonstrators in the streets and opposition leaders demanded the convening of "national conferences" to discuss necessary political changes. One of the common demands was for multiparty elections.

In Benin, President Mathieu Kérékou—military dictator for seventeen years—bowed to political pressure and convened such a conference, which then proceeded to strip him of his powers, appoint an interim president, call for a presidential election, and draft a new constitution. Kérékou accepted the decisions and, after losing the election to his opponent by a two-to-one margin in the March 1991 election, he became the first African ruler to be voted out of office.

Most of Africa's strongmen, however, were unwilling to go quietly. A case in point was Joseph Mobutu, the heavy-handed dictator of Zaire since 1965. In April 1990, he announced an end to one-party government and promised to accept the verdict of a free, multiparty election. But when the elections were held, Mobutu received over 99 percent of the votes, hardly the hallmark of a free election. In the Central African Republic, strongman president André Kolingba authorized opposition parties and scheduled an election for October 1992 but then abruptly arrested the opposition. Another holdout was President Daniel arap Moi of Kenya, who denounced the movement for multiparty elections as "garbage" and an invitation to chaos. In July 1990, Kenyan police opened fire on several hundred peaceful demonstrators calling for the legalization of opposition parties, killing at least twenty-six and jailing more than 1,000. After a year and a half of political agitation and after Western governments terminated economic aid to Kenya, arap Moi consented in December 1991 to legalize opposition parties. When elections were held, he manipulated the results, making certain he remained in power. In October 1990, demonstrations forced the president of the Ivory Coast, Félix Houphouët-Boigny, one of Africa's more benevolent dictators, in power since the early 1960s, to accept opposition parties. He made sure, however, to win decisively the subsequent election.

By the end of the twentieth century, freedom of the press existed in only three of Africa's fifty-five states: South Africa, Senegal, and Mali.[14] Not until 1986 did the OAU come up with an African Charter of Human Rights and the Rights of Peoples. The charter's interpretation of human rights, however, differed from the Western definition, which stresses the protection of the individual against the powers of the state. In Africa the traditional group—whether family or state—is more important and the rights of individuals are limited. The right of assembly, for example, is subject to "necessary limitations," and individual liberties must to be reconciled with the rights of others (that is, collective security, customs, and social interests). The OAU hesitated to condemn member states, even in the case of systematic human rights violations, as with Emperor Bokassa of the Central African Republic, who in 1972 led his soldiers into a prison to quell a disturbance and ended up massacring the prisoners and displaying their dismembered bodies to the crowds outside.[15]

## Flash Points in Africa in the 1990s

### Namibia, Angola, and Mozambique

The end of the Cold War was felt quickly in three war-torn countries in southern Africa: Namibia, Angola, and Mozambique. Soviet ruler Mikhail Gorbachev withdrew financial support for the leftist government in Angola and for the Cuban troops in Angola and in Namibia. In December 1988, under pressure from Washington and Moscow, Cuba agreed to evacuate its troops from Angola in exchange for a South African troop withdrawal from

Namibia. UN negotiators brought together opposing groups who (again with US and Soviet support) drafted one of Africa's most democratic constitutions and then held one of Africa's freest and fairest elections. In March 1990, the Namibian government, headed by SWAPO leader Sam Nujoma, celebrated the end of seventy-five years of colonial rule and twenty-three years of guerrilla warfare.

In Angola, in the meantime, the civil war and foreign intervention continued. The conflict pitted the Soviet/Cuban-supported MPLA government, headed by José Eduardo dos Santos, against the US/South African–supported UNITA guerrilla forces of Jonas Savimbi. Savimbi was a former self-proclaimed Maoist who compared his military campaigns to Mao's "Long March." Washington turned a blind eye to Savimbi's brutality (Human Rights Watch reported incidents of witches being burned alive) since he was fighting Soviet-backed Cubans. Indeed, Savimbi became the darling of the political and religious right in the United States. In 1986, President Ronald Reagan invited him to the White House and praised his struggle "for freedom." Once the Cold War was over and the belligerents exhausted, Portugal managed to serve as a peace broker. A precarious agreement was finally signed in May 1991, which called for the adoption of market-oriented economic reforms, the demobilization and integration of the two military forces into a national army, and an election by the end of 1992. The breakthrough ended (if only for the time being) sixteen years of continuous and crippling warfare that had devastated the country, claimed more than 300,000 lives, and given Angola the morbid distinction of having the world's highest number of amputees per capita.[16]

The new armistice held as Angola prepared for its first free multiparty presidential election in September 1992, one relatively free of irregularities. The victor was dos Santos, but Savimbi charged election fraud and disputed the election even before the results were counted. Savimbi, by now an isolated international pariah, continued his armed resistance until February 2002, when government troops hunted him down and shot him dead. The civil war was over.

A similar sequence of events unfolded in Mozambique, another former Portuguese colony in southern Africa. There, too, a long, bloody civil war between a Soviet-backed Marxist government and a South African–supported right-wing rebel force, Renamo (the Mozambique Nationalist Resistance), concluded with a negotiated settlement. The peace agreement between the government and Renamo, in September 1992, ended an extraordinarily brutal war that had claimed nearly a million lives. It set the stage for UN-supervised elections and opened the way for desperately needed foreign aid to reach the people of this blighted country. In 1990, Mozambique was the world's poorest nation. Its per capita GNP stood at $80, refugees represented one-quarter of its population of 15 million, and over 3 million people faced starvation.[17]

## Sudan, Ethiopia, and Somalia

The most war-ravaged and famine-stricken nations in Africa were Ethiopia and Somalia, where starvation, disease, and the displacement of peoples were endemic. In 1990, a drought in Sudan and Ethiopia caused crop failures and then famine and forced farmers to eat their remaining animals and seed grain. The main cause of misery, however, was the ceaseless civil wars.

War in Sudan—between the government, whose power was concentrated in the north, and the Sudan People's Liberation Army in the south—had deep-seated ethnic and religious roots. In the heavily Muslim north, Arab and Egyptian influence was strong; in the south, darker-skinned Africans, many of them Christians, resisted northern domination, including enslavement, something the government in Khartoum denied when it was brought to international attention. Prospects for a peaceful resolution suffered a setback in 1989 when a military junta, led by Omar al-Bashir, took power in Khartoum and set out to establish an Islamic state. As the fighting continued, some 8 million Sudanese were in desperate need of food. Many of them became refugees in regions beyond the reach of overland food shipments.

In April 2003, another catastrophe began to unfold in another part of Sudan, in Darfur. Between April 2003 and the summer of 2008, the United Nations estimated the number of dead at approximately 300,000—mainly by disease and famine. Another 2.2 million became refugees.

The conflict in Darfur (literally, "the land of the Fur [people]"), the western provinces of Sudan, pitted nomadic Arabs against the indigenous Fur who had long cultivated the land. The two had coexisted; they had intermarried, the Fur becoming Muslims centuries ago. In the mid-1970s, however, as a prolonged drought coincided with a population explosion,[18] farmers and herders engaged in sporadic clashes.[19] The military regime in Khartoum, dominated by Arabs, took the side of the herdsmen. In April 2003, the conflict took another bloody turn when Darfur rebels, organized as the Sudanese Liberation Army, alleging governmental discrimination and exploitation, attacked military garrisons, destroyed helicopters and airplanes, and killed about one hundred soldiers. The attacks came at a time when the Bashir government was still seeking to resolve its twenty-one-year-long conflict in the south.

Faced with two-front war, Khartoum turned to Musa Hilal, an Arab sheikh whose family had long been in conflict with blacks in Darfur. During the 1990s, the government had imprisoned Hilal for murder, armed robbery, and tax evasion. Now it released Hilal, who promptly created an army of marauders, the *janjaweed* (literally, "evil horsemen" or simply "bandits"), who were supported by the government and given immunity to engage in ethnic cleansing, plunder, murder, and rape in Darfur.

The conflict was more than just a dispute over land. Since the late 1980s, under the influence of Muammar Qaddafi of Libya, Arabs had sought to establish an "Arab belt" south of the Sahara. The *janjaweed* argued that they—and not the black Africans—were the original settlers of the land, that Arabs had brought civilization to the region, and that they were hardly bandits but rather *mujahidin* (freedom fighters) protecting their own people.

Gradually, the ongoing war began to make headlines around the world. In April 2004, US president George W. Bush criticized Khartoum for "the brutalization of Darfur." Kofi Annan, the UN secretary-general, spoke of the prospect of "military action."[20] In July, the US Congress, under the influence of evangelical Christians who had long sought to drum up international support against Khartoum's atrocities aimed at fellow Christians in the south of Sudan, passed a resolution condemning "genocide" in Darfur. This marked the first time that the US Congress had used that word to refer to an ongoing massacre. The US State Department would not go so far, but then in September 2004, Secretary of State Colin Powell spoke of genocide for the first time. In August 2004, the UN Security Council threatened Khartoum with economic sanctions unless it disarmed the *janjaweed* in thirty days. Khartoum responded that the demand was unreasonable, comparing it to the US inability to disarm the militants in Iraq. After the thirty days expired, neither the Bush administration—militarily overextended in Iraq—nor the United Nations had an answer to the violence in Darfur. Eventually, the United Nations and the African Union sent peacekeepers and relief workers into Darfur, but to little avail.

In July 2008, the prosecutor at the International Criminal Court, the Spaniard Luis Moreno-Ocampo, issued an indictment against Bashir—charging him with war crimes. Bashir, ensconced in Khartoum beyond Moreno-Ocampo's reach, contemptuously dismissed all accusations.

The violence in Darfur remained unresolved, but in July 2011, the long war between the Muslim north and the Christian and animist south ended with the establishment of Africa's newest state, South Sudan, which was carved out of the southern third of Sudan. Historically, the two peoples had been at the opposite end of the slave trade, the northerners preying on the southerners in what Arabs called "Sudan," the "land of the blacks." In the 1950s, Britain had intended to create a separate southern state, but then did nothing.

In the past, African leaders recoiled at the idea of any one nation breaking up into separate components. This time it was different. The heads of South Africa, Nigeria, and thirty-one other nations attended the independence ceremony. Even Bashir, the president of Sudan, attended, as did the secretary general of the United Nations, Ban Ki-moon, and lesser dignitaries from outside Africa (the United States, China, Norway).

For a generation, South Sudan had known little but war, during which an estimated 2 million people had died. Few knew how to govern or to develop the nation's mineral resources and agricultural land. South Sudan's main resource was oil, one reason why the north had been unwilling to give it up

and a major reason why the Chinese delegation attended the independence fes-
tivities. South Sudan's problem, however, was that its sole oil pipeline ran
through the north, which demanded exorbitant "transfer fees."[21]

A little over two years after its independence, however, South Sudan
stood on the threshold of suffering a fate similar to that of many of the other
newly independent African states. Two politicians, each representing their
own ethnic group (of which there were at least five dozen), went to war against
one another. Once again, the UN Security Council, amid reports of human
rights abuses and massacres, sent peacekeepers to a deeply troubled land, all
the while admitting there was no military solution to the continued fighting.

• • •

In September 1974, the eighty-two-year-old Christian emperor Haile Selassie,
who had governed Ethiopia since 1916 (first as regent, then as emperor), once
a symbol of African independence and resistance against colonialism, was
overthrown by a professedly Marxist military junta led by Haile Mariam
Mengistu. By now, the emperor—whom many Ethiopians saw as the reincarnation of Jesus—had become a symbol of Ethiopia's medieval past. Far from
saving his nation, however, Haile Selassie's reign had been marked by economic backwardness, famine, and political repression. He had done little to
avert Ethiopia's chronic famines and, instead, had gone to great lengths to suppress new reports of them.

The new government proved to be no better. The Soviet leader Leonid
Brezhnev saw a chance to extend Moscow's influence in Africa and thus
began to provide economic and military backing that eventually topped $11
billion. Economic disarray, Mengistu's brutality, and continued ethnic strife
ensured the further degradation of life in Ethiopia. Mengistu sought to carry
out an extensive land reform program, only to reap another agricultural disaster, the consequence not so much of his reforms as of many years of deforestation, overcultivation, and drought.

Arrayed against Mengistu were ethnic-based rebel armies such as the
People's Revolutionary Democratic Front in Tigre Province and the Eritrean
People's Liberation Front. The Eritrean fight for independence, Africa's
longest war, began in 1952, shortly after the United Nations transferred Eritrea
(previously an Italian colony along the shores of the Red Sea) to Ethiopia.
Ironically, the Eritrean rebel leaders were Marxists who fought the Marxist
government in Addis Ababa. Many of the Tigre rebels were Marxists as well.

In 1990, under the impact of Gorbachev's "new thinking," the Soviet
Union shut off military aid to Ethiopia, and soon thereafter rebel forces gained
the upper hand. In April 1991, as the rebels closed in on Addis Ababa and
Eritrean forces liberated their homeland, Mengistu fled Ethiopia. The statues
of Lenin came down in Addis Ababa. The new government of Meles Zenawi,

the head of the Ethiopian People's Liberation Front, agreed to accept the results of an internationally supervised referendum on Eritrean independence held in May 1993. With the outcome of the referendum a foregone conclusion, Eritrea finally gained its independence.

•  •  •

In neighboring Somalia, Mohammed Siad Barre maintained a semblance of order for twenty-one years. He did so by force of arms, first supplied by Moscow and then by Washington. When he lost control of the outlying regions, he was ousted in January 1991, leaving behind a government without central authority. As competing clans fought for control of the capital of Mogadishu, they turned Somalia into lawless land wracked by savage fighting, looting, and starvation. Jeeps roamed the streets of Mogadishu mounted with recoilless rifles, many of them manned by teenage soldiers. In a three-month period at the end of 1991, an estimated 25,000 people—mostly civilians—were killed or wounded in the fighting, and 250,000 residents of the capital were expelled.

The combination of drought and war produced in Somalia a famine as severe as any in modern times. Nongovernmental relief agencies such as the Red Cross, CARE, and Save the Children (a British-based charity) delivered thousands of tons of food each day, but many interior areas of Somalia and even some sections of Mogadishu were beyond reach. All too often warring forces seized food shipments. In mid-1992, the UN Security Council sent emergency food shipments protected by a token UN force of 500 armed guards. The UN relief missions came under attack at the airport, and ships laden with relief food were denied permission to unload at the docks. In December 1992, the United Nations agreed to a request from US president George H. W. Bush to send a UN military operation consisting primarily of 25,000 US personnel (CIA, Marines, Army) and another 13,000 troops from sundry other countries to oversee the distribution of food and medicine. By then, an estimated 300,000 Somalis had already died of starvation and one-third of the 6 million inhabitants of the country were in danger of succumbing to the same fate.

Bush envisioned a purely humanitarian mission of short duration. UN Secretary-General Boutros Boutros-Ghali, however, proclaimed a larger mission: to disarm the Somali warlords and establish political stability in the country. The new US president, Bill Clinton, accepted the expanded mission.

Initially, the US-led intervention was an admirable success. Food deliveries reached hundreds of thousands of ill and starving people. But then President Clinton authorized US soldiers to engage in a manhunt for the Somali warlord considered most responsible for the continued violence, General Mohammed Farah Aidid. His capture was deemed all the more important after his troops ambushed and killed twenty-four Pakistani UN soldiers in June 1993. In October 1993, an unsuccessful US Army Ranger raid on Aidid's headquarters led to the downing of two Blackhawk helicopters and a furious firefight that left eighteen US soldiers dead and eighty wounded. Worse yet, from a political standpoint, was the spectacle of Aidid's troops dragging the corpse of a US soldier through the streets of Mogadishu. The Clinton administration quickly cut its losses and withdrew since opposition to the intervention back home was already growing. In the end, the costly UN operation was a political and military failure. As a humanitarian gesture, however, it did mitigate conditions in Somalia. The UN's assistance, coupled with a plentiful harvest in 1994, finally ended the famine.

## Ethnic Violence in Burundi and Rwanda

The bloodiest confrontations between blacks in postcolonial Africa took place between Tutsi and Hutu in Burundi and Rwanda, in the Great Lakes region. The origins of the two peoples are not clear. The Hutu arrived in the area well before the Tutsi, who came from around the Horn of Africa, perhaps from Ethiopia, 400–500 years ago. The Tutsi were cattle herders, and the Hutu were cultivators. By the mid-nineteenth century, when the first reliable records were compiled, the two groups had developed a common culture (spirit faiths, cuisine, folk customs) and language. Occasionally, they intermarried. By that time, there were so few ethnic distinctions that one could not readily call them two different ethnic groups. Hutus and Tutsi often were unable to make the distinction. A Hutu who acquired cattle could become a Tutsi.

The Belgian colonialists, obsessed with race (as were many Europeans around the turn of the twentieth century), intensified the class and ethnic divisions between Tutsis and Hutus. The Belgians reinforced whatever differences existed between them by issuing ethnic identity cards. The Belgians treated the minority Tutsis (15 percent of the population) as a separate, superior ethnic entity and favored them for educational, professional, and administrative opportunities. The Belgians relegated the majority Hutus (85 percent of the population) to an inferior status. By the time the Belgians withdrew in 1962, the divisions ran deep. Moreover, the colonial system of using ethnic identity cards remained in force.

After the Belgian departure, the Hutu and Tutsi jockeyed for power. In 1965, after Tutsi extremists assassinated the Rwandan Hutu prime minister three days after his appointment, Hutu military officers attempted a coup. Tutsi reprisals were extremely brutal as they attempted to wipe out the first generation of postcolonial Hutu political leaders. In 1972, following another Hutu rebellion—this one in Burundi—Tutsis responded with what can only be called genocide. In a span of three months, they killed approximately 250,000 Hutus and purged the army, the government, and the economy of Hutu elements. Moreover, both sides became engaged in ethnic cleansing. By now, the Belgian myth of two different tribes had been turned into reality. Tutsis and Hutus feared each other and began to construct mythical versions of their pasts, which only further solidified division, fear, and hatred.[22]

In Burundi in 1987, the Tutsi general Pierre Buyoya attempted to reconcile the two peoples, but suspicion ran so deep that it proved impossible. In August 1988, a confrontation between Tutsi authorities and Hutus in northern Burundi sparked a renewal of violence. Hutu and Tutsi mobs again slaughtered each other indiscriminately. Tutsi control of Burundi continued until June 1993, when the country elected its first Hutu president, Melchior Ndadaye. Six months later, in December 1993, the Tutsi-dominated military assassinated him, touching off another round of bloodletting. In the first six months alone, the estimated death toll was between 50,000 and 100,000, and 600,000 refugees fled into neighboring countries.

Ethnic violence in Burundi was soon overshadowed by a far greater massacre in neighboring Rwanda. Under the banner of "Hutu Power," President Juvenal Habyarimana, who had ruled Rwanda since 1973, forced many Tutsis into exile in neighboring Zaire. In 1990, the exiled Tutsis formed the Rwandan Patriotic Front (RPF) for the purpose of reclaiming political power in Rwanda. An RPF invasion of Rwanda in October of that year unleashed another round of violence against Tutsis.

The immediate cause for the most serious outbreak of violence was the assassination of Habyarimana in April 1994, when his plane was shot down over Kigali, the Rwandan capital. Hutu soldiers blamed the assassination on Tutsis and immediately began to avenge Habyarimana's death with indiscriminate massacres of any and all Tutsis as well as moderate Hutus—particularly those who had married Tutsis. The militants forced other Hutus to join in this orgy of murder or be killed themselves. Mobs conducted house-to-house searches, hunting down and killing victims with whatever weapons they had at their disposal—machine guns, machetes, spears, knives, and clubs. People were herded into buildings, including churches, which were then set ablaze. In their genocidal fury, Hutus murdered an estimated 800,000 individuals, mostly Tutsis, over a period of three months.

One writer described Rwanda as "a tiny pebble dropped on the equator in the center of Africa, the continent that the rest of the world finds easiest to ignore." So it was this time. Clinton's ambassador to the UN, Madeleine Albright—although well aware of the magnitude of the massacre—ignored what was taking place in Rwanda, as did the rest of the world, including the United Nations.[23]

In the end, Tutsis, true to their military tradition, fought back and took revenge. Tutsis rallied to the RPF, which fought its way into Kigali and expelled the Hutu government and its army. In July 1994, RPF leader Paul Kagame set up a new government with a moderate Hutu as a figurehead president and himself as vice-president and defense minister. Kagame, who retained actual power, took steps to halt the violence. When the carnage ended in Rwanda, a country of 8 million people, between 800,000 and 1 million Rwandans lay dead, murdered in less than two months, the greatest-ever butchery in such a short period.[24] In Kigali alone, 100,000 had been slaughtered.

The bloodletting generated a refugee problem of immense proportion. Between 1.1 million and 1.5 million refugees—mainly Hutus fearing for their lives—streamed into neighboring Zaire, and another 350,000 poured into Tanzania, overwhelming relief workers. Donor nations and international relief agencies sent food and medicine. Although over $1.4 billion in aid was sent (one-fourth of total worldwide relief aid in 1994), it proved insufficient and tardy. Thousands of refugees died from hunger and disease inside refugee camps. The United Nations negotiated a repatriation agreement with the new government of Rwanda, which gave assurances to Hutu refugees that it was safe to return home, but few were persuaded to do so. Rwanda became a land of traumatized people who desperately wanted to forget the past. When asked about it, many would simply say, "I don't remember."

Neither the United Nations nor anyone else had intervened to stop the slaughter. Afterward, it established in Arusha, Tanzania, at the end of 1994, a court of justice modeled after the Nuremberg and Tokyo war crimes tribunals. The court was commissioned to undertake the herculean task of holding accountable more than 100,000 alleged *génocidaires*. After three years of taking testimony, it obtained its first convictions, in September 1998. Among those convicted were a small-town Hutu mayor, Jean-Paul Akayesu, for inciting fellow Hutus to kill Tutsis, and the former Rwandan prime minister Jean Kambanda, who became the first head of any government to be convicted of genocide. (Kambanda's conviction was used as a precedent for the 2008 indictment of President Bashir of Sudan.) The court also established a precedent in international law when it ruled that rape was an aspect of genocide.

The judicial process in Arusha was not only maddeningly slow, but also limited in scope. Tutsis complain that the prosecutions took too long and that only sixty-three individuals had been charged with genocide. The Tutsis, moreover, refused to permit the tribunal to investigate its own Rwandan Patriotic Front for crimes it may have committed.

President Paul Kagame sought to eliminate the source for the violence, the nation's artificial division into two ethnic groups. His people were to see themselves henceforth simply as Rwandans, part of a national, rather than ethnic, entity. For the time being it worked in the thoroughly exhausted and traumatized nation, but the question remained whether one can brush aside ethnic divisions with the stroke of a pen.

During the genocide, the world ignored Rwanda; afterward, to make amends, approximately 300 nongovernmental organizations (NGOs) descended on it, mostly from the United States and Britain. One of the consequences was that the Rwandan school system switched from French to English. Moreover, in November 2009, Rwanda joined the British Commonwealth as the second member (the other being Mozambique in November 1995) that had not been part of the British Empire.

## Conflict in Zaire

In 1996, the Hutu-Tutsi war spilled into Zaire, where Rwandan Hutu militants linked up with the Zairean army in an effort to oust Tutsis indigenous to the country's eastern region. The Zairean Tutsis, armed and supported by their compatriots from Rwanda and Uganda, fought back and routed the Hutus, thereby creating another flood of desperate refugees. The Tutsis of eastern Zaire linked up with Laurent Désiré Kabila, who for more than thirty years had sought Zairean leader Mobutu's overthrow. As a young man, Kabila had been a Marxist supporter of Patrice Lumumba and had gotten to know the Cuban revolutionary Ché Guevara. Guevara, however, had come away disenchanted from their meeting, noting in his diary that Kabila's forces lacked discipline and that Kabila himself was "too addicted to drink and women."[25] After Mobutu came to power in 1965, Kabila fled to eastern Zaire, from where he launched several unsuccessful attempts to overthrow Mobutu. He received a modicum of support from the Soviet Union and Communist China, but his main occupation consisted of the capitalist vices of trafficking in ivory, gold, diamonds, alcohol, and prostitutes.

By the mid-1990s, the corrupt regime of the aged and ailing Mobutu had little popular support. Under Mobutu, *The Economist* noted, Zaire had "experienced more than corruption." He had been engaged in the "systemic theft of the state, from top to bottom . . . his bank account indistinguishable from the national treasury." Zaire, the size of Western Europe, had only 200 miles of paved roads; in the capital of Kinshasa 90 percent of the population was unemployed. With few people left to defend him, Mobutu's regime collapsed like a house of cards.

Kabila promised to bring freedom and democracy. He also disavowed his Marxist past. "That was 30 years ago," he said; the Russian leader, Boris Yeltsin, "was a Marxist 30 years ago." As his troops entered Kinshasa, in May 1997, he proclaimed a new order and a new name for the country: the Democratic Republic of Congo. His long-suffering people, hoping for something better, welcomed the deliverance from thirty years of misrule. The joy did not last long, however. Kabila compared his long struggle against Mobutu to "spreading fertilizer on a field" and declared that now the "time to harvest" had arrived.[26] It was the turn of Kabila's men to collect the spoils of victory and to engage in human rights violations. Within a year, Kabila faced a rebellion out of the eastern provinces. Congolese Tutsis, now supported by Uganda and Burundi as well as Rwanda, turned against Kabila, their erstwhile comrade-in-arms. In Kinshasa, soldiers sympathetic to the rebels clashed with troops loyal to Kabila, who were supported by troops from Angola, Namibia, and Zimbabwe to keep him in power. It was the most complicated of all African wars since independence, one dubbed "Africa's first world war" or the "Great War for Africa."

By the end of 2000, Kabila lost the eastern half of the Congo to rebels and foreign invaders. The lion's share of partitioned Congo fell to Uganda. Rwanda benefited financially as Kigali became a market for gold and diamonds from Congo's Kivu Province.[27] In January 2001, Kabila's palace guard assassinated him. His son Joseph inherited a divided nation wracked by a continuing civil war, disease, dislocation, and famine.

By 2008, the war had taken the lives of an estimated 5.4 million Congolese. (Since 1945, only the thirty-year Indochina Wars claimed a higher toll.) UN peacekeepers proved to be ineffective, as they could barely manage to defend themselves. In October 2008, General Laurent Nkunda, a dissident Tutsi with a long history of atrocities (including the use of child soldiers), seized control of the province of North Kivu in eastern Congo. Nkunda sought to protect Tutsis against Hutus, but he was also after the riches that Congo had to offer, such as coltran, a scarce, valuable metal used in cellular phones and video-game players. When the UN troops had no answer to Nkunda's seizure of power, the result was another round of massacres, refugees, hunger, and disease (mainly cholera).

## Nigeria

In oil-rich Nigeria, General Sani Abacha seized power in a coup in June 1993. His greed knew no limit, his family's fortune estimated at between $3 billion and $6 billion. Political opponents languished in prison or were executed by firing squads or hanging. In November 1995, eleven activists, most famously among them the author and environmentalist Ken Saro-Wiwa, were hanged in defiance of vocal international protests. Saro-Wiwa and his men came from the small Ogoni ethnic group (of about half a million people) and were critical of Abacha's dictatorship and the despoliation of their region by Nigeria's oil industry.

Nigeria was one of the world's largest exporter of oil, yet many of its people lived in abject poverty. Most were without clean water, adequate health care, and reliable electricity. Abacha's successor, Olusegun Obasanjo, vowed to restore democracy and end corruption, but it was a tall order. Since independence, Nigeria had been under military rule for all but ten years, and the legacy of military rule was difficult to set aside. To complicate matters, Nigeria faced endemic poverty. According to World Bank figures, in 2010, one-third of the population subsisted on $1.25 per day and half subsisted on $2 per day or less, while the upper 10 percent shared nearly 40 percent of the nation's wealth.

In February 2000, violence in the northern province of Kaduna claimed 400 lives, mostly Christians, the result of the imposition of Islamic religious law—*sharia*—in the predominantly Muslim north. Starting in 2001, an Islamist offshoot, Boko Haram ("Western education is sinful"), an al Qaeda affiliate in northeast Borno state, took up the fight for a "pure" Muslim state. It targeted police stations, churches, bars, students attending secular schools, and international organizations. In August 2011, a Boko Haram suicide bomber blew himself up at the UN headquarters in Abuja, Nigeria's capital, killing twenty-one and injuring seventy-three. Boko Haram called for Islamic curricula in the schools, the amputation of a hand for theft, public flogging for other crimes, and an end to women working outside the home or even sharing public transportation with men.[28]

The government proved unable to deal with any of Nigeria's problems. Since Saro-Wiwa's execution, the pollution of the Niger Delta continued at an increasing rate. In the megacity city of Lagos, the population of which had doubled to 21 million in the past 15 years, living standards were falling. In the cities, the unemployment rate was nearly 50 percent. Nigeria's per capita gross national income in 2010 was $1,170.[29] Its population, nearly 170 million people strong in 2013, was projected to outstrip that of the United States by 2050.[30]

## Zimbabwe

Under the leadership of Ian Smith, the whites of Southern Rhodesia doggedly resisted the "wind of change" blowing through Africa. The result was a war of nearly twenty years' duration that claimed approximately 30,000 lives. In the end, the independence movement led by Robert Mugabe triumphed. A black majority government under Mugabe, after promising black-white reconciliation, took power in 1980 in what became known as Zimbabwe.

At the time, the presidents of neighboring Mozambique and Tanzania told Mugabe, "You have the jewel of Africa in your hands. Now look after it." Zimbabwe had a fine railroad system, good roads, and a functioning hydroelectric system. It produced vast amounts of food for export (maize, peanuts, pineapples, mangoes, apples) and raw materials (gold, chromium, platinum). Blacks had done fairly well economically, although they had no political power.[31]

After the white settlers lost their political dominance, their numbers dwindled from 278,000 in 1975 to 70,000 by 2000. Those who stayed behind retained their vast landholdings, however. An agreement in 1979 between the British government and Mugabe had stipulated that the white farmers were not to lose their lands without compensation, that all land transfers were to be based on the principle of a "willing buyer, willing seller," and that London would help finance the transfer of land to black farmers. The transfer funds, it soon became apparent, disappeared into the coffers of Mugabe and his allies.

The main focus of Mugabe and his supporters was the accumulation of wealth, not the nation's well-being. By the end of the 1990s, Zimbabwe was in ruins from neglect. The telephone system, once the best in Africa, functioned only sporadically. The indigenous agricultural sector remained primitive. Thirty-six percent of the population lived in poverty—on an income of less than $1 per day. And 26 percent of people between the ages of fifteen and forty-nine years suffered from AIDS. Per capita GNP stood at $620; inflation ran at over 25 percent. Unemployment was at 30 percent and those who had jobs saw their wages fall by one-third during the 1990s.[32] In August 1998, Mugabe committed the nation's scarce resources to the conflict in Congo, where the number of Zimbabwe's troops eventually reached 11,000.

To shore up his sinking popularity, Mugabe staged a referendum in February 2000 asking voters to give him additional powers. He sought authority to dispossess—without compensation—the remaining white farmers, who still controlled 4,500 large farms representing one-third of the nation's arable land. These farmers, however, also represented the most productive segment of Zimbabwe's economy. They produced 70 percent of the nation's agricultural exports and employed approximately 300,000 black workers. When the predominantly black voters rejected the referendum, Mugabe nonetheless declared the white farmers "enemies of Zimbabwe" and encouraged veterans of the war of liberation to seize white-owned farms, drive out their owners, intimidate the black workers, and, if need be, kill those who resisted. The veterans responded by murdering white settlers and Mugabe's black political opponents. By 2004, there were scarcely any white farmers left. The exodus led to a precipitous drop in agricultural output, and with it, foreign-currency earnings. The harvest of maize declined 67 percent, that of wheat 91 percent, and that of tobacco 75 percent.[33] By 2008, the economy of Zimbabwe was in shambles.

At the time of independence, the Zimbabwean and US dollars had traded roughly at par. Now they were trading officially at a rate of Z$30,000 to US$1. Life expectancy had dropped from sixty years to thirty-seven, the lowest in the world. The country faced a shortage of basic staples, including maize, cooking oil, gasoline, sugar, and salt. Unemployment was at 85 percent. One-third of the population had left the country, spilling mostly into South Africa, where they were not wanted. Still, Mugabe insisted that there was no crisis in Zimbabwe.

In March 2008, the eighty-four-year-old Mugabe lost the presidential election to Morgan Tsvangirai's Movement for Democratic Change. Initially Mugabe decided to step down and retire to his luxury villa, but the chief of the army, General Constantine Chiwenga, told Mugabe that the decision was not his alone. After a month's delay came the announcement that, on second thought, Tsvangirai had not won an absolute majority, only a plurality—48 percent to Mugabe's 43 percent—and that a runoff election was needed. In the meantime, the army initiated its plan known as "Coercion, Intimidation, Beating, and Displacement." First came the beatings of opponents. Then, in early May, Mugabe supporters rampaged through the streets of the remote farming village of Choana, whose residents had shown the effrontery of voting for Tsvangirai, leaving seven people dead. That pattern was repeated elsewhere with increasing frequency.[34] Hundreds of civilians and more than eighty members of Tsvangirai's party were murdered. Tsvangirai, who had been viciously beaten in the past, went into exile. When he returned he was arrested, released, and rearrested. In the end, he stopped campaigning and sought refuge in the Dutch embassy. In June, Mugabe won in a landslide and two days later took the oath of office for his sixth term.

The international community expressed outrage and eventually managed to broker a tenuous agreement after offering economic incentives, including a pledge to lift economic sanctions. By the agreement, in September 2008, Tsvangirai became prime minister, but Mugabe retained the all-important position of head of the army. It was far from a perfect solution, but it moved toward addressing the political deadlock. In 2013, when the eighty-nine-year-old Mugabe won reelection with 61 percent of the vote amid reported widespread irregularities, the outside world barely took notice.

### Sierra Leone and Liberia

While the Western world's attention was riveted on the fate of a small number of white settlers in Zimbabwe, a more gruesome spectacle, largely ignored, continued in Sierra Leone. It began in 1991, when Foday Sankoh, someone who claimed to possess supernatural powers, created the Revolutionary United Front (RUF). In the face of feeble government resistance, Sankoh gained control of Sierra Leone's source of gold and diamonds. Sankoh and his supporters made clear they would do anything to retain their power and wealth. In January 1999, they torched one-third of the capital city of Freetown and massacred 6,000 people. A UN force of 8,700 soldiers failed to disarm them; on the contrary, the RUF captured 500 UN peacekeepers before eventually releasing them.

Sankoh's troops engaged in systematic atrocities—torture, rape, arson, wholesale slaughter, and mutilation. They hacked off the arms and legs of an estimated 10,000 children. They pressed into military service children as young as ten years old. Fankoh dubbed one of his campaigns Operation Pay Yourself, encouraging his men to loot anything they could find. By 2000, between 100,000 and 200,000 people had perished in the conflict.[35]

None of that caused much of an outcry abroad. US president Bill Clinton—burned by the debacle in Somalia in 1993 and now engaged in Kosovo—and most of the rest of Africa and the world showed little interest in Sierra Leone. It was up to Britain to try and restore order in its former colony. In 2000, British troops with shoot-to-kill orders routed the RUF. Britain charged Fankoh with seventeen counts of war crimes, but before the trial began, Sankoh died of a stroke.

Sankoh had not acted alone in his murderous campaign. He had the support of a soldier of fortune, Charles Taylor of neighboring Liberia, a country with its own recent tragic history. In April 1980, a revolt led by Master Sergeant Samuel K. Doe overthrew the government of William Tolbert, an Americo-Liberian descendant of former slaves from the United States who had ruled Liberia since its formation in 1847. The former US slaves became the colonizers and oppressors of the native majority. When Doe, a native Liberian (from the Krahn ethnic group), murdered Tolbert, it marked the first time that a native Liberian had ruled the country. Doe quickly promoted himself to general and then consolidated his powers by carrying out mass executions. His Krahn supporters helped themselves to the spoils of war, seizing whatever they could.

When Taylor, another Americo-Liberian, challenged Doe in 1989, Liberia was plunged into the bloodiest of civil wars, briefly interrupted by Doe's brutal torture and execution (at the hands of yet another rival faction). After that it became Taylor's turn to plunder and terrorize Liberia. There was scarcely a crime that Taylor's men did not commit with near-total impunity in Liberia and nearby Sierra Leone. An estimated 150,000–200,000 people died in Liberia, and one-third of the population became refugees. UN economic sanctions in 2001 and the advance of seven rebel factions steadily weakened Taylor's hand. In the end, Taylor fled, accepting political asylum from the generals running Nigeria.

In response to recent genocidal brutality in Yugoslavia, the United Nations established in 2002 a new International Criminal Court (ICC), the first permanent war crimes tribunal. Its purpose was to bring to justice the worst of the worst. If their native countries were "unable or unwilling" to do so, the tribunal would. It took the tribunal nearly three years, but eventually the Nigerian government yielded to international pressure. In March 2006, it handed Taylor over to a Special Court for Sierra Leone in the capital of Freeport. Taylor became the first sitting African former head of state to be indicted. (Slobodan Milošević of Yugoslavia was the first overall to be indicted by the ICC.) Taylor was charged with eleven counts of war crimes committed in Sierra Leone. (The new government of Liberia, under Ellen Johnson Sirleaf, showed scant interest in putting Taylor on trial. Taylor still had a strong following in Liberia; besides, Johnson Sirleaf did not consider him a criminal, merely "someone who was human and who made some mistakes."[36]) Eventually, Taylor's trial was transferred to The Hague, where he did everything possible to drag out the process. It took until April 2012 before he was finally convicted and sentenced to fifty years in prison. Taylor challenged the verdict, charging that he had been convicted as part of a conspiracy by Western nations. An appeals court, however, upheld the verdict in September 2013.

• • •

In March 2011, the ICC charged Uhuru Kenyatta, the son of independence leader Jomo Kenyatta, with human rights violations, including murder and rape. The charges went back to the 2007 presidential election (in which Kenyatta had worked on behalf of a fellow Kikuyu candidate). In March 2013, Uhuru Kenyatta won the presidency in his own right, in another campaign filled with irregularities. Initially, Britain and the United States were slow to recognize the results of the 2013 election (the British even refused to mention Kenyatta's name), but after the Kenyan Supreme Court certified it, they came around and congratulated Kenyatta on becoming president. The African Union had long complained that the eight cases before the ICC all involved African leaders. It had a point. A score of heads of state outside Africa could readily have been indicted—such as Augusto Pinochet in Chile, Alberto Fujimori in Peru, and Kim Jong-Il in North Korea. The African Union also thought that sitting presidents should be exempt from prosecution. Kenyatta, however, had little to worry about. Kenya was doing well economically and foreign investors were satisfied with the political status quo, while the Pentagon saw it as a valuable base for its military operations in East Africa.[37]

## AIDS in Sub-Saharan Africa

During the 1990s, sub-Saharan Africa was ravaged by an epidemic of AIDS (acquired immune deficiency syndrome) reaching unprecedented proportions. In the two decades between the early 1980s and the end of 2000, more African people (19 million) had died of AIDS than in all the wars fought across the globe combined. About 6,000 Africans died from AIDS each day, and millions more were infected by HIV (human immune-deficiency virus), which weakens the natural immune system and is the root of AIDS. Sub-Saharan Africa, with 10 percent of the world's population, had 70 percent of the world's population infected with HIV (24.5 million out of 34.3 million total). Hardest hit were Zimbabwe, Zambia, Botswana, and South Africa. Botswana had the world's highest rate of infection—35 percent of the population.

South Africa was the last sub-Saharan African nation to be visited by AIDS. In the 1980s, the epidemic there was considered an illness that affected primarily white homosexuals. Within a decade, however, it had spread to more than a tenth of the South African population, and nearly all of the victims were black. By 2000, South Africa had more infected people than any nation in the world. During his five years as president, Nelson Mandela paid scant attention to the problem. When he finally did, in 1998, 20 percent of South Africa's pregnant women were already infected. Mandela's successor, Thabo Mbeki, and his health minister rejected the explanation that HIV caused AIDS and blamed it instead on drug and alcohol abuse, poverty, and underdevelopment. In the meantime, the disease spread. Among the breeding grounds for the virus were the communal residences of miners separated from their families for months at a stretch. There, sexual contact, the most common route of AIDS transmission, infected more than a third of the young adults—both men and women. When the men returned home, they spread the disease. HIV also contributed to the rapid spread of tuberculosis, particularly among miners. All the while, the topics of sex and AIDS remained taboo.

Mbeki's government refused to provide funds for AZT (Azidothymidin), a drug that suppresses the impact of the virus and that, in most cases, prevents the transmission of the disease to children borne by infected women. It was, moreover, an expensive drug that needed be taken in combination with other expensive drugs to be effective.

In January 2000, AIDS became for the first time a topic at the UN Security Council. In April, the IMF linked economic development with the fight against the disease. In May, the US government declared it a potential threat to national security. The bitter truth was that AIDS threatened first and foremost the poorer countries where the workforce—those between the ages of fifteen and forty-nine—were most at risk. Ninety-five percent of individuals infected with HIV lived in underdeveloped nations. The International Labour Organization estimated that, unless the epidemic was checked, by 2020 sub-Saharan Africa would suffer from a shortage of at least 24 million workers. UN studies predicted that eventually half of all fifteen-year-olds in sub-Saharan Africa would die of the disease. By the beginning of the twenty-first century, with the fate of the next generation at stake, AIDS education and prevention programs were finally becoming priorities for many governments in sub-Saharan Africa.[38]

Between 2009 and 2011, the United Nations program to eradicate AIDS in sub-Saharan Africa showed considerable progress. The number of those infected by the HIV virus dropped by 25 percent and mortality from AIDS-related causes declined by 32 percent. In twenty-one "priority nations," the United Nations reported that the percentage of newly infected children fell by 24 percent, the result of prenatal care of infected mothers. More people were tested for the HIV virus and became eligible for HIV treatment. Nonetheless, sub-Saharan Africa remained the world's most heavily infected region.

## Notes

1. *The World Bank Atlas, 1985* (Washington, DC: World Bank, 1985).

2. Cited in Arthur Agwuncha Nwankwo and Samuel Udochukwu Ifejika, *Biafra: The Making of a Nation* (New York: Praeger, 1970), p. 11.

3. The notable exceptions include Léopold Senghor of Senegal, Félix Houphouët-Boigny of the Ivory Coast, Jomo Kenyatta of Kenya, Julius Nyerere of Tanzania, Kenneth Kaunda of Zambia, Sekou Touré of Guinea, and Seretse Khama of Botswana—all of whom remained in power for fifteen years or more.

4. Ama Biney, *The Political and Social Thought of Kwame Nkrumah* (New York: Palgrave Macmillan, 2011), p. 87.

5. Reuters, "Ghana's Opposition Ahead in Early Election Returns," *New York Times*, December 8, 2000.

6. Moyibi Amoda, "Background to the Conflict: A Summary of Nigeria's Political History from 1919 to 1964," in Joseph Okpaku, ed., *Nigeria: Dilemma of Nationhood: An African Analysis of the Biafran Conflict* (New York: Third Press, 1972), p. 59.

7. David Lamb, *The Africans* (New York: Random House, 1982), p. 309.

8. Kwame Nkrumah, *Neo-Colonialism: The Last Stage of Imperialism* (New York: International Publishers, 1966), introduction.

9. Roland Oliver and Anthony Atmore, *Africa Since 1800* (New York: Cambridge University Press, 1981), p. 330.

10. World Bank, *Sub-Saharan Africa: From Crisis to Sustainable Growth: A Long-Term Perspective Study* (Washington, DC: World Bank, 1989). All data are from this source.

11. The figures are for all "reporting countries," which excluded the Soviet Union and most of its bloc—the inclusion of which, however, would not appreciably change the figures. See World Bank, *World Development Report, 1989* (Washington, DC: World Bank, 1989), p. 165.

12. Cited in "Democracy in Africa," *The Economist*, February 22, 1992, p. 21.

13. Cited in "Under Slow Notice to Quit," *The Economist*, July 6, 1991, p. 43.

14. Interview with the dissident journalist Charles Gnaleko from Ivory Coast, "Pressefreiheit gibt es nur in drei von 55 Staaten," *Frankfurter Rundschau*, April 13, 2000, p. 11.

15. Reinhard Muller, "Die Gruppe ist wichtiger: Die afrikanische Charta der Menschenrechte," *Frankfurter Allgemeine Zeitung*, May 24, 2000.

16. "Angola Moves to Put Aside the Devastation of War," *US News and World Report*, May 13, 1991, p. 50. During the sixteen-year war, Moscow had poured in 1,100 advisers, 50,000 Cuban troops, and between $500 million and $1 billion annually to prop up the leftist government; the United States provided at least $60 million per year to support Savimbi's guerrillas. Christopher Ogden, "Ending Angola's Agony," *Time*, June 3, 1991, p. 22.

17. World Bank, *World Development Report, 1992* (Washington, DC: World Bank, 1992), pp. 211, 218.

18. Sudan had one of the highest birthrates in the world; the CIA estimate for 2004 was 2.64 percent per year; CIA, *World Factbook* (Washington, DC: CIA, 2004).

19. From 1987 to 1989, 2,500 Fur and 500 Arabs died in clashes. Samantha Power, "Dying in Darfur," *The New Yorker*, August 30, 2004, p. 61.

20. Ibid., p. 68.

21. Jon Lee Anderson, "A History of Violence," *The New Yorker*, July 23, 2012, pp. 49–52.

22. Philip Gourevitch, "The Poisoned Country," *New York Review of Books*, June 6, 1996, pp. 58–60.

23. Tim Lewis, *Land of Second Chances: The Impossible Rise of Rwanda's Cycling Team* (Boulder, CO: Velo Press, 2013), p 8.

24. "Judging Genocide," *The Economist*, June 14, 2001.

25. "Laurent Kabila," *The Economist*, January 18, 2001.

26. Ibid.

27. Karl Vick, "Congo Looks for Leadership," *Washington Post*, October 30, 2000, pp. A1, A22.

28. Douglas Farah, "Islamic Law Splits Nigeria," *Washington Post*, August 31, 2000, pp. A24, A28.

29. Elisabeth Rosenthal, "Nigeria's Population is Soaring in Preview of a Global Problem," *New York Times*, April 15, 2012, p. 1; World Bank data.

30. "Nigeria Expected to Have Larger Population than US by 2050," *The Guardian*, June 13, 2013.

31. Samora Machel of Mozambique and Julius Nyerere of Tanzania, cited in Doris Lessing, "The Jewel of Africa," *New York Review of Books*, April 10, 2003, p. 6.

32. "Poorer and Angrier," *The Economist*, August 15, 1998; Simon Robinson, "Power to the Mob," *Time*, May 1, 2000, pp. 42–46.

33. Samantha Powers, "How to Kill a Country," *The Atlantic*, December 2003, pp. 86–100.

34. Craig Timberg, "Inside Mugabe's Violent Crackdown," *Washington Post*, July 5, 2008, A1.

35. "Human Rights Watch Report 2000," letter to Kofi Annan, November 29, 2000; Udo Ulfkotte, "Kurzsichtigkeit ist die Amme der Gewalt," *Frankfurter Allgemeine Zeitung*, May 20, 2000, p. 1.

36. John Lee Anderson, "After the Warlords," *The New Yorker*, March 27, 2006, p. 64.

37. Joshua Hammer, "In the Kenyan Cauldron," *New York Review*, May 9, 2013.

38. UN figures. Marion Aberle, "Sog des Verderbens," *Frankfurter Allgemeine Zeitung*, July 8, 2000. See also Brigitte Schwartz, "Fluch der Jungen," *Der Spiegel*, July 3, 2000. In contrast, North America and Europe combined had less than 1 percent of those infected.

# 14

# Latin America

**Latin America embraces the thirteen countries of the South** American continent, Mexico, the six countries that make up Central America, and the islands that dot the Caribbean Sea. Latin America is part of the global South and shares many of its features: economic underdevelopment, poverty, unequal distribution of wealth, high population growth rates, illiteracy, political instability, recurrent military coups, dictatorial regimes, intervention by outside powers, and fervent nationalistic pride. Several nations, such as Mexico, Brazil, and Argentina, have sustained impressive industrial growth and attained GNP levels that may qualify them as middle-income nations.

## The Colonial Heritage

Unlike the newly independent nations of Africa, the Latin American countries did not struggle to meet the challenges of nation-building. Most had won their independence from Spain early in the nineteenth century, and by 1945 they had experienced more than a century of nationhood. Still, Latin America's colonial experience haunts the present. The Spanish and Portuguese *conquistadores* came to the New World not to improve it; rather they were military men intent to plunder it. Along the way, they left behind complex multiracial societies with pronounced social cleavages between a traditional aristocracy and the underprivileged lower classes.

The privileged elite, mainly Spanish descendants who were later joined by newer immigrants from Europe, controlled the levers of economic, political, and military power and thoroughly dominated the remainder of the population, *mestizos* (racially mixed peoples), native Indians, and descendants of African slaves.

The great gulf between the privileged class, who may be thought of as an oligarchy, and the dispossessed lower classes is best seen in the landholding patterns. Nowhere in the world was the disparity in landownership as great. Traditionally, over two-thirds of the agricultural land was owned by only 1 percent of the population. The *latifundios*, huge estates owned by the elite, were so large—often more than 1,000 acres—that they were not fully cultivated. As a result, much of that land remained fallow. A 1966 study revealed that in Chile and Peru, 82 percent of the agricultural land was *latifundio* and that the average size of the *latifundio* was well over 500 times larger than the *minifundios*, the small parcels of land held by most farmers.[1] *Minifundios* were often too small to provide subsistence even for small families. In Ecuador and Guatemala, nine out of ten farms were too small to feed the owners' families. Moreover, in many Latin American countries the majority of the rural population owned no land at all, laboring instead for owners of the *latifundios*. Even after years of sporadic land reform efforts, the imbalance remained. Several Latin American countries (such as Mexico and Chile) enacted land reform programs, but they were seldom fully implemented, ensuring that little agricultural land was redistributed.

The wastefulness of the *latifundio* was a major cause of the failure of Latin American agriculture to meet the needs of its people. As a result, Latin America imported large amounts of food, and the high cost of such imports had a baleful effect on economic development. The depressed state of agriculture and the impoverishment of the rural population militated against industrial development because the majority of the people were too impoverished to be vigorous consumers of manufactured products.

## "Yanqui Imperialism"

Starting in the 1820s, the United States, the "colossus of the north," cast its long shadow over its neighbors to the south. Nationalism in Latin America characteristically focused on "Yanqui imperialism," an emotive term referring to the pattern of US (Yankee) domination and interference in Latin America.

With the Monroe Doctrine of 1823, the United States claimed for itself a special role in the Western Hemisphere as the protector of the weaker countries to the south. In the 1890s, Washington extended its unilateral right of direct intervention in Latin America (spelled out most famously in the Roosevelt Corollary of 1904). Washington began to prop up client governments and send the Marines to protect US investments. Inevitably, intervention produced fear and resentment. The strains in US–Latin American relations were somewhat ameliorated by President Franklin Roosevelt's "good neighbor" policy of 1933. It did not mean, however, that the United States rejected gunboat diplomacy; instead, it would employ it only as a last resort.

After World War II, Washington sought to strengthen its bonds with Latin American countries by plying them with military and economic aid. Washington's increasing preoccupation with the Cold War gave its hemispheric relations a distinct anti-Communist ideological cast. Washington pressured Latin American governments to cut their ties with the Soviet Union and to outlaw local Communist parties, and it altered its aid programs to give greater priority to bolstering the armies than to economic development.

President John Kennedy's ambitious 1961 Alliance for Progress program had two sides to it. For one, it was meant to take the steam out of leftist movements across Latin America by pledging $20 billion over ten years for economic investments. It also called for the establishment of democratic governments. Yet in the same breath it provided increased assistance to the military and police, two of the pillars propping up right-wing dictators. As it happened, Kennedy announced the Alliance for Progress in March 1961, during the final stages of preparation for the invasion of Fidel Castro's Cuba.

The Alliance for Progress produced increased financial dependency and indebtedness. It also caused confusion over priorities, over whether to focus on industrial projects, social reforms, and relief for the poor, or bolster the military to suppress leftist rebels—whether to be a "good neighbor" or engage in gunboat diplomacy.

Corporate US business interests invested heavily in Latin America. They bought land, mines, and oil fields and established industries to take advantage of the cheap labor. At the same time, the region became a market for US-manufactured products—automobiles, machinery, and weapons. In the 1950s, ITT owned every telephone in Latin America; when governments (such as that of Brazil and Chile) threatened its monopoly it did not hesitate to intervene against the offending parties. In Brazil, in the 1960s, foreigners (mostly from the United States) owned thirty-one of the fifty-five largest firms. In the 1970s, eight of the ten largest firms and 50 percent of the banks in Argentina were foreign-owned.[2] US business interests assumed that, as in the past, the US flag followed the dollar, and they lobbied for and expected Washington to protect their investments. Their interests dovetailed with Washington's ideological and strategic goals insofar as both gave priority to the maintenance of political stability and support to military strongmen.

## Economic and Political Patterns

After World War II, industrialization became an obsession in many Latin American countries. Postwar industrial progress in several of the larger countries was indeed impressive. Governments played an important role in this endeavor, investing in heavy industry and erecting high import tariffs, all for the purpose of ending foreign dependency. Industrial progress was, however, limited to only a few countries. Argentina, Brazil, and Mexico accounted for 80 percent of Latin America's industrial output in the late 1960s.

Although industrial growth produced higher GNP figures and contributed to a modest increase in the standard of living, it also produced frustration as it failed to meet expectations. It contributed to the growth of the middle class, which sought a larger share of the nations' wealth and a larger role in the political process. The middle class found political expression through political parties but remained generally too weak to challenge the traditional landowning elite, who had the support of the military.

The urban working class, too, grew in size but remained largely impoverished. It sought to advance its cause for higher wages through both trade unions and political parties. The growing radicalism of organized labor, however, aroused the fears of the middle class and caused it to side with the more conservative elements: the oligarchy and the military. The attempt to establish democratic governments was hampered by the weakness of the middle class, the entrenchment of the oligarchy and military, the lack of political involvement of the impoverished rural masses, and the radicalism of the growing labor class.

Military intervention in politics has a long history in Latin America. Since World War II, there have been scores of military coups, and in one short span (1962–1964) eight countries fell victim to military takeovers. The military, with few foreign wars to fight, assumed a domestic role as the guardian of the state. Officers, traditionally nationalistic and conservative, could be counted on to defend the status quo.

Military rule was reinforced by still another enduring colonial legacy: the rule by *caudillos*, charismatic strongmen with their cults of personality, such as Juan Perón in Argentina, Augusto Pinochet in Chile, Rafael Trujillo in the Dominican Republic, and Fidel Castro in Cuba. *Caudillos* first appeared in the early nineteenth century during the wars for independence. Their power was extraconstitutional, that is, outside the law and thus unchecked by law.

## South America:
## Oscillation Between Military and Civilian Rule

### Argentina
Postwar Argentina went through four distinct political phases: a decade of dictatorship under Juan Perón (1946–1955), a decade-long—largely unsuccessful—attempt to establish democratic governments (1955–1965), seventeen years of military dictatorship, briefly interrupted by the return of Perón (1965–1982), and a restoration of a semblance of democracy in 1983.

The rule of Juan Perón was distinctive for it simultaneously contained elements of populism, dictatorship, capitalism, and national socialism. A former army officer, Perón was elected in 1946 as president largely on the strength of votes from the working class, whose support he had cultivated in his previous post as labor minister. His quest to rid Argentina of foreign

**South America**

domination and attain self-sufficiency was initially successful, and as a result his popularity soared. He bought out foreign businesses, created a government board for marketing agricultural produce, subsidized industrial development, extended social services, expanded education, and strengthened labor's rights. All the while he increased his personal power by impeaching the supreme court, enacting a new constitution that broadened his authority, and purchasing the support of the army by vastly increasing the military budget. He also benefited from the immense popularity of his young, beautiful wife, Eva Perón, who had at her disposal a large budget for building hospitals and schools and dispensing food and clothing to the needy.

Perón's economic program began to sputter by 1950, however, and within a year Argentina was plunged into an economic crisis marked by falling agricultural and industrial production, wage reductions, layoffs, and runaway inflation. In response to protests, Perón became more dictatorial, silencing the press and political opposition. Frustrated by his loss of public support (occasioned in part by the death of Eva in 1952) and the mounting economic chaos, Perón became more erratic. His feud with the Roman Catholic Church, fueled in part by its refusal to canonize Eva, lost him additional support. The church also opposed his efforts to require the teaching in schools of his ideology, *peronismo,* as an alternative to its teachings. Perón responded by censoring Catholic newspapers, arresting priests, and forbidding church processions. Pope Pius XII excommunicated him. In September 1955, the military abandoned Perón and forced him into exile in Spain.

The army sought—with limited success—to purge Argentina of all Peronista influence. It outlawed the Peronista constitution and the party itself and arrested its leaders. Perón remained in exile for the next seventeen years, but he cast a shadow over Argentine politics, and his party—although officially outlawed—remained a force to be reckoned with.

The election of February 1958 brought to power Arturo Frondizi, who inherited a politically fragmented country with a struggling, inflation-ridden economy. Frondizi's invitation to foreign interests to take control of the stalled oil industry, provoked a nationalistic outcry. His relations with the military were strained, and when he looked to the left for support, army leaders, known as the *gorillas,* began to stir. In desperate need of support during the 1962 election, Frondizi legalized the Peronista Party. After the Peronistas won a smashing electoral victory, the army intervened. It seized power once again, arrested Frondizi, and again banned the Peronistas.

In 1972, none other than Perón's party ended the parade of military rulers when once again it won an electoral victory. When Perón died in office in July 1974, he left power in the hands of his third wife, Isabel, who just happened to be his vice-president. She proved unequal to the immense task of governing a troubled nation, and in 1976 the army again stepped in—for the sixth time since 1930.

The new regime, headed by General Jorge Rafael Videla, was the most ruthless in Argentine history. Videla suspended congress, the courts, political parties, and labor unions and vested all power in a nine-man military commission. The army set out on a witch-hunt against any subversives and critics. Only several hundred of those killed were leftist guerrillas; the vast majority were peaceful activists. "We will kill all the subversives," the military governor of Buenos Aires declared, and after that the collaborators, sympathizers, those who were neutral, and, finally, the merely timid. The military murdered up to 30,000; many of them were tortured and some simply "disappeared," including victims who were pushed out of airplanes over the Atlantic Ocean. Beginning in April 1977, mothers whose children had disappeared began to protest at the Plaza de Mayo in the center of Buenos Aires. (At least three of the mothers themselves eventually disappeared.)

In 1982, the military took Argentina to war in an attempt to draw people's attention away from their economic woes and the "dirty war," as the harsh government crackdown on dissent was known. The generals dusted off Argentina's historic claim to a group of islands, the Malvinas, a British possession known as the Falkland Islands, some 300 miles off Argentina's coast. When Argentina's army and navy suffered a costly and decisive defeat at the hands of the British, the military junta was further discredited. It was forced to call elections and relinquish power to a civilian government in October 1983.

Argentina's new president, Raul Alfonsín, head of the Radical Party, was the first to defeat the Peronistas in an open election. His election was seen as a mandate to restore order and civility. Cautiously, Alfonsín set in motion criminal proceedings against his military predecessors. Those convicted of crimes committed in the "dirty war" were sentenced to long jail terms. Alfonsín also succeeded in retiring fifty generals. But a series of barrack revolts put an end to further prosecutions. Congress enacted a new law that granted the accused the right to argue that they had only "obeyed orders," a spurious defense used unsuccessfully by Nazi war criminals at the Nuremberg trials following World War II.

Alfonsín also faced an economy saddled with one of the world's highest rates of inflation and largest debts. At the end of his presidency in 1989, inflation had risen to 7,000 percent annually—and the debt crisis remained unresolved. Moreover, between 1976 and 1989, personal income had shrunk more than 1 percent each year.[3]

The next president, Carlos Menem, in what he called an "act of reconciliation," granted the generals a blanket amnesty and after that a blanket pardon. With a stroke of the pen he sought to undo any and all attempts to hold the generals accountable for their crimes. Among those pardoned was the chief architect of the "dirty war," General Videla himself, who had been sentenced to life in prison.

But the issue would not go away. In June 1998, the courts overturned Menem's pardon, ruling that the pardons did not extend to officers such as Videla, who—among other crimes—had been charged with the abduction of children and the murder of their mothers. Survivors of the "dirty war"—mainly mothers and wives of the disappeared—continued through the years to demand justice as they sought to reclaim children who were stolen from them over thirty years earlier and then adopted by couples with connections to the military.[4]

Following the advice of the International Monetary Fund, Menem engineered a temporary economic turnaround when he pegged the Argentine peso (backed by the country's hard-currency reserves) to the US dollar. Menem sold off government property, such as the telephone system, airlines, railroads, electricity, water system, and even pensions. He also opened the Argentine economy to international investors. In return, the IMF provided new credits to help Argentina restructure its massive foreign debt. Between 1991 and 1997, the economy grew at an average rate of 6.1 percent, the highest in the region. Argentina briefly became one of the poster children for globalization.

The debt restructuring, however, had little effect because Argentina's foreign debt continued to increase, to $155 billion in 1998. Entry into the global economy produced a raft of bankruptcies of Argentine companies that could not compete with foreigners, leading to a rising tide of unemployment and a steady increase in public debt. Although Menem privatized the pension system, the state still had obligations to its remaining pensioners as well as to the unemployed. But hampered by an inefficient system of tax collection, it eventually ran out of money. The peso began a precipitous drop in 2001, as it was no longer backed by hard currency reserves, and by February 2002, it had lost half of its value against the dollar. The middle class lost much of its savings and depositors were unable to recover their money from banks that did not have the means to meet their obligations. Income per person dropped from $7,000 to $3,500 and unemployment rose to 25 percent. Among the consequences were a higher crime rate, the spread of *villas miserias* (shantytowns), higher divorce rates, and hunger. By February 2003, 58 percent of the population, according to the government's own figures, was designated as poor.[5]

The upshot was the biggest default on foreign debt in history. Argentina, which in 1913 had ranked among the ten richest nations—ahead of France and Germany—had hit rock bottom, suffering from an economic calamity without parallel, one of the steepest declines in recent history. A decade later, the economy was still sputtering along. Expensive energy imports greatly reduced foreign currency reserves, while inflation, estimated in 2013 at 25 percent a year, discouraged investments and further destroyed saving accounts. The gap between the rich and poor was as wide as ever. The poor sought help from the government; the rich wanted the government to protect them against the poor, many of whom lived literally only a stone's throw from their gated communities.[6]

## Brazil

Brazil stands out among the nations of South America both because of its Portuguese (rather than Spanish) background and because of its vast natural resources and immense size. Brazil covers one third of the South American continent and its population, just over 200 million in 2013, is the world's sixth largest. Ever since Portugal formally accepted Brazil's independence in 1825, the nation has been looking to the future.

When Brazil's democratically elected governments proved unable to cope with the struggling economy or attempted radical reforms, they followed the rest of South America and gave way to military strongmen.

In the first decade after World War II, democratically elected presidents wrestled with inflation fueled by heavy government borrowing. A case in point was the administration of Juscelino Kubitschek, who aggressively pursued industrial growth that depended on lavish government spending. His most extravagant project was the founding of a spectacular new capital city, Brasília, located away from the densely populated coast. A proud symbol of the nation's future, the new capital was also designed to spur the development of Brazil's interior.

Kubitschek's successors moved to the left of the political center. João Goulart proposed extensive land reform, enfranchised the nation's illiterate (40 percent of the population), and raised taxes to increase revenues. In 1964, he ordered the expropriation of some of the nation's largest estates. His measures earned him the support of the peasantry and the working class but raised the hackles of the landowning elite, the middle class, and the military. Goulart also antagonized Washington when he proclaimed a neutralist foreign policy, continued diplomatic relations with the Soviet Union (which his immediate predecessor had reestablished), legalized the Brazilian Communist Party, and began to woo that party's support. Goulart's free-spending policies, like those of Kubitschek, caused inflation, and this, in addition to his move to the left, eroded his support among the middle class. Once the Brazilian generals secured support from US president Lyndon Johnson, they forced his resignation in April 1964. On the next day, Johnson extended his recognition and good wishes to the new military dictatorship.

This time the generals came to stay for twenty years. Blaming free-spending civilian politicians for Brazil's ills, they silenced the opposition, forced an austerity program on the nation, banned the Communist Party, and carried out mass arrests of Communists and suspected Communists. A series of "institutional acts" incrementally restricted the powers of the congress, arrogated greater powers to the presidency, disenfranchised political parties, and sought to crush the labor unions.

The economy responded to the generals' stringent austerity program, and during the twenty years of military rule, Brazil realized its highest economic growth rates. In 1966, its annual rate of growth of GNP was 4 percent; in the early 1970s, it reached 10 percent. For the first time since World War II, Brazil had a favorable balance of trade. But the economic success could not be sustained, partly because of the severe impact of the oil crises of the 1970s and partly because of the large foreign debt the military leaders ran up. Moreover, industrial growth did not produce a higher standard of living for the majority of Brazilians since it was tied to keeping wages low. All the while the rise in the cost of living exceeded the growth in wages. In addition, the military had no interest in land reform and did nothing to improve the lot of the rural poor.

By South American standards, the Brazilian military's rule had been moderate. The generals executed 200 people (as compared with up to 30,000 in Argentina) and forced hundreds into exile. In Brazil's first free election in twenty-nine years, in March 1989, a civilian government returned to power. Fernando Collor de Mello, a young, winsome, articulate, conservative politician defeated the candidate of the left, Luiz Ignacio da Silva. Collor de Mello made the usual promises—democracy and prosperity—but his reign brought instead unprecedented personal corruption (largely in the form of selling government contracts), culminating in his resignation in 1992.

In October 2002, Brazilian politics saw a dramatic shift to the left. Luiz Ignacio da Silva—commonly known as Lula—in his fourth bid for the presidency, won a runoff election by a wide margin. His rise to power was literally from rags to riches. One of twenty-two children of an illiterate farm worker, Lula rose from shoeshine boy to the leader of São Paulo's militant auto workers' union. He then organized the Workers' Party, Latin America's largest left-wing party.

Lula inherited an economy in deep trouble. In 2003, the *real*, Brazil's currency, had lost 40 percent of its value, and as a consequence the public debt spiraled upward. The international financial community feared that Brazil would follow Argentina and default on its foreign debt. Immediately after the election, however, Lula put away his Ché Guevara tee shirts, put on a suit and tie, and stepped back from his previous pledge to renege on the debt. He had already brought under control the radicals in his party and had formed an alliance with the center-right Liberal Party. He reminded Brazilians, "There is no miraculous solution for such a huge social debt."[7]

Lula's former finance minister called him "the ultimate pragmatist." Indeed, he renewed Brazil's international financial obligations and repaid its IMF loans in full by the end of 2005, and then ran a surplus for the next two years. For decades, Brazil had been the largest debtor among the emerging nations, but in January 2008 it became a creditor nation for the first time. Under Lula's pragmatic guiding hand, Brazil became the world's eighth largest economy (and shortly became the sixth largest). As banks and foreign investors participated in the bourgeoning economy, Brazil's middle class grew from a little over one-third of the population to one-half.

Lula's foreign policy was equally conservative. He sought to play the role of an intermediary between adversaries, such as Hugo Chávez of Venezuela and the United States. Along the way, he drew criticism from both, but it did not deter him from trying to mediate tense standoffs. He caused a bit of a stir in the West when he told the British Broadcasting Corporation (BBC) that the world's problems were not caused by African or Latin American immigrants, as someone on the political right had charged. The global financial meltdown of 2007–2008, he said, was caused by the "irrational behavior" of financiers with blond hair and blue eyes who pretended "to know everything."

During Lula's presidency, Brazil was designated as the host for the two most prestigious international sporting events, the soccer World Cup in 2014 and the summer Olympic Games in 2016. Brazilians who have long suffered from a sense of inferiority—on a state visit, US president Ronald Reagan toasted "the people of Bolivia"—rejoiced at their upcoming moment in the sun. Brazil, they declared, was no longer an "emerging" nation. The games would be Brazil's coming-out party.[8]

Lula's presidency was tainted by scandals but they did not touch him directly. He had won the presidency with 61 percent of the vote; when he stepped down in December 2010, his approval rate stood at an astonishing 87 percent. Lula's successor was Dilma Rousseff, another former leftist (who had been imprisoned and tortured by the military) turned pragmatist.

Rousseff inherited a host of ills. Following a global pattern, the gap between the rich and poor continued to grow. Rio de Janeiro was famous for more than its beaches; overlooking them on the hillsides were the equally world-famous *favelas*, or shantytowns. Brazilians complained of First World taxes in return for Third World services—shoddy schools, health care, and roads.

A hike in bus and subway fares in São Paulo sparked spontaneous demonstrations that ultimately spread to eighty cities. One target was the tens of billions of dollars set aside for the World Cup and the Olympics. Brazilians, who uniformly believed that their political system was corrupt, were certain that politicians and contractors were reaping exorbitant profits. FIFA (Fédération Internationale de Football Association), the international soccer governing body, insisted, however, that the stadiums, such as Rio's Maracanã Stadium, be turned into first-class facilities.

## Chile

Chile stood apart from the rest of Latin America in that it did not succumb to military rule until 1973. Chileans were justly proud that theirs was the most orderly and democratic country in Latin America. Ultimately, however, it became Chile's fate to stand out as the most flagrant example of US interference in South America.

Nowhere in South America were US business interests more substantial than in Chile. US firms owned Chile's copper mines and many of its other industries. When Chilean politics moved to the left, it was not only the conservatives in Chile who were alarmed. Washington would not sit still as Chile edged closer to Communism.

In the 1960s, Washington favored moderate conservative governments in Chile, such as that of Eduardo Frei, the head of the Christian Democratic Party. The Chilean elite, however, considered Frei's gradualist reforms—reduction of illiteracy, expansion of social services, and a modest agrarian program—as too radical, while the working class and the parties on the left saw them as too modest. Only the middle class and Washington seemed happy with Frei.

The polarization of Chilean politics deepened during the election in 1970. The Marxist Salvador Allende, the candidate of a leftist coalition, Popular Unity, squeaked by with a narrow victory and became the world's first freely elected Marxist head of state. Allende, whose cabinet consisted mainly of socialists and Communists, rejected armed revolution and called instead for a peaceful transition to socialism. As such he had more in common with the West European Social Democrats that with the Communists in Moscow. Allende nationalized US and Chilean copper and nitrate companies and banks, extended the land reform begun by Frei, and placed a ceiling on prices while raising workers' wages. The latter was part of his "doctrine of excess profits," which US corporations took out of Chile while their workers received paltry compensation.[9] These measures were immensely popular with the majority of Chileans, but they alarmed US business in Chile, the political right, and Washington.

When Allende took office, Chile was already in an economic depression. By the second year of his term, the economy was in a tailspin, with inflation running out of control. Allende's policies contributed to these problems, but the major blow to the Chilean economy was a drastic drop in the international price of copper. By mid-1972, Allende's base of support dwindled to little more than the working class and the poor. Conservative elements—notably the military—began to organize a resistance. A crippling, nationwide truckers' strike—a measure secretly supported by CIA funds—had its impact, further polarizing the nation. Allende and his supporters, fearing the worst, began arming workers while the army prepared for a coup. On September 11, 1973, the air force bombed the presidential palace. Augusto Pinochet, the army's chief of staff, ordered his generals not to negotiate with Allende. Should he be captured alive, Pinochet said, "we . . . offer to fly him out of the country, but the plane falls in mid-flight."[10] Allende committed suicide as the army closed in on him.

Washington was deeply involved in the Chilean political arena. In 1970, the Nixon administration had sought to prevent Allende from coming to power and, failing to do so, joined in the efforts to destabilize his government. Even as the sins of Watergate were catching up with Nixon, he remained obsessed with Allende. Nixon's national security adviser, Henry Kissinger, regarded Allende as a threat to the entire region. "I don't see why we have to let a country go Marxist," he famously declared, "just because its people are irresponsible."[11]

The Nixon administration had funneled some $8 million through the CIA to Allende's opponents and cut off all loans, economic aid, and private investments to Chile. Speculation was rife of direct US involvement in the military coup, but Washington admitted nothing and kept the relevant documents classified until the late 1990s, when the Clinton administration declassified evidence supporting such speculation.[12] Several of the Chilean military officers, including Pinochet (like many others from Latin American countries), had received training at the School for the Americas, a US Army facility in Panama.

The new military junta, under the direction of Pinochet, swiftly carried out a relentless campaign against leftists and anyone suspected of being associated with Allende. It crammed a large soccer stadium and the jails with political prisoners, killing an estimated 4,000 of them. A "Caravan of Death" took soldiers throughout the country to engage in summary executions. It was under Pinochet that Latin America experienced the first cases of people simply "disappearing," a practice that then spread through the region. Pinochet was also the guiding force of Operation Condor, an effort on the part of military strongmen in six participating countries (Chile, Argentina, Brazil, Uruguay, Paraguay, and Bolivia) to track down opponents, not only in Latin America but also in Europe and the United States. In September 1976, Chilean operatives assassinated Allende's foreign minister, Orlando Letelier, in Sheridan Circle in Washington, DC. Kissinger knew of Operation Condor and, in fact, supported it against leftist Chilean exiles in Argentina. He urged the Argentine foreign minister to act "quickly" and then "get back quickly to normal procedure."[13] (Colonel Manuel Contreras, the former head of the Department of National Intelligence, the secret police, was sentenced to prison in 1993 for his role in the 1976 murder of Letelier. The court did not accept his defense that he had only followed Pinochet's orders.)

Pinochet invited US copper companies back in, halted the land reform program, broke up labor unions, banned all leftist parties, and dissolved congress. All the while, he enjoyed the support of Washington. The same, however, could not be said of his own people. Despite the ban against antigovernment demonstrations, thousands of people went into the streets starting in the late 1980s to protest the military dictatorship. Pinochet relented in 1990 by allowing a referendum on whether military rule should continue. In the first free election in twenty years, the people voted overwhelmingly to restore civilian rule. Pinochet, however, remained in command of the army by virtue of a clause in the constitution he had written. The constitution also had made the armed forces the "guarantor of institutionality," meaning that they had the right to step in whenever they felt necessary to do so.[14]

Pinochet relinquished his command of the army in March 1998 but then became "senator for life," a position that granted him immunity from criminal charges for atrocities committed under his seventeen-year rule. He returned to international attention when he was arrested in London, in October 1998, at the request of Spain, which wanted him extradited to try him on charges of human rights abuses against Spanish citizens in Chile. The eighty-three-year-old Pinochet languished in London under house arrest for over a year until January 2000, when a team of British physicians found him too ill to stand trial, thus clearing the way for his return to Chile.

In August 2004, Chile's supreme court, by a vote of 9-8, ruled that Pinochet was not immune from prosecution. Before he was brought to trial, he died in December 2006 at the age of ninety-one. The new government denied him a state funeral, as was customary for former heads of state, nor did it declare a national day of mourning. As a former chief of the armed forces, however, Pinochet did receive a military funeral.

### Peru

Perhaps nowhere in South America were social and economic inequities as wide as in Peru. A small, wealthy elite kept the Peruvian masses—mainly of native Indian stock—in dismal poverty. About 80 percent of the land was owned by a mere 1 percent of landowners, the richest owning over 1 million acres. Landless Peruvian peasants sporadically rose in rebellion to obtain land, only to be crushed by the army. Neither the early postwar military regime in Peru nor the civilian administrations that followed attempted land reform, even though much of the land of the *latifundios* lay fallow. As the country was seething with peasant unrest, a rural-based Communist movement began to spread.

Under the leadership of the left-wing general Juan Velasco (1968–1975), the government introduced state planning and modest social and economic reforms. Most noteworthy was land reform, which over a period of seven years expropriated and redistributed some 25 million acres—about 72 percent of Peru's arable land. The Velasco government also engaged in land reclamation to increase agricultural output and meet the needs of the land-starved Indians, and it nationalized foreign properties, including US-owned copper, petroleum, and sugar companies. Private enterprise remained legal, but industries were required to share profits with their workers. Despite its reformist efforts, however, the Velasco government failed to achieve either a fundamental social transformation or a significant improvement in the standard of living for most Peruvians.

An unlikely candidate won the July 1990 presidential election: Alberto Fujimori, an inexperienced politician of Japanese ancestry. When Fujimori took office, Peru had not made a payment for two years on its $23 billion debt; the inflation rate was over 40 percent per month; and the central government was unable to govern outlying regions, where hostile guerrillas stalked the countryside.

Fujimori first attacked the economic problem. By introducing "shock therapy"—that is, slashing government payrolls and subsidies and overhauling the tax system—he managed to break the inflationary cycle within six months. Elected by popular vote, Fujimori shortly became a front man for the military, however. When his "shock therapy" generated a public backlash, he suspended the constitution, closed the legislative assembly, and assumed emergency executive powers.

Fujimori won acclaim by winning a stunning victory in Peru's twelve-year war against the Sendero Luminoso, or "Shining Path," a Maoist-Marxist movement that combined violent revolution with drug trafficking. The Shining Path had organized poverty-stricken peasants to protect them against brutality by the police and the military, with the aim of ultimately bringing down the government. The result was a civil war with extraordinary savagery on both sides, causing the death of an estimated 69,000 Peruvians, killed outright or simply "disappeared," mostly impoverished native Quechuas in the high Andes. Its financial cost was estimated at $22 billion.[15]

The war ended with the arrest of the leaders of Shining Path, including its charismatic founder, Abimael Guzman, a former philosophy professor. They were sentenced to life in prison. Fujimori's defeat of the Shining Path and a measure of economic progress ensured his reelection in 1994.

Fujimori's austerity program, however, benefited only small segments of the population—among them the financial sector and international investors. Fujimori made sure to meet Peru's financial obligations as spelled out by the IMF. Meanwhile, real wages fell by 10 percent and the majority of Peruvians—about two thirds of them—remained mired in poverty. None of it prevented Fujimori from continuing to present himself as the champion of "true democracy" and the common man, even as he was doing the army's bidding.[16]

In July 1992, a military death squad operating under the direct orders of the commander-in-chief of the army, General Nicolas Hermoza—and ultimately under Fujimori's orders—abducted and murdered nine students and a professor at La Cantuta University. When the courts eventually convicted and sentenced twelve soldiers for the crime, Fujimori pushed through the pliant congress a blanket amnesty for those convicted of human rights crimes between May 1980 and June 1995.[17]

In December 1996, yet another leftist organization resurfaced, Túpac Amaru (which took its name from the last Inca ruler whom the Spanish had hanged in 1572 and a namesake whom the Spanish had tortured to death in 1781). Fujimori had proclaimed he had defeated their insurgency, but at a Christmas party hosted by the Japanese ambassador, Túpac Amaru took 400 hostages. It demanded the release of its imprisoned comrades, who had been sentenced by Peruvian military tribunals. The hostage crisis continued unresolved into April 1997, in part because the Japanese government insisted on a negotiated settlement. In the end, Peruvian commandos stormed the building, killing all Túpac Amaru members inside while losing one hostage and two commandos. For Fujimori, it was another feather in his cap.

In 1996, the Fujimori majority in congress reinterpreted the constitution, which restricted a president to two five-year terms, and granted him another term. Dissenting judges were dismissed. Newspapers became apologists for the Fujimori regime; editors who refused to fall into line felt the wrath of Vladimiro Montesinos, head of the National Intelligence Service, who controlled the death squads operating out of his headquarters, the "Little Pentagon." Montesinos was on the CIA payroll, despite its knowledge that he and Fujimori had long been engaged in extortion, larceny, drug trafficking, torture, and murder.[18]

In the April 2000 election, Fujimori faced a surprisingly strong contender in the person of Alejandro Toledo. Toledo, of Indian descent, was another political novice whose party, Perú Posible, promised a new dawn. Toledo came in a strong second, forcing a runoff election. Toledo refused to participate in the runoff unless it contained safeguards against rigging it. Fujimori refused to oblige him and went ahead with his third term, despite criticism from neighboring countries, the Organization of American States, and the United States, which heretofore had supported him.

Fujimori's grip finally began to slip in September 2000, when his right-hand man, Montesinos, was caught on videotape bribing an opposition politician. Ten days later, Montesinos fled the country. Unable to find political asylum abroad, he returning to Peru and went into hiding. Two weeks later, in November 2000, Fujimori fled to Tokyo, from where he resigned by fax. The Peruvian congress would not let him resign, however. Instead, it accused him of dereliction of duty and declared him morally unfit to govern. The government launched an investigation leading to charges against Fujimori and Montesinos—the running of death squads (such as one that perpetrated the La Cantuta University murders), embezzlement, and extortion. Montesinos was eventually arrested and got his day in court. He was found guilty and sentenced to twenty years in the Callao maximum-security prison, which, ironically, he and Fujimori had built, and which also housed Abimael Guzman, the former head of the Shining Path.

As a politician, Fujimori had emphasized his humble origins, even campaigning in the garb of the rural Indians. During his ten years in power, however, endemic poverty remained unchanged. During the 1990s, the poverty rate hovered around 50 percent and 41 percent of the people lived on $2 or less per day.[19] Montesinos and Fujimori, however, had no difficulty in making ends meet. Transparency International concluded that the two had engaged in "unprecedented looting of the resources" of Peru. Montesinos siphoned off an estimated $2 billion; Fujimori escaped with perhaps as much as $600 million.[20]

For five years, Fujimori lived in luxury in Tokyo beyond the reach of Peruvian law, a celebrity, particularly in Japanese right-wing circles. Japan granted him citizenship, ensuring that he would not be extradited. It would not hand over one of its own like a common criminal. Inexplicably, in November 2005, Fujimori returned to Peru, ostensibly to run for president again. It was likely that Tokyo found him an international embarrassment. Interpol (the International Criminal Police Organization) had him on its most wanted list, and Peru had repeatedly demanded his extradition. The honorable thing for the now sixty-seven-year-old Fujimori—"the last samurai," as he called himself—was to return to Peru and face the consequences. In the first trial, in December 2007, Fujimori, who denied all charges, was sentenced to six years in prison. In April and July 2009, Fujimori was again convicted for crimes against humanity—based in part on declassified US documents—and sentenced to a maximum 25-year prison term, for murder, kidnapping, and embezzlement.

Fujimori's last chance was his daughter, Keiko. As a member of the Peruvian legislature, she had been known as a law-and-order candidate, ready to punish all criminal wrongdoing. Now, however, she ran for president to spring her convict father from prison. All dictators leave behind a sizable following, and Fujimori was no different. In a close run-off election in June 2011, Keiko Fujimori lost to Ollanta Humala. Her father continued to languish in prison from where, in violation of Peruvian law, he used Twitter and YouTube to issue public pronouncements and personal insults directed at Humala.

## The Shift to the Left

In the late 1990s, the political pendulum in Latin America began to move to the left. The driving force was Hugo Chávez of Venezuela. In February 1992, he and 200 army officers launched a failed coup for which they spent two years in prison. In 1998, Chávez ran for the presidency as the candidate of the dispossessed, the vast majority of the population. He campaigned as the fervid champion of a "Bolivarian revolution," pledging a return to the ideals of "the Liberator," Simón Bolívar. In office, Chávez erected billboards that carried the image of Bolívar and his quote from 1829: "The United States seems destined by providence to plague the Americas with misery in the name of liberty."

Chávez, who was influenced less by Marxism than by nineteenth-century Venezuelan populists, was popular among those who lived in the barrios on the fringes of the capital city, Caracas. He lavished on them large sums of petrodollars to set up schools, soup kitchens, small cooperative businesses, and medical centers. Born into poverty at a time when oil money enriched the few and left the many to fend for themselves, he now focused on the redistribution of land and oil wealth. Oil was the linchpin of the Venezuelan economy. Up to 80 percent of Venezuelan exports, nearly 30 percent of its gross domestic product (GDP), and 50 percent of the state's revenue came from the sale of oil.

Chávez's revolution produced the inevitable confrontation with Venezuela's elites—the "rancid oligarchs," as Chávez called them—who were shocked by a "participatory democracy" that excluded them from power for the first time in their lives. Chávez also established close personal ties with Cuba's aged dictator, Fidel Castro, and provided Cuba with oil in exchange for more than 10,000 Cuban medical personnel, who went into barrios that had never before seen a doctor. The charismatic Chávez here followed in the foot-steps of South America's *caudillos*, constantly seeking to expand his powers—by extending favors, controlling the media, packing the courts, and drawing up blacklists. Chávez remained popular, however, winning seven national elections. But when he sought in December 2007, by way of a referendum, to amend the constitution designed to pave the way for unlimited presidential terms, the country voted against it. Chávez "wants a blank check," one of his supporters said, "and that's impossible." Nonetheless, in March 2009, the persistent Chávez won a second such referendum, which paved the way for the relatively young, fifty-four-year-old strongman to cling to power far into future.

In April 2002, the George W. Bush administration supported a failed coup to oust Chávez. When Chávez, in September 2006, addressed the UN General Assembly a day after Bush had done so, he remarked that "the devil came here yesterday, and it smells of sulfur still today."

When Chávez died in March 2013, he left behind a country with a spotty economic and human rights record. The rights of women and indigenous peoples had been expanded, but the courts and the press had seen their rights restricted. Venezuela had serious economic problems, a point his opponents never hesitated to make. Still, the rates of malnutrition and poverty were cut in half (the latter from 54 to 26 percent) and the poor had greater access to education and health care. These gains were a major reason why in his last election, his closest, Chávez still garnered 54 percent of the votes.

Chávez found a number of imitators in South America, although none of them was willing to go as far as he. The best known was Evo Morales, the first indigenous president of Bolivia, a forty-six-year-old Amaya Indian and former *cocalero*, or coca grower. It had taken the native Indians more than four centuries to put an end to serfdom (only in 1952), and it took them another half-century to put one of their own in the presidential palace.

Between the early 1990s and the December 2005 victory by Morales's Movement Toward Socialism party, Bolivia, the poorest of South American countries, had followed the dictates of the so-called Washington Consensus, which demanded cuts in social spending in exchange for private foreign investments and the promise of prosperity. The spending cuts were made (thus bringing hyperinflation under control) and the foreigners came, but prosperity remained elusive. Corruption remained rampant, per capita economic growth was a paltry 0.5 percent per year, and half of all Bolivians made do on less than $2 per day. Instead of continuing with the privatization of the economy, the holy grail of the Washington Consensus, Morales nationalized enterprises, notably oil and natural gas, which had primarily benefited foreign investors.

Other left-of-center Latin American presidents, who had been elected on the promise that they would invest heavily in social programs to close the wide gap between rich and poor, nonetheless took a more moderate approach as they sought to find a proper mix between state planning and the private market.[21]

## Mexico

The roots of Mexico's problems date back to the political and economic consequences of the bloody revolution of 1910–1917, during which 1.5 million people perished—approximately 10 percent of the population. Not until the late 1920s did the country enjoy a measure of stability when the Partido Revolucionario Institutional (the Institutional Revolutionary Party, or PRI) came to power and began to organize diverse groups in support of the state. It encouraged workers, peasants, bureaucrats, big-business executives, owners of small enterprises, and teachers to bargain with the party, which then became the arbiter between the various interest groups. The PRI skillfully formed political alliances, doled out patronage jobs, co-opted its opponents, occasionally carried out reforms within the party, controlled the media, and, when necessary, resorted to fraud and repression. Incumbent presidents usually selected their successors behind closed doors. The PRI-dominated governments produced a surface calm, but they did not address the underlying causes of social discontent that periodically bubbled to the top.

The revolution of 1910 began as a liberal challenge to the dictatorship of Porfirio Díaz, but it soon became more radical when the *campesinos* (the peasantry), led by Emiliano Zapata and Pancho Villa, demanded "Land and Liberty," the redistribution of land. At the time, 96 percent of the rural households owned no land, and fewer than 850 families owned 97 percent of Mexico's arable land.[22] The 1917 Constitution promised a redistribution of land, but until the presidency of the populist Lázaro Cárdenas (1934–1940), only 10 percent of the *campesinos* had benefited from land reform.

Cárdenas distributed more land than any other Mexican president. The campesinos' irrigated landholdings increased fourfold, but land distribution came to a halt in March 1938, after army generals complained that Cárdenas's reforms had gone too far.[23] Cárdenas then shifted his focus to "imperialist intervention," that is, foreign corporations that controlled sectors of the Mexican economy, notably oil. The time was ripe, Cárdenas declared, for the nationalization of these companies. This unleashed a massive outpouring of public support; millions of Mexicans contributed to a national indemnity fund to help pay off the $200 million the oil companies eventually received in compensation.[24]

Under the PRI's guidance, state capitalism, bolstered by a fourfold per capita increase in government expenditures, gave Mexico decades of sustained growth. Between 1940 and 1960, manufacturing rose by 365 percent, steel production by 934 percent, motor vehicle production by 451 percent, and agricultural output by 218 percent. During the same period, the population increased by 78 percent.[25] Yet the gap between the rich and the poor grew after World War II, leaving in its wake raised expectations, disillusionment, and dissent.

The economic downturn of the late 1960s had severe political repercussions. On October 2, 1968, tens of thousands of demonstrators—mostly students—congregated in Mexico City's Tlatelolco Plaza to protest police brutality, political corruption, and economic hardship. The army promptly put an end to the demonstrations by shooting dead at least 300 civilians. Ten days later, the Olympic Games began in Mexico City, the first such showcase in a developing country. As the torch was lit in Aztec Stadium, troops and tanks oversaw the proceedings just beyond the view of the television cameras.

The massacre did not solve the PRI's problems. It triggered, instead, a crisis of legitimacy for the party. During the 1970s and 1980s, the PRI conducted its "dirty war" against opponents, many of whom traced their anger back to the 1968 massacre. For thirty years, the PRI denied that the massacre (as well as others), had taken place. Eventually, Mexico began to come to terms with its past. In February 2002, pictures of the Tlatelolco Square massacre appeared in newspapers, and the courts began to grapple with the issue. The courts, however, were hopelessly divided on how to deal with Luis Echeverría, the interior minister at the time. The court ruled it had not been a case of genocide; moreover, the statute of limitations had expired.

When Echeverría became president in 1970, dissidents—among them students, reporters, guerrillas, and practitioners of "liberation theology"—set out to build grassroots social bases in the *barrios* and among the *campesinos*. Under pressure to create more jobs, Echeverría borrowed both time and money. To save jobs, the government ensured that bankrupt enterprises were keep running and borrowed increasing amounts of foreign money—without the revenue to repay it. When Echeverría took office, the nation's foreign debt was $5 billion; by the time his successor, José López (1976–1982), took office, it had quadrupled, to $20 billion. López came to power in the midst of the oil boom of the late 1970s, which made it possible for Mexico—sitting on top of vast oil reserves—to borrow still more money. During his presidency, the public and private sectors borrowed another $60 billion. By August 1982, Mexico was unable to pay its massive foreign debt, a condition that triggered a Latin American debt crisis.

In the early 1980s, elections in northern Mexico—free from the usual tampering by PRI functionaries—showed the weakness of the PRI, which lost several local races to the Partido Acción Nacional (National Action Party, or PAN), a center-right, business-based party. In the mid-1980s, an environmental protest movement emerged, partly in response to Mexico City's horrendous air pollution. Then came the massive earthquake of September 1985 (8.1 magnitude), which killed more than 10,000 people. In its aftermath, Cuauthemoc Cárdenas (the son of the revered Lázaro Cárdenas) broke with the PRI to become the candidate of a center-left coalition. In the 1988 presidential election, he challenged the PRI candidate, Carlos Salinas de Gortari. Two days before the election, two of Cárdenas's key aides were murdered (crimes that were never solved), and a few hours after the voting ended, the computer counting the votes crashed. When it came back online, Salinas had won the election with just over 50 percent of the vote. A few months later, the PRI destroyed the ballots.

By now, Mexico's economy was treading water during the country's worst recession in sixty years. Between 1980 and 1993, annual output declined by an average of 0.5 percent. Mexico worked out agreements with international lending institutions (such as the World Bank and IMF) that gave it access to additional credit. At the same time, it negotiated with Canada and the United States the terms of the North American Free Trade Agreement (NAFTA). Lazaro Cárdenas's "anti-imperialist" campaign of the 1930s was now but a dim memory.

The social price of Mexico's admission into the minefields of the global economy was high. It forced Mexico to carry out deep structural adjustments to satisfy creditors—the elimination of tariffs, deregulation of the economy, privatization of state enterprises, and labor "flexibilization" (literally, making labor more flexible, more amenable to the demands of factory owners). In short, workers were expected to work harder for lower wages. The state denied unions the right of free association and used police and the army against them. The once powerful unions lost both economic and political power.

### Chiapas

On January 1, 1994, Mexico faced yet another crisis, this time a rebellion by *campesinos*, mostly Indians, in the state of Chiapas, along the Guatemalan border. Organized as the Zapatista National Liberation Army in memory of Emiliano Zapata, one of the heroes of the 1910 revolution, the rebels seized control of several cities and *latifundios*, which they turned into communal farms. They insisted that the land belonged to them by virtue of the 1917 Constitution.

The Zapatistas of 1994 saw land as the core issue. Since the move toward privatization of the economy during the mid-1980s, the *campesinos*—who had little land to begin with—lost land to the *latifundistas*. When the Zapatistas seized the courthouse in San Cristobal de las Casas, they promptly burned the municipal archives that held the land titles. They denounced the government's electoral fraud, demanded regional autonomy, and declared that they would no longer endure abuses at the hands of the PRI, the police, the army, or the terrorist *guardias blancas* ("white guards") deployed by the *latifundistas*.[26]

Chiapas was the poorest state in a poor country. The federal government spent less than half of development money per capita in Chiapas than on the nation as a whole. Chiapas needed paved roads, adequate schools, electricity (the state contained large dams exporting energy to other states), and health facilities. A large percentage of Chiapas's population was of Mayan Indian origin (26.4 percent, compared to the national average of 7.5 percent); a third of its people did not speak Spanish. Nearly 60 percent of the workers earned less than the national minimum daily wage of $3.33. Nineteen percent of the labor force existed at a bare subsistence level. Food production barely kept up with a population that had doubled during the previous two decades, while prices for the main cash crop, coffee, fell drastically.

The rebellion broke out the very day NAFTA—the final indignity—went into effect. The Zapatistas saw the treaty with the United States and Canada as a "death certificate" for the Indians of Mexico, who would not be able to compete with manufacturers and food producers in the north. Led by the charismatic and mysterious Subcomandante Marcos, his face hidden by a ski mask, they declared they spoke for all Mexicans struggling for democracy, land, and autonomy. The Salinas administration, hamstrung by repeated scandals and mistrusted by the majority of its people, sent the army to end the rebellion. Estimates of those killed varied widely between 145 and 400. In the end, Salinas agreed to negotiate with the rebels, whose strength lay not so much in their military prowess but in their manifestos on the Internet, through which they rallied popular support.

For nearly two decades the Zapatistas developed their autonomous zones in Chiapas, home to between 120,000 and 150,000 people. They made significant gains in education, women's rights, and the standard of living. The Zapatista became part of an amorphous global protest movement against entrenched power (which included "Occupy Wall Street" in New York, the "Angry Ones" in Spain, and radical Mexican students). When the PRI returned to power in July 2012, the Zapatistas declared they would not give up their hard-won gains.[27]

### The PRI Defeated

The Zapatistas were hardly alone in venting their anger against the system. Two million members of the middle class—small shopkeepers, merchants, and farmers, hard hit by the recession of the mid-1990s—formed their own protest movement, El Barzon, showing up in large numbers to denounce foreclosure hearings. Another group, the Civic Alliance, sent election observers to polling stations to prevent PRI election fraud. The National Episcopal Conference supported the Roman Catholic bishop in Chiapas, Samuel Ruíz García, who served as intermediary in talks between the rebels and authorities.

The PRI's political monopoly was crumbling as it no longer fulfilled the functions for which it had been created—to arbitrate disputes among competing interest groups. Continued widespread corruption—including theft from the national treasury—and unresolved political murders in 1994 and 1995 further undermined its legitimacy. In 1996, PAN, the right-center party, elected four state governors and ruled about one-third of the population.

Growing dissatisfaction with the PRI was clearly expressed in the presidential election of July 2000. Vicente Fox, the PAN candidate and a wealthy businessman who campaigned for sweeping political and economic reforms, won a resounding victory against the PRI candidate, thus ending the PRI's seventy-one-year monopoly on power. For the first time, an independent commission oversaw a presidential election, thereby keeping the PRI from rigging it.

Under Fox and his successor, Felipe Calderón, the economy grew. Mexicans who had emigrated to the United States began to return home. As the bridge between the drug-producing regions to the south and the lucrative US market, Mexico fell prey to the growing power of its drug cartels. The well-armed and well-financed drug traffickers bought off officials and journalists or simply assassinated them (at times with the help of the police and army). Many of their victims simply disappeared. About 100,000 people perished during Calderón's six-year long war against the drug cartels.

The unstable conditions were a shot in the arm for the PRI. It returned to power when its candidate, Enrique Peña Nieto, won the July 2012 presidential election with a plurality of 38 percent.

## Revolution and Counterrevolution in Central America

Central America's political struggles, fueled by deep social divisions, dated back to the nineteenth century. They resurfaced with a vengeance during the 1970s when the region became part and parcel of the global struggle between the United States and Soviet Union. On one side were landowners, who enjoyed political power and had the backing of the army; on the other was the majority of the population, which possessed little land and even fewer political rights.

Direct US involvement in Central America began in the 1890s and increased after the Spanish-American War of 1898. Washington took on the role of police officer of the Western Hemisphere, especially in the Caribbean where, in the words of Theodore Roosevelt, it would not permit "chronic wrongdoing." It treated the region as its "backyard," a sphere of influence where its political, economic, and military interests needed to be protected.

Officially, the US goal in Central America was to champion the blessings of democracy. In 1913, President Woodrow Wilson famously stated that he would "teach the South American republics how to elect good men."[28] The military regimes in Latin America, however, had other ideas. Moreover, US commitments to the cause of democracy often took a backseat to the primary quest: political stability and the protection of US interests. In the early 1960s, President John Kennedy described the dilemma in Central America:

> There are three possibilities in descending order of preference: a decent democratic regime, a continuation of the Trujillo regime [a right-wing dictatorship in the Dominican Republic] or a Castro regime [a left-wing dictatorship in Cuba]. We ought to aim at the first, but we really can't renounce the second until we are sure that we can avoid the third.[29]

Washington's problem was the absence of Kennedy's "decent democratic regimes." Successive administrations had to choose between the likes of Trujillo and Castro, invariably coming down on the side of the Trujillos, whom they then declared to be part of the "free world." Indeed, Washington even opposed democratically elected reformist governments such as that of Jacobo Arbenz in Guatemala in the early 1950s.

The Cuban revolution of 1959 proved to be a particular thorn in the side of Washington. Fidel Castro, unlike other revolutionaries in Latin America, refused to accept Cuba's unequal relationship with the United States, which went back to 1898 when the United States seized Cuba from Spain. The mafia and US companies controlled large segments of the Cuban economy. The most powerful man in Havana was the US ambassador. Castro insisted on the nationalization (governmental takeover) of US property—with compensation—and the reorganization of the Cuban economy along socialist lines.[30] When talks stalled with Washington, Castro worked out a trade agreement with the Soviet Union, trading Cuban sugar for Soviet oil and machinery.

Unaccustomed to such a brazen show of defiance, Washington countered with an economic embargo and broke off diplomatic relations with Cuba. It then moved to overthrow Castro, an attempt that culminated in the fiasco at the Bay of Pigs in 1961 (see Chapter 4). The CIA tried to assassinate Castro who, with the help of Soviet assistance, consolidated his power. The Cuban missile crisis in 1962 led to a US pledge not to invade Cuba, but successive US governments, whether Democratic or Republican, were in no mood to tolerate other radical regimes in their "backyard." One Cuba was enough.

### Nicaragua

The next serious outbreak of revolutionary violence in Central America began in Nicaragua during the late 1960s. It became more volatile after a devastating earthquake in 1972 that leveled much of Managua, the nation's cap-

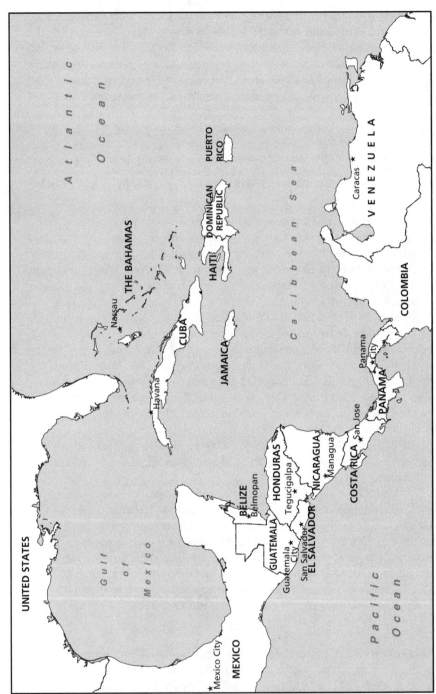

ital. Nicaragua was ruled by the Somoza family, which had come to power in the early 1930s with the help of US Marines (an occupying force in Nicaragua, off and on, from 1911 to 1932). President Franklin Roosevelt once remarked that Anastasio Somoza García, the founder of the dynasty, was an "s.o.b., but [he is] our s.o.b."[31] The greed of the Somozas became legendary. When the last of the Somozas, Anastasio Jr. ("Tachito"), fled the country in 1979, he took with him an estimated $100–400 million, most of it from the national treasury.

The 1972 earthquake highlighted the greed of Tachito Somoza and the National Guard, his private army. They had long been involved in the seizing of land and engaging in shady dealings—including construction kickbacks, prostitution, gambling, and taxation. When the devastation hit the capital, all discipline in the National Guard broke down. Its soldiers looted publicly while Somoza and his officers handled the foreign contributions for the relief of the earthquake victims, siphoning off large sums of money and selling relief supplies.

By 1974, Somoza had created powerful enemies, including the Roman Catholic Church and the middle class, neither of which had forgiven him for his conduct after the earthquake. In January 1978, Somocista hit men assassinated Pedro Joaquín Chamorro, an outspoken critic and the editor of the newspaper *La Prensa*. The murder of Chamorro sparked the first mass uprising against Somoza. Once Jimmy Carter became president in 1977 and made human rights a priority, Somoza could no longer count on the United States to bail him out (although it continued to sell him arms). The National Guard executed thousands, but it was too late. The rebellion gathered in strength; no amount of bloodshed could save Somoza's regime.

The violence in Nicaragua was brought home to the US public in June 1979, when the National Guard arrested ABC newsman Bill Stewart, forced him to kneel, and executed him. Stewart's camera crew recorded the murder on film, and hours later the scene was reproduced on US television screens. Only then did the Carter administration cut off arms sales to Somoza. A month later, in July 1979—after having looted the national treasury—Somoza fled Nicaragua, leaving behind a devastated country. The death toll was between 40,000 and 50,000, 20 percent of the population was homeless, and 40,000 children were orphaned. The industrial base was in ruins; the Somocistas, having plundered the country, left behind a foreign debt of $1.5 billion.

In Somoza's place, the Sandinistas, a coalition of revolutionaries, seized power. The Sandinistas took their name from the revolutionary Augusto Sandino, whom the first Somoza had murdered nearly fifty years earlier. Carter did not like the leftist orientation of the Sandinistas yet provided a modest amount of foreign aid in order to retain a bit of leverage. But as the Nicaraguan revolution continued to shift to the left, a disillusioned Carter suspended all economic aid.

The Sandinistas established a new order that included nationalization of land, press censorship, political imprisonment, nationalization of segments of industry, a militarized government, and a restricted electoral process. But they also extended health care, a fair measure of freedom of speech, a literacy campaign, the redistribution of land, and an economy of which half remained in private hands. In short, the Sandinista government became a typical example of a revolution consolidating its power while at the same time seeking to resolve pressing social and economic problems.

The war of nerves between Washington and Managua escalated in 1981 after President Ronald Reagan took office. Reagan canceled all aid to Nicaragua and launched covert CIA actions against the Sandinistas, who had committed the unpardonable sin of becoming recipients of aid from the Communist states of Eastern Europe, notably the Soviet Union (but also from West European states such as France and West Germany). Moreover, prior to March 1981 the Sandinistas had sent a small amount of arms to the leftist rebels in neighboring El Salvador. In the eyes of the Reagan administration, the Sandinistas had become a spearhead of Soviet expansionism in Central America.

The CIA organized and armed the opponents of the Sandinistas, a group known as the Contras. Headed by former members of the National Guard, the Contras were tainted by their past association with Somoza and therefore had little support in Nicaragua. Reagan had a difficult time selling his assistance to the Contras to Congress and the US public, who—after the Vietnam War— were leery of being drawn into another civil war in a land of which they knew little. But when Daniel Ortega, the dominant figure in the Sandinista government, flew to Moscow seeking economic aid, Congress approved financial assistance to the Contras, which was to be used only for "humanitarian" rather than military purposes.

Reagan's policy was to tighten the screws on the Sandinistas until they "cried uncle." A number of Latin American countries, the so-called Contadora group—Mexico, Panama, Colombia, and Venezuela—called for a political settlement instead. The group proposed a disengagement of all foreign advisers and soldiers—Cuban, Soviet, and US—from Central America, in short, the political and military neutralization of the region. It also pointed to the counterproductive nature of Washington's Central American military containment: By 1981, the Sandinista army had doubled in size, and the Salvadoran revolutionaries had tripled their forces.

The Sandinistas proclaimed their willingness to abide by the Contadora solution; the Reagan administration, however, rejected it because it would permit the Sandinista regime to remain in power. Instead, Reagan directed the CIA to arm and train the Contras holed up in nearby Honduras. Central America was now another Third World battleground in the East-West confrontation. In his address to Congress in April 1983, Reagan tied Nicaragua to the global Cold War:

If Central America were to fall [to Communism], what would be the consequence for our position in Asia and Europe and for alliances such as NATO? . . . Our credibility would collapse, our alliances would crumble.[32]

Despite US assistance, the Contras made no significant military progress. They lacked popular support and had virtually no prospect of defeating the Sandinista army. The US Congress, in response to the public's distaste for becoming involved in Nicaragua, suspended further aid to them. Reagan resolved to find other ways to fund them. Thus began the bizarre "Iran-Contra affair." Officials in Reagan's National Security Council worked out a complex scheme whereby profits from covert and illegal missile sales to Iran—through Israeli intermediaries—would be turned over to the Contras. Colonel Oliver North, who conducted this operation from the basement of the White House, also solicited money from private donors and from friendly foreign governments—all in violation of congressional laws that prohibited further military aid to the Contras and trade with Iran. These illegal and covert operations, detected in November 1986, remained in the news for several years—much like the Watergate scandal in the Nixon era—for they raised many questions about ethics, law, and power. Despite Reagan's persistent pleas, Congress, which earlier had vacillated on the issue of Contra aid, now firmly rejected further military support. In June 1986, the World Court (the International Court of Justice in The Hague, Netherlands) passed judgment for the first time against the United States when it ruled that it had violated international law by mining Nicaragua's harbors and by seeking to overthrow its sovereign government.

In 1987, Costa Rica's president, Oscar Arias, launched a new peace initiative that won the endorsement of the rulers of all five Central American nations. The Arias plan committed them to a cease-fire, a general amnesty, freedom of the press, free elections, the suspension of all foreign military aid, and a reduction in the level of arms. The unconditional acceptance of the Arias peace plan offered Ortega a diplomatic victory over Washington and spelled doom for the Contras, who now stood isolated.

But Ortega's problems were by no means over. The Sandinistas now had to deal with a crisis more threatening to their survival than either the Contras or the United States: the failing economy. Somoza's looting of the treasury, the war against the Contras, the US trade embargo, the loss of foreign credit, hyperinflation, and their own mismanagement all left their mark. Nicaragua's per capita GNP fell drastically, from over $1,000 in 1980 to $340 in 1993.[33]

In February 1990, the Sandinistas took a calculated risk by holding a free and unfettered election. The result was not what they had expected, however. A coalition of fourteen anti-Sandinista parties led by Violeta Chamorro—the widow of the publisher of *La Prensa* whom Somoza had murdered in 1978—

won fifty-two of the National Assembly's ninety seats. Nearly a dozen years of war and deprivation had taken their toll on the Sandinista revolution. Ortega grudgingly accepted the electoral defeat and agreed to transfer to the new government his movement's base of power, the 70,000 Sandinista troops.

Chamorro adopted a centrist and conciliatory policy, while keeping a wary eye on the army, which was still led by Sandinista officers, and the former Contras. Although peace—or at least the end of overt warfare—had its benefits, the incompetent Chamorro government showed little interest in economic reforms or in solving Nicaragua's insurmountable difficulties. The country remained heavily dependent on meager external financial aid. Meanwhile, incessant political violence continued as bands of "retread" revolutionaries—former Sandinista soldiers on the left and former Contras on the right—continued to fight each other. Nicaragua remained a blighted country with an estimated 60 percent of its people living in poverty. At the end of the century, it was among the poorest countries in the Western Hemisphere. Ortega tried to regain the presidency and did so on his third try, in 2006. At home he became more conservative, but his foreign policy retained a noticeable anti-Washington tilt.

## El Salvador

A scenario similar to the one in Nicaragua unfolded in El Salvador in the early 1970s. A rebellion in the countryside threatened to oust the governing oligarchy, one composed largely of *las catorce familias*, the Fourteen Families. Jorge Sol Costellanos, an oligarch and a former minister of the economy, defined the class structure in El Salvador as follows:

> It's different from an aristocracy, which we also have. It's an oligarchy because these families own and run almost everything that makes money in El Salvador. Coffee gave birth to the oligarchy in the late 19th century, and economic growth has revolved around them ever since.[34]

Sol went on to say that the Fourteen Families (or, more accurately, clans) controlled 70 percent of the private banks, coffee production, sugar mills, television stations, and newspapers. In 1984, the annual per capita GNP of El Salvador was around $710 (with the poor receiving much less than that), about 6 percent of the US figure.

The revolution in El Salvador had its roots in events forty years earlier. In 1932, deteriorating economic conditions—brought about by the Great Depression and falling farm prices—and Communist activities under the leadership of Augustín Farabundo Martí led to peasant uprisings. A lack of organization and arms proved to be fatal for the peasants, for machetes were no match against a well-equipped army. In a matter of days, the army, led by General Maximiliano Hernández, slaughtered 30,000 *campesinos*. Martí was captured and executed. The psychological impact of the uprising, however, remained deeply etched into the nation's collective memory. Hernández became the symbol of both deliverance and oppression, his ghost continuing to haunt El Salvador.

The 1932 massacre produced an uneasy stability until the 1972 national election. The civilian candidates of the Christian Democratic Party—José Napoleón Duarte and his running mate, Guillermo Ungo—advocating the redistribution of land, defeated the military candidates. The oligarchy and the generals responded by arresting Duarte, torturing him, and then sending him into exile.

The military deployed death squads on a rampage of indiscriminate violence, summarily killing thousands of men, women, and children. In March 1980, the Roman Catholic archbishop of San Salvador, Oscar Arnulfo Romero—a critic of the military—was gunned down at the altar while saying mass. The assassins, members of a death squad under the command of Roberto d'Aubuisson, were well-known to the CIA. The agency informed the Reagan administration that d'Aubuisson was the "principal henchman for wealthy landowners and a coordinator of the right-wing death squads that have murdered several thousand suspected leftists and leftist sympathizers." The CIA went on to say that d'Aubuisson was also involved in drug trafficking, arms smuggling, and the death of Romero—even providing details of how the men were selected to carry out the bishop's assassination.[35] The Reagan administration did not condone d'Aubuisson's crimes, yet continued to support him.

## Liberation Theology

Romero's assassination put into sharp relief a major political trend in Latin America. In the 1960s, the Catholic Church, traditionally the champion of the status quo, began to reexamine its mission. Many of its clergy moved toward a renewed commitment to improve the material lot of the faithful. Village priests in particular found they could not preach eternal salvation to their parishioners and at the same time ignore the violence visited upon them in this life. The upshot was a split between the traditional wing of the clergy and those, such as Romero, who championed what became known as "liberation theology." The movement may be traced to the encyclicals of Pope John XXIII and Pope Paul VI and to the Second Vatican Council (1963–1965). In 1968, 150 Latin American Catholic bishops embraced the movement at the Second General Conference in Medellín, Colombia. Marcos G. McGrath, archbishop of Panama, explained that the church's mission was meant to "integrate eternal salvation and revolutionary action for a just order in this world."[36] The bishops criticized the "institutionalized violence" that condemned the lower classes to poverty and hunger as well as foreign investors who benefited at the poor's expense. They were critical, however, not only of capitalism but also of Marxism, and thus looked for a third way. Capitalism and Marxism, they declared,

are affronts to the dignity of the human person. The first takes as a premise the primacy of capital. . . . in the pursuit of gain. The other, although
ideologically it may pretend to be humanist, looks rather to the collective
man, and in practice converts itself into a totalitarian concentration of
state power.[37]

In the villages, the priests formed base communities and cooperatives to
ameliorate the conditions caused by police and army brutality, poverty, illiteracy, and the lack of medical facilities. When the Third Conference of Latin
American Bishops convened in Puebla, Mexico, in 1979, a radicalized church
was already a fact of political life in much of Latin America. "Liberation theology" condemned state and guerrilla violence, capitalism, and Marxism, but
its harshest criticism was directed against corporations and their message that
poverty was a necessary phenomenon of economic development and that capitalism would eliminate it.

Maryknoll Sister Ita Ford, shortly before she and three other nuns were
murdered in El Salvador in 1980, noted that "the Christian base communities
are the greatest threat to military dictatorships in Latin America." It was a view
the military dictatorships—particularly that of El Salvador—readily shared.
As early as 1972, Salvadoran death squads began to murder members of the
clergy, at times leaving their bodies dismembered as a warning to others. The
oligarchs denounced the clergy as Communists and urged citizens "to be patriotic—kill a priest!" In the years between the Medellín and Puebla conferences
(1968–1979), military governments or their henchmen murdered, tortured,
arrested, or expelled an estimated 850 nuns, bishops, and priests in El
Salvador. The murder of Archbishop Romero was but the most dramatic act of
violence visited on the champions of liberation theology.[38]

• • •

The Reagan administration ignored the social, economic, and political roots of
El Salvador's violence. It preferred to see it as inspired from the outside. It saw
the rebels, organized as the Farabundo Martí National Liberation Front
(FMLN), as a Communist threat linked to Nicaragua, Cuba, and, ultimately,
the Soviet Union. It strengthened the military, all the while pretending to seek
a political solution. Under US supervision, El Salvador went through the
motions of holding presidential elections and, indeed, the 1979 election
returned Duarte to power. Duarte, however, ruled as the cat's paw of the generals, who needed him because without him Washington could hardly justify
supporting the military. Duarte's election enabled the Reagan administration
to argue that reforms were taking hold and that the army's human rights record
was improving. The violence, however, continued after the election of the hap-
less Duarte, who was powerless to stop it. The death squads continued to go
about with their grisly work.

By 1989, after nine years of fighting and despite \$3.3 billion in US economic and military aid, little had changed. The guerrillas, regarded by one observer as "the best trained, best organized and most committed Marxist-Leninist rebel movement ever seen in Latin America," controlled one-third of the country and made their presence felt by their periodic attacks in the capital and elsewhere.[39]

In November 1989, an army death squad burst into the rooms of six Jesuit priests who taught at Catholic University and murdered them, their cook, and her daughter. The newly elected president, Alfredo Cristiani, the candidate of the rightist National Republican Alliance party (ARENA), whose government received US military aid, assured Washington that it would conduct a thorough investigation and bring the killers to justice. In January 1990, his government arrested and charged eight military men for the murder of the priests. The ringleaders were convicted but then released in April 1993 under an amnesty law.

In March 1989, the FMLN agreed to participate in the electoral process. An FMLN offensive in November of that year showed the George H. W. Bush administration that military victory was beyond its reach. ARENA could count on US military aid only so long as its army was seen as holding at bay international Communism, but with the Cold War coming to an end, Washington's threat to discontinue aid to El Salvador became more credible, and ARENA became more amenable to compromise.

In May 1990, Moscow and Washington agreed to back UN-arranged Salvadoran peace talks, which finally produced a peace agreement in January 1992. It ended a brutal war that had claimed approximately 80,000 lives over twelve years. In exchange for an agreement to dissolve their military forces, the rebels secured government pledges to legalize the FMLN as a political party and to reduce by one-half the size of the Salvadoran army within two years. The agreement also called for land reform, as well as judicial and electoral reforms, and the creation of a UN Truth Commission to investigate the human rights violations.

The most appalling of these violations had been the December 1981 massacre of more than 700 peasants—evangelical Christians who did not support the rebels—by the US-trained elite Atlacatl Battalion in the remote village of El Mozote. In 1982, the Reagan administration angrily and repeatedly denied—although it knew better—that such a massacre had taken place. In El Salvador, El Mozote remained a metaphor for the army's ability to avoid responsibility for human rights abuses.[40] The Truth Commission's investigations produced reports, replete with damning evidence, of massacres by army officers and right-wing death squads, but the ARENA government ignored them. Instead, it passed a law in 1994 granting full amnesty to all army officers, despite the incontrovertible proof of massacres such as that of El Mozote. Civilian control of the military—a fundamental principle of democratic government—remained out of reach in El Salvador.

In May 1984, under pressure from the US Congress, which threatened to withhold aid, five enlisted members of the National Guard were convicted of the 1980 murder of four US nuns. It marked the first time in El Salvador's history that a member of the military had been found guilty of such a crime. Still, those who had given the orders, the director of the National Guard, Eugenio Vides Sasanova, and the minister of defense, José Guillermo García, escaped prosecution under a general amnesty. They retired to Florida, where they were tried under US law, but the prosecution was unable to establish a direct link between them and those who had committed the murders.

## Latin American Drug Trafficking

Since the early 1970s, when US president Richard Nixon first committed his country to a "War on Drugs," every administration spent increasingly more money on a losing effort. The main focus was on the interdiction of the flow of narcotics from Latin America, notably from Colombia. Famous for its powerful drug cartels, Colombia in the 1980s was responsible for about 80 percent of the cocaine entering the United States. Coca plants, from which cocaine is extracted, grow abundantly in the equatorial climate of Colombia, Bolivia, and Peru. Coca provided a living for the *campesinos* but it was also the source of corruption of law enforcement agencies by the fabulously wealthy criminal organizations. The cartel in the city of Medellín operated like a large multinational corporation. US Drug Enforcement Agency officials estimated that during the 1980s its profits were as high as $5 billion a year and that tens of thousands of people were on its payroll—growers, processors, couriers, politicians, police, judges. When bribes failed to obtain compliance, drug lords resorted to intimidation and violence.

In August 1989, the Colombian government launched its own highly publicized war on the drug cartels. President Virgilio Barco Vargas ordered the army into action, setting crops ablaze, destroying production facilities, and seizing the homes and properties of drug kingpins. The cartels responded by gunning down politicians and judges. In November 1989, the Medellín cartel claimed responsibility for the bombing of a Colombian jetliner, killing all 107 aboard. In the following month, it blew up the headquarters of the Department of Security, the agency most involved in the war against the drug operations. Half a ton of dynamite destroyed its six-story headquarters, killing fifty-two people and injuring about 1,000.

The drug lords' greatest fear was the extradition treaty with Washington, according to which they could be sent to the United States to stand trial. In February 1987, Carlos Lehder—one of the cofounders of the Medellín cartel and whose net worth was estimated at around $2.5 billion—was captured and extradited to the United States, where he was found guilty of an assortment of crimes and sentenced to life plus 135 years.

In June 1989, Pablo Escobar, the most powerful Medellín kingpin, surrendered to the authorities—but on his own terms, in exchange for immunity against extradition to the United States, where he was under indictment. He was permitted to select his own "prison"—a comfortable rural villa in his home province replete with Jacuzzi, fax machines, cellular telephones, and computers—and was allowed to dictate the security arrangements, even selecting his own armed guards. This arrangement permitted him to continue to run his drug empire. When he died during a shootout with Colombian police in 1994, it had little impact on the drug trade.

The apolitical cartels were not alone in the drug business. Leftist guerrillas, too, succumbed to the lure of this most profitable enterprise. The largest of the guerrilla groups was the Armed Revolutionary Force (FARC), 17,000 strong and in control of large areas of rural Colombia inhabited by several hundred thousand people—a state within a state. FARC was initially founded in 1964 as a movement for social change but since then had found a new calling: it sold protection to growers of coca, marijuana, and poppy (the source of heroin) and engaged in the lucrative business of "miraculous fishing," that is, kidnapping for ransom. By the end of the 1990s, its activities netted an estimated $500 million annually.[41] Another, smaller guerrilla group with a similar agenda was the National Liberation Army (known by its Spanish-language acronym ELN). Colombia's 11,000-man army proved generally ineffective against the well-financed guerrillas.

The early 1990s saw the emergence of another drug-running outfit, the Colombian Self-Defense Force, which deployed rightist paramilitary death squads between 5,000 and 7,000 strong. In their war against the left, they conducted their own reign of terror, murdering tens of thousands of individuals—mostly civilians—thought to be sympathetic to the guerrillas. They also succumbed to the lure of "miraculous fishing" and drug trafficking.[42] The army, too, became engaged in the torture and murder of civilians and in the drug trade.[43] Colombia became one of the most dangerous places on earth.

In August 1999, president Bill Clinton traveled to Colombia to present to the government an antidrug aid package of $1 billion that included 500 military advisers and transport and attack helicopters. During his visit, he was careful to avoid the capital of Bogotá, however. His eight-hour stay was limited to the coastal city of Cartagena, where he expressed confidence that this new round in the antidrug war would succeed where previous efforts had failed. Yet when he spoke, it was under heavy guard of 5,500 government troops, 350 US agents, four frigates, and eighteen patrol boats.

The magnitude of the profits from the drug business spoke against Clinton's optimism. At its source, 1 kilogram of coca paste already fetched $2,500; in Miami, after changing hands several times, the price was $20,000; by the time it reached New York City it was $80,000; and in Europe it was $120,000.[44]

Three years after Clinton's stopover in Cartagena, the George W. Bush administration introduced another ambitious antidrug initiative, Plan Colombia, under which its government launched a US-supported offensive against FARC. "The tide has turned," Colombia's defense minister announced, "and there is an end in sight," only to add that one "cannot expect a big [final] battle, a Waterloo."[45] That was putting it mildly. FARC continued its activities even after its founder, Manuel Marulanda, died in March 2008 at the age of seventy-seven.

Since Nixon launched the War on Drugs, it accomplished nothing of substance. In the United States it contributed to the vast expansion in the prison population (the highest per capita and in absolute terms in the world). Chemical spraying of coca fields and the destruction of labs were poor yardsticks by which to measure success. The fields were quickly replanted and the labs (often rickety structures) were rebuilt. "Colombia is the only country in the world where the problem of eradication has been resolved 10 times," a UN specialist on the drug war declared.

A surfeit of illicit drugs continued to flood the global market, producing a steady decline in prices. In the United States, cocaine prices fell from around $600 per gram in the early 1980s, to less than $200 in the mid-1990s, to around $100 by 2005. Global demand grew—notably in Europe—but the drug traffickers—whether in Colombia, Guatemala, Mexico, or Afghanistan—were able to meet it.

In June 2008, the World Health Organization reported that the United States, despite draconian antidrug laws, led the world in per capita cocaine use—and by a wide margin at that—as well as that of marijuana. The per capita use of marijuana in the United States was twice as high as that in the Netherlands where its personal use was decriminalized.

NAFTA, intended to facility the flow of goods between Mexico and its neighbors to the north, became a boon to drug smugglers. Mexico became the center of transshipment and thus a battleground for cartels seeking to carve out their empires. From Mexico, drivers (in 5 million trucks and 92 million cars in 2005) took small packages across the border into the United States.

The cost of the War on Drugs gradually rose. Forty years after its inception, it may have been as high as $40 billion per year. The United States appeared to have spent as much in this losing war as for the one in Vietnam ($600–800 billion, in 2007 dollars).[46]

## The Panama Connection

The first year of the George H. W. Bush presidency witnessed a bizarre war of words with Manuel Noriega, the military strongman of Panama. Previously an ally of the United States, Noriega was now suspected of being a conduit for

Colombian drugs en route to the United States. During the war against the Sandinistas, he had been on the payroll of the CIA, which had paid him $250,000 a year for Caribbean intelligence. The Reagan administration turned a blind eye to Noriega's human rights abuses. Torture, murder, rape, plunder, prostitution, drug trafficking, and the theft of elections—such as that in 1984—did not faze Washington. In 1987, however, Washington became aware that Noriega had transgressed the bounds of propriety when it learned he was also offering intelligence to Castro's Cuba. Ambler Moss, President Carter's envoy to Panama, explained that Noriega was "dealing with everybody—us, the Cubans, other countries. We used to call him the rent-a-colonel." The betrayal became too much for President Bush to bear. He now accused Noriega of being part of the international drug cartels. Knowledge in Washington of Noriega's drug connections, however, went all the way back to the Nixon administration.[47]

Noriega resisted US pressure to step down, presenting himself instead as the champion of small Latin American nations bullied by the "colossus of the north." In 1987, grand juries in Tampa and Miami indicted him on drug-trafficking charges. Just before Christmas 1989, Bush sent a posse of 20,000 troops to bring Noriega to justice. Operation Just Cause got its man, but the cost was high. Several hundred Panamanians—mostly civilians—and twenty-three US soldiers died in the fighting. The collateral damage of property and subsequent looting of stores in Panama City resulted in losses to small businesses totaling $1 billion.

The invasion of Panama was the first instance of US military intervention abroad since 1945 in which the anti-Communist theme was not central. It was a sign that the Cold War was winding down. Bush, however, stood in direct contrast to Soviet leader Mikhail Gorbachev, who had declared that no nation had a legal or moral right to interfere in the internal affairs of another.

In Miami, before a federal judge, Noriega—dressed in his general's uniform—presented himself as a "prisoner of war." The judge thought he was dealing with a common criminal. In April 1992, Noriega was found guilty on numerous charges, including the acceptance of millions of dollars in bribes from the Medellín cartel, and sentenced to a lengthy prison term. He became the first head of a foreign state to be convicted of criminal charges in a US court. He completed his sentence in September 2008, but his troubles were by no means over. He served additional time in France, where he had been sentenced in absentia to a ten years prison term for money-laundering. In December 2011, he was returned to Panama to serve out the rest of his sentence.

## Notes

1. Paul Harrison, *Inside the Third World: The Anatomy of Poverty*, 2nd ed. (New York: Penguin, 1984), cites a survey by the Inter-American Commission for Agricultural Development, pp. 108–109.

2. E. Bradford Burns, *Latin America: A Concise Interpretive History*, 3rd ed. (Englewood Cliffs, NJ: Prentice-Hall, 1982), p. 214.

3. "A Decline Without Parallel," *The Economist*, February 28, 2002.

4. Luis Marcus Ocampo, "Beyond Punishment: Justice in the Wake of Massive Crimes in Argentina," *Journal of International Affairs* (Spring 1999); "The Challenge of the Past," *The Economist*, October 22, 1998.

5. See "Argentina's Bottomless Pit," *The Economist*, August 8, 2004, and Peter Greste, "Argentina's Poor Hit New Record," *BBC News*, February 1, 2003.

6. "Reconstructive Criticism," *Economist.com*, October 28, 2013; "Barbarians at the Gate," *Economist*, October 26, 2013.

7. "From Pauper to President: Now Lula's Struggle Really Begins," *The Economist*, October 31, 2002.

8. Larry Rohter, *Brazil on the Rise: The Story of a Country Transformed* (New York: Palgrave Macmillan, 2010), pp. 224–225.

9. Oscar Guardiola-Rivera, *Story of a Death Foretold: The Coup Against Salvador Allende, 11 September 1973* (New York: Bloomsbury, 2013), pp. 91, 218–219, 313.

10. Ibid., pp. 329–330.

11. Cited in Walter Isaacson, *Kissinger: A Biography* (New York: Touchstone Books, 1993), p. 290.

12. Between 1998 and 2004, sixteen thousand documents in the US National Archives relating to Pinochet's reign were declassified. See Peter Kornbluh, "Chile Documentation Project," www.gwu.edu/~nsarchiv/.

13. Knight Ridder/Tribune, "Pinochet Is Not Immune, Chile's High Court Rules," *Baltimore Sun*, August 27, 2004, p. 18A.

14. Tina Rosenberg, "Force Is Forever," *New York Times Magazine*, September 24, 1995, p. 46.

15. "The Shining Path Revisited," *The Economist*, September 4, 2003.

16. Guillermo Rochabrun, "The De Facto Powers Behind Fujimori's Regime," *NACLA Report on the Americas* (July–August 1996), pp. 22–23. For the impact of economic reform on the population at large, see Manuel Castillo Ochoa, "Fujimori and the Business Class: A Prickly Partnership," ibid., pp. 25–30.

17. Enrique Obando, "Fujimori and the Military: A Marriage of Convenience," *NACLA Report on the Americas* (July–August 1996), pp. 31–36; also "Anatomy of a Cover-Up: The Disappearances at La Cantuta," a summary of a report by Human Rights Watch/Americas, ibid., pp. 34–35.

18. Kevin G. Hall, "CIA Paid Millions to Montesinos," *Miami Herald*, August 3, 2001.

19. World Bank, *World Bank Development Report 2000/2001: Attacking Poverty* (New York: Oxford University Press, 2000), p. 281.

20. Press release, "Transparency International Calls on Japanese Government to Extradite Fujimori," August 27, 2003; "Cleaner-Than-Thou," *The Economist*, October 7, 2004.

21. In 2006, there were seven such presidents, in Venezuela, Brazil, Chile, Bolivia, Uruguay, Argentina, and Nicaragua.

22. Judith Gentleman, "Mexico: The Revolution," in Barbara A. Tenenbaum, ed., *Encyclopedia of Latin American History and Culture*, vol. 4 (New York: Charles

Scribner's Sons, 1996), p. 15; Alma Guillermoprieto, "Zapata's Heirs," *The New Yorker*, May 16, 1994, p. 54.

23. James W. Wilkie, *The Mexican Revolution: Federal Expenditure and Social Change Since 1910* (Berkeley: University of California Press, 1970), pp. 193–194.

24. James D. Cockcroft, *Mexico: Class Formation, Capital Accumulation, and the State* (New York: Monthly Review Press, 1983), pp. 136–138.

25. Wilkie, *The Mexican Revolution*, pp. 222–225, 128–129, 195–197.

26. Paco Ignacio Taibo II, "Images of Chiapas: Zapatista! The Phoenix Rises," *The Nation*, March 28, 1996, pp. 407–408.

27. Ioan Grillo, "Return of the Zapatistas: Are Mexico's Rebels Still Relevant?" *Time*, January 8, 2013.

28. From a conversation with Sir William Tyrell, a representative of Britain's Foreign Office, November 13, 1913. Arthur S. Link, *Wilson, II, The New Freedom* (Princeton, NJ: Princeton University Press, 1956), p. 375.

29. Quoted in Arthur M. Schlesinger Jr., *A Thousand Days: John F. Kennedy in the White House* (Boston: Houghton Mifflin, 1965), p. 769.

30. Castro offered to pay for US property, but only on the basis of a low assessment the companies themselves had submitted for tax purposes. The US companies, however, had other figures in mind. Stephen E. Ambrose, *Rise to Globalism: American Foreign Policy, 1938–1970* (New York: Penguin, 1971), p. 269n.

31. "I'm the Champ," *Time* cover story on Somoza, November 15, 1948, p. 43.

32. Reagan to a Joint Session of Congress, *New York Times*, April 28, 1983, p. A12.

33. World Bank, *World Development Report: Workers in an Integrating World* (New York: Oxford University Press, 1995), p. 162.

34. Paul Heath Hoeffel, "The Eclipse of the Oligarchs," *New York Times Magazine*, September 6, 1981, p. 23.

35. Clifford Krauss, "US Aware of Killings, Kept Ties to Salvadoran Rightists, Papers Suggest," *New York Times*, November 9, 1993, p. A9.

36. Marcos G. McGrath, "Ariel or Caliban?" *Foreign Affairs* (October 1973), pp. 85, 87.

37. From the bishops' "Document on Justice," ibid., p. 86.

38. Walter LaFeber, *Inevitable Revolutions: The United States in Central America*, expanded ed. (New York: W. W. Norton, 1984), pp. 219–226; Tina Rosenberg, *Children of Cain: Violence and the Violent in Latin America* (New York: Penguin, 1992), pp. 219–270.

39. James Le Moyne, "El Salvador's Forgotten War," *Foreign Affairs* (Summer 1989), p. 106.

40. Mark Danner, "The Truth of El Mozote," *The New Yorker*, December 6, 1993, pp. 50–133; subsequently published in book form as *The Massacre at El Mozote* (New York: Random House, 1994).

41. Almo Guillermoprieto, "The Children's War," *New York Review*, May 11, 2000, p. 37; Patrick Symmes, "Miraculous Fishing: Lost in the Swamps of Colombia's Drug War," *Harper's* (December 2000), p. 64.

42. "Colombia's Overdose," *Harper's* (February 2000), p. 100. The paramilitaries committed an estimated 78 percent of Colombia's human rights atrocities. Serge F. Kovaleski, "Widespread Violence Threatens Colombia's Stability," *Washington Post*, March 1, 1998, p. A22; "Colombia in the Long Shadow of War," *The Economist*, July 17, 1999, p. 31.

43. "US Issues Rights Report Criticizing Colombia," *Baltimore Sun*, February 26,

2000, p. 1A; "Colombia's President Vows to Crack Down on Death Squads," *Baltimore Sun*, July 25, 2000, p. 12A.

44. Richard Wagner, "Kolumbiens illusionsloser Kampf gegen das Kokain," *Frankfurter Allgemeine Zeitung*, May 30, 2000, p. 4.

45. "Victories, but No Waterloo," *The Economist*, July 15, 2004.

46. Juan Forero, "Colombia's Coca Survives U.S. Plan to Uproot It," *New York Times*, August 19, 2006; Ken Dermota, "Snow Fall," *The Atlantic*, July/August 2007, pp. 24–25; Jordan Smith, "U.S. Ranks #1 in Consumption of Pot, Cocaine, Smokes," *Austin Chronicle*, July 23, 2008.

47. Tim Collie, "Noriega Played All Angles in Ascent," *Tampa Tribune*, December 25, 1989, pp. 22A, 25A.

# 15

# The People's Republic of China and Taiwan

**The twentieth century was an age of social and political experiments** and upheavals, and China, the world's most populous nation, had its share of both. The Chinese Communist efforts to transform China warrant an examination, not only because of the magnitude of the task but also because of the great lengths to which China's new leaders were willing to go. Their efforts to put Marxist theory into practice led to political and economic upheavals on an unprecedented scale.

## Mao Zedong's Quest for a Communist Utopia

The enormity of China's population sets it apart from other nations. Never before had there been a nation of more than 1 billion people. When the Communists took power in 1949, China was still primarily an agrarian nation, with about 90 percent of the peasants engaged in subsistence agriculture. Under Mao Zedong's leadership, the party emphasized both agrarian growth and industrialization as the key to improve the standard of living. Throughout, however, Mao insisted that China remain a revolutionary Communist society. The interplay of the economic and political objectives is the key to understanding China under Chairman Mao's leadership.

China's overriding problem in modern times (for at least the previous two centuries) has been how to feed itself. To complicate matters, the population grew rapidly after the Communists came to power in 1949. At the time, it was about 535 million; by 1970, it was 840 million; and in the early 1980s, it passed the 1 billion mark. Despite China's great size, there was a scarcity of arable land. Only about 20 percent of the land is suited for agriculture, with the remainder either too mountainous or too arid. China's population is heavily concentrated in the areas with arable land, mainly the coastal regions. Because of the unequal distribution of land, the bulk of the peasants either owned too little land or none at all. This set of conditions—the plight of the impoverished peasants and their exploitation by the landowning class—gave rise to the Communist movement, which was committed to putting an end to these conditions.

China had made some progress toward industrialization prior to Communist rule. The Nationalist regime's ongoing attempt to industrialize, however, was cut short by the eight-year war with Japan. The Communists inherited a country that had endured destruction during the war, followed by three years of civil war. China suffered from meager industrial development, uncontrolled inflation, an impoverished and illiterate peasantry, its cities swollen with jobless, desperate people. It also lacked many of the basic elements for modernization: capital, modern technology, skilled workers, and engineers.

To make matters worse, Mao decreed that politics—that is to say, Marxist ideology—had greater priority than economic growth. Mao's often-quoted dictum "politics take command" meant that every activity in China was to be defined in ideological terms. Whether it made practical sense was of secondary concern.

In their first three years in power, the Communists managed to establish economic and political order, control inflation, and restore production in the existing industries to their prewar level. Major industries were nationalized, foreign enterprises were confiscated, and private enterprise was gradually eliminated. The new regime also addressed the peasant question—an issue that could not wait—by instituting wholesale land redistribution, which was carried out swiftly and ruthlessly. It resulted in the transfer of millions of acres to over 300 million peasants and the elimination of the "landlord class." The party hailed the June 1950 land reform law as a long overdue measure that liberated the peasants from a 2,000-year-old feudal system. Capitalist landlords who once had lived off the peasants' rent payments, now had to work to survive.[1] Estimates of the loss of life vary greatly, but it appears that several million Chinese met their deaths during this upheaval.

By 1953, the Chinese government was ready to institute its First Five-Year Plan, modeled on that of the Soviet Union and guided by Soviet economic advisers. Economic assistance from the Soviet Union was of great importance to China—the technical aid more than the monetary loans, which were rather meager. As in the Soviet Union, the First Five-Year Plan stressed rapid development of heavy industry. China followed suit and its production of steel, electricity, and cement increased remarkably.

## The Great Leap Forward

As the Second Five-Year Plan was about to be launched, Mao questioned the effect it would have on the Chinese revolution. He feared it would result—as in the Soviet Union— in the entrenchment of a powerful bureaucracy, a new elite exploiting the masses. In early 1958, he suddenly called a halt to the plan. As he turned his back on the Soviet model, he called instead for a "Great Leap Forward." The Great Leap envisioned tapping the energies of the masses— China's greatest resource—to industrialize and collectivize at the same time. In the countryside, the collectives (initially formed in the mid-1950s), were to be reorganized into large communes embodying the basic Marxist principle "from each according to his abilities, to each according to his needs." In this fashion Mao hoped to mobilize the masses and thereby develop and sustain their ideological and revolutionary fervor. What Mao unleashed, however, was an excess of force coupled with poor planning that produced an economic disaster unprecedented in history. Matters were made worse by Soviet premier Nikita Khrushchev's withdrawal in 1960 of all Soviet technicians from China.

The Great Leap Forward proved to be a giant step back. It produced a four-year long man-made famine, the worst anywhere. It set into motion a devastating chain of events—widespread starvation, suicide, cannibalism, the birthrate cut in half, deforestation, soil erosion, floods, plagues, executions, 13 million party members purged as rightist deviants. An estimated 36-46 million people perished, 7 percent of the population.[2]

The disaster should have put to an end Mao's reliance on ideological purity. The more pragmatic members of the party raised their voices, but were beaten back. Mao's radical approach reflected the manner in which he had built the Communist movement in the 1930s. It stressed the "mass line," meaning—if only theoretically—the power of the people and their active engagement in the revolution. It called for intense ideological training of party cadres, the dedicated activists who served as a model for the masses. Mao's cult of personality became an important tool for politicizing the masses in the hope of creating a thoroughly revolutionary egalitarian society free from exploitation.

The pragmatists in the party played down ideology and revolutionary zeal and stressed instead planning and the development of skills and expertise—a rational, problem-solving, do-what-works approach. It was during the Great Leap Forward that Deng Xiaoping first uttered the heresy, at party meetings no less, proposing that ideology take a back seat to pragmatism. Instead of citing Karl Marx, he drew on an old Szechuan peasant expression. "What matters," he said, "is not whether a cat is white or black, but whether it catches mice."[3] In years to come, Deng paid a heavy price for his deviation from the Mao line. He and his family fell victims to Mao's next ideological upheaval, the Great Proletarian Cultural Revolution. His son was imprisoned and tortured, after which he tried to commit suicide. Deng was stripped of his party posts and, as part of his reeducation, was shipped off to work in a factory. It took the pragmatic foreign minister, Zhou Enlai, to convince Mao to rehabilitate him and bring him back into the good graces of the party.

## The Great Proletarian Cultural Revolution

After the Great Leap Forward fiasco, the moderates cleaned up the mess Mao had made. Gradually, during the first half of the 1960s, the economy recovered under the guiding hand of such moderate leaders as Liu Shaoqi and Deng Xiaoping. But once again, Mao was perturbed about the trend toward bureaucratic elitism. Using his immense prestige as "the Great Helmsman," he bypassed the party structure and, in July 1966, initiated a new political upheaval aimed at purging the party of its elitist leaders: the "Great Proletarian Cultural Revolution."

Mao was determined to eradicate once and for all what he called the curse of "bureaucratism." He charged his opponents with selfishly guarding and advancing their own personal power and privilege. He also accused them of the deadly sin of "revisionism," meaning they were guilty of revising (distorting) Marxism-Leninism. One of Mao's targets was the post-Stalin Soviet leadership, whom he accused of having taking the "capitalist road," thereby destroying the Communist revolution. His own party must not be permitted to travel that same road.

Mao enlisted the active support of the youth of China, who were dismissed from colleges and schools en masse, organized into the "Red Guards," and instructed to go out and attack all those who were guilty of selfish elitism. "Serve the people" was their slogan, and Mao's writings were their guidelines. Red Guards pressured people high and low—officials, soldiers, peasants, and workers—to reform their behavior through the arduous study of Mao's thought as presented in capsule form in the "Little Red Book," and they severely rebuked and punished those found wanting.

Mao's Cultural Revolution was unique—a revolution within an ongoing revolution, a people's revolt against the revolutionary party ordered by the head of that party. Mao called upon the masses to help him eliminate deviants in his own Communist Party and thereby put the revolution back on track. It was part and parcel of Mao's "permanent revolution"—a continuing struggle to rid the party of the enemies of the revolution and thus prevent backsliding toward capitalism.

To do so, force was needed because, as Mao explained, "dust never vanishes of itself without sweeping." The Cultural Revolution was proclaimed in the name of lofty ideals—a utopian, egalitarian society utterly free of class exploitation—yet it produced unimaginable mayhem. Its main product was terror, death, and destruction. The Red Guards rampaged throughout the country—wreaking havoc, destroying property, and capturing, condemning, brutalizing, and sometimes killing those deemed to be less than ideologically pure. Their excessive fervor rendered the Cultural Revolution into a terrifying witch hunt that destroyed the political order and disrupted the economy. Countless people died—probably in excess of 1 million; estimates run the gamut from half a million to eight million. (After Mao's death in 1976, the party condemned the Cultural Revolution and encouraged people to testify to its cruelty, but it remained reticent to reveal the number of lives it had claimed.)

When Red Guards met resistance, clashes occurred. In time, opposing bands of Red Guards, each claiming to possess the correct Maoist line, engaged in pitched battles against each other with weapons secured from the police or army units. As violence mounted, Mao found it necessary to call in the army to restore order.

Among the victims of the Cultural Revolution were the economy and education. The economy suffered from work stoppages, decreased production, and inflation. Education, science, and technology, however, may have suffered greater damage. High schools and universities were shut down for about five years; teachers and professors were taken to the countryside for political re-education that consisted of forced labor and the study of Mao's writings. Books and laboratory equipment were destroyed. The schools eventually reopened, but ideological content continued to take preference over academics. Students and teachers were evaluated not on the basis of acquired knowledge but on their dedication to Mao's version of Communism, a case of political correctness taken to the extreme. The disruption of higher education probably retarded China's economic development by a decade.

It took years for the Cultural Revolution to wind down. Officially, it did not end as long as Mao was alive, but it was nonetheless quietly scaled back in the early 1970s. By then, Mao was aged and ill, and leadership passed into the hands of the able and pragmatic Zhou Enlai. Zhou had managed to dodge the attacks by the Maoists and now, more than ever, Mao needed him. Zhou reinstated the moderates, including Deng Xiaoping, who had been expelled from the party.

Tensions between Maoists and moderates, however, continued to smolder and erupted in 1976, the eventful "Year of the Tiger," when Zhou and Mao died. Mao's designated successor, Hua Guofeng, quashed an attempt by the radicals to regain control of the party when he arrested their ringleaders, the so-called Gang of Four. One of the principal culprits was none other than Mao's wife, Jiang Qing. For several years, Mao's successors denounced the Gang of Four. By the end of the 1970s, Deng Xiaoping was in full control of the party and was secure enough to put its members on trial. Deng and his supporters orchestrated a prolonged political campaign denouncing the Gang of Four as a means of attacking the radicalism that Mao had preached. The Gang of Four was found responsible for the bloody nature of the Cultural Revolution and sentenced to long prison terms. Their conviction set the stage for Deng's sweeping economic reforms, which had little use for ideological purity.

It was far safer to make the Gang of Four the scapegoats for what ailed China, rather than Mao. The new leadership cautiously undertook the de-Maoization of China, even criticizing the once adored and infallible chairman for his "mistakes" (rather than crimes) during the Cultural Revolution. Mao's massive portrait continued to overlook the great plaza at Tiananmen Square in Beijing, but it was now the moderates' turn to reorganize Chinese society.

Deng's economic reforms opened China to the outside world and legalized capitalism. (For details, see Chapter 18.) It marked a remarkable departure from Maoism. Yet at the same time, a strong element of continuity prevailed. It was part of a long trajectory—China's "Road to Rejuvenation," the title of one of the few permanent exhibits in the National Museum in Beijing.

There is a circuitous line from China's early nineteenth-century reformers to the handiwork of Deng. The reformers differed over the means by which to restore China's wealth and power, but they shared a common bond that linked such diverse figures as Cixi (the Dowager Empress, 1835–1908), Jiang Jieshi, Mao Zedong, and Deng Xiaoping. The imprisoned Chinese dissident and 2010 Nobel Peace Prize laureate, Liu Xiaobo, noted that "the primary mind-set" that guided Deng's reforms "was neither 'liberation of humanity,' nor even 'enriching people,' but rather a sense of shame at China's . . . national humiliations." China's Communist revolution had not been on behalf of "liberty, equality, and fraternity," but for the sake of wealth, strength, and honor. When Xi Jinping (elected in 2012 as head of the party) spoke of a "Chinese dream," he mimicked the "American dream." Yet he did not dream of "life, liberty, and the pursuit of happiness" but of the restoration of China's past glory. During Xi's tenure, China rapidly approached the realization of his dream.[4]

### The Tiananmen Square Massacre

Deng's reforms paid extraordinary economic dividends, but they were not accompanied by a significant political liberalization. Deng had encouraged the Chinese to enrich themselves, in itself a dangerous bit of advice in a country that, if only theoretically, was still guided by Communist tenets. But with great wealth came great corruption. Corruption was nothing new; even Mao had admitted to it in private. But now, the nouveau riche, generally with party connections, flaunted their ill-gotten wealth. The demands for political reform came from the intelligentsia who, by dint of the Internet and a freer press, were aware of the political currents buffeting the world, particularly Mikhail

Gorbachev's "new thinking." In increasingly larger numbers, Chinese had been sent to study in the West, where they were exposed to ideas new to them. Some Chinese even took to them.

Deng's departure from Maoism would only go so far. The Politburo made sure to retain its political monopoly and all that it entailed. The last thing it wanted was a freewheeling political discussion. Deng, someone born in 1904, well remembered China's recent past plagued by nearly uninterrupted violence. The overthrow of the Manchu (or Qing) dynasty in 1911 was followed by civil strife that continued for nearly forty years. After that, Mao's ideologically charged campaigns continued to roil China. Deng was willing to open China to the Western economy, but not to its political ideas that threatened to roil China anew.

Deng rejected the notion that "bourgeois liberalism" was appropriate for China. A two-party system was out of the question. If anything, he did everything to ensure continuation of the rule of the party, first by its elders and then by their sons, or "princelings" as they became known. As demands grew for "democratization," the party began to tighten the screws. As a sign of the times, it condemned the new wave of Western-style popular culture (such as rock music) as "spiritual pollution."

The party, however, did become more responsive to public opinion. It permitted freer access to certain information and ideas, reduced censorship, permitted travel and study abroad, and allowed a measure of personal expression. But there was a limit how far people could go. The National People's Congress passed laws, but the party retained the right to rescind them. When one considers the changing nature of Chinese society, it was not surprising that it led to a clash of rising expectations.

The desire for additional change was made manifest by university students in large political demonstrations that began in 1986, first in Shanghai and then in Beijing and other cities. Students chafed under economic hardships and increasing evidence of widespread corruption by high-ranking officials and their families. Some even longed for a return to Mao and complained that the party that had abandoned Marxism. For others, state ideology had become irrelevant and the party had lost its moral authority—the "mandate of heaven"—to govern China.

The most dangerous demonstrations began in late April 1989, a day after the death of the former party chief, Hu Yaobang, the most outspoken advocate of "bourgeois liberalization." (It was the reason why two years earlier, the party—at the behest of Deng—had stripped Hu of his post of general secretary of the party.) Students from several Beijing universities defied government orders to disperse and instead gathered on Tiananmen Square in the heart of the city to commemorate Hu as their champion of democracy. In early May, their number in Tiananmen Square grew to more than 100,000. Invariably, they began to call for political reforms. Their posters demanded a respect for human rights, the release of political prisoners, a new democratic constitution, greater freedom of speech and press—and the right to hold demonstrations.[5]

As the students exploited Western press coverage they deluded themselves by thinking that the government would not risk damaging its international image by using force. The scheduled arrival of Soviet leader Mikhail Gorbachev on May 15—for the purpose of ending the Sino-Soviet feud—put the use of force on hold for the time being. Two days before Gorbachev's arrival, 2,000 students began a public hunger strike in Tiananmen Square. On the next day hundreds of thousands flocked to the square in support of the students, all the while ignoring the government deadline to clear the area.

The students hailed Gorbachev as a true champion of democratization and lampooned Deng as a stodgy old hard-liner. Gorbachev neither supported nor discouraged the students. He merely gave faint praise to the Chinese leaders for "opening a political dialogue with the demonstrators."[6] No sooner had he left Beijing than the government declared martial law. The students took heart when the soldiers deployed at Tiananmen Square seemed disinclined to use force against them. Emotions were heightened after students erected a "goddess of democracy" statue (resembling the Statue of Liberty in New York harbor) as a symbol of their cause. No longer satisfied with a dialogue with party leaders, they called for the dismissal of some of them.

Finally, under the cover of darkness in the early hours of June 4, columns of tanks rumbled toward the square and a massacre began. The extent of the carnage is not known, but estimates range from several hundred to several thousand deaths. The government used the controlled mass media to broadcast to the nation—and the world—its version of what had taken place and deny any other version. The army, it declared, had heroically defended the nation against an armed counterrevolution. As for the dead, no unarmed students were killed. In all, the government insisted, no more than 300 people had died in the clashes on the avenues approaching the square, and most of the dead, moreover, had been soldiers.[7]

Then came the reprisals. Dissidents were hunted down, arrested, and found guilty of treason. About forty were executed and eighteen were given long prison sentences. Chinese citizens who had witnessed the events in or near Tiananmen Square denied having seen anything at all. The party outlawed all talk of the massacre, particularly by the families of those killed. Chinese citizens reverted to the style of mutual self-protection that they had learned in Maoist times. They understood it was best not to discuss the unpleasant matter.

After the massacre, Washington pressured China—albeit only perfunctorily—about its human rights record. When a State Department official inquired into human rights violations, he was told that such inquiries constituted a violation of China's sovereignty. Those arrested, he was told, had been "offenders," not "dissidents." Washington briefly threatened to deny China most-favored-nation treatment (trade terms equal to those enjoyed by other nations), thus restricting its virtually unlimited access to the lucrative US market. In 1993, President Bill Clinton sided with the US economic interests in China when he separated human rights from economic issues and renewed China's most-favored-nation status.

China rejected any and all criticism of its crackdown on Tiananmen Square, its suppression in Tibet, its atmospheric testing of nuclear weapons, and its sale of missiles and nuclear technology to Pakistan. Beijing had its own list of grievances, including the continued US arms sales to Taiwan that included advanced jet fighters and US plans (still very much alive in 2014) to incorporate Taiwan under a proposed missile defense system.[8]

The crackdown cost China an estimated $2 to 3 billion in lost investments and developmental assistance and resulted in a decline in the economy's growth rate. By the second anniversary of the massacre, however, Beijing succeeded in wooing most major industrial democracies back into normal diplomatic and economic relations. The foreign investors hardly missed a beat. For them, it was strictly business.

$$\bullet \ \ \bullet \ \ \bullet$$

The party's legitimacy rested on its success in maintaining unprecedented economic progress and the political stability necessary for sustaining it. Its anxiety about instability was reflected in its reaction to the Falun Gong ("mind-body cultivation"), a popular movement that arose in 1992 and quickly attracted millions of followers. The movement combined elements of meditative religion and physical and spiritual training as reflected in China's traditional martial arts disciplines. The party viewed the Falun Gong as a source of instability, since the allegiance of its members was to their "master," Li Hongzhi, rather than to the state. Li preached that the Falun Gong embodied the original laws of the universe and that he possessed supernatural healing powers and the gift of prophecy that enabled him to predict the doom of Chinese civilization. In April 1999, some 10,000 Falun Gong members staged a defiant, silent protest against their treatment at the gates of the government leaders' compound in Beijing. The party broke up the gathering, denounced the Falun Gong as an "evil force," outlawed the group, and arrested thousands of its members.[9] In 1995, Li took his message to the West. He and his family became permanent residents of the United States. In 1999, the Chinese banned his movement altogether.

In the long run, however, the Falun Gong posed a minor problem compared to China's burgeoning overpopulation. Starting in the early 1960s, when the birth rate was 6 children per woman, the party promoted a successful birth control program that took the number down to 4.7 children by the early 1970s.

Yet that was not enough. By the end of the 1970s, the party moved from promoting to demanding stringent birth control, insisting that families have no more than one offspring. Families with more than one child were penalized. Among the most drastic measures were late-term abortions and sterilization. The "one-child" policy produced an increase in infanticide—with parents killing primarily unwanted female newborns—and overindulged their sons, known as "little emperors." Although draconian, the program held in check a population explosion that threatened to swallow up any increase in economic output.

The considerable imbalance between men and women of marrying age (122 men for every 100 women), Chinese researchers concluded, was a major factor for China's high household savings rate since 1990. The savings rate followed the law of supply and demand: In order to improve a son's chances of attracting a female partner, families with one male offspring (the supply), saved much more than families with a daughter (the demand). In short, families with sons were in competition with other such families. Researchers called it "keeping up with the Zhangs."[10]

The low birthrate also set the stage for a graying population, a serious impediment to future economic growth. In November 2013, the party granted parents who had grown up as single children the right to have a second child.

### Taiwan—The Other China

After the head of the Nationalist Party, Jiang Jieshi (Chiang Kai-shek), arrived on Taiwan in 1949 with 2 million soldiers and civilian supporters, he created the political myth that his government (the Republic of China) remained the only legitimate government of China. Although hailed for many years in the United States as the "democratic" alternative to the oppressive Communist regime on the mainland, "free China" under Jiang was anything but free or democratic. When the Jiang's army seized Taiwan from the Japanese after World War II, it was met with resistance by native Taiwanese. In February 1947, the army crushed an anti-Nationalist demonstration with enormous violence, killing between 5,000 (the Nationalist figure) and 20,000 Taiwanese (the Taiwanese figure). For four decades, Jiang's decree of martial law forbade anyone from speaking of this massacre on punishment of death.

Jiang maintained a one-party dictatorship. The National Assembly, made up entirely of Nationalist Party politicians who had been elected on the mainland in 1948, was a rubber-stamp legislature. It remained without Taiwanese representation until the 1980s. The Taiwanese majority, of about 13 million people in the 1950s, had no political voice. Until his last breath, Jiang remained ever vigilant against any and all challenges, and he ruthlessly suppressed all opposition. When he passed away in April 1975, his successor was his son, Jiang Jingguo (Chiang Ching-kuo), who continued for the time being in his father's footsteps.

Taiwan suffered a major diplomatic setback in 1972 when Washington normalized relations with the People's Republic, and again in 1979, when it broke off official relations with the Nationalist government. Economic ties with the United States, Japan, and other industrial countries remained intact, however.

It was not until the 1980s that Taiwan's economic growth accompanied by a rising middle class translated into political reforms. Liberalization became possible with the passing of the old guard; the lowering of Cold War tensions; the new prosperity, which strengthened the middle class; the spread of education; and the government's increased confidence in the nation's security. In 1986, a newly formed opposition party, the Democratic Progressive Party (DPP), was permitted to run candidates in the National Assembly election. The party's platform called for full implementation of democracy, social welfare, and self-determination for Taiwan. The party did not win, but it did gather a surprising 25 percent of the vote. In July 1987, the government, still led by Jiang Jingguo, finally lifted the thirty-eight-year-old martial law decree, granted freedom of the press, and legalized opposition parties. It also dropped the ban on travel to Communist China, for the first time permitting its people to visit families on the mainland. By 1993, over 1.5 million Taiwanese took advantage of this opportunity.

President Jiang Jingguo died in January 1988, thus ending the Jiang family's sixty-year reign. His successor was Vice-President Lee Teng-hui, who was not from mainland China but from Taiwan. Although Lee did not advocate independence for Taiwan, the fact that a native Taiwanese was now president encouraged those who did. Lee continued the political liberalization begun by Jiang Jingguo. The December 1989 National Assembly election was the first free, multiparty election in Chinese history. The election, in which 78 percent of eligible voters cast their ballots, gave Taiwan a legislative assembly far more representative than the previous one.

The first direct presidential election took place in April 1996. The incumbent Lee, the head of the ruling Nationalist Party, won the election, but his party's share of the vote decreased while the opposition parties made substantial gains. The Nationalist Party's rule finally ended in March 2000, when the DPP candidate, Chen Shui-bian, won the presidency.

## Taiwan and the People's Republic of China

Throughout the years, Taiwan's independence movement grew. Beijing, however, was vehemently opposed to even the idea of a permanent separation of the two Chinas. It considered Taiwan as a renegade province of China, to be reunited with the mainland sooner or later. Still, relations between Taiwan and the PRC improved. Beijing wanted Taiwanese investments and Taiwanese manufacturers welcomed the opportunity to enter the lucrative Chinese market. Economic contacts between the two Chinas increased vastly after Taiwan lifted its travel ban to China in 1987. Beijing and Taipei also opened a formal diplomatic channel, the so-called "cross-strait talks," for the purpose of negotiating economic and social issues.

Beijing offered assurances that, upon reunification, Taiwan would be an autonomous province of the People's Republic, retaining its capitalist economy. China offered something similar to Hong Kong. Hong Kong had no choice in the matter since its inclusion into China was a foregone conclusion. Taiwan rejected the offer of "one-country, two systems." It preferred not to take its chances in the folds of the Communist People's Republic. Taiwan's situation, its government explained, was different from Hong Kong's, for it was not a foreign-controlled colony.

China expressed concern that President Lee, as a Taiwanese, might succumb to political pressure to endorse the permanent separation of the two Chinas. It was not content, however, merely to register protests. It sought to intimidate Taiwanese voters by threatening military force. Prior to Taiwan's first presidential election of April 1996, China carried out large-scale military maneuvers—including missile tests with live ammunition—dangerously close to Taiwan's main port cities. This show of force, however, had little effect on the voters because Lee was reelected by a comfortable margin. It did provoke, however, a strong response from the United States, warning Beijing against any attack on Taiwan.

The return of Hong Kong by the United Kingdom to China in July 1997 and the reversion of the tiny Portuguese colony of Macao in 1999 served to quicken Beijing's insistence on the return of Taiwan. The intra-China feud heated up in July 1999, when Lee explicitly stated that further talks must be on a state-to-state basis, that is, between two sovereign governments negotiating on equal terms. Beijing rejected this position as anathema and again threatened that any attempt to create two Chinas would be met by force. An alarmed President Clinton warned Beijing against using force; at the same time, however, he urged Lee to stay with the fiction of "one China" so as not to ruffle Beijing's feathers. The winner of the March 2000 presidential election, Chen Shi-bian, the candidate of the pro-independence DPP, cautiously shied away from his party's independence agenda. In Beijing, the new leader, Hu Jintao, reiterated the call for "peaceful reunification" of Taiwan with the mainland, only to add an ominous caveat, that "we shall by no means . . . forsake the use of force."[11] If there was one immediate result of Beijing's saber rattling, it was an increase in the sale of sophisticated US weapons to Taiwan, which included improved air defense radar and missiles.

## Hong Kong

After World War II, the British crown colony of Hong Kong emerged as a budding Mecca of Asian capitalism. Britain's "gunboat diplomacy" had pried Hong Kong away from China in the mid-nineteenth century, and it remained in its control even after the Communists came to power. In its early years, the PRC was militarily too weak to attempt to recover Hong Kong by force. Eventually it took a pragmatic, rather than doctrinaire, view of the British presence there. It concluded that Hong Kong was not a threat to China but an opportunity to maintain profitable economic relations with the West.

The British governors of Hong Kong presided over a docile populace (6 million in 1990) and a prospering economy, said to be the freest in the world. A center of finance, trade, and insurance, Hong Kong also became highly industrialized in the 1980s. The thriving business environment attracted large investments from Western countries and Japan, further stimulating the colony's economic growth (averaging 5.5 percent between 1980 and 1992). Although it had a large number of poor people—mainly recent arrivals from the PRC—its per capita GNP reached $15,360 in 1992. Its center became resplendent with wealth, its gleaming skyscrapers soaring above Mercedes-Benz automobiles and free-spending shoppers crowding the streets below.

In the 1970s, London and Beijing began to discuss terms for returning Hong Kong to China by 1997 (as stipulated by agreement in the late nineteenth century). International business interests became nervous about their investments, and to head off the flight of capital and the attendant financial chaos, Britain was eager to secure an early agreement for an orderly transition. Similarly, it was in the PRC's interest to maintain the financial strength of Hong Kong, since it played an important role in China's economic plans.

In 1984, a joint declaration provided a framework for the Chinese takeover in 1997. It stipulated that Hong Kong would retain its capitalist system while maintaining "a high degree of autonomy" as a "special administrative region" of the People's Republic for fifty years after the reversion. By that formula, Hong Kong would preserve its political and economic stability. The agreement also stipulated that the ethnic Chinese of Hong Kong (98 percent of the population) would become citizens of China at the time of reversion, but they were free to leave the colony prior to that time.

The reversion agreement produced mixed results as the years ticked away. Economic growth did not decline appreciably. Unexpectedly, foreign and domestic investments actually increased. Even in 1996, with reversion to China only a year away, the Hong Kong government pumped record amounts ($21 billion) into a series of new projects, including a new international airport, a high-speed rail line to the airport, new superhighways, and a harbor tunnel.

But if investors remained confident about Hong Kong's future, a number of its residents were less so. In the late 1980s, about 50,000 people emigrated from Hong Kong annually (mainly to Canada, Australia, and the United States). The exodus of largely wealthy and well-educated residents of Hong Kong reflected a fear of the Chinese regime.[12] It caused consternation in Beijing, which sought to reassure Hong Kong's people of its benign intentions and avert a further hemorrhage of wealth and talent.

The long-awaited date for the return of Hong Kong to China came on July 1, 1997. The colorful ceremony was marked by nationalistic celebrations by China, nostalgia on the part of Britain (which witnessed the end of its long imperial presence in Asia), and unease on the part of Hong Kong residents. For the most part, the transition from British crown colony to Special Administrative Region went smoothly, however, and Hong Kong continued to prosper.

The PRC then started counting down to the reversion of the Portuguese colony of Macao at the end of 1999. That still left Taiwan out of the fold. Besides Taiwan, there was still the matter of China's territorial claims against India and Vietnam and a much larger claim, virtually the entire South China Sea, potentially a vast source of energy.

By dint of its expanding economy, China fulfilled many of the aspirations it had nurtured for decades. In Chinese eyes, the country was returning to its rightful status as the "Central Kingdom." In the summer of 2008, to worldwide acclaim and accompanied by lavish pomp and ceremony, China staged the summer Olympic Games in Beijing as yet another symbol of its newly gained prowess.

## China and Its "Autonomous" Western Regions

China's extensive railroad system tied two independence-minded peoples, the Turkic-speaking Uyghurs and the Tibetans, ever closer to the center. By 2000, the railroad reached Urumqui—the capital of the Xinjiang Uyghur Autonomous Region, the ancestral home of Sunni Muslim Uyghurs; by 2003, it extended to the city of Kashgar, at the far western frontier of China. The influx of overbearing—and from the Uyghurs' viewpoint, exploitative—Chinese was a contributing factor to the rise of militant Islam in western China. Uyghur resistance, generally ineffective, dated back to the nineteenth century. A particular violent outburst took place in 2009, followed by continuing sporadic acts of violence. From Beijing's perspective, the Uyghur militants were little more than terrorists, a view Washington shared. The separatist Uyghurs rejected that accusation. Their aim, they insisted, was independence from the heavy-handed Chinese.

In 2006, China extended the railroad to Lhasa, the capital of Tibet. The highest railway in the world, it was a marvel of engineering, traversing hundreds of miles of permafrost at elevations exceeding 13,000 feet. On the eighty-fifth anniversary of the birth of the Communist Party, on July 1, 2006, the first train left Golmund for its 700-mile journey to Lhasa. The railroad tied the "roof of the world" closer to Beijing and increased the pace of economic development in Tibet. It also brought an additional influx of ethnic Chinese, who were already the majority population in Lhasa and, indeed, all of Tibet (whereas in 1950 there had been virtually none).

China heralded the railroad as a symbol of progress. It poured huge investments into Tibet's "autonomous region" to improve its infrastructure—electrification, communications, transport, agriculture, commerce, public education, and health care. The educational reforms were designed to redress the widespread illiteracy of Tibetans, to prepare them for employment in the new economy, and to help them to escape from poverty. There was much to be said for what the Chinese did. Before its annexation in 1950, Tibet was a highly stratified feudal theocracy governed by Buddhist monks, a vast region plagued by illiteracy, economic inefficiency, and widespread human bondage, if not outright slavery. In the 1950s, the CIA recruited monks and landlords against the Chinese only to find that the Tibetan people in general did not rally to their former overlords, showing little desire to return them to power.

As the Chinese came in ever larger numbers, however, Tibetans saw their presence as an assault on their ancient culture. They pointed out that the exploitation of Tibet's resources served first and foremost the dominant Chinese. Massive deforestation and strip mining—for the world's largest reserves of uranium, borax, and lithium as well as copper, chromite, copper, bauxite, gold, silver, tin, and oil—was in the service of China's economic development. Tibetans also benefited, a point Beijing repeatedly made, but it was not enough to assuage their resentment. Tibetans remained marginalized and remained dependent on a painfully slow trickle-down effect. They charged that the Chinese had brought only vulgar materialism, as manifested in the dance halls at the foot of the Potala Palace, the former residence of the Dalai Lamas, their spiritual leaders.

China's actions in Tibet and in Xinjiang were strikingly similar to those of other colonizers. On the one hand, they exploited the local population and their resources; on the other, they touted their civilizing mission. China's argument was little different from the French *mission civilisatrice*, from the British carrying the "white man's burden," or the Japanese "co-prosperity sphere." Their pseudonyms masked the racial and exploitative aspects of colonization. So it was in Xinjiang and in Tibet.

Tibetans continued to worship their aged Dalai Lama, in exile in India, and looked toward the reincarnation of the next Dalai Lama—the transfer of the rarified mindstream of Buddha to a new mortal body. The Chinese response was a curious law, passed in August 2007, declaring that the reincarnation of the next Dalai Lama could only take place with the government's permission.

During the mid-1980s, the Dalai Lama, a firm champion of nonviolence, was still engaged in negotiations with Beijing. He was willing to acknowledge that Tibet was part of China—provided its ancient culture was protected. What the Dalai Lama proposed was similar to what other nations had granted their minorities. Canada had granted its French-speaking Québécois cultural and linguistic autonomy; after years of sporadic violence, Italy granted its German-speaking citizens in South Tirol, the right to their native tongue in their schools and elsewhere. To keep the Soviet Union together, Stalin granted similar concessions to his restless ethnic nationalities. Beijing, however, rejected all suggestions of local autonomy for Tibet, cultural or otherwise, and ended its talks with the Dalai Lama.

Upon returning from a 1980 fact-finding mission to Tibet, the reformer Hu Yaobang urged his government to respect Tibetan culture. Yet no one listened. Hu Jintao, who once had served as party secretary in Tibet (where he had not hesitated to use force), was in no mood to negotiate with a people he considered uncultured and dangerous.

Over the years, young Tibetans lost faith in the efficacy of nonviolent means. In March 2008, their mood turned ugly. First came the indiscriminate massacre of Chinese civilians in Lhasa, followed by the inevitable crackdown by the government, something it had sought to avoid, since it came just five months before the opening ceremonies of the Olympic Games. The Olympic torch completed its journey around the globe under tight security and even made its scheduled visit to Lhasa.[13]

Starting in February 2009, more than one hundred mostly young Tibetans resorted to the most dramatic form of protest imaginable—self-immolation. Some of the suicides—which Buddhists defended as altruistic acts of self-sacrifice—were captured on cell phones and made their way around the world. In Vietnam, such immolations caught the world's attention; this time the world merely shrugged. The Chinese government, nonetheless, responded by tightening controls on the Internet. Its foreign minister, Yang Jiechi, blamed the Dalai Lama—a "wolf in sheep's clothing"—for stirring up discontent in Tibet where its people lived in "happiness and in great freedom." It accused the Dalai Lama of separatism, of seeking to establish a "Greater Tibet on one quarter of Chinese territory."

## The South China Sea

As long as China's focus was on the economy, it made sure not to ruffle the feathers of its neighboring trade and investment partners. In due time, however, its foreign policy became more assertive. It leaned on its academics to dig up ancient Chinese documents to bolster its nationalistic claims, in preparation for claiming territory beyond its borders.[14] China's new passports contained a watermark map showing stretches of India's Arunachal Pradesh state and Kashmir as part of China. It was not only India that was unhappy with China's passport map. Other nations complained about China's claim to the entire South China Sea. As such, it claimed the Paracel and Spratly islands and sundry other outcroppings and shoals, potential sources of oil and natural gas.

To make its claim, China used a prerevolutionary map that featured a so-called "nine-dash-line" that extended its territorial claim right up to the shores of the Philippines, Vietnam, Malaysia, and Taiwan. The United States considered the South China Sea as an important international sea-lane used by its navy and the merchant ships of other nations such as Taiwan, South Korea, and Japan. Secretary of State Hillary Clinton spoke of "freedom of navigation"; China's foreign minister Yang Jiechi spoke of the importance of respecting "the sovereignty and territorial integrity of China."[15] Periodically, China backed off from its all-encompassing claim to the South China Sea, but not its claim to the islands.

China's relations with Japan, fueled by the memory of World War II, were not much better. In a confrontation over a group of uninhabited islands in the East China Sea (that the Japanese called Senkaku and the Chinese, Diaoyu), China and Japan deployed warships and scrambled military jets. In a game of brinkmanship, they unlocked their radar, suggesting an imminent attack. The Chinese government had no difficulty organizing anti-Japanese demonstrations. Occasionally, it had to break them up because they threatened to get out of hand, such as when crowds in the port of Qingdao set fire to a Panasonic factory and a Toyota dealership. In response to the Chinese demonstrations, the Japanese government organized "Senkaku memorial day" rallies.

In the dispute over the Senkaku/Diaoyu islands, the United States backed Japan, declaring the islands fell under their mutual defense treaty. The Pentagon, in its annual report to Congress in May 2013, accused the Chinese military of extensive cyber attacks against US government and defense contractors. (Ironically, the charge came from a government that had waged cyber warfare against Iran and, it was shortly revealed, had been spying on the rest of the world.) China dismissed the charges of cyber warfare as "groundless." Not just that, it declared, it would never engage in such activity.

Hegemonic aspirations of one power historically draw closer those it threatens. In response to China's increasingly ambitious foreign policy, the United States established in northern Australia an outpost manned by 2,500 Marines. Australia's dilemma was whether to side with the United States, its most important military partner since World War II, or with China, its most important trading partner.

• • •

The impressive Chinese economic turnaround lifted hundreds of millions out of poverty (if only according to the World Bank's artificially low definition of that term). But it also made a number of its citizens with the proper connections fabulously wealthy. There was never an attempt, the Communist-inspired rhetoric notwithstanding, of even a semblance of equal distribution of the new wealth. This was capitalism at its most basic. It made the party rich, but it also threatened to undermine its moral authority. It was a problem that had flared up during the Tiananmen Square demonstrations and would not go away. The behavior of party functionaries stood in conflict with the ancient Confucian admonition that "riches and honor without justice" are merely "fleeing clouds." A good ruler is synonymous with benevolence and virtue. The gap between the rich and poor threatened the breakdown of the Confucian precept of harmony.[16] At the party's Eighteenth Congress in November 2012, its outgoing leader, Hu Jintao, warned that corruption "could cause the collapse of the party and the fall of the state." Other officials urged the party to learn the "deeply profound" lesson inherent in the fall of the Soviet Union.

The party generally turned a blind eye to the doings of its wealthy members—unless they undermined the party's standing. A case in point was that of Bo Xilai, the party secretary of Chongqin, a leading contender to rule China in the near future. Bo offered himself as a populist, someone ostensibly still in the thrall of Mao's egalitarian rhetoric. He promoted the singing of "red songs," the airing of patriotic films on television, and low-cost housing. It turned out, however, that his main characteristics were greed, brutality, and a lust for power. His antimafia campaign enabled him to establish an extensive surveillance network that he used to wiretap other party officials, including China's president. In the party, he was more than disliked; he was also feared.

The worth of Bo's extended family was estimated at $2.7 billion. His glamorous wife was heavily involved in the profitable diamond and gem trade, but when a journalist reported on the family's doings, he spent five years in prison. The person who blew the whistle on Bo was none other than his police chief, Wang Lijun, whose family, too, had become extremely wealthy. Hitherto, Wang's claim to fame had been the efficient transplanting of organs from executed members of the Falun Gong. For reasons still not clear, Wang implicated Bo's wife in the murder of Neil Heywood, a British businessman and fixer, who had arranged their son's admission to Harrow, Oxford, and Harvard. Back home, the son drove a red Ferrari, and at Harvard, a more modest Porsche. The motive for Heywood's murder may have been a dispute over money or that he simply knew too much.

China did not have a tabloid press, but the authorities leaked enough about the strange case of Comrade Bo to keep the nation enthralled. Believing that all politicians were corrupt, the cynics were ready to believe the worst about Bo and his family. The investigation put a spotlight on the hidden wealth and power that the party's "princelings" enjoyed. Officially, China was a meritocracy, but few people believed it. Bo's father was Bo Yibo, one of the party's "Eight Immortals," who ruled under Deng Xiaoping in the 1980s and early 1990s. None of it was now of any help to the younger Bo, who was stripped of his party membership in March 2012 and not seen or heard from until his trial in September 2013. It was China's most sensational trial since that of the Gang of Four. In a perfunctory procedure lasting seven hours, Bo was sentenced to life in prison, as was his wife, who admitted to poisoning Heywood.[17]

In November 2012, the partly chose a new leader, Xi Jinping, another "princeling." Xi promised sweeping changes, yet his heart was not in it. For a while, observers (in China and abroad) had no clear idea where he stood politically until the party issued, in August 2013, a directive listing "seven perils" emanating from the West. The most dangerous threat was "Western constitutional democracy," followed by "universal values" of human rights, independent media and civic participation, opposition to one-party rule, pro-market "neo-liberalism," and "nihilist" criticisms of the party's painful past. To some it appeared that Mao's ghost was stirring. Indeed, to commemorate the one-hundred-twentieth anniversary of his birth, the party spent $1 billion to renovate commemorative sites in his hometown.[18]

Since the days of Deng, all Chinese leaders believed that the country was best served by its hereditary party oligarchy. What its members must not do, however, was to embarrass the party by their behavior, including ostentatious flaunting of their wealth. By 2013, China had 251 billionaires, as compared to only 15 in 2006. Less than half of one percent of China's families owned 70 percent of its wealth. Deng's son-in-law, part of a triumvirate that included the son of Mao's economic minister, headed state-controlled ministries valued at $1.6 trillion dollars. The seventy wealthiest members of the National People's Congress owned $89.9 billion—as compared to the 563 principal figures in the three branches of the US government (the 535 members of Congress, the president, his cabinet, and the Supreme Court), whose combined net worth was a paltry $7.5 billion, or $13.3 million each.[19]

For Xi Jinping to succeed, he would have to take on the "princelings" and nouveau riche. It was a tall order. China's wealthiest man, Zong Qinghou, thought that it would be a bad idea to focus on income inequality, among the highest in the world. The idea, Zong said, was to make everyone wealthy by lowering taxes. "If we had egalitarianism," he said, "we wouldn't have enough to eat."[20]

• • •

In the mid-1990s, Deng turned ninety and became increasingly feeble. But even in infirmity, he retained his authority as China's "paramount leader" until

1996, when he designated a successor, Jiang Zemin, as the country's president and general secretary of the party. When Deng died in March 1997, the transition to the next three heads of the Communist Party was smooth. Rapid industrialization and economic integration with the world would continue. (See Chapter 18.)

The history of the Chinese Communist revolution may be broken down into two parts: the rule of Maoism that prevailed for thirty years (1949–1979) and Deng's reforms, which by 2013 were already in place for an even longer period. But now, it was the Deng-inspired system that needed overhauling. China faced serious problems—the wealth gap (not only between the billionaires and the working poor but also between the urban and rural dwellers, between the rapidly industrializing coast and the inland regions), declining standards of living for some, joblessness, alienation, socially dysfunctional cities shoddily built and thrown up overnight, high suicide rates, corruption, pollution. The revolution remained a work in progress.

## Notes

1. "1950: The Land Reform," china.org.cn, September 15, 2009.

2. Frank Dikötter, *Mao's Great Famine: The History of China's Most Devastating Catastrophe, 1958–1962* (New York: Walker, 2010), pp. 324–334; Yang Jisheng, *Tombstone: The Great Chinese Famine, 1958–1962* (New York: Farrar, Straus and Giroux, 2012.)

3. Deng Xiaoping, addressing the Central Committee of the Chinese Communist Youth League, "Restore Agricultural Production," July 7, 1962, english.peopledaily.com.cn/dengxp/vol1/text/a1400.

4. Orville Schell and John Delury, *Wealth and Power: China's Long March to the Twenty-first Century* (New York: Random House, 2013); Ian Johnson, "Dreams of a Different China," *New York Review of Books*, November 21, 2013; Jung Chang, *Empress Dowager Cixi: The Concubine Who Launched Modern China* (New York: Alfred A. Knopf, 2013).

5. John Schidlovsky, "Strike Gains Momentum in China," *Baltimore Sun*, April 25, 1989.

6. Scott Shane, "Gorbachev Praises China for Dialogue with Demonstrators," *Baltimore Sun*, May 18, 1989.

7. Orville Schell, *Mandate of Heaven* (New York: Simon and Schuster, 1994), p. 154.

8. Michal Thim, "Taiwan in the Context of US Missile Defense Infrastructure in Asia," *Taiwan in Perspective*, August 24, 2012.

9. "Why the Exercisers Exercise China's Party," *The Economist*, July 29, 1999; "China's Trial of Faith," *The Economist*, November 4, 1999.

10. Shang-Jin Wei and Xiaobo Zhang, "The Competitive Savings Motive: Evidence from Rising Sex Ratios and Savings Rates in China," National Bureau of Economic Research, Cambridge, MA, Working Paper 15093, June 2009.

11. Cited in Richard Halloran, "How Will Hu Change China's Foreign Policy?" *Baltimore Sun*, September 29, 2004, p. 17A.

12. "New Record Set in Exodus," *Free China Journal*, December 22, 1988.

13. Pankaj Mishra, "The Quiet Heroes of Tibet," *New York Review of Books*, January 17, 2008, 39–40; Jonathan Mirsky, "How He Sees It Now," *New York Review*

*of Books*, July 17, 2008, pp. 4–6; Peter Hessler, "Tibet Through Chinese Eyes," *The Atlantic*, February 1999, 56–66; Jim Yardly, "Trying to Reshape Tibet, China Sends in the Masses," *New York Times*, September 15, 2003; International Committee of Lawyers for Tibet, "Human Rights and the Long-Term Viability of Tibet's Economy," November 1997.

14. William Wan, "Beijing Turns to Its Archival Arsenal," *Washington Post*, February 18, 2013, p. A8.

15. Ramsey a-Rikabi, "Dangerous Waters," *Energy Compass*, July 29, 2011, p. 3.

16. Orville Schell, "China's Quest for Moral Authority," *The Nation*, October 20, 2008, pp. 23–26.

17. Evan Osnos, "China's Crisis," *The New Yorker*, April 30, 2012, pp. 19–20; David Barboza, "As China Official Rose, His Family's Wealth Grew," *New York Times*, April 23, 2013; Lauren Hilgers, "The Unraveling of Bo Xilai," *Harper's*, March 2013, pp. 38–45; Peter Kwong, "Why China's Corruption Won't Stop," *The Nation*, April 22, 2013, pp. 17–21; Erich Follath and Wieland Wagner, "The Battle for China's Most Powerful Office," *Der Spiegel*, October 18, 2012.

18. Chris Buckley, "China Takes Aim at Western Ideas," *New York Times*, August 19, 2013.

19. Kwong, "Why China's Corruption Won't Stop," p. 18.

20. "China's Richest Man Says Wealth Gap Is Not a Priority," AFP news agency, July 17, 2013.

# 16

# The Indian Subcontinent and Southeast Asia

**The Himalayan Mountains separate the world's most populous** nations—China and India. After World War II, India shared many of China's problems, not the least of which was a burgeoning population. About one-fifth of the world's population lived on the Indian subcontinent, which consists mainly of India, Pakistan, and Bangladesh. In the postwar era, India and the other heavily populated nations of the subcontinent struggled to hold population growth in check and to elevate the standard of living. Although they shared many problems, these nations have not lived in peace with one another. Hostility between India and Pakistan has flared up several times, and both countries had to deal with violent internal disorders. The maintenance of large armies to deal with external and internal exigencies drained their limited resources.

To speak of India after World War II is to speak of population and poverty. At the time of the partition of India in 1947, its population was about 350 million, and it has grown steadily ever since at a rate of almost 3 percent a year. This meant an average annual increase of about 5 million people in the 1950s, 8 million in the 1960s, and 13 million in the 1970s. An electronic display in New Delhi reminded Indians that in mid-July 1992, the country's population stood at 868 million and was increasing by 2,000 people per hour, 48,000 per day, or 17.5 million per year.[1] In 2000, the population reached 1 billion, almost triple that of 1947; in 2013 it stood at 1.3 billion. Moreover, about 40 percent of the Indian people are concentrated in the Ganges River basin, where the population density is among the highest in the world. Although in the mid-1980s India had eight cities with over 1 million inhabitants, over 80 percent of the Indian people still lived in rural villages.

India's primary task was to feed its huge population. Population control was high on the government's agenda. Its birth control program, however, had minimal effect in rural areas. The largely illiterate and suspicious villagers clung to the ingrained, age-old notion that a large family was a blessing and that it represented wealth and security. Moreover, one way Indians combated the high infant mortality rate was simply to have more children. Birth control programs were responsible for a slight decrease in the birthrate, which, however, was offset by a declining death rate. Thus, the pressure of overpopulation on India's economy remained undiminished.

Food production increased steadily after independence, but it remained barely adequate. In general, the rate of increase of output was slightly higher than the rate of population growth. Indian agriculture featured small-scale, primitive subsistence farms, a most inefficient approach in terms of yield per acre. A shortage of farming machinery, a general lack of irrigation, a tradition-bound social system, and wide-spread malnutrition added to India's problem. The latter suggests a cruel cycle of cause and effect: Malnutrition and disease contributed to low agricultural productivity, which in turn led to greater poverty and hunger.

In India, as in the other agrarian nations, a wide gulf existed between the wealthy landowners and the far more numerous poor peasants, many of them landless. The practice of dividing land among sons contributed to making the average farm so small that it did not support the family; thus, the farmer was often forced to borrow money at high rates of interest to make ends meet. All too often, he was unable to repay the loan without selling what little land he had left. The result was a steady increase in landlessness and an increase in the land the wealthy owned.

The US-sponsored "Green Revolution" (introduced in 1965) and agricultural mechanization produced an increase in agricultural output. The Green Revolution introduced newly developed plants—high-yield varieties of wheat and rice—and new farming techniques (with considerable emphasis on irrigation) to grow the new types of grain.[2] In certain areas of India, wheat and rice production doubled between 1964 and 1972. The Green Revolution, however, turned out to be a mixed blessing. It benefited mainly the minority of India's farmers—the wealthy landowners who could afford the new seeds and the additional irrigation works, fertilizers, and labor required to grow the new high-yield grain. The majority of the rural population—small landholders, landless peasants, and dryland farmers—lacked the capital or the means to borrow enough money to grow the new crops. Not only were they unable to reap the benefits of the increased food production, but they were actually hurt by it. The increased yield lowered the price for grain crops, which meant a lower income for peasants who still followed traditional modes of farming. The Green Revolution made the rich richer and the poor poorer.

The mechanization of farming, meaning primarily the increased use of tractors, had a similar effect. On the one hand, it contributed to a rise in food production; on the other, mechanization benefited only those who could afford the expensive new equipment. Furthermore, the use of tractors greatly reduced the need for farm laborers and, by eliminating many jobs, increased the ranks of the unemployed. More and more impoverished villagers of India were reduced to collecting firewood and animal droppings to sell as fuel. Even progress can breed poverty.

Unable to make a living in the countryside, the landless migrated to the cities, where life was only little better than in the villages they had just left. Bombay and Calcutta (renamed Mumbai and Kolkata, in 1995 and 2001, respectively) were teeming with hungry and homeless people, many of whom literally lived and died in the streets. In the mid-1980s, of Calcutta's 11 million people, an estimated 900,000 people lived in the streets with scant shelter.

## India's Economic Development

India's efforts to increase industrial production met with moderate success in the first two decades after independence. It opted for a mixed economy, whereby major industries such as iron and steel, mining, transportation, and electricity were nationalized—that is, owned and operated by the government. The government's First Five-Year Plan, launched in 1951, met its relatively modest goals for increased industrial output. At the conclusion of the second plan, in 1961, Prime Minister Jawaharlal Nehru admitted that India "would need many more five-year plans to progress from the cow dung stage to the age of atomic energy."[3] Although some impressive large-scale, modern industrial plants were built, most of India's industry remained small in scale and lacked modern equipment.

The overall growth rate of India's economy was steady but not particularly high. India maintained an average annual GNP growth rate of between 3 percent and 4 percent.[4] A large gap existed between the incomes of the educated elites, technicians, and skilled laborers in the industrial sector and those of the unskilled laborers and peasants in the traditional sector—not to mention the many unemployed and underemployed city-dwellers.

India was handicapped by most of the problems of the global South: a lack of capital, difficulty in attracting foreign capital, illiteracy, and a lack of technology. To this list one might add India's unique social conservatism—the weight of tradition, especially a Hindu religious tradition in which much of Indian life was centered. The remnants of the ancient caste system militated against social mobility and advancement. Ethnic and linguistic diversity was another obstacle to economic modernization. Yet another factor retarding India's economic growth was the continual "brain drain" the country experienced. Many of India's best foreign-trained scientists and engineers chose not to return and remained in Western countries that provided career opportunities, modern technology, and creature comforts unattainable in their native land.

A prerequisite for economic development is a thriving market, either domestic or foreign. In India, the poverty of the masses meant a lack of purchasing power, which translated into a weak domestic market. The impact of the oil crisis in the 1970s and global inflation and recession made it virtually impossible to maintain a favorable balance of trade. Over the years, its trade deficit, its need of capital to finance continued industrialization, and its periodic food shortages forced India to rely heavily on foreign loans and the importation of food. With the increase in food production as a consequence of the Green Revolution, however, India became in the early 1980s a net exporter of food.

In 1971, US president Richard Nixon terminated US developmental aid to India, partly because of India's defeat of Pakistan in Bangladesh's war for independence, but also because he despised the "devious" Indians in general, particularly the prime minister, the "old witch" Indira Gandhi.[5] Moreover, although India was officially neutral in the Cold War, it tilted toward the Soviet Union because of the close military ties between the United States and Pakistan. As a result, the Soviet Union became India's primary source of foreign aid. In the decades since its First Five-Year Plan, India received more foreign aid (from the World Bank, the Asian Development Bank, and Japan) than any other developing country. Its per capita income, nonetheless, remained among the world's lowest.

Political stability is an important asset for developing nations, and India possessed a degree of stability—at least at the beginning. It had a functioning parliamentary system based on the English model. It also had prolonged rule by one dominant party—the Congress Party—and continuity of leadership in the persons of Jawaharlal Nehru, who ruled from independence (1947) until his death in 1964; his daughter, Indira Gandhi, who ruled (except for one brief interlude) from 1966 to 1984; and her son, Rajiv Gandhi, who ruled until 1989.

After independence, India's leaders faced the monumental task of binding together in nationhood the numerous subgroups of diverse ethnic, religious, and linguistic identities. Tensions were punctuated time and again by violent clashes between one or another of the ethnic and religious groups and the Hindu majority. In the mid-1970s, the Indian political consensus, guided by Nehru and then by Indira Gandhi, began to fray at the edges. As the economy suffered from the steep rise of oil prices in the early 1970s, dissent increased, railroad workers threatened to paralyze the vast railroad system, and popular agitation spilled into the streets. Indira Gandhi responded in June 1975 with a twenty-one-month-long "National Emergency," accompanied by the suspension of the constitution, stringent press censorship, and the arrest of political opponents. The emergency ended when Gandhi called for elections that she then lost, the Congress Party's first electoral defeat. The emergency cast a long shadow, for it weakened India's commitment to constitutional principles. The chief beneficiaries were far-right Hindu groups, which until then had carefully been kept out of politics. Among the Hindu jingoists Gandhi arrested in 1975 were members of what became the rightist ruling political coalition of the late 1990s, including the future prime minister, Atal Bihari Vajpayee.[6]

### India, Pakistan, and Bangladesh

In foreign affairs, Nehru sought to follow the dictum of "live and let live." He refused to be drawn into the Cold War and, instead, sought to exert the moral influence of India as a neutral peacemaker. It gained him considerable international prestige from some, but not all, quarters. President Dwight Eisenhower's secretary of state, John Foster Dulles, thought it was the height of immorality to stay neutral in the global struggle between good and evil. Nehru's neutrality, however, did nothing to mitigate India's troubles with its immediate neighbors, Pakistan and China. An ongoing border dispute with China led to large increases in military expenditures.

Indian-Pakistani relations were strained from the time of partition. India and Pakistan both claimed the remote, sparsely populated mountainous state of Kashmir. Despite UN efforts to keep the peace, India and Pakistan clashed over Kashmir in 1948 and 1949. India secured control of most of Kashmir and turned a deaf ear to Pakistan's continual demands for a referendum there. The Pakistani claim to Kashmir was based on the fact that the majority of its people were Muslim, which explains why Pakistan wished to settle the matter by a referendum. India's claim rested mainly on the expressed will of the local Hindu ruling elite (from which Nehru himself descended) of Kashmir to remain part of India.

China and India laid claim to the remote southern slopes of the Himalayan Mountains north of the Assam Plain, each staking its claim on different boundaries drawn by nineteenth-century British surveyors. India considered its claim as non-negotiable and turned down repeated diplomatic efforts by Beijing to settle the issue. In October 1962, India's forces suffered a humiliating defeat by China in a brief border war, after which Beijing redrew the border in the high Himalayas.

Tension between India and Pakistan remained high. Skirmishes along the cease-fire line drawn up after the wars of the late 1940s, occurred with increasing frequency. Shortly after Nehru's death in May 1964, Pakistan set out to force a military solution to the Kashmir issue. After its forces crossed the demarcation line in August 1965, the conflict quickly escalated into a brief, fierce but inconclusive war. The Pakistani air force relied on US-made F-86 Sabre and F-104 Starfighter jets; the Indians relied on an assortment of British fighter-bombers and Soviet-made Antonov-12 bombers and MiG-21s. If one country could claim to have won the war, it was India, but its victory was hardly decisive.

By now, the Indian-Pakistani conflicts had taken on important global dimensions. Moscow was more than willing to provide support to its Indian client and thus extend its influence into South Asia. Washington responded by increasing its long-standing military support to Pakistan. Pakistan's other source of support was the People's Republic of China. Ironically, Pakistan's patrons—the United States and China—were bitter Cold War foes during these years.

During the 1960s, Pakistan faced economic problems similar to those in India. It was beset by an additional problem stemming from its peculiar situation as a nation with two separate parts. West Pakistan, where the capital was located, was separated from East Pakistan by nearly 1,000 miles of Indian territory. The cultural and political distance between the two parts of Pakistan was even greater. The people of East Pakistan were Bengalis who, except for their Muslim religion, had little in common with the West Pakistanis, who belong to several ethnic groups—the largest of which is the Punjabi. Political and military power was concentrated in West Pakistan, despite the fact that the more densely populated East Pakistan contained the majority of the nation's population. According to the constitution, however, East Pakistan comprised only one of the nation's five provinces and thus had only 20 percent of the seats in parliament. Only about 35 percent of the national budget was earmarked for East Pakistan, which was, moreover, a captive market for West Pakistani goods.

Bengali frustration erupted in late 1970, when East Pakistan was hit by a terrible natural catastrophe, followed by a man-made disaster. In November, a powerful cyclone with an enormous tidal wave caused widespread flooding, leaving approximately 200,000 people dead and 1 million homeless. The lack of effective government relief was further proof for the Bengalis of their government's indifference toward their problems, and thus fed the flames of Bengali separatism. While still suffering the prolonged effects of the flood, East Pakistan fell victim to the second disaster, an assault by the military forces of West Pakistan to forestall secession.

In the December 1970 national election, Sheikh Mujibur Rahman, the head of the Bengali Awami League, a party that stood for elevating the status of East Pakistan, won a large majority. The government of General Yaha Khan and Zulfikar Ali Bhutto, head of the leading West Pakistan–based party, were shocked by the election results. Instead of accepting them, they imposed martial law on East Pakistan. In March 1971, Khan's army attacked East Pakistan, striking first at the leaders of the Awami League. After the arrest of Mujibur and his government, the Pakistani army turned on the Bengali people, killing an estimated 3 million civilians. Approximately 10 million terrorized Bengalis fled to India.

Bengali armed resistance consisted mainly in form of protracted guerrilla warfare. India, led by Indira Gandhi, seized the opportunity in December 1971 to deliver a blow against West Pakistan (it never had a quarrel with East Pakistan) and entered the fray. After two weeks of intensive combat, India drove West Pakistan's army out of East Pakistan. India's decisive victory over West Pakistan led to the birth of a new nation, Bangladesh.

Nixon and his national security advisor, Henry Kissinger, opposed independence for Bangladesh, denounced India for its "aggression," and supported West Pakistan, despite the latter's widely reported brutality. They downplayed reports of atrocities, even as other White House officials acknowledged a "reign of terror." Archer Blood, the US consul in Dacca, Bangladesh's future capital, spoke of genocide in his diplomatic cables.[7] Nixon and Kissinger, however, preferred to see the crisis in purely geostrategic terms. They were more concerned about India, a "Soviet stooge," flexing its military muscle. They ignored the local causes for the war, seeing it instead as one between proxies of Moscow and Washington. It did not sit well with them that their side was losing.

In a supreme act of recklessness, Nixon and Kissinger went so far as to urge China to intervene on the side of Pakistan. Such a step had the potential to touch off a war involving the great powers in South Asia. The Soviet Union would have been obliged to support India, and the United States to support Pakistan and China. The India-Pakistan war also gave Nixon, who suffered from an incurable fear of appearing weak, the opportunity to show his mettle. In the midst of extricating the US military from Vietnam, he wanted to show the Vietnamese—in Saigon and in Hanoi—his toughness and his resolve.[8]

At first, Washington and Beijing balked at extending diplomatic recognition to independent Bangladesh, but eventually they did so, setting the stage for its entry into the United Nations in 1975. With US diplomatic recognition came shipments of economic aid, something Bangladesh desperately needed.

For Pakistan, the 1971 war had a sobering effect. Now limited to what had been West Pakistan and with a population reduced by more than half, Pakistan turned to the tasks of rehabilitation and reorganization. Military government was ended when General Yahya Khan resigned and transferred power to Bhutto, whose Pakistan People's Party had come in second in the December 1970 election. One of Bhutto's first acts was to release Sheikh Mujibur from prison and arrange his return to Bangladesh, where he became its president. Bhutto also saw the wisdom of reducing tensions with India, and for that purpose he agreed to meet with Indira Gandhi in 1972. Indian-Pakistani relations substantially improved until May 1974, when India successfully tested what it called a "nuclear device." By demonstrating its nuclear capacity, India established even more conclusively its position as the dominant military power in South Asia, but at the same time it aroused Pakistani fears.

Bangladesh, born of disaster, learned that independence produced no significant improvement in the lives of its people. After the war, India ordered the return of the 10 million Bengali refugees to their ravaged homeland. The catastrophic flood damage and the war had left the country devastated and unable to cope with the hunger and disease. Mujibur's government faced not merely a destitute people but also crime, corruption, and general disorder. The government declared a state of emergency in 1974, and in 1975 the once popular Mujibur was killed in a military coup. In the years that followed, feuding military factions prolonged political instability.

One of the most densely populated nations in the world, Bangladesh became synonymous with poverty. No larger than the US state of Georgia, it was the home of nearly 165 million people in 2013, with an annual per capita GDP of $2,100.[9] There was simply too little land to support its swollen population; half of those who worked the land owned less than an acre of land—an amount insufficient to feed the average household of six. Since the mid-1990s, however, it was able to sustain an annual GDP growth rate of about 5 percent. Nevertheless, in 2010, nearly half of its people still lived below the World Bank's poverty line of $1.25 per day, its incidence of malnutrition remaining among the highest in the world.[10]

## South Asia Since 1980

### India

The 1980s brought to the Indian subcontinent a modest improvement in the standard of living. In India and Pakistan, one could witness the slow but steady growth of industry, increased urban construction, greater agricultural output, and the expansion of the middle class. Yet, due to continued population growth, both countries remained among the poorest in the world in terms of per capita GNP. Both sought to control population growth, which threatened their economic futures. Family-planning programs in past years, however, had produced little success. Activists hoped for a feminist revolt against the grain of societies dominated by men.[11]

In the 1980s, India faced a Sikh separatist movement in the northern state of Punjab. The Sikhs, whose religion consists of a mixture of Hinduism and Islam, made up about 2 percent of India's population, but they constituted the majority in Punjab where they sought to establish their own independent state. As the Sikhs became increasingly relentless in their demand for their separate state of Khalistan, the Indian police were equally relentless in their effort to ferret out Sikh militants, at times taking the law into their own hands by torturing and murdering suspects. A raid by Indira Gandhi's security forces on the Sikhs' Golden Temple in Amritsar, in June 1984, left 1,200 dead and as many prisoner (the number of fatalities remaining in dispute). Thousands of Sikhs

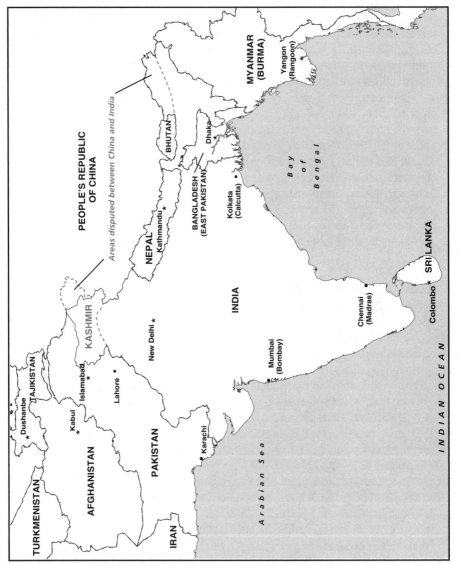

**The Indian Subcontinent**

became political prisoners, held with neither charges against them nor trials. In October 1984, two of Gandhi's Sikh bodyguards shot her to death. In the wake of the assassination, riots across India claimed the lives of thousands more Sikhs.

Indira Gandhi's successor was her son, Rajiv, who continued the repression of Sikhs. In May 1987, after four months of escalating violence during which security officers killed more than 500 Sikhs, he imposed direct rule over Punjab and ousted the elected state government made up of Sikh moderates.

After the Congress Party was narrowly defeated in the November 1989 parliamentary elections, Rajiv Gandhi resigned as prime minister. Two caretaker governments wrestled with India's faltering economy and divisive religious/ethnic disputes. While campaigning for reelection in May 1991, Rajiv Gandhi was assassinated, the victim of a terrorist suicide bomb, one of the first ever. He died as his mother had, the victim of an ethnic independence movement. His death was the work of the Hindu Tamil Liberation Tigers, who felt Gandhi had betrayed them in their war for independence against the Buddhist Singhalese majority on the island nation of Sri Lanka.

• • •

For more than a quarter of a century, the minority "Tamil Tigers" kept alive their dream of an independent Tamil state carved out of the northern and eastern stretches of Sri Lanka. Led and organized in 1976 by Vellupillai Prabhakaran, they began, against all odds, a long war for national liberation in 1983. As a small minority, 12 percent of Sri Lanka's population, the Tigers were reduced to relying on guerrilla war and the use of terror. It was they who apparently invented the suicide vests filled with explosives, which others then emulated. No group came close to the number of suicide bombers the Tigers sacrificed (estimated at nearly 200), far outstripping better known groups such as Hamas. Their dedicated "Black Tigers" squad had both male and female suicide bombers. They were the only terrorist group to assassinate two heads of state, Rajiv Gandhi and Sri Lanka's prime minister.

Although the Tigers were scions of Hindu families, their social and political orientation (in theory at least) was Marxist. Prabhakaran was influenced by Marx, the feats of Napoleon and Alexander the Great, and by Tamil nationalism steeped in part in legend, and in part in history. The type of Marxism the Tigers espoused, however, would have appalled Marx and Lenin, neither of whom had use for assassins.

In the end, after twenty-six years of terror, the Tigers had nothing to show for their efforts. After Prabhakaran was killed in a rocket attack in May 2009, they were utterly routed. Second-class citizens in their own land, the Tigers certainly had legitimate grievances. Their discrimination at the hands of the majority Singhalese (nearly three-quarter of the population) was all too real. But as they went about the business of addressing their grievances, their entire campaign became suicidal. The Tigers left no room for compromise and deemed moderation as act of betrayal. When it was over, 40,000 Tigers and perhaps an equal number of civilians were dead. After they laid down their arms, their political party, the Tamil National Alliance, finally gained something by winning landslide victories in local council elections, and with it a modicum of local autonomy.

• • •

In the early 1990s, India was burdened with a foreign debt of $71 billion and dwindling foreign reserves. By now, it could no longer count on the Soviet Union for support, as the latter was disintegrating. India thus took the historic step of abandoning its centrally planned economy, which Jawaharlal Nehru had established four decades earlier.

India sought to solve its balance-of-payments crisis by securing emergency loans from the International Monetary Fund and World Bank. In return, as these international agencies demanded, India slashed government spending, cut red tape, reduced import duties, invited foreign capital, and loosened interest rates to encourage private businesses. The upshot was sustained economic growth.

India was less successful, however, in reining in its religious extremists. In December 1992, it was wracked by a renewal of religious violence, this time between Hindus and Muslims. Fighting erupted in Ayodhya, the traditional birthplace of the Hindu god Ram, where Hindu zealots tore down a Muslim mosque built in 1528 by the Mogul emperor Babur on top of the ruins of a Hindu temple. It was the first time Hindus had razed a mosque since the 1947 partition. Violence soon spread to other cities. Before order was restored, over 1,200 lay dead and 4,600 were injured. It was the deadliest Hindu-Muslim clash since 1947.

Hindu nationalist fervor was such that, in March 1998, Congress lost its political monopoly to the Hindu Bharatiya Janata Party (BJP) under the leadership of Atal Bihari Vajpayee. The BJP—a linear descendant from the Hindu extremists of 1947—stood for making India a Hindu state and curbing the rights of Muslims and other religious and ethnic minorities. Its most extreme members openly expressed admiration for Adolf Hitler.

The BJP program called for a break with the tolerant political tradition championed by Nehru and Gandhi. That tradition had been enshrined in the Indian constitution for the past forty years, ever since Nehru rejected the notion of a "Hindu Pakistan." In the face of strong opposition, however, Nehru had his work cut out trying to forge a multiethnic, multireligious, and, officially, secular state. That opposition had never gone away, and now it was in power.

The BJP set out to rewrite the history of India with a vengeance. Its historians insisted that India was a Hindu nation, that the Vedas—the sacred, primary texts of Hinduism—were the only source of Indian culture, and that the Indus Valley (which happened to be in Muslim Pakistan) was the birthplace of India's civilization more than 5,000 years ago. The caste system, steeped in Hinduism, was the natural order of things. As for Islam, it had come to India only recently, and by force at that. Spokespersons for the BJP insisted that all Indians—including Muslims and Christians—should be reconverted to the Vedas.

The greatest blot on Vajpayee's tenure were the Gujarat riots of 2002, deadlier than the religious violence in Ayodhya a decade earlier. After fifty-nine Hindus perished on a train, apparently the result of an accident, Hindu extremists went on a rampage. They raped hundreds of women and girls, looted stores, killed approximately 2,000 Muslims, and generated a flood of refugees estimated at 200,000. Human Rights Watch accused the government of assisting the police engaged in the pogroms and of providing the Hindu killers the addresses of Muslim families.[12]

Vajpayee advocated a tougher line against Pakistan. He openly declared that India possessed a nuclear weapons arsenal—something all previous Indian governments had been careful not to do. The Pakistani government, which had been working for years on its own nuclear arsenal, responded by telling India and the world that it, too, had joined the nuclear club.

In May 1998, India put its nuclear prowess on display when it set off five underground nuclear explosions. Pakistan responded with six of its own. For a while, a nuclear war in South Asia appeared to be a distinct possibility. In the end, both sides backed off. The posturing had a sobering effect on Vajpayee. In April 2003, he made a stunning announcement in which he called for a dialogue with Pakistan over Kashmir. He also established closer ties with Beijing, no mean feat, and with Washington.

Under Vajpayee, India continued to tie its economy to that of the world at large. He continued to break down trade barriers, dismantle state monopolies, and sell off state assets to private investors. A rising middle class found employment in information technology, business-processing outsourcing, and biotechnology. Still, despite the growth of per capita income—from $370 to $480 in four years—it remained one of the world's lowest.

In the spring of 2004, Vajpayee, confident of winning reelection, suffered a surprising defeat. All the experts were caught off guard when the Congress Party returned to power. Its leader, Sonia Gandhi, the Italian-born widow of Rajiv Gandhi, however, rejected the post of prime minister after Hindu nationalists bitterly complained about a foreign-born prime minister. The party then turned to Manmohan Singh, a Sikh, the first prime minister from a religious minority. Singh, who as finance minister during 1991–1996 had begun the reform program, continued to open the economy to the outside world.

The election outcome was largely the result of the anger of those left behind, particularly the rural poor. Privatization had thrown many out of work, had reduced the number of government jobs, and had been accompanied by rising prices. The BJP slogan, "Shining India," was popular with the moneyed classes at home and abroad, but neoliberal policies caused havoc among the rank and file. Unchecked greed was at the root of stock market and banking scams, drug trafficking, and political corruption. There were nearly 35 million unemployed in 2002, and their numbers continued to rise. Even the educated had trouble finding jobs. The suicide rate—particularly among farmers who could not compete in the global market and were falling deeper into debt— was rapidly increasing. Forty percent of the population lived below the poverty line; 47 percent of children suffered from malnutrition; clean water was scarce; and the UN Human Development Index showed India slipping from 115th place in 1999 to 127th in 2001. Of the world's 800 million people living below the starvation line—defined as 1,960 calories a day—223 million lived in India.[13]

At the same time, however, another trend was in the making, the growth of a large middle class, variously estimated between 100 and 300 million people in 2012, between one-tenth and one-quarter of the population.[14] With their disposable income the middle class were increasingly able to purchase durable goods—appliances, electronic goods, and motorized vehicles. They were the beneficiaries of an economy that had sustained an annual growth rate above 6 percent since the early 1990s. By 2012, India's per capita GDP was estimated somewhere between $1,500 and $3,900—admittedly unevenly distributed.[15]

### Pakistan

Pakistan witnessed it own swings of the political pendulum in the late 1980s and the 1990s. Until 1988, it remained under the rule of military strongman General Mohammed Zia ul-Haq, who ignored critics calling for a return to civilian rule. The national emergency, Zia insisted, was necessary because of the ongoing war in Afghanistan across from Pakistan's northwestern border. The influx of hundreds of thousands of refugees from that war-ravaged country strained Pakistan's economy and threatened internal security. Zia also pointed to the perceived threat of Indian aggression, a constant Pakistani obsession.

Military rule ended abruptly in August 1988, when Zia died in an airplane explosion—an apparent assassination. Parliamentary elections in November resulted in a return to civilian rule. The election produced a stunning victory for the thirty-five-year-old Benazir Bhutto, who became the first female head of government of a Muslim state. She was the daughter of Zulfikar Ali Bhutto, Pakistan's last civilian ruler, who had been deposed in 1974 and executed in 1979 by the same General Zia she now succeeded.

Educated in the United States and Britain, Benazir Bhutto had returned from an extended exile early in 1988 for the express purpose of leading a national movement against Zia.

Bhutto's grip on power was tenuous. Opposition parties, the military, and the conservative clergy were watchful lest she make a slip. She had her work cut out ruling a nation beset with all the problems of the global South and at the same time satisfying Pakistan's military leaders, who remained distrustful of her. Bhutto sought to steer a careful course between delivering on promised increases in social spending and implementing an austerity program required by international lending agencies as the condition for granting desperately needed loans. During her first year, Bhutto's government played a key role in negotiating the terms by which the Soviet military withdrew from neighboring Afghanistan, while officially maintaining Pakistani support for Afghan rebels based in Pakistan.

Bhutto appeared on Pakistan's political scene as a self-proclaimed angel of democracy who was fond of the slogan "We the People" and who enjoyed support among younger Pakistanis. The army, however, was eager to find a pretext for her removal, lest she become too popular. Corruption and ethnic violence, although not new to Pakistan, were cause enough to try to get rid of Bhutto. In August 1990, she and her husband were charged with abuse of power and misconduct. The real force behind her demise was General Mirza Aslam Beg, who resented Bhutto's attempts to rein in the military.

The winner of the October 1990 parliamentary elections was Nawaz Sharif, who immediately set out to make good on his campaign pledge to establish an Islamic state in which the Koran became the supreme law and all aspects of life were subjected to its authority. Sharif's government, however, was ineffective in dealing with endemic corruption, recurrent violence (such as kidnapping for ransom), mounting foreign debt, and worsening relations with India. Pakistan, moreover, suffered a diplomatic and economic setback when the United States withdrew an annual $500 million in aid in protest of Pakistan's nuclear weapons program.

Waiting in the wings, Benazir Bhutto narrowly defeated Sharif in a bitter campaign in October 1993. As during her previous stint as prime minister, her government was insecure. Although she defended Pakistan's position on the two key foreign policy issues—the territorial dispute over Kashmir and Pakistan's development of nuclear weapons—her political adversaries faulted her for her lack of diplomatic toughness. Her position was made even more difficult when opposition party leader Sharif declared publicly in August 1994 that Pakistan had produced nuclear weapons and even threatened their use against India in the next war over Kashmir. In doing so, Sharif broke Pakistan's long silence regarding its nuclear capability and inflamed relations with India and, to a lesser degree, with the United States.

In February 1997, Bhutto once again traded places with Nawaz Sharif, the militant Muslim who now had the nearly impossible job of governing Pakistan. When Pakistan's supreme court began hearings on corruption charges against Sharif, he directed mobs to surround the court and then sacked the chief justice. Meanwhile, much of the country was in chaos, the result of violent feuds among rival ethnic, religious, and political groups. Sharif neglected the nation's infrastructure, and with that came a steep decline in such basic services as health care, education, and public transportation. An economic slump made matters worse.

To draw attention from his own corruption and domestic social chaos, Sharif allowed Islamic militants to pick another fight with India over Kashmir. In early 1999, Pakistani "freedom fighters" crossed the "Line of Control," a cease-fire line, which India and Pakistan had agreed on in 1972. The dividing line extended to the Siachen Glacier, high up in the Himalayas at an elevation 19,000. Taking the line into the glacier had been seen as pointless because, surely, no one could want it. Yet now, Pakistani "volunteers" and Indian soldiers were engaged in the most senseless of wars imaginable, fighting and dying over a desolate glacier in the dead of winter, in a region so bleak it was known as the "third pole." The Pakistani zealots, however, who Sharif insisted were outside his control, insisted on fighting in Kashmir "until the last drop of blood."

The army finally had enough of Sharif and arrested him, in October 1999, thereby ended twenty-two years of ineffective and corrupt civilian rule. The army chief of staff, General Pervez Musharraf, the head of the coup, was roundly criticized worldwide for having sacked a democratically elected ruler, but many Pakistanis expressed relief. Now it was the army's turn once again to attempt to make Pakistan governable.

### Southeast Asia

In their quest for security, and particularly in response to the perceived threat of Communism, five of Southeast Asia's non-Communist nations—Indonesia, Malaysia, Thailand, Singapore, and the Philippines—formed the Association of Southeast Asian Nations (ASEAN) in 1967. Its original purpose was "to promote regional peace and security."

Fear of Communist Vietnam was the glue that initially kept ASEAN together. The US withdrawal from Indochina in 1973, the Communist victories in Vietnam and Cambodia in 1975, and Vietnam's invasion of Cambodia at the end of 1978 raised concern of Communist expansion among ASEAN nations. That fear served as the impetus for building stronger diplomatic ties and for strengthening their respective armies without, however, establishing a regional military alliance.

Once the Cold War ended, ASEAN membership was expanded to ten—including Cambodia and Vietnam, the former locus of concern. The concentration was now on greater regional economic cooperation, such as tariff reductions among member states. Increased trade among them was a contributing factor to the remarkable economic growth for the region, especially in Indonesia, Thailand, and Malaysia.

### Indonesia

After independence in the late 1940s, Indonesia faced the daunting task of bringing together its large, ethnically diverse population (the fifth largest in the world), spread over thousands of islands, into a functioning national entity. The number of languages spoken and ethnic groups number more then 700. Understandably, Indonesia's national motto was "unity in diversity." With 86 percent of its population of more than 250 million people being Muslims, Indonesia has the distinction of being the world's largest Islamic nation. Besides their adherence to Islam, its many ethnic groups had little in common except that they had been under Dutch colonial rule for three centuries.

Indonesia's revolutionary leader and new president, Achem Sukarno, experimented for several years with a semblance of Western parliamentary democracy until he rejected it officially in 1957, replacing it with what he called "guided democracy," a system barely distinguishable from a dictatorship. Sukarno's regime failed to stimulate adequate economic growth, but he sought to quiet the growing discontent by harping on the theme of nationalism. Meanwhile, many disenchanted Indonesians joined the 2-million-strong and increasingly militant Communist Party of Indonesia (known by the acronym PKI). Support for Sukarno's "guided democracy" depended on an uneasy coalition of the army, the PKI, and religious (mostly Muslim) factions. Ostensibly, Indonesia was a part of the neutral Third World, yet it tilted heavily toward the Communist camp, accepting assistance from Moscow and Beijing.

Dictators either rule through the army or control it. When, in October 1965, a coup organized by Sukarno failed to decapitate the army command (although six generals were killed), the army, led by General Suharto (who, as many Indonesians, went by a single name), struck back with a vengeance. The generals convinced the public that the PKI had been behind the coup (and not Sukarno). The PKI's denial of complicity fell on deaf ears. Civilian and military officials belonging to or being sympathetic to the PKI were rounded up in a bloody purge. Over a period of six months, the army—with the ready help of civilians—massacred an estimated half million people alleged to belong to the PKI, to the point that rivers and canals were clogged with dead bodies. The CIA called it "one of the worst" mass murders of the twentieth century. It marked the end of Sukarno's "guided democracy" and the beginning of

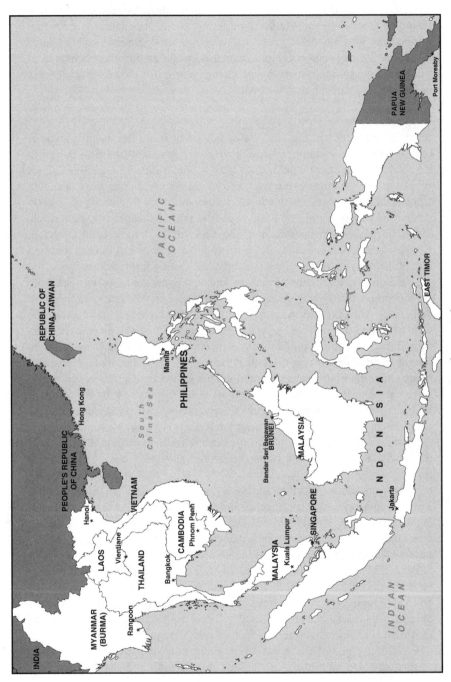

Southeast Asia

Suharto's "New Order," a pro-US military dictatorship that ruled Indonesia for the next three decades.

Earlier, a succession of US administrations had sought the overthrow of Sukarno. The CIA had provided covert aid to anti-Sukarno elements (notably the Suharto faction) and cut off economic aid to the Sukarno government. It did not help when, in March 1964, Sukarno told Washington to "go to hell with your aid." He would get it from somewhere else. The CIA recommended intervention in Indonesia "as a model for future operations" (one it followed elsewhere, notably in Chile during the early 1970s).[16]

In the mid-1970s, Suharto had his eye on the eastern half of the island of Timor, on the southeastern fringe of the Indonesian archipelago. East Timor was very much different from the rest of Indonesia. It had been a Portuguese colony for more than 400 years and had been granted its independence in 1974. The people there spoke Portuguese (besides their native tongues) and nearly all of them were Catholics. In December 1975, as rival leftist groups fought for power in East Timor, Suharto—with the support of Washington—sent in his army to claim the territory as Indonesian. The administration of Gerald Ford provided the Indonesian army with an array of weapons, but with the Congressional stipulation that they be used for "defensive" purposes only. In December 1975, Ford and his secretary of state, Henry Kissinger, met Suharto in Jakarta where, with a nod-and-a-wink—referred to as the "big wink" in State Department circles—they gave him the green light for an invasion, which began the day after *Air Force One* left Indonesian airspace. Kissinger gave Suharto the same advice he had given to the assassins of Latin America's Operation Condor: "It is important that whatever you do succeeds quickly."[17] For the next twenty-three years, five US presidents—from Ford to Clinton—backed Indonesia's extraordinarily brutal occupation of East Timor.

The Indonesian invasion of East Timor touched off a long and bitter war for independence. The resilience of the East Timorese and the massive use of force deployed by Suharto's army led to the death of more than 200,000 people over the next two decades. Insofar as the toll consisted of about one-third of the population of East Timor and most of the dead were noncombatants who were consciously targeted, the slaughter may well be considered genocide.

Suharto was more successful in fostering economic development. He courted foreign investment, especially from oil companies, which greatly increased Indonesia's production of petroleum. The high price of oil during the 1970s fueled continued economic development. By the early 1980s, oil accounted for 78 percent of Indonesia's export earnings. In the mid-1980s, when oil prices tumbled, the government introduced reforms that led to a reduction in government expenditures, diversification, less reliance on oil revenues, and even more foreign investment and joint ventures.

If Suharto's record as ruler of Indonesia were to be based on its GNP alone, he would receive decent marks, but the economic figures masked a grim reality of the military dictatorship's unbridled corruption, unabashed nepotism, and gross inequities in the distribution of wealth. Under Suharto the flow of money went mainly to the main island—"imperial Java," specifically to the capital of Jakarta—at the expense of the rest of the country. Hundreds of millions of dollars of the new wealth flowed into the hands of Suharto himself and his family members.[18] Still, even as the 1997 East Asian financial crisis (which began in Thailand) hit his country, Suharto (now seventy-six years old) was confident that his handpicked consultative assembly would elect him in March 1998 to his seventh five-year term as president. But with the economy in a meltdown and with Indonesia's currency, the rupiah, having lost 70 percent of its value against the dollar, there was a political cost to be paid. World Bank analysts pointed out that no nation in recent history "has ever suffered such a dramatic reversal of fortune" in such a short time.[19] (In contrast, the meltdown of the Soviet economy took place over several years.) Inflation reached 70 percent a year; widespread unemployment meant that an estimated two-thirds of the population were now living in poverty, unable to purchase the 2,000 calories of food per day necessary for a minimum diet. It led to looting and violence, particularly against ethnic Chinese who were singled out as scapegoats for the financial disaster.

Starting in January 1998, students demanding Suharto's ouster took to the streets day after day, where they clashed with police and army troops. As the crisis worsened, Suharto's privileged military, which had benefited handsomely during his tenure, abandoned him to save its own skin. In May, Suharto turned the reins over to an old crony, B. J. Habibie.

Habibie introduced political reforms aimed at mollifying the protesters and foreign critics. The parliamentary elections of June 1999 brought to power Abdurahman Wahid, an elderly, moderate Muslim scholar. His first order of business was to try and get the US-trained and equipped military out of politics. In February 2000, he dismissed the army chief (and defense minister) Wiranto, the man largely responsible for the "dirty war" in East Timor.

Early in 1999, after Suharto had stepped down, the government agreed to a referendum on independence for East Timor to be held in August under UN auspices. The Indonesian army commander in East Timor, however, threatened that in the event of independence "everything will be destroyed, so that East Timor will be worse off than it was 23 years ago."[20] Despite such threats and deadly assaults on civilians by heavily armed "militias" (instruments of the Indonesian army), nearly 80 percent of the East Timorese voted for secession. As promised, the "militias" went on a rampage, destroying much of East Timor's infrastructure, killing an estimated 3,000–7,000 people, and deporting to West Timor another 150,000–200,000. They also killed several unarmed UN workers, the remainder fleeing to nearby Australia. Indonesia's National Human Rights Commission later placed the blame squarely on the shoulders of Wiranto, who had done nothing to stop the massacres and thus was "morally responsible." When a helpless United Nations proved unable to stop the violence, Australia finally decided to act. Its troops landed on the island, expelled the Indonesian army and its militias, and restored order. Then came the difficult task of rebuilding devastated East Timor, the newest member of the United Nations.

Wahid then turned to another pressing problem, the growing independence movements in the provinces of Aceh and Irian Jaya. He offered them federalism, that is, a share of local control, a concession hitherto unthinkable. The greatest challenge was Aceh, the westernmost outpost of the far-flung archipelago. It was here, in "Mecca's verandah," where the first contacts with Islam had taken place in the eighth century. Its people remained particularly religious and resistant to outside control. It had taken the Dutch more than a quarter-century to conquer Aceh at the end of the nineteenth century, and even then it was never fully pacified. In 1945, its people were particularly enthusiastic for independence and thus their disappointment was much the greater when the heavy hand of Sukarno, and later of Suharto, came down on them. Aceh's wealth from its lucrative oil industry did not go to its people, schools, or hospitals, but to Jakarta. In 1976, the Free Aceh Movement (FAM) declared independence and the army reacted predictably; in the 1990s, it tortured and murdered an estimated 5,000 people in Aceh.

In December 2004, an earthquake in the Indian Ocean—at 9.0 on the Richter scale one of the largest ever recorded—triggered a massive tsunami that caused havoc in several nations. Aceh took the full brunt of it. Its devastation has been compared to that of Hiroshima. In the wake of the tsunami, in August 2005, a new Indonesian government and the FAM worked out a ceasefire that ended a twenty-nine-year civil war. Jakarta granted Aceh a high degree of autonomy; the FAM, in its turn, agreed to disarm.

Irian Jaya, the western half of the island of New Guinea, on the eastern fringe of the archipelago, nurtured its own dreams of secession that dated back to 1961 (when it was still under Dutch rule). After the Netherlands handed the region over to Indonesia in 1969, Suharto suppressed its independence movement. Irian Jaya holds substantial natural resources, including some of the world's most lucrative copper and gold mines. The mines, however, employed a scant 300 of the indigenous population; the other 11,000 workers came from other parts of Indonesia and from abroad. Wahid was not alone in believing that, particularly after East Timor, the loss of another province would mark the beginning of the end of Indonesia. Wahid had earlier spoken of federalism, only to backtrack in December 2000, when the army launched a crackdown in Irian Jaya, killing and jailing demonstrators who had hoisted their illegal separatist flag.

## Thailand

Thailand was an example of the axiom that "geography is history." Sandwiched in between the British colony of Burma and French Indochina, Thailand escaped colonization and thus was spared the pains and devastation of a war for independence after World War II. Moreover, its ruling dynasty survived the age of colonization. Thailand's political stability contributed to its economic growth, facilitated by increased agricultural production and foreign investment, the latter making possible the country's emerging industrial base.

The new prosperity was by no means enjoyed by all elements of society; indeed, the long-suffering, underpaid working class saw precious little of the national earnings its labor helped to generate. Moreover, Thailand's political tradition of deference to the king and entrenched patron-client relationships was more conducive to military rule than to democracy. In the 1930s, the military became the dominant political force and only occasionally gave way to civilian rule, which usually proved unstable.

Thus, when the generals took control of the government in February 1991, events followed a traditional pattern. The coup touched off angry antimilitary demonstrations in the capital of Bangkok. The demonstrators demanded an amendment to the constitution to protect society against military rule. As the demonstrations grew larger and more riotous, the highly revered Thai king, Bhumibol Adulyadej, who had occupied the throne since 1946, intervened, calling on all parties to accept the new constitution designed to strengthen civilian rule.

The military, led by General Suchinda Kraprayoon, however, refused to give in to the protesters. For three days in May 1992, 50,000 troops scattered unarmed civilians, firing live ammunition and killing over 100. The bloody spectacle was seen on television screens around the world—except in Thailand, where the army controlled the media. Once again, King Bhumibol interceded and helped put an end to the massacre.[21] Suchinda was forced to resign. The newly constituted civilian government sought to break the military's sixty-year hold on power. Its investigation of the recent massacre led to the sacking of four leading military officers.

The military influence was curtailed but by no means eliminated. Thailand had no tradition of civilian control of its military, which continued to keep its hands on many levers of power, including the police and important state industries (such as telecommunications, airlines, shipping, and trucking). When Prime Minister Thaksin Shinawatra, Thailand's richest man, was elected in 2001, he decided he was not rich enough and used his office to enrich himself further along with his cronies. The army could accept that, but not the replacement of senior military positions with Thaksin's allies and family members. When the army overthrew Thaksin in 2006, it brandished the monarchy's traditional colors and claimed to act on behalf of the king. The army may have done the nation a service by removing a dictator, but it also shredded the provision of the constitution designed to keep it out of politics.[22] The king's meddling in political affairs—largely on behalf of the military— over the years had also undermined the rule of law. In 2008, Thaksin's supporters—who had benefited from cheap health care, microcredit, and patronage appointments—again took to the streets, this time extending their protests against the once revered, but now feeble and aged king for repeatedly having backed military coups. Bangkok was treated to the spectacle of Thaksin's "red shirt" supporters demonstrating against the royalist "yellow shirts." Thailand faced a future with a weak parliamentary system, the illusion of a universally adored monarchy shattered, and an army always ready to step in.

## Malaysia

Once Malaya gained its independence in 1957, it gradually became one of the poster children for Third World economic progress. Blessed with natural resources—such as tin and gas, oil reserves, and agricultural products of all sorts—it also took pains to develop its manufacturing base, which in 1960 made up a scant 10 percent of its GDP, but rose to nearly 50 percent by 2008.

By the 1990s, manufactured goods accounted for half of Malaysia's exports, and it became the world's largest exporter of semiconductors (if only for a while). The showpiece of Malaysia's economic prowess was its gleaming capital city, Kuala Lumpur, which boasted at one time the world's tallest buildings, the 1,483-foot high Petronas Twin Towers. By 2012, the once overwhelmingly agricultural nation enjoyed a per capita GNP of $17,200.[23]

Malaysia's economic growth required political stability, which in turn required peace among its ethnic groups. Malaysia was born of the nation initially called Malaya, which encompassed the Malay Peninsula south of Thailand, the island city of Singapore at the southern tip, and the regions of Sabah and Sarawak on the island of Borneo, more than 1,000 miles to the east. In 1965, Singapore seceded to become an independent city-state, and the remainder of the federation was renamed Malaysia. Its population was made up of 50 percent Malay, 36 percent Chinese, and 9 percent Indian. Malaysia's parliamentary system was structured to maintain the Malays in power (by rigging elections and calling out the army when necessary) and to keep the ethnic minorities satisfied with economic growth and limited representation in parliament.

When the Malay-dominated Alliance Party lost its majority in the 1969 election, it led to four days of bloody clashes between ethnic Chinese and Malays. The government responded with a state of emergency, disbanded parliament, and brought in troops to restore order. Its "New Economic Policy" enshrined the Malays' privileged status at the expense of the Chinese and other ethnic groups. "Sedition acts" prohibited criticism of "sensitive issues," meaning the special rights granted to Malays.

During the mid-1970s, a sense of stability emerged as the economy—driven largely by petroleum and natural gas exports—grew at a rate of nearly 8 percent annually. The new wealth offered advantages for many educated Malays and Chinese and thus served to reduce ethnic tensions. The lower class benefited from trickle-down economics that included new schools, electrification projects, piped water, and paved roads. The upshot was a lessening of ethnic tensions. The minority Malaysians still had grievances, but they preferred not to take them into the streets. They preferred, instead, to "talk conflict, but walk cohesion."[24]

As Malaysia focused on boosting its exports, it increasingly became dependent on international trade and foreign investments. Prime Minister Mahathir Mohamad (1981–2003) was willing to join the global economy, but he was also a vocal critic of Western values. As such, he urged his people to "Look East." Asian problems, he said, demanded Asian solutions. He wanted little to do with Britain, Malaysia's former colonial master, urging his people to "Buy British Last." He preferred to look to Japan for inspiration. He was a harsh critic of the United States, even though it was Malaysia's main foreign investor. He was particularly critical of the double standards Western democracies practiced, saying one thing and doing something different altogether. Mahatir, in contrast, was a study in consistency. His "Asian" approach to governance included the rejection of the UN's 1948 Universal Declaration of Human Rights, press censorship, and the jailing of dissidents without a trial. He thought that Asians needed economic growth rather than civil liberties.

Early in his presidency, US president George W. Bush had criticized Malaysia's harsh security laws, saying that no country should imprison its people without a trial. But when Bush invited Mahatir to the Oval Office in May 2002, he described the Malaysian dictator as a valiant ally in the "global war on terror." As if to prove Mahatir's criticism of Western double standards, Bush took the opportunity at their meeting to castigate Cuba's Fidel Castro for failing to hold free election and releasing political prisoners, all the while ignoring Mahatir's remarkably similar record on these issues. When asked by a reporter whether he had changed his views on Malaysia's draconian laws, he replied with a straight face, as Mahatir sat by his side, "our position has not changed."[25] Mahitir did not bat an eye.

### Singapore

Singapore, with its overwhelmingly ethnic Chinese population, experienced its economic liftoff in the 1960s, about a decade earlier than most other East Asian nations. During the tenure of its prime minister Lee Kuan Yew (1959–1990), the city-state became one of the most prosperous countries in the world, with an estimated per capita GNP of $61,400 in 2012.[26] A combination of political stability, population growth control, high standards of education, a disciplined and skilled workforce, efficient economic management, export-oriented planning, and a free-market system worked miracles for its 5.3 million people in 2013. Strategically situated at the center of the Southeast Asian sea-lanes, Singapore was a conveyor belt for goods shipped to and from East Asian countries. It also became a major regional financial center.

Lee was a stellar example of the type of "Asian" leader that Malaysia's Matahir had in mind to emulate. (After World War II, virtually all leaders in East Asia held similar political philosophies, the sole exception being Japan under US tutelage, which was kept from sliding back into "Asian" habits.)

Lee's heavy-handed rule extended well beyond the bounds of conventional politics. He endeavored to make Singapore a spotless, crime-free, morally upright, and austere society (although vice was tolerated, it had to be kept in the shadows). He took it upon himself to dictate social and moral standards and to enforce them with harsh laws. There were prohibitions, for example, against men growing their hair too long and against littering. Offenders were subject to arrest, fines, or imprisonment. Lee had an abiding faith in the salutary effect of caning, having experienced it (to his benefit) as a pupil at a prestigious British boarding school. Possession of drugs, even small amounts, was subject to the death penalty. Nor did Lee allow dissent. He maintained that the curbs on individual freedoms were not regimentation but rather paternalistic guidance that made for a more disciplined and productive people whose work habits contributed to ever higher productivity and the betterment of society.

Upon stepping down from the post of prime minister, Lee was granted a newly formed title, "Minister Mentor of Singapore." From that post, he continued to exercise considerable influence, to the point that the Singaporean legislature briefly considered renaming the city-state in honor of the ninety-year-old Lee Kuan Yew.

## Dictatorship and Revolution in the Philippines

While most of East Asia registered impressive economic growth in the 1970s, the Philippines failed to do so. This nation of many islands, once a Spanish (1571–1898) and then a US colony (1898–1946), struggled to sustain economic growth and to maintain a semblance of democratic institutions after gaining independence in July 1946. Under a succession of dictators, the Philippines lost ground on both fronts, especially during the twenty-year rule of Ferdinand Marcos. When Marcos came to power in 1965, the country was developing apace with Taiwan, Singapore, and Thailand. When Marcos was driven from power in 1986, however, those nations had per capita incomes three to four times higher than that of the Philippines. The Philippines, moreover, had a foreign debt of $27 billion and had been unable to make payments on the principal since 1983.

Marcos was at the center of mismanagement and corruption. He had been elected president as a social reformer in 1965, but then succumbed to the pattern of patron-client corruption common to Philippine political tradition. Governing the Philippines became so lucrative for Marcos that he made certain he would stay in power despite a constitution that permitted only two four-year terms. As the end of his second term approached, he declared martial law, citing a mounting Communist insurgency as the reason for canceling elections.

He suspended the constitution and then wrote a new one that gave him a new term and broad powers. He rounded up and jailed political opponents and critical journalists. Along the way, Marcos and his wife, Imelda, became wealthy by pocketing foreign aid and demanding kickbacks from businesses.

Marcos promoted himself as the nation's indispensable leader. He claimed to be a lawyer who had never lost a case, a heroic military officer who had never lost a battle, a lover who had won the heart of the nation's beauty queen, a great athlete and marksman, a good father, a good Catholic, and an honest and modest man. Initially, the popularity of his wife, Imelda, a former Miss Philippines, was an added attraction to his cult of personality. Successive administrations in Washington turned a blind eye to what was taking place in Manila and instead honored Marcos as a stalwart opponent of Communism and a champion of democracy. When US vice-president George H. W. Bush visited the Philippines in 1981, this after nine years of martial law, he told Marcos, "We love your adherence to democratic principles and to the democratic processes."[27]

Washington remained tolerant as long as Marcos provided the political stability considered necessary to protect substantial US financial investments in the Philippines and to retain the two mammoth US military installations on the islands—Subic Bay Naval Station and Clark Air Base—considered vital to US strategic interests in East Asia. Marcos skillfully traded assurances for the bases in exchange for ever larger economic and military aid packages from Washington.

In the early 1980s—around the time of Vice-President Bush's visit—the Marcos regime began to unravel, however. In 1981, he released from prison his foremost political opponent, Benigno Aquino, to permit him to go to the United States for heart surgery. Aquino, the likely winner of the 1973 presidential election had it taken place, ended his exile in August 1983 to return home to lead a movement to unseat Marcos. As he was about to set foot on the tarmac at the airport in Manila, he was shot to death. In response to public outrage, Marcos appointed a commission to investigate the assassination. After lengthy deliberations, the commission reported the Aquino had been the victim of a military conspiracy reaching all the way to chief of staff General Fabian Ver, a cousin of Marcos. The verdict in an eight-month-long trial was predictable: Ver and twenty-four other military defendants were acquitted. Meanwhile, a vigorous opposition movement rallied around Aquino's wife, Corazon. As Marcos lost credibility at home and abroad, the economy deteriorated rapidly, largely because of the flight of capital triggered by Aquino's assassination. In the hinterlands, a Communist-led New People's Army stepped up its insurgency.

In response to mounting pressure, Marcos, the undaunted dictator who had won every election he had entered thus far, agreed to hold a presidential election in February 1986. The stage was set for a showdown that had all the makings of a morality play, the saintly Corazon Aquino against the discredited Marcos. Although the sixty-eight-year-old Marcos was visibly ill, suffering from kidney disease and roundly attacked by the press, he remained confident of victory. He appeared unfazed by the enormous throngs of people who rallied in support of Aquino. Aquino, who presented herself as Cory, a humble housewife, called for a return to democracy, decency, and justice. She did not hesitate to accuse Marcos of being "the No. 1 suspect in the murder of my husband."[28] As election day approached, it appeared that Cory's "people power" would sweep her to victory. Big business and the middle class were abandoning Marcos, and the Catholic Church openly supported Aquino. Many feared, however, that the cagey Marcos, who paid people to attend his political rallies, would find ways to rig the election results.

The election results were inconclusive, with each side claiming victory and charging the other with fraud. Despite evidence of election interference and fraudulent vote counting by the Marcos-appointed election commission, Marcos went ahead with plans for his inauguration ceremony. He was emboldened by US president Ronald Reagan's acceptance of the election results.[29] It put Reagan in opposition to the Catholic Church in the Philippines. At the encouragement of Jaime Cardinal Sin, hundreds of thousands of people went into the streets to express support for Aquino and to demand that Marcos step down. At this point, Marcos's defense minister and several high-ranking army officers switched sides. The climax came when pro-Marcos troops, as they advanced toward the protesters' encampments, were stopped by the human wall of Aquino supporters and nuns kneeling in prayer in front of stalled tanks. At that juncture, Reagan arranged for Marcos to be airlifted to Hawaii. Imelda and Ferdinand Marcos fled with the billions of dollars they had amassed. Cory Aquino proclaimed victory for a democratic revolution.

After the exultation over Aquino's triumph against dictatorship and corruption, the new and inexperienced president had to face the hard realities of governing the nation and restoring its shattered economy. She moved swiftly to restore civil rights, free political prisoners, eliminate pro-Marcos elements from the government, and enact political reforms. Aquino, whose family owned large stretches of land, had promised land reform during her campaign, but afterward she showed little interest in it. There would be no social revolution. The power of the old oligarchy and the old economic system remained intact. The nation was still saddled with a large foreign debt, the payment of which consumed about one-third of the country's export earnings. In 1988, the country was granted a $10 billion developmental grant from the combined sources of the IMF and several European and Asian nations, but to little avail. Affluence for the few and misery for the many remained the dominant trend. On the eve of Aquino's fourth anniversary in power in February 1990, people power was but a distant memory. She had lost support in virtually all segments of the population.

One of the issues Aquino faced was the status of the two large US military facilities, Subic Bay Naval Station and Clark Air Base. Nationalist groups saw them as an affront to Philippine sovereignty, a social blight, and potential targets in a nuclear war. Aquino was willing to renew the lease of the bases, which was due to expire in September 1991, but she made clear that the new constitution forbade nuclear weapons on Philippine territory.

Two events in 1991 intervened to cause an unanticipated resolution of the issues surrounding the military bases: the sudden end of the global Cold War and a powerful volcanic eruption. The former caused the United States to reconsider its Asian security needs, and the latter provided sufficient cause to vacate the bases. In June, Mount Pinatubo, a volcano dormant for 600 years, erupted, sending a towering plume into the air and blanketing the surrounding region—including the bases—with a thick layer of powdery ash. With Clark Air Base buried under volcanic debris, Washington decided to abandon it rather than spend the estimated $500 million to dig it out. Soon afterward, when the Philippines senate rejected a ten-year extension of the lease on Subic Bay Naval Station, Washington decided to pull up stakes there as well. The US military presence in the Philippines, which had existed since the Spanish-American War of 1898 (except from 1942 to 1944), was at an end.

The combination of the disastrous volcanic eruption and the loss of the two foreign bases dealt a severe blow to the Philippines economy, which was already stagnant and debt-ridden. The volcano and the base closings meant over 680,000 jobs lost.

The country remained in need of fundamental political and social reform and was still confronted with insurrections from both the right and the left. It was little wonder that the weary but still personally popular Aquino decided against running for reelection in 1992. The burden of pulling the Philippines out of its poverty, economic stagnation, and political corruption fell to her successors. It was not until after the turn of the century that the Philippines economy—fueled by business outsourcing, the telecommunications industry, computer chip manufacturing, and remittances from abroad—began to show substantial growth. But it had a long way to go; per capita GNP in 2012 was around $4,500.[30]

## Notes

1. "Population Commentary," *Baltimore Sun*, July 12, 1992, p. 2A.

2. The development of plants producing more grain and less stem was the result of years of scientific work financed by the Rockefeller and Ford Foundations. Under ideal conditions, the new rice plants produced twice as much grain per acre and reduced the growing period by half.

3. Quoted in Stephen Warshaw and C. David Bromwell, with A. J. Tudisco, *India Emerges: A Concise History of India from Its Origins to the Present* (San Francisco: Diablo Press, 1974), p. 132.

4. World Bank, *World Development Report, 1984* (New York: Oxford University Press, 1984). India's average annual rate of growth of GNP between 1955 and 1970 was 4.0 percent; during the 1970s, it fell to 3.4 percent. The rate of growth of GNP per capita for these two periods was 1.8 percent and 1.3 percent, respectively.

5. "Nixon Dislike of 'Witch' Indira," BBC News, June 29, 2005; for specifics, see Nixon's tape-recorded conversation with Kissinger, Nov. 5, 1971, shortly after meeting with Gandhi.

6. P. N. Dhar, *Indira Gandhi, the "Emergency," and Indian Democracy* (New Delhi: Oxford University Press, 2000).

7. Gary J. Bass, *The Blood Telegram: Nixon, Kissinger, and a Forgotten Genocide* (New York: Borzoi Books, 2013).

8. "Nixon/Kissinger Saw India as 'Soviet Stooge' in 1971 South Asia Crisis," *National Security Archive*, June 29, 2005.

9. CIA, *World Factbook*, 2013.

10. World Bank, "The World Bank in Bangladesh," September 2004; World Bank, "Poverty Headcount Ratio at $1.25 a day," 2013.

11. Steve Coll, "Burgeoning Population Threatens India's Future," *Washington Post*, January 21, 1990, p. H7.

12. Human Rights Watch, April 2002 report, *"We Have No Orders to Save You": State Participation and Complicity in Communal Violence in Gujarat.*

13. Pankaj Mishra, "India: The Neglected Majority Wins!" *New York Review of Books*, August 12, 2004, pp. 30–37.

14. Christian Meyer and Nancy Birdsall, "New Estimates of India's Middle Class," Center for Global Development, November 2012, p. 9.

15. Figures for Third World nations—on population growth, the economy, the middle class, the number of poor—are not even in the range of ballpark estimates. The widely discrepant figures for India's per capita GDP, for instance, are from the World Bank and the CIA, respectively.

16. Peter Dale Scott, "The United States and the Overthrow of Sukarno, 1965–1967," *Pacific Affairs* (Summer 1985), pp. 240, 253, 263, passim.

17. Jeffrey A. Winters, "US Media and Their Ignorance Partly Blamable for E. Timor's Misery," *Jakarta Post Online*, May 28, 2002. Also, John Pilger, "Journey to East Timor: Land of the Dead," *The Nation*, April 25, 1994. Kissinger here, perhaps unconsciously, drew upon Macbeth's contemplation of the murder of Duncan: "If it were done when 'tis done then 'twere well it were done quickly."

18. "Indonesia to Probe Riches Amassed by Suharto Since '66," *Baltimore Sun*, June 2, 1998, p. 10A. Estimates of the personal riches he and his family amassed vary greatly, but one estimate puts it at about $40 billion.

19. Floyd Norris, "In Asia, Stocks Melt Faster Than in '29," *New York Times*, January 11, 1998, p. BU1; "Indonesia Falls Rapidly from Riches to Rags," *Baltimore Sun*, October 8, 1998, p. 2A.

20. Colonel Tono Suratnam, cited in Erhard Haubold, "Verraten und verkauft?" *Frankfurter Allgemeine Zeitung*, September 18, 1999, p. 12.

21. The king learned of the massacre from his daughter in Paris, where she saw it on the TV news. "Months of Grace," *The Economist*, June 20, 1992, p. 32. The king summoned the general and members of the opposition for an audience. As they knelt before him, he demanded an immediate restoration of order—a scene seen on television screens around the world and this time in Thailand as well.

22. Joshua Kurlantzick, "Tanks Roll in Thailand," *Washington Post*, September 24, 2006, p. B3; Mark Beeson and Alex J. Bellamy, *Securing Southeast Asia: The*

*Politics of Security Sector Reform*, (London: Routledge, 2008), Chapter 5, "Thailand: Military Rule, There and Back Again?" pp. 97–126.

23. CIA, *World Factbook* 2012.

24. A. B. Shamsul, "No More Conflict, but Unity Remains Elusive in Malaysia," *East Asia Forum*, September 20, 2013.

25. David E. Sanger, "White House on Autocrats: Malaysian Sí, Cuban No," *New York Times*, May 15, 2002.

26. CIA, *World Factbook,* 2012.

27. Cited in William J. vanden Heuvel, "Postpone the Visit to Manila," *New York Times*, September 8, 1983, p. A23.

28. Cited in "A Test for Democracy," *Time*, February 3, 1986, p. 31.

29. William Pfaff, "The Debris of Falling Dictatorships," *Baltimore Sun*, February 17, 1986, p. 9A.

30. CIA, *World Factbook,* 2012.

# Part 5

# The Emergence of a New Landscape

**Historical processes are a combination of continuity and change.** It was inevitable, therefore, that a generation after World War II, the world would be a different place from the one the Big Three had helped to create in their moment of triumph in 1945. The new order, which arrived in what became known as "year zero," had considerable staying power, but it was bound to end one day. Since the French Revolution of 1789, none of the international configurations of power survived much longer than a biblical generation of forty years.[1]

Historic change often comes announced with a peal of thunder, such as the fall of Constantinople, the storming of the Bastille, and the end of World War II. Or it can steal in on cats' paws, barely noted at the time, but ultimately momentous nonetheless. The year 1979, the halfway point between the end of World War II and the present, ushered in striking changes, not readily apparent at the time, which created a "new [global] landscape," the title of Part 5.

The godparents of these changes, the historian Christian Caryl wrote, were "strange rebels" who had little in common—notably Deng Xiaoping of China, Margaret Thatcher of Great Britain, the Ayatollah Khomeini of Iran, and the Polish pope, John Paul II.

The year 1979 began with the overthrow of the shah of Iran, who was replaced by Khomeini's militant Islamic theocracy (a topic discussed in Chapter 21). It was followed by the hostage crisis, which further poisoned relations between Tehran and Washington for the next thirty-some years. The meddling on the part of Moscow and Washington in the internal affairs of Afghanistan in 1979 touched off a proxy war in one of the poorest nations in the world, the future haven of Osama bin Laden. In neighboring Pakistan, in the meantime, President Mohammed Zia ul-Haq, by aiding the Afghan rebels, intensified the Islamization of Pakistan. These events led directly to September 11 and the wars in Afghanistan and Iraq (Chapter 22).

It was in 1979 that Pope John Paul II took his first trip to his native Poland, an event that helped set the stage for the rise of Solidarity and the political destabilization of Eastern Europe (covered in Chapter 19). In the same year, Deng Xiaoping (with the blessing of the "Washington Consensus") initiated economic reforms in China that embraced the capitalist model, which launched its transformation to the world's second largest economy. In 1979, Margaret Thatcher, the supreme and most vocal Western apostle of "market reforms," came to power in Britain (followed by the election of the like-minded Ronald Reagan the following year). The story of the globalization of the economy, under the aegis of "market reforms," and the rise of East Asia is covered in Chapters 17 and 18, respectively. Those "reforms" were accompanied by what one journalist called the slow "the unwinding" of the United States and other industrial states, notably Great Britain.[2]

The Moral Majority, formed in the United States in 1979, was as yet another manifestation of the rise of religious dogmatism. It was also in 1979 that the Soviet Union's economy stopped growing. This worrisome trend touched off intense discussions by its intelligentsia and politicians, which proved to be the precursor to Mikhail Gorbachev's "new thinking" (a subject discussed in Chapter 19). The same year saw the breakdown of détente and the escalation of the nuclear arms race between the United States and the Soviet Union (see Chapter 20), a perilous trend that demanded a new approach to a seemingly intractable problem.[3]

The final chapter of the book discusses a new topic, seemingly emerging out of thin air, the "Arab Spring" that began in 2010. It remains a shifting target, however, an unfinished powerful challenge to the ancien régime. As of this writing, however, it remained a turning point that had yet to turn.

**Notes**

1. The French revolutionary system ended with Napoleon's defeat in 1815, and the "restored" conservative order lasted only until 1848. The wars for the unification of Germany and Italy rearranged the map of Europe by 1871, only to have that map be destroyed by World War I (1914–1918). The international system that came out of World War I lasted until the outset of World War II (1939–1945). Christian Caryl (see below) suggests that the order that came out of world war, one of thirty-four years' duration, began to fray at the edges starting in 1979.

2. George Packer, *The Unwinding: An Inner History of the New America* (New York: Farrar, Straus and Giroux, 2013). Packer discusses the thirty-five-year-long (ca. 1978–2013) unraveling of the Franklin "Roosevelt Republic" and the return to more traditional US norms. It was a process with global implications that included the shredding of social safety nets and increasing the powers of corporations, which were no longer merely too powerful to fail, but became too powerful even to prosecute.

3. This summary is an adaptation of Christian Caryl, *Strange Rebels: 1979 and the Birth of the 21st Century* (New York: Basic Books, 2013).

# 17

# The Globalization of
# the Economy

**The modern age—that is, since the days of European exploration—** witnessed an ever-increasing expansion of international trade. The Dutch city of Amsterdam, for instance, holds the distinction of being one of the pioneers in globalization, consumerism, and capitalism, more than a century before Adam Smith extolled the virtue of a free market. The central question was always over the nature of the organization of that trade. One school of thought insisted that commerce be regulated according to the principles of mercantilism, that is, for the benefit of the state. It coincided with the rise of the European nation-states ruled by absolute monarchs who sought to control trade to fill their royal treasuries. Mercantilism called for a favorable balance of trade as exemplified by the flow of gold and silver to the nations' capitals—Lisbon, Madrid, Paris, and London.

A competing school argued that commerce be relatively free, to serve primarily the interests of individual enterprise, as Adam Smith proposed in his classic *The Wealth of Nations* in 1776. It gave rise to the notion that private economic activity engage in unfettered competition. "Free" trade, so went the argument, was beneficial not only for the entrepreneur but for society as a whole. Gradually, the Western world (that is, Europe and its extensions overseas, such as the United States, Australia, etc.) moved in fits and starts toward the free-trade paradigm.

The debate between the advocates of mercantilism and free trade, however, was never resolved. Free trade was never absolutely free. It always had its national restrictions as countries repeatedly sought protection behind economic barriers—mainly tariffs—to keep out competitors, who were often demonized as exploiters.

Nowhere was this more evident than in the US response to the stock market crash of 1929. To protect the nation's economy, Congress passed the Smoot-Hawley tariff (1930), which raised tariffs by 50 percent. The trading partners of the United States responded in kind, and a trade war resulted. It was this, more so than the dramatic collapse of the overvalued stock market, that brought the Great Depression of the 1930s. Before World War II came to an end, the Western Allies took steps to ensure that history would not repeat itself. They were resolved to deal with the expected economic downturn after the war, but would do so without resorting to national solutions. In July 1944, at Bretton Woods, New Hampshire, the representatives of forty-four Allied nations met to facilitate the resumption of international trade after the war. They established the International Monetary Fund (IMF), which was designed to restore the system of multinational international payments that had broken down during the Great Depression. By 2012, 188 nations had joined the IMF.[1]

The IMF fund consists of a pool of money provided by member states, of which the United States is the largest contributor. For that reason, Washington is in a position to determine how IMF money is spent. When a debtor nation proves unable to meet its obligation, the IMF takes on the role of financial savior and steps in to eliminate the specter of "nonperforming" (that is, failing) loans and the subsequent breakdown of the international system of payments. As the lender of last resort, particularly for the poorest nations, the IMF lends money and lines up banks willing to extend additional credit. But the IMF also insists that borrowers remain in compliance with the lending terms. Its most potent weapon is its ability to withhold additional funds necessary to keep impoverished and indebted nations afloat. Over time, such heavy-handedness created much resentment in the global South, as the IMF appeared to be more interested in shoring up the international system of debt obligations and in bailing out private lending institutions in wealthy nations than in helping desperate borrowers.

The IMF became a lightning rod for peoples and politicians who felt victimized by the developed world. The IMF's defenders replied that it provided much-needed capital for ailing patients to restore them to financial health. But the patient must show fiscal maturity by keeping additional spending under control and meet the financial obligations to the lenders. By setting the terms of repayment, the IMF produced a backlash. For the IMF, it was a short path from savior to whipping boy.

The World Bank, another Bretton Woods institution, started operation in 1946 to finance specific projects across the world. Its original working capital came from members' contributions, but the bulk of its current capital now comes from borrowing in the world's money markets. It operates as any bank, that is, it borrows money (frequently at high rates) and then lends it at a markup.

The Allied victors created yet another international organization, the General Agreement on Tariffs and Trade (GATT), initially a small club of twenty-three members.[2] Through nine rounds of lengthy negotiations (the last one, the Doha Round, began in 2001), GATT was remarkably successful in reducing the average tariff on the world's industrial goods from 40 percent to 5 percent of market value. It marked the first multilateral agreement to reduce trade barriers since Napoleonic times.

Created as a temporary expedient, GATT lasted for nearly a half-century. In 1995, it was reorganized into the World Trade Organization (WTO), an agency designed to take the case of trade liberalization even farther. In 2013, its membership stood at 159. The WTO was established as a permanent institution with powers to arbitrate trade disputes. Its rules demand that countries deemed to be restricting free trade change their behavior or face sanctions. When China applied to join the WTO, in July 1986, it was in expectation that it would reduce its extraordinarily high tariffs, which ran as high as 100 percent on certain commodities.

## The European Union
The best example of free trade in practice is the European Union. It was the outgrowth of the European Coal and Steel Community, founded in 1952 to facilitate international trade in those commodities, the building blocks of postwar reconstruction. Its members were France, West Germany, Italy, Belgium, the Netherlands, and Luxembourg. By the 1957 Treaty of Rome, they became the original six of the European Community (EC)—also known as the Common Market—the first step on the road to eliminate all trade barriers and create a single integrated market.

The founding fathers of the EC were two Frenchmen, the foreign minister Robert Schuman and the economist Jean Monnet. Schuman was driven by political considerations; Monnet sought efficient trade. Their hope was that an interdependent Western Europe would lead to nothing less than a change in the psychological makeup of its citizens who were still digging out from the most devastating war in history. In his historic proclamation of May 9, 1950—five years to the day after the end of World War II—Schuman declared that the Coal and Steel Community's purpose was first and foremost to establish a lasting peace, particularly between Germany and France.

Schuman's proclamation became the birthday of what eventually became the European Union. For more than a half-century it did more than merely keep the peace among former bitter enemies; it also created a genuine peace of mutual understanding. Perhaps it should not have been surprising, therefore, that in September 2003—upon the fortieth anniversary of Schuman's death—the Roman Catholic bishop of Metz submitted to the Vatican a stack of documents to support a request for the beatification of Schuman. For Schuman to enter the pantheon of Catholic saints, however, the church would have to show that Schuman had worked a miracle. The mitigation of centuries-old national hatred might qualify as such.

The European Community broke down many of the formidable trade barriers among the nations of Western Europe. Many remained in place, however. Moreover, some nations had a tendency to turn at times to "national solutions" to solve their economic problems. The formation of "a more perfect union" remained elusive. But in the early 1980s, several factors came together: The French and Spanish socialists, who in the past had favored governmental regulations and control of the economy, acknowledged the superiority of the market over a planned economy. They began to extol the virtues of competition and the deregulation of the economy.

In March 1985, the European Council, whose members included the heads of the governments of the twelve member states, announced its intention to establish a single integrated market by the end of 1992. In its 1985 white paper, "Completing the Internal Market," the Council called for the removal of national rules and regulations in a host of areas in favor of supranational regulations. It was a mammoth task encompassing 279 areas—from the rights of labor and women to banking, transportation, communication, insurance, agricultural subsidies, border controls, immigration, pollution, and health standards. It even called for the creation of a common currency, the euro, designed to put an end to the eleven different national currencies. The euro was meant to streamline commerce and do away with the cumbersome and expensive practice of changing money. Travelers to all EC member nations, it was estimated, would lose 47 percent of their money after they changed it into local currencies.[3]

The first nation to take the road to a fully integrated market was France, which at the time was no longer ruled by the "nationalist" Charles de Gaulle but by the "European" François Mitterrand. In January 1984, Mitterrand became the president of the Council of Ministers of the EC, and in this capacity he became a convert to European economic and social integration. His term as president of the Council of Ministers, a French diplomat noted, became his "road to Damascus."[4] The chancellor of West Germany, Helmut Kohl, felt that the strong German economy could only benefit from the removal of national economic barriers. Margaret Thatcher, the prime minister of Britain, long an apostle of laissez-faire capitalism, had no reason to object to a free market.

The driving force behind full integration was the business elite. It was not a popular mass movement. In fact, many Europeans viewed it with misgivings. West Germans, for instance, feared an influx of immigrants from southern Europe. In the 1960s, West German industry had recruited a large number of "guest workers" from Turkey, Yugoslavia, and Greece, many of whom had not returned home. Northern workers feared competition from immigrants from countries in the south such as Portugal, Spain, and Greece, where the standard of living was less than half that in the north. Workers also feared that the removal of barriers could mean relocation of businesses to countries with lower wages and fewer social benefits (as indeed happened).

During the late 1980s, the four leading members of the EC—West Germany, France, Italy, and the United Kingdom—ranked third through sixth in the world in GNP. West Germany alone, with one half the population of Japan and one quarter that of the United States, had become the world's leading exporter in 1988, surpassing the United States for the first time and extending its lead in 1989. West Germany's 1989 commodity trade surplus of $61 billion equaled that of Japan and exceeded it in 1990.[5]

In their pursuit of full economic integration, the European Community nations agreed in December 1991, after lengthy sessions in the Dutch city of Maastricht, to a treaty that committed them to a "deepening" of their union. The treaty's centerpiece was the call for a monetary union with a single currency, the euro, and a common central bank. With the elimination of national currencies, national borders became anachronistic. Thus, border controls were slated to come down and foreigners were to be cleared at whatever border (or air or seaport) they arrived. Maastricht restated the goals of the 1985 white paper and added a few of its own. It was a typical European social democratic document. It called for standard economic and social practices regulating, among other areas, the environment, labor laws, minimum wages, vacations, and maternity leave. All citizens would be free to work and live anywhere they chose; they would even have the right to vote in local elections.

Before the Maastricht treaty could go into force, it to be ratified, however. In nine of the twelve nations, the governments quickly did so. But in Denmark, Ireland, and France ratification was by popular referendum. The voters of Denmark, the third-smallest member of the EC, rejected Maastricht in June 1992, by a narrow majority.

The Danish vote underscored a general unease with Maastricht. The "deepening" process, the handiwork of business and governing elites, clashed with the skepticism of the public, who felt that politicians had gone too far, too fast along the road to political, social, and economic integration by insisting, to an unprecedented degree, on the subservience of national sovereignty to a supranational community. The Danes were not necessarily against a unified Europe. But they were against granting faceless bureaucrats in Brussels—ensconced in one of the worlds' largest office building, fifteen floors high and encompassing three wings—the authority to decide, for example, on the maximum speed of a Danish moped.[6] There was also the danger of the EC being dominated by a resurgent Germany.

On this, the Danes were not alone in their fears. The plans for 1992 had been drawn up before German reunification, something no one had predicted, at a time when West Germany was first among equals (but equal nevertheless). Earlier, the French had used the metaphor of the French rider controlling the

German horse. With German reunification, however, the horse threw its rider and galloped off to the east to reclaim its former sphere of influence.[7]

Maastricht finally went into effect in November 1993 after Danish voters approved a modified version of the treaty in a second referendum. At this juncture, the European Community took a new name that reflected its commitment to integration. Henceforth, it would be known as the European Union (EU).

Despite the ratification of the Maastricht Treaty, a measure of pessimism over the deepening process remained. Britain's leaders, in particular, were having second thoughts about further integration. Moreover, the enlargement of the EU (to twenty-seven members in 2007) made the intergovernmental process more unwieldy. In subsequent years, public expressions of "euro-pessimism" became widespread. Many, particularly in Germany and Britain, wanted no part of a single monetary system—"esperanto money," as it was called derisively—preferring instead to retain their national currencies. Their sentiments, however, ran against the wishes and power of the politicians. The deepening process—that is, the granting of additional powers to the European Parliament at the expense of national legislatures—would continue.

The EU adopted the euro on January 1, 2002. Britain, Sweden, and ever-skeptical Denmark, however, kept their national currencies. The new bank notes featured open doors and windows and bridges, symbolic of the EU mission to integrate a continent that only recently had witnessed unprecedented bloodshed.

To join the monetary union, member states needed to meet the "euro convergence criteria." Their government budget deficits and debt needed to be manageable. When the time came, however, the rules were ignored and any of the then EU states was permitted to join the "euro-zone." Those that refused, did so on their own volition. The lax criteria meant that the heavily indebted southern tier—Greece, Spain, and Portugal, as well as Ireland—adopted the euro.

Even before Maastricht's ratification, the EU agreed to "broaden" its membership. The first to seek admission was Austria in July 1989, four months before the Berlin Wall, the symbol of European division, came crashing down. Austria's 1955 treaty with its former occupying powers had prevented it from joining any sort of association with Germany—economic or military. The major Western powers (the United States, Britain, and France) had no objection to Austria's membership in the EU. It was primarily the Soviet Union that did not want to see another German *anschluss*, or annexation, of Austria, creating another *Grossdeutschland*, or Greater Germany. Earlier, however, Mikhail Gorbachev had spoken of a culturally and economically unified Europe, "our common home." He had no objections to Austrian membership in the EU.

Sweden applied for membership in July 1991, and Finland and Norway followed suit in March 1992. Finland, however, had close trade and defense arrangements with the Soviet Union based on the treaty of 1948. But Finland suffered from an unemployment rate of 20 percent—its highest since World War II—and it saw the EU as a potential life raft. The EU, moreover, offered Finland the window of opportunity to formally become a part of Western Europe. Again, Moscow did not object.

In June 1994, Austrian voters approved EU membership by a wide margin. In Scandinavia, however, the votes were much closer. Farmers opposed opening their markets to imports from the south. Voters in Sweden and Finland ratified EU membership by narrow margins; in Norway, however, the voters (as they had done twenty years earlier) narrowly rejected EU membership, preferring to go it alone. Norway was self-sufficient in agriculture and energy (by virtue of North Sea oil), and its commercial fishers did not relish the thought of vessels from Portugal and Spain entering their country's coastal waters.

When the three new members—Austria, Finland, and Sweden—joined the EU on January 1, 1995, the population for EU member countries increased from 349 million to 370 million, and its GNP increased by 7 percent. The EU economy was now 10 percent larger than that of the United States. And still more applicants—mostly in Eastern Europe—were waiting in the wings. The projected expansion raised questions even among previous champions of the EU. For one, the EU operated on the principle of unanimity, something much more difficult to achieve in a greatly expanded union. There was the question of whether new applicants could meet the stringent entrance requirements— environmental standards, low unemployment, low state operating deficits, a viable private economy, and solid democratic institutions.

Former champions of the EU thought the focus should continue to be on integration, that is, the "deepening" of the union, rather than the "broadening" of it. Among them were Helmut Schmidt, the former chancellor of West Germany, and Jacques Delors, the former president of the European Commission. Delors feared that by expanding into Eastern Europe, the EU would become nothing more than a free-trade zone at the expense of the common social and political ideals as spelled out in the Maastricht Treaty. The skeptics, however, lost the battle. In May 2004, the EU accepted ten additional members—Poland, the Czech Republic, Slovakia, Lithuania, Latvia, Estonia, Slovenia, Hungary, Malta, and the Greek part of Cyprus; and in 2007, it accepted Romania and Bulgaria. Turkey had sought membership for decades, but its application remained on hold, in part because of the requirement that EU members be genuinely democratic. Moreover, many Europeans were not certain whether Turkey, with its Muslim population and situated primarily in Asia Minor, was a suitable candidate to join a *European* union.

The new members brought the EU population to 490 million (as compared to 305 million in the United States). Because of the relative poverty of its newest members, the overall per capita GDP among the EU membership dropped slightly to $32,900 (as compared to $45,800 in the United States).[8]

Since its formation, the EU underwent five enlargements. In the first four, the new members had to meet strict criteria. They needed to be fiscally sound (that is, no insurmountable debts) and had to be genuinely democratic (rather than merely pretend to be). During the fifth enlargement, between 2004 and 2007, however, the rules became lax. With the emphasis on expansion into Eastern Europe, the EU became an amorphous entity, a composite of developed and still-developing nations. It was a trend that had been seen previously with the admission of poorer countries, such as Spain and Portugal. These nations, however, had been able to count on large subsidies. Those days were over. Germans, who had been subjected to a huge increase in taxes to finance the absorption of East Germany, were no longer willing to subsidize poorer states.

In fifteen years, membership in the EU, once an exclusive club, more than doubled, from twelve to twenty-five. The expansion came at a time when European economic growth was stalled. The inevitable result was "euro-skepticism," accompanied by a rise in fervid nationalism. The EU had been formed specifically to overcome such tendencies, yet here they were again coming to the fore, particularly in the newly admitted states. Increasingly, people saw themselves as members of a tribe with their own customs, languages, and totems. Looking for scapegoats for their problems, they blamed others—among them immigrants, Jews, and Roma (gypsies). The smaller and poorer nations increasingly resented Germany's long shadow. In Greece, people dredged up the memory of their country's occupation by Hitler's army during World War II.

After "broadening" its membership, the EU returned to the more complex task of "deepening" the union. In October 2004, the heads of the twenty-five EU member states signed the European Constitution, scheduled for ratification by a popular vote in two years. The first such transnational entity in history was, in the eyes of many, an attempt to create the "United States of Europe."

The newly proposed constitution was steeped in the tradition of the Enlightenment. It granted citizens of the EU a host of civil liberties similar to those found in the Bill of Rights of the US Constitution. Yet there were differences, since the Europeans, heirs to a long tradition of social democracy, defined civil rights differently. The European Constitution specifically stressed the need for "peace, justice, and solidarity throughout the world." A right-to-life clause rejected the death penalty. In the United States, the future of social assistance, such as Social Security, was widely debated. The Europeans, however, saw "social help," such as universal health care, as an inalienable "right."

In the spring of 2005, increasingly skeptical voters in France and the Netherlands refused to ratify the dense and complicated constitution. The result was a redrawn, "streamlined" treaty (no longer called a constitution), signed in Lisbon in December 2007. In October 2009, the Irish voters, the last holdout, finally approved it. By now, the treaty resembled a catalogue of amendments, the nature of which few people understood, however.

As the EU grappled with the treaty, its most severe crisis began to unfold in Greece. Greece's government had never met the deficit and debt limits stipulated to join the euro-zone. Its public debt was high and rising (in part the result of widespread tax evasion) while its economy suffered from the effects of the global "Great Recession" that began in 2007. In Greece, however, the crisis created a veritable depression. The rates of unemployment reached levels not seen since the 1930s. (In May 2013, it stood at 27 percent.) When the government turned to the US investment firm of Goldman Sachs to manage its debt, it only made things worse. Greece fell further into debt while Goldman Sachs walked away with hundreds of millions in profits, the result of complicated cross-currency swaps that Greek officials did not understand. (Harvard University, Jefferson County in Alabama, and the German city of Pforzheim fell into the same trap).[9]

The German chancellor Angela Merkel insisted that Greece repay its extensive debts to foreign (mostly German) lenders. Tied to the euro-zone, Greece was trapped. Had it still possessed its old currency, the drachma, it could have reached for national solutions, such as devaluing its money. After Greece dropped the drachma for the euro in 2001, vacationing in Greece immediately became more expensive, this in a country where tourism is the main industry. Tourists went to Turkey instead, where the lira was cheap compared to the euro. Before accepting the euro, tourists to Greece outnumbered by millions those visiting Turkey; by 2012, two-thirds went to Turkey.[10]

The European Union's lending partners were willing to extend additional credit to Greece, but it came at a steep price: a draconian slashing of public expenditures—pensions, wages, school budgets, food allowances, and medical care. The public wound up paying the price for the profligacy of its bankers and politicians.

By 2013, after a five-year-long depression, Greece remained "ground zero" of the global economic crisis. In addition to its economic difficulties, the country was torn asunder by political polarizations, the very sort the EU had sought to eliminate. Neo-Nazi elements, such as the "Golden Dawn," who sought a return to Greece's ancient glory days, conducted xenophobic "national reawakening" sessions at which they peddled the diary of Josef Goebbels, Hitler's propaganda minister. The neo-Nazis and the political left took their differences into the streets, where they engaged in pitched battles. It reminded Europeans of the events of the 1920s and 1930s, which had brought the fascists to power in Germany and elsewhere.

Other members of the EU's southern tier experienced similar problems. Again, it was a case of indebtedness, of living beyond one's means. And again, someone had to pay, not necessarily those responsible for the crisis. Spain was a particularly painful case in point. Its economic meltdown was caused by the proverbial "smartest guys in the room," not the workers who subsequently found themselves unemployed. Spain had drastically overbuilt—much of it along the Mediterranean coast—for a foreign clientele that did not come in large enough numbers. When the warnings came, they were dismissed. Banks offered cheap loans to developers, using money they themselves had borrowed from foreign lenders, mostly German. The European Central Bank and the Spanish government did what they could to bail them out, yet banks continued to fail. Capital dried up and workers lost their jobs, leading to additional failed loans and foreclosures. In 2013, the unemployment rate was estimated at 26 percent. Among the young—last hired and first fired—the unemployment rate was 55 percent. Student protesters became known as *ninis—ni estudio no trabajo*—"neither studies nor work." They became part of an angry and lost generation, many of them looking to leave Spain.[11]

Spain's debt to banks and the IMF rose to over \$1 trillion, 80 percent of its GDP, with interest rates eating of up one-quarter of its GDP. Still, no one was held accountable.

## The 1980s: Three Economic Superpowers

At the end of the 1980s, the European Community's competitors, including the United States and Japan, increasingly took notice of the emerging structure. The EC sought to allay fears abroad that it was creating a "Fortress Europe" by stressing its commitment to international trade. Indeed, total exports of EC member nations (including exports to each other) amounted to 20 percent of international trade, compared to the United States with 15 percent, and Japan with 9 percent. To forestall the impact of European protectionism, Japanese and US companies sought to establish a foothold in EC countries. AT&T bought into Italtel in Italy to circumvent the rules of origin. Toyota invested \$1 billion in an automobile factory in Great Britain. For the Japanese the central problem was access. Should the walls go up, Japan's companies hoped to qualify as insiders by building industrial plants within EC nations. For this reason, Japan's direct investments in EC countries increased from \$1 billion in 1984 to about \$9 billion in 1989.

After 1987, the EC cracked down against "dumping" by East Asian firms, particularly Japanese companies. It drew up "rules of origin" and "local-content regulations" to determine the national origin of goods. These were meant to prevent the establishment of East Asian "screwdriver" assembly plants in Europe.

Europeans were divided over Japanese investment. Margaret Thatcher's government welcomed Japanese investment to shore up the economy of Britain, where in 1989, one hundred Japanese-owned factories employed over 25,000 workers. But many European industrialists feared that unrestricted Japanese investment could lead to Japan's domination of entire sectors of the economy.

In the 1960s, the United States accounted for 33 percent of the world's GNP, but by 1989 its share had slipped to 20 percent. The US current account trade deficit—that is, trade in goods and services *plus* income from US investments abroad *minus* payments to foreigners on their US investments—reached $125 billion that year, while Japan's surplus rose to $72 billion, Taiwan's to $70 billion, and Germany's to $53 billion. In the 1980s, Japan and the newly industrializing Asian countries, on the one hand, and West Germany and the EC, on the other, were gaining momentum while the United States was struggling. Its massive domestic debt was a recurring symptom of a nation that lived beyond its means, consumed too much and was unable to pay its bills.

During the 1980s, Japan ran up annual trade surpluses with the United States in the neighborhood of $50 billion, and such a large trade imbalance was bound to cause friction. Many of the economic problems that plagued the United States were of its own making: a huge defense budget (around $300 billion annually), the quest for short-term gain at the expense of long-term investments (which frequently led to shoddy craftsmanship and the attendant loss of market share, especially in automobiles), and the opening of its market to its competitors.

The oil crises of the 1970s hit the US automobile industry particularly hard as it produced gas-guzzling behemoths when the world demanded smaller, more fuel-efficient cars. Germany and especially Japan benefited handsomely because they already produced the smaller cars and efficient diesel automobiles now much in demand. Japan also profited from the production of other sought-after, relatively inexpensive consumer goods of high quality—cameras, television sets, stereo equipment, and VCRs.

The open US market—partly a product of the Cold War—served Japan well. The foreign policy establishment in Washington—the Pentagon and the State Department—favored a strong Japan allied with the United States, while the Commerce Department and Treasury Department fretted over the trade imbalance and the outflow of the nation's wealth.

For international trade to work smoothly, the flow of goods must be relatively even. An imbalance inevitably leads to friction. The US trade gaps, first with Japan and then with China, were a case in point. Since the late 1990s, China's trade surplus grew at an astonishing, unprecedented rate (see Table 17.1).

Still, the US economy remained the locomotive pulling other economies by purchasing vast amounts of goods from abroad. But it was not merely Japan and China that ran up huge trade surpluses with the United States. US trade deficits kept setting new records (see Table 17.2). In 1998, the deficit stood at $166 billion. It jumped to $265 billion in 1999, to $495 billion in 2003, and to $540 billion in 2012.[12]

In the 1980s, when "Japan-bashing" became a fashionable trend in the United States, many blamed declining US economic performance on

**Table 17.1  China's Current Account Balance, 1996–2010 (in US$ billions)**

| 1982 | 5.7 (first current account figures published) |
|------|-----|
| 1995 | 1.6 |
| 1996 | 7.2 |
| 1997 | 29.7 |
| 2003 | 45.9 |
| 2005 | 160.8 |
| 2006 | 249.9 |
| 2007 | 371.8 |
| 2008 | 426.1 |
| 2010 | 305.4 |

*Source:* State Administration of Foreign Exchange, People's Republic of China, www.chinability.com/CurrentAccount.

Japanese trade barriers. These barriers tended to be informal, "nontariff" constraints (including currency devaluation that made Japanese goods artificially cheaper abroad), which made it frustratingly difficult for US businesses to crack the lucrative Japanese market of more than 120 million buyers with deep pockets.

Europeans, too, complained about the restricted access to the Japanese market. In 1989 the leading West German news weekly, *Der Spiegel*, launched a broadside of articles in which it charged the Japanese with unfair, manipulative trading practices. The Japanese were not interested in trade but in ambushing their competitors, not merely to gain a share of the market but to dominate certain sectors completely—and all this by unfair means such as dumping, stealing technology, price manipulation, and excluding foreign competitors

**Table 17.2  US Current Account Trade Deficit with Its Most Important Trading Partners (in US$ billions)**

|         | 2001 | 2003 | 2005 | 2007 | 2012 |
|---------|------|------|------|------|------|
| China   | 83   | 124  | 202  | 258  | 315  |
| Japan   | 69   | 66   | 83   | 84   | 76   |
| Canada  | 52   | 51   | 78   | 68   | 31   |
| Mexico  | 30   | 40   | 49   | 74   | 61   |
| Germany | 29   | 39   | 50   | 44   | 59   |

*Source:* US Census Bureau

from their shores. The Japanese Ministry of International Trade and Industry, *Der Spiegel* went on to say, not only organized trade; it was the headquarters of an economic war machine on a mission to dominate the world.[13] It was not just *Der Spiegel* that took that interpretation. Starting in the late 1980s, a spate of books and articles put to rest the notion that Japan's success could be attributed to its superior free-market policies.

During the early 1990s, a rift emerged in the United States between those who pushed for greater integration of the world's economies and those who argued for measures against unfair competition. But interdependence was too deeply entrenched, and the proponents of the second argument were fighting an uphill battle.

Several examples illustrate the extent of global interdependence. General Motors no longer saw itself as a US corporation but as an international corporation. The Chrysler Corporation held 50 percent ownership in a joint venture with Mitsubishi Motors to produce cars in the United States as well as a 15 percent interest in Mitsubishi of Japan, which produced cars in Japan for Japanese and foreign markets. Other car manufacturers (General Motors, Ford, and several British corporations) entered into similar joint ventures with Japanese car producers. In 1998, Chrysler merged with the venerable German automobile manufacturer Daimler-Benz. The head of the new conglomerate was a German national. Many "US-made" or "British-made" cars had a large component of parts produced in Japan. Honda, the Japanese carmaker, shipped to Japan some of its cars manufactured in Ohio by US workers.

### NAFTA: North American Free Trade Agreement

In the early 1980s, the United States took the lead in negotiating the North American Free Trade Agreement (NAFTA) with Canada and Mexico. Its aim was to establish a free-trade zone encompassing more than 400 million consumers.

The roots of NAFTA may be traced back to the mid-1980s, when Mexico decided to join the global economy and began to open its economy to foreign goods and investors. By then, Mexico had accrued a staggering foreign debt of over $100 billion. Its creditors, among them US banks, urged the privatization of Mexico's state enterprises, some of which indeed were sold off to creditors. In 1986, Mexico joined GATT, leading to a reduction of its protective tariffs—some as high as 100 percent—to 20 percent or less. Foreign investments in Mexico began to increase. Between 1986 and 1991, US investments rose from $5 billion to $11.6 billion, and US exports to Mexico increased from $12 billion to $33.2 billion. NAFTA was meant to eliminate all tariffs among Mexico, the United States, and Canada (which already had a free-trade agreement with the United States, effective January 1, 1989). NAFTA was also designed to protect the rights of North American investors in Mexico, open it to foreign capital, lock it into the global economy, and foreclose radical political options in the future.

In June 1990, US president George H. W. Bush and Mexican president Carlos Salinas de Gortari first proposed NAFTA, hailing it as a "powerful engine for economic development, creating new jobs and opening new markets." There immediately arose an intense debate over the pros and cons of NAFTA. In corporate boardrooms across Mexico, the United States, and Canada, support for NAFTA was nearly unanimous. All five former US presidents and all former secretaries of state favored the agreement. Three hundred of the best-known US economists signed a letter of support. To obtain congressional ratification of the agreement, President Bill Clinton needed to persuade the public of its benefits.[14] He repeatedly promised that NAFTA would produce hundreds of thousands of new jobs in the United States—and high-skilled, well-paying ones at that.

There were those, however, who had misgivings about NAFTA. The rebellion in the state of Chiapas in Mexico began on the very day—January 1, 1994—that NAFTA went into effect, precisely because the agreement made it possible for foreigners to purchase ever more Mexican land. Canadian and US workers expressed concern that competing with lower-paid Mexican workers could lower their standards of living. Between 1989 and 1993, even before NAFTA, free-trade agreements with Mexico had already cost more than 360,000 US manufacturing jobs. The American Federation of Labor–Congress of Industrial Organizations (AFL-CIO, the major US labor union) estimated that under NAFTA the United States would lose 500,000 manufacturing jobs to Mexico, where the average wage was one-seventh of that in the United States. An AFL-CIO official correctly predicted:

> What is unstated . . . is that you are adding 50 million low-wage Mexican workers, many of them skilled, to the United States labor force. [They are] not located across the Pacific, but in a country that is attached to ours, as if it were another state.[15]

The concerns of US workers were not alleviated when, in October 1993, President Clinton asked large corporations to pledge that they would not outsource jobs to Mexico and found he had no takers. This came at a time when the Mexican state of Yucatan advertised that workers there could be hired for less than $1 per hour (including fringe benefits), an annual savings of $15,000 for every worker hired.

NAFTA went into effect on January 1, 1994, at a time when the Mexican economy already suffered from the effects of a deep recession and when the government of President Ernesto Zedillo introduced drastic measures to pay off Mexico's obligations. Mexicans had to swallow a very bitter pill. Zedillo raised taxes; clamped down on wages to make Mexican goods more competitive in the world economy (labor unions meekly accepted an 8 percent cut in real wages); raised interest rates; cut back on state-subsidized prices for basic items such as food, bus transportation, and gasoline; cut spending on social programs (such as pensions); and sold off state-owned enterprises—often at bargain prices—to cronies of politicians.

Zedillo's draconian measures, however, went a long way toward addressing the concerns of international investors. When he raised taxes in March 1995, Wall Street received the news enthusiastically. The US stock market rose, and the peso gained 18 percent in value. These steps also produced a deeper recession in Mexico during which 1 million workers lost jobs. Unemployment, fiscal austerity, and the decline of the value of the peso drove down the purchasing power of many Mexicans by as much as 50 percent. Members of the middle class, who had hoped for a better day, were particularly hard hit.

NAFTA drove down the wages of workers in the *maquiladoras*, the assembly plants established by foreign companies across the Mexican border. The *maquiladoras* were "restructured"—that is, wages were lowered and workers were dismissed—to become more competitive in the global economy. (After all, they competed not only with US workers, but with Chinese workers as well.) Mexican farmers also felt the impact of NAFTA when they suddenly faced competition from the efficient farms in the United States and Canada, which sent large amounts of processed meat, powdered milk, corn, and other commodities across the border.

NAFTA was an experiment that had never been tried before. It marked the first time that fully developed economies had agreed to eliminate all trade barriers with a low-wage, developing country that had a minimum daily wage of $4.20.

NAFTA primarily benefited investors who were granted a set of new rights and privileges that promoted the relocation of factories. NAFTA was first and foremost a free-investment agreement and *not* a free-trade agreement. It worked to the advantage of employers who, in a deregulated global market, could move from country to country and purchase labor essentially as a commodity at the lowest possible price.

After ten years under NAFTA, workers in Mexico and the United States had little to cheer. Investment in Mexico quintupled in size from 1994 to 2001, but the influx of money did not translate into jobs. Moreover, the wages of Mexican manufacturing workers dropped 13.5 percent. The minimum daily wage of $4.20 had not changed since 1994. In the United States, NAFTA contributed to the loss of nearly 880,000 jobs.[16] Clinton's well-paying jobs never materialized. NAFTA also contributed to the record-setting US trade deficits with Mexico and Canada.

The economy of Mexico, the chief beneficiary of NAFTA, improved in the first decade of the twenty-first century. The World Bank listed it as an "upper middle income" country, its economy strong enough to slow the exodus of its workers to the United States. It was a trend first apparent in the

2007–2008 economic meltdown. High unemployment rates and declining wages for blue-collar workers in the United States resulted in more Mexicans returning home than migrating to the United States. Despite improvements in Mexico's economy, in 2010 approximately half of its population still lived in poverty. Moreover, the country had one of the widest gaps between the rich and the poor in Latin America.

## Globalization: Remedy or Curse?

The integration of the international economy, long in place, intensified in the 1980s. "Globalization," as it was known, called for an unrestricted flow of goods and services across international borders. The promoters of "free trade" predicted prosperity for everyone around. US president Bill Clinton was particularly fond of preaching the gospel of globalization. He and others sold it as a cure-all: The removal of national barriers produces greater economic growth, makes more goods available at cheaper prices, and thus ultimately benefits everyone—consumers as well as businesses, poor nations as well as rich ones. "A rising tide," the promoters of globalization argued, "lifts all boats." Globalization, however, had nothing to do with the laws of physics, nor the laws of the marketplace. It had everything to do with the manipulation of the market.

Globalization depended on the conscious decisions made by those who controlled the levers of economic power. It called for deregulation (reduction of government controls of the economy), privatization (putting more state-owned property and operations under private ownership and management), austerity (reduction of government budgets), and trade liberalization (lowering of tariffs and other barriers to free trade). This formula became known as the "Washington Consensus." The IMF and World Bank used it as a yardstick for their financial-assistance operations. Nations applying for assistance had to meet the stringent and painful conditions. When their politicians and their public complained, they were assured that the pain was only temporary.

In 1997, several East Asian countries (South Korea, Indonesia, Thailand, and Malaysia) saw the value of their currencies drastically decline. The IMF, World Bank, and various industrialized nations came to their rescue with massive loans totaling over $100 billion to shore up the currencies. With the bailouts came the famous IMF "discipline," calling for recipient nations to undergo economic "liberalization," that is, the deregulation of their economies. In the IMF's view, the economies of these East Asian nations had suffered from overvalued currencies, heavily indebted banks, excessive government controls, and "crony capitalism" (close ties among politicians, big business, and bankers). In this case, the harsh medicine worked, and these nations pulled themselves out of recession.

Globalization in Latin America, as everywhere else, demanded the deregulation and privatization of the economy and a balanced budget. Governments slashed spending by cutting out "expendable" items—social programs such as health care, education, and welfare. This approach stimulated economic growth, but did not reduce poverty. In Latin America and the Caribbean, the percentage of those who lived on an income of $1 per day remained constant in the twelve years between 1987 and 1998.[17]

The World Bank acknowledged that poverty was "a global problem of huge proportions." Between 1990 and 1998, the number of people who lived on less than $2 per day rose from 2.1 billion to 2.8 billion—nearly half of the world's population—and that 1.2 billion lived on less than $1 per day.[18] (Poverty rates in emerging nations are notoriously difficult to calculate. The World Bank's rate of $1.25 and China's official rate of $1.80 per person per day give the misleading impression that those who live on $2 a day have escaped poverty.)[19] In Africa, the most impoverished continent, many countries had 80 to 90 percent of the population living on less than $2 per day.

The World Bank also pointed out that the combined wealth of the world's richest 200 *individuals* was greater than the combined incomes of the poorest 2 billion people. Two decades of aggressive globalization had not solved the problem of maldistribution of wealth but, instead, had contributed to it. In 2013, the wealth of the richest 300 individuals was equivalent to that of the world's poorest 3 billion people (out of a population of 7 billion).

One of the strongest opponents of globalization was organized labor. Unions lamented the loss of jobs for workers in their own country (after large firms relocated abroad to take advantage of cheap labor), while at the same time they decried the exploitation of workers abroad and their lack of union rights. Globalization was most destructive in countries where independent unions were not permitted to exist.

The wrath of antiglobalization groups—among them environmentalists, organized labor, human rights activists, and the so-called G-77 (that is, the world's poorest nations)—became manifest in huge protest demonstrations in November 1999 in Seattle on the occasion of a World Trade Organization conference. The protesters disrupted the proceedings, engaged in confrontations with the police and the National Guard, and grabbed headlines in their attempt to publicize their cause.[20]

As globalization picked up pace in the 1980s, workers' wages in the developed world generally declined. It became a race to the bottom. Between 2001 and 2007, the global economy grew at 4 percent. Wages, however, grew at only 1.9 percent. The lion's share of profits was distributed among investors (stockholders) rather than workers. This trend was facilitated by what one economist called the "great doubling" of the workforce—from 1.5 billion to 3 billion—after China, India, and the countries of the former Soviet bloc joined the capitalist system. This unprecedented widening of the labor pool in such a short time pitted workers against other workers across international borders and thus depressed wages overall.[21]

The defenders of the Washington Consensus continued to argue that economic growth will eventually solve the problems of poverty and the inequality of wealth distribution. They were challenged by those who argued that globalization had been responsible for the increasingly unequal distribution of wealth, a major cause of poverty, and that the World Bank and IMF only compounded the problem. Over time, the once solid World Bank–IMF consensus began to show cracks. Joseph Stiglitz, the World Bank's former chief economist, who had also served as an economic adviser to President Clinton, broke ranks with the consensus when he criticized deregulation, privatization, and austerity programs as panaceas for the developing world. The market alone, he insisted, will not abolish poverty. He advocated, instead, a "third way"—between the "free market fundamentalists" and outright governmental planning. Stiglitz acknowledged that the World Bank and the IMF had bailed out the East Asian economies in 1997, but he attributed the origin of the crisis to the reckless decisions by private investors pressured by World Bank and IMF bureaucrats.[22] Stiglitz, and others at the World Bank and the IMF, were moving toward the ideological camp of the protesters in the streets.

In 1998 and 2001, the Nobel Prize for Economics, which in the recent past had gone to the champions of the free market, now went to its critics, Amartya Sen and Joseph Stiglitz. In awarding it to Sen, an Indian economist who specialized in social welfare, the Nobel committee explained that Sen, whose writings focused on how little of the resources were allocated to the poorest members of society, "had restored an ethical dimension to the discussion of vital economic problems." Instead of relying on complicated computer-generated formulas (as other economists had done), Sen presented a simple thesis: poverty, not food shortages, caused famines. During the famine of 1974 in Bangladesh, he noted, workers simply did not have the money to purchase the food available to feed their families.[23] Sen's focus was on the great challenge for the twenty-first century: how to distribute more equitably the astonishing volume of wealth the world's economies produced.

Not only did the developing world suffer from income inequality. The developed world suffered from it as well. Among the world's developed nations, the United States had the greatest gap in income distribution. The matter came up at the November 2013 confirmation hearing of Janet Yellen as the new chair of the US Federal Reserve. Because a disproportionate share of the wealth was in the hands of the richest "ten percent," Yellen pointed out, it threatened the overall economy. It limited the purchasing power of the middle class, a necessary component for a strong economy. Yellen could have added that since the economic meltdown of 2007–2008, 95 percent of wealth generated had gone to the top 1 percent.[24] A report from the International Labour Organization put US inequality "off the chart."[25] In Japan, a similar trend was playing out. The changing nature of Japanese society—characterized by deregulation, cronyism, incessant competition, an increase in unemployment, a drastic reduction of the tax rate for the wealthy, and an aging population—led to previously unimagined inequality that ranked it among the highest in the developed world.[26]

Corporations were becoming not only wealthier, but also more powerful. In 2008, the outgoing George W. Bush administration proposed the world's most extensive free-trade zone, the Trans-Pacific Partnership (TPP), designed to further integrate the economies of the United States, Australia, Brunei, Canada, Chile, Japan, Malaysia, Mexico, New Zealand, Peru, Singapore, and Vietnam, with other nations expected to join over time. It was the most extreme—and most logical—example of globalization.

The deliberations of the nature of the proposed TPP were in secret, but once the details were leaked, opposition began to build. Voices from both the political left and the right complained that the agreement was being drawn up by lobbyists representing hundreds of international corporations. That was the reason, not "national security" as members of the US Congress were told, that the negotiations were conducted in strictest secrecy.

Under the presidential Trade Promotion Authority, first used in 2002, Barack Obama intended to "fast-track" the agreement, that is, ram it through Congress by majority vote, without amendments or without permitting it to die in committee. Congress would be left to rubber-stamp or reject it. Should Congress fail to act, the TPP would become law in 2014. That the Constitution granted Congress, not the White House, authority to regulate foreign commerce was now irrelevant.

When WikiLeaks published a draft of the agreement in November 2013, opposition to the TPP gathered steam in the United States and elsewhere. Smaller US trade agreements had been fast-tracked in the past (going back to the days of Nixon), but in this case Obama went one bridge too far. WikiLeaks confirmed what had been suspected. The TPP was slated to grant foreign corporations "preferred status" that included their right to sue sovereign governments and their citizens for "impeding" on their right to pursue a profit. A century earlier, US president Theodore Roosevelt had taken corporations to task when he dressed down the financier J. P. Morgan. Now corporations—foreign and domestic—were on the threshold of being able to sue sovereign states. The TPP called for private trade tribunals of three judges appointed by corporations to try and recover damages for them. Should the governments lose, taxpayers would pick up the bill. With the prospect of the will of corporations becoming the supreme law of the land, the TPP's critics referred to it as "NAFTA on steroids."

Under the TPP, sovereign states would be bound by decisions not of their own making. Public health, food safety, consumer protection, financial regulations, the environment, and labor's right to organize would fall under the purview of corporations. Earlier, corporations had been designated as "too big to fail"; now they were on the threshold of becoming "too big to regulate."

Some corporations were already "too big to prosecute." That issue came into focus in December 2012, when the US justice department declined to prosecute the officers of Britain's largest bank, HSBC, which was operating in the United States under a federal charter. The company admitted it had violated the Bank Secrecy Act by laundering hundreds of millions of dollars on behalf of narcotics traffickers in Mexico and Colombia and "outlaw" nations under international economic sanctions—Iran, Cuba, Libya and Burma. HSBC paid a huge fine—$1.25 billion, one it readily could afford, however, since it constituted roughly one month's profit. Its end of the year, the "performance" bonuses it paid for its top officials, were the same as the year before. Yet no HSBC official was charged with criminal wrongdoing. Doing so, the US attorney general explained, would have a negative impact on both the national and global economy.

## The Organization of Petroleum Exporting Countries

The apostle of free trade, Adam Smith, had argued that the free market worked best when regulated by the benevolent "invisible hand" of the market. This theory of a well-meaning, self-regulating market, however, often ran aground on the shoals of capitalist practice, which has traditionally sought to regulate the market for its own benefit. The oil shocks of the 1970s were such an example. In the fall of 1973, the world suddenly woke up to find that the supply of petroleum products did not meet the demand. The unprecedented oil shortages of the 1970s had an immediate and long-term destabilizing effect on economies all over the world, which since 1945 had become increasingly reliant on oil as the energy source for industry, transportation, and heating.

The Organization of Petroleum Exporting Countries (OPEC)—the association (some would say cartel) responsible for the shortages—argued that the finite amount of fossil fuel (particularly petroleum) was being consumed much too fast. Politicians across the globe hastened to legislate remedies such as conserving energy, diversifying energy sources, and reducing dependence on foreign oil. Automobiles, in particular, became more fuel-efficient. A second shortage in 1979 was not as severe as the first, but it added to the belief that the world indeed was running out of oil. The oil shortages, however, had been artificially created, led by Saudi Arabia, the shah of Iran, and the Western oil companies.

In the 1970s, OPEC consisted of the oil-exporting states of the Middle East (Saudi Arabia, Iran, Iraq, United Arab Emirates, Qatar, and Kuwait) as well as four African states (Algeria, Libya, Nigeria, and Gabon), two South

American nations (Venezuela and Ecuador), and Indonesia. Equally important were the oil-exporting nations that did not belong to OPEC but had the best of reasons to follow OPEC's lead: notably the Soviet Union (among the world's leading exporters of oil in the 1970s and 1980s), Mexico, and Canada.

When OPEC conspired to limit the supply of oil, the result was a fifteen-fold increase—from $2 to about $30 per barrel (at one point even to $40)—in the price of crude oil by the end of the decade. OPEC managed to dictate the price of crude oil by virtue of the fact that in the late 1970s, it produced 63.4 percent of the world's output.

OPEC dominance, however, began to weaken in the early 1980s, when a global oil glut was in the making and the bottom of the market began to drop out. The surplus was the result of conservation, a worldwide economic recession (which lessened the demand for all fuels), the discovery of new deposits (on the North Slope of Alaska, in the North Sea, and in Mexico), a worldwide increase in oil production once prices rose, and the cold, hard fact that even during the shortages at the pump there had always been a surplus of oil. By 1984, OPEC's share of oil on the global market dropped to 42.8 percent; by 1985 it fell to 30 percent. In the mid-1980s, as OPEC's market share continued to decline, its members, desperate for oil revenues, began to break ranks by surreptitiously selling more than their allotted quotas. The artificial shortages that OPEC had created gave way to competition based on the laws of supply and demand.

For years, Mexico (although not a member of OPEC) followed OPEC's pricing levels, but in the summer of 1985, it established its own pricing policy in direct confrontation with OPEC. The price of a barrel of crude oil now dropped to about $24. The Soviet Union followed Mexico's lead, thus placing additional pressures on OPEC. OPEC tried to cut back on production to reestablish an artificial scarcity, but it had little impact on prices. OPEC output declined to about 14.5 million barrels per day, its lowest level of production in twenty years. Saudi Arabia, the linchpin of OPEC, in order to shore up the price of oil, dropped its production to 2.3 million barrels per day (almost half of its quota allotted by OPEC), its lowest level since 1967. At the meetings of OPEC oil ministers in the summer of 1985, the debates centered on whether to cut prices or production. In the end, OPEC wound up doing both. No event underscored OPEC's dilemma as sharply as Ecuador's defection in September 1992, when it became the first member to leave the organization. (In 2009, Ecuador rejoined OPEC.) For Ecuador, membership in OPEC, with its quotas for members, had become pointless. Without OPEC restraints, Ecuador's oil industry expected to double its output.

In June 1998, the price for a barrel of oil dropped to rock bottom, to $10, the result of overproduction and a steep decline in demand caused by the Asian financial crisis of the year before. OPEC's income in 1998 of $80 billion—in real terms—was its lowest ever. To recover its losses, OPEC (supported by such nonmembers as Norway, Russia, and Mexico), cut production at a time of renewed rising demand and thus managed to drive up the price for a barrel of oil to $38 by the fall of 2000. Still, in real terms, the price per barrel was less than half of what it had been during the 1970s.

With the price of energy remaining relatively low, conservation once again became an afterthought. US vice-president Richard Cheney, a longtime oilman in charge of US energy policy during the George W. Bush administration, infamously declared in April 2001 that "conservation may be a sign of personal virtue" but it was "not a sufficient basis . . . for sound, comprehensive energy policy."[27]

The spike in the price of oil during 2007–2008 (at one time reaching nearly $150 per barrel) reflected a belief that the world's reserves might have reached a plateau, resulting in permanently high prices.[28] The world, it seemed, was finally *beginning* to run out of oil.[29] The primary reason for higher prices, however, was a growing demand across the globe, not only in the industrial world but also in the former Soviet bloc and developing nations. This was especially true for China and India, which, combined, made up one third of the world's population and whose economies were rapidly industrializing.

With the new demand and with wars and threats of war (including piracy on the high seas) promising to disrupt oil supply lines, speculators in the futures markets, betting that prices would continue to go up, drove up prices (adding perhaps 10 percent to the price for a barrel of oil).[30]

The precipitous decline of the price of a barrel of oil—from its high mark of $150 to below $50 by March 2009—came from an unexpected, and unwelcome, quarter: the global recession of 2008, which greatly lessened the demand for energy. Moreover, the US economy and homeowners were benefitting from a sharp increase in the production of natural gas, the result of "fracking" (short for "hydraulic fracturing"), a controversial method to extract gas from shale deep in the ground.

### Insurmountable Debts

The decline in the price of oil in the 1980s, deeply affected the economies of oil-exporting nations such as Mexico, Venezuela, and Nigeria. Not only did they receive less for their once precious commodity; they now had to deal with the large foreign debts they had incurred when times had been good, when they had been flush with "petrodollars"—money that oil producers had invested in Western banks. That money had made it possible to borrow additional money, but now it had to be repaid.

Western banks needed to recycle their surfeit of petrodollars, that is, they needed to find willing borrowers. They ultimately made them available to developing nations that, however, did not have the means to repay their obligations. By the mid-1980s, the combined debt of Africa and Latin America rose to more than $500 billion—Mexico and Brazil owing around $100 billion each. A default by any one of the large nations threatened to trigger an economic crisis with worldwide repercussions. It would led to an inevitable contraction of credit and with it a slowdown of international trade, perhaps even a global recession.

The indebted countries raised at times the specter of default, but they were at pains to avoid such a drastic measure and sought, instead, to meet their obligations. When, in early 1987, Brazil announced a halt to foreign debt payments, its government was careful to spell out that this was only a temporary emergency measure and that it eventually hoped to find a solution. In March 1987, Ecuador similarly suspended foreign debt payments temporarily after a devastating earthquake cut its main oil pipeline from the interior to the coast. In the summer of 1985, Peru's newly elected president, Alan García, declared that his nation would limit its foreign debt payments to 10 percent of export earnings. This was the first time a debtor nation had linked payments to its ability to repay its obligation. The leaders of the indebted nations understood, however, that a declaration of bankruptcy was a dangerous solution. It would cut their nations adrift, make them incapable of borrowing additional funds, and generate economic retaliation.

The staggering Latin American debt gave the Communist Fidel Castro of Cuba the opportunity to take center stage as the region's elder statesman. Castro urged Latin American countries to unite in a "debtors' cartel" to leverage better deals. Castro pointed to the example of the Soviet Union, which repeatedly had written off its assistance to Cuba.[31]

Donor nations eventually accepted that some debts could not be recovered, no matter what. In the late 1980s, a number of donors (including Canada, Finland, Germany, the Netherlands, Norway, Sweden, and Great Britain) converted some of their loans to grants (meaning the money did not have to be paid back). France wrote off $2.4 billion in loans to the thirty-five poorest African countries, and Belgium canceled debts of $200 million to thirteen African nations. The amount of money involved, however, was relatively small and affected only government-to-government loans.[32] In June 1999, Japan similarly wrote off $3.3 billion of its $8.2 billion in loans to some of the world's most impoverished countries. Private banks, however, were in no mood to write off their massive loans to debtor nations.

The debt crisis demanded a reevaluation of what had gone wrong with international lending practices and why some countries showed little (if any) economic growth and were therefore unable to repay their debts. In 1991, the World Bank study "Managing Development: The Governance Dimension" concluded that dishonest and inefficient governments were at the core of the problem. (Not wanting to stir up a hornet's nest, it was a topic the World Bank had avoided in the past.) Britain's Ministry of Overseas Development came to a similar conclusion. The ministry set aside substantial amounts of money to train efficient local officials in Commonwealth nations such as Zambia, Ghana, and India in an effort to mitigate widespread corruption. The ministry also increased its funding of private nongovernmental organizations (NGOs) in an attempt to bypass corrupt government officials. The British Red Cross, for instance, provided stellar contributions to health care on the local level. The World Bank similarly praised NGOs as the "eyes and ears" necessary for an effective and honest administration of aid.[33]

To repay the debts meant swallowing bitter medicine to put one's economic house in order. It meant first and foremost the raising of taxes, which could be achieved by various means: the elimination of subsidies on food, sales taxes on fuel, a limitation on imports (particularly luxury items), and the devaluation of money. Such steps, however, promised political repercussions, for they invariably lower living standards. Resentment was particularly great when the repayment of international debt obligations—as demanded by the IMF—led to an increase in food prices. Such increases produced riots in the streets—in Sudan, Tunisia, the Dominican Republic, Jamaica, Bolivia, and Argentina. The Egyptian president Hosni Mubarak touched a responsive chord when he famously referred to the IMF as the "International Misery Fund."

The poor nations were caught between two unpalatable choices. Default promised economic repercussions and political unrest. But so did compliance with IMF demands. Either way, the impoverished global South was not a place to look for political stability, a necessary component of economic progress.

The mid-1980s witnessed another phenomenon that compounded the plight of the debtor nations: the flight of capital from the poorer to the wealthy nations. In Mexico, the high rate of inflation undermined the value of money on deposit in Mexican banks. Depositors, therefore, sought safer havens—Western Europe and the United States—where inflation was under control. Since the mid-1980s, the South changed from a net importer of capital to a net exporter, a trend that served to widen the gap between the rich and the poor nations, the North and the South. Thirty years later, the problem remained unresolved.[34]

The reassessment of reckless lending practices to poor nations scarcely able to repay their loans brought the bankers back to the fiscal conservatism of earlier days. The World Bank's second president, Eugene Robert Black (1949–1962), had not been interested in providing money to bring Southern political leaders into the Western ideological camp. He had insisted that money be lent for projects that created income, which then would be used to repay the loans. Black's fiscal conservatism had made possible the lending of billions of dollars by the World Bank without a default, a basic lesson that the lending spree of the 1980s forced the international lending institutions to relearn.[35]

Zambia was a textbook case of the predicament of a poor nation trying to repay its foreign debt. The IMF and World Bank worked out a program of debt relief under a plan known as the Heavily Indebted Poor Countries (HIPC) initiative. The lending agencies agreed to restructure Zambia's debt and provide an additional infusion of money—provided Zambia agreed to "structural adjustments," that is, drastic cuts in domestic spending. The savings would be passed on to the foreign creditors.

Under the terms of the HIPC initiative, Zambia increased its debt payments from $70 million per year to $200 million. The additional outflow of $130 million meant the curtailment of vital social services. The World Bank, a beneficiary of the new payment schedule, praised Zambia's "reformed" health care system as a model for the rest of Africa. The "reforms" had indeed eliminated long lines in the hospitals, yet it was not because of more efficient services but because people could not afford treatment there. The reforms also contributed to malnutrition, an increase in preventable disease, and a decrease in life expectancy. In Zambia, 20 percent of children died before they reached the age of five. Children, particularly girls, were withdrawn from school and put to work to augment their families' meager incomes. Primary-school enrollment dropped from 96 percent to 77 percent. When the Zambian government reduced its payroll, unemployment rose.[36] The problems, one should add, were not the making of the IMF and World Bank alone. Zambia's dilemma was compounded by government corruption, political instability, and human rights abuses. But in each instance, the problems were created by conscious decisions by individuals in power.

## Global Environmentalism

Toward the end of the twentieth century, industrialized nations increasingly became concerned with climate change caused by global warming. Records showed that the planet's temperature had been steadily rising in the twentieth century, the warmest on record. Since the 1990s, new records became annual occurrences. The chief cause was the emission of carbon dioxide, mainly from the exhaust of the increasing number of motor vehicles, as well as "greenhouse gases" that trapped heat in the atmosphere. That the earth was warming was not a matter of debate among scientists. Some even thought that temperatures could increase by as much as 6 degrees Fahrenheit by 2100. If so, the effects could lead to widespread droughts and desertification, more frequent devastating storms, and a rise in ocean levels by as much as 3 feet, submerging heavily populated and cultivated regions.

Environmental organizations, such as the Sierra Club in the United States, were among the most persistent opponents of the drive for pell-mell industrial expansion. They faulted industrialists for their voracious consumption of the earth's raw materials and their unrestricted pollution (particularly in the South) of the land, water, and air. China became a poster child for environmental degradation. After three decades of rapid industrialization, it had seven of the world's ten most polluted cities.

Well into the twenty-first century, the United States remained the world's largest polluter, with China rapidly gaining. To deal effectively with pollution, all nations would have to do their part, particularly the larger and wealthier ones. The first halting agreement to cut emissions came out of the Kyoto international conference on climate change, in October 1997. In attendance were the representatives of 150 nations.

The highly publicized Kyoto Protocol called for reducing emissions by at least 5 percent by 2012. Shortly after taking office, the newly elected US president, George W. Bush, bluntly announced in April 2001 his administration's flat rejection of the Kyoto Protocol, claiming that its provisions would be harmful to the US economy. The world's number one polluter simply checked out of the process. Nonetheless, Kyoto went into effect when Russia ratified it in November 2004, becoming the 127th nation to do so. Still, the world's insatiable appetite for internal-combustion engines remained undiminished. Moreover, China (as a developing nation) was granted an exemption, and the United States stood on the sidelines. As China prepared to host the 2008 Olympic Games, there was fear that the heavily polluted air in Beijing would impact negatively on the competition, especially endurance events. The Chinese authorities solved the problem by shutting down smokestacks in Beijing and banning most vehicles from the city's streets. It worked as a short-term solution, but the root of the problem remained after the competitors returned home.

## The Global Economy and the Great Recession

The multifaceted global crisis that gripped worldwide markets starting in 2007 came at a time when the US economy—the engine that drove global consumption—was already in recession. It was a predicament long in the making. The sins of the past—overlending, speculation, and toxic assets known as subprime mortgages that were sold to unsuspecting buyers as sound investments—eventually caught up with Wall Street. The result was a decline in productivity, employment, and purchasing power.

The roots of the crisis went back to the early 1980s, when a new economic orthodoxy gradually replaced that of the New Deal of the 1930s. The New Deal, put in place to mitigate the effects of the Great Depression, set out to eliminate the economic boom-and-bust cycles of the past. The new "neoliberal" orthodoxy, in contrast, called for a market free of cumbersome restrictions. The "invisible hand" of the market, it was again argued, would essentially govern itself for the benefit of all. In reality, however, the hidden hands of bankers and money managers controlled the market.

The free-market advocates rejected the notion that the government should play a major role in the economy, except for the regulation of the money supply. The politicians most closely identified with returning the economy to private interests were British prime minister Margaret Thatcher and US president Ronald Reagan. Government was not the solution, Reagan famously insisted, but was instead the problem. Others wanted government to get out of people's lives altogether, to see it shrunk "down to the size where we can drown it in the bathtub." The "free-market fundamentalists," as their critics called them, became deeply entrenched in the 1980s in Washington's corridors of power. The highly respected chairman of the Federal Reserve, Alan Greenspan, who was among their gurus, had served for twenty years (1987–2006) under four presidents, yet had paid no heed to repeated warning that a tidal wave was gathering momentum off-shore.

As financial institutions became unregulated, it left them free to engage in high-risk and unsupervised transactions. Banks extended credit to the riskiest of applicants who lied about the their incomes on their loan applications. The banks repackaged the "liar's loans" and resold them to Wall Street investors under the rubric of "securitization." The selling of subprime mortgages as AAA-rated investments, critics charged, was reminiscent of the work of medieval alchemist who tried to turn lead into gold.[37]

The recycling of toxic mortgages was a profitable business, but it also helped create an unsustainable bubble in the US housing market. As many had predicted, overextended borrowers, unable to make their payments, walked away from their mortgages and defaulted en masse. Overextended banks (unable to collect on the mortgages and holding unsalable houses) and investment firms (now in possession of the toxic assets) went bankrupt. Loans became scarcer, thereby undermining the capitalist system, which cannot function without the well-managed circulation of capital. The specter of deflation—the contraction of money in circulation—not seen since the Great Depression, became a possibility. Across the globe, markets plummeted and unemployment rose.

The firms facing bankruptcy included some of the world's most venerable investment, banking, and insurance companies. The crisis started on Wall Street but soon spread abroad. Governments scrambled to save (and to reregulate) their financial institutions and stock markets. French president Nicolas Sarkozy, who had won his recent election as the darling of the free-market proponents, now lurched to the left. He thought (prematurely as it turned out) that "laissez-faire is finished, the all-powerful market that is always right, that's finished."[38]

International financial institutions were overextended to such a degree that they were unable to meet their obligations to stockholders as well as to customers in need of capital. They were in danger of going under unless a higher power bailed them out. Treasury Secretary Henry Paulson—with the help of two presidents and the US Congress—obliged them. Because the corporations were "too big to fail," he called on the US Congress to allocate massive sums of taxpayers' money to shore them up. The Congress, prodded by the outgoing president George W. Bush and supported by president-elect Barack Obama, approved bailout packages running to trillions of dollars.[39]

The large financial institutions were happy to accept the money but chafed at any restrictions. Paulson, a former head of Goldman Sachs, an investment firm with its own severe financial problems, saw little reason to impose undue hardships on the companies. Six weeks after Congress voted for an initial $700 billion bailout, and after Paulson had allocated nearly $300 billion to various firms, the rules and regulations were yet to be written. Paulson was adamant that the officers of the companies responsible for the global financial meltdown be given a free pass.

The Bush and Obama administrations had no clear idea of how to deal with the meltdown. A telling example was their approach to American Investment Group (AIG), the world's largest insurance company. Starting in 2000 one of AIG's subdivisions, the Financial Products Group, took full advantage of the lack of regulations and insured banks and investment houses—foreign and domestic—against reckless lending practices. Its chief officer, Joseph Cassino, boasted as late as August 2007 that it was "hard for us . . . to even see a scenario within any kind of realm of reason that would see us losing $1 in any of those transactions."[40] Within twelve months, however, AIG had to make good on more than half a trillion dollars in credit insurance—money it did not have—to cover the toxic loans held by venerable global financial institutions such as the Bank of America, Citibank, Goldman Sachs, Société Generale, Deutsche Bank, and Barclays.

AIG's bankruptcy threatened to bring down the institutions it had insured against losses. Its obligation to European banks alone was $307 billion. In September 2008, France's finance minister, Christine Legarde (who became the head of the IMF in June 2011), pleaded with Paulson to shore up AIG—and with it France's banking system. The US treasury's bailout of AIG made possible AIG's bailout of European and US investment houses.

The AIG bailout (ultimately running to $178 billion by 2009), meant that the US government owned 80 percent of AIG's depreciated assets. The company, however, continued to operate as an independent, private entity—throwing lavish parties and extending even more lavish bonuses to the same people who had brought it to ruin. These individuals understood that Wall Street and large corporations could count on bailouts, but the same could not be said of Main Street, that is, small businesses and homeowners.

US automakers (General Motors and Chrysler) received a bailout of $25 billion; in November 2008 they asked for and received another $25 billion. It did not help that the auto executives, as they appeared hat in hand before Congress, had arrived in corporate jets and had no specific answers for how they would spend the money. Still, the board of General Motors expressed full confidence in its management team, as if the company had just set record sales.

As discretionary spending by jittery consumers slowed, it led to rising unemployment across the globe. In Detroit, automakers laid off tens of thousands of workers; in Moscow, construction stopped on Europe's tallest building; in China, factories closed their doors. Indebtedness (both public and private) and massive job losses further eroded confidence in the economy. Emerging economies, their debt estimated at $4–5 trillion, were unable to repay their obligations. The "free-market fundamentalists," once certain of their understanding of the economy, had no idea when—or under what conditions—the "Great Recession" would end.

The depression of the 1930s ended when the purchasing power of workers and farmers rose, followed by vast government deficit spending as it financed the armament industry in preparation for World War II. Since the early 1980s, however, the trend was in another direction. Government fiscal stimuli were down to a trickle. Workers saw their purchasing power diminished while the wealthy became wealthier still. In a span of thirty years, the United States witnessed an unprecedented imbalance of wealth, greater than during the era of the late nineteenth-century robber barons or during the Roaring Twenties. The broad middle class, at one point the vast majority of the population, shrunk to about 50 percent. As workers saw their share of the nation's wealth decline, the economy increasingly depended on the purchasing power of the well-to-do. It was an inefficient way to stimulate growth.

## Notes

1. The sole major exceptions were Cuba and North Korea (as well as the principalities of Andorra, Monaco, Liechtenstein, and Nauru).

2. By the time of its dissolution in 1995, GATT membership stood at 125 nations.

3. Belgium and Luxembourg had a common currency. Stanley Hoffmann, "The European Community and 1992," *Foreign Affairs* (Fall 1989), p. 28.

4. Andrew Moravcsik, "Negotiating the Single Act: National Interests and Conventional Statecraft in the European Community," Cambridge, MA, Harvard University, Center for European Studies, Working Paper Series 21, n.d., pp. 14–15.

5. Organization for Economic Cooperation and Development (OECD), December 1989; Hobart Rowen, "Bonn Next in Line as Power Center," *Washington Post*, January 7, 1990, pp. H1, H8.

6. *Berliner Zeitung*, June 5, 1992, in "Pressestimmen zum dänischen EG-Referendum," *Deutschland Nachrichten*, June 5, 1992, p. 3.

7. Conor Cruise O'Brien, "Pursuing a Chimera: Nationalism at Odds with the Idea of a Federal Europe," *Times Literary Supplement*, March 13, 1992, pp. 3–4.

8. "European Union Economy 2008," CIA, *World Factbook*, 2008.

9. Beat Balzli, "How Goldman Sachs Helped Greece to Mask Its True Debt," SpiegelOnline, Feb. 8, 2010; Nicholas Dunbar and Eliza Martinuzzi, "Goldman Secret Greece Loan Shows Two Sinners as Client Unravels," *Bloomberg News*, May 5, 2012.

10. Greg Palast, "My Big Fat Greek Minister," *Vice Magazine*, May 21, 2013.

11. Nick Paumgarten, "The Hangover," *The New Yorker*, Feb. 25, 2013, 38–47.

12. US Census Bureau, Foreign Trade Division, "FT 900: U.S. International Trade in Goods and Services," March 13, 2009, www.census.gov/foreign-trade, Exhibit 1; Robert E. Scott, "U.S. Trade Deficit Declines in 2012," *Economic Policy Institute*, February 11, 2013.

13. "Der Krieg findet längst statt" ("The War Began Long Ago"), *Der Spiegel*, December 6, 13, and 20, 1989.

14. NAFTA was not a treaty (which the Senate would have to ratify by a two-thirds vote) but a "trade agreement," which needed a majority vote from both houses of Congress.

15. Cited by Clyde N. Farnsworth, "What an Earlier Trade Pact Did Up North," and Louis Uchitelle, "NAFTA and Jobs: In a Numbers War, No One Can Count," *New York Times*, November 14, 1993, p. 1E.

16. David Bacon, "NAFTA's Legacy—Profits and Poverty," *San Francisco Chronicle*, January 14, 2004; James Cox, "10 Years Ago, NAFTA Was Born," *USA Today*, December 30, 2003.

17. World Bank, *World Development Report 2000/2001: Attacking Poverty* (New York: Oxford University Press, 2000), p. 23.

18. Ibid., pp. vi, 3–6, 23, 280–282; Joseph E. Stiglitz, *Globalization and Its Discontents* (New York: Norton, 2002), p. 259.

19. "World-Class Poverty," *The Economist*, February 27, 2013.

20. G-77 is in contrast to another group, the G-7, representing seven of the leading capitalist nations. (With Russia's addition, it became the G-8.)

21. International Labour Office, *Global Wage Report 2008/09: Minimum Wages and Collective Bargaining* (Geneva: International Labour Office, November 2008), pp. 59–60; for the "great doubling," see the writings of Richard Freeman, such as "The Great Doubling: The Challenge of the New Global Labor Market," 2005 Usery Lecture in Labor Policy, University of Atlanta, 2005.

22. Stiglitz, cited in Doug Henwood, "Stiglitz and the Limits of Reform," *The Nation*, October 2, 2000, pp. 20, 22.

23. Wire reports, "Expert on Welfare Who Studied Famine Wins Economic Nobel," *Baltimore Sun*, October 14, 1998, p. 14. See also Amartya Sen, *Poverty and Famines: An Essay on Entitlement and Deprivation* (New York: Oxford University Press, 1981).

24. Annie Lowrey, "The Rich Get Richer Through the Recovery," *New York Times*, November 18, 2013. In 2012, the top ten percent took more than half of the nation's income (with the top one percent taking 24 percent), the highest disparity since record keeping began a century earlier.

25. Salvatore Babones, "US Inequality Now Literally Off the Chart," Inequality.org, June 8, 2013.

26. Toshiaki Tachibanaki, "Inequality and Poverty in Japan," *Japanese Economic Review*, March 2006, pp. 4–5.

27. Cited in Michael T. Klare, "Anatomy of a Price Surge," *The Nation*, July 7, 2008, p. 6.

28. Matt Piotrowski, "Oil Sets New Records: 'This Is Not a Speculative Bubble,'" *Oil Daily*, Energy Intelligence Group, October 11, 2004.

29. Michael T. Klare, "Beyond the Age of Petroleum," *The Nation*, November 12, 2007, pp. 17–21; US Census Bureau, Foreign Trade Division.

30. "Are Speculators Sending the Right Signals?" *Petroleum Intelligence Weekly*, June 30, 2008.

31. Joseph B. Treaster, "Cuban Meeting Stokes Emotions on Latin Debt," *New York Times*, August 1, 1985, p. D1.

32. World Bank, *Sub-Saharan Africa: From Crisis to Sustainable Growth: A Long-Term Perspective Study* (Washington, DC: World Bank, 1989), pp. 176–179.

33. Barbara Crosette, "Givers of Foreign Aid Shifting Their Methods," *New York Times*, February 23, 1992, p. 2E.

34. Shamim Adam, "Emerging Markets Act to Stem Capital Flight," *Bloomberg Personal Finance*, June 13, 2013.

35. "Eugene R. Black Dies at 93; Ex-President of World Bank," *New York Times*, February 21, 1992, p. A19.

36. World Bank, *World Bank Development Report, 2000/2001*, p. 315; Oxfam International, press release, September 18, 2000, "HIPC Leaves Poor Countries Heavily in Debt: New Analysis," www.oxfaminternational.org; Mark Lynas, "Letter from Zambia," *The Nation*, February 14, 2000.

37. Joseph Stiglitz, *Freefall: America, Free Markets, and the Sinking of the World Economy* (New York: W. W. Norton, 2010), p. 6.

38. Elitsa Vucheva, "'Laissez-Faire' Capitalism Is Finished, Says France," euobserver.com, September 26, 2008.

39. *Bloomberg News*, a financial publication, calculated that the US government, at the end of November 2008, pledged $7.7 trillion (equivalent to $24,000 for every US resident) to bail out the financial sector; Mark Pittman and Bob Ivry, "U.S. Pledged Top $7.7 Trillion to Ease Frozen Credit (Update 2)," *Bloomberg.com*, November 24, 2008, www.bloomberg.com.

40. From a tape obtained by ABC News; Jay Shalor, Lauren Pearle, and Tina Babarovic, "AIG's Small London Office May Have Lost Big," March 10, 2009, www.abcnews.go.com.

# 18

# The Rise of East Asia

**The recovery of East Asia from the ashes of World War II began** in Japan. Between the late 1940s and the late 1970s, Japan underwent an astonishing "economic miracle." No larger than the state of California, lacking in virtually all the raw materials needed for modern industry, Japan grew in the space of thirty years to become the world's second-largest economic power.[1] Only the United States had a larger GNP. But Japan's industrial productivity—in terms of output per person—was already as efficient as that of the United States.

In 1953, Japan's economic output reached its prewar level. It was the result of US assistance, Japan's own assets and hard work, and some good luck as well. The luck was the timely outbreak of the Korean War in 1950, which provided Japan the opportunity to sell its light industrial goods to the UN forces in Korea and thereby earn capital to invest in the rebuilding of its heavy industries.

US assistance came in various forms, such as $2 billion in direct economic aid (spread over a span of five years). Washington also persuaded its Western wartime allies to drop their demands for reparations from Japan, pressured Japan to curb inflation and regain fiscal solvency, provided modern technology by making US patents available cheaply, opened the US market to Japanese goods, persuaded other countries to resume trade with Japan, tolerated Japan's protective tariffs for its industries, and took up the burden of Japan's defense. This assistance was not mere kindness to a former enemy but was also designed to strengthen a new, strategically located Cold War ally. The appreciative Japanese took full advantage of what the United States offered. Without the diligent work of the Japanese themselves, however, the economic recovery would not have been possible.

Japan's economy began its skyrocket growth in the late 1950s, and it continued through the 1960s. The average annual growth rate of Japan's GNP in the 1960s was about 11 percent, far higher than other industrialized nations. The double-digit growth rate continued into the 1970s, until Japan's economic drive was thrown off track in 1974 by the global oil crisis. Detractors were quick to point out the fragility of Japan's economy because of its resource dependency, and some declared that Japan's miracle had ended. But the Japanese made adjustments, reduced their oil consumption and diversified their energy sources, and were back on track by 1976. Until the late 1980s, Japan's average annual growth rate was about 4.5 percent, still the highest among the world's industrialized nations.

Japan surged past most European industrial leaders—Italy, France, and Britain—in the 1960s, and then in the early 1970s it surpassed West Germany, whose postwar economic recovery was also impressive. By 1980, Japan ranked first in production in a number of modern industries. It had long been first in shipbuilding; in fact, it has built more than one-half of the world's ships by tonnage in the last quarter of the century. It outpaced the United States in the production of electronic equipment such as radios, televisions, and video recorders. Japanese automobiles captured an increasing share of the world's markets, so that in 1980 Japan became the world's leader in automobile production. In the 1970s, it had the world's most modern and efficient steel industry. By 1980, Japan was poised to mount a challenge to US leadership in the new, all-important high-tech industries, especially in the computer and microelectronics fields.

Many in the West tended to belittle Japan's success and explained it away with self-serving excuses or outdated, if not entirely erroneous, notions—for example, Japan's cheap labor. Japan, they argued, was competitive because its people were willing to work for very low wages. Such an assertion was certainly accurate during the 1950s and early 1960s, but by the early 1970s Japan's wages reached the level of most industrial nations. It was also said, accurately, that Japan also benefited from its low level of defense spending because the United States guaranteed its security.[2]

Other factors, however, were more important in explaining Japan's economic growth. Scholars specializing in Japan studies have adduced a host of factors of Japan's remarkable economic advance, many of them unique to Japan.

1. *The government-business relationship in Japan was complementary and cooperative rather than antagonistic.* The Ministry of International Trade and Industry (MITI) charted a course for the economy and coordinated industrial growth. Government and industrial firms engaged in long-term planning, which made for policy continuity. It targeted specific industries for growth and designated declining industries to be scaled down or dismantled. It also targeted foreign markets on which the Japanese would concentrate their attack.

2. *The labor-management system in Japan stressed mutual harmony between the workers and management rather than confrontation.* Japan's "lifetime employment" system, with its built-in rewards for worker seniority, provided job security to the workers, who developed strong identity with and dedication to their firms. The companies, in turn, were able to count on the services of a well-trained and loyal workforce. Worker morale and motivation were increased by various management programs, such as a generous bonus system, educational benefits, housing, insurance, and recreational facilities. There were labor unions in Japan, but they were rather weak, and their relations with management tended to be cooperative rather than confrontational. Worker participation in management decisionmaking and in quality-control circles also contributed to the mutual benefit of employer and employee.

3. *The state-controlled Japanese educational system maintained uniform, high standards and was extremely competitive.* University entrance examinations determined a person's future, and only the best of the best were admitted to the best universities, whose graduates obtained the best jobs. Therefore, students at all levels studied intensely in preparation for entrance examinations or, as they were called in Japan, "examination hell." The result was a highly educated society with well-developed work habits. On the whole, the Japanese students received more, if not better, education than their counterparts in other countries. The Japanese school year was sixty days longer than in the United States, and Japanese schoolchildren typically studied many hours a day after school with tutors or in private schools. The Ministry of Education stressed high standards, especially in math and science. This and the fact that Japanese universities turned out more engineers (even in absolute terms) than the United States helped to explain Japan's technological progress.

4. *The Japanese aggressively sought new technology.* They were swifter than many foreign competitors to modernize their steel plants with the most recent, efficient, and cost-saving technologies. When the oxygen-burning type of steel furnace was developed in Austria in the early 1960s, the Japanese quickly purchased the patents and invested large sums to rapidly convert their plants to the new technology. This explains, in part, why the Japanese were able to compete with US-made steel, even though they had to import their iron ore and ship their finished product across the Pacific. Japan swiftly gained the lead over the rest of the world in robotics and in automating the production line. By the late 1980s, Japan had twice as many industrial robots in operation as the rest of the world combined.[3]

5. *The high rate of personal savings by the Japanese played a significant role.* Wage-earners saved a remarkable 18 percent of their salaries, compared to about 6 percent for US workers.[4] Banks then invested this surplus capital in industry and commerce. Japanese firms sold stocks, but a great portion of their capital came from banks, which, unlike stockholders, did not insist on quarterly profits. Instead, the banks financed long-term business enterprises, which at times operated in the red for several years

before turning a profit. The ready availability of capital also made possible continuous plant modernization.

6. *Japan developed superior mechanisms for marketing its products abroad.* Japanese comprehensive trading companies set up branch offices around the world where they collected data and engaged in thorough market research. They also worked with MITI to arrange the most advantageous trade agreements, secure long-term supply of vital raw materials, and direct Japanese investment abroad. Japan became indispensable to nations supplying natural resources, both as a reliable buyer and as a supplier of technology and capital.

7. *There were also intangible factors unique to Japan—and to other East Asian countries—that contributed to economic growth.* The Japanese were served well by historically conditioned cultural traits, such as the Confucian acceptance of authority, paternalism, an emphasis on group harmony, loyalty, discipline, and a sense of duty. Group consciousness prevailed over individualism. Without these traits, Japan's labor-management system would hardly have been possible. Additionally, there were certain historical circumstances that fortuitously benefited Japan, such as the timing of its industrial development during a period of global economic expansion and guaranteed access to lucrative markets and resources.[5]

Japan's relatively low level of defense spending worked to its advantage. It was an important factor in the critical first two decades after World War II (when the United States saw fit to protect the nation it had just demilitarized).[6] Only in 1986 did Japanese spending on defense exceed 1 percent of its GDP; by 2005, it rose to 3 percent, only to decline again.[7]

A more important explanation for Japan's economic success was the preferential treatment Japan received from the United States throughout the Cold War years. Japan was strategically important to Washington's policy of containment, and for that reason it tolerated Japan's protectionist policies and threw its doors wide open to Japanese products. As Japan's industrial competitiveness improved and its trade surpluses increased, US politicians and the public became less tolerant. By that time, another explanation for Japan's economic success became commonplace: its trading practices that bent the rules of the free market.

## Strains in US-Japanese Economic Relations

### The 1980s: Japan's Economic Boom

Bilateral trade between the United States and Japan in the 1980s became, up to that point, the largest volume of overseas trade between any two nations in history. (Only US-Canada trade, which is not overseas commerce, was larger.) Japan had a trade deficit with the United States until 1964; that is, it exported less than it imported. From that point, the US trade deficit with Japan rose to

$1 billion in 1972, $12 billion in 1978, and then to $56 billion in 1987.[8] This was the largest trade imbalance ever between two nations (until Communist China broke all records in the first decade of the twenty-first century).

In the 1980s, "Japan bashing" became one of Washington's favorite pastimes, even though many economists and government officials recognized that declining US industrial competitiveness was an important cause of the trade imbalance. Consumers found Japanese products, especially cars and electronic equipment, superior and less expensive than US-made products.

Still, Japan did engage in trade practices such as "dumping" (selling its products abroad at a loss or at lower prices than in Japan) while protecting its own market from foreign imports by instituting high tariffs, import quotas, and various nontariff barriers. US politicians called for "get-tough" trade policies and economic sanctions against Japan. If the Japanese did not lower their trade barriers, they argued, then the United States must erect barriers against the flood of Japanese products. President Reagan, like his predecessors, opposed taking this protectionist route, knowing that it could lead to a mutually damaging trade war.

Washington joined Tokyo in accentuating the positive aspects of US-Japanese relations, which the US ambassador to Japan, Mike Mansfield, liked to call "the most important bilateral relationship in the world, bar none."[9] But despite the talk of partnership and cooperation, Washington maintained pressure on Tokyo, which grudgingly gave in to some of its persistent demands. On the one hand, Tokyo agreed "voluntarily" to quotas on its exports to the United States; on the other, Washington endeavored to pry open Japan's doors to US products by removing Japan's trade barriers. In the 1960s, Japan agreed to quotas on its textiles exports to the United States, in the 1970s to limitations on steel exports, and in 1981 to a voluntary ceiling on US-bound automobiles. Japan also began building auto-manufacturing plants in the United States in order to quiet the argument that Japanese car manufacturers robbed US workers of their jobs. Starting in the late 1960s, Tokyo gradually reduced its own tariffs and quotas to make foreign goods more competitive in Japan.

Japan, however, persisted in the continued protection of its farmers from foreign suppliers of such foodstuffs as beef, oranges, and especially rice. After years of hard bargaining, the two sides achieved an interim agreement on beef and oranges. Tokyo continued to hold out on rice, however, even if it meant that the Japanese continued to pay as much as seven times the world price for their homegrown staple. Japan tried to deflect criticism by pointing out that it was already by far the world's largest importer of US agricultural commodities.

Washington was convinced that Japan kept US goods out of its market through various nontariff barriers such as restrictive licensing, burdensome customs-clearing procedures, rigid safety standards, a uniquely cumbersome distribution system, and nettlesome purchasing regulations. It particularly targeted *keiretsu*, Japan's informal but powerful corporate network that controlled the distribution system and excluded foreign suppliers. These were complicated matters involving peculiarities of the Japanese business system as well as cultural patterns, and in any case they proved difficult to change.

The Reagan administration hoped that a weak dollar (which lowered the prices of goods produced in the United States) would make US goods more attractive in Japan. The weak dollar, however, also lowered the cost of Japanese investments in the United States. This, as well as high interest rates in the United States, attracted Japanese investors. The Japanese, who had accumulated a tremendous amount of capital, went on a buying spree, purchasing US banks, businesses, and real estate. Most conspicuous were the highly visible acquisitions by Japanese investors in Hawaii, California, and New York City. US senator Ernest F. Hollings, an advocate of retaliatory sanctions against Japan, remarked that Reagan's monetary approach transformed the United States "into a coast-to-coast yard sale, with our assets available to foreigners at cut-rate, foreclosure-sale prices."[10]

By 1982, Japan briefly gained an edge on US competitors in the production and sale of microchips (particularly the 64K RAM chips—which at the time were cutting-edge).[11] In the early 1980s, Japan found a booming market in the United States for VCRs (video cassette recorders), a product that had been invented in the United States but abandoned as commercially impractical. The Japanese also won increased shares of the US market for industrial products such as precision tools, musical instruments, and power tools. Meanwhile, Japan surpassed the United States in nonmilitary technological research and development expenditures, and its research programs either gained the lead or challenged the US lead in a number of new and important fields, particularly robotics, magnetic levitation, fiber optics, and superconductivity.

In the mid-1980s, the United States swiftly fell from the status of the leading creditor nation in the world to the largest debtor. Japan just as swiftly became the world's leading creditor. Japan's assault on the money market of the United States in the late 1980s was breathtaking. By the end of the decade, eight of the ten largest banks in the world were Japanese, and 20 percent of US government bonds were purchased by Japanese financial firms. The Tokyo Stock Exchange surpassed the New York Stock Exchange in capital value, while the Osaka Exchange surpassed the London Stock Exchange.[12]

## The 1990s: Japan's Long Economic Downturn

During the January 1991 Persian Gulf War, Japan's constitution barred it from sending military forces to support the UN coalition. Many in the West thought that Japan should participate in a war that was fought, in part, to protect its main source of oil. After months of parliamentary debate, the Japanese government pledged $13 billion toward the cost of the war, and it offered a token contribution to the post–Gulf War peacekeeping effort by sending a fleet of minesweepers to the Gulf. The Gulf War touched off a heated debate in Japan over the use of its Self-Defense Forces to participate in UN peacekeeping operations. When the Japanese Diet passed legislation permitting it to do so, it prepared the way for Japan to play a role in the UN operation in Cambodia aimed at ending its decade-long civil. It marked the first time since World War II that Japanese military forces were deployed abroad.

US criticism of Japan persisted into the early 1990s, when polls showed Japan's popularity in the United States plummeting.[13] Contributing to the growing acrimony were media coverage of the fiftieth anniversary of Pearl Harbor in December 1991 and several tactless (actually racist) remarks by Japanese political leaders critical of the US work ethic. A best-selling novel (and later movie) by Michael Crichton, *Rising Sun*, painted an unfavorable portrait of a Japan covertly seeking to destroy the US economy.

Moreover, a new "revisionist" view of US-Japanese economic relations found favor in the United States and Europe. Writers such as Karel van Wolferen, Lester Thurow, James Fallows, and Clyde Prestowitz argued that the Japanese political economy was fundamentally different from the Western market economies and that it operated in ways that gave it distinct advantages in international economic competition. Japanese business activity, they argued, was driven primarily by mercantilist, that is by national considerations, as if in a war with the rest of the world. It was not enough for Japanese businesses merely to make a profit; they sought, instead, to control the market. Japan's success, James Fallows argued, depended in part in rigging "the market, to 'get prices wrong,'" a central feature "of catching up in the industrial race."[14]

The acrimony in US-Japanese relations over trade abated in the early 1990s when Japan fell into a lengthy economic recession. The economic bubble—the overheated economy—had burst. The real estate and stock markets that had soared to dizzying heights declined sharply, leaving Japan's financial institutions with a massive debt problem, the result of billions of dollars' worth of "nonperforming" loans. The annual growth rate of GDP barely showed economic growth, averaging 0.9 percent for the next two decades. During this time unemployment averaged well above 4 percent, which was unusually high for Japan.[15] Industrial production and investments declined, as did savings and interest rates. Businesses tightened their belts and reduced payrolls, fraying the social contract between employers and their workers. Japan's "lifetime employment" system began to dissolve, increasingly resembling the arrangement in the United States.[16]

By one estimate, in the five years between 1992 and 1996 alone, Japanese businesses and households suffered a combined capital loss of $7.2 trillion, forcing the government to shell out about $1 trillion in economic stimulus packages by the end of the 1990s.[17] Still, Japan had a huge current account surplus and foreign currency reserves and a large and sophisticated industrial capacity driven by world-class technology. Moreover, during the two-decade-long downturn, the value of the yen against foreign currency held fairly steady and there was only a marginal decline in living standards. Oddly, the prolonged recession had surprisingly little effect on Japan's trade imbalance with the United States. In fact, Japan's bilateral trade surplus crept further upward. As Japanese cut back on purchases of goods—foreign as well as domestic—the US appetite for Japanese goods remained strong.

Japan also faced an increasingly urgent demographic issue: its aging population. It had the world's largest proportion of people over age sixty-five and the smallest age fourteen and under. This was the result of Japan's declining birthrate—the lowest in the world, in 2007 down to 1.25 children for every female, with 2.07 needed to keep the population steady—and increasing longevity, the highest in the world at eighty-two years. Should the trend hold, Japan would have 20 percent fewer people in 2040 as compared to 2010.[18] The decline in population was caused mainly by decades of birth control as well as a rise in the age of marriage, with females tending to delay marriage until their late twenties—or not marrying at all. The result was a shrinking workforce, a detriment to continued economic growth. There was talk that labor shortage might be remedied by opening the doors to immigration, but Japan's political leaders—in the thrall of inertia and procrastination—and the majority of its people, determined to safeguard their ethnic purity, remained firmly against that idea.

· · ·

In March 2011, Japan suffered a horrible natural disaster exacerbated by man-made disaster. A 9.0 earthquake, one of the largest ever recorded, erupted off the coast of northern Japan causing a mammoth tsunami wave that devastated heavily populated coastal cities, killing an estimated 20,000 people. The tsunami also knocked out the Fukushima Daiichi Nuclear Power Plant, causing a nuclear crisis of enormous proportions. In the hours and days that followed, Tokyo Electric Power Company (TEPCO) workers frantically attempted to prevent a meltdown of the plant's six reactors. But it was to no avail. Flooding had knocked out the electrically powered generators used to cool the reactors. Two of the six reactors overheated and exploded spewing radioactive material into the air. New generators were brought in to pump ocean water in to cool the remaining reactors, resulting in an ever-increasing amount of radioactive water pumped back into the Japanese Current. The problem remained unresolved, as did the far more difficult task of removing the radioactive rods from the reactors. Fukushima remained a far more difficult challenge than Chernobyl in 1986, where the problem was resolved, however inelegantly, by covering the reactor with concrete.

This was not the first time that TEPCO, the world's largest private power company, had failed to properly attend to its nuclear power plants, or had to deal with the consequences of an earthquake. A July 2007 earthquake had forced it to shut down its nuclear plant at Kashiwasaki-Kariwa, the world's largest. (As of this writing, it is still not fully functioning.) It turned out that the plant had not been built to withstand an 8.15 earthquake, this in a land famous for its earthquakes. Afterward, TEPCO denied any radiation leaks—only to have to backtrack later on.

In August 2009, just as the World Nuclear Association, an industry lobbying group promoting nuclear power, was about to honor one of TEPCO's former executives, Japan's nuclear regulatory agency announced that the company had been falsifying safety records for at least a decade. TEPCO later admitted that between 1977 and 2002, it had submitted doctored safety records on 200 occasions.[19]

As was its corporate culture, TEPCO again denied after the Fukushima disaster the extent of the problem and again had to admit it had not been telling the truth. This environmental disaster of the first magnitude once again put into question the future of nuclear power. In several countries, notably Germany, the decision had already been made to move to other sources of energy.

Residents in the immediate vicinity of the Fukushima power plant were ordered to evacuate beyond a 30-kilometer radius and within two days as many as 150,000 did so, settling down far from what had been home. Land as far as 200 miles away was contaminated by nuclear fallout, causing a nationwide fear of unsafe farm produce. After the meltdown, most of the remaining nuclear plants were shut down for over a year. Because over 50 percent of Japan's energy was nuclear powered, a rationing of electric power had to be initiated which forced factories to operate on a reduced basis. It caused a loss in production and everything that came with it—diminished export earnings and reduction of workers' income and buying power. Meanwhile, the Fukushima area remained an uninhabitable wasteland.

### The Four Tigers of Asia

By the 1980s, four other prospering nations emerged on the Asian shores of the Pacific Ocean: South Korea, Taiwan (the Republic of China), Hong Kong, and Singapore. These "Four Tigers" of Asia followed Japan's example to produce their own economic miracles. Their performance, especially their vigorous export-oriented industrial development, together with that of Japan, gave rise in the 1980s to predictions of the coming "Asian century." The Four Tigers became the source of a flood of imports into the United States and a major source of its mounting trade deficit. The US trade gap with the four countries grew from $3.6 billion in 1980 to over $35 billion in 1987.

The Four Tigers shared with Japan certain features that accounted for their remarkable economic performance in the 1970s and 1980s, averaging about 8 percent annual growth. They shared a Chinese historical and cultural heritage, particularly the ingrained Confucian value system. It appears that this philosophy—long ridiculed by the West (and by Westernized Asians) as antiquated and a barrier to modern progress—was a major source of such traits and attitudes as harmony, discipline, and a respect for education. The Confucian legacy became a vital ingredient for making capitalism work in East Asia.

Other factors were no doubt involved in the economic success of the Four Tigers, including the model of Japan and the investments and technology flowing from abroad. They also benefited from their ready supply of cheap labor. Their authoritarian governments made economic development their highest priority and marshaled the power of the state toward that end. They emphasized public education, the development of technology, and birth control.[20] Like Japan, they stressed export-oriented industrial development and took advantage of the global trade system with its unimpeded access to lucrative markets.

South Korea and Taiwan shared the experience of facing continuing serious threats to their security by Communist opponents—North Korea and the People's Republic of China, respectively. The persistent threat fostered a sense of urgency and national purpose that facilitated the mobilization of people and resources to strengthen the military and the economic base. In both cases, these Cold War exigencies fostered dictatorships, but after a couple of decades of strong economic growth and modernization, a prosperous middle class asserted itself, demanding political liberalization.

### South Korea

South Korea catapulted from a miserably poor, war-torn, Third World nation in the 1950s to the status of a rapidly industrializing nation by the early 1990s. North and South Korea both suffered from the division of the country because most of the minerals and electric power were located in the north and most of the agricultural land was in the south. After World War II, Korea, as a whole, had a better economic infrastructure—particularly in terms of transportation and communications—than most Third World countries, owing to construction done by the Japanese before World War II. But the Korean War devastated both parts, particularly the north where the US aerial campaign laid waste to the countryside below.

South Korea began its economic takeoff in the mid-1960s, a decade after the end of the Korean War. Its annual rate of economic growth rose above 14 percent in the early 1970s, and after a brief slowdown in the early 1980s, it climbed again to the rate of 12 percent in 1986 and 1987. In 1964, the per capita GNP of South Korea had been a mere $103; by 1994 it had soared to $8,260.

South Korea's resurgence occurred mainly during the nineteen-year dictatorship of General Park Chung Hee. Park, who came to power as a result of a coup in 1961, made economic growth his highest priority. His government-led industrialization drive supported the large state-supported industrial firms, financed by generous development loans from the United States and Japan. Park, having been trained in the Japanese army, was familiar with Japanese organizational methods, and he assiduously employed the Japanese model for economic development.

Park's assassination in 1979 did not end military rule since his replacement was another general, Chun Doo Hwan. When students protested vehemently against the continuation of the military dictatorship, Chun expanded martial law, closed universities, dissolved the national assembly, banned all political parties, and for good measure threw student leaders into prison. The most vicious act of repression came in the city of Gwangju (Kwangju) in May 1980, where perhaps as many as 3,000 civilian protesters were gunned down by security forces. The event took place with the implicit approval of President Jimmy Carter's administration, which knew the military's heavy hand was about to come down. Washington's aim at the time was to prevent South Korea from becoming another Iran, where demonstrations in the streets had helped to bring down another US-supported dictator the year before (see Chapter 21).[21] Although there was no letup in student agitation in the 1980s, South Korea's economic industrialization continued on its rapid course. Its industries continued to churn out quality goods competitive in the world market.

### Halting Steps Toward Korean Democracy

The showcase of South Korea's emergence as a modern nation was the summer Olympic Games in Seoul in September 1988. In anticipation of the event, there was concern over the possible disruption of the games either by acts of terrorism by North Korea or by violent student demonstrations. After Chun rejected the pleas of opposition parties for reform of election laws—to allow the direct election of the president—he faced still larger and more volatile demonstrations, spearheaded by university students now joined by many of the country's new middle class. To head off a bloody confrontation that could result in the cancellation of the Olympics, Chun backed down. In June 1987, he appointed his military academy classmate, Roh Tae Woo, as his successor, and Roh announced a general election to be held in December in which he would run as candidate for president. In Korea's first free presidential election, Roh won a narrow victory, but only because the two popular opposition candidates, the "two Kims," Kim Dae Jung and Kim Young Sam, split the opposition vote.

A political lull prevailed during the summer and fall of 1988 as South Korea basked in the international limelight of the Olympics. But the political rancor resumed soon afterward. In the national assembly, Roh's political opponents demanded that his predecessor, General Chun, be put on trial for corruption. Students demanded Chun's head because of his role in the Gwangju massacre. They also protested the continued presence of US forces, which they saw as the guarantor of the military government. On the diplomatic front, Roh achieved some startling breakthroughs, establishing diplomatic and economic relations with both the Soviet Union and Communist China.

The December 1992 presidential election established a precedent when two civilian candidates—Kim Dae Jung and Kim Young Sam—competed for the office. The winner was Kim Young Sam, who then took bold steps to introduce much needed political reforms. He curbed the power of the internal security agency and arrested military officers charged with corruption.

Kim sought to pacify the students by pledging a full-scale investigation of the 1980 Gwangju massacre and promised compensation for its victims' families. By now, however, the students wanted more. They demanded that former presidents Chun and Roh be punished for the massacre and for corruption. In November 1995, Roh was arrested after he admitted receiving huge contributions from the chiefs of some of the most powerful business groups (among them Hyundai and Samsung) and operating a $653 million slush fund. In a sensational trial, Chun was found guilty and sentenced to death (subsequently commuted to a lengthy prison term) for his role in the 1979 military coup and the Gwangju massacre. Roh was sentenced to a twenty-two-month prison term for accepting $500,000 in bribes.

Forty years after the Korean War, a semblance of democracy had finally arrived in South Korea, all without appreciable support from Washington.

It was finally the other Kim's turn to lead South Korea. Long the country's leading dissident and democracy's most fervent advocate, Kim Dae Jung won the presidency in December 1998. (Kim had previously been kidnapped by the Korean CIA, imprisoned on sedition charges, and sentenced to death. He was later exonerated and freed by his predecessor.) Kim inherited an economy that had been hard hit by the recession that had swept across East Asia in 1997. In that year alone, the value of Korean currency against the dollar fell 54 percent, GDP fell by 5.8 percent, and large companies went bankrupt, including banks that became insolvent when they were unable to collect on loans they had issued.

The IMF, World Bank, and eight donor nations put together a huge bailout package of $57 billion. Kim then took the difficult steps the donors demanded. He regulated the financial industry, held down inflation, granted foreign investors additional legal protection, and liquidated weak businesses. The reforms revived the economy within two years to the point that, by 1999, South Korea's industrial production saw its largest surge in twenty years.

### Divided Korea: North vs. South

After the Korean War, North and South continued to arm themselves against attacks by the other. In the North, Kim Il Sung consolidated his power over a Stalinist regime, which by the early 1960s had achieved a fairly impressive economic and military recovery. Kim occasionally sent commandos across the DMZ, and in 1968 he went so far as to send agents to assassinate President Park. Their shots missed Park, but killed his wife.

North Korea's policy toward the south was marked, on the one hand, by a bewildering fluctuation between threats and provocations and, on the other, by appeals for talks. The North Koreans dug tunnels under the 2.5-mile-wide DMZ that were wide enough to infiltrate efficiently large numbers of troops into the south. They attacked US border guards, killing two of them with hatchets at Panmunjom in 1978. They attempted to assassinate President Chun on a state visit to Burma in 1983; they failed in their attempt, but the bomb they detonated killed seventeen South Korean officials, including four cabinet members. In 1987, they set off a bomb on a South Korean airliner, killing all 115 people onboard. The reckless provocations brought talk of war in the south and assurances of support from Washington. One of North Korea's long-standing major objectives was the removal of US troops from South Korea. Attacks on South Korea, however, could only ensure that the US forces, about 40,000 strong through the 1980s, would remain. The US contingent was armed with tactical nuclear weapons, which Washington made clear it would use in the event of an all-out North Korean attack.[22]

After Mikhail Gorbachev came to power in the Soviet Union in March 1985, the international climate improved drastically as he sought to end the Cold War. With it came opportunities to resolve the Korean conflict. Moscow and Beijing became less willing to support the dangerous and erratic regime in Pyongyang, North Korea's capital. Moreover, they sought to do business with the prosperous south. South Korean president Roh met with Gorbachev in June 1990 and secured an agreement establishing diplomatic ties and trade relations between their countries. He also won Gorbachev's support for South Korea's admission to the United Nations. North Korea had consistently opposed the entry of either of the two Koreas into the United Nations and had been able to count on a Soviet veto. In September 1991, both Koreas were admitted to the UN.

Roh pressured the North Korean ruler, Kim Il Sung, to join negotiations for the peaceful reunification of Korea. Direct talks in 1990 between the two Koreas produced some surprising results when they signed a nonaggression pact and an agreement banning nuclear weapons from the Korean peninsula. The latter agreement was especially remarkable, since North Korea's clandestine nuclear bomb project was a major concern. Washington and Seoul insisted that Pyongyang submit to inspections by the International Atomic Energy Agency (IAEA), but Kim steadfastly denied that he was building a bomb and refused to comply.

Kim suddenly reversed himself in August 1992, and agreed to open his nuclear facilities to inspections. IAEA examiners determined that North Korea had built a plutonium-reprocessing plant but had not produced enough material to make an atomic bomb. Pyongyang, however, refused to allow inspectors to see all of its nuclear facilities and was thus able to perpetuate uncertainty in Seoul and Washington.

In July 1994, the eighty-two-year-old Kim Il Sung, the world's longest-surviving ruler, died. His successor was his fifty-two-year-old son, Kim Jong Il, of whom little was known. Like his father, Kim Jong Il became the object of the state-promoted cult of personality, the omniscient and infallible "Dear Leader."

This unproven and mercurial leader was soon to be tested by a cluster of dilemmas, not the least of which was a failing economy. As it was, North Korea's per capita income was one-fifth that of South Korea.[23] For years, North Korea's frail economy was propped up by assistance and preferential trade arrangements with the Soviet Union. With the Soviet Union in its own financial meltdown, Gorbachev slashed that support and terminated it altogether by the end of the 1980s. As a result, the already impoverished northern economy took a nosedive, shrinking by one-half in the 1990s.

Next came a natural disaster of biblical proportion when, in 1995, a deluge of floods inundated North Korea. Torrents of water destroyed reservoirs, farms, livestock, roads, bridges, schools, and more than 1 million metric tons of food reserves. UN officials declared the food situation the worst in the world. Rations were set at 450 calories per day, but not everyone had access to even that meager amount.[24] North Korea was reduced to accepting a donation of 150,000 tons of rice from South Korea. It took pains, however, not to reveal to its people the source of the handout. In the spring of 1996, the United States, South Korea, and Japan provided an additional $15 million in food. For the next several years Pyongyang swallowed its pride and accepted food shipments, fertilizer, and other aid from its capitalist enemies.

Still, Kim Jong Il was not ready to abandon his belligerence toward South Korea and continued thumbing his nose at the United States and Japan. In August 1999, he tested a medium-range missile over Japan. He declared that it was not a military missile but rather a rocket for launching satellites that had "inadvertently" flown off course.

In South Korea, the newly elected president, Kim Dae Jung, was determined to find a way to make peace with the north. From the day he took office, he pledged a "sunshine policy" toward North Korea, for the purpose of a peaceful reunification of Korea. In February 1998, Kim Jong Il suddenly responded to the "sunshine policy" with a surprising peace overture of its own. It called for "co-existence, co-prosperity, common interests, mutual collaboration, and unity between fellow countrymen."[25] Soon afterward, the diplomatic ice between the United States and North Korea was broken when Pyongyang agreed to receive a visit from a special envoy from Washington in May 1999. It also agreed to send a high-ranking diplomat for talks in Washington. In response, South Korea sent additional amounts of food relief, fertilizer, and other aid to the north, where the famine was worsening. To negotiate and administer the aid program, South Korean officials and businessmen traveled into North Korea, something that had been impossible before. Contacts among North Korean, US, and Japanese officials increased.

The historic "Kim-meets-Kim summit" in Pyongyang in June 2000, appeared to signal a major breakthrough. The democratically elected South Korean president Kim Dae Jung and the reclusive dictator Kim Jong Il of North Korea met face-to-face and declared a willingness to bury the hatchet. They discussed a range of issues, including a willingness to work toward the eventual reunification of Korea. They also called for reuniting thousands of families that had been divided by a border closed since 1953. South Korea declared a willingness to invest in the northern economy. The meeting was mostly diplomatic theater, yet it was followed by a series of confidence-building gestures by both sides, such as conducting the first exchange of visits by separated families, the first meeting of the respective defense ministers, the preparation to open highways and railroads across the heavily armed border, and the mutual cessation of propaganda attacks against each other.

The 2000 summit paved the way for the north's talks with the United States. US secretary of state Madeleine Albright's visit to Pyongyang was hailed as a diplomatic breakthrough. Both sides acknowledged, however, that it was but a first step and that the road to reunification would be long and difficult. Kim Dae Jung's "sunshine policy" helped him garner the Nobel Peace Prize in 2000. That honor was greatly diminished, however, when, in 2003, investigations confirmed that he had secretly and illegally bribed Kim Jong Il to agree to the heralded summit. Kim Jong Il's newfound reasonableness, it turned out, had been purchased with huge sums of money (perhaps as much as $500 million) rather than coming from the heart.[26]

The tentative negotiations between Pyongyang and Washington ran into a roadblock when George W. Bush was inaugurated president in January 2001. Bush wanted no part of the "sunshine policy," nor negotiations with Kim Jong Il. In the wake of the September 11 terrorist attacks on the United States, he lumped North Korea together with Iraq and Iran into his "axis of evil." Along the way, he claimed the right to wage preventive war against North Korea (the so-called Bush Doctrine of preemption), just as he was about to do against Iraq. Chagrined at having his peace efforts chopped off at the knees, Kim Dae Jung was at pains to make certain that Bush understood that a war with North Korea was the last thing South Korea wanted. Its capital, Seoul, a scant 30 miles from the DMZ, was highly vulnerable to attack, within easy range of North Korea's massive array of rocket launchers.

Kim Jong Il responded to Bush by playing the only card he held. In October 2002, he made the stunning announcement that he was restarting North Korea's uranium and plutonium processing programs. Preoccupied with Afghanistan and Iraq, Bush had no meaningful answer except to shrug off the significance of this sensational disclosure. He steadfastly rejected Kim's call for bilateral talks with Washington at which Kim hoped to secure, among other things, a peace treaty officially ending the Korean War and a mutual nonaggression pact. In October 2006, North Korea exploded its first nuclear weapon, a plutonium bomb. That got the attention of Bush, who agreed to resume the talks that the Clinton administration had initiated a decade earlier. The new round of talks led to some successes. In June 2008, the North Koreans blew up the cooling tower of their reactor in Yongbyon that produced plutonium only to threaten, in February 2009, to test-launch a new rocket capable of reaching Alaska and Hawaii.

## Taiwan's Economic Growth

Starting in the 1960s, Taiwan underwent a remarkable economic transformation. Its GNP rose from $8 billion in 1960 to $72.5 billion in 1986, and for most of the 1970s it maintained double-digit growth rates. Its annual volume of foreign trade increased from $2.2 billion to $100 billion between 1969 and 1988. By virtue of its burgeoning exports, Taiwan by 1988 had accumulated a foreign exchange reserve in excess of $70 billion, second in the world only to Japan.

South Korea and Taiwan, had several common characteristics that set them apart from the other two "tigers of Asia." Both were highly militarized, with each facing threats to its security—from Communist North Korea and from the Communist mainland, respectively. Like South Korea, Taiwan thrived on adversity. Their large military establishments and the burden of large military budgets seemed to have the effect of spurring economic development rather than dragging down the economy. Moreover, the presence of an outside threat produced a sense of national urgency and purpose that was useful to these governments as well as to the government-supported industries.

Taiwan's economic success can be attributed to additional factors unique to the island, including the infrastructure the Japanese had built, the influx of highly educated Chinese from the mainland in 1949, a quarter-century of US economic aid, an open US import policy for Taiwanese goods, the growth-oriented economic policies of the Nationalist government, and Taiwan's industrious people. In the 1950s, a sweeping land reform was carried out and agricultural production grew steadily, paving the way for capital accumulation and the investment necessary for industrial development. By the 1960s, Taiwan's industries shifted from domestic consumption to export-oriented production. Lured by Taiwan's cheap, high-quality labor, US and Japanese companies made substantial investments, and Taiwanese industrialists and workers rapidly absorbed modern technology. In the late 1970s, Taiwan gravitated toward capital-intensive and knowledge-intensive industries, a shift that paid huge dividends in the 1980s. By the end of the 1980s, electronics replaced textiles as the leading export, and Taiwan became one of the world's leaders in micro-computers and computer parts.

## Deng Xiaoping's Economic Reforms

In 1979, a scant three years after Mao's death, the Communist Party took a radical turn when it invited foreign capitalists to set up shop in China. China had much to offer—an orderly society, no environmental standards, no labor unions or laws protecting labor, and a disciplined and cheap labor pool. In 2003, hourly wages averaged the equivalent of 62 cents an hour; by the end of the decade, wages had more than tripled, yet were still far below the pay scales in industrialized countries. The "outsourcing" of jobs, as the process became known, was by no means new. In the past, international companies had shipped their factories abroad. US firms had a long history of manufacturing their goods in Latin America. What happened in China, however, was unprecedented in scope.

As impressive as the economic performances of Japan and the Four Tigers had been, that of China was nothing short of phenomenal. Never before, in such a short period of time, in no more than a third of a century, has such great wealth been created. In 1979, China's per capita income was $182, its trade deficit 11.2 percent. Since then, its annual GDP growth averaged nearly 10 percent. Its growth in international trade, at 16.3 percent per year, was even

*Embassy of the People's Republic of China*

*Chinese leader Deng Xiaoping, chairman of the Chinese Communist Party Advisory Commission, December 14, 1985*

more impressive. By 2009, China had become a "middle-income country," its per capita GDP at \$3,688.[27]

The reforms began in 1979 with a new agrarian program called the "responsibility system." Peasants signed contracts with the state whereby they received land, seeds, and tools. After they repaid their obligations, they kept the surplus harvest, which they then sold on the newly created open market. The incentive for personal profit led to more efficient farming and served to increase overall production.

The new system struck observers as more like capitalism than Communism. It represented indeed a radical departure from the party's previous emphasis on egalitarianism. Deng Xiaoping, the dauntless pragmatist, was determined to pursue any course that would speed China's economic development. Under his tutelage, the party proclaimed that, rather than ideology, "practice is the sole criterion of truth."[28] The new approach dovetailed with Deng's earlier statement that what interested him was not the color of the cat but whether it caught mice. Soviet leaders, who had once criticized Mao for moving too far to the left, now thought that Deng was going too far to the right. A Soviet visitor was said to have remarked, "If this is Marxism, I must reread Marx."[29] The Chinese Communist Party called it "socialism with Chinese characteristics." The authoritative *People's Daily*, China's party organ, admitted in December 1984 that the party had redefined Marxism. The party, it declared, must study other economic theories. After all, Marx wrote his treatises

> more than 100 years ago. Some of his ideas are no longer suited to today's situation, because Marx never experienced these times, nor did Engels or Lenin. So we cannot use Marxist and Leninist works to solve our present-day problems.[30]

After China repaid its loans to the Soviet Union by the mid-1960s, it had no foreign direct investment (FDI) of any sort. When Deng came to power, the Chinese economy was completely isolated from the world's economy. All this was to change, and quickly at that. That capitalists—and foreigners no less—could set up shop in Communist China remained an outlandish idea. Indeed, the law prohibited it. In the fateful year of 1979, however, a new foreign investment law legalized FDI. At first, FDI was limited to China's "Four Special Economic Zones," where limited joint equity ventures were given a test run. Further changes in the law, in 1984, set the stage for an accelerated growth in FDI.

China's economic growth was fueled primarily by its own capital investments, its high savings rate, and the plowing back of profits into further development. Foreign capital played a substantial role as well, much of it coming from Japan and the Four Tigers, their earlier economic miracles underwriting that of China. The extent of FDI in China is difficult to measure with precision. Some of it was intended, but never used; some came from Hong Kong where bank capital from the mainland was recycled back to China. But the sums were vast and steadily growing, topping $100 billion in 2010. In the thirty years between 1984 and 2013, the sum of "utilized" investments ran to more than $1.3 trillion.[31] In the early twenty-first century, one-half of all FDI by the industrialized OECD nations went to China.

Once Deng opened China's door to outside capital, multinationals (foreign global corporations) flocked to China. One after another, foreign companies pulled up stakes at home and planted them firmly on Chinese soil. Traditional US brands—Sunbeam, Apple, Nike—no longer carried the label "Made in the USA." "Italian" handbags carried the label "Made in China," but they were buried deep inside the smallest side-pockets. Foxconn, the largest private employer in China, was of Taiwanese origin.

For three decades the global companies were a major factor in China's industrial growth. During 1995–2007, they were responsible for nearly 60 percent of China's exports. The sum of foreign equity capital flowing into China was the most extensive in history. The Chinese Ministry of Commerce calculated that FDI enterprises accounted for 30 percent of China's industrial output (and 22 percent of industrial profits) and accounted for more than half of its exports and imports. FDI was a major component of China's high growth rate, adding perhaps as much as 3 to 4 percentage points.[32] China was also the recipient of cheap World Bank loans and grants and received the lion's share of the bank's international contracts in the developing world.[33]

To maximize profits, the companies had to keep wages low. When a new 2006 labor law made it more difficult for employers to cheat workers of their already meager wages, the American Chamber of Commerce in Shanghai and the United States–China Business Council resolutely opposed it. After they threatened to relocate US enterprises to other countries, the Chinese legislature accommodated them and rescinded the law.

Foreign invested enterprises (FIEs) were another contributing factor to China's economic growth. At the end of the 1990s, FIEs were responsible for more than half of China's exports; in electronics and telecommunication, it was 95 percent. In contrast, only 17 percent of the output by "non-FIEs" (that is, domestic companies) was for export. Between 1995 and 2004, FIEs employed a small percentage of the workforce, but their productivity contributed an estimated 20–30 percent to China's GDP.[34]

The FIEs also played a role in the accelerated transfer of technology and managerial expertise. FIEs created better-paying jobs than those offered by local companies and their on-the-job training contributed an increasingly more efficient labor pool. They also forced domestic companies to study the management practices of their joint venture partners and foreign competitors.

It was initially expected that the Chinese would produce cheap goods for the US market (even if it cost US manufacturing jobs) and would buy sophisticated US goods. It appeared to be a win-win situation, but the Chinese were not buying as expected. They retained a high savings rate, their households saving 25 percent of their income, as compared to less than 4 percent in the United States. It was one of the reasons for the trade imbalance; US consumers bought $35 billion in Chinese goods and services each months and sold China $11 billion.[35]

Economic liberalization transformed China from a drab and poor proletarian society into a lively consumer society. The Chinese people became generally more prosperous, and better fed, dressed, and housed than at any time in the past. Private enterprise, profit-seeking, capital investment, and the pursuit of private wealth were no longer taboo but were encouraged instead. Indeed, Deng declared, "to get rich is glorious." Enterprising Chinese succeeded in private business ventures and displayed their newfound wealth in conspicuous ways, purchasing large homes and automobiles and taking trips abroad. Although the authorities were concerned about the resentment their behavior caused, they nonetheless encouraged people to pursue the profit motive.

The year 1993 was a particularly good year for China. Its GDP grew by 13 percent, industrial output by 21 percent, and foreign trade by 18.2 percent. In that year alone, China received $27 billion in foreign capital—at the time the largest sum for any nation—and 140,000 new foreign-funded businesses were created.[36]

China's new wealth led to a building binge. Modern high-rises sprouted up in cities large and small linked by high-speed railroads and highways. Small towns and fishing villages suddenly morphed into boomtowns with large factories surrounded by towering, impersonal apartment buildings for workers newly arrived from the distant countryside. Shanghai's transformation was especially spectacular. By 1993, it had more than 2,000 new projects, involving more than $3.5 billion in foreign investments. More than 120 multinational corporations set up shop there.[37] The Three Gorges Dam on the Yangtze River, the world's largest power station, epitomized the enormous scale of China's industrial leap forward. It was the world's largest man-made structure, five times larger than the Hoover Dam, holding back a reservoir 370 miles long.

The economic surge served to dim the memory of Tiananmen and to divert attention away from politics. But there were problems attendant with such rapid growth. Chinese politicians understood that attendant corruption and the concentration of wealth in the hands of the few threatened social stability. It was a point even recognized by the wealthiest and most corrupt among them. In 2004, Xi Jinping, who would take the party's helm in 2012, warned its members to "rein in your spouses, children, relatives, friends and staff, and vow not to use power for personal gain." He understood that it was best that his daughter study at Harvard under an assumed name and he made sure that his family's vast assets were not in his, but in his sister's name.[38]

Rapid industrialization also brought with it a serious environmental problem. Pollution levels from coal-fired power plants were so severe that the Chinese cities became the most polluted in the world, the air barely fit for humans. London's "Great Smog of '52" (which caused thousands of premature deaths) and the biologically dead rivers and lakes in the United States of the 1960s had served as wake-up calls. The Chinese government, however, could only do so much, even though pollution in China dwarfed anything seen before. In the summer, Beijing was engulfed by sandstorms blowing from the encroaching deserts; in the winter, the coal-generated smog presented a serious health hazard. In the city of Harbin, in October 2013, the level of pollution was literally off the charts. There was little point in the government "shaming" the polluted cities, since it had been the government that had created the problem in the first place.

Its single-minded focus on growth meant that China had no effective means of dealing with the crisis. Handan, China's steel city, arguably the most polluted place on earth, was plagued with high mortality rates. Hansteel, however, found it cheaper to pay nearby residents a "pollution fee" of several hundred dollars per year rather than mend its ways.[39]

Trade relations with the United States remained contentious. Complaints about China's enormous trade surpluses, however, came from "Main Street" rather than "Wall Street," which had a stake in perpetuating the trade imbalance. China was also criticized for pirating intellectual property (computer software, videos, compact disks, scientific papers, etc.) and manipulating its currency to keep the prices of its exported goods artificially low.

Each month, US consumers demanded large quantities of Chinese goods priced in the Chinese currency, the renminbi (RMB, also known as the yuan). Meanwhile, Chinese consumers demanded far fewer goods priced in the stronger dollar. In the natural order of the marketplace, as directed by the laws of supply and demand, the RMB should have appreciated and the dollar should have depreciated. A cheaper dollar would make US-made goods cheaper, while a stronger RMB would raise the price of Chinese goods, thereby creating a more equitable trade balance. To ensure that Chinese goods remained cheap, however, the Central Bank of China bought US bonds, thus creating an artificially high demand for the dollar, which then remained artificially strong vis-à-vis the RMB. The beneficiaries were China's exporters, including the foreign companies doing business there. The Chinese currency, devalued at one point by an estimated 40 percent, was a subsidy to China's exporters and a tax on imports by making them more expensive. It was one of the reasons foreign companies shifted their production to China. Between 2000 and 2012, the US industrial sector lost an estimated six million jobs, about one half of its capacity. Every president since Ronald Reagan sought to persuade China to float its currency, but to no avail.[40]

In 2006, China surpassed Britain as the world's fourth largest economy (after the United States, Japan, and Germany); by 2010, it trailed only the United States. Its gigantic surplus in foreign trade (in 2007, over $250 billion with the United States alone) signified it had become the world's factory. Its most industrialized province, Guangdong (adjacent to Hong Kong), employed a workforce of approximately 18 million industrial workers, larger than that of the entire United States (14 million). One particular industrial firm in Guangdong—the Taiwan-based Foxconn, the world's largest manufacturer of electronic components—employed over 200,000 workers.[41]

Historical transformations of this scale and speed cannot be the result of a single cause. Invariably, a number of factors are involved. China's rise could not have been possible without its capable entrepreneurs, engineers and planners, but also the normalization of relations with the United States, its entry into the vast US market, and its admission to the World Trade Organization (WTO) in November 2001. Foreign corporations provided models for industrialization, capital investment, technology, and financial institutions.

The sustained rapid growth of economies is historically a modern phenomenon. Before the Industrial Revolution, innovations came in slow doses, barely changing the lives of peoples over centuries. But once the Industrial Revolution moved into high gear, innovation followed innovation, fueled by experimentation in scientific laboratories. The process sped up in the nineteenth and twentieth centuries.

To catch up with other economies became a—relatively—easy process. The newly industrializing states tapped inexpensively into the earlier innovations and into available capital. Starting from a low level of development, their economies grew more rapidly than those of the more established countries. The United States and Germany closed the gap with Britain and then surpassed it at the end of the nineteenth century. After World War II, Japan closed the gap with the United States. After that, South Korea closed its gap with Japan. Once it was invited to join the global economy, it was China's turn to close the gap with the industrialized world.[42]

For thirty years, Chinese wages were kept low. Starting in 2007, however, a long-predicted trend came to fruition. A shortage of labor led to a 10–30 percent rise in assembly-line wages, depending on skills. Vietnam, with an average wage of one-quarter of that in China, was thus able to attract increasingly larger amounts of foreign capital. As in China, its one-party government promised stability and greater profits. Still, China remained the main destination for foreign capital. In 2007, it attracted $83 billion in investments. Vietnam, however, with but one-sixteenth the population of China, drew an impressive $17.86 billion.[43]

## Notes

1. The size of the GNP of the Soviet Union was not known for certain, but it was generally believed in the West that Japan's was as large and probably larger by 1980. Its per capita GNP was far larger.

2. From the 1950s, Japan steadily increased its defense spending; by the 1980s it was about 6 percent of the annual budget, or 1 percent of its GNP, compared to US defense expenditures of approximately 6–8 percent of its GNP.

3. Robot Institute of America, *Japan 1989: An International Comparison* (Tokyo: Keizai Koho Center, 1988), p. 27.

4. This high rate of savings was accounted for in part by the government taxation laws and the relatively low pensions for Japanese workers. Other factors included the huge lump-sum biannual bonuses Japanese workers received and traditional habits of saving. Similar saving habits were found in other Asian countries, such as South Korea and Taiwan.

5. Washington made sure that certain nations, particularly Germany and Japan, had "equal access" to cheap raw materials, the quest for which was a major reason for their aggressive foreign policy leading to World War II.

6. Chalmers Johnson, *MITI and the Japanese Miracle: The Growth of Industrial Policy, 1925–1975* (Stanford: Stanford University Press, 1982), p. 15, argues that for nations where investment rates were high, such as Japan, South Korea, and Taiwan, "very high defense expenditures have had little or no impact on economic performance."

7. "Japan Drops Its Symbolic Ceiling on Defense Spending," Inquirer Wire Services, December 31, 1986; Neil Weinberg and Kiyoe Minami, "The Front Line," Forbes.com, September 19, 2005.

8. Japan also built up a large surplus—$20 billion in 1987—through its trade with the European Community, where the demand for protection against Japanese imports was even stronger than in the United States. Japan also had large trade surpluses with most Asian nations.

9. John E. Woodruff, "Veteran Envoy Mansfield to Retire from Tokyo Post," *Baltimore Sun*, November 15, 1988.

10. Ernest F. Hollings, "We're Winning the Cold War While Losing the Trade War," *Baltimore Sun*, December 17, 1989, p. 4N.

11. See Clyde V. Prestowitz, *Trading Places: How We Are Giving Our Future to Japan and How to Reclaim It*, 2nd ed. (New York: Basic Books, 1989), chapter 2. By August 1982, the Japanese had captured 65 percent of the world market for microchips. In 1980, when the United States was still trying to get its 64K chip out of the lab, the Japanese had already produced prototypes of the 256K chip.

12. Richard W. Wright and Gunter A. Pauli, *The Second Wave: Japan's Global Assault on Financial Services* (New York: St. Martin's Press, 1987).

13. Edwin Reischauer, Center for East Asian Studies, *The United States and Japan in 1992: A Quest for New Roles* (Washington, DC: Johns Hopkins University Press, 1992), pp. 51–58.

14. James Fallows, *Looking at the Sun: The Rise of the New East Asian Economic and Political System* (New York: Vintage, 1995), p. 203.

15. data.worldbank.org/indicators

16. Rick Wartzman, "Japan: Rethinking Lifetime Employment," Bloomberg Businessweek, September 4, 2009.

17. Shigeyoshi Kimura, "Japan Blames Inaction for Economy," Associated Press, December 12, 1998.

18. "Japan's Depopulation Time Bomb," *Japan Times*, April 17, 2013.

19 Stephanie Cooke, *In Mortal Hands: A Cautionary History of the Nuclear Age* (Melbourne: McPherson, 2009), pp. 388, 391.

20 The World Health Organization rated Taiwan's birth control program first among developing nations in 1989. Singapore rated second, South Korea third, and Hong Kong fifth. The PRC was fourth. "ROC Rated Top for Birth Curbs by World Group," *Free China Journal*, December 21, 1989.

21 See Chalmers Johnson, *Blowback: The Costs and Consequences of American Empire* (New York: Henry Holt, 2000), pp. 112–116. Johnson bases his account on the work of US journalist Tim Shorrock. The South Korean government admitted to only 240 deaths.

22. David Rees, *A Short History of Modern Korea* (New York: Hippocrene Books, 1988), p. 168. In 1975, US secretary of defense James Schlesinger stated explicitly that in the event of a North Korean attack the United States would not become involved in "endless ancillary military operations" but would "go for the heart" of its opponent.

23. "Placing Bets on a New Korea," *The Economist*, December 21, 1991, pp. 27–28. In 1990, South Korea had over five times higher per capita income and twenty times more foreign trade than the north; the north spent more than 20 percent of its meager GNP on its military, whereas the south spent only 4 percent of its burgeoning GNP on its military.

24. Walter Russell Mead, "More Method Than Madness in North Korea," *New York Times Magazine*, September 15, 1996, p. 50.

25. "North Korea Makes Overture to South," *Baltimore Sun*, February 26, 1998, p. 14A.

26. Anthony Faiola, "As Tensions Subside Between Two Koreas, US Strives to Adjust," *Washington Post*, July 25, 2004, p. A16; Sung-Yoon Lee, "Engaging North Korea: The Clouded Legacy of South Korea's Sunshine Policy," American Enterprise Institute, April 19, 2010.

27. Justin Yufi Lin, "The China Miracle Demystified," presentation at the Econometric Society World Congress in Shanghai, August 19, 2010, p. 1.

28. Immanuel C. Y. Hsu, *The Rise of Modern China* (New York: Oxford University Press, 1983), p. 804.

29. Quoted in John F. Burns, "Canton Booming on Marxist Free Enterprise," *New York Times*, November 11, 1985, p. A1.

30. Deng Xiaoping in a front-page commentary in the December 7, 1984, edition of *People's Daily*, quoted in "China Calls Rigid Adherence to Marxism 'Stupid,'" *New York Times*, December 9, 1984.

31. World Bank, World Development Indicators.

32. Data.worldbank.org; World Bank, "Foreign Direct Investment—The China story," July 16, 2010; John Whalley and Xian Xin, "China and Foreign Direct Investment," *Brookings Trade Forum*, 2007, pp. 61–62, 73; Ouyang Jianyu, "Foreign Direct Investment in China and Its Impact on Manufacturing Growth" (The Hague: Institute of Social Studies, Working Paper Series No. 237, January 1997).

33. Howard Schneider, "Patronizing China, at U.S. Expense," *Washington Post*, October 15, p. A15.

34. Whalley and Xian, "China and Foreign Direct Investment," pp. 63–64; Shuxun Chen and Charles Wolf, Jr., *China, the United States, and the Global Economy* (Santa Monica, CA: Rand Corporation, 2001); Yasheng Huang, "The Role of Foreign-Invested Enterprises in the Chinese Economy," pp. 147, 155–158.

35. Adam Davidson, "Come On, China, Buy Our Stuff," *New York Times*, January 25, 2012.

36. Orville Schell, *Mandate of Heaven: A New Generation of Entrepreneurs, Dissidents, Bohemians, and Technocrats* (New York: Simon and Schuster, 1995), p. 433.

37. Ibid., p. 433.

38. "Xi Jinping Millionaire Relations Reveal Fortunes of Elite," *Bloomberg News*, June 29, 2012.

39. Ian Johnson, "In the Air: Discontent Grows in China's Most Polluted Cities," *The New Yorker*, December 2, 2013, pp. 32–73.

40. Davidson, "Come On, China, Buy Our Stuff."

41. James Fallows, "China Makes, the World Takes," *The Atlantic*, July/August 2007.

42. Lin, "The China Miracle Demystified," pp. 2–5.

43. Keith Bradsher, "Investors Seek Asian Options to Costly China," *New York Times*, June 18, 2008; Brendan Smith, Tim Costello, and Jeremy Brecher, "Chinese Heat Is on US Sweatshop Lobby," *Asia Times Online*, April 5, 2007, www.atimes.com.

# 19

# Russia:
# The Legacy of Soviet Empire

**After Leonid Brezhnev came to power in the Soviet Union in 1964,** he showed little taste for reform. Innovations in the economic sector that his predecessor, Nikita Khrushchev, had introduced were quickly shelved, and the Soviet Union entered a seventeen-year-long "era of stagnation" (as its critics called it) that only a change in leadership could reverse. In 1979, the Soviet ministries ceased publishing statistics to avoid revealing that the country was falling farther behind the West in productivity, health care, and standard of living. In March 1985, the Communist Party elected as general secretary Mikhail Gorbachev, who immediately took a number of highly publicized steps to try and transform the Soviet Union in the hope of saving it.

Gorbachev advocated a new openness, or "glasnost," giving Soviet citizens and officials alike the freedom to discuss not only the nation's strengths but also its weaknesses. *Pravda*, the newspaper of the Communist Party, began to cover disasters such as the nuclear accident at Chernobyl, floods, collisions between ships in the Black Sea, corruption, cover-ups, shoddy workmanship, and police abuse. Motion pictures never before shown to the public played to sold-out crowds. The Gorbachev revolution was on its way.

## Gorbachev's "New Thinking"
When the party turned to Mikhail Gorbachev, the Soviet public and the West knew little about him. In December 1984, he had made his successful debut on the world stage during a visit to London, where he had behaved unlike previ-

ous Soviet visitors. Khrushchev's visit in 1955 had turned sour when he reminded his hosts ominously of the Soviet Union's potentially devastating nuclear arsenal. Gorbachev spoke, instead, of the need to disarm and reminded his British hosts of their wartime alliance with the Soviet Union and their losses at Coventry. Instead of the customary visit to Karl Marx's grave at Highgate Cemetery, Gorbachev visited Westminster Abbey. Margaret Thatcher, Britain's conservative prime minister, said: "I like him. We can do business with him."

Gorbachev soon caused another stir with his speech in February 1985, in which he declared that the Soviet Union needed a radical transformation. "Paper shuffling, an addiction to fruitless meetings," and "windbaggery" would no longer do.[1] He proved to be a reformer who understood that politics is the art of the possible. In his first speech as general secretary of the party, he placated the right wing with his reaffirmation of the old values, but as time went by he showed that he intended to carry through a radical "perestroika," or reconstruction. To that end, "new thinking" was required.

Among Gorbachev's targets were the centrally planned industrial complex and the collective farms Stalin had introduced starting in the late 1920s. He ended the long and debilitating conflict between the state and organized religions, ended the isolation of his country's intellectuals, invited those who had been expelled to return to their native soil, sent an unprecedented number of Soviet citizens abroad, permitted the sale of Western publications, forced the Soviet Union's conservative historians to come to grips with the past, and broke the party's monopoly on political power. He also redefined the Soviet Union's position vis-à-vis China, Eastern Europe, the West, and the global South and took the Soviet army out of Afghanistan. By doing what had been thought no leader in the Kremlin could or would even try to do, Gorbachev turned the science of "Kremlinology" on its head.

Gorbachev called for an open and honest discussion, "to call things by their name." To this end, he had to give society, not just the party, a voice. Glasnost, from the Russian word for "voice," therefore, became the first order of business. The most severe test of glasnost came in April 1986, when an atomic reactor in Chernobyl, in the Ukrainian Republic, suffered a meltdown and an explosion, spewing radioactive matter into the Belorussian Republic, Scandinavia, down into Germany, and as far south as Italy. Soviet technology was contaminating what Gorbachev earlier had called "our common European home." The recognition of mistakes, Gorbachev said, was the "best medicine against arrogance and complacency." But for the first nineteen days after Chernobyl, no acknowledgment of the disaster came out of the Kremlin. When Gorbachev finally spoke on national television, he admitted that a nuclear plant—a symbol of Soviet technological prowess—was burning out of control.

Gorbachev used Chernobyl to weaken the conservative wing of the party, the chief obstructionists to perestroika. He repeatedly used political, natural, and man-made disasters—on the surface, setbacks—to his advantage.

Artists and writers quickly tested the limits of glasnost. The consequence was a veritable flood of works that had been written years before "for the drawer," waiting to see the light of day. Among them were Anatoli Rybakov's *Children of the Arbat*, a novel set in 1933–1934 at the beginning of Stalin's terror, and films such as *Our Armored Train*, a critical dissection of Stalin's legacy.

The acid test of glasnost would be how the Kremlin treated the writings of the exiled Alexander Solzhenitsyn, whose novel *One Day in the Life of Ivan Denisovich* had been the Soviet literary sensation of 1962. Khrushchev had used Solzhenitsyn's exposé of the Soviet prison system to discredit Stalin. In his later writings, however, Solzhenitsyn, notably in his three-volume *Gulag Archipelago*, laid the blame squarely at the feet of the revered Lenin—whose stature in the Soviet Union was no less than that of a saint. Gorbachev and his Politburo initially opposed the publication of *Gulag Archipelago* on the grounds that it undermined "the foundation on which our present life rests." But public pressure, expressed in thousands of letters and telegrams, had an unprecedented impact on Soviet cultural history. In June 1989, Gorbachev told his Politburo that the decision whether to publish Solzhenitsyn should be made by editors, not the party. After an absence of twenty-five years, Solzhenitsyn was reintroduced to Soviet readers.[2]

Soviet historians generally wanted no part of Gorbachev's "new thinking." Early 1988, however, saw the purge of the editorial boards of the leading historical journals. The lead article in the February 1988 issue of *Voprosy istorii* (Problems of History) announced that the time had come to discuss events hitherto taboo, such as Stalin's purges of the party, the "tragedy" of collectivization in Kazakhstan, and the nationality problem. Historical journals began to participate in the political rehabilitation of Khrushchev and victims of Stalin's purges and went so far as to publish Leon Trotsky's essay, "The Stalin School of Falsification of History." In the huge Lenin Library in Moscow, "new" books were made available to readers—books that had been published decades earlier and then suppressed.[3]

Most intellectuals, freed from the constraints of the past, expressed distinctly liberal, Western values. They supported Memorial, an organization honoring the memory of those who had fallen victim to Stalin's purges. But glasnost also gave writers of an anti-Western, anti-liberal persuasion a voice and showed that the nativist tradition still ran deep. Their organization, Pamiat (Remembrance), recalled history differently from Memorial. Pamiat did not consider the Stalinist legacy to be the nation's source of difficulty; instead it blamed Zionists. In Pamiat's view, Stalin had played the role of the good tsar, terrible but righteous, who had punished the wicked and brought the nation to its military and industrial power.

## Industry

When Gorbachev spoke of an economic perestroika, he expected an orderly process. It became clear, however, that reconstruction would be extraordinarily difficult, compounded by the fact that many workers and managers of factories and collective farms looked upon the Gorbachev revolution with skepticism, even resentment. They had learned to fulfill the plan as spelled out by the ministries and saw few reasons to embrace a new approach that threatened to punish those who failed. In the mid-1960s, Premier Alexei Kosygin similarly had sought to reorganize the economy so that factories would have to sink or swim on their own. In 1965, "accountability" became the watchword of the Kosygin-led reforms. The conservatives, however, soon brought this experiment to a halt.

The majority of the population expected the state to solve their problems, an attitude that had seeped into their blood. When Gorbachev suggested that government subsidies—for bread, milk, apartments, education, health care, transportation, and so on—come to an end and spoke of closing down inefficient factories and raising prices, he hit a raw nerve. Perestroika threatened to bring not only higher prices but also unemployment. The relative security of the past began to give way to an uncertain future.

## Farming

In his speech on November 3, 1987, commemorating the seventieth anniversary of the October Revolution, Gorbachev—under pressure from conservatives—still defended the necessity of Stalin's collectivization. In October 1988, however, in a televised address, he proposed radical changes. Farmers, he insisted, must once again become "masters of their land." Five months later, in March 1989, he took his case to the party's decisionmaking body, the Central Committee, where he summarized the failure of Soviet agriculture. Stalin, he explained, had bled the farmers by setting artificially low farm prices. Khrushchev and Brezhnev subsequently spent huge sums to improve productivity and eliminate waste on collective and state farms, but to little avail. The time had come to abandon decisionmaking at the top and to learn from experimentation and from the lessons that could be gleaned from the United States, China, India, and the Green Revolution.[4]

On April 9, 1989, the government passed a law permitting private individuals and collectives to lease land, buildings, mineral deposits, small factories, and machines from the state "for up to 50 years and more." TASS, the Soviet news agency, acknowledged that the law intended to promote the establishment of private family farms.

## The Role of the Party

When, in the spring of 1989, Gorbachev established a new legislative body, the Congress of People's Deputies, not only were the majority of the delegates freely elected, but many were non-Communists. The weakness of the party became glaringly apparent when many of its candidates failed to receive a majority of votes, even though they ran unopposed.

Gorbachev, however, did not call for the abolition of Article 6 of the 1977 Constitution, which granted the Communist Party a monopoly of political power. He still lacked the votes in the party's Central Committee to do so. Yet, the sentiment to scrap Article 6 ran deep. During his January 1990 visit to Vilnius, Lithuania, where the republic's Communist Party had already legalized a multiparty system and elections, Gorbachev declared "we should not be afraid [of a multiparty system], the way the devil fears incense."[5] In early February 1990, during an emergency session of the party's Central Committee, after three days of debates, the party did the unthinkable when it legalized opposition parties. Lenin's legacy, the Communist Party as the sole driving force in the Soviet Union, became the casualty of the "February Revolution" of 1990.

## The Nationality Question

Gorbachev's emphasis on glasnost set in motion a discussion of the Soviet Union's nationality question. Russians made up 145 million of the Soviet Union's 282 million people; of the other Slavs, 51 million were Ukrainians, and 10 million were Belorussians. Over centuries, Ukrainians and Belorussians had developed their own national consciousness, and many among them sought independence from Moscow.

The Communist revolution of 1917 had taken place in an empire of well over 100 nationalities, which in the course of the last four centuries had been incorporated into the Russian state. According to the official Soviet interpretation, however, the revolution had forged a new social consciousness among the varied ethnic groups, which now voluntarily resided in the new Soviet state. The fact that none had requested to secede from the Soviet Union—as permitted under the constitution—was proof that a new Communist consciousness had obliterated national antagonisms, that the Soviet citizens made up one happy family.

Glasnost blew the official theory apart. Discussions revealed deep-rooted grievances among national minorities, and they were directed not necessarily against the dominant Russian majority but against each other. At a minimum, the fourteen non-Russian republics sought economic and political autonomy, perhaps something on the order of the Swiss model—a nation of four nationalities with four official languages. Gorbachev favored this approach, as it would keep the Soviet Union together.

That proposal found little traction among the non-Russian peoples. They called instead for the dismemberment of the empire, that is, a 180-degree reversal of Russian history. It was no coincidence that the Russian monarchs who had been granted the appellation "Great"—Ivan III, Peter I, and Catherine II—had earned it by virtue of expanding their empire's borders. All this was now in jeopardy.

The most serious challenge came from the Baltic republics—Lithuania, Latvia, and Estonia—where nationalists began to test the limits of Gorbachev's "democratization." First, they demanded economic autonomy, stating they were merely supporting perestroika—that is, the decentralization of the top-heavy economy. Then they insisted on—and gained—the right to fly their old flags, openly practice their religions, and rewrite their histories. They spoke of fielding their own teams for future Olympic Games and their Communist parties insisted on their right to act independently from Moscow. Then came the inevitable talk of secession.

The reason for the radicalism in the Baltic states can be found in their recent history. They had been part of the Russian empire for over 200 years, but in the wake of World War I, they became independent. Their independence, however, lasted only until 1940. On the eve of World War II, Hitler and Stalin agreed on a nonaggression pact and for good measure decided—on the basis of a secret protocol—to divide Eastern Europe. The Baltic states fell to Stalin who then deported or murdered hundreds of thousands of suspected nationalists. Glasnost's critical reassessment of the Stalin era could not ignore the infamous Hitler-Stalin pact. After much soul-searching and hesitation, official Soviet historians finally admitted that, yes, there had been a secret protocol in violation of international law.

The Communist Party of Lithuania voted in December 1989, to establish its independence from Moscow. The mass movement Sajudis demanded (1) "freedom and independence" and the repeal of the Hitler-Stalin pact, (2) the removal of the "occupant Soviet Army," (3) compensation for "the genocide of Lithuanian citizens and their exile" and for Soviet-caused environmental destruction, and (4) the reestablishment of friendly relations between Lithuania and the Soviet Union on the basis of their 1920 peace treaty.

In January 1990, Gorbachev took a highly publicized trip to Lithuania to convince the people there of the dangers of secessionism. He pleaded, cajoled, and issued thinly veiled threats, all to no avail. As his limousine departed for the airport, the crowds jeered him. In Moscow, the spokesman for the foreign ministry, Gennady Gerasimov, remarked that the divorce between Lithuania and Russia must follow an orderly course. Lithuanians quickly replied that there had been no marriage, only an abduction and rape. Two months later, on March 11, 1990, the newly and freely elected parliament of Lithuania unilaterally declared its independence.

Not all nationalist grievances were directed against the Russians. As Lithuanians demonstrated against the Russians, the Polish minority in Lithuania demonstrated for incorporation into Poland. Nearly every Soviet republic had territorial claims against a neighbor. The bloodiest clashes were between the Christian Armenians and the Turkic-speaking Shiite Muslims of Azerbaijan. When Gorbachev gave the Armenians a voice, they immediately demanded the return of a piece of their historical territory, Nagorno-Karabakh, which Stalin had placed under Azeri administration in 1923.

Armenian national consciousness was deeply affected by the 1915 massacre at the hands of the Turks, in which 1.5 million Armenians perished.[6] The Turks then seized what once had been Armenians lands and as a result, the symbol of Armenian nationalism, Biblical Mount Ararat, is inside Turkey, just across the border from Armenia's capital, Yerevan.

In February 1988, over a period of several days, an estimated 100,000 people demonstrated in Yerevan against Azerbaijan—and against Moscow and Communism. At the end of the month, Azeris responded with a pogrom in Sumgait, a city north of Baku, the capital of Azerbaijan, murdering thirty-two Armenians.

In June 1988, the Armenian Communist Party voted to reconquer Nagorno-Karabakh, while the Azeri Communist Party voted to defend it. For the first time, Communist parties of the Soviet Union split along national lines and then went to war against each other. Only Moscow's intervention minimized further bloodshed, but the fear and hatred remained. When, in December 1988, an earthquake destroyed much of eastern Armenia, killing tens of thousands, Azeris rejoiced over the misery of their despised neighbors.

On January 13, 1990, in a replay of the Sumgait pogrom—this time in Baku—Azeris murdered at least sixty Armenians. Gorbachev decreed a state of emergency in the region. When it had no effect, he sent the Soviet army and troops of the Interior Ministry into Baku, explaining that he had no choice because "neither side listened to the voice of reason."[7]

• • •

Gorbachev's revolution was the product of historic processes. The social conditions that had lent support for Lenin and Stalin had undergone significant changes since 1917. Between 1964 and the mid-1980s, the number of Soviet citizens with a high-school education or better had increased from 25 million to 125 million.[8] When de-Stalinization began with Khrushchev's 1956 speech, more than half of the nation's population still lived in the countryside; that figure was down to about one-quarter by the late 1980s. Gorbachev inherited a nation with a sizable and largely urbanized middle class. His generation (he was born in 1931) came to political maturity during Khrushchev's "thaw" and his attacks on Stalin. Gorbachev's perestroika became a battle between reformers and the dead weight of history, the legacy of centralization and intolerance bestowed on the nation by generations of tsars and commissars.

In December 1988, the prestigious West German news weekly *Der Spiegel* named Gorbachev its "Man of the Year: Man of the Hour"—the first time it had bestowed such recognition on anyone. It compared him to the Westernizer Peter the Great, the Protestant reformer Martin Luther, and the emancipator Abraham Lincoln. In January 1990, *Time* magazine named him "Man of the Decade." The applause, however, was for a tightrope walker who was only half-way across Niagara Falls.

## The End of the Soviet Union

Gorbachev's perestroika alienated those on the right, who thought he was irrevocably disrupting Soviet society, as well as those on the left, who felt the reforms were not going far enough. By autumn 1990, both the left and the right wanted him out.

After years of hesitation, Gorbachev and his economic advisers concluded that the freeing of prices (determined by supply and demand) and the right to make a private profit were not merely necessary evils but positive economic forces. In other words, the Soviet Union would legalize capitalism. At the end of 1990s, Gorbachev was prepared to accept a radical proposal by Stanislav Shatalin, an economist long opposed to the Soviet centralized economy. The Shatalin Plan called for a sudden 500-day transition from the Soviet system to what was still called a "market" economy, a pseudonym for capitalism. Shatalin, however, was unable to answer basic questions about the economic, social, and political consequences of his bold proposal.

At this juncture, Gorbachev moved to the right. He feared the so-called "democratic opposition" on the left, led by Boris Yeltsin, a fellow Politburo member who, in July 1990, had staged a dramatic exit from the party. Yeltsin's aim was nothing less than the dissolution of the Soviet Union. To protect himself against Yeltsin, Gorbachev surrounded himself with conservatives uncomfortable with perestroika.

In April 1991, Gorbachev and Yeltsin worked out a formula for the decentralization of the Soviet Union. The republics would be able to exercise virtually unlimited power on the local level, while Moscow would continue to handle matters such as currency, diplomacy, and defense.

The following June, Yeltsin won a historic victory at the polls when he was elected president of the Russian republic, the largest component of the Soviet Union. He was the first popularly elected Russian head of state. As the political tide moved to the left, Gorbachev commissioned the economist Grigorii Yavlinskii, with the help of economics professors from Harvard and the Massachusetts Institute of Technology, to launch a full-blown capitalist experiment.

These events triggered a military coup by desperate party members who saw their power slipping away. On August 19, 1991, while Gorbachev vacationed in the Crimea, the leaders of Soviet military and paramilitary organizations—Defense Minister Dmitrii Yazov, the chief of the secret police (the KGB) Vladimir Kriuchkov, and Minister of the Interior Boris Pugo—sent tanks into the streets of Moscow and declared a state of emergency. Two of Gorbachev's recent appointees, Gennadii Yanaev and Valentin Pavlov, declared that Gorbachev had fallen ill and thus was unable to fulfill his duties as president. At a live news conference later that day, Yanaev stated that "his good friend Gorbachev" would some day return to political life in another capacity. Virtually no one believed his account, particularly as neither Gorbachev nor his physician was present to confirm Gorbachev's illness. A subversive camera operator instead focused on Yanaev's trembling hands.

Since the days of Lenin, Communist ideology had stressed unity of action. During the attempted coup, however, there was none. The conspirators had acted in desperation and haste, without planning or coordination.[9] They failed to enlist a unified military. Some commanders were deeply unhappy with the state of affairs to which perestroika had brought them, but even they were unwilling to use force against their fellow citizens. Other commanders openly opposed the coup. A similar division was apparent in the KGB and the party. The coup collapsed with scarcely a shot fired. The conspirators had but one hope: that Soviet society would tacitly accept the transfer of power. Back in 1964, when the party had changed leadership, the KGB was surprised to find out that not a single demonstration or voice of support was heard on behalf of Khrushchev. This time it was different. President Yeltsin, standing on top of a renegade tank in front of the "White House," the parliament building, denounced the coup and demanded Gorbachev's return.

The conspirators had gone after Gorbachev, the head of both the party and the Soviet government, without taking into account the fact that political power had already become diffused throughout the Soviet Union. Yeltsin's election as president of Russia in June 1991 had already created a situation of "dual power": Yeltsin and Gorbachev were in effect coequals. Had Yeltsin been arrested and had Gorbachev accepted the transfer of power (as he was pressured to do for three days), the coup might have succeeded.

Yeltsin held the Communist Party—and indirectly Gorbachev, its general secretary—responsible for the coup and suspended the party's activities indefinitely. The conspirators had hoped to preserve the Soviet Union; instead, they hastened its demise. By the end of 1991, the red flag with its golden hammer and sickle, the symbol of the Bolshevik seizure of power in 1917, came down from the buildings of the Kremlin and was replaced with the old flag of imperial Russia.

The now independent republics inherited a disintegrating economy. By 1990, the Soviet Union was already in a depression as severe as that the West had experienced in the 1930s. It was in the midst of this depression that Yeltsin committed Russia to the full embrace of capitalism. The network of resource allocation was disrupted and factories had to fend for themselves to obtain necessary supplies. Ethnic tensions added to the economic chaos. Armenians no longer provided parts to machine-tool factories in Moscow, and Russians refused to deliver steel to the huge truck factories of independence-minded Tatarstan on the Volga River. The result was increased idleness in factories, empty stores, and a continued decline in the standard of living.

The collapse of the Communist regimes in Eastern Europe brought an end to COMECON, the Kremlin-imposed system of economic integration. It meant, for instance, that the former Soviet Union, which had obtained about half of its medicines from COMECON trading partners, saw a drastic decline in its already perilous health care system. Hungarians were still willing to sell their buses to Russia, but now only for hard—that is, Western—currency.

To cushion the shock of higher prices, Yeltsin's government printed ever more money. The result was an inflation rate of 2,000 percent and a government budget deficit of 25 percent in 1992. Wages declined relative to the newly freed prices to the point where, during winter 1991–1992, 90 percent of Russians lived below the official subsistence level.[10]

Yeltsin and his economic advisers were committed to a "grand bargain," the entrance into the global market economy and membership in the International Monetary Fund. It was predicated on obtaining aid from the capitalist nations, which were basking in the glow of their ideological victory over the Soviet Union. Unfortunately, the money markets had dried up. US president Ronald Reagan's push for military superiority had produced a binge of borrowing. A worldwide economic recession and the collapse of the Japanese stock market—a decline of approximately 60 percent of its value since 1986—ended the era of cheap capital. The German government provided more assistance to the former Soviet Union than did any other nation, but it, too, had little money to spare because of the heavy cost of German reunification.

The IMF was willing to lend money to the former Soviet republics, provided they balanced their budgets, repaid their debts, and adopted convertible currency to permit foreign investors to take their profits out of the country. The IMF demanded, moreover, the freeing of prices (notably of energy), letting unprofitable businesses fail, and protecting the sanctity of foreign investments. Once the price of oil—previously sold to the Soviet Union's consumers at $3 per barrel—was raised to the world market's price of $19, Western investments and technology arrived.

Russia's transition to capitalism produced a class of private entrepreneurs (who only recently had been called capitalist exploiters), as well as an impoverished, humiliated, and embittered mass of people who could not understand how their great nation had reached this juncture in its history. When the Communist Party went on trial in fall 1992, the Russian people were more concerned with their economic lot. A political commentator remarked that even to dream of such a trial in the past could have led to arrest—but now no one cared.[11]

. . .

After the dissolution of the Soviet Union, the nationality problems remained. Armenia had the most homogeneous population, as approximately 90 percent of its citizens were Armenians. But in Latvia, 34 percent were Russian, as were 38 percent in Kazakhstan and 13 percent in Ukraine.[12]

Georgia witnessed the most serious political problems among any of the former Soviet republics. Abkhazia in western Georgia and South Ossetia (which Stalin had separated from North Ossetia inside Russia proper), provinces with their own history and languages distinct from Georgian, declared their independence.

In May 1991, the anti-Communist Georgian nationalist Zviad Gamsakhurdia became the first democratically elected president of a former Soviet republic. He was also the first dissident to come to power who, in the past, had expressed admiration for Western political ideals. Within months, however, Gamsakhurdia began to arrest political opponents, whom he denounced—in language reminiscent of his countryman Joseph Stalin—as spies, bandits, and criminals, "enemies of the people" all. In a fit of chauvinism and paranoia, he sought to ban interracial marriages, by which, he charged, the Russians sought "to dilute the Georgian race."[13] In September 1991, he declared a state of emergency. In the ensuing civil war between Gamsakhurdia loyalists and his opponents, heavy fighting destroyed the center of the capital, Tbilisi. After Gamsakhurdia fled, the victorious faction turned to Eduard Shevardnadze, Gorbachev's former foreign minister, to bring stability to Georgia.

Yeltsin, who had frequently criticized Gorbachev for refusing to grant the Baltic states their independence, had to deal with his own secessionists in Russia when the Muslim Chechen-Ingush (in November 1991) along the Georgian border and the Tatars (in March 1992) along the Volga River declared their independence.

An even more ominous development began to appear: the call for "ethnic cleansing." Russians demanded the expulsion of Jews and Azeris from Moscow, Chechen-Ingush were driven out of Volgograd, and in Stavropol attempts were made to force out Armenian families. In the Kuban, north of the Caucasus Mountains, Russian Cossacks appeared in their traditional dress, insisting on the ouster of Turkic-speaking Meskhetians.[14]

## The Yeltsin Presidency

The most prominent feature of Yeltsin's embrace of capitalism was the transfer of state property to individuals with connections to his government. The oil and gas industry, once the Soviet Union's chief source of Western currency, fell into private hands busy milking state-owned properties. The situation was corrupt even by Soviet standards.[15] In the struggle for the spoils of victory, theft, extortion, and even murder became widespread—while the devil took the hindmost. Those left behind found that the former Soviet safety net contained increasingly larger holes as state subsidies were eliminated one by one. Inflation wiped out the savings of millions of citizens. Cynics remarked that "we thought the Communists were lying to us about [the glory of] socialism and [the evils] of capitalism, but it turns out they were lying only about socialism."[16]

The economic disaster triggered a rebellion by Russia's parliament. When, in early spring 1993, Yeltsin considered dissolving the parliament and holding new elections, parliament countered with an attempt to impeach him. The issue was settled with violence. On September 22, 1993, Yeltsin—already accustomed to ruling by fiat—issued Decree No. 1,400, ordering the dissolution of parliament. Parliament refused to go quietly, and its building—the so-called White House—became a defiant armed camp surrounded by concertina wire. In early October, 10,000 anti-Yeltsin demonstrators overwhelmed the police and then marched to the state television complex (which was heavily biased in favor of Yeltsin) to try and seize it. Yeltsin responded by shelling the White House—the same building that had served as a symbol of democracy and resistance to the Communists in August 1991. Russia's short-lived democratic experiment was over.

Yeltsin disbanded parliament, suspended the Constitutional Court, and banned the opposition press and television. The top half of the once gleaming White House was charred by tank artillery fire, and 144 Russians lay dead. Throughout, the Western powers refused to condemn Yeltsin and continued to refer to him as a "democrat," declaring that the radicals had forced his hand. The new constitution promulgated later in 1993 gave Yeltsin the power to rule virtually without the legislature.

### The First Chechen War

Then came the violence in Chechnya. It began at the end of 1994, when Yeltsin decided he could no longer tolerate claims of independence by Chechnya, one of Russia's eighty-nine regional subdivisions. Yeltsin, the chief architect of the dissolution of the Soviet Union, would not permit a breakup of his Russian Federation.

The Muslim Chechens, along the northern slopes of the Caucasus Mountains, had been brought under Moscow's control in the mid-nineteenth century after a lengthy campaign by the Russian army to subdue them. During World War II, when the Germans pushed into the Caucasus, a number of Chechens—acting on the time-honored principle that "the enemy of my enemy is my friend"—collaborated with them. The Chechen population paid a heavy price for it. Stalin meted out collective punishment that included the deportation of Chechens (along with other ethnic groups in that region) to Central Asia and Siberia. In his Secret Speech of 1956, Nikita Khrushchev listed the deportation of the Chechens as one of Stalin's crimes, and in 1957 he permitted Chechens to return to their ancestral home. But the Chechens never forgot what the Soviet state had done to them, and at the first opportunity they declared their independence.

For three years, Yeltsin ignored Chechen claims to independence. But then Dzhokhar Dudayev, the leader of the Chechen rebels, reminded the Russians that the northern Caucasus was one of the great fault lines where the Christian and Muslim worlds meet. He predicted that all Muslims in the Caucasus would rebel, Siberia would secede, and the Russian Far East would align itself with East Asia. "Russian racism in the Caucasus," he added ominously, "will not go unpunished."[17]

Yeltsin decided to act. Instead of quickly reasserting control, however, Russian troops walked into deadly ambushes set by Chechen rebels, particularly in Grozny, the capital city. The heavy-handed Russian response reduced the city to ruins; by the end of 1996, an estimated 45,000 people had died in Chechnya, and almost 2 million had become refugees.[18] Television images from Grozny reminded Russians of the devastation of World War II.

When the Chechen resistance proved to be much tougher than anticipated, Yeltsin sought a negotiated solution. The best he was able to obtain, in August 1996, was an interim five-year cease-fire. Independence, however, remained the Chechens' goal. The Chechen chief of staff, Aslan Maskhadov, flatly declared, "No Chechen has ever signed any kind of document saying that Chechnya is part of Russia and there will never be such a Chechen."[19]

## The Election of 1996

Few gave Boris Yeltsin much chance of winning the 1996 presidential election. Opinion polls showed that a scant 10 percent of voters planned to cast their ballots for him. The unpopular war in Chechnya, a drastic increase in the crime rate, Yeltsin's poor health, and money and political power in the hands of the nouveaux riches, commonly known as the "mafia," took their political toll. The Communist Party candidate, Gennadii Zyuganov, appeared the likely winner.

Yeltsin and his advisers, however, would not accept defeat. In March 1996, when Yeltsin's prospects for a victory were dim, he contemplated a so-called "forceful option." Under the pretext of a bomb threat, he would dissolve parliament and cancel the election. In the meantime, he followed the "softer option": television controlled by the government (running footage of Communist atrocities) and money spent to curry favor with the voters. As one of Yeltsin's advisers bluntly declared, "If Yeltsin loses, he will not give power to the Communists. He has said that more than once."[20] Zyuganov would not be permitted to win.

In April 1996, Yeltsin overtook Zyuganov in the polls and won the election by a comfortable margin. Voters—even those who suffered hardships because of the new economic order—ultimately proved reluctant to place their future in the hands of a Communist who unabashedly praised Stalin and promised a return to economic policies that had been tried and had failed. Zyuganov had offered no new ideas, not even bothering to change the name of his party.

In the ten weeks before the election in June, Yeltsin unabashedly used the power of the incumbent. He issued decrees that doubled the minimum pension—effective immediately—and compensated those who had lost their savings because of hyperinflation. He bestowed his largesse on students, teachers, war veterans, single mothers, small businesses, and the agro-industrial, military, and aviation complexes. His aides blatantly handed out cash. One region after another was singled out for special treatment and subsidies—from the heart of Russia to the farthest reaches of Siberia.

A woman who worked for a coal mine in Vorkuta asked for and received from Yeltsin a car, an event carried on national television. Yelstin's generosity cost the hard-strapped Russian treasury the astonishing sum of $11 billion. It was, until then, the most expensive political campaign ever conducted. The IMF—which had a stake in keeping the capitalist reforms of Yeltsin on track—underwrote his spending spree with a new $10.2 billion loan.[21]

Throughout, Washington turned a blind eye to the political and economic conditions in Russia, the Clinton administration arguing that they were part of the growing pains of the transition from a planned to a market economy. By the end of the decade, however, approximately one-half of the population still lived below the official poverty line of $30–35 a month, and perhaps another 25–30 percent were close to it. "In modern peacetime," the political scientist Stephen Cohen noted, "never have so many fallen so far."[22]

## The Putin Presidency

In 1999, Yeltsin, now physically ailing and prohibited by law from serving a third term, began to look for a way to retire and at the same time avoid a criminal investigation of his finances and sundry other transgressions, as one of his prime ministers threatened. After dismissing one prime minister after another, he finally settled on a man to his liking, the obscure Vladimir Putin, a product of the KGB, the Soviet Union's secret police. Under Yeltsin, Putin had risen to head the KGB's successor, the FBS. Putin had no qualms about giving Yeltsin a free pass. And thus, on New Year's Eve 1999, came the stunning announcement that Putin had replaced Yeltsin and would serve as acting president until the election in March 2000. Yeltsin obliquely apologized for past "mistakes," for which he would not be punished, however.

## The Second Chechen War

After the first Chechen war, the Chechen rebels behaved as if they governed an independent—although scarcely functioning—state, now a training ground for criminal activities—trading in slaves, smuggling narcotics, operating stolen-car rings, counterfeiting, and taking hostages. Putin came to power two days after a radical fringe group of Chechens launched an attack on neighboring Dagestan to establish the "independent Islamic state of Dagestan" in hopes of sparking an Islamic anti-Russian uprising. Putin responded to the challenge. Five days later the Russian bomber jets arrived, an omen of things to come. Three weeks later a series of explosions shook Moscow. There was no question in the minds of most Russians that the bombings had been the work of Chechen terrorists. Although it remained unclear who had been responsible for the bloody deeds, Putin had his justification to go to war. He set out to avenge not only the recent bombings but also Russia's defeat in the first Chechen war.

This time, the Russian military did not walk into Grozny in the expectation of a quick victory. It prepared, instead, a massive assault, which left tens of thousands of Chechens dead, mostly civilians. Little was left standing of Grozny and other rebel strongholds. The world stood by idly, wringing its hands, unwilling to become involved in a war in the distant Caucasus. After the rebels lost Grozny, they retreated into the mountains, vowing to continue their fight. The conflict became more than merely a war of secession: It took on ethnic and religious connotations, Russians against Chechens and Christians against Muslims.

Putin had no discernible foreign policy except to argue that Russia must once again play the role of a great power. With that in mind, he emphasized the need for a strong state and patriotism. The stress was on executive power and discipline, not democracy. He offered his people a "dictatorship of the law," adding, "as I choose to rewrite it."[23]

In October 2002, forty-one Chechen terrorists, including several "black widows" (women who had lost relatives to the Russian terror), seized 700 hostages in a Moscow theater. The rescue attempt went terribly awry when 129 hostages perished (as did the terrorists, who were summarily executed). In the months to come, Chechens bombed a train in southern Russia, Moscow's military command base in Grozny, and a subway station in Moscow. At the end of summer 2004, "black widows" on suicide missions brought down two Russian airliners, and then in September 2004 came the shocking spectacle of Chechens seizing a school in Beslan in southern Russia. Putin, who refused to negotiate with renegade Chechens, sent the army to carry out what became another ill-fated rescue attempt. Among the 335 dead, most were children. Immediately thereafter, Putin issued a decree ending popular elections of regional governors and established a "single chain of command" to strengthen the "unity of the country and prevent further crises." The Chechen resistance was gradually ground down, permitting the Russian government to declare—overoptimistically—that its counterterrorist operations were officially over in April 2009. In late December 2013, six weeks before the Sochi winter Olympic Games, two suicide bombings a day apart killed at least 34 people in a Volgograd trolley, bus, and train station.

Under Yeltsin the news media had been left alone. Putin, however, quickly declared war on the independent voices in Russia. When Andrei Babitsky, a reporter for Radio Free Europe/Radio Liberty, dwelled on the brutality of the second Chechen war, Putin arranged Babitsky's kidnapping. Babitsky was "on the side of the enemy," Putin charged; what he did was "much more dangerous than firing a machine gun."[24] It was largely because of an international outcry that Babitsky was eventually released. Other journalists were less fortunate. In October 2006, Anna Politkovskaia, a scathing critic of both the Chechen warlords and Moscow's brutality in Chechnya, was—after receiving a number of death threats—finally gunned down. Putin also turned against Media-Most, a company that published a daily newspaper and owned a radio station and NTV, the only Russian television network not controlled by the government. In June 2000, the company's owner, Vladimir Gusinsky, was arrested and briefly jailed. His exposure of corruption in the Kremlin had hit too close to home; moreover, Gusinsky's television station had satirized Putin.

Not even the high and mighty escaped Putin's wrath. Public criticism of Putin came to an end in October 2003, after the arrest of Mikhail Khodorkovsky, the chief executive of the YukosSibneft oil company, one of the world's richest men. Officially, Khodorkovsky was charged with tax evasion; the real reason was his political ambition, his temerity to challenge what he called Putin's corrupt "managed democracy." After Khodorkovsky was sentenced to nine years in prison (with additional years tacked on later), other tycoons quickly expressed their fealty to Putin. (In December 2013, in the weeks before the Sochi Olympics, Putin, to burnish Russia's image, released Khodorkovsky and other political prisoners.)

In November 2006, a former KGB-FSB officer, Alexander Litvinenko, suffered an agonizing death, succumbing after twenty-two days to Polonium-210 radiation poisoning. Litvinenko, a vocal dissident in the ranks of the FSB, had been fired, briefly jailed, and then made his way to London where he obtained British citizenship. From what he considered a safe haven, Litvinenko continued to criticize Putin, charging him and the FSB of having ties to the al Qaeda terror network and of masterminding violent acts in Russia and blaming the Chechens. Scotland Yard determined that Litvinenko's assassin was Andrei Lugovoi, who managed to make his way back to Moscow, where he became a hero in the eyes of ultranationalist circles, even winning election to the Duma. London sought Lugovoi's extradition; Moscow denied that he had played any role in Litvinenko's murder.

In Putin's eyes, Russia's greatness was tied to its military prowess. He was photographed flying an Su-27 fighter jet into Grozny and aboard the ill-fated submarine *Kursk*. In August 2000, seismologists in Norway noted two powerful blasts in the Barents Sea. The *Kursk*, Russia's state-of-the-art, nuclear-powered, missile-launching submarine, commissioned only five years earlier, had been ripped apart (by its own torpedoes, it was later learned). Putin reacted slowly to the catastrophe. Surviving sailors inside the submarine continued to hammer on the hull until they ran out of oxygen. The disaster, the slow response, and the inability of Russian divers to open the hatch shed a light on the sorry state of Russia's military forces.

Over time, the Russian economy began to recover—thanks largely to the phenomenal rise of the cost of energy—and the Kremlin began to play a more confident—at times belligerent—role in international affairs. The Russian constitution limited the popular Putin to two five-year terms as president. Unwilling to go gently into retirement, he simply switched jobs with his protégé, Prime Minister Dmitri Medvedev. When, in March 2008, Medvedev was elected president as the candidate of Putin's United Russia party, Putin moved into Medvedev's former office of the prime minister—from where he continued to exercise his enormous influence. As expected, Putin once again became president in May 2012.

### The Non-Russian Successor States

A number of Soviet republics—notably Estonia, Latvia, and Lithuania—managed to establish functioning democracies. But in most instances, the road to democracy proved to be difficult. The Caucasus and Central Asia were plagued by ethnic strife and wars for political supremacy. When elections were held, they were often tampered with or fixed outright. The president of Uzbekistan, Islam Karimov, for instance, was reelected in September 1996 with 99.6 percent of the vote—in a country that had neither freedom of speech nor freedom of the press.

In July 1994, voters in Belarus elected a conservative president, Alexander Lukashenko, a Communist functionary who had no taste for change. Lukashenko instead called for a return to the not-too-distant past. He saw privatization as stealing from the state and insisted on preserving collective farming and state control of factories. Among his heroes was Felix Dzherzhinski, the legendary dreaded founder of the Soviet secret police.

The proper form of governance for Belarus, Lukashenko announced, was by "one strong man." He fired the editor of the country's largest newspaper and demanded that citizens who sought to travel abroad register with the proper authorities. He denounced demonstrators as "enemies of the people" and blamed the US State Department for a subway workers' strike in the capital of Minsk. In a rigged October 2004 referendum, he gained the right to amend the constitution, permitting him to run for a third presidential term. After that, he won a fourth term in 2010 with nearly eighty percent of the vote. When demonstrators protested voter fraud, the police dispersed them.

In 2003, manipulated elections were held in Azerbaijan, Armenia, and Georgia. In November, Georgian president Eduard Shevardnadze, who had come to power as a champion of democracy in 1991, rigged the parliamentary election. After twelve years, corruption and the violation of the rule of law had taken their toll. When he faced large, hostile demonstrations, neither the army nor the police backed him. In January 2004, Georgia's bloodless "Rose Revolution" brought to power Mikheil Saakashvili, a thirty-five-year-old US-trained lawyer, who, as it turned out, was another Georgian with a penchant for unlimited power.

## The Retreat from Empire

A cursory glance at the Soviet Union's global position in the mid-1980s revealed a powerful presence in Europe and Asia. Yet a restless population in Eastern Europe showed no signs of coming to terms with their status subordinate to Moscow's interests. In Asia, a hostile Communist China tied down more than one-third of the Soviet Army along the Sino-Soviet border. Ayatollah Khomeini's Islamic government in Iran did not hide its distaste for the secular, atheistic government in Moscow, and Afghanistan, governed by a socialist regime since the early 1970s, remained torn asunder by a bloody civil war that threatened to topple the Kremlin's clients in the capital of Kabul.

### The Afghan Crisis

In December 1979, in an act that stunned the world, the Soviet Union sent 80,000 troops into Afghanistan. For the first time since the end of World War II, the Soviet Union had sent troops into a region beyond its sphere of influence.

Since 1973, the political orientation in Afghanistan had been toward the left, yet it was generally considered a neutral nation, a part of the Third World outside the spheres of any of the world powers. Until 1973, both the United States and the Soviet Union jockeyed inconclusively for influence in Afghanistan, one of the poorest nations on earth, with an annual per capita GNP in 1979 of $170.[25]

### The US Reaction

The Soviet invasion came at an unfavorable time for the United States. For one, the recent defeat in Vietnam did not sit well with many in the United States. Second, 1979 saw the second oil shortage of the decade. Third, the Iranian hostage crisis (which had just begun on November 4) highlighted the limits of US power. Collectively, they produced a sense of frustration and belligerence.

Domestic political pressures demanded that US president Jimmy Carter respond to the invasion. On the eve of the 1980 presidential election, he could ill afford to be blamed for "losing Afghanistan." A country of extraordinary poverty and of little significance in the international balance of power, Afghanistan suddenly took on an importance unmatched in its modern history.

There was scarcely a debate in the United States of the motives behind the invasion. The CIA explained that the Soviet Union faced an "extremely painful" decline in oil supplies and that the invasion of was intended to move the Soviet army closer to the lucrative oil fields in the Persian Gulf region. "Moscow is already making the point," said CIA director Stansfield Turner, "that Middle Eastern oil is not the exclusive preserve of the West." (The CIA later retracted its statement when it acknowledged that the Soviet Union was not likely to suffer from oil shortages in the near future.[26]) A Soviet thrust through Afghanistan against the oil refineries near the Gulf, however, made little sense. Why take a 500-mile detour through rugged terrain and at the same time tip off your enemy?

Carter had no good options. A direct military challenge to the USSR was out of the question. He was reduced to denying US athletes the opportunity to participate in the 1980 summer Olympic Games in Moscow unless the Soviets withdrew from Afghanistan. The Soviets were stung by the boycott, for they had envisioned the Olympics as validating their country as one of the world's two great powers. They ignored Carter's ultimatum and held the Olympics without the participation of the United States and other Western nations. Carter also halted US grain sales to the Soviet Union. The glut on the world market in agricultural commodities, however, meant that the Soviets shifted their orders to more reliable sources. Carter's search for clients willing to help him contain the Soviet Union drew the United States a bit closer to Communist China. Together and in secret, they provided weapons to Afghans fighting the Soviets, with Saudi Arabia underwriting much of the cost. The Soviets responded by beefing up their forces, which soon numbered more than 100,000.

The invasion of Afghanistan finished off détente. The Soviets could not expect a thaw in the Cold War and at the same time intervene in the internal affairs of other nations. The Soviets replied that détente would not prevent the Kremlin from playing the role of a great power, from carving out its own sphere of influence—as the United States had done in Vietnam. The Soviets replied that détente and playing the role of a great power—carving out its own sphere of influence—were not antithetical. It was only following the example of the United States during the Vietnam War.

## Soviet Objectives in Afghanistan

The reason the Soviet Union intervened in Afghanistan was to bring order to a chaotic political situation in a neighboring socialist country. Moscow did not want to lose Afghanistan because, according to the simple arithmetic of the

Cold War, a setback for one side meant a victory for the other. The purpose was to avoid a sense of loss of prestige and image rather than by rational analyses of national security. It rested on what conclusions others might draw from one's own misfortune.

Political instability has long been the hallmark of Afghanistan. In 1973, the leftist Prince Muhammad Daoud exiled his cousin, King Zahir Shah. In April 1978, Daoud was killed in a coup by the Marxist People's Democratic Party under the leadership of Nur Muhammad Taraki, who established closer ties with the Soviet Union. In his turn, Taraki was murdered in the course of a third leftist coup led by Hafizullah Amin. It was Amin who was the target of the Soviet invasion. All this bloodletting took place within Afghanistan's Communist factions.

It is here that one can find another clue to Moscow's decision to invade Afghanistan. Taraki and Amin had a falling-out, with Taraki looking to Moscow for support and Amin looking to Washington. Amin, it was known, had met a number of times with the US ambassador, Adolph Dubs. What transpired between them was not clear, but the Soviets feared the worst. To the Soviets, Amin was at the threshold of following in the footsteps of Anwar Sadat, the Egyptian head of state who, in 1972, had ousted the 20,000 Soviet military advisers in Egypt and then invited in the US military. More than anything else, it was the fear of an Afghan diplomatic revolution—from Moscow to Washington—that prompted the Soviet invasion.

The Kremlin's concerns were not unfounded. CIA director Robert Gates confirmed in his memoirs that the United States had begun to assist Afghan rebels six months before the Soviet invasion. President Carter's national security advisor, Zbigniew Brzezinski, similarly acknowledged that Carter had signed on July 3, 1979, the first directive providing assistance to the rebels in the hope that this provocation would lead to a Soviet invasion.[27] Washington did not have to wait long.

Taraki had asked Moscow for military assistance thirteen times in 1979, only to be turned down each time. Brezhnev told him: "We must not do this. It would only play into the hands of enemies—both yours and ours." But after Taraki's murder at the hands of Amin, the Kremlin, against its better judgment, sent the Soviet army into Afghanistan to restore order and extract revenge.[28] Soviet commandos killed Amin and replaced him with his rival, Babrak Karmal. The Kremlin then announced that it had acted on an invitation from the government of Afghanistan.

In the name of freedom, Islam, and anti-Communism, the *mujahidin*— or freedom fighters, as they called themselves—rose against a succession of Marxist governments in Kabul. Resistance against the center has long been a feature in Afghanistan, where local rulers in outlying regions jealously guarded their autonomy. This time they had other grievances, the social and economic transformation of their tradition-bound society, untouched even by colonial rule. Resentment against social reforms ran deep. The establishment of coeducational schools, for instance, touched off a rebellion in western Afghanistan in March 1979. The elimination of the Muslim veil and bridal dowries, carried out with brutality, did not help matters.

The Kremlin feared the spread of radical Islam into Central Asia, where most of the Soviet Union's 50 million Muslims lived. As the Soviet army crossed into Afghanistan, it mobilized recruits from Central Asia, a step in line with the standard procedure of using the most readily available reserves. Muslim soldiers, however, showed little inclination to fight their ethnic and religious counterparts. Some deserted, while others went over to the rebels. Within three months, the Soviet army started to bring in politically more reliable Slavic troops.

Unlike guerrilla movements in other parts of the world, the Afghan rebels had no program of social, political, or economic reform. There was no literacy campaign (in 1979, primary-school enrollment stood at 30 percent, mostly in the cities; the adult literacy rate was 15 percent), no declaration of the rights of women, no medical programs (life expectancy at birth was thirty-six years; in the industrial nations of the West it was twice that), and no political experiments such as elected village councils. Gerard Chaliand, a French specialist on guerrilla movements in the global South, concluded: "The current Afghan resistance movement looks [more] like a traditional revolt [against the capital] . . . than like modern guerrilla warfare. Among contemporary guerrilla movements, only the Kenyan Mau Mau [of the early 1950s] are less sophisticated in their strategy and organization."[29] In a strange twist of fate, the United States, the standard-bearer for the industrial revolution and parliamentary democracy, became the main arms supplier for the Afghan rebels, who drew their inspiration from seventh-century Arabia.

Soon foreign Islamic *jihadists* began to flock to Afghanistan, recruited largely through the efforts of Saudi Arabia. The CIA and US State Department looked with favor upon their arrival and, in fact, sought ways to increase their numbers, despite repeated warnings of their anti-US sentiment.[30]

## The Soviet Exodus from Afghanistan

Mikhail Gorbachev inherited a war his army was unable to win. The determined rebels were too well equipped. Their deadly, effective, US-made Stinger ground-to-air missiles, for example, brought down numerous Soviet aircraft (including passenger planes). Unwilling to accept a defeat along the southern flank of the Soviet Union, Gorbachev escalated the war. But he understood that if he wanted to end the Cold War, his army would have to leave Afghanistan. When the Soviet army finally did so, he stated that the invasion had not been merely another one of Brezhnev's many mistakes; it was also a sin.

But the Soviet retreat would not be unilateral. Gorbachev insisted—and Ronald Reagan agreed—that Afghanistan must not be allied with the West. The last Soviet troops marched out of Afghanistan on February 15, 1989, leaving behind a client government led by President Mohammad Najibullah.

Earlier, Gorbachev had declared his opposition to the Brezhnev Doctrine, Moscow's right to interfere in the internal affairs of other Communist countries. The retreat from Afghanistan marked the end of that doctrine. The war claimed the lives of approximately 1 million Afghans (out of a population of 15 million). Between 5 million and 6 million people became refugees in Pakistan and Iran; another 2 million were displaced inside Afghanistan. The estimated physical damage—to agriculture, industry, power stations, schools, and hospitals—was an estimated $20 billion, a tidy sum for such an impoverished country.[31]

### The Aftermath: Civil War

Still, weapons and ammunition continued to pour into Afghanistan from a variety of sources. The government in Kabul survived the withdrawal of the Soviet army—if only for the time being—because of the extraordinary fragmentation among the Afghan resistance. In December 1991, however, Moscow stopped supplying arms to Najibullah, and Washington ended its arms deliveries to the *mujahidin*, who were nevertheless able to obtain weapons from Iran, Pakistan, and Saudi Arabia. Najibullah was on his own. When he proved incapable of suppressing an army mutiny in January 1992, his generals, sensing vulnerability, began to switch sides. In April 1992, Najibullah negotiated the transfer of political power to the *mujahidin* and then took refuge inside a UN compound in Kabul.

As the *mujahidin* closed in on Kabul, the doomed Najibullah prophetically told reporters that the secular leaders of Afghanistan, the United States, and "the rest of the civilized world" faced a "common task," a "joint struggle" against Islamic fundamentalism: "If fundamentalism comes to Afghanistan, war will continue for many years. Afghanistan will turn into a center of world smuggling for narcotic drugs . . . [and] into a center for terrorism."[32] Few in the West, however, paid attention to Najibullah's warning.

Kabul fell to the Islamic fundamentalist Shiite, Gulbuddin Hekmatyar, one of the chief recipients of US aid. In April 1992, a coalition led by the ethnic Tadzhik, Ahmad Shah Masoud, entered Kabul from the north and expelled Hekmatyar. Hekmatyar, now supported by Shiite Iran, continued to fight from entrenched positions in the hills south of Kabul. In August 1992, he launched a deadly artillery barrage in which over 1,200 residents lost their lives. In the war between rival warlord armies, Kabul suffered greater death and destruction in the single year after the fall of Najibullah than during the previous fourteen years of revolution, foreign invasion, and civil war. Continued bombardments over the next three years turned the city of 1 million inhabitants into rubble, killing as many as 10,000 and turning over half the population into refugees.

For a time, a succession of corrupt and brutal Islamic governments vied for control of Kabul. But then Afghanistan witnessed the emergence of yet another—the most extreme—Muslim movement, the Taliban, created in August 1994 with the help of the Inter-Services Intelligence, Pakistan's military intelligence arm. The Taliban consisted, in part, of former Islamic seminary students—indeed, Taliban means "students" in Pushtun—many of them from across the border in Pakistan and other Islamic countries. Led by its supreme leader, the one-eyed Mullah Muhammad Omar, the Taliban had become disgusted with the corruption and factional infighting by warlords who were not particularly interested in Islam. The Taliban, in contrast, called for an Afghan government subject to the laws of the Koran as codified in the seventh century. As the Taliban represented an alternative to the lawless warlords, it quickly gained popular support. In the regions where it ruled, it closed girls' schools, confined women to their homes, and carried out public executions. Thieves were punished by cutting off their left hand.

In September 1996, the Taliban—already in control of more than half of Afghanistan—began its final push toward Kabul. Upon taking the city, its first act was to seize Najibullah inside the UN compound, castrate him, beat him to death, and hang his blood-soaked torso from a traffic post as a warning to any and all who opposed it.

The Taliban's second act was to forbid women to work outside the home. Should they step outside their homes, they were ordered to cover themselves with the traditional *burqa*, a garment covering them from head to toe. It also ordered government officials to grow beards, closed Kabul's sole television station (because Islam equates the reproduction of images of humans with idolatry), and banned Western music and other amusements such as flying kites.

The Taliban eventually controlled more than three-quarters of Afghanistan, but the fighting was not over. The history of Afghanistan—a struggle between the center and the provinces—continued. When the Taliban moved to enter the Panjshir Valley, ninety miles north of Kabul, Uzbek and Tadzhik forces blocked their way.

## Poland and Solidarity

The Polish Communist Party elected Edward Gierek as first secretary in December 1970, and he inherited an increasingly radicalized country. Gierek's tenure coincided with Willy Brandt's *Ostpolitik*, which was marked by an easing of tensions between East and West. With détente came an increase in East-West trade, underwritten by Western bankers who made available increasingly larger amounts of "petrodollars"—money deposited by the oil-rich nations.

Gierek, unlike his frugal predecessor, Wladyslaw Gomulka, began to borrow heavily. In 1973, Poland owed $2.5 billion to Western banks; by 1982 the debt had risen more than tenfold, to $27 billion. With the influx of Western capital and goods—machinery, grain, and consumer items—the standard of living rose, but the day of financial reckoning had to come.

That day came in July 1980, when the Gierek government, in order to pay off the foreign debt, decreed an increase in food prices. The announcement led to illegal strikes and demonstrations. It also led to the emergence of Solidarity.

In the past, the government had bought off striking workers with economic concessions. This time, however, the workers refused to take the bait. Workers at the mammoth Lenin Shipyard in Gdansk instead insisted on concessions from the government that were nothing short of revolutionary. They demanded that any settlement would have to cover the country's workers as a whole, rather than merely a single group. Their demand gave rise to Solidarity, a union that at one point represented 10 million people in a country of 35 million. Lech Walesa, the head of Solidarity, became one of the most powerful men in Poland.

Solidarity, with the support of the vast majority of the population as well as the Roman Catholic Church, wrung concession after concession from the government. During the next sixteen months, the attention of the world was riveted on Poland, where the impossible was taking place. According to Marxist ideology, Polish workers were striking against themselves because, in theory, they were the owners of the "means of production," the factories. Strikes by workers against their places of employment were, therefore, both illogical and illegal. Yet the right to strike was the first and most important concession Solidarity wrenched from the Communist Party. Solidarity became the only union in Eastern Europe not controlled by government.

Solidarity then escalated its demands. It broke the government's monopoly of the information media. It received the right to put out an uncensored daily newspaper; it even gained access to radio and television. It wrested from the state the materials necessary to erect monuments in honor of workers the state had gunned down during the riots of 1956 and 1970. Finally, Solidarity obtained the right to free parliamentary elections with a secret ballot.

The Polish Communist Party was paralyzed in the face of Solidarity's demands. It was also deeply split. Some members openly supported Solidarity; others even quit the party to join Solidarity. The party began to look for a savior, a Napoleon Bonaparte, to bring the revolution under control. It turned to a man of considerable moral authority, General Wojciech Jaruzelski, who in 1970 and 1976 as minister of defense had refused to use force against workers, declaring that "Polish troops will not fire on Polish workers." The party promoted him to prime minister in 1980, and after that to first secretary of the party in October 1981.

Jaruzelski understood the precariousness of his position. He now held the three paramount political positions in Poland and yet was unable to govern effectively. Lech Walesa, the head of Solidarity, who held no government position, was his coequal.

Party hard-liners resented the concessions granted to Solidarity. Solidarity hard-liners, in turn, argued there could be no coexistence with the party. One of them, Jacek Kuron, long a bitter critic of the party, put it succinctly: The regime either "must die, or it must destroy Solidarity. There is no other solution."[33]

On December 12, 1981, a radicalized Solidarity called for a popular referendum—one it was sure to win—on the fate of the Communist Party. The Polish and Soviet governments warned against an attempt by Solidarity to seize political power.

Brezhnev's Politburo in Poland knew that the cost of intervention would be high. It could lead to a war between the two most important members of the Warsaw Pact, this at a time when the Soviet army was already bogged down in Afghanistan. Moreover, when the Soviet army mobilized troops along the Polish border in November 1980 to intimidate Solidarity, it proved to be a disaster. Reservists could not be found; others failed to answer the call, and so many deserted and went home that the authorities gave up trying to punish them.[34]

The day after Solidarity's call for the referendum, Jaruzelski's security forces arrested its leadership and declared martial law—effectively outlawing Solidarity and reestablishing the primacy of the party. The commonly held view in the West was that the Soviet Union bore direct responsibility for Jaruzelski's actions. But there was no clear proof of this. No doubt, Jaruzelski did what the Soviet Union had demanded all along, restore order. But he also knew that either he would do it or the Kremlin would do it for him.

Solidarity's extraordinary gains of the previous sixteen months were now largely erased. Poland's security forces acted with remarkable efficiency in restoring order, which astonished most observers, including Solidarity itself. Jaruzelski and the party, however, did not win the hearts and minds of the nation. This chapter of Polish history was far from closed.

### *Annus Mirabilis*

In Europe, 1989 became known as *annus mirabilis*, the "year of miracles." When it began, all of Moscow's satellite Communist parties appeared firmly in its control. By year's end, however, the ring of Communist states along the Soviet Union's western borders, which Stalin had created in 1945, was no more.

**Eastern Europe (1995)**

The events of 1989 underscored the reality that the governments of Eastern Europe had little popular support. In the past, whenever a Communist party had shown signs of being overwhelmed by its own people, Moscow had intervened—as in East Germany in June 1953, in Hungary in 1956, and in Czechoslovakia in 1968. Intervention and threats had maintained a deceptive calm.

Early in his reign, Gorbachev declared several times that the Brezhnev Doctrine was dead, that no nation had the right to impose its will on another people. When he delivered his message to the United Nations in December 1988, the Communist parties in Eastern Europe understood they now stood alone, that Moscow was unlikely to bail them out.

The economies of Eastern Europe had done tolerably well in the first decade or so when the Communist parties established large factories. The test was whether the Communist system could sustain productivity, absorb new technology, and produce a wider range of sophisticated products. When it could not, the result was that in 1989 every East European country was much poorer compared to the West than it had been in the 1970s. In 1987, per capita GNP for Poland and Hungary, for example, was 14 percent of West Germany or Sweden.[35] By this time, moreover, the Iron Curtain had long ceased to be a barrier to the flow of information. Many East Germans regularly watched West German television—via cable, no less. That and the steady flow of visitors from the West gave the East Europeans a clear picture of how far they had fallen behind.

## Poland

The dam cracked first in Poland. After Jaruzelski declared martial law, he found out that he could not rule Poland without Solidarity, particularly as the economy continued to deteriorate. In January 1989, Jaruzelski had little choice but to resume talks with Solidarity's jailed leaders. In April, the party granted Solidarity legal status once again. More significantly, it agreed to parliamentary elections in June. When the party insisted that Solidarity's representation in parliament be limited to 35 percent of the seats, Solidarity balked. The deadlock was broken after the party agreed to create an upper house, or Senate, that would be elected democratically. Solidarity would win the Senate elections, the party reasoned, but in the lower house the party was guaranteed to keep its majority.

The Senate elections gave Solidarity 99 of the 100 contested seats. The result showed that support for the Communist Party had sunk to record low levels. Cynical Poles called it "the only known crucifixion in which the victim has nailed himself to the cross."[36] After Solidarity's smashing Senate victory, the Peasant Party, which during the previous forty years had been little more than a front for the Communists, suddenly bolted and joined Solidarity in the lower house. Together, they formed a majority coalition. Under the parliamentary system, the two parties were now entitled to create a new government. In August 1989, the new parliament elected Tadeusz Mazowiecki as prime minister, the first non-Communist leader in Eastern Europe since shortly after World War II.

Mazowiecki flew to Moscow to assure Gorbachev that his government did not plan to leave the Warsaw Pact, as the Hungarian Communists had attempted to do in 1956. Solidarity, moreover, agreed to refrain from the incendiary language it had used in 1981, suggesting the abolition of the Communist Party, which, in any case, had become largely irrelevant. Gorbachev told Mazowiecki that he had no intention of invoking the Brezhnev Doctrine. Instead, he welcomed the events in Warsaw.

The Mazowiecki government now had to manage an economy deeply in debt and run aground on the shoals of central planning. On New Year's Day 1990, it abolished numerous subsidies to which Poland's citizens had long become accustomed. The price of bread rose by 38 percent and that of coal, which many used for heating, went up 600 percent. A drastic increase in gasoline and auto-insurance prices forced some Poles to turn in their license plates.[37] The primary advocates of such "shock therapy" were the Western banks and governments and the IMF, all of which insisted that Poland put its fiscal house in order to be eligible for aid.

Poland's plan for dismantling its centralized economy was the boldest in Eastern Europe. By the summer of 1991, however, the government began to roll back some of its free-market policies to stave off a popular rebellion. It checked the rising rate of unemployment by keeping afloat state-owned factories and by levying protective import tariffs on certain goods. Economists who had envisioned a "big-bang" transformation to capitalism began to speak of an evolution over ten years.

### East Germany

In the late summer of 1989, Hungarian soldiers went to work to dismantle the fortifications along the Austro-Hungarian border, the first example of the physical demolition of the Iron Curtain. The Communist Hungarian government already had granted its citizens the right to a passport and with it the freedom of travel and emigration. Hungary, moreover, made no effort to keep East Germans from taking the same road to the West. Although officially still a Communist country, Hungary became a hemorrhaging wound that threatened to bleed Communist East Germany, which for the first time since 1961—when the Berlin Wall was built—was losing tens of thousands of its citizens. In September 1989, 12,000 East Germans crossed into Austria in the span of three days. Other East Germans left through Czechoslovakia and Poland. East Germany's Warsaw Pact allies had become the road by which East Germans abandoned what they considered a sinking ship.

East Germany's rigid Communist Party chief, Erich Honecker, declared that he would ride out the storm. But in May 1989, after the party had rigged local elections, the voices of protest by civic groups grew louder. Protestant church leaders, in particular, grew increasingly critical of the regime. Then came the summer exodus. More importantly, the summer of 1989 saw demonstrations in many cities, notably in Leipzig, where increasingly larger crowds demanded change while insisting, "we're staying here." Honecker promised "another Beijing" (in reference to the massacre in Tiananmen Square in June) and ordered the security police, the despised and dreaded Stasi, to use "any means" to put down the "counterrevolution." The showdown came in Leipzig on the night of October 9, 1989, one month after Hungary had become an unimpeded escape route and the day after

*Between November 9 and 12, 1989, more than 1 million East Germans walked or drove into West Berlin, where they received a joyous reception*

Gorbachev's visit to East Berlin to commemorate the fortieth anniversary of the East German state. Gorbachev made clear that he had not come to support Honecker but to say good-bye to him. He reminded the East German Politburo that a leadership that isolates itself from its people loses the right to exist. During the demonstration on October 9, the party did not resort to the use of force. Nine days later, the Politburo forced Honecker to step down in favor of his protégé, Egon Krenz.

Krenz's first trip as head of the party was a visit to Moscow, where he took pains to describe himself as a disciple of Gorbachev's "new thinking." Mass protests, Krenz now insisted, were a healthy sign of change. The demonstrators, he said, wanted "better socialism and the renovation of society."

On November 6, 1989, 500,000 people showed up in Leipzig, on a cold, rainy night. There were also rallies in Dresden, Erfurt, Schwerin, Halle, Cottbus, and Karl-Marx-Stadt. The Dresden march was sanctioned by authorities and led by the mayor and the reformist local party chief. The march was the first officially approved antigovernment demonstration in that city. What only a short time ago would have been sensational concessions by the government were no longer enough. On November 9 came the historic announcement that East Germans wishing to emigrate to the West could do so by applying for passports. In addition, East Germans who wanted to visit West Berlin would be able to pass unimpeded through the checkpoints separating the two parts of the city. The Berlin Wall was crumbling.

The logic of revolution, however, demands that halfway measures are not enough. Dissidents now demanded the abolition of Article I of the constitution, which granted the party its political monopoly. The party caved in and scuttled Article I on December 1, 1989, clearing the way for free elections.

## German Reunification

The breach in the Berlin Wall put the unification of Germany on the agenda. Washington, Moscow, and the nations of Europe were bracing themselves for the inevitable.

After the creation of the West German government in May 1949 and that of East Germany in October 1949, the division of Germany had taken on an aura of permanence. Officially, however, the West German government rejected the notion of a permanently divided Germany that, moreover, had been divided not just into two but into three parts. There was still the issue of Silesia, Pommerania, and East Prussia—under Polish and Soviet "administration" since 1945.

When West German chancellor Helmut Kohl spoke of unification in November 1989, Moscow declared that just because East Germans were able to visit West Germany, it did not mean the automatic unification of the two Germanies. Kohl's remarks received a cool reception in the West as well. The World War II allies and most Europeans did not relish the re-creation of a strong and unified Germany in the heart of Europe. Such an eventuality dredged up unpleasant memories of Germany's past.

When the West German government arranged the unification of Germany in October 1990 and decided to move the capital from Bonn to Berlin, it did so without much consultation with its allies. Germany calmed the fears of its neighbors, particularly Poland, when it officially accepted the borders the victors of World War II had drawn up and, concomitantly, the loss of East Prussia and the lands beyond the Oder and Neisse Rivers.

With the decline of the Soviet empire, the economy of a united Germany became the most powerful in Europe. After the failed coup in Moscow in August 1991, it was Germany that took the lead in recognizing the independence of the Baltic states. In Yugoslavia, Germany broke ranks with the European Community (EC) and the United States when it recognized the breakaway republics of Slovenia and Croatia and convinced its reluctant EC partners to do the same. During the Gulf War, Germany sent troops abroad for the first time since 1945, an air squadron to Turkey. In the summer of 1992, the German navy showed its flag in the Adriatic Sea off the coast of Yugoslavia to help the UN enforce its embargo against Serbia, a matter-of-fact step the government did not even deem worth discussing in the parliament.

Germany took the lead in providing economic assistance to Eastern Europe. It was in part to prevent the dreaded consequences of a collapse of the

East European economies—a flood of refugees westward. West Germany was already grappling with the unpopular fact that approximately 10 percent of its population consisted of foreigners. As residents—whether as workers or refugees—they were entitled to services from a government whose resources were stretched to the limit. The result was an antiforeigner backlash; in 1992, there were 2,000 assaults—including a number of fatalities—against Turks, black Africans, and Jews. The attackers were generally young males who unabashedly proclaimed themselves as neo-Nazis. By the end of 1992, the euphoria of German reunification gave way to bitterness, violence, and economic stagnation.

After unification, nearly all physical traces of the Berlin Wall were erased. But the psychological gulf between the Easterners and the Westerners remained. The Easterners had lived since 1933 under two consecutive dictatorships, first the Nazis and then the Communists. Their past experience being different from those in the West, many of them were strangers to open democratic political discourse. Unification also meant that East German economic enterprises were thrown into a marketplace in which they had little chance of surviving. Economic recovery in East Germany came slowly, assisted by the infusion of massive sums the result of drastic, unpopular tax increases. At the time of the twentieth anniversary of unification, the cost stood at nearly $2 trillion.[38]

### Hungary

At the time that Solidarity in Poland conducted its noisy challenge to the Communist Party, events in Hungary, though quieter, brought similar results.

János Kádár had come to power in 1956 after the Soviet army crushed the Hungarian rebellion. By the late 1960s, however, Kádár and his party began a cautious program of domestic innovation that, by East European standards, was remarkable. While gradually moving away from the Soviet model, Kádár assured the Soviets that he had no intention of disrupting their East European empire.

Kádár's innovations included experiments in small-scale capitalism, producing a mixed economy. The "commanding heights" of the economy—heavy industry, transportation, and banking—remained in the hands of the state. At the same time, however, small private enterprises—such as artisan shops, restaurants, bars, food stands, and garages employing no more than three persons—were permitted to operate for private profit. Western journalists called it "goulash Communism." Hungarians spoke of "Communism with a capitalist facelift."

From a rigid Marxist point of view, the Hungarian innovations were acts of heresy. But at no time did Karl Marx waste his time discussing the malfeasance of the man running a barbershop or the woman selling flowers on a street corner. His *Das Capital* was an expose of what the poet William Blake had called the "dark Satanic mills" of the early industrial revolution.

On June 8, 1985, Hungarian voters cast their ballots for representatives to parliament and local councils, in which at least two candidates ran for nearly all seats. This was the first election under a 1983 law that offered a choice for the voters, something unique for a Soviet bloc country.

In May 1988, the reform wing of the party nudged the seventy-six-year-old Kádár aside as its leader. It paved the way for the political, posthumous rehabilitation of Kádár's victims. For the first time since 1956, it became possible in Hungary to mention the names of Imre Nagy, Hungary's party chief at the time of the 1956 revolution, and Pal Maleter, the general who had fought the Soviets. They had been among those Kádár had executed and dumped, hands still tied behind their backs, in an unmarked mass grave. Their names had disappeared from the official histories but not from the collective memory of the nation. Their rehabilitation culminated in the solemn June 1989 reinterment of Nagy and his associates, a ceremony broadcast live on national television.

In September 1989, the Communist Party renamed itself the Socialist Party, and parliament rewrote the constitution to permit multiparty elections the following spring. On October 23, 1989, the thirty-third anniversary of the beginning of the 1956 uprising, parliament declared Hungary no longer a "People's Republic." It became the Republic of Hungary, and the red star on top of the parliament building came down. Two rounds of elections, in March and April 1990, shattered whatever illusions the Socialist Party still had of clinging to power. The voters gave the Hungarian Democratic Forum, a populist, nationalist umbrella organization with a right-of-center orientation, a plurality of the seats in parliament. Its leader, Jozsef Antall, then created a coalition with the other conservative parties. The Socialist Party won but 8 percent of the parliamentary seats. The Communist experiment in Hungary was over.

## Czechoslovakia

The fourth Communist domino to fall in 1989 was Czechoslovakia. The initial driving force against the Communist regime consisted of intellectuals and students. In the center of the opposition stood Charta 77, named after a January 1977 typewritten petition demanding civil rights. Its leaders were Jiri Hajek, the country's foreign minister during the Prague Spring, and the dissident writer Václav Havel. Since June 1989, another petition, signed by 40,000 citizens, circulated throughout the country demanding the release of all political prisoners, freedom of expression and assembly, and an independent news media. Czechoslovakia's "Velvet Revolution" was under way.

As long as the demonstrating crowds remained relatively small—2,000 in January 1989 and still only 10,000 at the beginning of November 1989—the police were able to maintain a semblance of order with arrests and occasional beatings. The workers who enjoyed a relatively high standard of living were slow to join. When they did, they swelled the number of the demonstrators on Saint Wenceslas Square in Prague. At the end of November 1989, the Communist regime folded like a house of cards.

Virtually the entire nation stood in opposition to the Communist Party. Not even a bloodbath could save it. After the party agreed to abandon its ruling monopoly on November 29, 1989, events moved quickly. The opposition established a provisional government until voters were able to choose the country's first freely elected government since 1948. Havel, who earlier in the year had been arrested and jailed for antistate activities, became the new prime minister. Alexander Dubček one of the architects of the 1968 Prague Spring, became the country's new president.

At a Warsaw Pact meeting in December 1989, the five participants in the 1968 invasion of Czechoslovakia—the Soviet Union, East Germany, Poland, Hungary, and Bulgaria—formally admitted that the invasion had been "illegal" and pledged in the future strict noninterference in each other's internal affairs. It marked the formal repudiation of the Brezhnev Doctrine. The Gorbachev government issued a separate statement admitting that the reasons for intervention had been "unfounded" and "erroneous."[39]

Havel, in a pointed reminder that Czechoslovakia was a part of Central and not Eastern Europe, went on his first official state not to Moscow, but to Berlin and then to Warsaw. "It's not good-bye to Moscow," a foreign ministry official explained, "but it's a new orientation toward West and Central Europe."[40]

In the summer of 1992, militant Slovaks in the eastern part of the country urged secession from their Czech cousins. Czechoslovakia had come into existence in 1918 as a federation of Czechs and Slovaks under the leadership of the Czech Tomas Masaryk. From the outset, Slovaks resented Czech domination, particularly the fact that they never received the autonomy the Czechs had promised. Remarkably, there was little sentiment among Czechs to preserve the union with their ungrateful cousins. The breakup into the states of the Czech Republic and Slovakia became official on New Year's Day 1993.

## Bulgaria

Next in line was Bulgaria, the most loyal member of the Warsaw Pact. The seventy-eight-year-old boss of the Communist Party, Todor Zhivkov, in power since 1954, showed no signs of stepping down. But his long rule had bred widespread opposition. He had been responsible for reviving the ancient quarrel between Bulgarians and Turks in 1984 when he forced the 1-million-strong Muslim Turkish minority to adopt Slavic names. In May 1989, he pressured 310,000 Turks to emigrate. Not only did he damage Bulgaria's international standing, but the exodus also wrought havoc with the nation's economy. When Zhivkov promoted his son to the Central Committee's Department of Culture in 1989, even his old allies deserted him and the Politburo demanded his resignation.

To placate the population, the authorities charged Zhivkov with corruption and nepotism. It was too little, too late. Increasingly larger and more defiant crowds now demanded political change. On January 15, 1990, the Communist Party caved in to popular pressure and agreed to give up its leading political role and to hold free elections. In September 1992, after an eighteen-month trial, the now eighty-one-year-old Zhivkov was found guilty of embezzling nearly $1 million and sentenced to seven years in prison (commuted to house arrest due to ill health and old age). Zhivkov became the first former Soviet bloc leader to be judged by a post-Communist court.

## Romania

The last and least likely of the Communist dictators to be toppled in 1989 was Nicolae Ceaușescu, who had been in power since 1965. Ceaușescu carved out a foreign policy independent of Moscow without, however, leaving the Warsaw Pact. Romania reserved the right to skip the pact's annual war exercises, continued to recognize Israel after the 1967 Six Day War, and refused to join in the invasion of Czechoslovakia in 1968. In 1984, Ceaușescu defied the Moscow-led boycott of the summer Olympic Games in Los Angeles, where the Romanian team received a standing ovation at the opening ceremonies. The West rewarded maverick Romania with most-favored-nation treatment, and US presidents Richard Nixon and Jimmy Carter paid highly publicized visits to Bucharest. They spared no words in heaping praise on the Romanian dictator, ignoring the fact that Ceaușescu's regime was by far the most repressive within the Warsaw Pact.

Ceaușescu decided what few dictators dared to contemplate. Romania would pay off its $10 billion foreign debt, never mind the social consequences. The result was a sharp drop in the standard of living. Large amounts of food were exported; the work week was increased to six days; the price of gasoline was raised; apartments were kept at about 50 degrees Fahrenheit in the winter; electricity was rationed; hospitals lacked supplies. The 24 million people of Romania, an agrarian land, were reduced to a meager diet. Pigs' feet, commonly known as "patriots," remained in abundance; they were the only part of the pig that stayed behind after the rest had been exported.

Ceaușescu's style was reminiscent of that of Stalin and the fascist Benito Mussolini of Italy. He dropped the label "comrade" and began to call himself "Conducator," or leader. Ceaușescu ruled not through his party but, similar to Stalin, through the secret police, the Securitate. The party existed merely to legitimize Ceaușescu's rule. The most prominent feature of Romanian television was the glorification of Ceaușescu and his wife, Elena, the nation's second-most-powerful figure. Their son, Nicu, was groomed to follow in his father's footsteps. Forty other relatives were on the government payroll.

In June 1989, Ceaușescu sent a congratulatory message to Deng Xiaoping for crushing the Chinese student demonstrations. He promised to respond likewise should dissidents take to the streets. A party official explained Ceauşescu's method of governance: "All the systems of the world are based on reward and punishment. Ceauşescu works only with punishment. It is a reward that there is no punishment."[41]

After the foreign debt was largely repaid, economic conditions in Romania did not change. Ceauşescu continued to bleed his people to fund a massive building program, a monument to his megalomania. Fifteen thousand workers labored on the thirteen-story, 1,000-room, white marble House of the Republic on the Avenue of Socialist Victory. To make room for the palace, nearly 40,000 people were moved and many historic buildings were destroyed—among them the sixteenth-century Monastery of Michael the Brave, the ruler who in 1600 had unified Wallachia, Moldavia, and Transylvania into modern Romania. Ceauşescu personally supervised the project, visiting it two or three times a week. His other projects included the razing of entire towns in Transylvania, many inhabited by ethnic Germans and Hungarians whose ancestors had built them over the span of seven centuries.

The city of Timişoara, in Transylvania, lit the spark that brought down the seemingly impregnable Ceauşescu dictatorship. In early December 1989, the government decided to deport a little-known dissident Hungarian Protestant priest, Laszlo Tokes. After Tokes' parishioners defied the authorities, they were joined by a cross section of the people of Timişoara. Economic considerations played a part. In October, additional food had been rationed—this in a city that contained large food-processing factories and bakeries. Workers who knew nothing of Tokes, but who handled the food destined for export, joined the swelling ranks of the demonstrators.

The fall of the other East European Communist parties had taken place without a single fatality. Romania, however, was destined to be different. Ceauşescu took a page from the Chinese book by sending the Securitate into Timişoara. The Conducator, the "hero of the nation, the brilliant son of the people," began to murder his own people.[42] Brute force might have worked had the police ended the practice of refusing to return the bodies of those it had killed. Adding insult to injury, the police dumped the bodies into a mass grave on the outskirts of the city. "Give us our dead," the demonstrators demanded.

In a speech in Bucharest, Ceauşescu vowed to punish the "terrorists and hooligans." That speech—before what appeared to be a traditionally docile crowd assembled by the authorities—became a disaster as it turned into an anti-Ceauşescu demonstration. Ceauşescu never finished it and fled the presidential palace. At that point, he also lost control of the army. He had never trusted the military, and for good reason. After initially firing into the crowd, soldiers turned their guns on the police. Ceauşescu and his wife fled, only to be captured.

The Ceauşescus were put before a military tribunal and charged with genocide—the murder of 60,000 Romanian citizens—theft, and looting the state treasury. Elena Ceauşescu termed the last accusation a "provocation." The unrepentant Conducator denied all charges and still claimed to be the leader of Romania. A firing squad ended the discussion on Christmas Day 1989. Romanian television showed a tape of the trial and the elegantly dressed corpses of the Ceauşescus.

The head of the new provisional government was Ion Iliescu, Gorbachev's classmate in Moscow in the 1950s and party boss in Timişoara in the late 1960s. Iliescu had become popular with many party members for speaking out against Ceauşescu's economic measures. On the surface, the new government followed the precedents established in the other East European countries. It declared that Romania was no longer a socialist state, stocked the stores with food, reduced the workweek to five days, cut the price of electricity by more than half, permitted each farm family an acre of land for private cultivation, abolished the death penalty after the Ceauşescus' execution, dissolved the Securitate, and promised free elections in April 1990. The government also arrested Ceauşescu's closest associates, including the entire Politburo and ranking officers of the Securitate, promising punishment for "all evildoers from the old regime."

What had taken place in Romania, however, was neither a political nor a social revolution. The Ceauşescus were executed by their own henchmen, among them Iliescu, who now tried to save their own necks. Their aim was to eliminate the dictator but not the dictatorship. The "red aristocrats," as the party leaders were known, then made sure to stress the myth of a political revolution.[43]

Still, Romania had set out on road to becoming a workable democracy. The country had never known a modern party system, a responsible political intelligentsia, or an autonomous church. Romania's political culture was steeped in intrigue, conspiracy, and subservience to authority.

Six months after the death of Ceauşescu, the Marxist Iliescu found solace in fascism. He announced the formation of a national guard reminiscent of the fascist Iron Guard of World War II and arrested opposition leaders. All along, he insisted he was defending democracy.[44]

By the beginning of the twenty-first century, Romania remained a society in transition to democracy. It was plagued with widespread economic and political corruption. It sought to join the European Union, but that organization always insisted that its members follow the rules of democracy.

Democracy and economic hardship do not mix well. The death of Ceauşescu was followed by a brutal economic collapse. Forty percent of the population lived on less than $35 per month, below the international poverty line of $2 per day. The giant Craiova heavy machine and tool complex, for instance, which once had employed 7,000 workers, ten years later only employed 800.[45]

The presidential election of 2000 pitted the discredited Ion Iliescu against Corneliu Vadim Tudor, once Ceauşescu's court poet, the head of the ultra-nationalist Greater Romania Party. Tudor declared that Romania could be governed only at "the point of a machine gun" and promised to end corruption "with a Kalashnikov." He continued to call Ceauşescu a "great patriot" and his party's publications were filled with articles and cartoons railing against "dirty Jews," "fascist Hungarians," and "criminal Gypsies." Iliescu, the lesser of two evils, handily defeated Tudor. With Tudor, Romania had no choice of joining the EU; with Iliescu its chances improved a little. Still, when the EU added ten new members in 2004, Romania was not among them. It had to wait until 2007, after it instituted several rounds of reforms.

## Albania

The Communist state of Albania, the creation of Enver Hoxha in 1944, became the next casualty. Hoxha's regime, a fusion of the worst features of Stalinism and Maoism, was even more oppressive than that of Ceauşescu. Poverty-stricken and isolated, Albania was the world's only official atheist state. Defendants were often executed without trials or simply disappeared and their relatives were punished for good measure. After Hoxha's death in April 1985, Ramiz Alia continued his policies. After 1989, however, Alia introduced reforms to an increasingly restless population. He rescinded, for example, the "crime" of religious propaganda and granted free elections, which ended Communist rule in March 1992.

## Yugoslavia

Communist Yugoslavia was a patchwork of eight major ethnic regions made up of six republics—Bosnia, Croatia, Macedonia, Montenegro, Serbia, and Slovenia—and two officially autonomous provinces within Serbia, Kosovo and Vojvodina. Josip Tito, whose father was a Croat and mother a Slovenian, did what he could to convince his people to see themselves primarily as members of the nation rather than of an ethnic group. To that end, he established a federation in which no one people would dominate another, particularly the numerically and historically dominant Serbs.

Tito understood the danger that ethnic strife posed for Yugoslavia—literally "South Slavia"—an artificial nation formed in 1918 after the collapse of Ottoman Turkish control. The 1974 constitution granted the ethnic regions a measure of autonomy. The Serbian nationality, because of its size, remained first among equals but an equal nevertheless. As long as Tito lived, Yugoslavia retained a remarkable degree of cohesion. After his death in 1980, Yugoslavia began to unravel.

The new head of the Communist Party, the Serb Slobodan Milošević, stripped the Albanian majority in Kosovo Province of its autonomy. Milošević gave notice that he sought a Greater Serbia dominating the other nationalities.

**Yugoslavia and Its Successor States**

On June 28, 1989, he added fuel to the fire when he led a Serb demonstration of 1 million people into Kosovo to commemorate the 600th anniversary of the Battle of Kosovo Field, in which the Muslim Turks had defeated the Christian Orthodox Serbs. The time had come, Milošević declared, to restore Serbia to its former greatness.[46]

Although most Yugoslavs were of Slavic origin, there were serious divisions among them. Slovenes and Croats in the west had fallen under the influence of Roman Catholicism, while the Slavs farther to the east, including Serbs and Macedonians, belonged to the Eastern Orthodox Church. Yugoslavia also had a sizable Muslim population—Albanians and Bosnians—the legacy of centuries of Turkish control. To complicate matters, the diverse populations were interspersed. Yugoslavia represented an uneasy patchwork of Western and Eastern Christianity and Islam.

Assertive Serbian nationalism produced a fearful reaction from other nationalities. Taking their cue from the independence movements in the Soviet

Union, they began to secede. The first to do so, in June 1991, was Slovenia—with a population of 2 million—tucked away in Yugoslavia's northwestern corner. The larger and more powerful Republic of Croatia followed suit, as did Bosnia. Germany became the first nation officially to recognize Slovenia and Croatia in January 1992, and the other members of the EC followed suit. The United States still held out hope that a united Yugoslavia could somehow remain a viable option. But in April 1992, the administration of George H. W. Bush came into line with the EC when it recognized Slovenia, Croatia, and Bosnia.

The stage was set for a bloody war—the first on the European continent since 1945—when the Serbian-dominated Yugoslav army invaded Croatia. The United Nations brokered a cease-fire that took effect in January 1992. Blue-helmeted UN troops—14,400 from thirty-one nations—became the first such deployment on the European continent. But the troops did not have a combat role. They were sent there merely to keep the belligerents apart.

### Bosnia

The ethnic makeup of Bosnia was the most complex of all the republics—92 percent were of Slavic origin, but 44 percent were Muslim, 31 percent were Orthodox Serbs, and 17 percent were Catholic Croats.[47] Stymied in Croatia, Milošević turned against Bosnia, ostensibly to protect the threatened Orthodox Serb minority. He provided weapons for Serbian militia forces in Bosnia, who then laid siege to the capital, Sarajevo. The siege lasted more than 1,000 days, one of the longest in history.

It became a war of extraordinary brutality. Serbs established concentration camps and engaged in "ethnic cleansing," accompanied by rapes, tortures, massacres, and forced deportations of civilians in freight cars. It was reminiscent of crimes last committed in Europe by Stalin and Hitler. Serbian perpetrators were aware that they faced potential charges of war crimes, and for that reason they often wore ski masks. By 1992, Yugoslavia had approximately 2.5 million refugees, the most on such a scale in Europe since 1945.

The Serbian chauvinist Milošević had become the destroyer of Yugoslavia, its peoples, cities, economy, as well as its currency (inflation, at 25,000 percent per year, rendered the Yugoslav dinar worthless). As recently as 1989, Europeans had exulted in the spiritual rebirth of the continent. Yet in 1992, the EC, the UN, and the United States were confronted by a defiant, virulent Serbian chauvinism.

Yugoslavia was reduced to five separate entities: a rump state of Yugoslavia (that included Serbia, the once autonomous provinces of Kosovo and Vojvodina, and the Republic of Montenegro), Slovenia, Croatia, Bosnia, and Macedonia.

A UN weapons embargo ensured that the Bosnian Muslims received little help from the outside world. The Bosnian Serbs, in contrast, obtained large quantities of arms from their kinsmen in Serbia. The Bosnian Serbs, led by their president, Radovan Karadžić, and the commander of their forces, General Ratko Mladić, proclaimed a secessionist Serbian Republic carved out of what had been the republic of Bosnia.

But that was not enough for the homicidal Mladić who saw himself as the vindicator of Serbian history. To him, there was hardly a difference between the past and the present. He saw the violence of the 1990s as part of the continuum of Serbian history. Serbs were again fighting to save Europe from an Islamic tide.[48]

It became increasingly difficult for the United Nations and NATO to stand by idly as the evidence of atrocities mounted. In February 1994, as Serbs made gains in eastern Bosnia, the United Nations declared several regions as "safe" havens. NATO air power would protect them. But when NATO carried out its first air strikes against Serb forces near Goražde in April 1994, the Serbs attacked the "safe" areas. In 1995, they seized 270 UN peacekeepers and shackled them to potential bombing targets. French general Bernard Janvier, whose troops made up more than half of the hostages, arranged their release. But the price was a halt to further air strikes on the Serbs. The deal left the UN powerless, and the 40,000 Bosnian Muslims in Srebrenica—officially still under UN protection—were now left defenseless.

In early summer 1992, Washington collected evidence that the Serbs were conducting widespread massacres of Muslims. Its spy satellites showed that in the northern town of Brčko, Serbs had herded 3,000 Muslim men into an abandoned warehouse and tortured and murdered them. It had even intercepted telephone conversations in which Mladić spoke of his intentions to cleanse Goražde and Žepa.[49] In July 1995, Serbs carried out yet another massacre, this one in Srebrenica, killing between 6,000 and 8,000 Muslim men and boys. According to eyewitnesses, Mladić was present at the killings. This time, Madeleine Albright, at the time the US ambassador to the United Nations, revealed photographs of fresh graves taken by US spy planes.

In May 1993, the UN Security Council established the International Criminal Tribunal for the Former Yugoslavia, the first such court since the Nuremberg and Tokyo trials in the aftermath of World War II. In May 1996, a young Croat, Dražen Erdemović, who had fought for the Serbs, became the first person to plead guilty to war crimes. He confessed to the murder of scores of unarmed Muslim men at Srebrenica. His defense was that, fearing for his life, he had only followed orders.[50]

At the end of summer 1995, the tide turned against the Serbs when Croat forces wrested control of southeastern Croatia, causing more than 170,000 Serbs to flee in fear. In October, the three warring sides—by now thoroughly exhausted—agreed to a cease-fire and to hold talks in the United States.

Bosnian Muslims pleaded with the international community not to recognize the partition of Bosnia, one that had been accompanied by genocide and "ethnic cleansing." But it was to no avail. The November 1995 Dayton Agreement accepted an even division of Bosnia, between the Serbian-controlled Serbian Republic and the Bosnian Federation of Croats and Muslims. Its preamble spoke of "human dignity," "justice," and "tolerance," but in effect it rewarded Serbian genocide. A small NATO force was left behind to monitor a precarious cease-fire.

Officially, Bosnia remained a single country divided into two republics. As of June 1996, 1,319,250 Bosnian refugees had made their way to European nations that did not want them. They were unable to return to their former domiciles that had been "ethnically cleansed."[51] Muslims in Bosnia remained bitter that the world had done little to protect them.

### Kosovo

After the partition of Bosnia, the focus shifted to the Yugoslav province of Kosovo. Ninety percent of its people were Albanian Muslims, who were ruled by a Serb minority under the protection of Milošević in Belgrade. Early in 1999, deadly violence between the Albanian Kosovo Liberation Army (KLA) and the Serbian authorities began to escalate.

This time, the Clinton administration—prodded primarily by Secretary of State Madeleine Albright—decided to act. It would not stand by idly as it had in the other recent Balkan wars. Previously, Third World leaders had criticized the West for doing nothing while Hutus had gone about their business of exterminating Tutsis in Rwanda. This time the West would act.

Clinton knew he could not count on the UN, because Russia was certain to exercise its veto in the Security Council. Russia has historic ties to Serbia: Russians and Serbs are Slavs, they tend to be of the Orthodox faith, and in the past Russia had come to the assistance of Serbia against the Turks, Austrians, and Germans. Moreover, the Kremlin was unhappy with NATO's recent eastward expansion. It took the Clinton administration some doing to persuade its NATO allies to join the fray in Kosovo, but in the end they came onboard, agreeing that the alliance could not ignore another potential case of genocide in Europe.

When Milošević rejected Clinton's demand that he withdraw his army from Kosovo, NATO began an air war that lasted for seventy-eight days (March 24 until June 9, 1999). NATO here went into combat for the first time, even though Yugoslavia posed no threat against any of its members. At best, it was a war to uphold the self-esteem of NATO's member nations.

The war touched off precisely what the West had feared and had sought to avoid, the ethnic cleansing of Albanians—accompanied by arson, rapes, and mass executions. An estimated 850,000 refugees headed for the Albanian and Macedonian borders.

The air war involved 1,100 airplanes flying 38,000 sorties, the largest concentration of airpower in history. The Serb army in Kosovo was subjected to a hail of thousands of "smart" bombs and cruise missiles. NATO did not suffer a single combat fatality in what was the first war ever won solely by airpower. It became known as the first "telecommunications war," the first "virtual war," waged by remote control, with pilots using state-of-the-art computer displays to guide their bombs to their targets.

NATO was at pains to insist that it was not waging a war against the Serbian people, only against the government of Milošević. "Collateral damage" among Serb civilians was relatively small, particularly when one considers the scale of the sustained air attacks. One hundred sorties that went astray killed about 500 civilians. After the war, it became the KLA's turn to exact revenge. In the eight months after the war, 250,000 Kosovo Serbs were driven from their homes.

The fighting ended when Milošević agreed to withdraw from Kosovo. Under political pressure at home, Milošević agreed to hold a presidential election in September 2000. The winner, to his surprise, was the candidate of the Socialist Party, Vojislav Koštunica. At first Milošević refused to acknowledge defeat, but when street demonstrations became uncontrollable, he finally stepped down.

Koštunica was no more inclined than Milošević to accept the loss of Kosovo and the ongoing expulsion of Serbs from lands they considered to be theirs. In December 2000, the two sides were still trading mortar rounds across the three-mile buffer between Kosovo and Serbia. Koštunica warned that a declaration of independence by ethnic Albanians in Kosovo would touch off yet another Balkan war.

Officially, NATO had not gone to war to create a separate state of Kosovo. Once the Serbian army departed, however, an independent Kosovo was just a matter of time. An interim civilian government of a de facto independent Kosovo, headed by Ibrahim Rugova, was able to counterbalance the KLA, an army with a proclivity for violent and illegal behavior—including the smuggling of drugs and guns, extortion, and murder. After Rugova died in January 2006, the KLA seized power. The new prime minister was Hashim Thaçi, a former KLA guerrilla leader known for his ruthlessness.

Western leaders took the curious position that to contain the sporadic violence in Kosovo, it had to be granted de jure independence. With virtually no public debate, George W. Bush's administration—joined by Germany, France, and Britain—crossed its fingers and, in February 2008, extended diplomatic recognition to the poorest and most unstable nation of Europe, now known as the Republic of Kosovo. The dismemberment of what since 1919 had been the patchwork of Yugoslavia was now complete. Serbians—who considered Kosovo to be part of their patrimony—denounced the United States. Some of them broke into the US embassy in Belgrade and torched several rooms.[52]

Of the three men primarily responsible for the violence, only one was quickly apprehended. In 2001, Milošević became the first head of state since

World War II to face charges of war crimes and genocide. Acting as his own lawyer at the Hague International Criminal Tribunal, Milošević dragged out the proceedings for years until he died of a heart attack in March 2006.

The Bosnian Serb leaders, Karadžić and Mladić, indicted for the crime of genocide in 1995, went into hiding. When Karadžić was finally apprehended in July 2008, he followed Milošević's example and tied up the trial for years. A verdict was expected by 2014. Mladić eluded capture for sixteen years, until May 2011. But as his trial began, in November 2013, a prosecution error led to an indefinite suspension of the case against the ailing and aged general.

## Notes

1. "On a Course of Unity and Solidarity," *Pravda*, February 21, 1985; *Current Digest of the Soviet Press*, March 20, 1985, p. 7.

2. David Remnick, "Solzhenitsyn—A New Day in the Life," *Washington Post*, January 7, 1990, p. B3.

3. B. Minonov, "'Otkryvaia dver' v 'spetskhran,'" *Pravda*, September 10, 1988, p. 6.

4. "On the Agricultural Policies of the Communist Party of the Soviet Union Under Present Conditions," *Pravda*, March 16, 1989.

5. Cited in Ester B. Fein, "Gorbachev Hints He Would Accept Multiparty Rule," *New York Times*, January 14, 1990, p. 1.

6. The exact number is unknown. The Turkish government resents any mention of a massacre, denying it ever took place, merely admitting to Turkish-Armenian violence in which both sides suffered fatalities.

7. Esther Schrader, "Baku Refugees Celebrate Deaths of Azerbaijanis," *Baltimore Sun*, January 23, 1990, p. 4A.

8. Jerry F. Hough, "Gorbachev's Politics," *Foreign Affairs* (Winter 1989–1990), p. 30.

9. See the interrogations of the conspirators in V. A. Zatova and T. K. Speranskaia, eds., *Avgust-91* (Moscow: Politizdat, 1991), pp. 253–271.

10. Leslie Gelb, "The Russian Sinkhole," *New York Times*, March 30, 1992, p. A17; Steven Greenhouse, "Point Man for the Rescue of the Century," *New York Times*, April 26, 1992, section 3, pp. 1, 6.

11. Aleksandr Pumpianskii, "Sud na partiei, kotoraia byla pravitel'stvo," *Novoe vremia*, no. 42 (1992), p. 5.

12. *Baltimore Sun*, April 28, 1991, p. 11A; based on *Europa World Yearbook*, 1989 Soviet Census, and *World Almanac*.

13. Joe Murray in an interview with Gamsakhurdia, "Outside the Stronghold," *Baltimore Sun*, October 30, 1991, p. 9A.

14. Galina Kovalskaia, "Kavkaztsam v Stavropole doroga zakazana," *Novoe vremia*, no. 28 (1992), pp. 8–9.

15. Zhores A. Medvedev, "Property Rights," *In These Times*, April 19, 1993, p. 29; Stephen F. Cohen, "American Policy and Russia's Future," *The Nation*, April 12, 1993, p. 480.

16. Cited by Stephen F. Cohen, *Failed Crusade: America and the Tragedy of Post-Communist Russia* (New York: W. W. Norton, 2000), p. 115.

17. Cited in Michael Specter, "From Mother Russia with Brute Force," *New York Times*, January 21, 1996, p. 6E.

18. The estimated fatalities vary widely. Among the highest, 80,000, is that of Michael Specter, "The Wars of Aleksandr Ivanovich Lebed," *New York Times Magazine*, October 13, 1996, p. 44.

19. "Chechnya Will Never Be Part of Russia, Top Rebel Leader Says," *Baltimore Sun*, October 7, 1996, p. 7A.

20. Comment by Sergei Karaganov to David Remnick, "The War for the Kremlin," *The New Yorker,* July 22, 1966, p. 50. In October 2000, Yeltsin, in his third book of memoirs, confirmed this scenario.

21. Remnick, "The War for the Kremlin," p. 49. Daniel Treisman, "Why Yeltsin Won," *Foreign Affairs* (September–October 1996), pp. 64–77.

22. Cohen, *Failed Crusade*, p. 49. According to World Bank figures, about one-third lived in poverty; *World Development Report 2000/2001: Attacking Poverty* (New York: Oxford University Press, 2000), p. 281.

23. Andrew Meier and Yuri Zarakhovich, "Putin Tightens His Grip," *Time*, May 29, 2000, p. 24.

24. Cited by Amy Knight, "Hit First and Hit Hard," *Times Literary Supplement*, June 9, 2000.

25. World Bank figures for Afghanistan in 1979 put it among the "low-income developing countries . . . with incomes below about a dollar per person per day." World Bank Atlas, www.worldbank.org.

26. Associated Press, "Soviets Facing Oil Crunch, CIA Director Says," *Baltimore Evening Sun*, April 22, 1980, p. A5. In September 1981, the CIA announced that the Soviet Union's energy prospects looked "highly favorable for the rest of the century." Bernard Gwertzman, "Soviet Is Able to Raise Production of Oil and Gas, US Agency Says," *New York Times*, September 3, 1981, pp. A1, D14.

27. Raymond L. Garthoff, *Détente and Revolution: American-Soviet Relations from Nixon to Reagan* (Washington, DC: Brookings Institution, 1985), pp. 887–965; Chalmers Johnson, "Abolish the CIA!" *London Review of Books*, October 21, 2005, p. 25.

28. Michael Dobbs, "Secret Memos Trace Kremlin's March to War," *Washington Post*, November 15, 1992, pp. A1, A32; Christian Parenti, "Ideology and Electricity," *Nation*, May 7, 2012, p. 32. See also the memoirs of KGB colonel Alexander Morozov, the deputy of intelligence operations in Kabul during 1975–1979, "Kabul'skii rezident," *Novoe vremia*, nos. 38–41 (1991); and "KGB i afganskie lidery," *Novoe vremia*, no. 20 (1992).

29. Gerard Chaliand, *Report from Afghanistan* (New York: Penguin, 1982), p. 49.

30. Steven Coll, *Ghost Wars: The Secret History of the CIA, Afghanistan, and bin Laden, from the Soviet Invasion to September 10, 2001* (New York: Penguin, 2004), pp. 155–156.

31. "Spravka 'NV,'" *Novoe vremia*, no. 17 (1992), p. 26.

32. Coll, *Ghost Wars*, p. 234.

33. Michael Dobbs, K. S. Karol, and Dessa Trevisan, *Poland, Solidarity, Walesa* (New York: McGraw-Hill, 1981), p. 70.

34. Andrew Cockburn, *The Threat: Inside the Soviet Military Machine*, 2nd rev. ed. (New York: Random House, 1984), pp. 111–114, 178–180; Michael T. Kaufman, "Bloc Was Prepared to Crush Solidarity, a Defector Says," *New York Times*, April 17, 1987, p. A9.

35. World Bank, *World Development Report, 1989* (Washington, DC: World Bank, 1989), p. 165.

36. "A Survey of Eastern Europe," *The Economist*, August 12, 1989, p. 10.

37. Craig Whitney, "East Europe Joins the Market and Gets a Preview of the Pain," *New York Times*, January 7, 1990, p. E3.

38. Reuters, "Study Shows High Cost of German Unification: Report," November 7, 2009.

39. For the statements, see *New York Times*, December 5, 1989, p. A15.

40. Diana Jean Schemo, "Soviet Troops to Leave Czech Soil," *Baltimore Sun*, January 6, 1990, p. 2A.

41. Cited in William Pfaff, "Change in a Vulnerable Land," *Baltimore Sun*, December 22, 1989, p. 17A.

42. Mary Battiata, "State's Violence Sparked Rebellion," *Washington Post*, December 31, 1989, p. A1.

43. Edward Behr, *Kiss the Hand You Cannot Bite: The Rise and Fall of the Ceauşescus* (New York: Villard Books, 1991), chapter 13, pp. 251–268. Behr cites a Romanian proverb: "A change of rulers is the joy of fools." Antonia Rados, *Die Verschwörung der Securitate: Rumäniens verratene Revolution* (Hamburg: Hoffmann und Campe, 1990); Bartholomäus Grill, "Revolution der Funktionäre," *Die Zeit*, January 11, 1991, p. 30.

44. William Pfaff, "Romania Moves Forward to the Past," *Baltimore Sun*, June 21, 1990, p. 11A; Associated Press, "Iliescu Inaugurated with Pledge to Defend Democracy," *Baltimore Sun*, June 21, 1990, p. 4A.

45. New York Times News Service, "Romanian Voters Look Both Left and Right," *Baltimore Sun*, November 26, 2000, p. 29A.

46. June 28 is St. Vitus' Day. It was on that day in 1914 that Gavrilo Princip, a member of the Serb nationalist group the Black Hand, assassinated the heir to the Austrian throne, Francis Ferdinand, touching off World War I.

47. Helsinki Commission on Security and Cooperation in Europe, *The Referendum on Independence in Bosnia-Herzegovina, February 29–March 1, 1992* (Washington, DC: US Government Printing Office, 1992), p. 3.

48. Robert Block, "The Madness of General Mladić," *New York Review of Books*, October 5, 1995, pp. 7–9.

49. Charles Lane and Thom Shanker, "Bosnia: What the CIA Didn't Tell Us," *New York Review of Books*, May 9, 1996, pp. 10–15.

50. Commission on Security and Cooperation in Europe, "Prosecuting War Crimes in the Former Yugoslavia: An Update," *CSCE Digest* (May 1996), pp. 13, 21–27.

51. Figures by the United Nations High Commissioner for Refugees, "Doors Slam," *The Economist*, September 28, 1996, p. 64.

52. Mark Kramer, "Welcome to Kosova, the Next Failed State?" *Washington Post*, March 2, 2008, p. B3.

# 20

# The Nuclear Arms Race

**The Cold War produced an unchecked nuclear arms race in which** neither the United States nor the Soviet Union dared fall behind the other. An increase in one side's nuclear arsenal or advances in weapons technology had to be matched by the other. Various studies in the first three decades of the arms race concluded that 200–300 nuclear warheads could utterly destroy each side. By the late 1950s, the strategic nuclear arsenal of the United States took on an irrational dimension and the Soviet Union was not far behind. The weapons, however, were useful only as deterrents, for they could not be used offensively in a first strike without inviting certain retaliation. "Overkill," the ability to destroy the enemy several times over, became institutionalized—and thus rationalized. The stockpiling of nuclear weapons became an end in itself.

Secretary of Defense Robert McNamara acknowledged in 1964 that a nuclear force of 400 megatons (the equivalent of 4,000 million tons of TNT) was enough to sustain a balance of terror that became known as MAD, short for Mutually Assured Destruction. Yet, when McNamara spoke, the United States already possessed 17,000 megatons, or more than forty times the amount deemed necessary to destroy the Soviet Union.

For decades, it was believed that nuclear weapons were relatively cheap, as compared to the costs of maintaining, equipping, and deploying large armed forces. These bombs, it was said in the United States, provided "more bang for the buck." The bombs themselves, indeed, were relatively cheap. The nuclear deterrent, however, entailed more than merely building bombs. A 1998 Brookings Institution study calculated that the various components of the nuclear program—research, development, manufacture, deployment itself, command and control, defense, and dismantlement—had cost the

United States a staggering $5.8 trillion since 1940, an average of $21,646 per citizen.[1]

Throughout the arms race, the United States maintained the lead despite political rhetoric of bomber and missile gaps favoring the Soviet Union. As a presidential candidate, John Kennedy charged that the Eisenhower administration had been asleep at the helm and had permitted the Soviets to forge ahead in the missile race. As president, Kennedy laid that myth to rest after the Pentagon's civilian leadership announced in 1961 that the United States possessed a second-strike capability—that is, the ability to retaliate—that was more powerful than a potential Soviet first strike. The hard cold fact of US supremacy, coupled with the Soviets' humiliation during the Cuban missile crisis the following year, put two items on the Kremlin agenda: closing the missile gap favoring the United States and negotiating with Washington to establish a rough nuclear parity between the two superpowers.

The Cuban missile crisis had a sobering effect, leading to a gradual improvement in East-West relations. Détente led to several US-Soviet treaties to limit a further escalation of the nuclear arms race. The first such treaty was a partial Nuclear Test Ban Treaty in 1963, which prohibited nuclear testing in the atmosphere, in outer space, and on the high seas. The United States and the Soviet Union then took their nuclear weapons tests underground, thus limiting environmental contamination. More than 100 other nations also signed the treaty. Notable exceptions were France, already a nuclear power, and Communist China, soon to become one in 1964. Both countries joined the treaty in 1992.

Additional agreements followed. They included the Outer Space Treaty (1967), which banned nuclear weapons in space and in earth orbit; the Nuclear Non-Proliferation Treaty (1968), by which the Soviet Union, United States, Great Britain, and eighty-three other nations pledged to prevent the spread of nuclear weapons and technology; the Seabed Pact (1971), which prohibited nuclear arms on the ocean floor beyond a nation's twelve-mile limit; and the Biological Warfare Treaty (1972), which outlawed the development, production, and stockpiling of biological weapons.

### The SALT Treaties

Still, the superpowers continued to add to their nuclear arsenals by developing and testing new weapons and by deploying additional warheads. Toward the end of the 1960s, Washington and Moscow agreed on the need to control the open-ended arms race, leading to the Strategic Arms Limitation Talks (SALT), the purpose of which was to limit the costly and potentially catastrophic nuclear arms race. When negotiations began in the late 1960s, both sides had more than enough weapons to destroy the other side many times over. The SALT negotiations were meant to bring an element of control and rationality to the arms race.

## Glossary of Nuclear Weapons Terms

**ABM** Antiballistic missile; a defensive missile to destroy incoming enemy missiles

**ASAT** Antisatellite missile; a missile to neutralize satellites in Earth orbit; a central component of SDI

**ICBM** Intercontinental ballistic missile

**INF** Intermediate-range nuclear forces; see "theater weapons," below

**IRBM** Intermediate-range ballistic missile (such as the Pershing II and the SS-20)

**MIRV** Multiple independently targeted reentry vehicle; a missile carrying several smaller missiles, each capable of reaching a different target

**NMD** National Missile Defense; US program for an antimissile defense system; a scaled-down version of SDI

**NPT** Nuclear Non-Proliferation Treaty

**payload** Destructive power of a warhead, measured in megatonnage (1 megaton equals 1 million tons of TNT; 1 kiloton equals 1,000 tons of TNT); a bomb with an explosive force of about 12 kilotons destroyed Hiroshima, where at least 70,000 people died; in the 1970s, US strategic warheads carried an average payload of more than 4 megatons, or more than 300 times the Hiroshima bomb; the warheads of the Soviet Union were even larger

**SALT** Strategic Arms Limitations Treaty; the emphasis is on strategic and limitations

**SDI** Strategic Defense Initiative; the official name of Star Wars

**SLBM** Submarine-launched ballistic missile

**START** Strategic Arms Reduction Treaty; the emphasis is on reduction rather than merely limitation

**strategic weapons** Warheads carried over long distances (usually over 3,000 miles); they include intercontinental missiles, bombers, and submarine-launched missiles

**tactical weapons** Short-range nuclear battlefield weapons (such as artillery shells)

**theater weapons** Intermediate-range weapons for use in a specific global region, or theater (such as Europe or the Far East); also known as INF

**warhead** A nuclear bomb

President Richard Nixon and Communist Party chief Leonid Brezhnev signed the first SALT Treaty (known as SALT I) in Moscow in May 1972. Its aim was modest: a limit on the deployment of strategic weapons with a range of 6,000 miles or more. They included the intercontinental bomber forces, intercontinental ballistic missiles (ICBMs), and submarine-launched ballistic missiles (SLBMs). SALT I, however, did not put a dent in either side's arsenal; it merely placed a ceiling on the their destructive powers. But SALT I marked the beginning of a process of mutual consultation. The negotiators expressed hope that subsequent treaties would address the more difficult problem of actually *reducing* the number of nuclear weapons.

SALT I froze the existing number of land-based ICBMs, leaving the Soviet Union with a numerical advantage in ICBMs: 1,398 to 1,052. The Nixon administration, to appease domestic critics, argued that the agreement prevented the Soviet Union's from deploying additional surface-to-surface missiles, notably its latest, the powerful SS-9.[2] Moreover, the treaty offered the United States several advantages. It ignored the questions of US intercontinental bombers (in which the United States always enjoyed a marked superiority), US intermediate-range missiles in Europe (which became a major issue during the early 1980s), and the French and British arsenals. Moscow also accepted, if only for the time being, Washington's two-to-one advantage in the number of strategic warheads.

But the treaty did not limit MIRVs (multiple independently targeted reentry vehicles), which gave missiles the capability to carry several warheads, which could be directed at separate targets. When MIRVed, the missile—the expensive component—carries multiple warheads, the less expensive components. During the SALT I negotiations, the United States had refused to discuss the Soviet proposal to ban MIRVed missiles, as it saw no reason to give up its most significant nuclear weapon advantage. US negotiators soon had reasons to regret their decision, however.

SALT I was not expected to halt the arms race. For one, it did not prevent improvements in the quality of weapons, which continued to become increasingly more sophisticated and destructive. The emphasis on limiting launchers (that is, bombers, missiles, and submarines) made less and less sense, since the launchers carried ever more warheads, the component that actually causes the damage.

After the Soviet Union deployed its own MIRVed missiles in the mid-1970s, MIRV technology worked to its advantage. The Soviet ICBMs were larger and much more powerful than the US ICBMs, and thus were able to carry up to thirty independently targeted warheads. In contrast, the heaviest US ICBM, the Minuteman III, carried only three warheads. What the United States needed was a second SALT agreement that put a limit on the number of MIRVed warheads on each ICBM.

In June 1979, Leonid Brezhnev and Jimmy Carter met in Vienna to sign SALT II. The treaty established a ceiling of 2,400 missile launchers, of which only 1,320 could be fitted with MIRVed warheads. Moreover, the number of warheads on each missile was limited to ten. SALT II thus created a cap to blunt the Soviet Union's strategic strength, its land-based ICBMs. But it also perpetuated the Soviet Union's 5:2 advantage in ICBM warheads. US proponents of SALT II argued that the gap would have been much wider had it not been for the treaty. To offset the Soviet Union's powerful land-based nuclear arsenal, SALT II gave the United States a decisive advantage in other categories, particularly submarine-launched ballistic missiles (SLBMs).

The signing ceremony proved to be the last act of détente. By that time a climate of mutual suspicion was again on the rise. US critics of negotiations with the Soviet Union were becoming increasingly vocal. They argued that the Soviet Union could not have it both ways: It could not expect normal relations with the West while also supporting revolutionary movements in Africa and Asia. Détente, these critics insisted, must be tied to improved Soviet behavior, especially abroad. The international climate worsened when US embassy personnel were taken hostage in Iran in November 1979. Some even blamed the Soviet Union for it. Eight weeks later, the Soviet army invaded Afghanistan.

Washington's version of détente was always linked to a change in Soviet behavior, particularly in Afghanistan. Moscow, however, defined détente as the Western acceptance of its status as a major power on par with the United States. After all, the Soviets argued, they had normalized US-Soviet relations when the United States was engaged in a war against "international Communism" in Vietnam. For them, they tried to explain, détente had been more important than Vietnam; but for the United States, Afghanistan was more important than détente.[3]

In the United States, the suspicion lingered that détente and the SALT treaties had made it possible for the Soviet Union to forge ahead in the nuclear arms race. The most vocal critic of détente by 1980 was the Republican presidential hopeful Ronald Reagan, who declared that the SALT treaties had opened a "window of vulnerability" and that only one side, the Soviet Union, was engaged in the arms race. The United States, he declared, had in effect disarmed unilaterally. Reagan gained considerable traction with this political argument. In reality, however, the United States had doubled its strategic arsenal in the 1970s. By the time of the 1980 presidential election, the Soviet Union had narrowed the gap, but the United States continued to lead. It was never a race with only one contestant.

Nuclear arms negotiations became a casualty of the renewed Cold War. The US Senate never ratified SALT II, in part because critics such as Reagan had hammered home the point that it favored the Soviet Union. Once Reagan became president, however, he gave tacit recognition to the fact that SALT had, after all, placed a limit on the Soviet Union's strategic strength. The Joint Chiefs, too, acknowledged as much when they urged the treaty's ratification, calling it "a modest but useful step."[4] Reagan agreed to abide by the unratified terms of SALT II for the next five years. Even as US-Soviet relations deteriorated during the early 1980s, a succession of Soviet leaders abided by SALT II, even though they had no legal obligation to do so.

## The Correlation of Forces

By the mid-1980s, the United States and Soviet Union had roughly the same number of deliverable nuclear warheads. The configurations of their delivery systems, however, were different.

The Soviet nuclear "triad" consisted of 65 percent of its warheads deployed in land-based missiles, 27 percent in submarines, and a scant 8 percent (an amount sufficient to destroy the United States, however) in intercontinental bombers. The Soviets relied largely on their powerful land-based ICBMs carrying up to ten warheads. US missiles were smaller and contained less powerful, but more accurate, warheads. Because their missiles were less accurate, the Soviets counted on larger warheads and thus enjoyed an advantage in "payload," or "megatonnage." (As missiles became increasingly accurate, however, both sides reduced the explosive power of their warheads.) If one focused on payload, then the Soviet Union was ahead in the nuclear arms race; but if one took into account accuracy, then the advantage went to the United States.

The better balanced—and thus more sensible—US strategic "triad" ensured that 51 percent of its warheads were deployed in submarines, 30 percent in its intercontinental bomber force, and only 19 percent in land-based missiles. Should the Soviets choose to knock out any single leg of the US triad, the retaliatory power of any one of the other two legs provided a credible and powerful second-strike deterrent. Unlike Soviet warheads, most US warheads were not stationary targets on land, whose location was known to spy satellites in orbit, but instead were constantly on the move in the world's oceans.

The different compositions of the respective triads posed a problem for determining an equitable formula to stem the nuclear arms race. The Soviet Union, with its massive land-based force, was not about to negotiate away its strength.[5] Yet its missiles deployed in land-based silos were vulnerable targets. Moreover, its ground-based ICBMs used liquid fuel and were thus slow to fire. US missiles, in contrast, used a solid-fuel propellant and therefore could be fired virtually at will. It was for this reason that the Soviet Union eventually managed to solve the riddle of how to build smaller, mobile, solid-fuel ICBMs. The mobile ICBMs added a new element to the arms race, the increasing difficulty in verifying their location.

During the first half of the 1980s, both sides produced greater numbers of ever more accurate nuclear weapons at a furious pace. In December 1981, the Soviet Union walked out of arms-reduction talks in Geneva when it failed to halt the deployment of US intermediate-range missiles (Pershing IIs) as well as cruise missiles. Talks were not resumed until March 1985. During the intervening forty months, both sides added approximately one new warhead every day to their strategic arsenals (2,000 in all during the first half of the 1980s). That did not include intermediate-range weapons, which both sides continued to deploy as well.

In the mid-1980s, the United States possessed the ability to destroy the Soviet Union fifty times with its strategic arsenal alone (see Table 20.1). As a result, US strategic planners ran out of targets. The surfeit of atomic warheads forced them to look for new targets, such as grain elevators in Ukraine and open fields that Soviet bombers could conceivably use—their airfields having been destroyed—on their return trips from the United States.[6] The Soviet Union's ability to destroy the United States was little different. The pointlessness of continuously adding to the nuclear arsenals had led Henry Kissinger to ask, in 1974: "What in the name of God is strategic superiority? . . . What do you do with it?"[7]

### Intermediate-Range Weapons

The introduction of a new generation of sophisticated intermediate-range missiles by both sides, starting in the mid-1970s, made matters worse. For the Europeans, these weapons suggested that they just might become the first casualty in a nuclear war.

**Table 20.1  US and Soviet Strategic Arsenal, 1985**

|  | Number of Warheads | Percentage of Strategic Arsenal |
|---|---|---|
| *United States* | | |
| 1,035 ICBMs | 2,125 | 19 |
| 36 submarines with 640 missiles | 5,728 | 51 |
| 263 B-52 bombers, 98 of which carry | | |
| 12 cruise missiles each | 3,072 | 27 |
| 61 FB-111 bombers | 366 | 3 |
| Total | 11,291 | 100 |
| | | |
| *Soviet Union* | | |
| 1,398 ICBMs | 6,420 | 65 |
| 62 submarines with 924 missiles | 2,688 | 27 |
| 173 bombers, 25 of which carry | | |
| 10 cruise missiles each | 792 | 8 |
| Total | 9,900 | 100 |

*Source: New York Times*, October 4, 1985. All figures are estimates of classified information. Compiled from Pentagon publications, the International Institute for Strategic Studies, the Arms Control Association, and the Center for Defense Information.

The Europeans, as well as the Soviets, with their record of suffering and defeat, had a better understanding than most individuals in the United States that history is all too often tragedy. The destruction wreaked by World War II, a conventional war fought with primitive weapons by modern standards, remained a recent memory in Europe. Berlin, Stalingrad, and many other cities retained in place selected ruins as museum pieces serving as a reminder of the war. The persistence to negotiate, if only to limit the arms race, was a mute tribute to the uncomfortable fact that a nuclear war could have no winners. The ruins in Germany and the Soviet Union did not reveal which country had won and which had lost World War II.

Initially, the focus had been on strategic, long-range nuclear weapons. Starting in the 1950s, however, both sides began to accumulate an arsenal of intermediate-range arms. In the mid-1970s, the Soviets began to deploy their most sophisticated medium-range missiles—the mobile SS-20s—capable of devastating every capital city in Europe. The SS-20 was a significant improvement over the older, single-warhead, liquid-fuel SS-4s and SS-5s. It had a range greater than 3,000 miles, it was mobile, it contained three independently targeted warheads, and it used a solid-fuel engine that could be fired quickly. This new addition to the Kremlin's military might produced a psychological shock among Western military strategists. The SS-20 did not change the nuclear balance, but it did give the appearance of a Soviet escalation of the arms race, a perception that was largely correct.

The United States responded, predictably, with its own intermediate-range weapons in Europe, the Tomahawk cruise missile and the Pershing II ballistic missile. Slow-moving, cruise missiles hug the ground during target approach and are therefore difficult to detect and destroy in flight. With a range of approximately 2,000 miles, the Tomahawk cruise missiles were capable of reaching the Soviet Union from West European soil. The Pershing II was a fast-flying missile with a range greater than 1,100 miles. Its mobility, range, accuracy, and speed made it one of the premier weapons in the US arsenal. It was a potential first-strike weapon suitable for the elimination, or "decapitation," of Soviet command structures. The distinction between "strategic" and "theater" missiles became increasingly blurred. What was the difference, for example, between a Minuteman missile fired from Wyoming (thirty minutes' flying time to a Soviet target) and a Pershing II missile fired from West Germany (six minutes' flying time)?

The nuclear arms race was becoming increasingly illogical. The atomic bomb had given the United States the "ultimate weapon," only to face the prospect of its own nuclear annihilation within ten short years. Similarly, the SS-20 briefly gave the Kremlin an advantage in case of a nuclear exchange in Europe—provided the war could be limited to Europe, a most unlikely prospect. When the United States countered with cruise and Tomahawk missiles, the Soviet Union became less secure.

To be effective, the cruise and Tomahawk missiles had to be stationed on European soil. Presidents Carter and Reagan had their work cut out in selling their deployment to their NATO allies. The Europeans understood all too well that the Soviet and US arsenals threatened to turn their continent into a nuclear shooting gallery. Reagan did not help matters when he said, "I could see where you could have the exchange of tactical weapons in the field [in Europe] without it bringing either one of the major powers to pushing the [strategic] button."[8] The prospect of fighting a limited nuclear war in Europe split NATO on whether to accept the missiles. Still, the United States was able to convince several NATO allies to accept 464 cruise missiles and 108 Pershing IIs.[9]

This round of escalation produced a series of discussions in Geneva beginning in the spring of 1981. Each side sought to eliminate the other side's missiles while holding on to its own arsenal. It was a prescription for deadlock. Instead of seeking compromises, negotiators played to larger audiences, to their people back home and the nervous Europeans. Propaganda and accusations of bad faith became the order of the day.

The two chief negotiators, Yuli Kvitsinsky for the Soviet Union and Paul Nitze for the United States, eventually came up with a compromise, the so-called "walk-in-the-woods" proposal (named after their stroll through a wooded park in Geneva during which they came up with it). It called for a rough balance between the Soviet Union's seventy-five SS-20s (each carrying three warheads) and the United States' seventy-five Tomahawk cruise missiles (each with four warheads). By this proposal, the Soviets would have had to curtail, but not scrap, the deployment of their SS-20s, while the United States would have had to forgo the deployment of its Pershing IIs. Hard-liners in Moscow and Washington quickly denounced the compromise. In December 1981, the Soviets left the conference table when the United States deployed on schedule the first cruise missiles and Pershing IIs in Great Britain and West Germany, respectively. The deadlock lasted three and a half years; in the meantime, missile deployment accelerated.

In April 1985, about a month after the Soviet and US negotiators had resumed talks in Geneva, the new Soviet leader, Mikhail Gorbachev, announced a six-month freeze on further deployment of SS-20s, provided the United States halt the deployment of its missiles in NATO countries. There was nothing in Gorbachev's proposal, however, suggesting a reduction of the Soviet arsenal. If anything, the Soviet deployment was largely completed. The Soviet gesture was too little, too late. Instead of facing seventy-five slow-moving cruise missiles, as proposed during the "walk in the woods," the Soviets now faced fifty-four deadly Pershing IIs and forty-eight cruise missiles, with the prospect of more to come. Western Europe, in turn, faced 250 of the Soviet Union's 414 SS-20s.

## Star Wars: The Strategic Defense Initiative

In March 1983, the arms race took another twist when President Reagan went public with a military research program long on the drawing board. It was a missile defense system officially called the Strategic Defense Initiative (SDI), commonly referred to as "Star Wars." Its purpose was to protect US land-based missiles in the event that the Soviet Union struck first with its powerful and accurate land-based ICBMs, notably the SS-18s. With this pronouncement, Reagan officially committed the United States to creating an entirely new and futuristic defense system designed to disarm the Soviet nuclear missile arsenal.

Thus far, the avoidance of all-out nuclear war had been based on deterrence—the balance of terror—based on the assumption that neither side wanted to commit suicide. Mutually Assured Destruction had kept the peace.

In the late 1960s, the Soviets had entertained the idea of creating their own defensive shield, which was unacceptable to the United States for the same reason the Soviets found Star Wars unacceptable. US officials warned that a Soviet anti-missile shield would lead to US countermeasures. The United States could simply increase its number of warheads to overwhelm the Soviet defenses. The Soviet shield promised a new round of escalation. Washington prevailed upon Moscow to abandon its missile defense program. The resultant compromise accord, the Anti-Ballistic Missile (ABM) Treaty (1972), permitted both sides to create two *limited* defensive systems each, which neither bothered to develop fully.

The ABM Treaty became part and parcel of SALT, without which SALT I would have been impossible. The United States was not about to sign any agreement whereby it agreed to freeze its missile strength while sitting by as the Soviets put in place a defensive shield designed to neutralize the US strategic arsenal. The simple, brutal deterrent of Mutually Assured Destruction remained intact.

In March 1983, however, eleven years after the ratification of the ABM Treaty, Reagan announced his plans for Star Wars, a highly complex defensive system slated for completion within twenty-five years. Reagan had never been comfortable with arms agreements that accepted Soviet parity with the United States. That and his unlimited faith in US ingenuity and know-how led him to opt for a program that, he argued, would protect the United States and its allies and not cause an escalation of the arms race.

Reagan's proposal would nullify Mutually Assured Destruction, which he regarded as immoral, since it was a strategy predicated on the potential annihilation of the United States. A high-tech barrier capable of shooting down missiles before they reached their targets, he argued, would make nuclear war impossible. He even suggested that once US scientists had solved the riddle of how to intercept incoming Soviet ICBMs, the United States would hand over the technology to the Soviet Union. Nuclear war would then become impossible and peace would prevail. The ultimate goal, Reagan said, was "to eliminate the weapons themselves."[10]

Star Wars played to mixed reviews. Its theoretical underpinnings could not be faulted. But there were serious problems in implementing a missile defense of such staggering complexity. First, to be effective it would have to be nearly perfect. Since merely 2 percent of the Soviet Union's existing strategic arsenal could destroy the United States, a 90 percent efficiency in the Star Wars defense system—which, according to some scientists, was the best that could be gained—would not do. Mutually Assured Destruction would continue to prevail, for 10 percent of the Soviet Union's 10,000 nuclear warheads would destroy the United States several times over. Still, from the Kremlin's perspective, Star Wars threatened to neutralize the bulk of its nuclear arsenal, something it could not abide.

Star Wars threatened another escalation of the arms race. The Soviets were being given the choice of accepting US nuclear superiority or of deploying additional missiles and warheads weapons capable of overwhelming the Star Wars defense system. Predictably, they threatened to invoke the latter option.

Then there was the staggering cost of Star Wars. Despite already running a record federal deficit of more than $200 billion per year, Reagan requested a budget of $30 billion ($3.7 billion for fiscal 1986) for research and development during the first five years.

Another problem was the complexity of the system. Star Wars called for a new generation of sensors for the surveillance, tracking, and destruction of enemy missiles. They would have to work flawlessly to be able to discriminate among thousands of incoming warheads and decoys. The program also envisioned the deployment of energy weapons, primarily powerful lasers, based either on the ground (and deflected by huge mirrors circling the planet) or in orbit. It would militarize space in violation of the 1967 Outer Space Treaty, part of international space law. The most crucial part of the entire program, "systems concepts and battle management," called for an error-free computer system that instantaneously linked the system's diverse elements.[11]

Star Wars was intended to protect the United States against incoming missiles, but the program's components, too, would need to be defended. Mirrors and spy satellites in orbit would be inviting targets that could easily be neutralized.

Finally, Soviet scientists were sure to work overtime to find ways over, under, around, and through any missile defense envisioned by their US counterparts.

In light of these obstacles, it was little wonder that Pentagon officials told Congress, which had to finance Star Wars, that this was a long-range program of at least twenty-five years' duration. There was soon talk, however, of an "interim deployment" to protect land-based missiles. This put first things first; civilians would have to wait. Former defense secretary Harold Brown admitted, "technology does not offer even a reasonable prospect of a population defense."[12]

Domestic critics of Star Wars feared that it would result in an open-ended contest in space that would give neither side added security. Reagan's secretary of defense, Caspar Weinberger, when asked how he would view a unilateral deployment of a Soviet version of Star Wars, replied that such an act "would be one of the most frightening prospects I could imagine."[13] That was precisely the reason why the Kremlin repeatedly threatened that it would not accept Star Wars and, if necessary, would join in the militarization of space.

## Gorbachev's Peace Offensive

Mikhail Gorbachev, upon coming to power in March 1985, launched a "peace offensive." He was determined to bring about not only domestic perestroika but one in foreign relations as well. "We will rob you of your enemy," he told the West. His proposal to freeze the deployment of Soviet SS-20 intermediate-range missiles was his first move.

Soon the world witnessed a number of summit meetings between Gorbachev and Reagan, who had previously resolutely refused to sit down with his Soviet counterparts. Soviet leaders Brezhnev, Andropov, and Chernenko were clearly dying men; moreover, Reagan felt there had been nothing to talk about with the leaders of what he had called the "evil empire." The first meeting between Reagan and Gorbachev was a successful get-acquainted session in November 1985, in neutral Geneva. Several factors played a role in Reagan's turnabout. He had been criticized at home as being the first president since 1945 who had not met with Soviet leaders. He also came to realize he was dealing with a new type of Soviet man.

The first order of business was the recent nuclear arms escalation in the heart of Europe: the deployment of intermediate-range nuclear forces (INF) such as US Pershing IIs and cruise missiles and Soviet SS-20s. Gorbachev surprised Reagan when he suddenly dusted off an old US proposal, the "zero-option," that Reagan had proposed to Brezhnev in November 1981, on the eve of the first deployment of the Soviet Union's SS-20 missiles: If Moscow did not deploy the SS-20s, Washington would not counter with its cruise and Tomahawk missiles. Gorbachev would undo Brezhnev's error; he would take Soviet INF forces out of Europe if the United States did the same. Gorbachev called Washington's bluff: If Reagan rejected the zero-option to eliminate all INFs, the US position would be exposed as another example of Cold War propaganda.

Reagan responded positively. The result—after a year of difficult negotiations—was the INF Treaty of May 1988, which eliminated an entire category of nuclear missiles, those with a range between 310 and 3,400 miles. Under the watchful eyes of onsite inspectors, the superpowers dismantled their costly weapons—1,752 Soviet and 867 US missiles.[14]

Reagan was then able to turn to one of his favorite programs, the Strategic Arms Reduction Talks (START). Early in his presidency, he had argued—correctly—that SALT had accomplished little. SALT merely kept the nuclear arms race within broad parameters, making it possible, nevertheless, for both sides to increase their strategic arsenals. When the INF Treaty was signed, the US arsenal still contained 13,134 strategic warheads, and the Soviet arsenal contained 10,664.[15] Reagan believed the time had come to reduce both.

Reagan found a responsive partner in Gorbachev. Earlier, in October 1985, Gorbachev had already proposed a 50-percent reduction of strategic nuclear forces, which would lessen the Soviet threat to US land-based missiles. In October 1987, at their summit in Reykjavik, Iceland, Gorbachev went so far as to offer Reagan the elimination of all strategic nuclear weapons. A surprised Reagan was on the verge of accepting before his suspicious advisors interfered. They feared that a world free of nuclear weapons would leave Western Europe at the mercy of superior Soviet conventional forces.

Gorbachev was not finished with his surprises, however. On December 7, 1988, he launched another volley in his peace offensive. He announced—unilaterally and without precondition—the reduction in the Soviet armed forces by 10 percent (500,000 soldiers), as well as the elimination of 800 airplanes, 8,500 pieces of artillery, and 5,000 tanks within two years. Included in the offer was the promise to dissolve six of the fifteen Soviet divisions in East Germany, Hungary, and Czechoslovakia by 1991. But most important, Gorbachev pledged the withdrawal from central Europe of Soviet assault troops and mobile bridges designed for crossing rivers. Gorbachev's speech marked a 180-degree turn in Soviet military doctrine as it had existed since the early 1960s. The Soviet conventional military threat against Western Europe was about to be dismantled. The East German party chief Erich Honecker immediately recognized what he called the "immense historical significance" of the Soviet troop withdrawal.[16] Gorbachev's speech also shocked many in the US defense community; some saw it as a propaganda offensive designed to disarm the West, even comparing it to Pearl Harbor.

The critics of Gorbachev's speech of December 7, 1988, were partly correct. The first casualty of that speech was the US program of "modernizing" the short-range Lance missile, a tactical nuclear weapon. The Lance II, a new weapon with a range of just under the 310-mile limit stipulated by the INF Treaty, made possible the circumvention of the spirit, if not the letter, of that treaty. The Lance II would give the United States a backdoor to maintaining an INF arsenal.

West German politics torpedoed the Lance II "modernization" program. The powerful Social Democratic opposition party insisted that the shorter-range rockets, too, must go. "The shorter the rockets, the deader the Germans" became the West German catchphrase. In February 1989, Egon Bahr, the national security expert of the Social Democratic Party, explained to Brent Scowcroft, US president George H. W. Bush's national security advisor, that the United States had no chance of deploying the Lance II. If the conservative government in Bonn capitulated to US pressure and accepted the weapons, his party would win the next election and take them out.[17] West German foreign minister Hans-Dietrich Genscher, who was born in Halle, East Germany, and whose relatives still lived there, declared: "I have sworn an oath to avert harm from the German people and that includes East Germany."[18]

East German scientists joined the debate. Even in the case of conventional war, they argued, Europe would still be contaminated with nuclear fallout. The continent contained 220 civilian nuclear reactors that, if damaged, could turn into radioactive infernos. Because of the type of fuel they used, they would emit greater doses of radiation than atomic weapons. The large concentrations of chemical plants—along the Rhine River in Western Europe and in cities such as Halle and Leipzig in East Germany—would spew deadly poisons upon humans, plants, and animals. Even a conventional war would turn Europe into an "atomic, chemical and genetically contaminated desert." It would lead to the "destruction of what the aggressor would seek to conquer."[19]

Gorbachev stood in stark contrast to the cautious newly elected US president George H. W. Bush, who was slow to accept the idea that he, too, could play a role in affecting the course of history. The demise of the Communist parties in Eastern Europe led to demands, in January 1990, from Czechoslovakia, Hungary, and Poland that the Soviet army leave those states by the end of 1991. It became a question of when, not if, the Soviet troops would depart. It was at this point that Bush took the initiative and proposed the reduction of US and Soviet forces to 195,000 each in Central Europe. Even the hawks in the Pentagon had to admit that in the fourteen months since Gorbachev's speech of December 7, 1988, the Soviet Union had dismantled its capability to invade Western Europe. Bush's speech was welcome news in Warsaw, Budapest, and Prague, as well as in Moscow, because it facilitated the Soviet army's withdrawal from its forward positions in Eastern Europe. The military confrontation in the heart of Europe was coming to an end.

After the last Russian combat troops stationed in Poland pulled out in October 1992, Polish president Lech Walesa declared: "Polish sovereignty has finally been confirmed." Problems related to logistics, and a lack of adequate housing in Russia for its returning troops, produced a longer timetable for withdrawal from the newly independent Baltic states and East Germany (completed by 1994).

## START

The START negotiations, begun in 1982, proceeded at a snail's pace for eight years, during which the intricacies of balanced reductions in Soviet and US arsenals were debated in twelve rounds of formal negotiations, thirteen foreign ministers' meetings, and six summits. It was not until July 1991 that the treaty was ready to be signed by the heads of state.

Oddly, the signing of the treaty in Moscow was attended with little fanfare—certainly not what had been expected at the completion of one of the most important nuclear disarmament treaties, one that had reversed the forty-five-year-old strategic nuclear arms race. START seemed anticlimactic because it had been so long in coming and its main features had long since been known. Moreover, the deteriorating situation in the Soviet Union and the fading of the Soviet military threat made the treaty seem less significant.

START, however, broke new ground by calling for a reduction rather than merely a limit on the growth of strategic weapons. The US arsenal would be cut from 12,646 warheads to 8,556 and the Soviet Union's from 11,012 to 6,163 by 1999. To the distinct advantage of the United States, START reduced the Soviets' heavy ICBMs by 50 percent, yet it allowed the United States to retain a three-to-one advantage in SLBMs. The treaty, however, did not place limits on nuclear weapons modernization. It left the United States free to continue to develop its state-of-the-art US B-2 stealth bomber and Trident submarine.

By the end of 1991, the Soviet Union ceased to exist, and Washington now had to deal with Boris Yeltsin, the president of the new Russian Federation, and with the heads of the other fourteen successor states of the former Soviet Union. Yeltsin proclaimed his commitment to stand by START and the disarmament pledges made by Gorbachev. In addition to Russia, however, three of the new sovereign republics—Belarus, Ukraine, and Kazakhstan—had nuclear weapons stationed on their soil. All three announced their intention to get rid of them. Confident that Russia had a sufficient nuclear deterrent, and greatly needing to slash military costs and attain Western economic assistance, Yeltsin declared his intentions to scrap even more nuclear weapons.

At the first US-Russian (as opposed to US-Soviet) summit in Washington in February 1992, Yeltsin joined Bush in signing a "Declaration of Friendship" and agreed to new negotiations. Four months of talks produced another startling agreement, one that proposed far deeper cuts in strategic nuclear forces than the yet-to-be-ratified START had called for. Yeltsin, given to grandstanding, made an offer that Bush could not reject. The result was START II, a spectacular agreement that called for the reduction, over ten years, of strategic nuclear weapons down to 3,000–3,500. This was approximately one-half of what START I called for and amounted to a reduction of 73 percent of the existing strategic nuclear warheads. The most extraordinary feature of the Bush-Yeltsin agreement was its call for banning all MIRVed land-based missiles, leaving each side with 500 single-warhead, land-based strategic missiles.

It represented Russia's abandonment of its long-held advantage in heavy land-based missiles, which Washington had long regarded as Moscow's first-strike capacity. In announcing this concession, Yeltsin stated that Russia needed only a "minimum-security level" of nuclear forces. Moreover, the quest for nuclear parity, he went on to say, had caused Russia "to have half its population living below the poverty line."[20] In return for Yeltsin's concession, Bush agreed to a ceiling on SLBMs of 1,744, a 70-percent reduction.

It remained to be determined which delivery systems were to be destroyed. By the end of 1992, the two sides reached a compromise. Russia agreed to the conversion of US strategic bombers to conventional use, rather than destroying them altogether. The United States, in its turn, agreed that Russia, as a cost-cutting measure, could keep 90 of its SS-18 silos for conversion to be used by single-warhead SS-25 missiles, and that it could keep as well 105 of its 170 SS-19s, provided they were refitted with single warheads. Similarly, the United States would convert its Minuteman III missile to carry but a single warhead.

Reagan had been fond of the Russian proverb, "trust, but verify."[21] So it was this time. The compromise became possible only after each side accepted unprecedented verification procedures.

Bush and Yeltsin signed START II in Moscow in January 1993, pledging their nations to return by 2003 to where they had been in the early 1970s, before MIRVing and stockpiling their missiles. As such, it was a tacit admission of the mindlessness of the nuclear arms race. Table 20.2 provides comparative data on the size of the arms reductions called for in START.

### Table 20.2  Strategic Warhead Levels and Reduction Proposals

| | Land-Based (ICBMs) | Sea-Based (SLBMs) | Air-Launched (bombers) | Totals |
|---|---|---|---|---|
| **Levels in 1991** | | | | |
| US | 2,450 | 5,760 | 4,436 | 12,646 |
| USSR | 6,612 | 2,804 | 1,596 | 11,012 |
| | | | | 23,658 |
| **START I, to be implemented by 1999; a reduction of 38% from the 1991 levels** | | | | |
| US | 1,400 | 3,456 | 3,700 | 8,556 |
| USSR | 3,153 | 1,744 | 1,266 | 6,163 |
| | | | | 14,719 |
| **START II, to be implemented by 2003; a reduction of 73% from the 1991 levels** | | | | |
| US | 500 | 1,728 | 1,272 | 3,500 |
| Russia | 500 | 1,744 | 752 | 2,996 |
| | | | | 6,496 |

*Source:* Strategic Arms Control Association, Washington, DC. Cited in John F. Cushman, Jr., "Senate Endorses Pact to Reduce Strategic Arms, *New York Times*, October 2, 1992, pp. 1, 6.

The ratification of the agreements proved to be a difficult matter, however. Ratification of START I was delayed mainly by complications caused by the breakup of the Soviet Union. Both Washington and Moscow wanted to be certain that all four former Soviet republics in possession of strategic weapons abided by the treaty. In May 1992, four successor states to the Soviet Union—Russia, Belarus, Ukraine, and Kazakhstan—signed a protocol making them parties to START I. They agreed to place their strategic weapons under Russian control, to remove them in accordance with the terms of the treaty, and then to sign the Nuclear Non-Proliferation Treaty. Satisfied with these arrangements, the US Senate finally ratified START I in October 1992, and one month later the Russian parliament did so as well.

Ukraine, in contrast to earlier professed intentions of becoming a nuclear-free nation, had second thoughts about giving up its nuclear weapons without something in return, namely, substantial financial assistance for its struggling economy. The Ukrainian demand to be paid to disarm pointed to an additional, unforeseen problem: the high cost of removing and destroying thousands of missiles and recycling of what had once been nuclear bombs. The former Soviet republics (Russia included) could ill afford the cost of dismantling so many missiles. In order to complete the process, a consortium of nations (led by the United States) underwrote the cost. At the end of 2013, the United States quietly completed the recycling of more than 475 metric tons of Russian bomb-grade uranium for use by US nuclear power stations.

There was still the matter of the high cost of environmental cleanup. One estimate to clean up the nuclear weapons environmental mess in the United States alone ran to $300 billion.[22] In the former Soviet Union, environmental pollution at many of its nuclear weapons sites had reached crisis proportions.

The US Senate ratified START II in January 1996; in Russia, however, the treaty ran into opposition. Nationalists and Communists insisted that START II sold out Russian interests. The ultranationalist Vladimir Zhirinovsky, leader of the Liberal Democratic Party—the second largest in the Duma (parliament)—glossed over the fact that the treaty called for parity between the United States and Russia. Instead, he argued, the reduction of nuclear weapons "makes Russia a secondary state." His party would not ratify an agreement that would "humiliate, insult or limit Russia as a great nation."[23] It was not until after Vladimir Putin's election as president in March 2000 that the Duma ratified START II. Putin also managed to obtain the ratification of the Comprehensive Nuclear Test Ban Treaty.

### The Expansion of NATO into Eastern Europe

When Mikhail Gorbachev agreed to withdraw Soviet troops from Eastern Europe, he insisted—and George H. W. Bush agreed—that the region remain a neutral buffer between the NATO nations and the Soviet Union. NATO was not to expand into a military vacuum that the Warsaw Pact had once occupied. But then came the sudden end of the Soviet Union, after which Poland, Hungary, and the Czech Republic asked for membership in NATO as insurance against renewed Russian military ambitions.

Washington and its NATO allies tried to present the expansion into the formerly Soviet bloc nations as benign, meant largely to shore up democracy in Eastern Europe and somehow "strengthen European security." But the Russians well remembered the numerous invasions in the past launched from Germany and Poland. In June 1996, at a Berlin meeting of the foreign ministers of the sixteen NATO nations, Russian foreign minister Yevgeny Primakov warned that NATO expansion was "unacceptable."

Although he no longer held office, Gorbachev joined the debate by pointing out that the agreement regulating the Soviet withdrawal from East Germany had demanded that East German troops not be integrated into the unified German army. The "borders" of NATO, he said, must not expand eastward. The expansion of NATO could have only one meaning—the isolation of Russia from Europe, resulting in "highly unpredictable consequences."[24]

US president Bill Clinton paid no heed to these warnings, and in 1999 NATO completed its first expansion into the former Soviet bloc when it offered full membership to Poland, the Czech Republic, and Hungary. There was not much Moscow could do except to temporarily put on hold the ratification of START II. NATO's ambitious move came at a time when Russia still suffered from severe economic problems, when much of its military-industrial complex was in disarray and its conventional forces severely reduced.

NATO had been created to check the Soviet military across the Iron Curtain, but now it assumed a new, amorphous mission at a time when there was no longer an Iron Curtain, a Soviet military in Eastern Europe, or a Soviet Union. What it did achieve was to create a new military line dividing Europe, this one farther to the east. Yeltsin (as well as Gorbachev) bitterly complained, but with Russia still suffering from the consequences of a historic economic meltdown, there was little anyone in Moscow could do. All Yeltsin managed to obtain was a pledge from Clinton that NATO would not expand all the way to the borders of Russia.

Critics of NATO expansion were not given a hearing in Washington. In June 1997, the conservative Arms Control Association sent an open letter to Clinton warning that an expansion of NATO was "a policy error of historic proportions." Russia did not "pose a threat to its western neighbors." An enlargement could draw NATO into "countries with serious border and national minority problems."

The next US administration, under George W. Bush, heedless of the consequences, pushed for yet another round of NATO expansion, this one up to Russia's border. The new members enlisted in NATO, in March 2004, included the former Soviet republics of Lithuania, Latvia, and Estonia, as well as

Slovenia, Slovakia, Romania, and Bulgaria. In April 2009, Obama brought aboard Albania and Croatia.

One of the arguments used to justify NATO's eastward expansion was that it would shore up the fledgling democratic institutions in Eastern Europe. The European Union, however, with its insistence that its members be democracies (never a criterion for NATO membership), was a better vehicle to that end. Putin had no choice but to swallow this bitter pill since again there was little Russia could do about it. But then came a further attempt by the Bush administration to push NATO ever farther eastward when it offered membership to Georgia and Ukraine. By this time, Russia's economic and military fortunes had undergone a recovery. Putin announced that he would take measures—unspecified—to prevent further NATO expansion. This was a line, Putin insisted, that NATO must not cross.

US-Russian relations suffered additional setbacks after the Bush administration initiated talks with the Czech Republic and Poland to deploy on their soil anti–ballistic missile systems. Ostensibly it was directed against Iran, but Russia's leaders were unwilling to accept that explanation. They saw it as another NATO initiative directed at them. (In 2009, the Obama administration scrapped the system.) For good measure, the Bush administration inexplicably unilaterally withdrew from the Anti-Ballistic Missile Treaty in June 2002 (without which there could have been no strategic arms limitation and reduction treaties).

In 2008, a resurgent Russia (primarily thanks to rising energy prices) repeated the warning that Russia would not tolerate NATO expansion into Georgia or Ukraine. Even Mikhail Gorbachev accused the Bush administration of deliberately undermining hopes for a permanent peace with Russia. He recalled the pledges of the past that NATO would not expand beyond Germany. "What happened to their promises?" he asked. It appeared to him that "every US president has to have a war."[25]

At the April 2008 NATO meeting in Budapest, West European member states (led by Germany) blocked Georgia's entry into the alliance. Their decision had no impact on Bush, however, who continued to press for Georgian and Ukrainian membership. Mikheil Saakashvili—the US-educated president of Georgia who treated Vladimir Putin with disdain, a feeling Putin openly reciprocated—insisted that Georgia needed NATO protection to keep it from suffering the same fate as Czechoslovakia in 1938.

The issue was put to the test by the Russo-Georgian war of August 2008. The immediate issue was South Ossetia and Abkhazia, the de facto independent breakaway provinces of Georgia openly backed by Russia. For reasons difficult to fathom, Saakashvili, the president of a country of 4.6 million people—and fewer yet if one excludes the residents of Abkhazia and South Ossetia—sent his army into South Ossetia. Russian tanks had little difficulty in scattering the Georgian army (which had been trained in part by US special forces). After the war, Putin declared that Abkhazia and South Ossetia were now independent nations. Putin explained that Russia was only doing what NATO had done in the former Yugoslavia, where the Western military alliance, prodded by Clinton, had wrested the province of Kosovo from the control of Serbia, historically an ally of Russia. At the urging of the Bush administration, European nations had recognized Kosovo as a sovereign state earlier that year, in February 2008.

Tied down in Afghanistan and Iraq, Bush was in no position to act. Direct military assistance to Georgia could lead to war in the Trans-Caucasus, one the overextended US military could not conceivably win. Bush was left with the tacit acceptance of Moscow's authority in what for centuries had been its sphere of influence. The expansion of US military power across the globe had not taught the Russians the lessons that US geopoliticians had wanted them to learn.

## National Missile Defense

With the end of the Cold War, Star Wars appeared to be dead, although successive administrations continued to fund the research project at about $3–4 billion per year. But then a coalition of political conservatives, the aerospace industry, and the Pentagon sought to develop a more modest version of it, now dubbed the National Missile Defense (NMD) system. The cost of NMD, projected at about $60 billion, was not cheap, yet it was a far cry from the estimated price tag for Star Wars—up to $1 trillion. Its aim was also more modest. It was meant to intercept a few dozen warheads launched by "rogue states" such as North Korea, Iran, and Iraq. As Clinton's term in office came to an end, he left his successor with the decision of whether to go forward with the controversial weapons system.

In tests, the system did not perform as well as advertised. Tests showed that inexpensive decoys could fool the costly interceptor missiles. The NMD, moreover, violated the 1972 Anti-Ballistic Missile Treaty with the Soviet Union, without which other nuclear arms reduction treaties would be put into jeopardy. The Russians warned that they would not reduce their arsenal while the United States further "disarmed" them by means of the NMD system. China, with a nuclear deterrent of only eighteen to twenty single-warhead ballistic missiles, opposed the system as well.

None of that made an impression on President George W. Bush. He declared that the United States would deploy the system, the main purpose of which was to guard against North Korean missiles. It was at this point, in December 2001, that Bush gave Russia notice of the US withdrawal from the ABM Treaty. Reaction from Russia and the People's Republic of China was relatively mild. For one, neither wanted a renewal of tensions with Washington; moreover, both had more than enough weapons to deal with a poorly functioning ABM system.

## Proliferation of Weapons of Mass Destruction

Among the different types of weapons of mass destruction (WMD), nuclear weapons remain by far the most dangerous. Chemical and biological weapons instill a particular horror because of their nature. The very idea of such weapons arouses a deep revulsion. When US president George W. Bush went to war against Saddam Hussein in Iraq, ostensibly to eliminate his chemical and biological arsenals, he struck a responsive chord among his fellow citizens, despite that in the past conventional weapons produced by far much greater "mass destruction."

Chemical weapons are not well suited for the battlefield. In World War II, Germans used poison gas, but they did so against defenseless prisoners, not enemy soldiers, as part of the Nazis' "final solution," the Holocaust of the Jews. Saddam Hussein also used it against defenseless civilians—75 percent of them women and children—in Halabja in March 1988, but he had less success with poison gas against Iranian troops.

To use chemical weapons on the battlefield, conditions have to be just right. When the Germans launched their devastating poison gas attack at Ypres in April 1915 that killed 5,000 French soldiers, it was the fifth such attack during World War I, but the first to succeed. The Germans had to wait six weeks for the wind to blow in the right direction at the right speed. The wind could not be more than seven miles per hour, otherwise it would disperse the poison's effectiveness. Among the Western troops in that war, chemical weapons caused fewer than 1 percent of all battlefield deaths. They

**Table 20.3  Estimated Nuclear Warheads, Selected Countries**

|                    | Early 1990s   | 2008      | 2012                       |
| ------------------ | ------------- | --------- | -------------------------- |
| United States[a]   | 9,680         | 3,575     | 1,700–2,200[b]             |
| Russia[a]          | 10,996        | 3,340     | 1,700–2,200[b]             |
| Britain            | 260           | 160       | 160                        |
| France             | 100–200       | 348       | 300                        |
| China              | 100–200       | 200       | modernizing                |
| India              | not available | 50–60     | building more              |
| Pakistan           | not available | 30–50     | following India's example  |
| Israel             | 100–200       | 100–200   | never officially declared  |
| Iran               | none          | none      | 2–10 years away            |
| North Korea        | 1–2           | up to 10  | up to 10                   |

*Sources: Bulletin of the Atomic Scientists;* International Institute for Strategic Studies; Stockholm International Peace Research Institute; *The Economist,* "Just How Low Can You Go?" March 27, 2008.

*Notes:* a. Strategic warheads only.

b. Maximum permitted under the Strategic Offensive Reductions Treaty (SORT), signed by Vladimir Putin and George W. Bush in May 2002; ratified in 2003.

quickly learned that protective clothing and masks readily negated the impact of chemical weapons. Biological weapons are even more difficult to employ effectively in time of war.[26] Nuclear bombs remain by far the most potent WMD.

· · ·

As the superpowers rushed to eliminate thousands of their nuclear weapons, other countries worked surreptitiously to develop such weapons. Suddenly, in the early 1990s, nuclear proliferation began to replace superpower confrontation as the leading threat to international security.

The 1968 Non-Proliferation Treaty (NPT) required signatory nations *without* nuclear weapons not to produce or receive them and to open their nuclear power facilities to inspection by the UN's International Atomic Energy Agency (IAEA). Signatory nations *with* nuclear weapons were treaty-bound not to make such weapons available to non-nuclear nations. Only in 1992 did China and France sign the NPT, thereby bringing all five declared nuclear powers under its regime. By that time, 149 nations had signed the treaty. There were holdouts, however—notably India, Pakistan, Israel, Argentina, Brazil, and Algeria, all of which had nuclear weapons programs in various stages of development. These nations were thus beyond the pale of IAEA inspectors. Several nations that had signed the NPT, such as Iraq, North Korea, South Africa, Iran, and Libya, had nonetheless acquired nuclear materials and had begun weapons programs.

South Africa, which had begun its nuclear weapons project in secret in the 1970s, closed its nuclear plants in 1990, signed the NPT, and opened its nuclear facilities to IAEA inspectors. It was the only nation to abandon its nuclear weapons program voluntarily. In March 1993, South Africa admitted that by 1989 it had built six nuclear bombs, which, however, it had destroyed prior to signing the NPT. Brazil and Argentina both built large uranium-enrichment facilities in the 1980s and thus had the potential for producing nuclear weapons. In December 1990, however, they accepted IAEA inspection of their nuclear stockpiles and facilities.[27]

The danger of nuclear proliferation increased with the collapse of the Soviet Union and the prospect that its critical nuclear material, technology, and technicians might become available to the highest bidder. In 1991, the Soviet Union still had over 40,000 nuclear weapons. Of the 700,000 people who worked at its nuclear weapons plants, over 2,000 had access to key technical information. Since the 1940s, the Soviet Union had produced some 100–150 tons of weapons-grade plutonium and 500–700 tons of enriched uranium (only a pound of which is needed for a Hiroshima-size bomb). The problem was how to keep nuclear fuel and technology out of unauthorized hands or the hands of rulers with past records of, or the propensity for, military aggression.

Although Israel never confirmed that it had nuclear weapons, its arsenal was estimated at well over one hundred warheads in the 1990s. It was the product of an effort that began in the early 1960s. At the same time, Israel made sure no other Middle Eastern country acquired a nuclear weapons capability. In 1982, Israeli fighter planes destroyed a nuclear reactor that Iraq had purchased from France, the centerpiece of Saddam Hussein's nuclear weapons program. In September 2007, Israel destroyed a nuclear reactor in Syria, a facility that apparently had the potential of producing atomic bombs. When the United States invaded Iraq in 2003, ostensibly to rid the country of "weapons of mass destruction," which included atomic weapons, it found that Saddam had not rebuilt what the Israelis had destroyed twenty-two years earlier. When it was argued that Iran was working on a nuclear bomb, it was Israel more than anyone other country that urged preemptive strikes against Iran.

### Pakistan's Role in Nuclear Proliferation

In December 2003, the United States and Libya ended their twenty-year-long confrontation, which had begun during the Reagan administration and then reached crisis proportions when Libyan agents blew up a TWA airliner over Lockerbie, Scotland, killing all 259 onboard as well as 11 on the ground (see Chapter 21). The settlement between the United States and Libyan strongman Muammar Qaddafi included the opening up of Libya to inspections by the IAEA.

The inspections revealed that Qaddafi had a primitive nuclear bomb program. For a paltry sum—estimated at between $60 million and $100 million—Libya had purchased from Pakistan enriched uranium, plutonium, centrifuges to enrich uranium, and warhead designs. One US official called it "the complete package." It was useless, however, because Libya did not know how to use it.

Libya's nuclear project had come courtesy of Abdul Qadeer Khan—the chief of the Khan Research Laboratories, the father of the Pakistani bomb, a national hero. In addition to Libya, Khan had provided nuclear assistance to more technologically sophisticated nations, such as Iran and North Korea.

The head of the IAEA described Khan's operation as "a veritable Wal-Mart." Khan did it mostly for money, but in the case of North Korea, he traded nuclear know-how for missile technology. These were not private transactions, however. None of this could have been arranged without the assistance of Pakistan's military, which provided the cargo planes for transport.

Pakistan's role in nuclear proliferation had long been suspected in the West. Still, there was little that President George W. Bush could do when he heard the stunning news. He had enlisted Pakistan in his war against the Taliban and al Qaeda in Afghanistan and he was still looking for Osama bin Laden in Pakistan's rugged North-West Frontier Province. He did not challenge, therefore, the explanation of Pakistan's military dictator, General

Pervez Musharraf, that his military, too, had been shocked by the deeds of a lone wolf. Musharraf, however, was more annoyed by the duplicity of his Libyan "Muslim brothers" who had revealed Khan's operation. Without a word of public rebuke, Musharraf then pardoned Khan.[28]

## The Case of North Korea

Another severe challenge to the NPT system was North Korea's nuclear weapons project, another beneficiary of Khan's black-market dealings. In the 1980s, North Korea had built nuclear reactors and a plutonium-processing plant capable of turning spent nuclear fuel into weapons-grade plutonium. What was not known to the West was whether North Korea had succeeded in producing plutonium and, if so, how much. North Korea's dictator, Kim Il Sung, remained tight-lipped. He denied possession of a bomb or the intention of building one and skillfully created uncertainty by playing on the fears of others. There was indeed much to fear. A nuclear-armed North Korea could threaten South Korea and Japan, both of which had forsworn nuclear weapons (but were under US nuclear protection). Moreover, the prospect of North Korean nuclear bombs, missiles, or technology exported to other nations posed a danger to global nonproliferation efforts.

North Korea had signed the NPT in 1985, but then, in September 1993, Kim barred all further monitoring by IAEA inspectors. In exchange for a promise of direct high-level talks with the United States, Kim agreed in January 1994 to allow the inspectors to continue their work. Yet two months later, when the inspectors returned to North Korea, they were prevented from entering the key plutonium-processing plant and from testing samples.

Tensions escalated rapidly. The Clinton administration sounded the call for UN sanctions and began talks with China and other nations to rally support for such a move. North Korea warned that sanctions were tantamount to an act of war. A visit by former US president Jimmy Carter to Pyongyang in June 1994 served to cool things off. Carter secured from the North Korean dictator a pledge not to expel IAEA inspectors as long as good-faith negotiations continued between the United States and North Korea. Clinton declared that talks would resume only if North Korea would "freeze" its plutonium weapons program and accept international safeguards. Kim agreed and a new round of high-level talks began. These talks had barely opened when the eighty-two-year-old Kim Il Sung died. The negotiations were suspended while the North Korean government regrouped under its new ruler, Kim Jong Il, son of the long-lived dictator.

Negotiations resumed in August 1994. They produced an agreement whereby North Korea pledged to freeze its plutonium production and the United States promised to replace North Korea's graphite rod nuclear reactors with light-water reactors, which have far less potential for producing plutonium. Until the new reactors went in operation, the United States, Japan, and

South Korea would supply North Korea with fuel oil to meet its energy needs. In effect, the agreement rewarded North Korea handsomely for ceasing its violations of the NPT.

Within four years of the signing of the agreement, however, Kim Jong Il began to circumvent its terms when he acquired from Pakistan the means to build a uranium bomb, something he kept a secret for a while. After September 11, 2001, President Bush included North Korea, along with Iraq and Iran, as part of an "axis of evil." North Korea's uranium bomb became Kim Jong Il's ace in the hole. In October 2002, the "Dear Leader" volunteered the stunning news that North Korea had joined the select nuclear club. Engaged in Afghanistan and preparing to invade Iraq, Bush had no answer.

As his father had done, the younger Kim wanted to engage the United States in bilateral talks. High on his agenda was a nonaggression treaty, a US pledge not to attack North Korea, thereby officially ending the Korean War. Bush, however, refused to sit down with a man he loathed. Instead, Bush threatened Kim with preventive war. Bush's secretary of defense, Donald Rumsfeld, already had announced that the United States had the means to fight a two-front war against Iraq and North Korea, two nations Bush had singled out as possessing WMD. Events in Iraq, however, belied Rumsfeld's confident claim. When it became clear that the United States had no adequate military option against North Korea, Bush changed course and pretended that it hardly posed a problem.

Meanwhile, North Korea proceeded with its uranium and plutonium weapons projects. In 2005, Kim Jong Il proposed to end his nuclear weapons program in return for economic assistance and improved relations with Washington. When Bush was slow to respond, Kim went ahead, in October 2006, with an underground test of a plutonium bomb. That got the attention of the Bush administration. Bush accepted an agreement similar to the one Clinton had hammered out, an arrangement he once had treated with unconcealed contempt. In return for economic assistance and North Korea's removal from the US State Department's terror list, Pyongyang agreed to end its plutonium enrichment program. As a token of good faith, it blew up the cooling tower of its plutonium reactor in Yongbyon in June 2008. Still, a number of problems remained unresolved, such as the amount of processed plutonium still in North Korea's possession, as well as a full accounting of its uranium-processing capabilities. There was also the issue of North Korea's missile program. In April 2009, it launched a missile test over the Pacific, followed seven weeks later by a second nuclear bomb test and another test of rockets that fell into the sea near Japan. It all served to underscore the uncomfortable fact that three successive US administrations had no ready answer of how to deal with North Korea.

After Kim Jong Il suddenly died in December 2011, he was succeeded by his son, Kim Jong Un, an untested, young, and erratic head of state who carried out the threat of a third nuclear test (in February 2013) and continued to test North Korea's long-range missiles. He even declared, in March 2013, that he was no longer bound by the Korean War cease-fire in place since July 1953. Two weeks later, the US military carried out long-range maneuvers near North Korea by B-2 stealth bombers capable of carrying nuclear weapons. On the next day, Kim Jong Un put his missiles on high alert. The Pentagon sped up its missile defense program on Guam. Throughout, both sides attempted, in fits and starts, to resume negotiations.[29]

### The Cases of India and Pakistan

India, which had refused to sign the NPT, developed and tested a "nuclear device" as early as 1974. On the one hand, India thereby touted its possession of a nuclear bomb, while on the other denied having one. Pakistan, seeking a deterrent to India's bomb, finally succeeded twenty years later, in the mid-1990s, with some assistance from China, in developing its own nuclear bomb. It kept it a secret until May 1998, when in rapid succession both India and Pakistan carried out underground tests of their nuclear weapons. After India exploded five nuclear bombs, its nationalistic prime minister, Atal Bihari Vajpayee, explained that the tests had been purely defensive in character. The events caused jubilation in India but caused strong rebukes around the world. The major nuclear powers, as well as other nations, called upon India to halt its nuclear program. India had no intention of going that far, but it did declare a moratorium on further testing. The major powers warned Pakistan against matching India with tests of its own weapons, but Pakistan was in no mood to listen. Within two weeks, Pakistan answered with six underground nuclear bomb tests. Now the Pakistanis rejoiced. As India had done, Pakistan declared its tests as defensive in nature.

The tests triggered the fear that the low-intensity warfare still going on in Kashmir might trigger a South Asian nuclear war. Animosity between India and Pakistan was deep-seated, and their nuclear face-off created a sense of urgency, particularly since both had missiles capable of delivering nuclear weapons. Yet the tests had a sobering effect. They revealed an Indian-Pakistani balance of terror that demanded confidence-building measures that, indeed, gradually led to an improvement in their relationship.

### The Case of Iran

Iran began a nuclear weapons program in the early 1970s, during the days of the shah, and in 1970 it joined the NPT, thus permitting inspections without prior notice. The Islamic revolution of 1979 suspended the nuclear program. To a degree, the resumption of Iran's nuclear program was a problem of Washington's own making. It had installed the shah, who had embraced nuclear power as a symbol of prestige and modernity. Washington's support of Saddam Hussein's invasion (replete with chemical weapons of mass destruction) underscored to the Iranians that they stood alone, particularly after the repeated threats of regime change emanating from Washington. In 1984, the Khomeini government resumed in secret the nuclear program it had inherited from the shah.

With the assistance of the Soviet Union (and later Russia), North Korea, and Pakistan, Iran began to develop a secret weapons program. It would admit, however, only to a civilian nuclear power program, not that it was working on a nuclear bomb. After September 11, 2001, Bush declared Iran—with which the United States had no diplomatic or economic relations since 1979—as part of the "axis of evil" and repeatedly threatened preemptive war. Despite US threats and economic sanctions imposed by the UN, the United States, and the European Union, Iran remained defiant. In October 2004, Hassan Rouhani, Iran's chief nuclear negotiator, declared "no other country can stop us exploring technology, which is the legal right of Iran."[30] Under the terms of the NPT, Iran indeed had the right to a nuclear program, provided it did not lead to a nuclear bomb.

Toward the end of the Bush presidency, Iran had a nuclear weapons program of indeterminate quality. In December 2007, the US National Intelligence Estimate concluded that Iran had suspended its program in 2003, but that did not stop the Bush administration's constant drumbeat that Iran still sought to build a nuclear arsenal. Bush kept repeating that "all options"—including a military attack—were "on the table." During the US presidential campaign of 2008 all the major candidates took a hard line on Iran, repeating Bush's position that Iran was a threat that had to be confronted. It was the generals in the Pentagon, more than anyone else, however, who took steps to scotch the notion of a preemptive war. Tied down in Iraq and Afghanistan, they showed little enthusiasm for another war in the Middle East, one they knew would be more difficult than the other wars. War with Iran was also bound to complicate the US mission in Iraq. Iran had allies in Gaza (Hamas), Lebanon (Hezbollah), and even in Iraq (the Mahdi Army, the Badr Organization, and the Maliki government). Iran had the capability to disrupt the shipping lanes out of the Persian Gulf at a time when the price of fuel at the pump in the industrial world had reached—if only briefly—record levels. The generals who had meekly followed Bush into Iraq in 2003, seduced by the promise of a short war, now paid closer attention to the truism that even the most meticulous plans for military operations fall by the wayside once the shooting starts.

Admiral William Fallon, chief of US Central Command, declared on his own volition that a war with Iran "isn't going to happen on my watch." (For his unauthorized statement, Secretary of Defense Robert Gates announced Fallon's "voluntary" retirement in March 2008.) Gates and the chairman of the Joint Chiefs of Staff, Admiral Mike Mullen, publicly supported Bush's stance on Iran. Nonetheless, they urged a political solution.[31]

The chances for a negotiated solution remained slim as long as the belli-cose George W. Bush and Mahmoud Ahmadinejad remained in office. Famous for his anti-Israel rhetoric, Iranian president Ahmadinejad denied the Holocaust had happened and insisted that Iran's nuclear program was its own business. His successor, Hassan Rouhani, Iran's former nuclear negotiator, took a different tack. He expressed a willingness to discuss with the West a number of issues. Instead of denying the Holocaust, he took to Twitter to wish all Jews "a blessed Rosh Hashanah." Israel's skeptical prime minister, Benjamin Netanyahu, however, was not charmed by Rouhani, calling him a "wolf in sheep's clothing."

After months of secret negotiations between the United States and Iran, the foreign ministers of Iran and the P5+1 (UN's Big Five plus Germany), agreed in November 2013 on a six-month preliminary agreement. In it, Rouhani (with the blessing of Iran's Supreme Leader, Ali Khameini), declared Iran's willingness to permit UN inspectors on its soil to keep an eye on its nuclear program, making sure it did not entail building a bomb. But he insist-ed that under the terms of the NPT, Iran had a right to its civilian nuclear pro-gram. The problem was that there was no real dividing line between a military and a peaceful nuclear program.

Although not foolproof, UN inspections promised to make it most difficult for Iran to enrich weapons-grade uranium—the heart of the landmark accord—necessary to build a nuclear bomb. Another question was what to do with Iran's ten tons of enriched uranium that could only be used for a nuclear weapon. Iran's sole reactor generating electricity for civilian use, built and supplied by the Russians, had no use for it since it reportedly had enough fuel to last it ten years. Iran also agreed to stop work on its Arak heavy-water reactor suited for weapons-grade plutonium production. Finally, swallowing its nationalistic pride, Iran accepted daily monitoring of its nuclear facilities by UN inspectors.[32]

In exchange, during the six-month trial run, Iran received the first install-ment of modest relief from the crippling international economic sanctions. The sanctions had contributed to a severe contraction of the Iranian economy, with inflation running at 40 percent and unemployment as high as 30 percent. Indeed, the plight of the economy had been a major reason why Rouhani had won the presidential election in the first place. The choice for the West, an *Economist* editorial concluded, was not "between the good and the bad, but between the bad and the less bad."[33] Netanyahu, supported by Obama's critics in the United States, called it a "historic mistake."

## The Quest for a Comprehensive Nuclear Test Ban Treaty

As a result of the partial Nuclear Test Ban Treaty of 1963, three of the five declared nuclear powers—the United States, Britain, and the Soviet Union—

**Table 20.4  Known Nuclear Tests, 1945–1996**

|  | Atmospheric | Underground | Total |
|---|---|---|---|
| United States | 215 | 815 | 1,030 |
| USSR | 219 | 496 | 715 |
| France | 50 | 159 | 209 |
| Britain | 21 | 24 | 45 |
| China | 23 | 22 | 45 |
| India | 0 | 1 | 1 |

*Sources:* UN; Physicians for Social Responsibility; Barbara Crosette, "U.N. Endorses a Treaty to Halt All Nuclear Testing," *New York Times,* September 11, 1996, p. A3.

took their tests underground. The other two—China and France—however, continued to test in the atmosphere. The tests were crucial to the production of reliable nuclear weapons (although computer simulations were becoming increasingly accurate). To curtail nuclear proliferation, a comprehensive test ban treaty was needed to end all tests by declared as well as undeclared nuclear powers. To that end, in 1996 the United Nations proposed a Comprehensive Nuclear Test Ban Treaty (usually abbreviated as CTBT).

India repeatedly resisted such an arrangement. It argued that a test ban preserved the division between the nuclear haves and have-nots, and the CTBT did not commit the haves to getting rid of their weapons. When the issue came before the UN General Assembly in September 1996, the vote was 158-3 in favor of the treaty. India (along with Libya and Bhutan) voted against it. For it to become international law, the legislatures of all forty-four countries with nuclear reactors had to ratify it.[34]

By September 2004, 116 nations had ratified the treaty, including Russia. The US Senate, however, rejected it in October 1999 after the Senate Foreign Relations Committee, headed by the conservative Republican senator Jesse Helms of North Carolina (also known as "Senator No"), denounced it, citing the potential need for future testing and problems with verification. President George W. Bush showed no interest in taking up the treaty's ratification, another piece of unfinished business his successor, Barack Obama, inherited. Obama sought the treaty's ratification, something he could only obtain with the support of the opposition Republican party. The Republicans, however, had taken a pledge not to agree with him on anything.

As of September 1996, the nuclear powers had conducted 2,045 tests of nuclear weapons. To these figures must be added the more recent tests by India, Pakistan, and North Korea. (See Table 20.4.)

## Notes

1. Walter Pincus, "US Has Spent $5.8 Trillion on Nuclear Arms Since 1940, Study Says," *Washington Post,* July 1, 1998, p. A2.

2. SS (surface-to-surface) is the US designation of Soviet missiles. As soon as a Soviet missile was tested, the Pentagon assigned it a number.

3. Georgy Arbatov, director of the Institute of US and Canadian Studies of the Academy of Sciences of the Soviet Union, in Arthur Macy Cox (with a Soviet commentary by Georgy Arbatov), *Russian Roulette: The Superpower Game* (New York: Times Books, 1982), pp. 177–178, 182.

4. George McGovern, "SALT II: A Political Autopsy," *Politics Today* (March–April 1980), p. 64.

5. This was the basis of Ronald Reagan's "window of vulnerability": The increasingly accurate Soviet land-based arsenal was capable of overwhelming the US missiles in their silos and thereby threatened the existence of the United States. It ignored the fact that US submarines and bombers were more than enough to keep the Soviets honest. Reagan promised that, if elected president, he would close the window. In 1984, he declared that he had closed it—without, however, having done anything to protect US land-based missiles.

6. Thomas Powers, "Nuclear Winter and Nuclear Strategy," *The Atlantic,* November 1984, p. 60.

7. Kissinger, cited in Lawrence Freedman, *The Evolution of Nuclear Strategy* (New York: St. Martin's Press, 1981), p. 363.

8. Leonid Brezhnev and Ronald Reagan, "Brezhnev and Reagan on Atom War," transcripts of statements, *New York Times,* October 21, 1981, p. 5.

9. Great Britain accepted 160 cruise missiles; West Germany, 108 Pershing II and 96 cruise missiles; Italy, 112 cruise missiles; Belgium and Holland, 48 cruise missiles each.

10. Ronald Reagan, quoted in "President's Speech on Military Spending and a New Defense," *New York Times,* March 24, 1983, p. A20.

11. Wayne Biddle, "Request for Space Weapons Reflects Early Goals," *New York Times,* February 4, 1985, p. A10. The fate of the world would be in the hands (or the chips and software) of computers. "Perhaps we should run R2-D2 for president in the 1990s," Senator Paul Tsongas (D-MA) quipped at a congressional hearing. "At least he'd be on line all the time. Has anyone told the President that he's out of the decision-making process?" George Keyworth, President Reagan's science advisor, replied, "I certainly haven't." Philip M. Boffey, "'Star Wars' and Mankind: Consequences for Future," *New York Times,* March 8, 1985, p. A14. In January 1987, the Office of Technology Assessment concluded that the software could not be property tested and would have to be written "without the benefit of data or experience from battle use." It would have to rely on theoretical "peacetime testing," which, however, would offer "no guarantee that the system would not fail catastrophically . . . as a result of a software error . . . in the system's first battle." Office of Technology Assessment, *SDI: Technology, Survivability, and Software* (Princeton, NJ: Princeton University Press, 1988), p. 249.

12. Harold Brown, December 1983, quoted in Boffey, "Star Wars," p. A14.

13. Caspar Weinberger quote, ibid., p. A14.

14. The Soviet SS-20 rockets carried three warheads each; thus the Soviet Union gave up more than three times as many warheads as the United States.

15. Arms Control Association, from data supplied by the US Defense Department, the Joint Chiefs of Staff, and the Arms Control and Disarmament Agency, *New York Times,* May 26, 1988, p. A12.

16. "Wir werden euch des Feindes berauben," *Der Spiegel*, December 12, 1988, p. 22.

17. Christian Schmidt-Häuer, "Die Armee gerät unter Beschuss," *Die Zeit*, November 11, 1988, p. 8.

18. "Unsere Antwort wird Nein sein," *Der Spiegel*, May 1, 1989, p. 21.

19. Wolfgang Schwarz of the Institute for International Politics and Economy in East Berlin, in a report to the East German Council of Ministers, "DDR-Wissenschaftler warnt vor Atomverseuchung Europas," *Frankfurter Rundschau*, June 21, 1989, p. 2.

20. John F. Cushman Jr., "Senate Endorses Pact to Reduce Strategic Arms," *New York Times*, October 2, 1992, pp. A1, A6.

21. When Reagan again referred to the Russian proverb at the signing of SALT I, Gorbachev remarked, "You repeat it at every meeting." To which Reagan replied, "I like it."

22. George Petrovich, "Counting the Costs of the Arms Race," *Foreign Policy* (Winter 1991–1992), p. 87.

23. Cited in David Hoffman, "Russian Says Arms Treaty Vote Should Follow Election," *Washington Post*, February 1, 1996, p. A17.

24. Mikhail Gorbachev, "'Geroi' razrusheniia Sovetskogo Soiuza izvestny . . . ," *Novoe vremia*, nos. 2–3 (1995), p. 27.

25. Adrian Blomfield and Mike Smith, "Gorbachev: US Could Start New Cold War," *Daily Telegraph*, May 7, 2008.

26. William K. Blewett, "Chemical and Biological Threats: The Nature and Risk," *HPAC Engineering* (September 2004), pp. 2–4; William Blewett, "75 Years of Chemical Warfare," *Baltimore Sun*, April 20, 1990.

27. Leonard S. Spector, "Repentant Nuclear Proliferants," *Foreign Policy* (Fall 1992), pp. 26–27.

28. Seymour M. Hersh, "The Deal: Why Is Washington Going Easy on Pakistan's Nuclear Black Marketers?" *The New Yorker*, March 8, 2004, pp. 32–37. Khan was released from house arrest in February 2009.

29. "Timeline of North Korea's Nuclear Program," *New York Times*, August 6, 2013.

30. Associated Press, "Iran Threatens to End Nuclear Talks with Europeans," *Baltimore Sun*, October 28, 2004, p. 14A.

31. Thomas Powers, "Iran: The Threat," *New York Review of Books*, July 17, 2008, pp. 9–11.

32. Stephanie Cooke, "Perspective: Bringing Iran's Nuclear Program in the Fold," *Energy Compass*, November 29, 2013.

33 "The Best v the Not-Too-Bad," *The Economist*, October 19, 2013.

34 "A Nice Red Afterglow," *The Economist*, March 14, 1992, p. 43.

# 21

# The Emergence of Political Islam in the Middle East and North Africa

The Cold War was largely a bipolar struggle between Western liberalism and the Soviet variant of Communism, with much of the world trying to stay out of harm's way. In the 1970s, however, a new political force took center stage: militant Islam. The militants sought to resurrect the "house of Islam," a term that come into use after Muslim armies had completed the conquest of the Middle East, North Africa, and much of the Iberian Peninsula in the eighth century. Eventually, the "house of Islam" stretched from the Atlantic shores of Africa to the easternmost tip of the Indonesian archipelago in Asia, from Central Asia to the Sudan. In the 1980s, its population was nearly 1 billion people. Its aim was to free Islam from the debilitating and overbearing influence of outside forces—Communism, secularism, and above all, the West.

## Islam: Theory and Practice
Islam is the third of the world's great religions to come out of the Middle East. To Muslims, it is the third and last of the "true revelations" by a divinity whom the Jews call Jehovah, the Christians call God, and the Muslims call Allah.

This final revelation came in the seventh century of the Christian era when Allah spoke to his prophet, Mohammed of Mecca, Islam's holiest city, in what today is Saudi Arabia. Mohammed was born into a society of idol worshipers, Jews, and Christians, and he fell under the influence of Arabia's two dominant monotheistic faiths, Judaism and Christianity. In fact, these two faiths were the starting point of Mohammed's teachings. He was always at pains to acknowledge that God had revealed himself to his prophets of another age—Abraham, Moses, and Jesus Christ among them. In fact, Islam recog-

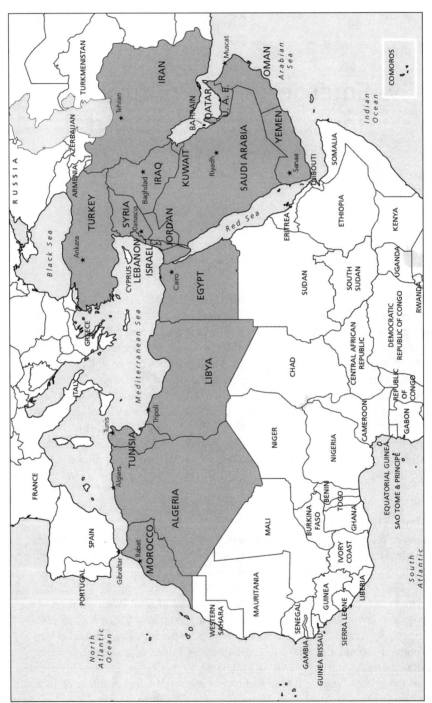

**The Middle East and North Africa**

nized that Jews and Christians were "people of the book," that is, God's revelations in the Old and New Testaments. Mohammed held the view that uncorrupted Judaism and Christianity were early manifestations of Islam (literally "submission" to God) and that Abraham had been the first Muslim. Mohammed also insisted, however, that Christians and Jews had gone astray, had ignored God's commandments, and thereby had corrupted the original scriptures. God then revealed himself to the last in the long line of prophets, Mohammed. The links between Islam and Christianity were such that several seventh-century Christian theologians believed that Islam was a heterodox Christian doctrine, similar to Nestorianism (an interpretation that attributed to Jesus two natures—divine and human).[1]

Islam is an offshoot of Judaism and, to a lesser degree, Christianity. Its linear relationship to Judaism resembles Christianity's link to Judaism. At one time, Muslims, including Mohammed, faced Jerusalem when they prayed. All three religions stress justice and compassion. Islam has a heaven and a hell; God spoke to Mohammed through the Archangel Gabriel (as he did to the Virgin Mary); Islam has its Day of Resurrection and Judgment, "and the hour is known to no one but God." Believers who are created "from an essence of clay . . . shall surely die hereafter, and be restored to life on the Day of Resurrection," a "day sure to come."[2]

Arabs and Jews both claim Abraham as their ancestor. The Jews descended from Abraham's second son, Isaac, born of his wife Sarah; the Arabs descended from the first son, Ishmael, born of Hagar, Sarah's Egyptian maid. The Bible prophesied that great nations would descend from the two sons of Abraham. The biblical account, however, stresses that God renewed with Isaac the covenant he had made with Abraham, while the Muslims make no distinction between the sons of Abraham. Islamic scholars argue that it is inconceivable that God would favor one son over the other. In Islamic teachings, the conflict between Jews and Muslims takes place in a family divided against itself. Since Muslims and Jews both trace their religious lineage to Abraham, it was not surprising that both sought control of the West Bank city of Hebron, which contains the tombs of Abraham and his family (notably his wife, Sarah, and his son Isaac).

God's revelations to Mohammed were codified in the Koran (literally "recitation" of the word of God), the holy, infallible book of the Muslims, which contains God's commands to the faithful. The Koran is God's word, last in time and the completion and correction of all that had been written before.

Deviation from an established faith is no trifling matter, since it attempts to replace the established faiths with one that claims to be the only true or, in this case, final revelation from God. The conflict between Muslims and Jews began in Mohammed's day and has lasted centuries down to our time. Neither Judaism nor Christianity has ever recognized the validity of Islam. Western scholars have used the label "Mohammedanism" to describe Islam, a term insulting to Muslims because it suggests that it is an invention of one man rather than God's final word. And Islam, in its turn, has denied the Holy Trinity, and thus the divinity of Jesus Christ, which amounts to a demand, as one historian put it, for "the unconditional surrender of the essence of Christianity."[3] Islam does, however, recognize Jesus as one of God's revered prophets.

A Muslim is someone who "submits" to the will of God. Islam is thus a religion that encompasses the totality of one's existence. It is a complete way of life, both secular and religious. There can be no separation between one's spiritual and secular existence. In an Islamic nation, therefore, a believer cannot make a distinction between secular and religious laws. All laws must be based on the Koran; it cannot be otherwise. Muslim societies must be governed according to the word of Allah. Islam, as the Koran makes clear, is a religion of laws.

There is an elemental simplicity to the fundamental laws, the "five pillars" of Islam. They include, first and foremost, an affirmation of one of the shortest credos of any religion in the world: "There is no god but God and Mohammed is the Prophet of God." All that a convert to Islam has to do is to state this attestation in the company of believers. No other rite or ceremony is required. (The very simplicity inherent in the act of conversion explains in part why Islam was the fastest-growing religion in Africa at the end of the twentieth century.) Second, a Muslim is obliged to pay an alms tax (the *zakat*) of around 5 percent. Islam emphasizes the importance of charity: "Whatever alms you give . . . are known to Allah . . . and whatever alms you give shall be paid back to you in full."[4] In an Islamic state, the alms tax is also a source of revenue for the government. Third, a Muslim must say five daily prayers while facing toward Mecca. The *muezzin* (crier) calls the faithful to prayer from the minaret (a slender tower) of a mosque at various times during the day: at sunset, during the night, at dawn, at noon, and in the afternoon. Fourth, Islam demands abstention from food, drink, and sexual intercourse from dawn to sundown during the lunar month of Ramadan, which commemorates Allah's first revelation of the Koran to Mohammed. Fasting here becomes a spiritual act of renunciation and self-denial. Last, a Muslim must attempt to make at least one pilgrimage, or *haj*, to the holy city of Mecca.

After the death of Mohammed in 632, Islam spread quickly throughout the Middle East and North Africa. With Islam came the establishment of some of the world's great civilizations, centering on the cities of Damascus and Baghdad. Yet, ultimately, this golden age of Islam gave way to a European ascendancy, which may be dated to the Crusades of the Middle Ages. In more recent times, Western powers (notably Britain and France) established their presence in the Muslim lands of the Middle East, only to find their grip weakening after World War II. Militant Islam seeks to free the Muslim world from the continuing overbearing influence of the Christian

West and to reassert the sovereign status denied to it over the past centuries. As with many independence movements, it seeks the restoration of what in retrospect was a golden age.

## The Shiites and the Sunnis

In the 1970s, the most visible and radical advocates of resurgent, militant Islam were the Shiites, the smaller of the two main branches of Islam. The other wing, the Sunnis, represents what is generally called the mainstream of Islam and, in fact, makes up approximately 90 percent of all Muslims. Shiites are little known in Africa, whether among the Arabs in the north or among the blacks in sub-Saharan Africa. The same is true of southern Asia, in countries such as Indonesia, Malaysia, Bangladesh, India, Turkey, and Pakistan. The keepers of the holy places in Mecca and Medina, the Saudi royal family, and their subjects are mostly Sunnis. In Iran, however, nearly all Muslims belong to the Shiite branch; in fact, Shiism became a state religion there. The majority of the Muslims of Iraq and of the former Soviet Republic of Azerbaijan are Shiites. Shiites may also be found in large numbers in all the states of the Persian Gulf, as well as Syria, Lebanon, Yemen, and Central Asia.

The split in Islam came two decades after Mohammed's death. The first four caliphs, the Rightly Guided, who succeeded Mohammed, were selected from the ranks of his associates; after that, the line became hereditary. From the very outset there were strains in the Muslim community over the question of succession. As the caliphs became more tyrannical, they increasingly appeared as usurpers. There were those who insisted that Ali, the husband of Mohammed's daughter Fatima, was the true successor. The assassination of the reigning caliph in 656 set off a civil war between Shiites—from *shia*, or party (of Ali)—and Sunnis—from *sunna*, meaning "practice" or "custom"— who sided with the caliphs. The war continued for a quarter century until the Battle of Kerbala in 681, in today's Iraq. During the fighting, Ali died a martyr's death. It was here that the Sunnis established their domination and the Shiite resistance went underground. The struggle was both political and religious in nature. The Sunnis represented authority, while the Shiites opposed privilege and power and championed the oppressed. The Shiites found their inspiration in the actions of Mohammed in Mecca, where he first made his mark as the advocate of the downtrodden. The Shiites of Iran, for example, waged a long conflict with the shah's regime in their quest to re-create a social and political order in line with the teachings of the Koran.

Politics and religion, in the Shiites' eyes, cannot be separated. Obedience to civil authority has never been a hallmark of Shiite behavior. In their challenge to entrenched political power, Shiites time and again have elevated political disobedience to a religious duty. When, in 1963, the shah of Iran offered his uncompromising critic, the Ayatollah Ruhollah Khomeini, his freedom on the condition he leave politics to the politicians, Khomeini replied: "All of Islam is politics." Khomeini became the shah's most vocal opponent, accusing him of having sold his country into bondage on behalf of US interests. In 1964, Khomeini was briefly detained for having publicly refused to recognize the government, its courts, and its laws. Ten days after his release, Khomeini delivered the first of his political sermons. In one of them, he denounced a law, passed in October 1964, which had granted US citizens in Iran the right of extraterritoriality, that is, the right to be tried according to US law, instead of Iranian law. Khomeini called the law "a document for the enslavement of Iran," reducing it to a colony of the United States. At the end of 1964, he was rearrested and then exiled.[5]

Sunnis and Shiites both accept the Prophet's promise of the return of one of his descendants who will "fill the world with justice and equity."[6] For Shiites, the spirit of messianism is central to their creed. They look to an *imam*, a divinely appointed descendant of Mohammed, whose mission is the spiritual—as well as political and at times insurrectional—guidance of the faithful.

The Sunnis, the party of custom and practice, stand—as a rule—for the continuity of the social, political, and religious order. They emphasize consensus and obedience to civil and religious authority. In contrast to the Shiites, Sunnis look for inspiration to Mohammed's work in Medina, where he created the first Muslim state and ruled as a military commander, judge, and teacher to whom Allah's word was revealed.

Radicalism in the name of Islam, however, is not a Shiite monopoly. The Shiites have a lower boiling point when it comes to dealing with corruption and oppression. The militant Muslims in Iran, Iraq, Lebanon, and Saudi Arabia are generally Shiites; the Islamic radicals in Algeria, Hamas in Gaza, the Taliban in Afghanistan, and al Qaeda are Sunnis. What militant Islam—whether Shiite or Sunni—sought was the elimination of foreign influences that humiliated and degraded the "house of Islam." The militants in Algeria fought a military dictatorship still heavily dominated by French culture; those in Iran combated Western (at first largely British and later US) influence; and the Soviet Muslims (whether Shiite Azeris or Sunni Chechens or Uzbeks) sought to free themselves from Moscow's rule and dreamed of a restoration of their once glorious civilizations.

## The Revolution in Iran

### The Shah and the United States
From the end of World War II until the late 1970s, Iran stood in sharp contrast to its Arab neighbors. Shah Mohammed Reza Pahlavi appeared to be a rock of

stability in the turbulent Middle East, a bulwark against political radicalism, Islamic fundamentalism, and Soviet expansionism. Even after the shah's rule had been shaken by violent protests, US president Jimmy Carter still praised him for his stabilizing influence in the Middle East. Surely, there was no solid reason to believe that the shah, still apparently a vigorous man in middle age, would not continue to rule and that his young son would not succeed him on the Peacock Throne.

But Iran turned out to be another case of US involvement in a foreign land of which few people in authority in Washington had an adequate understanding. The outward stability of Iran only masked the volatile undercurrents, which had deep historic roots. The shah had ruled for a long time, since 1941, but his reign had been plagued by instability, an inconvenient fact that US policymakers preferred to overlook. The militant clergy was a nuisance, they reasoned, but they certainly appeared to be no threat to the shah.

Resistance to Iran's shahs by militant Shiites was a constant thread running through Iranian history. This was particularly the case when shahs made deals with foreigners, granting them favorable economic concessions. In 1872, Nasir ed-Den Shah, for example, granted Paul Julius de Reuter, a British subject, such comprehensive monopolies that the shah, in effect, had sold him the country. De Reuter received monopolies in the construction of railroads, canals, and irrigation works; the harvesting of forests; the use of all uncultivated lands; and the operation of banks, public works, and mines. The British leader Lord George Curzon called this "the most complete and extraordinary surrender of the entire industrial resources of a kingdom into foreign hands that has ever been dreamed of, much less accomplished."[7] In 1892, the shah faced an angry mob demanding the repeal of a monopoly granted to a British firm in the production, sale, and export of tobacco. The demonstrators were able to bring about the repeal of the concessions. Nasir ed-Den Shah's troubles persisted, however, and in 1896 he was assassinated. His reign points to a recurring pattern of Iranian politics: royal complicity with foreign nations, the mobs in the streets, and the inability of most shahs to cling to power. During the previous 360 years, only four shahs died natural deaths while still on the throne. The rest were either dethroned or assassinated. Shiite Iran was not a likely place to look for political equilibrium.

After Nasir ed-Den Shah's assassination, the practice of selling favors to foreigners—British, French, and Russian—nonetheless continued. In 1906, the Iranian parliament, the *majlis*, took away this privilege from the shah. But the practice continued. It was a contributing factor to a legacy of bitterness and resentment directed toward the Qajar dynasty (1779–1925) that ultimately led to its demise. In its stead, a military officer took power, Colonel Reza Khan, who crowned himself Reza Shah Pahlavi in 1926.

Reza Shah did not act differently from the previous monarchs when it came to dealing with foreign powers. In 1933, he granted new favorable concessions to the Anglo-Iranian Oil Company, an enterprise that was largely controlled by the British. His close association with the British continued until World War II, when he leaned toward Nazi Germany at a time when it threatened to take the Soviet Union's oil fields north of the Caucasus Mountains, on the western shores of the Caspian Sea, notably around the city of Baku. The Germans appeared to be on the threshold of linking up with Iran. The upshot was the joint occupation of Iran by the Soviets (who took control of the northern part) and the British (who occupied the southern regions). The British and Soviets forced the shah to abdicate in favor of his young son, who turned out to be the second and last of the Pahlavi dynasty.

Iran's oil reserves were the greatest source of wealth for the Pahlavi dynasty. After World War II, Iran became one of the largest producers of oil in the Middle East. Iran's own share of the oil profits increased, but many nationalists were not satisfied, particularly after the Arab-American Oil Company, a US concern, offered Saudi Arabia more favorable terms. More importantly, the lion's share of the Iranian profits still went to the foreign investors, mostly British.

Reza Khan's son, Mohammed Reza (who ruled from 1941 to 1979), sought to identify his ruling house with the glories of Persia's past. In 1971, he staged an elaborate ceremony in Persepolis, the ancient city of Cyrus the Great. Guests from far and wide attended the gala celebration. In March 1976, a dutiful parliament created the "monarchy calendar," dating from the coronation of Cyrus, 2,535 years earlier. Its purpose was to link the shah to Iran's glorious past and to suggest millennia of historic continuity. It did not sit well with most Iranians since the new calendar replaced the Islamic calendar based on the date of the *hegira* (flight) of Mohammed from Mecca to Medina in 622.[8] Nominally a Muslim, the shah became the Shahansha (King of Kings), the Light of the Aryans, who ruled by divine right, a man who claimed to have experienced religious visions.[9]

This spectacle impressed the world, but many Iranians, particularly the Shiite clergy, saw the shah in a different light. They considered him an usurper—only the second in the short line of the Pahlavi dynasty—who had been educated in the West and who had sent his son to study there.

In 1951, the Iranian parliament, headed by Prime Minister Mohammed Mossadegh, in a challenge to the shah, voted for the nationalization of the oil industry. The British declared the law illegal. US president Harry Truman sought to mediate the dispute, eventually siding with the British, but he refused to become involved in Iran's internal affairs. The new US administration under Dwight Eisenhower, however, had no such qualms. Its secretary of state, John Foster Dulles, and his brother, Allen, the chief of the CIA, decided to act. Truman had thought that Mossadegh constituted a barrier against the aspirations of the Communist Tudeh Party; the Dulles brothers thought that Mossadegh was contributing to an eventual Communist takeover.

Mossadegh's challenge to the West struck a responsive chord in Iranian society. As tensions rose, the CIA and British intelligence plotted to oust Mossadegh. Washington put economic pressure on Iran by cutting off aid and refusing to buy Iranian oil. The use of an economic weapon only inflamed the militants in the capital of Tehran. Street riots forced the shah to flee to Rome in August 1953.

The CIA and British intelligence moved quickly and decisively. With the help of the Iranian army and other elements opposed to Mossadegh, the United States and Britain managed to return the shah after only three days in exile. Demonstrations in the streets had ousted the shah; counterdemonstrations in these same streets created a political climate enabling his return.

The shah now owed his throne to a foreign power, something he always resented. Still, his ties with the United States grew. Oil exports to the West increased, enabling Iran to become one of the best overseas customers for US products. The shah took steps to modernize Iranian society by launching his conservative "White Revolution." The transformation, however, came at a price. It created a gulf between a new privileged class, which benefited from the shah's close link with the West, and much of the rest of the country. Too many were left out, and it was inevitable that the shah's actions would breed resentment. The influx of Western technicians, engineers, military advisers, and sales representatives disturbed many Iranians. The uneven distribution of the country's enormous wealth and the attendant Westernization led to a distortion of traditional Iranian social patterns. Traditional Iranian self-sufficiency became a thing of the past. By the 1970s, Iran became greatly dependent on foreign imports; it even bought food from abroad. Since Iran based much of its wealth on a one-product economy (80 percent of its export earnings came from the sale of oil), its dependency on the West appeared to be total.

Much of the money the shah spent on foreign products went for the purchase of modern military equipment, most of it US-made. Between 1972 and 1978, he ordered $19.5 billion in US arms. The greater the oil revenues, the more weapons he bought. After 1973, about one-third of the government's spending went for armaments.

Richard Nixon's administration applauded such a course: Iran, armed to the teeth, would preserve stability in the Middle East, particularly in the Persian Gulf, the waterway through which passed much of the oil on which the industrial powers depended. It was here that the "Nixon Doctrine" appeared to work best. First formulated at the end of the war in Vietnam, the Nixon Doctrine called for client states to be armed (and at times financed) by the United States to engage in the actual fighting on behalf of US interests. In South Vietnam the doctrine collapsed in 1975, when its army took to its heels. In Iran the doctrine seemed to be working to perfection.

In the early 1970s, it was not clear how Iran would pay for the massive military equipment the shah demanded. But good fortune intervened. October

1973 saw the fourth Arab-Israeli conflict, the Yom Kippur War, which led to an oil embargo by OPEC and a doubling of oil prices. The shah took the lead in demanding an increase in the price of oil. Even though it caused grave damage to the US economy, the Nixon administration saw a silver lining. Iran's military strength would be achieved without raiding the US treasury. Henry Kissinger, Nixon's secretary of state, explained in his memoirs: "The vacuum left by British withdrawal [from Iran during the early 1950s], now menaced by Soviet intrusion and radical momentum, would be filled by a power friendly to us. . . . And all of this was achievable without any American resources, since the Shah was willing to pay for the equipment out of his oil revenues."[10]

This scenario fell apart in a most unexpected way when Islamic militants drove the shah from power. Rather than being ruled by a servant of the "Great Satan" (the United States), Iran henceforth was ruled by the Shiite clergy.

### The Return of Khomeini
The best-known practitioner of militant Islam in the 1970s was Ruhollah Khomeini, who carried the honorific title of ayatollah. Khomeini demanded that the "House of Islam" be purged of Western, infidel influence. In the eyes of Khomeini and the *mullahs*, the Muslim clergy, the shah stood in direct violation of the history and religion of Islam. With the trappings of Western civilization all around him, the shad appeared little different from the tens of thousands of Western technicians he had invited to Iran.

Khomeini's denunciations of the shah had little effect at first. They were regarded merely as the raving and ranting of an old man in exile. But as dissatisfaction with the shah grew, Khomeini's sermons, distributed on audiocassette tapes smuggled into Iran, began to have an effect. By January 1979, it became apparent that the shah would maintain his throne only if the notoriously brutal SAVAK (the secret police established in 1957 with the help of the CIA) and the army were willing to suppress the rising tide of discontent. Civil war loomed on the horizon. The shah, unsure of the loyalty of the army and unable to obtain a clear-cut US commitment from the Carter administration, decided to leave the country. Corruption, favoritism, police brutality, poverty and luxury side by side, the lack of justice, the influence of foreigners—all contributed to the demise of the Pahlavi dynasty.

The events of the late 1970s showed that the shah had merely maintained an illusion of power. In February 1979, Ayatollah Khomeini returned in triumph from exile in Paris. Under the leadership of the Muslim clergy, Iran would now undergo a spiritual and national rejuvenation. There was little doubt that the support for Khomeini's regime was massive in those heady days when the shah was put to flight.

But the shah had not officially abdicated. When he left in January 1979, he emphasized that he and his family were going abroad for an unspecified period. In effect, he promised to return.[11] It was no secret that the United

*Embassy of Iran*

*Ayatollah Ruhollah Khomeini,*
*Shiite leader of the Iranian*
*revolution, 1979*

States preferred the shah over the anti-US militants who now governed Tehran. The militants feared a repetition of the events of 1953, when the CIA had returned the shah to power from his brief exile in Rome. Radicals, bitterly hostile to a US government on which they blamed all of Iran's ills, stirred up deep emotions. Anti-US street demonstrations became daily affairs, and two weeks after Khomeini's return from exile, the first attack by militants on the US embassy took place. The organizers of the attack claimed—correctly—that the embassy housed the CIA. Khomeini's police dispersed the attackers this time.

Instead of concentrating on the consolidation of power, the Khomeini government sharpened the differences between the Islamic revolution and Washington when it repealed the 1947 law authorizing the US military mission in Iran. Tensions were already high when, in October 1979, the shah arrived in New York for medical treatment. The militants saw it as the first step by the CIA to try and bring him back to power. They refused to believe the shah was ill and in need of treatment.

On November 4, a group of radical students took matters into their own hands. They climbed over the walls of the US embassy compound in Tehran, seized its diplomatic personnel, and demanded that the United States extradite the shah to Iran to stand trial. Only then would they release their fifty-two hostages, who were kept bound and blindfolded in the embassy. There was no evidence that Khomeini had ordered them to engage in an act that clearly violated international law. The huge crowds who gathered daily in the square in front of the embassy in support of the students limited Khomeini's options. On the plus side, however, from Khomeini's objective, it further radicalized the politics of Iran.

The hostage crisis came when memories of US helicopters departing from the embassy in Saigon were still fresh in the US public's mind. Moreover, eight weeks after the hostage crisis began, the United States was hit with yet another jolt when the Soviet Union sent 80,000 troops into Afghanistan—a country bordering Iran—to bail out a Communist government barely hanging on. The United States had lost a sphere of influence in Iran, and the Soviet Union had expanded its sphere of influence. Washington's loss in Iran and what appeared to be Moscow's gain in Afghanistan gave Carter a foreign policy headache that ultimately played a major role in his defeat in the presidential election of 1980. As for Afghanistan, he was unable to do much except to refuse to sell the Soviets grain and boycott the 1980 Olympic Games in Moscow.

Since Carter could not shake the damaging perception that he was indecisive and a "wimp," voters gave the tough-talking Republican Ronald Reagan the chance to handle the nation's foreign policy.[12] After a failed rescue attempt, Carter, however, did manage to obtain the release of the hostages after 444 days in captivity. He struck a deal with the Khomeini government by returning to Iran most of its frozen assets abroad (mostly money in Western banks) in exchange for the hostages' release. Khomeini, however, whose feud with Carter had become personal, refused to return the hostages as long as Carter was president. Minutes after Reagan was inaugurated, they were set free.

Khomeini set out to establish an "Islamic Republic of Iran" according to the strictures set down in the Koran. Iran's secular Constitution of 1906 gave way to a new one based on Islamic laws. As sovereignty was transferred from the shah to the clergy, its leading ayatollah was designated as the "Supreme Leader." The upshot was bloody civil strife between the Shiite clergy and the secular parties. The challenge to the revolution came mainly from the numerous splinter groups on the left—Marxists, Maoists, and socialists—who feared the replacement of one dictatorship by another. Waves of revolutionary terror led to the execution of an estimated 10,000 Iranians; another half million, many of them from the professional classes, went into exile. The revolution swept aside all remnants of the Pahlavi dynasty and much of the Western influence it had introduced.

Khomeini's revolution brought about a redistribution of land and broadened health care and educational opportunities for the poor. Since the revolution, women saw an increase in university enrollment and employment in the civil service. From Washington's perspective, however, the most important aspect of the revolution was the threat of the spread of militant Islamist zeal beyond the confines of Iran. Indeed, Shiite communities in Lebanon, Iraq, the

Gulf states, and Saudi Arabia began to look to Iran for guidance. Khomeini's revolutionary message in support of the downtrodden masses and his virulent opposition to the West found traction across the Middle East. Before the revolution, Washington had believed that Communism posed the greatest danger to its position in the Middle East. Afterward, the alternatives were no longer between Western liberalism and Soviet-style Communism, neither of which, in any case, had found much traction in the Middle East. Militant Islam, in direct challenge to the Soviet Union and the West, became a force to be reckoned with.

Revolutionary movements have a tendency to run their course. The fervor that makes a revolution possible cannot be sustained indefinitely. As long as Khomeini was alive and was able to inspire his followers, the revolution appeared secure. After his death in June 1989, however, many Iranians were ready for change and for normalization of relations with the outside world. Shiite-led Iran was isolated diplomatically, economically, spiritually, and intellectually from the rest of the world. Branded a "terrorist state," some of its officials were sought to stand trial abroad for criminal complicity in terrorist acts. The clergy stifled open discussions, enforced religious laws, regulated private affairs, and imposed strict press censorship. (The newspaper editor Abdullah Nouri, for example, was declared a heretic and sentenced to a five-year prison term after he had enraged the religious hierarchy by questioning their absolute power.) It was a country in which many of the young were second-class citizens who faced an uncertain future.

## The Iran-Iraq War

With Iran in the throes of its revolution and civil strife, Saddam Hussein of Iraq availed himself in September 1980 of the opportunity to invade Iran. Hussein had three objectives. He sought (1) to destroy Khomeini's revolution, which he feared might spread to his subjects, most of whom were Shiites; (2) to secure disputed territory at the confluence of the Tigris and Euphrates Rivers, the Shatt el-Arab; and (3) to emerge as the paramount leader in the Arab world.

By securing the Shatt el-Arab, Hussein sought to capture Iran's oil ports on the other side of the river and then drive eastward into Iran. He calculated that Iran was unprepared for war because of extensive losses to its officer corps and pilots caused by purges and desertions. Iran, however, still had many loyal middle-grade officers and pilots. Moreover, it was able to rally its people to a conflict that for Iranians echoed a resumption of the ancient wars between Persians and Arabs.

Iran managed to build up its Revolutionary Guard (regular forces) from 7,000 to 200,000 men and to form a new militia of more than 350,000 troops ready to fight a "holy war." Iran thereby was able to offset Iraq's initial advantage of a better-trained and better-equipped army. With the two sides evenly matched, neither side was able to score a decisive victory. The war became a stalemate after Iran's 1982 counteroffensive regained lost territory and captured almost 60,000 Iraqi troops on the battlefield.

The United States, the Soviet Union, and the European nations officially declared their neutrality in the conflict. But as the war dragged on, over forty countries supplied weapons to one side or the other, and several, including the United States, covertly sold weapons to both. Israel and the United States provided weapons to Iraq to keep the war going. In 1983, Reagan sent a special envoy, Donald Rumsfeld, for the purpose of reestablishing diplomatic relations—which had been broken off in 1967—and offering economic and military assistance.[13] The Reagan administration's assistance included billions of dollars of credits, satellite surveillance of Iranian troop movement, cluster bombs, and poison gas. It was all designed to ensure that Iraq would not lose.[14] Israel's defense minister, Yitzhak Rabin, stated frankly, "We don't want a resolution of this war."[15] Iraq also received financial support from nations that feared Iran's ideological revolution, such as Saudi Arabia and other oil-exporting Arab states on the Gulf.

Both sides understood the importance of oil in financing the war, and each targeted the other's oil-producing and -shipping facilities in the Gulf. A primary US aim was to keep open the Straits of Hormuz, the passageway from the Gulf to the Arabian Sea through which much of the industrialized world's oil flowed. For that reason, the US Navy accepted, in December 1986, a request by the Kuwaiti government to protect its oil tanker fleet. Kuwaiti tankers were then "reflagged," that is, placed under the US flag and escorted by US naval vessels.

The war also saw the first extensive use of chemical weapons—by both sides—since World War I. But as long as the belligerents were only killing each other, the outside world did not care. Toward the end of the stalemated war, in March 1988, Hussein launched a poison gas attack on his own citizens. The target was the city of Halabja, which was populated by Kurds, a non-Arab Islamic people hostile to Hussein's regime. The lethal chemicals killed as many as 5,000 civilians. This time, the use of chemical weapons brought strong worldwide rebuke, for it underscored the new potential danger the world faced from "the poor man's atomic bomb," as some called it.

The long war of attrition left its mark on both sides. In the summer of 1987, Hussein accepted a UN Security Council resolution calling for an armistice. Khomeini held out for another year, demanding that Hussein first step down and that Iraq pay $150 billion in reparations. But after suffering a series of military setbacks and a decline in oil profits, Khomeini reversed himself, announcing in July 1988 that he must take "the bitter drink of poison" and accept the UN peace formula.[16]

There was no winner of the absurd eight-and-half-year-long war. Each side suffered almost a million casualties and enormous economic losses. Iraq, it may be said, emerged from the war with the stronger military forces. (It also emerged heavily indebted to lender nations such as Kuwait.) But Iran was not defeated, and its Islamic revolution remained very much intact.

### Terrorism in Lebanon and Libya

In Lebanon, extremists inspired by Islamic fundamentalism and frustrated by setbacks at the hands of Israel, resorted to desperate, at times suicidal, attacks against Israeli troops still in Lebanon. They considered terrorism as a moral act, whatever the cost to themselves, their enemies, or, for that matter, innocent parties. In some instances, they acted to gain specific ends, such as the return of prisoners taken by Israel. Israel responded with a show of force.

The United States, by its military intervention on behalf of the Phalangist government of Lebanon in 1983 and its naval bombardment of Muslim strongholds in the mountains, made itself the target of terrorism as well. In retaliation, radical Islamists took Westerners as hostages. In March 1984, in Beirut, a pro-Iranian Shiite group, the Islamic Jihad, kidnapped CIA agent William Buckley and tortured and killed him. During the next two years, at least twenty others—college teachers, journalists, businessmen, and priests from Western countries—were taken hostage by the Islamic Jihad and other revolutionary groups in Lebanon. Lacking knowledge of the identity of the kidnappers or the location of the hostages, Western governments were unable to rescue them. In January 1986, Terry Waite, an envoy of the Church of England, went to Beirut to negotiate the release of foreign hostages, only to be kidnapped himself by the Islamic Jihad. Although most of the hostages were eventually released, at least ten were killed.[17]

Exasperated by the continuing wave of terrorism and determined to stop it, the Reagan administration vowed to retaliate. It found a likely target in Muammar Qaddafi, the dictator of Libya. Qaddafi, a strident pan-Arab extremist, had already raised Reagan's ire for his support of the Palestine Liberation Organization and for his brash threats against the United States for trespassing in what he claimed to be Libya's territorial waters, the Gulf of Sidra. Moreover, Qaddafi had maintained terrorist training camps in Libya and had provided financial support for Lebanese extremist groups suspected of terrorism.[18] In April 1986, a terrorist bomb ripped through a discotheque in West Berlin, killing two people, among them a US soldier, and leaving 204 injured. Reagan blamed Qaddafi and ordered a punitive air attack on the Libyan cities of Tripoli and Benghazi. One bomb landed yards away from Qaddafi's residence, leaving him unharmed but, Qaddafi claimed, killing his adopted infant daughter. The US attack was little more than an act of frustration and vengeance and was of questionable deterrent value. Terrorism in the Middle East continued unabated.

Two years later, in December 1988, a terrorist attack blew up a US commercial jetliner, Pan Am flight 103, in flight over Lockerbie, Scotland, killing all 259 people aboard and 11 on the ground. After three years of masterful detective work, investigators were able to identify two suspects, agents in the Libyan secret service. In the interim, Qaddafi sought improved relations with the West by renouncing and apparently refraining from terrorism. He refused, however, to hand over the suspects to be tried, no doubt fearing that they might point the finger at him. Britain and the United States sought their extradition, later joined by France, which itself was investigating an explosion of a French airliner over Niger in September 1989 that killed 170.

Cornered, Qaddafi made the best of a bad situation. UN economic sanctions and diplomatic isolation had their impact. After stalling for nearly a decade, he agreed to hand over the two men charged in the Lockerbie bombing to be tried in the Netherlands under Scottish law. Two years after their conviction, in August 2003, Qaddafi admitted responsibility for the bombing and agreed to pay compensation of nearly $2 billion to the families of the 270 victims. The next month, he also agreed to pay compensation to the families of those killed over Niger. The settlements set the stage for Libya's reestablishment of normal relations with other nations, which were willing to let bygones be bygones and carry on business as usual with a mass murderer. The "mad dog of the Middle East," as Reagan called Qaddafi, had been turned into a statesman. Speaking to a Western reporter in May 2006, Qaddafi declared that he and Bush were both on the same page, "fighting for the cause of freedom."[19]

## The Gulf War

In 1990 the Persian Gulf—long a site of Western colonialism, internecine conflict among Muslims, and now one of the world's wealthiest regions—became a flash point of violence when Iraq's Saddam Hussein threatened and then invaded neighboring Kuwait.

### A War of Nerves

On August 2, 1990, Hussein launched a full-scale invasion of Kuwait and quickly conquered this small, virtually defenseless, oil-rich nation. The ruler of Kuwait, the Emir Sheikh Jabir al-Sabah, his cabinet, and his family fled to Saudi Arabia. Four days later, the UN Security Council voted unanimously to impose a worldwide trade embargo and three weeks later approved the use of armed force to execute it.

US president George H. W. Bush, a former oilman, at first was not alarmed. It mattered little to him who owned the oil reserves in Kuwait, as long as it made its way to the international market. After British prime minister Margaret Thatcher warned him that "this was no time to go wobbly," he took the lead to oust Hussein.[20] He responded to a request from Saudi Arabia for protection by ordering Operation Desert Shield, a massive airlift of US ground troops, aircraft, and naval vessels, to guard that country and its oil fields against further Iraqi aggression. Meanwhile, Arab League nations held an emergency meeting at which twelve of its twenty-one members voted to send troops to protect Saudi Arabia.

In the weeks prior to the invasion, Hussein had accused Kuwait of cheating on its OPEC-approved quota of oil production. By dumping large quantities of oil on the market, Hussein complained, Kuwait drove down the price of oil, thereby depriving Iraq of badly needed revenue. He also accused Kuwait of stealing oil from the Ramaila oil field, which straddled the Iraqi-Kuwaiti border, and complained that Kuwait refused to cancel the billion-dollar loans it had granted Iraq during its war against Iran. Three days after Kuwait rejected Hussein's demands for some $14 billion compensation for lost oil revenue, Hussein ordered his massed troops into action. Hussein then revived old Iraqi claims to all of Kuwait and proclaimed it Iraq's nineteenth province.

When Bush moved against Hussein's "naked aggression," virtually no government took Iraq's side. Statesmen recalled Hussein's unsavory past, his political beginnings as an assassin, his summary execution of political

*Iraqi Office, Embassy of Algeria*

*Saddam Hussein, former president of Iraq*

opponents, and his use of poison gas in his recently concluded war against Iran and against his own Kurdish population. They charged him with violating international law by annexing Kuwait; Bush even equated him with Hitler.

By virtue of the fact that the Cold War was over, Bush had little difficulty bringing the UN's Big Five on board, which permitted him to build a powerful international coalition. He also ambitiously spoke of creating a "new world order," reflecting the US status as the only superpower after the Soviet Union had ceased to exist. Bush projected a vision of a new era in which the United Nations—led by the United States—maintained international peace and order. Bush also came to see the Gulf crisis as a means of restoring the prestige of the US military and of purging the United States of its "Vietnam syndrome."

Bush's outrage against Hussein masked concerns about his position toward Iraq prior to the attack on Kuwait. In September 1990, Baghdad released a transcript of US ambassador April Glaspie's final talk with Hussein, on July 25, one week before he attacked Kuwait. In the transcript, which the US State Department confirmed as 80 percent accurate, she was quoted as saying: "I know you need funds. We understand that and . . . you should have the opportunity to rebuild your country. But we have no opinion on the Arab-Arab conflicts, like your border disagreement with Kuwait."[21] The ambassador seemed to suggest that Washington would not stand in Hussein's way should he invade Kuwait.

Revelations after the Gulf War also indicated that the Bush administration had been far less than candid about its pre–August 1990 relations with Hussein. It had consistently provided substantial economic, military, and intelligence support to Hussein, part of a policy begun by the Reagan administration in the early 1980s when Iraq was at war with Iran. Washington persistently ignored Hussein's record of human rights violations, took Iraq off the State Department's list of terrorist nations, and suppressed warnings regarding Iraq's atomic bomb project.

Once Bush decided to become involved in getting Hussein out of Kuwait, he rejected economic sanctions in favor of all-out war. At his urging, the UN Security Council, on November 29, 1990, passed (by a 12-2 vote) Resolution 678 authorizing the use of force if Iraq did not leave Kuwait by January 15, 1991. It now became a forty-eight-day countdown during which allied forces readied for a war sanctioned by the United Nations. By mid-January 1991, a thirty-one-member coalition massed in the Gulf region, led by more than 530,000 US, 35,000 Egyptian, 25,000 British, 22,000 Saudi, 19,000 Syrian, and 5,500 French fighting forces—in all nearly 700,000 troops. Hussein responded that if war occurred, it would be a horrible "mother of all wars" with "columns of dead bodies that may have a beginning but which would have no end."[22]

## A Most Unusual War

The Gulf War, code-named Desert Storm, was fought almost exclusively from the air. Iraqi pilots chose not to engage coalition aircraft in battle and instead fled with their planes on a one-way trip to Iran. (They did so because no other country would grant them sanctuary. After the war, the grateful Iranians refused to return them.) Absent an Iraqi air force, coalition fighter planes struck at Iraqi targets at will. In the first fourteen hours they flew more than 2,000 sorties. The round-the-clock bombing of Baghdad and other cities of Iraq continued until the end of the war. Television coverage of the war provided viewers with an impressive display of the new, seemingly pinpoint-accurate high-tech weaponry deployed against defenseless Iraqi targets.

Iraq answered the air attacks with ineffectual Scud missile attacks against Israel. Although no one was killed, the Scud attacks caused great anger in Israel. Especially frightful was the prospect that the next Scuds might be armed with chemical weapons. Hussein hoped that this diversionary attack would draw a military response from Israel, which might cause Arab nations to withdraw from the coalition. Washington restrained Israel by promising to destroy the Scud missile sites and providing Israel protection with US Patriot antimissile batteries.

The anticipated, potentially bloody ground war against Hussein's army had yet to be fought, however. When it came, it lasted only 100 hours. Under the command of US Army general Norman Schwarzkopf, the coalition forces met far less resistance than expected. Iraq's vaunted Republican Guard forces retreated from the battle, leaving the weaker, poorly trained, poorly fed, and exhausted regular troops to absorb the brunt of the invasion.

It left Hussein little choice except to comply with UN Resolution 660, which called for a cease-fire and Iraqi withdrawal to the pre-invasion lines. His defeated, retreating, and demoralized army was massacred on the "highway of death," a stretch of road running sixty miles from Kuwait to Basra. US airplanes trapped the retreating convoy by disabling the vehicles at the front. After that, a US pilot explained, it was like "shooting fish in a barrel." Tens of thousands of Hussein's retreating soldiers perished on that highway.[23]

Before the last of Hussein's troops departed Kuwait, they engaged in acts of sheer vandalism, opening the valves of oil pipelines and creating a major oil spill. For good measure, they also torched some 700 Kuwaiti oil wells.

Despite the decisiveness of the coalition military victory, the war's outcome was ambiguous. Before and during the war, Bush had spoken of removing Hussein from power, of trying him as a war criminal, and of completely destroying his military, including its weapons of mass destruction. Only the first of these objectives was achieved. Removing Hussein would have meant a march into Baghdad. As Bush later wrote in his memoirs:

> Trying to eliminate Saddam . . . would have incurred incalculable human and political costs. . . . We would have been forced to occupy Baghdad and, in effect, rule Iraq. . . . There was no viable "exit strategy" we could see. . . . Had we gone the invasion route, the United States could conceivably still be an occupying power in a bitterly hostile land.[24]

After Vietnam, the Pentagon concluded that the next war would have to be fought differently. The result was the Powell Doctrine, named after General Colin Powell, at that time the chairman of the Joint Chiefs of Staff: In the next war, the United States must define its objectives clearly—including a clear "exit strategy." Unlike in Vietnam, the military must marshal its resources to achieve victory here and now. In the 1991 Gulf War, the Powell Doctrine worked to perfection. The UN-sanctioned coalition consisted of more than 530,000 US troops—accompanied by a vast array of airpower—and another 160,000 allied soldiers. Moreover, again unlike Vietnam, the United States had an "exit strategy." After Hussein was driven out of Kuwait, the United States withdrew while the UN kept an eye on Hussein's military capability.

The United States took the lead in the war, but it did not have to carry the burden of paying for it. Several Gulf nations and wealthy nonparticipants (among them Germany, Japan, and Saudi Arabia) ended up paying nearly the entire bill. For the US public, still suffering from the Vietnam hangover, the war was short and cheap, in terms of both money and lives. The UN coalition lost fewer than 300 on the battlefield; the United States lost 148 troops, two-thirds from "friendly fire."

### The Aftermath

The war left behind a devastated Kuwait. The ruling emir, his family and government, and the wealthy Kuwaiti elite returned from exile to reclaim their homeland, now darkened by the smoke from the oil wells still on fire. But there was no significant political change, as some in the West had hoped. As before, the emir's new cabinet was composed almost entirely of members of the ruling Sabah family.

In Iraq, a spontaneous rebellion by the majority Shiites, 55 percent of the population, threatened the battered Hussein regime when they briefly seized control of the bombed-out city of Basra. To complicate matters for Hussein, Kurds asserted their authority in northern Iraq where they were in the majority. Bush had openly encouraged such uprisings during the war. But now, with the war over, they were on their own. According to the terms of the UN resolution that ended the war, the southern third of Iraq, the Shiite stronghold, was in a "no fly zone" for Iraqi aircraft. The US military warned Hussein that if "you fly, you die." But when he used helicopter gunships, neither the United States nor the UN moved to stop him.[25] Within less than three months, Hussein crushed the Shiite insurrection in the south, killing perhaps as many as 30,000 Shiites and driving more than 1 million into Iran.

## The Kurds

The Kurds suffered a similar fate. When Kurdish leaders proclaimed that the "whole of Kurdistan [in Iraq] had been liberated," they spoke too soon. A week later, Iraqi forces using helicopter gunships drove Kurdish troops out of their strongholds. Hussein's forces killed an estimated 50,000 Kurds and turned more than 1 million into refugees. The best Bush could do was to follow the lead of British prime minister John Major in sending food and supplies and attempt to create a UN-sponsored "safe haven" for the refugees in northern Iraq.

The defeat of the Kurds was but another chapter in the long and tragic history of an ancient people whose Indo-European language and distinct culture set them apart from their neighbors who speak Semitic languages. At the end of World War I, US president Woodrow Wilson proclaimed in his Fourteen Points that the ethnic minorities of Ottoman Turkey should have "absolutely unmolested opportunity of autonomous development." The Treaty of Sèvres (1920), by which the Ottoman Empire was carved up, called for an independent Kurdish state. The Turkish government of Kemal Ataturk, however, refused to accept that provision. In 1990, approximately 10 million Kurds lived in eastern Turkey, 5 million in western Iran, 4 million in northern Iraq (where they made up about 20 percent of the population), and 1 million in northeastern Syria. If there was one thing these nations were always able to agree on, it was that there must be no independent Kurdistan. Since 1961, Kurds fought Iran and Iraq whenever the opportunity availed itself, only to be defeated by one or the other and sometimes both. In the 1970s, the United States supported the Kurds, only to drop them after the shah and Hussein worked out an agreement to bring the Kurds to heel. When in 1971 the Kurds asked for US aid, Henry Kissinger, Nixon's national security advisor, ignored their request, saying covert US involvement in that region "should not be confused with missionary work."[26]

Turkey, in particular, wanted no part of a successful Kurdish rebellion in Iraq. In the past, Kurds in Turkey had been prevented from speaking their language in public. Indeed, the government denied their very existence, classifying them as "mountain Turks." Turkish politicians and newspaper publishers were sentenced to long prison terms for even mentioning the Kurds. It was no surprise that Bush obliged Turkey, a NATO ally and participant in the Gulf War, when he delivered the Kurds into the arms of Hussein.

Tens of thousands of Iraqis—whether Shiites, Sunni, or Kurds—died during and in the aftermath of the war. Allied bombing raids had destroyed electric power plants, transport facilities, and water purification and sewage treatment plants. Subsequent UN sanctions, which continued until George W.

Bush's war in 2003, claimed an even larger number of lives. US secretary of state Madeleine Albright, when asked (on the CBS program *60 Minutes* in 1996) whether the death of half a million Iraqi children, "more" than the number who "died in Hiroshima," had been worth the price of the continued containment of Saddam Hussein, she said, "Yes, we think the price is worth it."

• • •

The UN-brokered cease-fire with Iraq was accompanied by severe economic sanctions. Moreover, Iraq agreed to destroy its chemical, biological, and nuclear weapons and production facilities. For the next seven years UN weapons inspectors endeavored to gain Iraq's compliance with the cease-fire weapons inspection regimen. Hussein opened some weapons-producing facilities and some of these were dismantled, but he continued to thwart full inspection. That issue was brought to a head in December 1998, when Hussein ordered all US members of the inspection teams out of Iraq. As a result, still another test-of-wills crisis was played out. President Bill Clinton launched a series of bombing attacks in an unsuccessful attempt to force the defiant Hussein into compliance. In October 1998, a frustrated US Congress went so far as to pass the Iraq Liberation Act, calling for the overthrow of Hussein by "the Iraqi opposition." Clinton signed it without preparing for an invasion of Iraq. After September 11, 2001, however, the resolution was still on the books.

## Notes

1. Some Western scholars have argued that Mohammad did not believe he was "founding a new religion" as much as bringing to "fullness . . . divine revelation . . . granted to earlier prophets." Richard Fletcher, *The Cross and the Crescent: Christianity and Islam from Muhammad to the Reformation* (New York: Viking, 2004), cited in William Dalrymple, "The Truth About Muslims," *New York Review of Books*, November 4, 2004, p. 32.

2. N. J. Dawood, trans., *The Koran*, 4th rev. ed. (New York: Penguin, 1974), p. 220, Surah 23:14–16; p. 375, Surah 4:87.

3. Alfred Guillaume, *Islam*, 2nd rev. ed. (New York: Penguin, 1956), p. 38.

4. Dawood, *The Koran*, pp. 362–364, Surah 2:261–265, 270–277.

5. Khomeini citations in Bernard Lewis, "How Khomeini Made It," *New York Review of Books*, January 17, 1985, p. 10.

6. The basis of the Shiite creed, in Bernard Lewis, "The Shi'a," *New York Review of Books*, August 15, 1985, p. 8. Shiites point to Allah's will "to favour those who were oppressed and to make them leaders of mankind, to bestow on them a noble heritage and to give them power in the land." Dawood, *The Koran*, p. 75, Surah 28:5.

7. Robert Graham, *Iran: The Illusion of Power* (New York: St. Martin's Press, 1979), p. 33.

8. Ibid., p. 61.

9. "Aryans" here is in reference to the Farsi-speaking peoples of Iran, originally from northern India. It was an attempt to identify the shah with the nation's earliest history.

10. Henry Kissinger, *The White House Years* (Boston: Little, Brown, 1979), p. 1264.

11. After the shah's death in 1980, his son became the claimant to the throne, and many Iranian exiles pinned their hopes on him.

12. It came as a surprise to the US public, therefore, when in November 1986 it was revealed that Reagan, who for six years had bitterly denounced any and all terrorists and had vowed never to deal with any of them, was found to have paid ransom to terrorists in Lebanon who were holding US hostages and even sent antitank missiles to the government of the Ayatollah Khomeini, which was at that time engaged in a long and bloody war with Iraq.

13. In April 1984, the Reagan administration gave the Bell Helicopter Corporation the green light to sell helicopters to the Iraqi ministry of defense, provided that they "can not be in any way configured for military use." National Security Archive online, www2.gwu.edu/~nsarchive, National Security Archive, Electronic Briefing Book No. 83, February 27, 2003, Document 55.

14. Shane Harris and Matthew M. Aid, "Exclusive: CIA Files Prove America Helped Saddam as He Gassed Iran," *Foreign Policy*, August 26, 2013.

15. Quoted in Mansour Farhang, "Iran-Iraq Conflict: An Unending War Between Two Despots," *The Nation*, September 20, 1986.

16. Graham E. Fuller, "War and Revolution in Iran," *Current History* (February 1989), p. 81.

17. Seventy hostages were finally released between August 1991 and June 1992; some had been in captivity for more than ten years.

18. In October 1989, Qaddafi admitted to having bankrolled terrorist groups but added: "When we discovered that these groups were causing more harm than benefit to the Arab cause, we halted our aid to them completely and withdrew our support." "Kadafi Admits Backing Terrorists, Says He Erred," *Baltimore Sun*, October 26, 1989.

19. Scott MacLeod, "Why Gaddafi's Now a Good Guy," *Time*, May 16, 2006.

20. Margaret Thatcher, *The Downing Years* (New York: HarperCollins, 1993), pp. 823–824.

21. Cited in Jim Hoagland, "Transcript Shows Muted US Response to Threat by Saddam in Late July," *Washington Post*, September 13, 1990, p. A33. In March 1991, before the Senate Foreign Relations Committee, Glaspie refuted the Iraqi version of her conversation with Hussein; the State Department, however, refused to make public its transcript of the meeting or its correspondence with Glaspie.

22. Cited in Robert Ruby, "Security Council OKs Military Force," *Baltimore Sun*, August 26, 1990, p. 1A.

23. Joyce Chediac, "The Massacre of Withdrawing Soldiers on 'The Highway of Death.'" From her report at the New York Commission hearing, May 11, 1991, deoxy.org/wc/wc-death.htm.

24. George Bush and Brent Scowcroft, *A World Transformed* (New York: Knopf, 1998).

25. "You Fly, You Die," *Time*, August 31, 1992.

26. Quoted in Raymond Bonner, "Always Remember," *The New Yorker*, September 28, 1992, p. 48.

# 22

# September 11, Afghanistan, and Iraq

On September 11, 2001, nineteen young Arabs, fifteen of them from Saudi Arabia, led by the Egyptian Mohamed Atta, hijacked four US airliners. Two of them slammed into the twin towers of the World Trade Center in New York City, bringing the skyscrapers down within minutes. Another airplane plowed into the Pentagon across the Potomac River from the White House. A passenger revolt caused the crash of the fourth airplane in a field near Shanksville, Pennsylvania. In all, almost 3,000 individuals perished, nearly all of them civilians.

Within hours, the US government identified the hijackers as members of al Qaeda, a shadowy organization led by Osama bin Laden, an exile from Saudi Arabia living in Afghanistan under Taliban protection. This had not been al Qaeda's first attack against US targets. Previously, in February 1993, it had sought to topple the twin towers, and in August 1998 it carried out simultaneous suicide bombings of US embassies in Nairobi, Kenya, and Dar-es-Salaam, Tanzania, killing 224 and injuring over 5,400 (mostly Africans, many of them Muslims, as well as 12 US citizens).

After the attacks on the embassies, the administration of President Bill Clinton quickly identified al Qaeda as the perpetrator and then lashed out with cruise missiles against al Qaeda facilities in Afghanistan that missed their targets, however. Embroiled at the time in the Monica Lewinsky scandal, Clinton could only do so much; besides, there was little public outcry for more drastic action. Then came a suicide attack against the USS *Cole* in October 2000 in the harbor of Aden, Yemen, which claimed the lives of seventeen US sailors. Eleven months later came the September 11 attacks.

In his first speech after September 11, US president George W. Bush vowed to find the perpetrators and bring them to justice. In what he dubbed a "global war on terror," he called on all nations to join the fight, adding, "you are either with us or against us."

It was difficult to understand what drove nineteen young, educated Arabs to commit mass murder while committing suicide. Bush could offer nothing better than "they hate us for our freedoms." The Islamic militants, Bush and others suggested, were driven by resentment, hate, irrationality, and a flawed religion. Some individuals saw it as part of a "clash of civilizations."

Israeli intelligence tried for years to come up with a typical profile of suicide terrorists, only to conclude that they could not establish one. Not surprisingly, then, every statement about suicide terrorists is speculative. Attempts to comprehend the motives of the terrorists, moreover, ran into a social taboo against trying to understand them. Comprehension, it was argued, only dignified the terrorists. In the United States, publishers of the collected works of bin Laden were accused of promoting "al Qaeda's evil."[1]

Some terrorists have personal problems, while others are deeply affected by the deaths of relatives or friends at the hands of the enemy. The majority— 55 percent—of Palestinian suicide bombers, for example, had witnessed their father's humiliation by Israelis. They often mentioned a specific event for which they sought revenge. Once life becomes unbearable, suicide becomes an option.

When a conflict becomes cloaked in religious arguments—absolute and dogmatic—killing and dying become easier. The struggle for Palestine, for instance, initially a secular conflict over territory between socialist Zionists and the secular Palestine Liberation Organization (also in part socialist), became a holy war on both sides that made it easier for true believers to kill and die for.

Geographic displacement—that is, an alienated existence in a foreign land—affected many of the terrorists. Terrorists become the champions of their own people's rightful place in the sun as they call for the redemption of history—the return of territory and to a golden age, particularly glorious when compared with the current unbearable situation.[2]

Suicide bombings are part of what has been described as "asymmetric warfare," the weapon of last resort by the poor and weak. The bombs the "martyrs" use are cheap to produce and—guided by human intellect—highly accurate. Between 1980 and 2003, suicide attacks accounted for 48 percent of those killed in terror attacks, even though they made up only 3 percent of the attacks launched.[3]

The September 11 attacks were the consequence of political Islam's conflict with Western imperialism, which, in the eyes of the militants, had brought its "filth of disbelief" and "moral bankruptcy" to the House of Islam. As a graduate student in urban planning in northern Germany, Mohamed Atta had dedicated his master's thesis to the preservation of the ancient, vast market, the *souk*, in Aleppo—perhaps the world's oldest continuously inhabited city—a living symbol of the Arab world. Despite the Syrian government's best efforts to preserve the *souk*, it was dying, under siege by the Western imprint, replete with fast-food restaurants and concrete-block tourist hotels. In Cairo and Aleppo, Atta fell under the influence of the Muslim Brotherhood. Living in Hamburg among the prostitutes and heroin dealers in the city's red-light district, an alienated Atta came to accept the noble obligation of martyrdom.[4]

George W. Bush was in part correct when he asserted that Islamic terrorists hated what US society represented. Al Qaeda's war against the West, however, was not against the Bill of Rights but against the West's presence in the House of Islam. Islamic militants singled out the West's support of apostate and corrupt, tyrannical governments, such as in Iraq, Syria, and Saudi Arabia. They also decried Western support for Israel; US troops on the Arabian peninsula; support for Russia, India, and China in their suppression of Muslims in Chechnya, Kashmir, and Central Asia; and the pressure on Arab oil suppliers to keep prices low.

Terror is the choice of last resort by the weak against the powerful—whether in Vietnam, Algeria, Chechnya, Iraq, or Sri Lanka. In the 1965 motion picture *The Battle of Algiers*, a terrorist in the dock is asked: "Isn't it cowardly to use your women's baskets to carry bombs that have killed so many innocent people?" To which he replies: "And you? Is it less cowardly to drop napalm on defenseless villages, killing thousands more? With planes, it would have been easier for us. Let us have your bombers and you can have our women's baskets."[5]

Islam does not permit suicide. A Muslim's life belongs to Allah and only Allah has the right to take it. But it does encourage martyrdom. A Hamas official explained the difference between suicide and martyrdom: "If a martyr wants to kill himself because he is sick of being alive, that's suicide. But if he wants to sacrifice his soul in order to defeat the enemy and for God's sake—well, then he's a martyr."[6]

The hijackers came from established, well-to-do families and had grown up in the shadow of the culture, wealth, power, and overbearing presence of the West. Their resentment of the West eventually turned into the conviction that little had changed since the days when the Crusaders first descended on the Muslim world at the end of the eleventh century. After the 1991 Gulf War, bin Laden denounced the US occupation of "the most sacred lands of Islam: the Arab Peninsula . . . stealing its resources, dictating to its leaders, humiliating its people."[7] History must not repeat itself. Ayman al-Zawahiri, bin Laden's chief lieutenant, declared that "we will not accept [in Palestine] the [repetition of the] tragedy of Al Andalus," that is, the Arabs' traumatic expulsion from Andalusia (today's Spain) in 1492, after having been there for 700 years.[8]

*Osama bin Laden, spiritual and operational chief of al Qaeda, was the inspirational leader of the September 11 terror attacks.*

Bin Laden's aim was to rearrange the unequal relationship between the West and the Islamic world. Five weeks after the deadly bombings of Madrid railway stations in March 2004 (which claimed the lives of 191 people and injured another 1,800), he offered the Europeans reconciliation that "will start with the departure of the last soldier from our country."[9] In late October, he made the same offer to the United States.

After World War II, as the Arabs gained their independence from France and Britain, they looked to a new beginning, a renaissance that would restore the Arab world to its previous grandeur. In most Arab nations, socialist movements came to power with the promise of such a revival. In fact, the Ba'ath Party, which seized power in Syria and Iraq, took its name from the Arabic word for "rebirth." But it was not to be. Arab governments—whether socialist or monarchist—became corrupt, propped up by oil money, secret police, or armies equipped by infidel nations such as the United States and the Soviet Union. It was particularly true in the very heart of the Arab world—Syria, Lebanon, Iraq, Egypt, and Saudi Arabia.

The disenchantment, particularly among young Arabs, was heightened by the fact that they had limited professional opportunities at home. Some went abroad, some sought solace in religion, and some joined terrorist organizations. The problem was especially acute in Saudi Arabia. Between 1980 and 1998, it had the highest population growth rate in the world, at the phenomenal annual rate of 4.4 percent. By 2002, its population had swollen from 6 million to 22 million; 43 percent were fourteen years of age or younger. The number of princes, widely viewed as hypocrites who feigned piety while serving foreign interests and engaging in foreign vices (pornography, alcohol, prostitution), rose from 2,000 to 7,000. At the same time, oil revenues declined from $227 billion in 1981 to $31 billion in 1986. Saudi Arabia's per capita income peaked at $19,000 in 1981, only to drop to $7,300 in 1997 (in constant US dollars). As universities produced far more graduates than the economy needed, it was not surprising that Saudi Arabia became a hotbed for Islamic militancy. Saudi Arabia is, after all, the only modern Muslim state created by Wahhabi warriors, who espoused a particularly strict interpretation of Islam, with an emphasis on *jihad*, one aspect of which is the sacred struggle against infidels. It was also one of but a handful of Muslim countries that had escaped European imperialism, Afghanistan being another. The Saudi royal family, having come to power with the assistance of the Wahhabi clergy, was now forced to spend lavish sums on placating it in the vain hope of tempering its anti-Western militancy.[10]

Militant Islam's quest to purify society and return it to its former glory has a long history. In the recent past, it was the Muslim Brotherhood that played the leading role in the revival of Islam. Founded in Egypt in 1928, the Brotherhood was in response to what the Islamic world saw as the calamity of the destruction of the caliphate, which had ruled the House of Islam since after Mohammed's death. In the wake of the caliphate's demise, the European powers had returned. The Brotherhood rejected nationalism, Communism, socialism, and liberalism and dreamed, instead, of the creation of Islamic states— perhaps even another caliphate—guided by the laws and daily behavior as spelled out in the Koran. The Brotherhood's founder, Hassan al-Banna, railed against the West's corruption of Islam with "their half-naked women . . . their liquors, their theaters, their dance halls." The Brotherhood's credo is,

> God is our objective, the Koran is our constitution, the prophet is our leader, the struggle is our way, and death for the sake of God is the highest of our aspirations.[11]

By the late 1940s, the Westernized Egyptian government (headed by the scandalous King Farouk) and the Brotherhood were in a deadly embrace; after the Brotherhood assassinated the prime minister in 1949, the police shot Banna dead.

The mentor of the late-twentieth-century Arab radicals was the Egyptian Sayyid Qutb. In his magnum opus, *Milestones* (1964), Qutb popularized the view that the Arab world lived in the state of *jihaliya*, a darkness that had existed before Mohammed's revelations. The prevailing apostasy must—and will—give way to a true Muslim state after the purification of "the filthy marsh of the world." Qutb developed his views in part as the consequence of a two-year stint among the *kuffar*, the unbelievers, at the Colorado State

College of Education. A student of US literature and popular culture, Qutb became repulsed by aspects of US society, such as dances in church recreation halls—organized by ministers no less—and by a people who attended the numerous churches in Greeley, Colorado, yet appeared uninterested in spiritual matters.[12]

The quest to return to the Prophet's teachings led to a vicious war between the Muslim militants and the socialist/militarist government of Egypt. President Gamal Abdel Nasser arrested members of the Brotherhood and in August 1966 had Qutb hanged. Upon hearing his death sentence, Qutb replied: "Thank God. I performed jihad for fifteen years until I earned this martyrdom."[13] In October 1981, the Brotherhood, after having infiltrated the Egyptian army, assassinated the "pharaoh" Anwar Sadat for having signed a peace treaty with Israel.

Sadat's successor, Hosni Mubarak, introduced a permanent state of emergency. Tens of thousands of Islamicists and other political dissidents filled Egypt's prisons, where they were subjected to systematic torture. The terrorists responded with assassinations that ended only after a crackdown in the wake of the Brotherhood's murder in 1997 of sixty-two people in Luxor—mostly foreign tourists. By that time, however, Arab Islamic militancy—born in the mosques and coffeehouses and nurtured in the prisons of Egypt—had already begun its migration to the far corners of the earth.

In the 1980s, the attention of the Islamicists was diverted to Afghanistan. After the Soviet invasion, Ayman al-Zawahiri, a scion of one of the most prominent Egyptian families who was deeply affected by Qutb's worldview, was one of the first Arabs to arrive in Afghanistan. There he linked up with the charismatic Osama bin Laden, the son of one of the most prominent—and wealthy—Saudi families. Their organizations merged into one. Zawahiri was vital to bin Laden because of his organizational abilities. At the tender age of fifteen, he had already helped form an underground cell. An expert in clandestine work, it was Zawahiri who plotted the attacks on US targets, including that of September 11. Zawahiri was also responsible for bin Laden's new focus on corrupt Arab governments. An Egyptian lawyer for the Brotherhood explained that, in the early 1980s, bin Laden already "had an Islamic frame of reference, but he didn't have anything against the Arab regimes."[14] Zawahiri would change that.

Bin Laden spent much of his time shuttling between Saudi Arabia and Peshawar, Pakistan, raising money for the anti-Soviet cause. He imported bulldozers for civilian and military projects, and in April 1987 he participated in a battle against Soviet troops. It was here that he earned the reputation as a *jihadist* warrior. There is no evidence that he worked directly with the CIA, but US officials looked favorably on his recruitment of Arab *mujahedin*. In fact, the CIA sought ways to increase the jihadists' participation in the war. Yet at the same time, it ignored rumors of anti-US sentiment among the Arabs.

With considerable help from its jihadist proxies, the United States won in Afghanistan a historic Cold War victory over the Soviet Union. After the last Soviet soldier departed in 1989, the CIA's station chief at the US embassy in Islamabad, Pakistan, Milt Bearden, cabled Washington, "WE WON," turned out the lights, and joined the celebration at the embassy.[15] But it was a costly victory. The CIA left behind a network of jihadists—stronger and wealthier than ever—who now trained their gun sights on the US presence in the Islamic world.

The Arab-Israeli conflict was a contributing factor to the rise of Arab resentment against the West, particularly against the United States for its role in backing Israel. Washington professed to be an honest broker in the conflict, but no Arab believed it. In the Yom Kippur War of 1973, the Nixon administration openly sided with Israel, and in 1983 Reagan sent the Marines into Lebanon, ostensibly in the capacity of neutral peacekeepers, only to have the battleship *New Jersey* train its 16-inch shells on Arab targets. In his videotape of October 2004, bin Laden stated that it was this event, the destruction of "towers in Lebanon," that made him determined to give the United States a taste of its own medicine.

Al Qaeda began its work shortly after the Gulf War of 1991, when bin Laden sharply criticized the Saudi royal family for granting the United States a permanent military base in Saudi Arabia. Eventually, bin Laden crossed the line in his criticism and was ordered to leave. He went first to Sudan, at that time a haven for terrorists. In 1996, he wrote an open letter to King Faud of Saudi Arabia in which he again denounced the US presence in the land of the Prophet. After that, he left for Afghanistan, where the Taliban had just come to power.

Al Qaeda's first attempt to challenge the West came during the Serbian-Bosnian conflict. Militant Arabs arrived in Bosnia to help their fellow Muslims to fight the Orthodox Christian Serbs. They brought with them the military expertise acquired in Afghanistan, and money they laundered with the help of cultural and benevolence societies set up in places such as London, Milan, Chicago, Hamburg, and Saudi Arabia. Their engagement in Bosnia proved to be a failure, however, in part because the Bosnians resented them for their viciousness.

### Afghanistan: The War Against al Qaeda

Before September 11, Bush was not all that concerned about al Qaeda, although the outgoing Clinton administration—notably the national security advisor, Sandy Berger, and terrorist expert Richard Clarke—had warned Bush's national security team that they would spend more time on terrorism than on anything else. Four days into the Bush administration, Clarke wrote a memo to Bush's national security advisor, Condoleezza Rice, stating that a review of al Qaeda was needed most *"urgently"* (emphasis in the original). Clarke tried to explain that al Qaeda was an international, "active, organized, major force," and thus should be a "first order issue" for the administration.[16] Rice ignored the warning. Clarke stayed on as terrorist expert, but he lost his cabinet-level status and now reported to Rice, who showed little interest in what he had to say.

On July 10, 2001, the director of the CIA, George Tenet, briefed Rice on al Qaeda at a meeting she was unable to recall in 2006. Shortly after his inauguration, Bush appointed Vice-President Dick Cheney to chair a task force on terrorism, one that never met, however. The attorney general, John Ashcroft, rejected on July 5, 2001 a request from the acting head of the FBI, Thomas Pickard, for another $59 million to combat al Qaeda, adding that he was tired of hearing about it.[17]

Even after Bush received the CIA's now famous Presidential Daily Brief ("Bin Laden Determined to Strike in US") of August 6, 2001, warning of a potential al Qaeda attack using airplanes against government buildings, he continued his vacation in Texas. In the meantime, as early as late March 2001, in the words of Clarke, the "system was blinking red." In the summer, Clarke cancelled all vacation leave for his staff in a desperate attempt to stave off an attack. As a member of the Clinton staff, he had participated in the successful disruption of the "millennium plot" against the Los Angeles international airport by "shaking the trees"—pursuing every lead and working with various US as well as foreign authorities, notably in Canada and Jordan.[18] This time, however, despite repeated warnings, the White House showed little concern.

September 11 called for an immediate and forceful response. Bush rallied a stunned and angry nation and vowed to go after bin Laden, to pursue him to the four corners of the earth, and to capture him "dead or alive." A CIA agent even requested a box with dry ice in anticipation of bringing home the supreme war trophy, the head of bin Laden. Bush dismissed Clinton's earlier response to al Qaeda, the "launching [of] a cruise missile into some guy's . . . tent," as a "joke."[19] He would do it right.

Global support for the United States was nearly universal; for the first time, NATO declared an attack on one of its members had taken place. Bush demanded that Mohammed Omar, the head of the Taliban, hand over bin Laden. When Omar refused, Bush took the fight into Afghanistan, starting on October 7, 2001. First came the bombs, dropped by state-of-the-art jet fighters from nearby carriers and B-2 bombers from as far away as Missouri. Then came a highly mobile, efficient contingent of special forces supported by the latest computers, CIA agents, air force personnel, soldiers, sailors, and NATO forces. The United States, however, initially relied on too small a number of "boots on the ground," 110 CIA officers and 316 special forces.[20] It would need much more.

Afghan warlords of the Northern Alliance—primarily Tadzhiks and Uzbeks—who had held out against the Pushtun Taliban during the previous five years, assisted the United States. It was an uneven contest—one between the richest and strongest nation with powerful allies on its side against the poorest. By early December 2001, the Taliban and al Qaeda were beaten, their surviving forces streaming toward the Pakistani frontier from where the Taliban had originally come.

Bush's secretary of defense, Donald Rumsfeld, held a series of press conferences where he basked in the adulation of a grateful nation. Yet it was at this point that matters began to go sour. The enemy had been mauled, but when the United States and its NATO allies reached bin Laden's redoubt in the caves in the steep mountains of Tora Bora, they did not have sufficient troops to trap and capture him. Omar and bin Laden disappeared into the rugged terrain along the Afghan-Pakistani border, surviving to fight another day.

Bin Laden was not captured because General Tommy Franks, the US commander in Afghanistan, relied on Afghans to do the job. They were either not up to the task or, worse, collaborated with the fleeing al Qaeda fighters. It was something Franks—already hard at work planning the invasion of Iraq from his command center in Tampa, Florida—grasped too late. It did not prevent Bush from proclaiming victory. Bin Laden, he explained on March 14, 2002, had "met his match" and had been "marginalized," that he "may even be dead," before adding, "I truly am not that concerned about him."[21] After that, the administration's references to the still-at-large bin Laden became fewer and fewer.

Early in the war, Franks told Pakistani president Pervez Musharraf, "We won't stop until we get" bin Laden.[22] Yet two months into the war, with Osama bin Laden still at large, Franks shifted his resources to Iraq, leaving behind a scant 4,000 troops in Afghanistan, augmented by 5,000 NATO soldiers. In his memoirs, Franks spoke of a "historic victory" in Afghanistan, skipping over the fact that the perpetrators of September 11 remained at large.

In all likelihood, the Taliban and al Qaeda escaped to Waziristan, across the border from Tora Bora, in Pakistan's impenetrable North-West Frontier Province. The Waziris, ethnic Pushtuns who claim to be descendants of King Saul, have held off since 600 B.C. any and all invaders—among them Alexander the Great, Genghis Khan, and Great Britain—to keep their realm "pure and clean." When the Pakistani army—at the urging of the Bush administration—entered Waziristan in March 2004, it ran into a wall of silence and came away empty-handed, this despite the FBI's $50 million bounty on the head of bin Laden.

During the Soviet war in Afghanistan, Waziristan fell under the thrall of radical Islam. It became the home of at least ninety schools—*madrassas*—preaching a radical strain of Islam for which the Taliban were known. Before the Soviet invasion, the Waziris had considered themselves primarily as

Pushtuns; afterward, they increasingly saw themselves as Muslims and Pushtuns. In October 2003, an exclusively Islamist government took power in Waziristan, a region that by this time had become an exporter of radical Islam as well as heroin. By Islamic law, heroin was *haram* (forbidden), but if heroin killed a single non-Muslim, it was defensible.[23]

### Detour to Iraq

Even before September 11, the Bush administration had its eyes on Iraq and, before the smoke cleared in Afghanistan, it prepared to invade. Richard Clarke warned that an invasion of Iraq just might fulfill al Qaeda's "dream" of a "Christian government attacking a weaker Muslim region," allowing it "to rally jihadists from across the globe to come to the aid of the religious brethren."[24] Prominent government officials and military officers tried to warn Bush about the pitfalls awaiting him in Iraq, including his own father and his father's foreign policy advisers (Brent Scowcroft and James Baker), Republican leaders in Congress, top military officers (Eric Shinseki and Anthony Zinni), CIA analysts, and foreign heads of state. The venerable diplomat and historian George Kennan warned, "if we went into Iraq . . . you know where you begin. You never know where you are going to end."

The Bush administration, however, was certain that whatever the pitfalls in Iraq they would emerge from them unscathed—and victorious. During the feverish build-up to the war in the summer of 2002, one of Bush's aides (apparently Karl Rove, the architect of the "Mission Accomplished" aircraft carrier moment), chided a reporter for being part of "the reality-based community" who "believe that solutions emerge from . . . [a] judicious study of discernible reality." That was "not the way the world really works anymore," he explained:

> We're an empire now, and when we act, we create our own reality. And while you're studying that reality—judiciously, as you will—we'll act again, creating other new realities, which you can study too. . . . We're history's actors . . . and you, all of you, will be left to just study what we do.[25]

It was nation-building at its boldest. In Vietnam, US officials had harbored similar illusions, but not even their most optimistic spoke in such audacious fashion.

Bush paid no attention to the voices of caution. He obliged bin Laden with the invasion of Iraq. As for the jihadists, he challenged them in July 2003: "Bring 'em on." Soon jihadists from across the Middle East descended on Iraq. "If Osama bin Laden believed in Christmas," a CIA intelligence official declared, "this is what he'd want under his Christmas tree." In October 2003, seven months after the war began, the London-based International Institute for Strategic Studies concluded that al Qaeda, despite having suffered considerable losses in Afghanistan, was now "fully reconstituted" with an estimated strength of 18,000 members and with a "new and effective modus operandi," operating in as many as ninety countries.[26] Al Qaeda–sponsored acts of terrorism spread beyond Iraq to Spain, Morocco, Indonesia, Tunisia, Pakistan, Kenya, Turkey, and Saudi Arabia.

In the months prior to September 11, Bush and his cabinet focused on Iraq and its vast oil reserves. When Vice-President Cheney convened his secret sessions on energy in February 2001, maps of Iraq, with its oil fields marked, were rolled out. After the invasion of Iraq, Cheney's office, the Pentagon, the CIA, and Iraqi exiles pushed for the privatization of the oil industry. The *Wall Street Journal* called the quest for Iraq's oil "one of the most audacious hostile takeovers ever." Iraq's determined resistance (which included the oil workers) was so strong that it became evident that, in the words of the satirist P. J. O'Rourke, it was "much cheaper to buy oil than to steal it."[27]

In the early 1990s, Dick Cheney, secretary of defense at the time, had issued a document, "Defense Planning Guidance," that called for the permanent expansion of US power abroad. After he returned to power in January 2001, Cheney and others, in the span of two months, drew up plans to invade Iraq without knowing as yet how to sell such a war to a jittery public. Six hours after the September 11 attacks, Rumsfeld ordered the Pentagon to prepare for war against both Osama bin Laden and Saddam Hussein. "Sweep it all up," one of Rumsfeld's aides wrote in the margin of the orders, "things related and not."[28]

Bush was aided and abetted by his foreign policy advisers, a group known as the neoconservatives, or "neocons." Its leading members were Cheney, Rumsfeld, Deputy Secretary of Defense Paul Wolfowitz, and Condoleezza Rice. Many of them had gotten their start in the 1970s as members of the Committee on the Present Danger and the CIA's B Team under George H. W. Bush, committees that persistently had exaggerated the Soviet threat.

Still smarting from the defeat in Vietnam, the neocons remained optimistic about US power and dismissive of warnings about a military overreach. Fond of advocating preemptive war, they disdained the realpolitik of Richard Nixon and Henry Kissinger, who had pursued détente and had negotiated with the Soviet Union and Communist China. They were certain the United States was capable of bringing progress and morality to a world wracked by evil. The United States remained the "city on the hill," the shining—Christian—beacon for other nations, an idea their hero Ronald Reagan had frequently expressed. In Iraq, the neocons insisted, they would be received with open arms, sweets, and flowers. The British general Stanley Maude had suffered from the same delusion when he told the Iraqis, in March 1917: "Our armies do not come into your cities and lands as conquerors or enemies, but as liberators." At the end of his presidency, George W. Bush was still unable to understand why the ungrateful Iraqis had not thanked him personally and publicly for their liberation.[29]

The neocons argued assiduously that Hussein had been part of the September 11 conspiracy and that, moreover, he possessed weapons of mass destruction that could arrive any day on US soil, even in the shape of a nuclear mushroom cloud. It did not matter that in the months before September 11, Bush's secretary of defense, Colin Powell, and Condoleezza Rice had publicly stated that Hussein had lost his war-making capacity of a decade earlier and had not been able to rebuild his armed forces. Richard Clarke's conclusion that there was no link between bin Laden and Hussein fell on deaf ears.

As the neocons prepared for war, they convinced the public—as well as the press, whose job it was to ask questions—that the war on terror demanded regime change in Baghdad.[30] They insisted that Hussein still possessed chemical and biological weapons, the capability to produce nuclear weapons, and the will to use them. More ominously, Hussein was about to make his WMD available to al Qaeda.

This bleak scenario ignored that bin Laden and Hussein were mortal foes. When bin Laden spoke of apostate Arab governments, he also had Hussein in mind. When the United States went to war against Hussein for the first time, in 1991, bin Laden sought—unsuccessfully—Saudi backing to unleash a jihad against Hussein.[31] It was no secret to Hussein that the greatest domestic threat he faced was militant Islam, whether of the domestic Shiite or al Qaeda Sunni variety. In 2004, the *9/11 Report* pointed out that Hussein had not responded to bin Laden's request to establish terrorist camps in Iraq. Reports by the CIA and the Senate Intelligence Committee (in 2005 and 2006, respectively) came to the same conclusion. The *9/11 Report* noted that other nations had provided assistance to al Qaeda—either officially or unofficially—not just Afghanistan but also pro-US nations such as Pakistan, Saudi Arabia, and the United Arab Emirates. Iraq, however, had not.

To make their case for war, the neocons turned to Ahmed Chalabi, a US-educated Iraqi whose family, once one of Iraq's wealthiest, had been dispossessed by the Ba'athist revolution of 1958. In the early 1990s, Chalabi had joined a conservative think tank, the American Enterprise Institute, created the Iraqi National Congress (INC), and began to lobby for a US invasion to return him to Iraq. Chalabi's INC was the primary force behind a 1998 US congressional resolution calling for "regime change" in Baghdad. Chalabi charmed high-level officials in Washington to the degree that between 1992 and 2004 three administrations funneled at least $100 million to his organization. The CIA and State Department, however, considered him a charlatan. A court in Jordan sentenced him *in absentia* to twenty-two years at hard labor for embezzling large sums of money. None of that kept him from cultivating powerful patrons in high places in Washington—Rumsfeld, Wolfowitz, and Cheney.

The Bush administration used Chalabi's disinformation—channeled through the Pentagon—to sell the war. When the question arose whether Hussein had mobile chemical and biological laboratories, Chalabi chimed in, saying that Hussein indeed did have them and that he could provide their location. He also circulated stories of al Qaeda terrorist camps in Iraq.

When Chalabi insisted that it would take only 1,000 US troops to topple Hussein, the US Marine Corps commander, Anthony Zinni, dismissed his scenario as a "pie-in-the-sky fairy tale." Bush, however, preferred to listen to Chalabi than to his own general. When Chalabi's Free Iraqi Fighters arrived in Baghdad, they joined the looting in progress, except that they focused on villas, SUVs, and the like. When the time came to establish an interim government, the UN opposed Chalabi's candidacy. The Bush administration subsequently dropped Chalabi when it discovered that he had sold intelligence to Iran.

During his January 2003 State of the Union address, Bush accused Hussein of having enough biological and chemical weapons (500 tons of sarin, mustard, and nerve gases) "to kill several million people" as well as enough botulinum toxin to kill another million.

Shortly thereafter, Bush's respected secretary of state, Colin Powell, offered the clinching arguments for war. Before the United Nations—and the world—Powell offered "incontrovertible" proof of the existence of these weapons. Powell, who initially had refused to present the report, swallowed his pride and, as a good soldier, came onboard—and converted many a doubter.[32] His "evidence" consisted of photographs and specific addresses where the weapons were allegedly produced and stored. He held up a small vial, the contents of which, he claimed, could kill thousands. Yet nearly everything Powell said that day was a tale of half-truths or outright misrepresentations.

The neocons had insisted that Hussein's son-in-law, Hussein Kamal, who had defected to Jordan, had alleged in August 1995 the existence of WMD. In his speech before the UN, Powell invoked Kamal's name. Only after Kamal's testimony found its way to the Internet did it become evident that he had made no such claim. If anything, he had told the CIA that Hussein had destroyed his WMD in 1991. The war was launched on the basis of Rumsfeld's famous rationale that "the absence of evidence is not evidence of absence." The *New York Times* journalist Thomas Friedman, who had originally beaten the drums for war, stated that the invasion had been the handiwork of twenty-five individuals who worked within "a five-block radius" of his office in Washington. "If you had exiled them to a desert island a year and a half ago," he wrote, "the Iraq war would not have happened."[33]

Bush initially sought UN approval for the invasion, but all he was able to obtain was a resolution authorizing the return of UN weapons inspectors, whom Hussein had kicked out in 1998. Under the direction of the Swedish diplomat Hans Blix, the inspectors set out to find the WMD. After Blix's team issued intermediary reports that they had found no evidence of WMD, Bush started the war before they could complete their task. After the invasion, the Pentagon's Iraq Survey Group, a force of 1,500 inspectors led by David Kay, failed as well to come up with the evidence the neocons hoped to find.

When the United Nations called for the continuation of the economic, military, and diplomatic containment of Iraq, Bush decided to go it alone. Of all the major nations, only Great Britain—whose government, too, had hyped the imminent threat from Iraq—offered meaningful assistance by sending 10,000 troops. Britain's prime minister Tony Blair thought that support of Bush would earn him a measure of influence in Washington. In the end, Blair had nothing to show for his efforts except a disillusioned electorate, which increasingly saw him as "Bush's poodle." In May 2005 came the revelation of the so-called Downing Street memo, a report by British intelligence—written eight months before the invasion—that warned Blair that Bush had already decided on war. The memo explained that "intelligence and facts were being fixed" to provide the rationale for war.

The Downing Street memo also pointed out what later became painfully obvious, that "there was little discussion in Washington of the aftermath after military action." The Powell Doctrine had focused on an "exit strategy" in future wars. When Powell asked Cheney about it, the vice-president reportedly replied, "We have no exit strategy. We stay." Kissinger, who attributed the defeat in Vietnam to a loss of national will, advised the Bush administration, "Victory is the only meaningful exit strategy." In April 2005, Rumsfeld echoed Kissinger's sentiments when he reminded the troops in Baghdad, "We don't have an exit strategy, we have a victory strategy."[34]

No one doubted that the United States would be able to make short shrift of Hussein's depleted army. Hussein had virtually no air force and approximately one-third the troops, artillery, and armor that he had 1991. His inventory contained Soviet T-55 tanks nearly fifty years old. Colin Powell nonetheless warned the administration that if it intended to occupy Iraq, it must not go in "light." It must not repeat the mistakes of Vietnam. The army chief of staff, Eric Shinseki, and General Anthony Zinni spoke of the need for 400,000 troops, not the 75,000 the civilian leadership at the Pentagon (notably Rumsfeld and Wolfowitz) had in mind. (The 150,000 troops ultimately deployed were the result of a compromise between the military and the civilians in the Pentagon.) The academician Wolfowitz publicly ridiculed Shinseki, whose estimates, he declared, were "wildly off the mark." "It's hard to conceive," he said, "that it would take more forces to provide stability . . . than it would take to conduct the war itself." It marked the first public dressing-down of a four-star general since the Harry Truman–Douglas MacArthur clash more than fifty years earlier. Zinni fared even worse, being called a traitor in meetings in the Pentagon.

Many of the problems the United States later faced stemmed from the fact that it did not have sufficient "boots on the ground." The comparison with the 1991 Gulf War is instructive. There, a coalition force of 690,000 troops was given but one task: drive Hussein out of Kuwait. In 2002, in contrast, a force less than one-quarter that size was deployed to defeat the Iraqi army, dismantle it, occupy a resentful nation of 25 million people the size of Texas, and administer and rebuild it.

Powell also warned that the United States was responsible for the destruction it caused. He invoked what became known as the "Pottery Barn rule"—if you break it, you own it. Powell's warning was dictated not only by common sense but also by international law: The occupier is responsible for the well-being of the citizens it controls. It was something that could not be done by going in "light." The first casualty of this war, as always, was truth; the second was the Powell Doctrine.

Events quickly proved Powell, Shinseki, and Zinni correct. Hussein's army did not stand and fight; instead, it melted away to fight another day. Determined to sweep away the symbols of the old order, US troops pulled down statues and portraits of Hussein, and US "ambassador" Paul Bremer went so far as to disband the 400,000-strong Iraqi army, dissolve the police, dismiss Ba'athist bureaucrats, and begin to privatize the state sector of the Iraqi economy. In one fell swoop, Bremer not only threw hundreds of thousands of Iraqis out of work but also tore apart the complex fabric of Iraqi society that the Ba'ath Party had stitched together over thirty-five years.

As the United States dismantled the old order, Iraqis were no longer under any sort of constraint, and they began to loot stores, museums, hospitals, all of the government ministries, and—most important—army depots, carting off vast stores of weapons and explosives. US troops made no effort to stop the looting. At first US tanks controlled the bridges across the Tigris and the plundering was confined to eastern Baghdad. When they withdrew, western Baghdad was looted as well.[35] Rumsfeld dismissed reporters' concerns, saying, "Free people are free to make mistakes and commit crimes and do bad things."

### "Mission Accomplished"

Bush announced that the United States would withdraw as soon as its objectives—never specifically spelled out—were accomplished. In the meantime, the Pentagon began to build permanent military bases. On May 1, 2003, three weeks after the fall of Baghdad, President Bush, donning an aviator's suit, was dropped off on the aircraft carrier USS *Lincoln*. Standing under a banner proclaiming "MISSION ACCOMPLISHED," he declared that "major combat" in Iraq had ended. The number of US dead at that point stood at 139.

Policymakers in Washington expressed the hope that the political and economic reconstruction of Iraq would follow the lines of the postwar occupations of Germany and Japan. The citizens of these countries, however, understood why they were under foreign occupation. With the exception of the Kurds in the north, Iraqis generally did not see the US invasion as an act of liberation. Even the Shiites, finally free of Saddam Hussein's brutality, viewed the US bases as symbols of a permanent occupation. Iraqis, with their keen sense of history, well remembered other occupations—most recently by the Ottoman Turks and the British. They saw the US invasion as an act of recolonization by foreigners who neither understood nor respected their language, customs, or religion.

In postwar Germany and Japan there had been no resistance to occupation. Their people focused, instead, on clearing the rubble and on rebuilding their cities and factories. Perhaps even more importantly, the victorious Allies did not dismantle the efficient bureaucracies of these nations. In Japan, in particular, the government scarcely skipped a beat as it continued to run the country under the US occupation.

Bush's first envoy to Iraq, General Jay Garner, saw the country as "our coaling station in the Middle East," on the model of Cuba and the Philippines. Garner thought the United States should fix the economic infrastructure, hold quick elections, and leave economic shock therapy to the International Monetary Fund. Garner lasted but three weeks. The neocons wanted more than a coaling station. They wanted a transformation of Iraq's economy and political structure from the ground up. Iraq was to become the poster child for free markets and democracy in the Middle East.

On May 12, 2003, Bush replaced Garner with Paul Bremer, who began to hand out contracts to US companies poised to establish their control of the Iraqi economy. Every economic sector, with the exception of oil (for the time being), was now up for grabs by foreigners who assumed the right to take their profits out of the country. Iraq now belonged to the true believers who initiated the most drastic economic shock therapy anywhere. *The Economist* called Iraq "a capitalist's dream." US businessmen anticipated an economic climate that would permit a well-stocked 7-Eleven store to knock out thirty Iraqi family-owned stores. Yet it was illegal. The Geneva Conventions of 1907 and 1949 stipulated that an occupier must abide by the nation's laws and has no right to its assets. The Iraqi popular resistance was over this issue.

Because of escalating violence, US companies were slow to set up shop in Iraq. Few of the individuals the Bush administration recruited had the requisite expertise in either running Iraq or rebuilding its economy; they were chosen, instead, on the basis of political loyalty. In 2003, the US Congress appropriated nearly $20 billion for reconstruction, yet the money went to Western corporations at the exclusion of Iraq's state-owned enterprises, which were now operating at 50 percent capacity. The ubiquitous concrete barriers (derided as "Berlin walls" or "Bremer walls"), for example, were available from Iraqi contractors for $100 each; instead, they were imported at $1,000 each. Workers, out of a job, joined the ranks of the unemployed—and the resistance. Estimates of the number of unemployed in the summer of 2004 ranged between 50 percent and 70 percent.

The resistance targeted foreign business interests—US, South Korean, Japanese, Italian, Turkish—by kidnapping, ransoming, and killing hostages. By November 2004, more than 170 foreigners had been kidnapped; more than three dozen of them were murdered or "disappeared." Iraq, the neocons' dream laboratory, became the most dangerous place to do business.

Iraq attracted an indeterminate number of foreign jihadists, the most important of whom was Abu Musab Zarqawi, a Jordanian who it was said to have been personally responsible for the decapitation of two US contractors in September 2004 and who, the US military claimed, led the foreign contingent in the city of Fallujah. Zarqawi, the head of his own organization that previously had caused bloodshed in Europe and the Middle East, was both a rival and an ally of al Qaeda. As with so many of the Islamic militants, he had cut his teeth in Afghanistan, where he first made contact with al Qaeda and where he began to construct a distinct network, called Monotheism and Jihad. In Iraq, Zarqawi was particularly effective in the conservative Sunni city of Fallujah, where he called for a holy war against the United States and the heretic Iraqi Shiites.

Shiite clergy were among the early critics of the occupation. The most vociferous of them was Moqtada al-Sadr, a young ayatollah who had inherited the mantle of his revered father, who had been assassinated in 1999, presumably by Hussein's agents. The Shiite quarter of Baghdad, home to more than 2 million impoverished residents, formerly known as "Saddam City," became "Sadr City" (renamed in honor of the father). In March 2004, Bremer padlocked the offices of Sadr's weekly newspaper after it charged, "Bremer Follows the Steps of Saddam."[36] He issued a warrant for the arrest of the "outlaw" Sadr for his alleged complicity in the April 2003 murder of a rival Shiite cleric, Abdel Majid al-Khoei, the son of a grand ayatollah, whom the CIA had brought back from exile.

Sadr's resistance movement, the Mahdi Army, was a classic example of "blowback." Its members were the young, the unemployed, the disillusioned. "Sadr took Bremer's economic casualties," a Canadian journalist explained, "dressed them in black and gave them rusty Kalashnikovs."[37] The US military considered Sadr a priority because of his stature and uncompromising militancy. Repeated flare-ups of pitched battles between the Mahdi Army and US troops ended in a stalemate after a final round of fighting in the Shiite holy city of Najaf, the burial place of the founder of the Shiite branch, Mohammed's son-in-law, Ali. Grand Ayatollah Ali al-Sistani, the most influential cleric in Iraq, brokered a truce under the terms of which US troops withdrew from Najaf and the militia agreed (without doing so) to give up their weapons.

The troubles in Fallujah, the "city of mosques," a conservative Sunni religious center of approximately 300,000 inhabitants thirty-five miles west of Baghdad, began early. At the end of April 2003, US troops commandeered a local school to use as a military base, which did not sit well with the city's residents. The resistance gained momentum after US troops, in the course of a confrontation, killed thirteen Iraqis, several of them children.

A year later came the disturbing images on television and the Internet of four US "contractors" working for the Pentagon, who had been trapped in Fallujah and then killed, their dismembered bodies strung up from one of the city's bridges. US forces sought to retake the city with the help of a US-trained militia—the Fallujah Brigade—only to see it go over to the other side. Fallujah became a symbol of national and religious resistance and a haven for jihadists, many of them foreigners, under the command of Zarqawi.

Immediately after the 2004 US presidential election, 10,000 US Marines, augmented by 5,000 Iraqi soldiers, retook Fallujah after a bloody, weeklong battle, leaving behind thousands of casualties, a flood of refugees, and much of the city in ruins. Once again, the United States proclaimed victory, but many of the resistance fighters had escaped.

The US image in Iraq suffered a serious blow when, in late April 2004, photographs on the Internet showed US troops engaged in systematic torture of Iraqis at the Abu Ghraib prison, just west of Baghdad. Amnesty International and the International Red Cross had already reported on the abuses, but their complaints had been ignored. Rumsfeld had dismissed the initial reports of torture as "isolated pockets of international hyperventilation." This time the shocking photographs could not be readily dismissed. Ironically, the Abu Ghraib prison had first gained notoriety for torture, rapes, and executions under Hussein. The Pentagon and the White House feigned shock that US troops would behave in such fashion and placed the onus on a few low-ranking "bad apples." It soon became evident, however, that the decision to use torture had been made at the highest levels of the Bush administration.

In other wars, the United States had long been engaged in torture, but it had generally done so surreptitiously through intermediaries, such as South Vietnamese and Latin American soldiers who had applied the lessons learned at the School of the Americas in Fort Benning, Georgia. Torture began in Afghanistan when the Bush administration lumped the Taliban and al Qaeda together in a new category of "enemy combatants," not enemy soldiers, and thus not subject to the protection of the 1949 Geneva Convention that prohibited torture of any and all prisoners "at any time and in any place whatsoever." For the first time, the United States denied prisoner-of-war status to enemy soldiers.

Beginning in February 2002, White House counsel Alberto Gonzales declared that the Geneva Conventions had become "irrelevant" and that the president, acting as commander-in-chief, was not bound by any law—US or international. Inflicting pain on prisoners, Gonzales went on to say, was justified as an act of "self-defense." In the Pentagon, Rumsfeld signed off on several similar such expositions. Torture migrated from Afghanistan to the Guantánamo Bay Naval Base, to which the Taliban and al Qaeda prisoners had been taken, and from there to Iraq.

As the Iraqi resistance grew in the summer of 2003, US forces became desperate to gain information about the ubiquitous insurgents. Soldiers began to arrest civilians at the site of attacks, often raiding homes and wrecking furniture. Eventually the number of detainees reached 50,000, who were guarded by understaffed, ill-prepared National Guard troops. Few of the detainees had information to give; fewer still were released.

Torture became institutionalized at the end of August when Major General Geoffrey Miller, commander of the detention camp at Guantánamo, arrived in Baghdad. Miller demanded "actionable intelligence" any way possible—by beatings, sexual humiliation, "water-boarding" (near-drowning of detainees), and the use of attack dogs. The commander of US forces in Iraq, General Ricardo Sanchez, sanctioned Miller's tactics. The system was self-defeating, however, because it generated much hostility and little information. In June 2004, at Friday prayers in Baghdad, imams charged that the only freedom the United States had brought to Iraq was the freedom to abuse Iraqis, "the freedom of rape, the freedom of nudity and the freedom of humiliation."[38]

Iraq's ethnic complexity proved to be another vexing problem. When Bremer began to draw up the first transitional laws, he stated that ethnicity had no place in the new Iraq, that the country's citizens were all Iraqis. It was a tall order. The Kurds did not see themselves as Iraqis. By now, 75 percent of Kurdistan's adult population had signed a petition demanding independence. Even before the invasion Kurdistan had become de facto independent. Kurds flew their own flag, paid no Iraqi taxes, controlled their own borders, and maintained their own army. To complicate matters, most Shiites—the majority of the population—wanted an Islamic state, while the Sunnis saw the Shiites as heretics and believed that it was their right to govern Iraq. The potential for ethnic and religious violence was particularly great in the northern oil center of Kirkuk, a city of 850,000 people, roughly evenly divided among Kurds (35 percent), Sunni Arabs (35 percent), and Turkomen (26 percent) of Turkish descent hostile to both Kurds and Arabs. Each had their historic claims to the city and its oil.[39]

None of the neocons expected that nearly 4,500 US troops would die in Iraq, with another 32,000 seriously wounded. (In Afghanistan, as of January 2014, nearly 2,200 US and another 1,100 allied troops were killed.) As for Iraqi civilian casualties, the Pentagon did not bother to count them. "We don't do [civilian] body counts," General Tommy Franks declared. By the end of 2008, a conservative tally put the number at around 125,000.[40]

As regular and National Guard units had their tours of duty extended, they were stretched to the breaking point. The cost in dollars, once estimated at a paltry $30 billion, shot past $850 billion by the end of 2008. Estimates for the final cost—after everything was added up, including veterans' benefits and health care and interest on borrowed money—ranged up to $3 trillion. President Clinton's budget surplus was a distant memory wiped out by September 11, homeland security, the wars in Afghanistan and Iraq, and tax cuts—the first in history, anywhere, in time of war. In another historical first, the wars were waged entirely on borrowed money (largely from Japan and China), down to the last cent.

When the United States retaliated against the Taliban, the world, including many Muslims and even Arabs, believed its cause was just. Iraq, however, quickly drained the reservoir of goodwill. Clerics at Cairo's Al-Azhar University, an esteemed center of Muslim thought, who had condemned the attacks of September 11, now preached that every Muslim had an obligation to defend Iraq.[41]

The Bush administration sought an Iraqi government that would accept a permanent US presence. Once elections were proposed, Iraq's most revered Shiite cleric, Ali al-Sistani, insisted on a direct election—one person, one vote—in contrast to an indirect election that the Bush administration hoped to manipulate. Under Sistani's proposal, the majority Shiite, for the first time in their history, going back to the late seventh century, were destined to take power. When one of their own, Nouri al-Maliki, became prime minister, he worked with the Bush administration, which provided money and military training. The other winner was the Islamic Republic of Iran, which obtained what it had always wanted: a Shiite government in neighboring Iraq. The head of Iran's powerful Guardian Council thought that the "election results are very good."[42]

The new Iraqi government had close ties to Tehran. Maliki, who headed the Islamic Dawa Party, was a sworn enemy of Hussein going back to the 1960s. But the party also opposed the West's presence in the Arab world. (In 1983, for instance, Dawa bombed the US and French embassies in Kuwait.) In 1980, Hussein had sentenced Maliki to death; in December 2006, it was Maliki who gladly signed Hussein's death warrant. Iran also had close ties to Shiite blocs, such as the Badr Organization, which had been founded in Tehran during Hussein's war with Iraq and whose godfather was the Ayatollah Khomeini. Iran also supported the Mahdi Army, a Shiite militia led by the nationalist Moqtada al-Sadr. Iran's influence went a long way to explain why Maliki was in no position to give the Bush administration what it sought—fifty-eight permanent bases, control of oil, and immunity from prosecution of US troops. These requests were subject to parliamentary ratification by the Shiite majority.

In the meantime, a civil war between Sunnis and Shiites spun out of control. The violence was fanned initially by the nihilistic brutality of Zarqawi, who was responsible for the death of an estimated 6,000 Shiite Iraqis. In February 2006, Zarqawi poured additional gasoline on the fire by blowing up one of Iraq's holiest Shiite shrines, the golden dome of the Al-Askari Mosque in Samarra, the burial place of two revered ninth-century Shiite imams. The savage Shiite retaliation convinced many Sunnis that Zarqawi was leading them down the path of destruction. His violence appalled even bin Laden and his lieutenants. Can Zarqawi's men "kill all the Shia in Iraq?" Zawahiri asked, "has any Islamic state ever tried that?"[43] Residents of the "Sunni triangle," the region to the north and west of Baghdad, on whose behalf Zarqawi was fighting, began to turn against him. In June 2006, acting on a paid informer's tip, US troops tracked him down and killed him.

## The Sunni "Awakening"

Sunni insurgents concluded that their best chance of survival against the US-supported Shiite tide was cooperation with the US military. The result was the Sunni "Awakening." The US military, under the command of General David Petraeus, gained a new ally in the war against al Qaeda. More than 100,000 so-called Sons of Iraq—who until then had been killing US troops—were put on the Pentagon's payroll and entrusted to guard checkpoints, to set up barriers to prevent roadside bomb explosions and suicide car attacks, and to patrol neighborhoods.

Three years after Bremer's disastrous decision to dismantle the Sunni-dominated Ba'athist state, Hussein's men were gradually returning to power. The city of Fallujah gained a new police chief, Colonel Faisal Ismail al-Zobaie, once a member of Hussein's Republican Guard and, after the invasion, a supporter of al Qaeda. After al Qaeda murdered members of his family, he joined the Awakening. The Marine Corps website touted Fallujah's newly found stability as a success, but it came at a heavy price. Zobaie was more than the new police chief. He was the law in Fallujah—judge, juror, jailer, torturer, and executioner. One of his interrogators, who had honed his methods under Hussein, saw no need to change them. "Iraq obeys only force," he explained. What Zobaie wanted was for the United States to leave Fallujah, giving him full control of the city. Then "I'll be tougher with the people."[44] His ultimate aim, however, was the destruction of Shiite power.

The Awakening solved one problem—the drastic reduction of US fatalities—but created another. The Sunni leaders—rehabilitated, financed, and armed by the Pentagon—posed a direct challenge to the Shiite-dominated government. Petraeus found himself trying to square the circle, satisfying the claims of two mortal enemies. His counterintelligence adviser obliquely spoke of "balancing competing armed interest groups." A former senior member of President Clinton's national security staff put it more succinctly, and more accurately. By virtue of this "balancing" act, he said, "we're mid-wifing the dissolution of the country."[45] In due time, events proved him to be correct.

## The "Surge"

The Awakening coincided with an increase in US troop deployment. This escalation—prudently called a "surge" so as not to invoke unpleasant memories from the Vietnam War—added another 30,000 troops (bringing the total to 146,000). Their new task was to "clear and hold" neighborhoods (a concept inherited from the latter stages of the Vietnam War) to deny them to the insurgents. Violence abated in part because of the surge and in part because ethnic cleansing by Iraqis had been largely completed and neighborhoods were divided, kept apart by concrete barriers. On the eve of the 2008 US presidential election, with US fatalities at record lows, Bush announced that the troops would remain in Iraq, thereby kicking the issue down the road to his successor, Barack Obama.

Bush had believed that regime change in Iraq would be the foundation of a democratic Middle East. The scenario, however, played out very much differently than expected. It was not that Arabs did not warn Bush. The Egyptian

*Barack Obama declares his presidency. It was a historic moment—an African American started his successful run for the presidency in Springfield, Illinois, before the old state capital, where Lincoln made his political career*

dictator Hosni Mubarak predicted that the war would spawn "100 bin Ladens." The secretary-general of the Arab League warned it would "open the gates of hell." As Mubarak had predicted, the war became a boon for the Muslim Brotherhood, with many of its radicalized recruits winding up in Iraq. Mubarak, well aware of the threat he faced, responded with the most extensive crackdown in a decade against the Egyptian branch of the Brotherhood.

More than a decade into the "global war on terror," the United States was unable to escalate the conflict because of fiscal constraints and a shortage of additional troops. It had reached a dead end. No one wanted to call it a *quagmire*, the term the journalist David Halberstam had popularized in his reports from Vietnam. Once more, historians wrote about the limits of US power. Bush's moral clarity—shored up by 725 US bases abroad and another 969 at home[46]—meant to rid the world of evil, was replaced by frustration and doubt.

Even UN secretary-general Kofi Annan, who tended to see things from Washington's point of view, stated his opposition to the war—albeit a year and a half after it began. Absent an authorization from the UN Security Council, Annan argued, the US presence in Iraq was "illegal." Several UN resolutions, however, eventually granted Washington the temporary right to be in Iraq. Resolution 1790 (December 2007) extended that right "one last time" for one more year, but it also asserted the "right" of Iraqis "to determine their own political future and control of their national resources."

In November 2008, the Iraqi parliament passed an agreement with the Bush administration that emphasized Iraqi sovereignty and called for a "withdrawal" of US forces by 2011. It undermined the neocons' fond hope of a permanent US presence in Iraq. Still, the purposely vague compromise agreement held open the possibility of extending the US military footprint.

Both Bush and Obama wanted to retain a residual force in Iraq, but for political reasons, Maliki could not give them what they wanted—permanent bases and civilian contractors and US troops immune to Iraqi law. Obama had to settle for what was known as the "zero-option." The US mission ended in mid-December 2011. At a ceremony at Fort Bragg, Obama told the troops they had left behind "a sovereign, stable and self-reliant Iraq." It was anything but that, however.

The Bush administration, as it intended, did create a new reality in Iraq, but not the one it wanted. Because of the invasion, Iran and Iraq drew closer together. And by bringing the Shiites to power, the invasion overturned the political order in place since the Sunni victory over the Shiites in the late seventh century. Sunnis, however, continued to believe that it was their birthright to govern Iraq. The Awakening had given them a new lease on life and they intended to make the best of it. After the last US troops departed, civil strife gradually picked up in intensity. Within two years, bombings and shootings were a common occurrence, particularly in Anbar province, a Sunni stronghold. The UN estimated that in the first two years of the US withdrawal, 8,000 Iraqis died in sectarian violence.[47]

By 2013, al Qaeda had staged a comeback. From bases in Iraq, its fighters infiltrated Syria to join the insurrection against the Syrian government of Bashar Assad. After establishing a beachhead in Syria, they turned their attention to Anbar Province. The Maliki regime had always dreaded a revival of Sunni power, the ultimate goal of the Awakening. "Once Anbar [Province] is settled," a Sunni tribal leader explained, "we must take control of Baghdad, and we will."[48] An alarmed Maliki government began to round up prominent members of the Awakening. What Petraeus had wrought, Maliki intended to undo.

When Maliki moved against Anbar's two most important cities, Fallujah and Ramadi, it revealed his army's weaknesses.[49] By early 2014, three factions vied for control of Anbar, which the United States had brought under control at vast expense. It had been Anbar where it suffered the bulk of its casualties. When al Qaeda took control of Fallujah and Ramadi, the independent-minded tribes of Anbar again rose in rebellion. They were not ready to yield the province to either al Qaeda or Maliki's government. For the time being, as a political expedient, they sided with Maliki's army even thought they had only recently fought against it.

## Kurdistan

In the north of Iraq, the status of autonomous Kurdistan remained unresolved. In September 2008, the *peshmerga*, soldiers of Kurdistan's regional government, advanced along a 300-mile front into territories claimed by Arabs and Turkomen. Along the way, they seized control of the cities of Kirkuk and Mosul and their adjacent oil fields. Iraqi Arabs always resented Kurdistan's autonomy, but now, in one fell swoop, the Kurdish state had increased its territory by 70 percent.

There was little the relatively weak Maliki government could do to challenge the *peshmerga,* whose checkpoints extended 75 miles south of the official Kurdish border. In the regions the Kurds controlled, Hussein's policy of "Arabization" was replaced by "Kurdification," accompanied by ethnic cleansing, torture, and killings. Kurds justified their actions as self-defense against the Maliki government, which, they claimed, had its eyes on Kurdish territory. Kurds went on to say that they were only reclaiming what had historically been their land. Arabs replied they would not permit the Kurdish "Gestapo" to "steal" their land and oil.

By virtue of the 1991 and 2003 wars against Saddam Hussein, Washington had made possible a de facto independent Kurdistan (although officially it remained an autonomous region of Iraq, governed by a "regional government"). The Bush administration looked with favor upon Kurdistan's reasonably democratic government, its economic recovery, and its powerful army. Paradoxically, the US government was officially committed to a unified Iraq under the Maliki government. As always, Kurdistan's other neighbors—Syria, Iran, and Turkey—remained hostile to the idea of an independent Kurdistan.

## Afghanistan

In December 2001, on the eve of the Taliban's overthrow, the UN convened an Afghan council in Bonn, Germany, to choose an interim head of state. The Bush administration engineered the selection of Hamid Karzai, a royalist who had gone into exile after the Soviet invasion and who had established close ties to the CIA and the US oil giant Unocal. When Karzai returned to Kabul, he came courtesy of Washington, as a president who had no army of his own and little authority beyond the capital. His safety was ensured by US mercenaries, private "contractors" paid by the Pentagon.

After the Taliban were driven from Kabul, an economic recovery of sorts took place. In three years, the annual per capita GDP doubled from $123 to $246 and daily wages rose from $2.70 to $6.25. Primary-school enrollment, a more significant measure of progress, rose from 1 million to 3.5 million. Progress, however, was limited largely to Kabul.

Much of the new wealth came from the production of opium, the raw material for heroin. Banned by the Taliban and virtually nonexistent in 2001, opium production now increased drastically. Among the chief beneficiaries were the Taliban and the other militias still operating in Afghanistan. In 2006, the UN reported that Afghanistan grew 95 percent of the world's poppy crop. Washington now had another front in its already ineffective global "war on drugs." The opium trade threatened to turn Afghanistan into a narcostate on the Colombian model.

Meanwhile, the Taliban and al Qaeda were rebuilding their strength. Mohammed Omar, the still at large head of the Taliban, smuggled seditious "night letters" into Kabul urging Afghans to resist the infidel foreigners and their Afghan lackeys—"dog washers," in popular parlance (that is, individuals who looked after the dogs—considered dirty creatures in the Muslim world—of the infidel occupiers). The endless Afghan war demanded increasingly greater resources that the United States could only afford by borrowing more money. The Brookings Institution's "index of state weakness" ranked Afghanistan just ahead of Somalia, the poster child for failed states. In the index's "annual corruption perceptions index," Afghanistan ranked near the bottom.[50]

Obama took a lesson from Bush's surge in Iraq when he increased US troop levels in Afghanistan from 32,000 to nearly 100,000 (augmented by additional allied forces). After pledging to "bring the troops home" by 2014, he reduced their level to 45,000 by the end of 2013. He tried to avoid, however, the "zero option" for Afghanistan. Thus, in November 2013, came the surprising announcement that the Pentagon sought to retain a footprint in Afghanistan. A preliminary draft of the agreement with the Afghan government called for a continuing US presence, its size still undetermined (perhaps as many as 20,000 troops), until "the end of 2024 and beyond." Before Karzai would accept a final agreement, however, a number of issued needed to be resolved, including a "total ban" against US troops entering Afghan homes.

Afghanistan remained a country in transition, but in which direction remained unclear. It remained a nation seething with xenophobia, as attested by the murder of US troops by the soldiers they were training. The killing of Afghan civilians by airplane and drone strikes bred additional resentment. Karzai was willing to step down from the presidency but not relinquish power. He had leveraged bribes from the Iranian government to extract bribes from the CIA that the agency spent with virtually no oversight. The Afghan government was riddled with double-agents, warlords, heroin traders, and politicians openly soliciting bribes.[51]

In the meantime, Mullah Omar ominously spoke of a repetition of history. He compared Karzai to the ill-fated Shah Shuja, whom the British had brought to power after thirty years in exile. It was an episode well known to Afghans. Omar reminded them that Karzai was a tribal descendant of the reviled Shuja, while he and most of the Taliban leadership were descendants of the Ghilzai clan, which drove the British out of Afghanistan.[52]

## Pakistan

The Taliban's revival was tied directly to the unstable political situation in Pakistan. After the US invasion of Afghanistan, the Taliban and al Qaeda made their way back to Pakistan's rugged North-West Frontier Province, where they reconstituted their organizations. They were greatly assisted by the fact that Pakistan's military and its intelligence branch, the Inter-Services Intelligence (the ISI, under whose auspices the Taliban had come into existence), showed little zeal in joining the Bush administration's war on terror. For years, the ISI was more concerned about the threat from India.

When president Obama made the dramatic announcement of the assassination of bin Laden by the US Navy "Seal Team Six" in May 2012, it turned out it had taken place at bin Laden's house in Abottabad, a city with a major Pakistani military base. The violation of Pakistani territory by the Seal commandos did not go over very well with the Pakistani military government. The Pakistani physician who had helped the United States find bin Laden was denounced as "the lowest of traitors" and charged with murder in an unrelated malpractice suit.[53]

The close relationship between the Pakistan military and radical Islamists went back to the days of the Soviet invasion of Afghanistan. At the time, Pakistan's strongman, General Zia ul-Haq, became a hero in Washington for supporting the US effort in Afghanistan. With the blessing of the CIA, Zia cemented a close relationship between the ISI and the reactionary anti-Soviet mullahs. When Pervez Musharraf seized power in a military coup in October 1999, he saw no reason to go to war against the Taliban. To the conrary, in September 2006 he signed a peace treaty with the Taliban holed up in North Waziristan. Officially, Musharraf was part of Bush's "global war on terror," yet he did little to warrant the largesse that Washington bestowed upon his military.

Popular pressure—from the middle and professional classes, Islamic radicals who railed against Western cultural pollution, and the traditional landowning *zamindars*, who owned vast stretches of land and traditionally exercised considerable political powers—forced Musharraf into retirement. Once it became clear that his days in power were numbered, the old guard returned from exile. Among them was Benazir Bhutto, a woman from the wealthy landowning class who was educated at a convent run by Irish nuns and at Harvard and Oxford. She had previously served two terms as prime minister (see Chapter 16), and was still under investigation for corruption (along with her husband, Asif Ali Zardari, known as "Mr. Ten Percent" for the kickbacks he allegedly received for government contracts). Before they could return home, however, Bhutto and Zardari were granted immunity from further prosecution. In December 2007, as Bhutto campaigned for the presidency, she was assassinated by assailants unknown. Her death was but one of a number of unsolved political murders in recent Pakistani history. In the West, the tendency was to blame al Qaeda since she had returned to Pakistan at the prodding of the Bush administration. But she was also a threat to the military establishment. Before her death, she had stated publicly that she considered General Musharraf as the major threat to her safety.

Asif Ali Zardari completed the family's political comeback when he was sworn in as president in September 2008. His first test came two months later when an Islamic suicide squad of ten men launched an audacious assault in India's financial center, the city of Mumbai (formerly known as Bombay). It began at a railway station and then shifted to two luxury hotels and a restaurant catering to foreigners, a Jewish center, and even to a hospital. The terrorists killed more than a dozen policemen, including the city's chief counterterrorism official, more than 170 people in all. Their primary targets were US and British citizens and Jews.

This was the eighth Islamic attack in Mumbai since 1993. In the first attack, the terrorists set off thirteen bombs, killing more than 250 people. The November 2008 attack, however, was of such sophistication that, so Indians argued, it had to have been organized with foreign assistance. Indeed, the evidence pointed to Pakistani terrorist groups with ties to al Qaeda, who had threatened strikes against India in the past.

When India demanded the extradition of twenty terrorists from Pakistan (including the mastermind behind the 1993 bombings), Zardari promised cooperation. But the ISI intervened, making clear that there would be no handover of Muslims to India. It underscored what was already known, that Pakistan's powerful army, which had aided and abetted terrorist organizations in the first place, was beyond the control of a civilian president, particularly one whose family been had long engaged in a feud with the military. All Zardari managed to extract was a promise to shut down the terrorist camps.

Pakistani politicians of every stripe insisted that an Indian attack on Pakistani soil (including terrorist facilities) was tantamount to an act of war. Pakistan would retaliate and, in the process, would withdraw its troops from the North-West Frontier Province, where it was doing the bidding of the Bush administration by ostensibly keeping an eye on the Taliban and al Qaeda. It appeared briefly that for the first time two nuclear powers were about to go to war against one another. That prospect set off a flurry of diplomatic missions. India's foreign minister hurried off to Washington, and US envoys (including the secretary of state and the chairman of the Joint Chiefs) flew to New Delhi and Islamabad to defuse the issue.

## Notes

1. Jacqueline Rose, "Deadly Embrace," *London Review of Books*, November 4, 2004, pp. 21–24; Raffi Khatchadourian, "Behind Enemy Lines," *The Nation*, May 15, 2006, p. 24.

2. Avishai Margalit, "The Suicide Bombers," *New York Review of Books*, January 16, 2003; Jessica Stern, *Terror in the Name of God: Why Religious Militants Kill* (New York: Ecco Press, 2003).

3. Christian Caryl, "Why They Do It," *New York Review of Books*, September 22, 2005; Scott McConnell, "The Logic of Suicide Terrorism: It's the Occupation, Not the Fundamentalism," *American Conservative*, July 18, 2005.

4. Jonathan Rabin, "My Holy War," *The New Yorker*, February 4, 2002; Steven Coll, *Ghost Wars: The Secret History of the CIA, Afghanistan, and bin Laden, from the Soviet Invasion to September 10, 2001* (New York: Penguin, 2004), pp. 470–474.

5. *The Battle of Algiers*, written and directed by Gillo Pontecorvo (Rialto Pictures Release and Janus Films, 1965).

6. Abdel Aziz al-Rantissi, cited in Rose, "Deadly Embrace," p. 24.

7. Cited in Coll, *Ghost Wars*, p. 380.

8. Lawrence Wright, "The Terror Web," *The New Yorker*, August 2, 2004, p. 47.

9. Ibid., pp. 40–53.

10. David B. Ottaway and Robert G. Kaiser, "Marriage of Convenience: The US-Saudi Alliance," *Washington Post*, February 12, 2002, p. A10; Max Rodenbeck, "Unloved in Arabia," *New York Review of Books*, October 21, 2004, pp. 22–25.

11. Cited in David Remnick, "Letter from Cairo: Going Nowhere," *The New Yorker*, July 12 and 19, 2004.

12. Lawrence Wright, "The Man Behind bin Laden," *The New Yorker*, September 16, 2002; Karen Armstrong, *The Battle for God* (New York: Ballantine Books, 2000), pp. 239–244; Rabin, "My Holy War."

13. Wright, "The Man Behind bin Laden."

14. Montasser al-Zayat, cited in ibid.

15. Coll, *Ghost Wars*, pp. 87, 155–157, 162–163, 185.

16. Clarke memo to Rice, "Presidential Policy Initiative/Review—The *Al-Qaeda* Network," January 25, 2001.

17. Lisa Meyers, NBC News, "Did Ashcroft Brush Off Terror Warnings?" June 22, 2004; Dan Eggen and Walter Pincus, "Ashcroft's Efforts on Terrorism Criticized," *Washington Post*, April 14, 2004.

18. *The 9/11 Commission Report: Final Report of the National Commission on Terrorist Attacks upon the United States* (New York: W. W. Norton, 2004), pp. 174–182, 254–277.

19. Bob Woodward, *Bush at War* (New York: Simon and Schuster, 2002), pp. 38, 141, 143.

20. Ibid., p. 314.

21. Barton Gellman and Thomas E. Ricks, "US Concludes Bin Laden Escaped at Tora Bora Fight," *Washington Post*, April 17, 2002.

22. Tommy Franks, *American Soldier* (New York: Regan, 2004), p. 309.

23. Eliza Griswold, "Where the Taliban Roam," *Harper's* (September 2003), pp. 57–65; Eliza Griswold, "In the Hiding Zone," *The New Yorker*, July 26, 2004, pp. 34–42.

24. Richard Clarke, *Against All Enemies: Inside America's War on Terror* (New York: Free Press, 2004), chapter 6, "Al Qaeda Revealed," pp. 133–154.

25. Ron Suskind, "Faith, Certainty and the Presidency of George W. Bush," *New York Times Magazine*, October 17, 2004.

26. Peter Bergen, "Backdraft," *Mother Jones* (July–August 2004), pp. 40–45.

27. Bill Moyers and Michael Winship, "It Was Oil, All Along," *Bill Moyers' Journal*, June 27, 2008; "US Pushing for Privatized Iraq Oil Sector," *Petroleum Intelligence Weekly*, April 21, 2003; Greg Palast, "Secret US Plans for Iraq's Oil," *OfficialWire*, March 17, 2005; "Blood for Oil," *London Review of Books*, April 21, 2005, p. 13; James A. Baker III, Lee H. Hamilton et al., eds., *Iraq Study Group Report* (New York: Vintage, 2006), p. 2 and Recommendation #63, pp. 85–86; P. J. O'Rourke, "The Backside of War," *The Atlantic*, December 2003.

28. Cited in Paul Krugman, "Osama, Saddam, and the Ports," *New York Times*, February 24, 2006.

29. On the eve of Paul Bremer's departure for Iraq in May 2003, Bush told him, "it's important to have someone willing to stand up and thank the American people for their sacrifice in liberating Iraq"; L. Paul Bremer III, *My Year in Iraq: The Struggle to Build a Future of Hope* (New York: Simon and Schuster, 2006), p. 359. In his interview with Bob Woodward five years later, Bush returned to that sentiment.

30. For a scathing indictment of the press, see Michael Massing, "Iraq: Now They Tell Us," *New York Review of Books*, February 26, 2004.

31. Coll, *Ghost Wars*, p. 380.

32. During the first of five rehearsal sessions, Powell tossed the papers in the air, saying, "I'm not reading this. This is bullshit." Bruce B. Auster, Mark Mazetti, and Edward T. Pound, "Truth and Consequences: New Questions About US Intelligence Regarding Iraq's Weapons of Mass Terror," *US News and World Report*, June 9, 2003.

33. Cited by Danny Postel, "Look Who's Feuding," *American Prospect* (July 2004), p. 22.

34. Caroline Alexander, "U.S. Has No Exist Strategy for Iraq, Rumsfeld Says," *Bloomberg News*, April 12, 2005; AP, "Woodward: Kissinger Advising Bush," September 29, 2006.

35. Alexander Cockburn, "Because We Could," *The Nation*, November 8, 2004, p. 46.

36. Pamela Constable, "Paper Closed by US Is Back in Business," *Washington Post*, July 25, 2004, p. A15.

37. Naomi Klein, "Baghdad Year Zero: Pillaging Iraq in Pursuit of a Neocon Utopia," *Harper's* (September 2004), p. 51.

38. Cited in Mark Danner, "Abu Ghraib: The Hidden Story," *New York Review of Books*, October 7, 2004, p. 44.

39. Galbraith, "Iraq: The Bungled Transition," pp. 72–73 and David Ignatius, "Kirkuk as Car Bomb," *Washington Post*, July 20, 2004, p. A17.

40. Figures are from www.iraqbodycount.org.

41. Peter Bergen, "Backdraft," pp. 40–45.

42. Steven Simon and Ray Takeyh, "Iran's Iraq Strategy," *Washington Post*, May 21, 2006, p. B2.

43. Lawrence Wright, "The Terrorist," *The New Yorker*, June 19, 2006, p. 31.

44. Sudarsan Raghavan, "In Fallujah, Peace Through Brute Strength," *Washington Post*, March 24, 2008.

45. Nir Rosen, "The Myth of the Surge," *Rolling Stone*, March 6, 2008; Steven Coll, "The General's Dilemma," *The New Yorker*, September 8, 2008, p. 37.

46. Tony Judt, "The New World Order," *New York Review of Books*, July 14, 2005, p. 16.

47. "Malaki Under Fire as Iraq Violence Continues," Al Jazeera, December 31, 2013.

48. Jon Lee Anderson, "Inside the Surge," *The New Yorker*, November 19, 2007, p. 62.

49. Yasir Ghazi and Tim Arango, "Qaeda-Aligned Militants Threaten Key Iraqi Cities," *New York Times*, January 2, 2014.

50. Brookings Institution, *Afghanistan Index*, www.brookings.edu/afghanistanindex.

51. Matthew Rosenberg, "With Bags of Cash, C.I.A. Seeks Influence in Afghanistan," *New York Times*, April 28, 2013.

52. William Dalrymple, "The Ghosts of Afghanistan's Past," *New York Times*, April 14, 2013.

53. M. Amad Razi, "Shakil Afridi: The Lowest of Traitors," *The Express Tribune Blogs*, February 22, 1012.

# 23

# The Arab Spring:
# Turning to Winter?

The countries most seriously affected by the uprisings known as the "Arab Spring" had much in common. They had languished under the Ottoman Empire and then had been Western colonies. After independence they had turned to the Arab version of socialism (Morocco excepted), only to wind up being ruled by repressive and corrupt military dictators whose primary aim was to avail themselves of their nations' wealth and transfer power to their offspring. They also had similar social problems, such as rapidly growing populations, high rates of unemployment, rising expectations for a better future, and radicalized Islamic factions.

## Tunisia

After more than three decades in power, Tunisia's independence leader, Habib Bourguiba, was ousted in November 1987 in a military coup by army general Zine el-Abidine Ben Ali. (For the Arab independence movements, see Chapter 7.) By this time, Bourguiba had long ago outworn his welcome, and Tunisians were looking for positive changes. Indeed, Ben Ali promised a return to democracy, but it turned out he was more interested in enriching himself and consolidating his power. He had no intention of stepping down, nor did he tolerate criticism. He cracked down on both militant Islamists and the secular opposition.

The Arab Spring began unexpectedly in Tunisia, on December 17, 2010, after a twenty-six year old street vendor, Mohammed Bouazizi, set himself on fire in the central town of Sidi Bouzid in protest of police harassment and extortion. Bouazizi was not alone in his grievances. Tunisia's young tended to be well educated but found it difficult to find gainful employment, yet they were expected to accept their lot quietly. Bouazizi's agonizing death, after three weeks in a hospital, touched off widespread protests. For eleven days security forces killed dozens of unarmed civilians, but on the twelfth day they refused to shoot. At that point, Ben Ali and his family fled on a private jet to Saudi Arabia.

Bouazizi's suffering coincided with Wikileaks revelations of deep-rooted corruption in Tunisia. The main culprits were members of Ben Ali's family. The revelations confirmed what most Tunisians already knew. According to the leaked documents, US ambassador Robert Godec had stated that he could not help but notice that after more than twenty years of misrule by Ben Ali, the public "chorus of complaint" had turned into vehement "dislike, even hate." In a series of diplomatic dispatches, which became widely known in Tunisia, the ambassador spoke of Ben Ali's "sclerotic regime" and compared his inner circle to the mafia. He was particularly critical of the president's wife and her

*Tunisians defy a nighttime curfew in a "Liberation Caravan" protesting the regime of Ben Ali during the Arab Spring, Tunis, January 23, 2011*

extended family, whom, he explained, Tunisians reviled for "their lack of education, low social status and conspicuous consumption." Upon attending a dinner party at the beachfront mansion of one of Ben Ali's daughters, Godec came away appalled by her "over the top" opulence as manifest, in particular, by the her pet tiger. It reminded him of Uday Hussein's lion cage in Baghdad. "Whether it's cash, services, land, property, or yes, even your yacht" (stolen from a vacationing French businessman), Godec wrote, the family "gets what it wants."[1]

As soon as Ben Ali fled Tunisia, the Islamists flexed their muscles. Since 1991, Ben Ali had arrested 25,000 of them, but now, recently released, they began to clash with the authorities. They killed politicians, policemen, and soldiers. They called for a state based on *sharia* (Islamic) law, sought to take over universities, attacked moderate Sufi Muslims, protested outside synagogues, besieged the US embassy, and burned down an adjacent American school and the US Information Agency library. In Tunisia's rugged mountains, they battled security forces to a standstill. At Al-Qayrawan, Tunisia's ancient historic center of Islamic learning, militants pledged to "finish what we started" with the overthrow of Ben Ali. To deal with the rising Islamic militant threat, the government began to arrest members of Ansar al-Sharia, a group loosely tied to al Qaeda.

The militants called for *sharia* law, yet the bars and beaches remained open. They remained an affront to Islamist militants, who targeted the symbols of Tunisia's ties to the West. Tunisia's first suicide bomber killed himself (and no one else) at a beach resort hotel frequented by Westerners. Another suicide bomber sought to blow up the mausoleum containing the remains of Habib Bourguiba, the French-educated founder of the modern Tunisian state.

To strengthen the hand of reformers who continued to look to the West for inspiration, French president François Hollande paid Tunisia a state visit in July 2013 and offered aid for its struggling economy. Despite Tunisia's travails, by the beginning of 2014 the glass appeared to be half full. Tunisia held its first free election, kept a series of relatively moderate struggling governments in power, held the militants at bay, and kept the army out of politics. Unlike Egypt, Tunisia did not have to choose between militant Islamists in power imposing *sharia* law and a return to military rule.

## Libya

In Libya, strongman Muammar Qaddafi had managed to retain his powers for more than four decades, since 1969. Until the Arab Spring, Qaddafi posed as a pan-Arab statesman and a socialist reformer who had lifted Libyans out of poverty. But corruption, police brutality, the prospect that his detested sons would succeed him, an unemployment rate of 30 percent, and exorbitant food prices left Qaddafi with a shrinking base of support.

As soon as disturbances commenced in Tunisia, Qaddafi saw the hand-writing on the wall. Heavily reliant on his army, he purged it of potentially dis-loyal elements. Fearing the worst, he offered Libyans both the carrot and the stick. To forestall unrest, he reduced food prices, which had been a problem for several years. Because Libya imported 80 percent of its food, the increased cost of food on the global market hit it particularly hard.[2]

All the while, Qaddafi made clear he would not hesitate to use force. He linked the demonstrators in the streets to al Qaeda—whose presence in Libya, however, was still minimal at best—and he vowed to hunt them down, "street by street, house by house." But his army, even after killing hundreds, proved unable to restore order in Benghazi, the center of the resistance. From there, the resistance spread westward, toward the capital of Tripoli. The loss of Benghazi, the capital of Cyrenaica, King Idris's ancestral home, proved to be a serious blow to Qaddafi. People there remembered Idris's ouster by Qaddafi, forty-three years before. It was no coincidence that many of the rebels in Cyrenaica fought under Idris's old flag—as well as the black flags of militant Islam.

In the end, Qadaffi was reduced to defending the capital of Tripoli. Under domestic pressure to intervene, US president Barack Obama and British prime minister David Cameron invoked NATO. For domestic political reasons, how-ever, ground troops were out of the question. As it turned out, NATO naval and airpower proved to be enough. NATO fighter-bombers strafed strategic tar-gets, even hoping to kill Qaddafi. With the help of other nations (Qatar and the United Arab Emirates), the rebels on the ground had sufficient weapons to push into Tripoli. After eight months of fighting, Qaddafi was trapped.

When Qaddafi announced a willingness to negotiate a transfer of power, it was too late. His opponents wanted more than to get rid of him; they wanted their pound of flesh. Fearful for his life, hiding in abandoned houses, and scav-enging for scraps of food, Qaddafi was captured in October 2011, beaten to a pulp, and lynched, as were scores of his supporters, including black guest work-ers from sub-Saharan Africa.[3] It was all documented on video for posterity.

The new government inherited a country with much of its infrastructure in ruin and armed militias dictating the agenda. In September 2012, rebels attacked a CIA safe house in Benghazi, killing the US ambassador Christopher Stevens, two former Navy Seals, and a security contractor. During Qaddafi's reign Islamists had no visible presence in Libya (although flashes of Islamic anger occasionally could be seen in Benghazi), but now they set up shop there. The Libyan branch of Ansar al-Sharia was created in Sirte, in September 2011, on the eve of the final, decisive battle of the civil war. After the battle, they did not hesitate to join in the mass killing of Qaddafi loyalists.

In was possible that Ansar al-Sharia was responsible for the murder of Ambassador Stevens in Benghazi, although the likely culprit was a militia under the leadership of Ahmed Abu Khattala, who had openly declared that the

United States ranked just below Qaddafi as the enemy of Islam. (Abu Khattala, who had spent most of his adult years in Qadddafi's prisons, became notorious in Libya for killing a fellow rebel general for being insufficiently committed to establishing a Muslim theocracy.) The militias, having played a leading role in Qaddafi's overthrow, had no intention of laying down their arms. As they took aim at their new target, the United States, the situation became eerily reminiscent of what had transpired in Afghanistan in the 1980s, where militant Islamists, having defeated the Soviets, turning on their former comrades in arms.

Anger at a blasphemous video ridiculing Islam, produced by a Baptist minister in Gainesville, Florida, who had earlier won notoriety by burning a copy of the Koran, played a role as well in generating the violence in Benghazi. The residents of the city were well aware of the video, courtesy of television broadcasts. As in Cairo, where the video generated attacks on the US embassy, it now galvanized public opinion against the US presence in Benghazi. The attack appeared to have been a mix of spontaneous anger and spur-of-the-moment planning by Abu Khattala. Once the attack on the CIA safe house began, the Libyans on whom the United States had counted for protection simply melted away or joined the mob in looting it, rushing to carry out television sets, clothing, and food, before someone torched it.[4]

Whatever authority the government had, it was largely in name only. In Benghazi, a city awash in weapons, militias destroyed virtually every police station. In Tripoli, Prime Minister Ali Zeidan promised to bring the rival militias under control, but instead *jihadist* gunmen (thought to be on the payroll of the interior ministry) took Zeidan hostage. It was a rival militia, not the government, that secured Zeidan's release. The incident underscored the central authority's obvious weakness. While rebel militias vied for control of the nationalized oil industry, Libya's chief economic asset, oil workers went on strike. Two years after the death of Qaddafi, Libya still had no constitution and divisions between the secular National Forces Alliance (that the West had supported) and the renascent Muslim Brotherhood paralyzed the National Congress.[5]

## Morocco

After 9/11, the king of Morocco, Mohammed VI, was among the first Muslim rulers to side with the Bush administration in its global war on terror. That and the fact that Morocco was ostensibly a "constitutional monarchy" endeared him to Western observers. When the Arab Spring began, the king said all the right things and declared a commitment to much needed reforms. The constitution was revised and a moderate Islamist government was elected. And, indeed, Morocco withstood the shockwaves emanating from the upheavals throughout the Arab world.

Despite the reforms, Morocco's political system remained largely intact. Mohammed VI retained his powers, which included the right to govern by decree. In September 2013, for instance, the police arrested Ali Anouzla, an independent online journalist known for his opposition to al Qaeda. But he was also known for his criticism of the royal family. Anouzla's troubles began when he drew his readers' attention to an article in a Spanish newspaper that mentioned an al Qaeda video critical of Mohammed VI, charging him for presiding over "a kingdom of corruption and despotism." Anouzla's alleged crime consisted of posting a link to the Spanish newspaper that, in turn, offered a link to the al Qaeda video. By directing his readers, albeit in a circuitous way, to an al Qaeda pronouncement, he was charged with "knowingly providing material support" to terrorists. His real crime, however, was his past criticism of the king's doings. Morocco's constitutional monarchy, much hailed in the West, remained very much a work in progress. For the king, the Arab Spring turned out to be just a minor inconvenience.

## Egypt

Eleven days after Ben Ali fled Tunisia, on January 25, 2011, demonstrations commenced in Cairo's Tahrir Square to protest the three-decade-long military reign of the "pharaoh" Hosni Mubarak. As the ranks of the demonstrators swelled, security forces responded with force, killing hundreds of them. Yet the unrest spread. On February 11, after seventeen days of escalating demonstrations and a scant four weeks after Ben Ali had fled Tunisia, Mubarak was forced to step down. At that heady moment, everything seemed possible in the Middle East and not just in Egypt. A hopeful dawn appeared to be rising.

In May 2011, Mubarak, along with two of his sons, was arrested and ordered to stand trial. The bill of particulars included "intentional murder" of demonstrators, a charge that carried the death penalty. He was also accused of theft, of "unlawfully making private financial gains and profits."[6]

In June 2012, voters elected as their new president Mohammed Morsi, the candidate of the long-suppressed Muslim Brotherhood. The well-organized Brotherhood attracted devout Muslim voters, but also, perhaps more important, a vote for Morsi meant a vote against Ahmed Shafrik, Mubarak's last prime minister and a marshal in the Egyptian air force. Morsi and the Brotherhood became the beneficiaries of a backlash against the toppled regime. The political pendulum had swung from one extreme to the other. The question was how far it would go and whether it would generate a backlash.

Despite his relatively narrow victory (52–48 percent), Morsi treated it as a mandate to establish an Islamic state. The new constitution sought to enshrine the Brotherhood's permanent political domination. Human rights abuses—including murder, public lynching, and torture—were as egregious under the Brotherhood as under the old regime. "The police state," a Human Rights Watch official concluded, remained "alive and kicking with Morsi's blessing." Meanwhile, the economy, heavily dependent on tourism, remained in a tailspin. Throughout, the army stood in the wings, ready to participate in the rectification of recent trends.

The demonstrators had not risked their lives on behalf of an Islamist monopoly. Opposition to political Islam, even by practicing Muslims, had set Egypt apart from much of the Arab world. A year after Morsi's election, a groundswell of opposition—facilitated by online communication—grew even larger than the protests against Mubarak. Tamarod ("Rebellion"), an online movement launched by no more than half a dozen activists at the end of June 2013, brought millions of demonstrators—widely estimated at between 17 and 33 million people—into the streets and squares of Egypt. Tamarod also claimed to have collected 15 million online signatures demanding Morsi step down.

The Brotherhood increasingly stood alone while the army bided its time. In early July, the head of the army, Abdel Fattah el-Sissi, demanded that Morsi resign. When Morsi balked, the army arrested him two days later and outlawed the Brotherhood. Once more it became a crime to belong to the Brotherhood. The military—cheered by Egyptians who only recently had protested Mubarak—was back in power and Mubarak was released from prison. Egypt's first experiment in democracy had lasted only a year.

Following Morsi's arrest, the first confrontation between Islamists and the army claimed the lives of more than 1,000 demonstrators. Thereafter, violence continued unabated, with both sides committing atrocities.[7] After security forces killed more than fifty protesters at a large "anticoup" rally in early October, Islamists killed nine soldiers and police officers. Clashes between Islamists and the army were already a common occurrence, except that for the first time the insurgents used rocket-propelled grenade launchers, weapons eminently suited for guerrilla warfare.[8]

Throughout, the Obama administration, the self-appointed beacon of hope to the world, tacitly sided with the army. It refused to label its return to power as a military coup because US law forbade foreign aid to a government that had seized power in such a manner. Obama's secretary of state John Kerry went so far as to label Morsi's ouster as "restoring democracy."[9]

The events in Egypt reminded political analysts of how revolutions had played out in the past, particularly in nineteenth-century Europe. The bourgeoisie, the middle class, would topple the ancien regime with the help of the radicalized proletariat, the working class. But when the proletariat appeared to be getting ready for its bid for power, the frightened middle class would rally to the side of law and order.

## Syria

Between 1920 and 1946, France ruled Syria as part of its post–World War I mandate. After independence, Syria was plagued by a succession of unstable governments until the ostensibly socialist Ba'ath (Renovation) Party took power in 1963. By that time, however, the party was already an extension of the army. The Ba'athist seizure of power was essentially a military coup. In 1970, an Alawite faction in the army, led by Hafez Assad, the commander of the air force, took control of the Ba'ath Party and then purged it of its non-Alawite elements—primarily Sunni Muslims (three-quarters of the population) and Greek Orthodox Christians.

The roots of the civil war that began in Syria in March 2011 go back to days when the minority Alawites came to power. The Alawites understood that they were resented, even reviled, by the majority of Syrians. Their primary task, therefore, was to cling to power at all cost. When the Muslim Brotherhood seized the city of Hama in 1982 and murdered its Alawite-appointed officials, Assad sent 12,000 Alawite troops into Hama, who then leveled the city and massacred virtually all—perhaps as many as 30,000—Sunni Muslims.

The rise of Hafez Assad has been described as being as unlikely as a Jew becoming the tsar of Russia.[10] Assad came from Syria's most-hated religious group, the Alawites, approximately 12 percent on the population. In the West, Alawites (literally "followers of Ali") are generally described as Shiites. The Alawites, however, had split from Shia Islam more than a thousand years ago, after their leading theologian had pronounced the divinity of Ali. In the eyes of Islam, however, there is only one God. To suggest otherwise is sheer heresy.

Alawites keep their rites a secret from outsiders, but they appear to worship an amalgam of divine emanations—among them Adam, Zoroaster, Socrates, Plato, Christ, Simon Peter, Mohammed, and Ali. Some of their rituals resemble the Christian mass, including the consecration of bread and wine. Alawites celebrate Christmas and believe in reincarnation. Not surprisingly, Sunni Muslims refer to Alawites as "more infidel than Jews and Christians" and accuse them of past collaboration with the French and the crusaders. During the Ottoman reign, the Alawites were close to extinction.[11]

It should be noted, however, that there are Shia theologians who still consider the Alawites part of Shia Islam. That interpretation facilitated cooperation between the Assad regime and Shiite Hezbollah in Lebanon, Shiite-led Iran, and the Shiite Iraqi government, all whom were engaged in a bitter struggle against Sunnis, particularly those who had rallied to the al Qaeda cause.

When Hafez Assad died in June 2000, his Western-educated son, Bashar Assad, followed in his father's footsteps. There was initially talk of reforms, but mostly in the West. Alawites feared that reforms could unleash forces threatening them with genocide. The memory of Hama served as a reminder—to both the Alawites and their enemies—of the past sins of the Assad regime.

The Syrian uprising, it has been said, began as a Facebook revolution. Syrians were well educated, aware of the Arab Spring, and fed up with a hereditary dictatorship now forty years old. It began as a civil war against the Assad dictatorship but, as in all civil wars, it drew outside intervention. Iran, Iraq, Hezbollah, and Russia (its arms deliveries dating back to Soviet times) supported Assad. On the other side were militias tied to al Qaeda and supported by oil money from the Gulf states. There were also so-called "moderates" with a pro-Western orientation who, however, remained fairly weak.

Inevitably, there was talk in the United States about arming the rebels. But the question was, which faction? Many a rebel leader would tell reporters anything to obtain Western weapons. It became clear that the various rebel groups pursued their own interests, not necessarily those of the United States. After more than two years of fighting, the *New York Times* reported, "Nowhere in rebel-controlled Syria is there a secular [pro-Western] fighting force to speak of." A defeat of Assad threatened to bring to power jihadists who fought under black flags evocative of those of al Qaeda.[12] Their well-documented atrocities, which they themselves videotaped, served as a reminder of what was in store for Syria, and not just for the Assad regime, should they emerge victorious. The Alawites, in particular, understood that should they lose, genocide awaited them.

By the fall of 2013, jihadists carved out fiefdoms in several parts of Syria. "Al Qaeda in Iraq," a group that had cut its teeth fighting US troops in Iraq, now called itself the Islamic State of Iraq and Syria (ISIS). It first appeared in April 2013; by the end of the year, it was in control, of large stretches in northern Syria, where it swept aside all who stood in its way, including moderate Islamists. One of its goals was a pan-Arab state reminiscent of the caliphate. ISIS changed the nature of the Syrian war. It forced the West to reconsider its primary aim of getting rid of Assad.[13]

ISIS was by no means the only extremist Islamist group in Syria. Another such faction was Jabhat al-Nusra, yet another offshoot of al Qaeda. It, too, envisioned a pan-Arab state under Sunni *sharia* law. Competing jihadist factions ran schools, provided rudimentary medical care, effectively spread their message, and attracted recruits. As part of their propaganda, they videotaped the executions of Alawites. By reopening oil wells and natural gas plants, they served notice they were in Syria for the long haul. Unlike the weak pro-Western factions, they did not lack in outside support, much of it coming from the wealthy Gulf states. Their funding, fighters, and weapons entered Syria unimpeded through Turkey.[14]

John Kerry and his Russian counterpart, Foreign Minister Sergei Lavrov, hoped to broker a cease-fire leading to a political solution between Assad and pro-Western rebels. The latter, however, wanted no part of it. Instead, they lobbied for US intervention on their behalf. Obama, who earlier had said that Assad must go, understood that there was little to be gained by ousting Assad, but domestic politics drove him to declare that he would join the fray should Assad cross a "red line," the use of poison gas.

After 1,400 civilians (nearly 400 of them children) were killed by poison gas (ostensibly by Assad's troops) in August 2013, Obama faced a take-it-or-leave-it choice. If he went to war in Syria, it would be his war and everything that came with it—the casualties, the financial cost, the inevitable domestic and international outcry—would be his as well. If he did not act, he would be criticized for a lack of leadership. Opinion polls showed that the US public, still reeling from the effects of the wars in Iraq and Afghanistan (the latter still not yet over), wanted no part of another war. Thus, in a departure from recent history, Obama decided to leave the final decision to Congress. Congress gave the hot potato right back to the president.

As the hawks pushed Obama—who previously had declared that he was not against war per se, only against stupid wars—US naval and aerial forces prepared to attack. (Ground troops were never seriously considered.) Since Congress was not about to sanction war, Obama would have to go it alone. But then, in September, Kerry (who was chomping at the bit to start the bombing) was asked at a news conference what it would take to avoid a war. Assad could hand over his chemical arsenal, Kerry airily declared, but he was certain it would never happen. Moscow immediately responded, however, saying Assad was ready to hand over his chemical weapons to UN inspectors.

By now, the civilian death toll was already past the 100,000 mark and much of Syria's infrastructure was destroyed. The ancient city of Aleppo, its historic *souk* (market) still undergoing renovation under UN sponsorship, was largely in ruins. The relief agency CARE anticipated that by the end of 2013, the number of refugees who had fled Syria (not counting those internally displaced) would reach 3.4 million people (out of 22 million) and expected that half of Syria's population would be displaced or in need of assistance.[15] In the refugee camps, the scourge of polio returned, an illness thought to have been largely eradicated across the globe.

Assad's decision to permit UN inspectors on Syrian soil gave him a reprieve. It made it extremely difficult for the West to intervene. By the end of 2013, the Assad regime was holding its own, even as jihadist groups were gaining in strength across the Middle East. Ayman al-Zawahari, Osama bin Laden's successor as the overall leader of al Qaeda, saw Syria as key in the struggle for the Middle East. He envisioned it as an al Qaeda staging ground, similar to the role that Afghanistan had played in the years prior to 9/11.

In times like these, doctrinal differences generally are set aside. The Western democracies and the Soviet Union, for instance, made common cause against Hitler and Japan. In a rational world, the United States would have been on the side of Assad, who had rendered it assistance earlier during its global war on terror against al Qaeda. But these were not normal times.

Few officials in Washington were willing to discuss publicly what the retired veteran diplomat Ryan Crocker, the former US ambassador to Syria, suggested. The United States, Crocker explained, had mistakenly assumed that Syria would be like Tunisia or Egypt, where dictators were quickly replaced. Instead, Syria became a magnet for jihadists from far and wide, including from Western nations. Washington, Crocker said, needed to talk to Assad about issues of shared concern, namely counterterrorism. It would have to be done "very, very quietly," he went on to say, "but as bad as Assad is, he not as bad as the jihadis who would take over in his absence."[16]

Such a step would mean a remarkable shift. The United States, only recently on the verge of going to war against Assad, would have to embrace him as an ally against radical Islam. The domestic repercussions in the United States would be severe. But, as the chairman of the Joint Chiefs, Martin Dempsey, explained, the United States might not have much of a choice since the "al Qaeda brand" was "clearly expanding its affiliates, both in numbers and . . . capability."[17]

And it was not just Syria that was drawing terrorists. In Yemen, according to one of its officials, al Qaeda operated in a "perfect environment," taking hostages for ransom and ambushing government troops. In Lebanon, Shiite Hezbollah—hostile to the United States, Israel, and al Qaeda—was fighting for its survival. Its leader, Hassan Nasrallah, understood that if Assad fell, Hezbollah would be the next logical Shiite domino to fall. In the streets and neighborhoods of Beirut, Shiites supported by Iran and Sunnis supported by Saudi Arabia were killing each other. As Assad prepared to send long-range missiles to Hezbollah, the Israeli air force bombed the Syrian military base in Latakia (and for good measure Damascus). On the southern border of Lebanon, Hezbollah and the Israeli army were poised to resume their war.

In Egypt, the military was back in power, but in the Sinai Peninsula, well-armed jihadists were fighting back. Their arsenal included surface-to-air missiles, courtesy of the chaos in Libya. Jihadists were gaining in strength in the remote south of Libya. "The worm has turned in the Middle East," a former senior State Department adviser remarked. Counterterrorism was once again becoming a focal point of US foreign policy.[18]

## Notes

1. "Wikileaks Might Have Triggered Tunis' Revolution," *Al Arabiya News*, January 15, 2011; Steven Coll, "Democratic Movements," *The New Yorker*, January 31,

2011, pp. 21–22; the US embassy cables were published in *The Guardian*, December 7, 2010.

2. "Libya's Gaddafi Worried by Food Price Rises," Reuters, April 17, 2008.

3. Mark Urban, "Inside Story of the UK's Secret Mission to Beat Gaddafi," *BBC News Magazine*, January 19, 2012.

4. David D. Kirkpatrick, "Deadly Mix in Benghazi: False Allies, Crude Video," *New York Times*, December 29, 2013, pp. 1, 12–14.

5. Ibid.; Ghaith Shennib and Ulf Laessing, "Libyan PM Briefly Held by Gunmen Angry at U.S. Qaeda Capture," Reuters, October 10, 2013.

6. Yasmine Saleh and Dina Zayed, "Mubarak to Be Tried for Murder of Protesters," Reuters, May 24, 2011.

7. Yasmine El Rashidi, "Egypt: The Misunderstood Agony," *New York Review of Books*, September 26, 2013.

8. David D. Kirkpatrick, "Egyptian Attacks Are Escalating Amid Stalemate," *New York Times*, October 7, 2013.

9. Michael Birnbaum, "Egypt Orders End to Sit-Ins," *Washington Post*, August 2, 2013, p. A8.

10. Robert Kaplan, "Syria: Identity Crisis," *Atlantic*, February 1993.

11. Malise Ruthven, "Storm over Syria," *New York Review of Books*, June 9, 2010, p. 19; Robert F. Worth, "The Trap of Loyalty," *New York Times Magazine*, June 23, 2013, pp. 30–47.

12. Ben Hubbard, "Islamist Rebels Created Dilemma on Syria Policy," *New York Times*, April 28, 2013, p. 1.

13. Sarah Birke, "How al Qaeda Changed the Syrian War," *New York Review of Books*, December 27, 2013.

14. Loveday Morris, Joby Warrick and Souad Mekhennet, "Jihadist Gains Hurt West's Syria Plans," *Washington Post*, October 14, 2013, pp. A1, A15; "Rebel Atrocities," economist.com, October 13, 2013.

15. www.care.org

16. Robert F. Worth and Eric Schmitt, "Jihadist Groups Gain in Turmoil Across Middle East," *New York Times*, December 3, 2013; Michael Krever, "Syria Can Only Be Contained, not Extinguished Former U.S. Diplomat Ryan Crocker Tells CNN's Amanpour," CNN, September 11, 2013.

17. Worth and Schmitt, "Jihadist Groups Gain in Turmoil."

18. Ibid.

# Recommended Readings

## Chapter 1: The End of World War II and the Dawn of the Nuclear Age

### World War II

Beevor, Anthony. *The Second World War*. New York: Little, Brown, 2012.
  A comprehensive account of not merely the battles, but also of the human toll; its focus is on the irrationality and brutality of that conflict.

Buruma, Ian. *Year Zero: A History of 1945*. New York: Penguin, 2013.
  A well-received, truly global history of the aftermath of the war.

Dower, John W. *War Without Mercy: Race and Power in the Pacific War*. New York: Pantheon, 1986.
  A frank analysis of the racial nature of the war.

Hart, B. H. Liddell. *History of the Second World War*. New York: Putnam, 1971.
  One of the most highly regarded single-volume studies of World War II.

Saburo, Ienaga. *The Pacific War: World War Two and the Japanese, 1931–1945*. New York: Pantheon, 1978.
  A strong indictment of Japanese militarism.

Werth, Alexander. *Russia at War, 1941–1945*. New York: Dutton, 1964.
  Excellent look at the Soviet Union's wartime experience, by a British war correspondent, a native of St. Petersburg.

Wright, Gordon. *The Ordeal of Total War*. New York: Harper and Row, 1968.

### The Atomic Bomb

Alperovitz, Gar. *Atomic Diplomacy: Hiroshima and Potsdam*. New York: Simon and Schuster, 1965.
  An early revisionist interpretation arguing that the atomic bombs were used for diplomatic reasons, to influence the behavior of the Soviet Union.

———. *The Decision to Use the Atomic Bomb*. New York: Knopf, 1995.

Bernstein, Barton J., ed. *The Atomic Bomb: The Critical Issues*. Boston: Little, Brown, 1976.
  An excellent anthology of excerpts from the writings of some of those involved in the atomic bomb project and specialists on the topic.

Committee for the Compilation of Materials on Damage Caused by the Atomic Bombs in Hiroshima and Nagasaki. *Hiroshima and Nagasaki: The Physical, Medical, and Social Effects of the Atomic Bombs*. New York: Basic Books, 1981.
  The definitive study on the subject from the Japanese perspective.

Frank, Richard B. *Downfall: The End of the Imperial Japanese Empire*. New York: Penguin Books, 1999.
Argues that the use of the atomic bombs on Japan was necessitated by the "massive" build-up of Japan's forces on its home islands in the summer of 1945.

Hasegawa, Tsuyoshi. *Racing the Enemy: Stalin, Truman and the Surrender of Japan*. Cambridge, MA: Harvard University Press, 2005.
Further develops the Alperovitz theses (see above); based on sources not available to Alperovitz four decades earlier.

Hersey, John. *Hiroshima*. New York: Bantam, 1959.
A reporter's classic account of the destruction caused by the first atomic bomb attack.

Nobile, Philip, ed. *Judgment at the Smithsonian: The Bombing of Hiroshima and Nagasaki*. New York: Marlowe, 1995.
The Smithsonian's catalog for its controversial 1995 exhibit, before veterans' organizations and Congress banned it on grounds it challenged the orthodox interpretation.

Rhodes, Richard. *The Making of the Atomic Bomb*. New York: Simon and Schuster, 1986.
The first of a trilogy by a foremost authority on the topic, followed by *Dark Sun: The Making of the Hydrogen Bomb* (New York: Simon and Schuster, 1996) and *Twilight of the Bombs: Recent Challenges, New Dangers, and the Prospects for a World Without Nuclear Weapons* (New York: Vintage Books, 2010).

Sherwin, Martin J. *A World Destroyed: The Atomic Bomb and the Grand Alliance*. New York: Knopf, 1975.
Among the best studies of politics and diplomacy affecting the decision to drop the atomic bomb on Japan.

## Chapter 2: The Cold War Institutionalized

Andrzejewski, Jerzy. *Ashes and Diamonds*. London: Weidenfeld and Nicholson, 1965 [orig. 1948].
The classic novel on life in Poland at the very end of World War II.

Applebaum, Anne. *Iron Curtain: The Crushing of Eastern Europe, 1944–1956*. New York: Doubleday, 2012.
Primarily on the harsh fate of the people of Poland, the initial bone of contention of the Cold War.

Clemens, Diane Shaver. *Yalta*. New York: Oxford University Press, 1970.
Discusses Yalta not as an ideological confrontation but as an exercise in horse-trading.

de Zayas, Alfred M. *Nemesis at Potsdam: The Anglo-Americans and the Expulsion of the Germans: Background, Execution, Consequences*. 2nd rev. ed. London: Routledge and Kegan Paul, 1979.
Focuses on the refugee problem after the war, a topic generally ignored in Cold War histories.

Fleming, D. F. *The Cold War and Its Origins, 1917–1960*. 2 vols. Garden City, NY: Doubleday, 1961.
By one of the first practitioners of the revisionist school of history of the Cold War.

Halle, Louis J. *The Cold War as History*. New York: Harper and Row, 1967.
One of the few early books on the Cold War that put it into historical perspective.

Ulam, Adam B. *The Rivals: America and Russia Since World War II*. New York: Viking, 1971.

Discusses the first phase of the East-West confrontation.

————. *Expansion and Coexistence: Soviet Foreign Policy, 1917–1973.* 2nd ed. New York: Praeger, 1974.

Volkogonov, Dmitri. *Stalin: Triumph and Tragedy.* Rocklin, CA: Prima Publishing, 1991.
A product of Gorbachev's "new thinking" and glasnost, a critical reassessment of the reign of Stalin.

## Chapter 3: The Cold War in Asia: A Change of Venue

### Japan

Dower, John W. *Empire and Aftermath: Yoshida Shigeru and the Japanese Experience, 1878–1954.* Cambridge, MA: Harvard University Press, 1979.
An in-depth analysis of the politics of the US occupation authorities and the government of occupied Japan.

Kawai, Kazuo. *Japan's American Interlude.* Chicago: University of Chicago Press, 1960.
A firsthand account of the occupation by a Japanese American scholar who edited an English-language newspaper in Japan during the period.

Minear, Richard. *Victor's Justice: The Tokyo War Crimes Trials.* Princeton, NJ: Princeton University Press, 1971.
Argues that the war crimes trials were unjust.

Perry, John C. *Beneath the Eagle's Wings: Americans in Occupied Japan.* New York: Dodd, Mead, 1980.

Reischauer, Edwin O. *Japan: The Story of a Nation.* 4th ed. New York: Knopf, 1988.

### China

Bianco, Lucien. *The Origins of the Chinese Revolution, 1915–1949.* Palo Alto, CA: Stanford University Press, 1971.
Focuses on the strengths of the Communists and the failures of the Nationalists.

Fairbank, John K. *The United States and China.* 4th ed. Cambridge, MA: Harvard University Press, 1979.

Pepper, Suzanne. *Civil War in China: The Political Struggle, 1945–1949.* Berkeley: University of California Press, 1979.

Purifoy, Lewis M. *Harry Truman's China Policy: McCarthyism and the Diplomacy of Hysteria, 1947–1951.* New York: New Viewpoints, 1976.
Strongly critical of the US policy of supporting Jiang Jieshi.

Tsou, Tang. *America's Failure in China, 1941–1950.* Chicago: University of Chicago Press, 1963.
Argues that the United States had neither the means nor the will to achieve its goals in China.

Tuchman, Barbara. *Stilwell and the American Experience in China, 1911–1945.* New York: Macmillan, 1970.
A criticism of Jiang Jieshi and of US support for him.

### Korea

Cumings, Bruce. *The Origins of the Korean War: Liberation and the Emergence of Separate Regimes, 1945–1947.* Princeton, NJ: Princeton University Press, 1981.

————, ed. *Child of Conflict: The Korean American Relationship, 1943–1953.* Seattle: University of Washington Press, 1983.

Essays by revisionist historians that refute orthodox Western interpretations of the origins of the war.

———. *The Origins of the Korean War: II, The Roaring of the Cataract, 1947–1950.* Princeton, NJ: Princeton University Press, 1990.
The best scholarly analysis of the background and the early stages of the war.

Halberstam, David. *The Coldest Winter: America and the Korean War.* New York: Hyperion Books, 2007.
The war from the US side, by one of America's premier journalists.

Rees, David. *Korea: The Limited War.* Baltimore: Penguin, 1964.
Focuses on the uniqueness of this conflict as the first US limited war.

Spanier, John W. *The Truman-MacArthur Controversy and the Korean War.* New York: Norton, 1965.

Stone, I. F. *The Hidden History of the Korean War.* New York: Monthly Review Press, 1952. A provocative early revisionist version of the Korean War.

Whiting, Alan S. *China Crosses the Yalu: The Decision to Enter the Korean War.* New York: Macmillan, 1960.

## Chapter 4: Confrontation and Coexistence

### Western Europe

Judt, Tony. *Postwar: A History of Europe Since 1945.* New York: Penguin, 2005.
The magisterial, detailed treatment of the first sixty years.

Williams, Philip, and Martin Harrison. *Politics and Society in de Gaulle's Republic.* New York: Doubleday, 1971.
A focus on the politician most responsible for the political orientation of postwar France.

### The Cold War, 1953–1962

Beschloss, Michael. *Mayday: Eisenhower, Khrushchev, and the U-2 Affair.* New York: Harper and Row, 1986.
An analysis of the U-2 incident and its impact on US-Soviet relations.

———. *The Crisis Years: Kennedy and Khrushchev, 1960–1963.* New York: HarperCollins, 1991.
Detailed account of the Cold War confrontations of the early 1960s.

Bundy, McGeorge. *Danger and Survival: Choices of the Bomb in the First Fifty Years.* New York: Random House, 1988.
By the assistant to Secretary of War Henry Stimson and national security advisor to Lyndon Johnson.

Dallin, David. *Soviet Foreign Policy After Stalin.* Philadelphia: Lippincott, 1961.

Lebow, Richard Ned, and Janice Gross Stein. *We All Lost the Cold War.* Princeton, NJ: Princeton University Press, 1994.
A discussion of the resolutions of three East-West confrontations: the Cuban missile crisis, the Yom Kippur War of 1973, and the management of the nuclear deterrent.

Ra'anan, Uri. *The USSR Arms the Third World: Case Studies in Soviet Foreign Policy.* Cambridge, MA: MIT Press, 1969.
On the debates in the Kremlin over foreign policy after Stalin's death.

### Iran, Guatemala, and Cuba

Abel, Elie. *The Missile Crisis.* Philadelphia: Lippincott, 1966.
A journalist's account of the nuclear confrontation.

De Bellaigue, Christopher. *Patriot of Persia: Muhammed Mossadesh and a Tragic Anglo-American Coup.* New York: Harper Perennial, 2013.
A full-length study on the roots of the US-Iranian confrontation.

Dobbs, Michael. *One Minute to Midnight: Kennedy, Khrushchev, and Castro on the Brink of War.* New York: Knopf, 2008.
The definitive account of the crisis.

English, T. J. *Havana Nocturne: How the Mob Owned Cuba—and Then Lost It to the Revolution.* New York: Morrow, 2008.

Kennedy, Robert F. *Thirteen Days: A Memoir of the Cuban Missile Crisis.* New York: Norton, 1969.
By the president's brother, what may be called the official US view.

Kinzer, Stephen. *All the Shah's Men: An American Coup and the Roots of Middle East Terror.* Hoboken, NJ: John Wiley and Sons, 2003.
How the CIA overthrew Mossadegh's elected government in Iran.

Schlesinger, Stephen, and Stephen Kinzer. *Bitter Fruit: The Untold Story of the American Coup in Guatemala.* Revised and expanded. Cambridge, MA: Harvard University Press, 2005.
The definitive account of the CIA's coup of 1954.

Szulc, Tad. *Fidel: A Critical Portrait.* New York: Morrow, 1986.
A detailed biography that offers the thesis that Castro was already a Communist before seizing political power.

Walton, Richard J. *Cold War and Counterrevolution: The Foreign Policy of John F. Kennedy.* New York: Viking, 1972.
Contains two chapters highly critical of Kennedy's handling of the Bay of Pigs and the missile crisis.

Wyden, Peter. *Bay of Pigs: The Untold Story.* New York: Simon and Schuster, 1979.
On the CIA's ill-fated attempt to overthrow Fidel Castro.

## Chapter 5: Decolonization in Asia

### India and Pakistan
Brown, W. Norman. *The United States and India, Pakistan, Bangladesh.* 3rd ed. Cambridge, MA: Harvard University Press, 1972.

Burleigh, Michael. *Small Wars, Faraway Places: Global Insurrection and the Making of the Modern World, 1945–1965.* New York: Viking, 2013.
On the difficulty of suppressing anticolonial insurrections during the Cold War.

Hutchins, Francis G. *India's Revolution: Gandhi and the Quit India Movement.* Cambridge, MA: Harvard University Press, 1973.

Merriam, Allen H. *Gandhi vs. Jinnah: The Debate over the Partition of India.* Calcutta: Minerva, 1980.

Scott, Paul. *The Raj Quartet.* Published in various editions between 1966 and 1975.
A novel examining the dark side of the British Raj—its legal and moral pretensions; the questions of race, ethnicity, religion; sexual mores guiding the rulers and their subjects; and the independence movement—at the time of its demise, 1942–1947.

### Vietnam
Duiker, William J. *Ho Chi Minh.* New York: Hyperion, 2000.
Definitive biography that emphasizes Ho's nationalism, not Communism, as the wellspring of Ho's ideology.

Fall, Bernard B. *Hell in a Very Small Place: The Siege of Dien Bien Phu.*
Philadelphia: Lippincott, 1966.
By one of the leading Western authorities on Indochina until his death in
Vietnam in 1967.
————, ed. *Ho Chi Minh on Revolution: Selected Writings, 1920–66.* New York:
Praeger, 1967.
A collection of primary sources.
Joint Chiefs of Staff. *The Joint Chiefs of Staff and the War in Vietnam: History of the
Indochina Incident, 1940–1954.* Washington, DC: Joint Chiefs of Staff, 1955,
declassified 1981.
The Pentagon's assessment of why the French lost.
Patti, Archimedes. *Why Vietnam? Prelude to America's Albatross.* Berkeley:
University of California Press, 1980.
By a US OSS officer who established a working relationship with Ho Chi Minh
in 1945.
Vo Nguyen Giap. *People's War, People's Army.* New York: Praeger, 1962.
Vo Nguyen Giap's discussion of the nature of wars for national liberation and
the reasons for his victory at Dien Bien Phu.

## Chapter 6: Decolonization in Sub-Saharan Africa

### Black Africa

Anderson, David. *Histories of the Hanged: The Dirty War in Kenya and the End of
Empire.* New York: Norton, 2005.
Based largely on the official record in London.
Brendon, Piers. *The Decline and Fall of the British Empire, 1781–1997.* New York:
Knopf, 2008.
A reminder that the history of empires, as the historian Edward Gibbon put it,
"is the history of human misery," rebellion, and decline.
Cartey, Wilfred, and Martin Kilson, eds. *The African Reader: Independent Africa.*
New York: Random House, 1970.
A anthology of writings by participants in the African independence move-
ment.
Davidson, Basil. *Black Star: A View of the Life and Times of Kwame Nkrumah.*
London: James Currey Publishers, 2007.
Reprint of the 1973 edition; still among the best political biographies of Nkrumah.
Elkins, Caroline. *Imperial Reckoning: The Untold Story of Britain's Gulag in Kenya.*
New York: Henry Holt, 2005.
A history based to a great extent on the stories of the survivors.
Hochschild, Adam. *King Leopold's Ghost: A Story of Greed, Terror, and Heroism in
Colonial Africa.* Boston: Houghton Mifflin, 1999.
The tale of unchecked colonialist exploitation, slavery, and the murder of millions.
McQueen, Norrie. *The Decolonization of Portuguese Africa: Metropolitan Revolution
and the Dissolution of Empire.* London: Longman, 1997.
Mazrui, Ali A. *The Africans: A Triple Heritage.* Boston: Little, Brown, 1986.
An introduction to the culture and politics of Africa by a native of Kenya whose
emphasis is on the European colonial heritage; a companion volume to the
BBC/WETA television series.
Mazrui, Ali A., and Michael Tidy. *Nationalism and New States in Africa.* London:
Heinemann Educational Books, 1984.
A survey of the decolonization process in Africa, focusing on Ghana.

Nkrumah, Kwame. *The Struggle Continues*. London: Panaf Books, 2006.
  Reprints of six pamphlets discussing topics such as "positive action," "black
  power," and economic sovereignty.

### South Africa
Boraine, Alex. *A Country Unmasked: Inside South Africa's Truth and Reconciliation
  Commission*. New York: Oxford University Press, 2001.
  By the deputy chair of the commission, a former president of the South African
  Methodist Church and antiapartheid activist.
Breytenbach, Breyten. *The True Confessions of an Albino Terrorist*. New York:
  Farrar, Straus and Giroux, 1984.
  By a poet from a well-known Afrikaner family who became a revolutionary
  activist.
Lelyveld, Joseph. *Move Your Shadow: South Africa, Black and White*. New York:
  Times Books, 1985.
  A *New York Times* reporter explains the South African racial divisions.
Malan, Rian. *My Traitor's Heart: A South African Exile Returns to Face His Country,
  His Tribe, and His Conscience*. New York: Atlantic Monthly Press, 1990.
Mandela, Nelson. *The Struggle Is My Life*. New York: Pathfinder Press, 1986.
  A collection of Mandela's speeches and writings.
———. *The Long Walk to Freedom: The Autobiography of Nelson Mandela*. Boston:
  Little, Brown, 1995.
Shea, Dorothy. *The South African Truth Commission: The Politics of Reconciliation*.
  Washington, DC: United States Institute of Peace, 2000.
Thompson, Leonard. *The Political Mythology of Apartheid*. New Haven, CT: Yale
  University Press, 1985.
  On the origins of apartheid.
Woods, Donald. *Biko*. New York: Paddington Press, 1978.
  A white South African's sympathetic treatment of Steve Biko.

### Chapter 7: Decolonization in the Arab World
Fanon, Frantz. *A Dying Colonialism*. New York: Monthly Review Press, orig. 1959;
  English edition, 1965.
  By a native of the West Indies, a psychiatrist, on the psychological disorientation
  French colonialism created in Algeria.
———. *The Wretched of the Earth*. New York: Grove Press, 1963.
  Fanon's most influential book on the psychological impact of colonialism.
Ginat, Rami. *Egypt's Incomplete Revolution: Lutfi al-Khuli and Nasser's Socialism in
  the 1960s*. London: Routledge, 1997.
  Charts the evolution of Nasser's version of Arab socialism.
Horne, Alistair. *A Savage War of Peace: Algeria, 1954–1962*. New York: New York
  Review Books, 2006 [orig. 1977].
  After more than thirty years, still the authoritative history of the war.
Lobban, Richard Andrew, Jr., and Christopher H. Dalton. *Libya: History and
  Revolution*. New York: Praeger, 2014.
Miller, Susan Gilson. *A History of Modern Morocco*. Cambridge, UK: Cambridge
  University Press, 2013.
  The second half covers events since 1945.
Murphy, Emma C. *Economic and Political Change in Tunisia: From Bourguiba to
  Ben Ali*. New York: Palgrave Macmillan, 1999.
Nasser, Gamal Abdel. *Egypt's Liberation: The Philosophy of the Revolution*.

Washington, DC: Public Affairs Press, 1955.

Seale, Patrick. *Asad: The Struggle for the Middle East.* Rev. ed. Berkeley: University of California Press, 1999.

_____. *The Struggle for Arab Independence: Riad el-Solh and the Makers of the Modern Middle East.* Cambridge, UK: Cambridge University Press, 2010.
Carefully researched history of the decline of French influence and the making of the modern Middle East through the life of Lebanon's first prime minister.

Talbott, John. *The War Without a Name: France in Algeria, 1954–1962.* New York: Random House, 1980.

Wilford, Hugh. *America's Great Game: The CIA's Secret Arabists and Shaping of the Modern Middle East.* New York: Basic Books, 2013.
How the CIA switched from working with Arab nationalists to opposing them by mistaking them as budding Communists.

Zeine, Zeine N. *The Struggle for Arab Independence: Western Diplomacy and the Rise and Fall of Faisal's Kingdom in Syria,* 2nd ed. Ann Arbor, MI: Caravan Books, 1971.

## Chapter 8: The Arab-Israeli Conflict

Avineri, Shlomo. *The Making of Modern Zionism: The Intellectual Origins of the Jewish State.* New York: Basic Books, 1981.
An explanation of the intellectual climate of the nineteenth century that produced the Zionist movement.

Elon, Amos. *The Israelis: Founders and Sons.* New York: Holt, Rinehart and Winston, 1971.
On the roots of Zionism and the first two decades of the existence of Israel.

Fisk, Robert. *The Great War for Civilization: The Conquest of the Middle East.* New York: Knopf, 2007.
By arguably the best-informed Western reporter on the Middle East, writing for Britain's *Independent.*

Kimmerling, Baruch, and Joel S. Migdal. *Palestinians: The Making of a People.* New York: Free Press, 1993.
How a clan-centered Arab population acquired a national collective character.

Lilienthal, Alfred M. *The Zionist Connection: What Price Peace?* Rev. ed. New Brunswick, NJ: North American, 1982.
An account critical of Zionism.

Oz, Amos. *In the Land of Israel.* New York: Random House, 1983.
By an Israeli novelist who dwells on Israel's contradictions.

Peters, Joan. *From Time Immemorial: The Origins of the Arab-Jewish Conflict over Palestine.* New York: Harper and Row, 1984.
An ambitious, controversial attempt to prove that the Jews did not displace the Arabs in Palestine but instead that Arabs had displaced Jews.

Rabinovich, Abraham. *The Yom Kippur War: The Epic Encounter That Transformed the Middle East.* New York: Schocken, 2004.
An Israeli journalist's definitive account of the war told from the Israeli side; The Arab view of the "Ramadan" War is covered only sketchily.

Said, Edward W. *The Question of Palestine.* New York: Random House, 1980.
By a US scholar of Palestinian descent, this is the classic study championing the Palestinian cause.

———. *The End of the Peace Process: Oslo and After.* New York: Pantheon, 2000.
Collection of essays highly critical of both the Palestinian and Israeli leaderships.

Segev, Tom. *1949: The First Israelis.* New York: Free Press, 1985.

A controversial best-seller in Israel, a reinterpretation, particularly of the origin of the refugee problem.

———. *One Palestine, Complete: Jews and Arabs.* New York: Henry Holt, 2000.
    A revisionist, also known as "post-Zionist," treatment of the British mandate period from the Zionist and Palestinian perspective by an Israeli journalist and historian.

Shavit, Ari. *My Promised Land: The Triumph and Tragedy of Israel.* New York: Spiegel & Grau, 2013.
    A Zionist's recognition that the "miracle" of the state of Israel was "based on denial" that others occupied the land.

Shehadeh, Raja. *Samed: Journal of a West Bank Palestinian.* New York: Adama Publishers, 1984.
    Life on the West Bank from a Palestinian's perspective.

## Chapter 9: The Communist World After Stalin

Bethell, Nicholas. *Gomulka: His Poland, His Communism.* New York: Holt, Rinehart and Winston, 1969.
    An explanation of the Polish road to socialism.

Chen Jian. *Mao's China and the Cold War.* Chapel Hill: University of North Carolina Press, 2001.

Clubb, O. Edmund. *China and Russia: The "Great Game."* New York: Columbia University Press, 1971.
    A comprehensive and evenhanded analysis of the Sino-Soviet split by a US diplomat-turned-scholar.

Crankshaw, Edward. *Khrushchev: A Career.* New York: Viking, 1966.

Deutscher, Isaac. *Stalin: A Political Biography.* Rev. ed. New York: Oxford University Press, 1966.
    The classic biography by a Trotskyite.

Hinton, Harold C. *China's Turbulent Quest.* 2nd ed. New York: Macmillan, 1973.
    An analysis of the Sino-Soviet rift.

Kecskemeti, Paul. *The Unexpected Revolution: Social Forces in the Hungarian Uprising.* Stanford, CA: Stanford University Press, 1961.

London, Kurt, ed. *Eastern Europe in Transition.* Baltimore: Johns Hopkins University Press, 1966.
    A study of the force of nationalism in Eastern Europe.

Medvedev, Roy A. *Let History Judge: The Origins and Consequences of Stalinism.* New York: Knopf, 1971.
    An indictment of Stalin by a Soviet "Leninist" historian.

Medvedev, Roy A., and Zhores A. Medvedev. *Khrushchev: The Years in Power.* New York: Norton, 1978.

Shipler, David K. *Russia: Broken Idols, Solemn Dreams.* New York: Times Books, 1983.
    A discussion of Soviet society at the end of the Brezhnev era, by a correspondent of the *New York Times.*

Solzhenitsyn, Alexander. *One Day in the Life of Ivan Denisovich.* New York: Praeger, 1962.
    An exposé of Stalin's forced-labor camps, the novel that brought Solzhenitsyn international acclaim.

Tatu, Michel. *Power in the Kremlin: From Khrushchev to Kosygin.* London: William Collins Sons, 1968.
    A well-received study of Soviet politics by a French expert.

Taubman, William. *Khrushchev: The Man and His Era.* New York: Norton, 2003.
    The definitive biography.

Ulam, Adam. *Stalin: The Man and His Era.* New York: Viking, 1973.

A highly readable, detailed biography written from a Western perspective.

Valenta, Jiri. *Soviet Intervention in Czechoslovakia in 1968*. Baltimore: Johns Hopkins University Press, 1979.

An analysis of the Kremlin's reasons for ending the Czechoslovak experiment in liberalization.

## Chapter 10: The War in Indochina

Appy, Christian G. *Patriots: The Vietnam War Remembered from All Sides*. New York: Penguin, 2003.

An oral history consisting of approximately 140 interviews of participants, US as well as Vietnamese.

Arnett, Peter. *Live from the Battlefield: From Vietnam to Baghdad, 35 Years in the World's War Zones*. New York: Touchstone, 1994.

By an AP reporter from New Zealand.

Fall, Bernard B. *Vietnam Witness, 1953–1966*. New York: Praeger, 1966.

One of several books by a French historian, widely considered the West's leading authority on Vietnam.

FitzGerald, Frances. *Fire in the Lake: The Vietnamese and the Americans in Vietnam*. New York: Random House, 1972.

Places the US intervention in a context of Vietnamese history.

Halberstam, David. *The Best and the Brightest*. New York: Random House, 1972.

By a former *New York Times* reporter, still the best account of how Washington was drawn into the war.

———. *The Making of a Quagmire: America and Vietnam During the Kennedy Era*. Rev. ed. New York: Knopf, 1988 [1964].

Reportage at its best.

Hersh, Seymour. *My Lai Four: A Report on the Massacre and Its Aftermath*. New York: Random House, 1970.

Isaacs, Arnold R. *Without Honor: Defeat in Vietnam and Cambodia*. Baltimore: Johns Hopkins University Press, 1983.

Just, Ward, ed. *Reporting Vietnam: American Journalism, 1959–1975*. New York: Library of America, 1998.

Excellent selection of articles.

McNamara, Robert S. *In Retrospect: The Tragedy and Lessons of Vietnam*. New York: Times Books/Random House, 1995.

The mea culpa of the secretary of defense for Presidents Kennedy and Johnson.

Moyar, Mark. *Triumph Forsaken: The Vietnam War, 1954–1965*. Cambridge, UK: Cambridge University Press, 2006.

One of several post-revisionist histories arguing the United States actually had won the war, only to abandon certain victory.

Shawcross, William. *Sideshow: Kissinger, Nixon, and the Destruction of Cambodia*. New York: Simon and Schuster, 1979.

A discussion of the widening of Nixon's war into Cambodia.

Sheehan, Neil. *A Bright Shining Lie: John Paul Vann and America in Vietnam*. New York: Random House, 1988.

A critical account of the US conduct of the war in Vietnam.

Sheehan, Neil, et al., eds. *The Pentagon Papers*. New York: Bantam, 1971.

A useful, abridged version of the official Pentagon collection of documents and interpretation.

Turse, Nick. *Kill Anything That Moves: The Real American War in Vietnam*. New York: Macmillan, 2013.

Discusses the arbitrary violence visited on South Vietnam, an aspect of the war generally given short shrift in most histories.

## Chapter 11: Détente and the End of Bipolarity

Bueler, William M. *US China Policy and the Problem of Taiwan.* Boulder: Colorado Associated University Press, 1971.
> An analysis of the Taiwan issue on the eve of Nixon's visit.

Fairbank, John K. *The United States and China.* 4th ed. Cambridge, MA: Harvard University Press, 1983.
> A standard work that provides a historical account of Sino-US relations as well as a survey of Chinese history.

Garthoff, Raymond. *Détente and Confrontation: American-Soviet Relations from Nixon to Reagan.* Washington, DC: Brookings Institution, 1985.
> A most detailed analysis of a complex relationship.

Griffith, William E. *Peking, Moscow, and Beyond: The Sino-Soviet Triangle.* Washington, DC: Center for Strategic International Studies, 1973.
> Discusses the implications of Nixon's visit to Beijing.

Hersh, Seymour M. *The Price of Power: Kissinger in the Nixon White House.* New York: Summit Books, 1983.
> A devastating analysis of Kissinger's foreign policy.

Schaller, Michael. *The United States and China in the Twentieth Century.* New York: Oxford University Press, 1979.
> A useful study that takes the story well beyond the Nixon visit to China.

Ulam, Adam B. *Dangerous Relations: The Soviet Union in World Politics, 1970–1982.* New York: Oxford University Press, 1983.
> On the rise and fall of détente.

## Chapter 12: The Challenges of Economic Development

Barnet, Richard J. *The Lean Years: Politics in the Age of Scarcity.* New York: Simon and Schuster, 1980.
> A study of the political factors involved in sharing limited global resources.

Brown, Lester R., et al. *State of the World, 1986.* New York: Norton/Worldwatch Books, 1984–2012.
> Annually updated reference on global issues.

Ehrlich, Paul E., and Anne H. Ehrlich. *The Population Explosion.* New York: Simon and Schuster, 1990.
> Sequel to Paul Ehrlich's *The Population Bomb* (1968), warning of the dangers of rampant population growth.

Emerson, Steven. *The American House of Saud: The Secret Petrodollar Connection.* Danbury, CT: Franklin Watts, 1985.

George, Susan. *Ill Fares the Land: Essays on Food, Hunger, and Power.* Rev. and expanded ed. London: Penguin, 1990.
> A sociological inquiry into what went wrong with agricultural planning in the South.

Graebner, David. *Debt: The First 5,000 Years.* New York: Melville House, 2013.
> A history of debt forgiveness serving as a spur to economic development.

Harrison, Paul. *Inside the Third World.* 2nd ed. New York: Penguin, 1984.
> An excellent, highly readable survey of the dilemmas facing the South.

Lacey, Robert. *The Kingdom: Arabia and the House of Sa'ud.* New York: Avon, 1983.

Sampson, Anthony. *The Sovereign State of ITT.* 2nd ed. New York: Fawcett, 1974.
> By an English muckraking reporter who wrote several popular books on global

economic issues. This book discusses ITT's reach, particularly into Latin America.

———. *The Seven Sisters*. New York: Viking, 1975.

On the doings of the major international oil companies.

———. *The Money Lenders: The People and Politics of International Banking*. New York: Penguin, 1982.

World Bank. *World Development Report: Development and Environment*. New York: Oxford University Press, 1992.

Fifteenth in an annual series, it discusses the link among economic development, population pressures, and the environment.

## Chapter 13: Africa

Bayart, Jean François, and Stephen Ellis. *The Criminalization of the State in Africa*. London: Oxford University Press, 1999.

A critical look at Africa's major political problem.

Biney, Ama. *The Political and Social Thought of Kwame Nkrumah*. New York: Palgrave Macmillan, 2011.

A study of Nkrumah's contradictions.

Gourevitch, Philip. *We Wish to Inform You That Tomorrow We Will Be Killed with Our Families: Stories from Rwanda*. New York: Farrar, Straus and Giroux, 1998.

A reporter's account of the genocide in Rwanda.

Leys, Colin. *Underdevelopment in Kenya: The Political Economy of Neo-Colonialism*. Berkeley: University of California Press, 1975.

Lewis, Tim. *Land of Second Chances: The Impossible Rise of Rwanda's Cycling Team*. Boulder, CO: Velo Press, 2013.

On Rwanda digging out from under the rubble after the genocide.

Lloyd-Jones, Stewart, and Antonio Costa Pinto, eds. *The Last Empire: Thirty Years of Portuguese Decolonization*. Bristol, UK: Intellect Books, 2003.

Meredith, Martin. *The Fate of Africa: A History of the Continent Since Independence*. Rev. updated ed. New York: Public Affairs, 2011.

A sweeping survey from the "Gold Coast experiment" to "somewhere over the rainbow."

Neuberger, Ralph Benyamin. *National Self-Determination in Postcolonial Africa*. Boulder, CO: Lynne Rienner Publishers, 1986.

On the impact of colonialism on postcolonial African nationalism and secession.

Soyinka, Wole. *The Open Sore of a Continent: A Personal Narrative of the Nigerian Crisis*. New York: Oxford University Press, 1996.

By the Nigerian Nobel laureate for literature.

## Chapter 14: Latin America

### Latin America—General

Gill, Leslie. *The School of the Americas: Military Training and Political Violence in the Americas*. Durham, NC: Duke University Press, 2004.

Rosenberg, Tina. *Children of Cain: Violence and the Violent in Latin America*. New York: Penguin, 1991.

Wolf, Eric R., and Edward C. Hansen. *The Human Condition in Latin America*. New York: Oxford University Press, 1974.

### South America

Blanco, Hugo. *Land or Death: The Peasant Struggle in Peru*. New York: Pathfinder Press, 1972.

A longtime revolutionary argues his case for radical land reform.

Burns, E. Bradford. *A History of Brazil.* 2nd ed. New York: Columbia University Press, 1980.

Guardiola-Rivera, Oscar. *Story of a Death Foretold: The Coup Against Salvador Allende, 11 September 1973.* New York: Bloomsbury, 2013.
Focuses on the US role.

Rohter, Larry. *Brazil on the Rise: The Story of a Country Transformed.* New York: Palgrave Macmillan, 2010.
Brazil on the rise, both as an economic power and in its self-esteem.

Valenzuela, Arturo. *The Breakdown of Democratic Regimes: Chile.* Baltimore: Johns Hopkins University Press, 1978.
Strongly critical of the militarist intervention in Chile.

Whitaker, Arthur P. *The United States and the Southern Cone: Argentina, Chile, and Uruguay.* Cambridge, MA: Harvard University Press, 1976.

### Central America and Mexico

Berryman, Phillip. *Inside Central America: The Essential Facts Past and Present on El Salvador, Nicaragua, Honduras, Guatemala, and Costa Rica.* New York: Pantheon, 1985.
By the Central American representative of the American Friends Service Committee.

Chace, James. *Endless War: How We Got Involved in Central America and What Can Be Done.* New York: Vintage, 1984.
A brief, popular, but insightful historical analysis.

Corchado, Alfredo. *Midnight in Mexico: A Reporter's Journey Through a Country's Descent into Darkness.* New York: Penguin Press, 2013.
On Mexico's social and economic problem in the eve of the PRI's return to power in 2012.

Danner, Mark. *The Massacre at El Mozote.* New York: Random House, 1993.

Diedrich, Bernard. *Somoza and the Legacy of US Involvement.* New York: Dutton, 1981.

LaFeber, Walter. *Inevitable Revolution: The United States in Central America.* Expanded ed. New York: Norton, 1984.
By a well-known revisionist historian on the role of the United States in the Cold War.

Lopez Vigil, José Ignacio. *Rebel Radio: The Story of El Salvador's Radio Venceremos.* Willimantic, CT: Curbstone Press, 1995.
An oral history of the "Voice of the Voiceless," which broadcast nightly from the mountains of El Salvador from 1981 until the peace accord of 1992.

Schlesinger, Stephen, and Stephen Kinzer. *Bitter Fruit: The Untold Story of the American Coup in Guatemala.* Garden City, NY: Doubleday, 1982.
The best-seller on the CIA's 1954 coup in Guatemala.

### Chapter 15: The People's Republic of China and Taiwan

Bergston, C. Fred. *China: The Balance Sheet: What the World Needs to Know About the Emerging Superpower.* Washington, DC: Public Affairs, 2006.

Evans, Richard. *Deng Xiaoping and the Making of Modern China.* London: Penguin, 1992.

Hsu, Immanuel C. Y. *The Rise of Modern China.* 6th ed. New York: Oxford University Press, 2000.
An excellent, evenhanded, and comprehensive history.

Jung Chang and Jon Holliday. *Mao: The Untold Story.* London: Jonathan Cape, 2005.

An unflattering, carefully researched biography of Mao, dedicated to his victims.

Meisner, Maurice. *Mao's China and After: A History of the People's Republic*. New York: Free Press, 1986.

Assesses Chinese politics on its own Marxist terms.

Schell, Orville. *In the People's Republic*. New York: Random House, 1977.

An eyewitness account of the PRC shortly after Mao's death.

———. *Mandate of Heaven: The Legacy of Tiananmen and the Next Generation of Chinese Leaders*. New York: Simon and Schuster, 1994.

Schell, Orville, and John Delury, *Wealth and Power: China's Long March to the Twenty-first Century*. New York: Random House, 2013.

Puts Deng's reforms in the context of the past two centuries.

Yang Jisheng. *Tombstone: The Great Chinese Famine, 1958–1962*. New York: Farrar, Straus & Giroux, 2012.

A reinterpretation of the Great Leap Forward: far worse than previously thought.

Zhang Liang, Perry Link, and Andrew J. Nathan. *The Tiananmen Papers: The Chinese Leadership's Decision to Use Force Against Their Own People—In Their Own Words*. New York: New York Review of Books, 2003.

## Chapter 16: The Indian Subcontinent and Southeast Asia

### South Asia

Ali, S. Mahmud. *The Fearful State: Power, People, and Internal War in South Asia*. London: Zed Books, 1993.

A study of insurrection in South Asian separatist groups, such as the Sikhs and the Tamils.

Barnds, William J. *India, Pakistan, and the Great Powers*. New York: Praeger, 1972.

Bhatia, Krishan. *The Ordeal of Nationhood: A Social Study of India Since Independence, 1947–1970*. New York: Atheneum, 1970.

Brecher, Michael. *Nehru: A Political Biography*. London: Oxford University Press, 1959.

Dhar, P. N. *Indira Gandhi, the "Emergency," and Indian Democracy*. New Delhi: Oxford University Press, 2000.

A combination of memoir and history, critical of Indira Gandhi, by one of her close advisors at the time of the "Emergency."

Kangas, G. L. *Population Dilemma: India's Struggle for Survival*. London: Heinemann, 1985.

Margolis, Eric S. *War at the Top of the World*. New York: Routledge, 2000.

On the extension of the India-Pakistan conflict into the glaciers of the Himalayas.

### Southeast Asia

Ali, Anuwar. *Malaysia's Industrialization: The Quest for Technology*. Singapore: Oxford University Press, 1992.

Crouch, Harold A. *The Army and Politics in Indonesia*. Ithaca, NY: Cornell University Press, 1988.

Diamond, Larry, Juan Linz, and Seymour Martin Lipset, eds. *Democracy in Developing Countries: Asia*. Boulder, CO: Lynne Rienner Publishers, 1989.

Kulick, Elliot, and Dick Wilson. *Thailand's Turn: Profile of a New Dragon*. New York: St. Martin's Press, 1992.

Palmer, Ronald D., and Thomas J. Reckford. *Building ASEAN: 20 Years of Southeast Asian Cooperation*. New York: Praeger, 1987.

Taylor, John G. *Indonesia's Forgotten War: The Hidden History of East Timor.*
    London: Zed Books, 1991.
    An exposé of Indonesia's ongoing effort to suppress the Timorese nationalist
    movement.
Wurfel, David. *Filipino Politics: Development and Decay.* Ithaca, NY: Cornell
    University Press, 1988.

## Chapter 17: The Globalization of the Economy

Bhagwati, Jagdish. *In Defense of Globalization: With a New Afterword.* New York:
    Oxford University Press, 2007.
    A Columbia University professor's reply to, *Globalization and Its Discontents*
    by his colleague Joseph Stiglitz (see below.)
Chang Ha-Joon. *Bad Samaritans: The Myth of Free Trade and the Secret History of
    Capitalism.* New York: Bloomsbury Press, 2008.
    A rejection of unfettered capitalism's the "world-is-flat" thesis by the *New York
    Times* columnist Thomas Friedman, a fervent booster of globalization, as the
    answer for the world's poor nations.
Dinan, Desmond. *Ever Closer Union: An Introduction to European Integration.* 4th
    ed. Boulder, CO: Lynne Rienner Publishers, 2010.
Frank, Thomas. *One Market Under God: Extreme Capitalism, Market Populism, and
    the End of Economic Democracy.* New York: Doubleday, 2000.
    A critical view of the negative consequences of globalization.
Galeano, Eduardo. *Upside Down: A Primer for the Looking-Glass World.* New York:
    Henry Holt, 2000.
    By a Guatemalan writer who tells the story of globalization from the perspective
    of the South.
Harrison, Paul. *Inside the Third World: The Anatomy of Poverty.* 2nd ed. New York:
    Penguin, 1981.
    An English journalist's introduction to the realities of the Third World.
Kuttner, Robert. *The End of Laissez-Faire: National Purpose and Global Economy
    After the Cold War.* New York: Knopf, 1991.
    An argument on behalf of a US national economic strategy.
Reid, T. R. *The United States of Europe: The New Superpower and the End of
    American Supremacy.* New York: Penguin, 2004.
Sen, Amartya. *Inequality Reexamined.* Cambridge, MA: Harvard University Press,
    1995.
    One of several books by the recipient of the 1998 Nobel Prize for Economics;
    its focus is on the downside of globalization, that is, on its impact on those left
    behind.
Stiglitz, Joseph E. *Globalization and Its Discontents.* New York: Norton, 2002.
    By the former chief economist at the World Bank, a critique of how the major
    institutions of globalization failed many of the developing nations.
Stiglitz, Joseph E., and Shahid Yusuf, eds. *Rethinking the East Asian Miracle.* New
    York: Oxford University Press, 2000.
    A collection of articles on the pitfalls of globalization.

## OPEC

Blair, John M. *The Control of Oil.* New York: Pantheon, 1976.
Emerson, Steven. *The American House of Saud: The Secret Petrodollar Connection.*
    Danbury, CT: Franklin Watts, 1985.
    Discusses the link between the US oil companies and Saudi Arabia.

Lacey, Robert. *The Kingdom: Arabia and the House of Sa'ud*. New York: Avon, 1983.

Yergin, Daniel. *The Prize: The Epic Quest for Oil, Money, and Power*. New York: Simon and Schuster, 1990.
The definitive history of the geostrategic quest to control the world's supply of oil.

## Chapter 18: The Rise of East Asia

### Japan

Christopher, Robert. *The Japanese Mind*. New York: Fawcett, 1983.
One of the most readable of the many books on Japan's "economic miracle."

Dower, John. *Embracing Defeat: Japan in the Wake of World War II*. New York: Norton, 1999.
A definitive study by a first-rate scholar of modern Japanese history.

Johnson, Chalmers. *MITI and the Japanese Economic Miracle: The Growth of Industrial Policy, 1925–1975*. Palo Alto, CA: Stanford University Press, 1982.
A superb analysis of the role of government in Japan's economic growth.

Nakamura, Takafusa. *The Postwar Japanese Economy: Its Development and Structure*. Tokyo: University of Tokyo Press, 1981.

Reischauer, Edwin O. *The Japanese Today: Change and Continuity*. Cambridge, MA: Harvard University Press, 1986.
A masterful survey of modern Japan by one of the foremost Japanists in the United States.

Vogel, Ezra. *Japan as Number 1: Lessons for America*. Cambridge, MA: Harvard University Press, 1979.

### US-Japan Relations

Forsberg, Aaron. *America and the Japanese Miracle: The Cold War Context of Japan's Postwar Economic Revival, 1950–1960*. Durham: University of North Carolina Press, 2000.
On the US role and the importance of the Cold War in Japan's postwar economic recovery.

Johnson, Chalmers. *Blowback: Costs and Consequences of American Empire*. New York: Henry Holt, 2001.
A provocative and sharply critical analysis of both US and Japanese economic policies.

Kuttner, Robert. *The End of Laissez-Faire: National Purpose and Global Economy After the Cold War*. New York: Knopf, 1991.
Argues that since Japan and the EU have close government-business cooperation, strategic economic planning, and managed trade, the United States must also develop a national strategy.

LaFebre, Walter. *The Clash: A History of US-Japanese Relations Throughout History*. New York: Norton, 1997.
An excellent survey by a seasoned diplomatic historian.

McCraw, Thomas K., ed. *America Versus Japan*. Boston: Harvard Business School Press, 1986.
A comparative analysis of economic policies in the United States and Japan.

Prestowitz, Clyde V. *Trading Places: How We Are Giving Our Future to Japan and How to Reclaim It*. 2nd ed. New York: Basic Books, 1989.
A revisionist interpretation of the twin causes of Japan's economic rise: Japan's strategic, long-range program and the US "flight from reality."

Van Wolferen, Karel. *The Enigma of Japanese Power: People and Politics in a Stateless Nation*. New York: Knopf, 1989.
   By the dean of the revisionist school.

### Korea
Amsden, Alice. *Asia's Next Giant: South Korea and Late Industrialization*. New York: Oxford University Press, 1989.
   On South Korea's economic surge starting in the 1960s.
Cumings, Bruce. *Korea's Place in the Sun: A Modern History*. New York: Norton, 1997.
   A comprehensive and critical survey of modern Korean history focusing on the postwar period.
Oberdorfer, Don. *The Two Koreas: A Contemporary History*. Rev. ed. New York: Basic Books, 2001.
Vogel, Ezra. *The Four Dragons: The Spread of Industrialization in East Asia*. Cambridge, MA: Harvard University Press, 1991.
   On the common causal factors for economic growth of the Four Tigers.

### China
Eichengreen, Barry, Charles Wyplosz, and Yung Chul Park, eds. *China and the New World Economy*. New York: Oxford University Press, 2008.
   China as the most significant global economic factor at the outset of the twenty-first century.
Fishman, Ted C. *China Inc.: How the Rise of the Next Superpower Challenges America and the World*. New York: Scribner, 2006.

## Chapter 19: Russia: The Legacy of Soviet Empire

Brown, Archie. *The Gorbachev Factor*. New York: Oxford University Press, 1996.
   On Gorbachev's role in the perestroika of the Soviet Union.
Cohen, Stephen F. *Failed Crusade: America and the Tragedy of Post-Communist Russia*. New York: Norton, 2000.
   A critical assessment of the US role in urging the Yeltsin government to accept capitalism and to dismantle Soviet institutions.
Goldman, Marshall I. *Gorbachev's Challenge: Economic Reform in the Age of High Technology*. New York: Norton, 1987.
   A discussion of the magnitude of Gorbachev's economic problems.
Gorbachev, Mikhail. *Perestroika: New Thinking for Our Country and the World*. New York: Harper and Row, 1987.
———. *The August Coup: The Truth and the Lessons*. New York: HarperCollins, 1991.
Hollander, Paul. *Political Will and Personal Belief: The Decline and Fall of Soviet Communism*. New Haven, CT: Yale University Press, 2000.
   Focuses on the lack of faith in Communism as an all-encompassing ideology.
Karny, Yoav. *Highlanders: A Journey in Quest of Memory*. New York: Farrar, Straus and Giroux, 2000.
   A Israeli journalist's discussion of the ethnic complexities in the Caucasus.
Matlock, Jack F., Jr. *Autopsy of an Empire: The American Ambassador's Account of the Collapse of the Soviet Union*. New York: Random House, 1995.
Medvedev, Zhores A. *Gorbachev*. New York: Norton, 1986.
   By a dissident Soviet historian.
Reddaway, Peter, and Dmitri Glinski. *The Tragedy of Russia's Reforms: Market Bolshevism Against Democracy*. Washington, DC: United States Institute of Peace, 2000.

Schmidt-Häuer, Christian. *Gorbachev: The Path to Power.* Boston: Salem House, 1986.
A Moscow-based West German journalist's account of how the party elected Gorbachev as its chief.

### Eastern Europe

Ascherson, Neal. *The Polish August: The Self-Limiting Revolution.* New York: Viking, 1982.
On the political climate in Poland that set the stage for the rise of Solidarity.
Ash, Timothy Garton. *The Polish Revolution: Solidarity.* New York: Charles Scribner's Sons, 1984.
———. *The Magic Lantern: The Revolution of '89 Witnessed in Warsaw, Budapest, Berlin, and Prague.* New York: Vintage, 1993.
A British journalist's eyewitness account of the historic events of 1989.
Behr, Edward. *Kiss the Hand You Cannot Bite: The Rise and Fall of the Ceauşescus.* New York: Villard Books, 1991.
Political biography that focuses on the deep social and cultural roots of the dictatorship.
Brumberg, Abraham, ed. *Poland: Genesis of a Revolution.* New York: Random House, 1983.
A collection of essays by Polish activists.
Carre d'Encausse, Helene. *Decline of an Empire: The Soviet Socialist Republics in Revolt.* New York: Harper and Row, 1978.
An introduction to the ethnic complexity of the Soviet empire.
Djilas, Aleksa. *The Contested Country: Yugoslav Unity and Communist Revolution, 1919–1953.* Cambridge, MA: Harvard University Press, 1993.
An analysis of why Tito's concept of a unified Yugoslavia eventually failed.
Glenny, Misha. *The Balkans: Nationalism, War, and the Great Powers, 1804–1999.* New York: Viking, 2000.
By a BBC correspondent who covered the disintegration of Yugoslavia.
Stokes, Gail. *From Stalinism to Pluralism: A Documentary History of Eastern Europe Since 1945.* New York: Oxford University Press, 1996.
Sullivan, Stacy. *Be Not Afraid, for You Have Sons in America: How a Brooklyn Roofer Helped Lure the US into the Kosovo War.* New York: St. Martin's Press, 2004.

## Chapter 20: The Nuclear Arms Race

Bottome, Edgar M. *The Balance of Terror: A Guide to the Arms Race.* 2nd rev. ed. Boston: Beacon Press, 1986.
Broad, William J. *Teller's War: The Top-Secret Story Behind the Star Wars Deception.* New York: Simon and Schuster, 1992.
How Edward Teller, the "father" of the US hydrogen bomb, sold SDI to the Reagan administration.
Bundy, McGeorge. *Danger and Survival: Choices About the Bomb in the First Fifty Years.* New York: Random House, 1988.
John Kennedy's national security advisor on how successive US governments developed a "tradition of nonuse."
Cockburn, Andrew. *The Threat: Inside the Soviet Military Machine.* New York: Random House, 1983.
A sober assessment of Soviet capabilities and weaknesses.
FitzGerald, Frances. *Way Out There in the Blue: Reagan, Star Wars, and the End of the Cold War.* New York: Simon and Schuster, 2000.

Freedman, Lawrence. *The Evolution of Nuclear Strategy.* New York: St. Martin's Press, 1981.

Gervasi, Tom. *The Myth of Soviet Military Supremacy.* New York: Harper and Row, 1986.
Challenges the Reagan administration's claim that the Soviet Union had overtaken the West in the arms race.

Holloway, David. *Stalin and the Bomb: The Soviet Union and Atomic Energy, 1936–1956.* New Haven, CT: Yale University Press, 1994.
The definitive work on the topic.

Matlock, Jack F. *Reagan and Gorbachev: How the Cold War Ended.* New York: Random House, 2004.
By Reagan's ambassador to the Soviet Union.

McDougall, Walter A. *The Heavens and the Earth: A Political History of the Space Age.* New York: Basic Books, 1984.

Newhouse, John. *Cold Dawn: The Story of SALT.* New York: Holt, Rinehart and Winston, 1973.

Office of Technology Assessment. *SDI: Technology, Survivability, and Software.* Princeton, NJ: Princeton University Press, 1988.
A study for the House Armed Services Committee and Senate Foreign Relations Committee, concluding that SDI would fail in case of war.

Rhodes, Richard. *Arsenals of Folly: The Making of the Nuclear Arms Race.* New York: Vintage Books, 2008.
The third volume of previous, well-received books on the topic, taking the story to the end of the Cold War.

Schell, Jonathan. *The Fate of the Earth.* New York: Knopf, 1982.
The popular best-seller on the consequences of nuclear war.

Schlosser, Eric. *Command and Control: Nuclear Weapons, the Damascus Accident, and the Illusion of Safety.* New York: Penguin, 2013.
On the hazards of the arms race, which had its share of accidents, carelessness, and miscalculations.

Smith, Gerard. *Doubletalk: The Story of SALT I.* Garden City, NY: Doubleday, 1980.
By the chief US arms negotiator at the talks.

Talbott, Strobe. *Endgame: The Inside Story of SALT II.* New York: Harper and Row, 1979.

———. *Deadly Gambits: The Reagan Administration and the Stalemate in Nuclear Arms Control.* New York: Knopf, 1984.
By a former *Time* correspondent, detailed and lucid treatments of arms negotiations in the 1980s.

Union of Concerned Scientists. *The Fallacy of Star Wars.* New York: Vintage, 1984.

US Department of Defense. *Soviet Military Power.* Washington, DC: US Government Printing Office, six editions, 1981–1987.
The Pentagon's exaggerated assessments of the Soviet threat.

Zuckerman, Solly. *Nuclear Illusion and Reality.* New York: Random House, 1982.
A critical view by a former scientific adviser to the British Ministry of Defence: Neither side can gain nuclear advantage.

## Chapter 21: The Emergence of Political Islam in the Middle East and North Africa

*Islam*

Guillaume, Alfred. *Islam.* 2nd rev. ed. New York: Penguin, 1956.

The classic analysis of the theological basis of Islam by one of the West's recognized scholars in the field.

Jansen, G. H. *Militant Islam.* New York: Harper and Row, 1979.
 Explains to Western readers the philosophic foundations of Islam and the reasons for its militant form in Iran.

Pichthall, Muhammad Marmaduke. *The Meaning of the Glorious Koran.* N. J. Dawood, trans., New York: Penguin, 1956.
 A translation of the Koran for Western readers; contains a valuable introduction to the early history of Islam by an English convert to the faith.

### Iran and Its Revolution

Bakhash, Shaul. *The Reign of the Ayatollahs: Iran and the Islamic Revolution.* New York: Basic Books, 1984.

Kapuscinski, Ryszard. *Shah of Shahs.* San Diego: Harcourt Brace Jovanovich, 1985.
 By a veteran Polish journalist, an embellished eyewitness account of the Iranian upheaval.

Rubin, Barry. *Paved with Good Intentions: The American Experience and Iran.* New York: Oxford University Press, 1980.
 On what went wrong with the US scenario for the shah's Iran.

Said, Edward W. *Covering Islam: How the Media and the Experts Determine How We See the Rest of the World.* New York: Pantheon, 1981.
 By a US citizen of Palestinian descent, a critical analysis of how the US press covered the Iranian hostage crisis.

Salinger, Pierre. *America Held Hostage: The Secret Negotiations.* Garden City, NY: Doubleday, 1981.
 By someone involved in settling the crisis.

Sick, Gary. *All Fall Down.* New York: Random House, 1985.
 A member of President Carter's National Security Council offers a firsthand account of the hostage deliberations.

### Iraq and the Gulf War

Bush, George, and Brent Scowcroft. *A World Transformed.* New York: Knopf, 1998.
 The memoirs of the US president and his national security advisor.

Gordon, Michael R., and Bernard E. Trainor. *The General's War: The Inside Story of the Conflict in the Gulf.* Boston: Little, Brown, 1994.

Schwarzkopf, H. Norman. *It Doesn't Take a Hero.* New York: Bantam, 1992.
 The memoirs of the commander of UN forces in the Gulf War.

## Chapter 22: September 11, Afghanistan, and Iraq

### Militant Islam

Armstrong, Karen. *The Battle for God.* New York: Ballantine Books, 2000.
 A discussion of the force of fundamentalism in Judaism, Christianity, and Islam since 1492.

Kepel, Gilles. *The War for Muslim Minds: Islam and the West.* Cambridge, MA: Belknap, 2004.

Stern, Jessica. *Terror in the Name of God: Why Religious Militants Kill.* New York: Ecco Press, 2003.
 Based on interviews of zealots—Muslims, Jews, and Christians.

Wehrey, Frederic M. *Sectarian Politics in the Gulf: From the Iraq War to the Arab Uprising.* New York: Columbia University Press, 2013.

On the political complexity of the Arab Gulf states and the Shia challenge to Sunni authority.

### The War on Terror Under George W. Bush

Bacevich, Andrew J. *The Limits of Power: The End of American Exceptionalism.* New York: Metropolitan, 2008.

Blix, Hans. *Disarming Iraq.* New York: Pantheon, 2004.
By the head of the UN weapons inspection team.

Clancy, Tom, with Tony Zinni and Tony Koltz. *Battle Ready.* New York: G. P. Putnam's Sons, 2004.
A biography of Gen. Tony Zinni, the former commander of the US Marines.

Clarke, Richard A. *Against All Enemies: Inside America's War on Terror.* New York: Free Press, 2004.
The memoirs of the antiterrorist chief who served both Bill Clinton and George W. Bush.

Coll, Steven. *Ghost Wars: The Secret History of the CIA, Afghanistan, and bin Laden, from the Soviet Invasion to September 10, 2001.* New York: Penguin, 2004.
The definitive account.

Hersh, Seymour M. *Chain of Command: The Road from 9/11 to Abu Ghraib.* New York: HarperCollins, 2004.
By an investigative journalist who was among the first to break the Abu Ghraib story.

Johnson, Chalmers. *The Sorrows of Empire: Militarism, Secrecy, and the End of the Republic.* New York: Metropolitan, 2004.

Mann, James. *The Rise of the Vulcans: The History of Bush's War Cabinet.* New York: Viking, 2004.
On the rise of the neocons, by a former correspondent of the *Los Angeles Times*.

Scheuer, Michael. *Imperial Hubris.* New York: Potomac Books, 2004.
By the operative in charge of the CIA's bin Laden unit, 1996–1999.

Woodward, Bob. *Bush at War.* New York: Simon and Schuster, 2002.
The first of four books by the *Washington Post* correspondent who had considerable access to Bush and his cabinet. It was followed by *Plan of Attack* (2004), *State of Denial* (2007), and *The War Within: A Secret White House History, 2006–2008* (2008).

### Chapter 23: The Arab Spring: Turning to Winter?

Lynch, Marc. *The Arab Uprising: The Unfinished Revolutions of the New Middle East.* New York: Public Affairs, 2013.
By a staffer of *Foreign Policy*, who places the Arab Spring in the context of the Middle East's broader history, notably its religious and political divisions.

Noueihed, Lin, and Alex Warren. *The Battle for the Arab Spring: Revolution, Counter-Revolution and the Making of a New Era.* New Haven, CT: Yale University Press, 2012.
An early attempt by scholars to zero in on a moving target.

Prashad, Vijay. *Arab Spring, Libyan Winter.* Edinburgh, UK: AK Press, 2012.
The focus is on the unreliable nature of revolutions and how they appear to head in one direction only to turn in unexpected ways.

# Index

# About the Book

New emphasis on the impacts of globalization, events in the Middle East, and political and economic changes in East Asia—as well as new information and maps throughout—are among the features of this thoroughly revised edition of The World Since 1945.

The text traces the major political, economic, and ideological patterns that have evolved in the global arena from the end of World War II to the present, providing the background needed for a solid understanding of contemporary international relations. Written to be student friendly, it has made its place as the text of choice in scores of introductory IR and world history courses.

**Wayne C. McWilliams** and **Harry Piotrowski** are emeritus professors in the Department of History at Towson University.